Contents

Contents

Contributors

Tanveer Ahmad is currently an Assistant Professor at the Department of Law, North South University, Bangladesh. He holds a Doctor of Civil Law (DCL) degree and a Master of Laws (LL.M.) degree from the Institute of Air and Space Law, McGill University, Canada. He completed his Bachelor of Laws (LL.B.) (Honors) degree and Diploma in Law degree from the University of London, UK. He is the recipient of the prestigious International Civil Aviation Organization Assad Kotaite Graduate and Postdoctoral Fellowship of 2013, and the Boeing Fellowship in Air and Space Law of 2013 and 2014. During his doctoral and master's studies, McGill University awarded him, among others, the Provost's Graduate Fellowship in 2009, the Principal's Graduate Fellowship in 2009, the Graduate Excellence Fellowship in 2012, the Robert E. Morrow, QC, Fellowship in 2012, and the Graduate Excellence Award in Air and Space Law in 2013.

Jimena Blumenkron worked as a legal clerk in the Supreme Court of Justice of Mexico (2000–04) and as a General Counsel of the Retirement Fund in Mexico (2004–07), before she obtained her LL.M. in Air and Space Law at McGill (2007–09). She then proceeded to intern at IFALPA (2007–08), then ICAO for four months (2008–09). She also practiced as an Independent Legal Advisor from 2007 to 2011 while working at ICAO as a Safety and Policy Expert (2010–11) and as a Technical Officer (2011–13). She remains at ICAO as an Aviation Safety Officer, a position she occupied in 2013, and remains to do so.

Paul Stephen Dempsey, with a BA in Journalism and an Juris Doctor in Law from University of Georgia, went on to acquire an LL.M. in International Law from George Washington University and a DCL in Air and Space Law at McGill University. He was Vice Chairman of Frontier Airlines Holdings, Inc., and Chairman of Lynx Aviation, Inc. He served as Attorney-Advisor to the Interstate Commerce Commission's Office of Proceedings (1975–77), Attorney-Advisor to the former Civil Aeronautics Board's Office of General Counsel, and its Bureau of Pricing and Domestic Aviation (1977–79), and the Legal Advisor to the Chairman of the US Interstate Commerce Commission (1981–82). He was also the Director of the Transportation Law Program at the University of Denver in Colorado and Director of the National Center for Intermodal Transportation. From 2012 to 2016 he served as Tomlinson Professor of Global Governance in Air and Space Law and Director of the Institute of Air and Space Law at McGill University.

Martine De Serres works as a lawyer in regulatory and international law at Air Canada and is an Adjunct Professor at McGill University, where she teaches Government Regulations of Air Transportation. She also sits on the board of various non-profit organizations. She holds an

LL.M. in Air and Space Law and a B.Sc. in Physics from McGill University, as well as an LL.B. in Civil Law from the University of Sherbrooke. Prior to joining Air Canada, she practiced commercial litigation at a reputable Montreal litigation boutique. The views and opinions expressed here are her own and do not reflect the views or policies of Air Canada.

Peter van Fenema, with an LL.M. (thesis on Satellite Communications) from Leiden, an LL.M. (thesis on The 1972 Convention on International Liability for Damage caused by Space Objects), and a Doctoral (thesis on The International Trade in Launch Services: The Effects of US Laws, Policies and Practices on its Development) from Leiden, worked as the Assistant Legal Advisor to the Air Staff at Royal Netherlands Air Force (1969–71), an Advisor/Expert on International Aviation Law Policy in the Netherlands (2000–present), and a trainer at JAA Training Organization (2006–present). He was also the vice president of Foreign Relations and Cooperation at KLM Royal Dutch Airlines (1990–97), is a co-editor in *Air and Space Law* at Kluwer Law International (1993–present), and an Adjunct Professor of Air and Space Law at McGill (1995–present).

P.P.C. Haanappel, with a Master's degree in aviation and space law and a Doctor of Civil Law (thesis on IATA Tariffs), was a Professor of Law at McGill (1976–90). He was also Associate Dean (Academic) of the Faculty of Law (1985–87), Associate Dean (Graduate Studies and Research) of the Faculty of Law (1988–90), and Associate Director of the Institute of Air and Space Law (1989–90) at McGill. In 1990, he was appointed Director, European Aeropolitical Affairs at the International Air Transport Association (IATA) in Geneva until 1996, when he was also appointed Professor of Air and Space Law at the Faculty of Law of Leiden University. From 1997–2000, he was IATA's Director, and from 2000–02, he was Senior Aero-Political Advisor (IATA). From 2003 to 2007, he was Head of the Department/International Institute of Air and Space Law at Leiden, and Director of the Master's programme in aviation and space law. He retired early in 2009, and is currently an Emeritus Professor in Leiden. In 2010, he remained an Adjunct Professor of Law at McGill. He also remains a member of the Editorial Board of the *Annals of Air and Space Law* (McGill), a member of the Editorial Board of the *Zeitschrift für Luft- und Weltraumrecht* (University of Cologne), acts as consultant and is on the list of aviation legislation experts to ICAO, is the Associate Legal Adviser at CAAi (UK), and is a member of the European Aviation Club and of the International Foundation for Public Aviation (IFPA).

Jiefang Huang graduated from McGill with an LL.M. in Air and Space Law (1985) and currently works as a Legal Officer of International Civil Aviation Organization. He was a Board Member of the Canada-China Network Council and the Canadian Branch of the International Law Association before becoming the Vice President of the latter.

Ram S. Jakhu, with an LL.M. and a DCL in Air and Space Law and the Law of Outer Space and Telecommunications, respectively, at McGill, has maintained an Associate Professor position at the Institute since 1998, and a position as Associate Director of the Research Centre of the Institute since 2006. He maintained the position of Director of the Centre for the Study of Regulated Industries (1999–2004) following his position as a Professor, Head of School Social Sciences and Management, and the First Director of the Master's Program of the International Space University in Strasbourg (1978–94). He has also held multiple positions at the Institute of Air and Space Law at McGill. He is a Member of the World Economic Forum's Global Agenda Council on Space Security, Research Director for Space Security Index Project, a 'Fellow' and the Chairman of the Legal and Regulatory Committee of the International Association for the Advancement of Space Safety, Managing Editor of the Space Regulations Library Series, a

Member of the Editorial Board of the *Annals of Air and Space Law* and the German *Journal of Air and Space Law*, and a Member of the Board of Directors of the Institute of at McGill.

Isabelle Lelieur enrolled at McGill to obtain a Master's degree in Air and Space Law (2000–02) as she pursued a traineeship at Air France's International Affairs Department (2000). After completion of her studies at the Institute, she pursued another traineeship at the European Commission in Brussels (2002), followed by a position as the Head of the Legal Department at the French Airport Association (2002–07) alongside maintaining a position as an academic speaker (2002–14). Currently, she holds a position as the Head of the Legal Department at VINCI Airports in France (2007–present).

George Leloudas is an Associate Professor at the Institute of International Shipping and Trade Law (IISTL) of Swansea University. He is a graduate of the National and Kapodistrian University of Athens. He holds LL.M. degrees in Commercial Law from the University of Bristol (England, 2002) and in Air and Space Law from the Institute of Air and Space Law of McGill University (Montreal, Canada, 2003). He also completed his PhD degree in air law with emphasis on liability and insurance at Trinity Hall, Cambridge University in 2009. Before joining the Institute, he worked as a Solicitor at Gates and Partners in London for several years where he advised on aerospace liability and airlines' regulatory matters. He is also an instructor at the Training and Development Institute of the International Air Transport Association (IATA) where he teaches international air law for lawyers and legal professionals, law of aviation insurance and air cargo liability. He is a contributing editor to *Shawcross and Beaumont Air Law*. He is an active researcher and his most recent article is entitled '"Door to Door" Application of the International Air Law Conventions: Commercially Convenient, but Judicially Dubious' and has been published in the August 2015 issue *of Lloyd's Maritime and Commercial Law Quarterly* (pp. 368ff.). He is also authoring a book together with Professor Malcolm Clarke of Cambridge University entitled *Air Cargo Insurance* (Informa law from Routledge) that will be published in June 2016.

Kate Markhvida holds a BA in economics and statistics from the University of British Columbia (2007), an MA in economics from Carleton University (2008), and a graduate diploma in Air and Space Law from McGill (2012). She is also a recipient of the Social Sciences and Human Research Council (SSHRC) graduate scholarship. She worked at Canada's federal antitrust agency (2008–11), and has since served as Manager of Economic Analysis and consulted with InterVISTAS Consulting Inc., while conducting courses in aviation economics and law to students and professional audiences. Her areas of expertise include competition assessments, regulatory and policy analysis, demand analysis and forecasting, economic modeling and cost–benefit analysis.

Yaw Nyampong worked as External Counsel for the Ghana Civil Aviation Authority while he practiced law as a pupil and an associate in the Ghanaian law firm G.A. Sarpong and Co. (2000–03). This ignited an interest for aviation in him, which after pursuance led him to obtain an LL.M. (2003–05) and Doctorate (2006–11) in Air and Space Law at McGill. He then became Assistant to the Director of the Bureau of Administration and Services (ICAO) (June to November 2011). During his time at McGill, he worked as a research and teaching assistant under the supervision, on multiple occasions, of Professors Paul Dempsey and Ram Jakhu, he held the position of Editor of the *Annals of Air and Space Law* (2007–12), was a Postdoctoral Fellow at the Institute from 2011–12, was a Boulton Junior Fellow (visiting Scholar) (2012–13), and Executive Director (Academics) (2013–14). At present, he occupies the position of Senior Legal Officer at Pan-African University, which he acquired in September 2014.

Christopher M. Petras acquired an LL.M. in Air and Space Law at McGill University in 2001. He has over 22 years' experience in the practice of law, with expert knowledge of international Air and Space Law and governmental policy related to air and space operations. With a strong background in governmental acquisition and utilization of commercial air transport, space-based telecom and remote sensing services, he worked as the chief of Operations Law at NORAD–US Space Command (2001–02), the Senior Legal Advisor at Peterson Air Force Base (2002–03), where he also worked as the Chief of International Air and Space Operations Law (2003–05). He also served as the General Counsel at the Fairchild Air Force Base (2005–08), as Chief of Operations and International Law at the Scott Air Force Base (2008–10), where he was also the Senior Legal Advisor at Tanker Airlift Control Center (2010–11). He is also an Adjunct Professor at the University of Mississippi School of Law since 2013 and a Legal Officer at ICAO since 2011.

Juan Carlos Salazar, with a Master's (LL.M.) in Air and Space Law from McGill University, worked as the Secretary and Chief Legal Counsel of a Colombian airline for five years, the Colombian Civil Aviation Authority for six years, and, currently, with UAE GCAA for three years. He specializes in economic regulation of air transport, bilateral and multilateral air transport affairs, and air transport policy.

Charles E. Schlumberger graduated with a Master's degree from Basel Law School, focusing on Aviation Law and Bankruptcy Procedures (1982–86), acquired an MBA from Harvard Business School (1987–89), and a Doctorate degree in Civil Law from the Institute of Air and Space Law at McGill (2006–09). He was also the Vice President of UBS, a financial services company, from 1995–98. At present, he is a Lead Air Transport Analyst at the World Bank (1998–present) and he is also an active FAA and EASA licensed pilot and certified flight instructor, and a 'Fellow' at the Royal Aeronautical Society.

Francis Schubert, with a PhD in International Aviation Law from the University of Geneva and a Diploma in Higher Studies in International Relations from the Graduate Institute for International Studies in Geneva, has lectured on ANS matters at several universities and contributed to numerous legal studies conducted by international organizations and research institutions. As the previous President of the Swiss Air and Space Law Association, he presently serves as Chairman of the CANSO Legal and Policy Committee and Chairman of the FABEC Institutional, Regulatory and Legal Standing Committee.

Mathieu Vaugeois, with an LL.M. in Air and Space Law at McGill (2015), interned at the Legal Affairs and External Relations Bureau of ICAO for five months between 2012 and 2013, where he also worked as a Consultant for seven months in 2013. In August 2014, he was awarded the MRI Fellowship at the Legal Affairs and External Relations Bureau of ICAO, which lasted until January 2015.

Ludwig Weber is Adjunct Professor of Law at McGill University, where he teaches Comparative Air Law. He was Legal Counsel of the International Air Transport Association (IATA) in Geneva (1992–95), Director of the Legal Bureau of the International Civil Aviation Organization (ICAO) in Montreal (1995–2004), and Consultant to ICAO on a number of projects. He is a Senior Civil Aviation Policy and Management Advisor to ICAO, and also a Member of the Board, Institute of Air and Space Law Center for Research at McGill University.

Preface

As part of the initiative of renowned academic publisher Routledge to develop their legal research program, Professor Ram S. Jakhu and I have assumed the role of editors for the *Routledge Handbook of Public Aviation Law*. This unique treatise is the first book of its kind. A Routledge Handbook is a prestige reference work providing an overview of a whole subject area or sub-discipline. A Handbook is an edited collection surveying the state of the discipline, including emerging and cutting-edge areas.

We have assembled a team of international experts with widely recognized professional expertise and academic credentials in the field. They are leading scholars and professionals – all of whom, incidentally, are either McGill University Institute of Air and Space Law graduates or Professors at the Institute – in producing a prestigious work that summarizes topics of current international research and identifies emerging issues of interest. The end product is a Handbook that is both practical and theoretical in scope, that we believe will prove to be an invaluable research tool and reference material for academics, students, researchers, lawyers, and policy makers alike.

Renowned globally, the McGill University Faculty of Law spearheaded trans-systemic studies in legal education. Benefiting from this unique approach to legal education, the Institute and Centre for Research of Air and Space Law has over the course of several decades published numerous studies, reports, and compendia, as well as the *Annals of Air and Space Law*, the highly regarded peer-reviewed journal in the domain. With our interest in pursuing advanced research and dissemination of the knowledge of air and space law, and on the invitation of Routledge, we undertook this *Handbook of Public Aviation Law*, and its companion, *Handbook of Space Law*, to be published by one of the world's leading publishers.

This Handbook comprises 14 chapters covering several topics and subject matters. Each chapter focuses on a specific topic. It is fitting that McGill University produces such a collection, for the University is located in Montreal, the center of the universe of Public International Aviation Law. It is Montreal in which the UN Civil Aviation Organization is headquartered, and where it produces Annexes to the Chicago Convention and has hosted many diplomatic conferences creating numerous Montreal Conventions on various aspects of aviation law in areas of safety, security, and liability. Also in Montreal are the major industry organizations – the International Air Transport Association and Airports Council International – as well as major aircraft and component manufacturers and aircraft service organizations.

This treatise is a labor of love. Author royalties are donated to establishing the George S. and Ann K. Robinson Space Law Graduate Fellowship at McGill University Institute of Air and Space Law. We are proud to have produced a seminal work that will contribute to the continuing development and research in the domain of public aviation law.

Paul Stephen Dempsey
Ram S. Jakhu

1

Introduction

Multilateral conventions and customary international law

Paul Stephen Dempsey

1.1 Introduction

International Air Law (or, if you prefer, Aviation Law) is divided into two broad categories: Public and Private. In this book, we review several of the major issues Public International Air Law likely will confront during this century.[1]

1.2 The Chicago Convention

Because so much of aviation is inherently international in scope, early in its development the world community assembled and drafted major multilateral conventions attempting to unify international rules governing safety and navigation and other aspects of civil aviation to ensure protection of the public.

The "magna carta" of Public International Air Law is the Chicago Convention of 1944.[2] The Chicago Convention is both an organic constitution of an international organization and the source of major principles of Air Law. Established by the Chicago Convention, the International Civil Aviation Organization (ICAO) was given responsibility for regulating the many

---

1 See Paul Stephen Dempsey, *Public International Air Law* (McGill 2008). The sources of Public International Air Law are:

- multilateral conventions;
- ICAO SARPs;
- bilateral agreements (e.g., traffic rights, safety, security);
- customary International Law;
- intergovernmental decisions and regulations (e.g., those of the European Union);
- national legislation and regulation;
- administrative practice and procedure;
- contracts (e.g., air carrier alliance agreements, airport agreements);
- judicial opinions; jurisprudence of courts interpreting all the above in cases and controversies brought before them.

2 Convention on International Civil Aviation, Opened for signature, December 7, 1944, 61 Stat. 1180, T.I.A.S. No. 1591, Art. 7 (hereinafter Chicago Convention).

technical aspects of the international civil aviation. Consequently, the jurisdiction of ICAO was extended to such matters as aircraft licensing, airworthiness certification, registration of aircraft, international operating standards, and airways and communications controls. Beyond safety and navigation, ICAO also has taken the lead on environmental and security issues, jurisdictional areas not originally contemplated when the Chicago Convention was drafted. ICAO has promulgated Standards and Recommended Practices (SARPs) which its 191 Member States are obliged to implement uniformly, unless they find it impracticable to comply.[3] Moreover, the Chicago Convention provides that: "over the high seas, the rules in force shall be those established under this Convention."[4] Hence, ICAO has law-making authority over 72 percent of the Earth's surface. This jurisdictional scope, which is unparalleled by any other international organization, in effect, makes ICAO a paradigm of global governance.[5] Today, ICAO is one of the largest, and most successful, specialized agencies in the United Nations family.[6]

The Chicago Convention set forth many of the guiding principles of Public International Air Law. Among them are:

1   *Territorial Sovereignty.* Every State has, to the exclusion of all other States, the unilateral and absolute right to permit or deny entry into the area recognized as its territory and similar right to control all movements within such territory.
2   *National Airspace.* The territory of a sovereign State is three dimensional, including within such territory the airspace above its national lands and its internal and territorial waters.
3   *Freedom of the Seas.* Navigation on the surface of the high seas and flight above such seas are free for the use of all.
4   *Nationality of Aircraft.* Aircraft have the characteristic of nationality similar to that developed in maritime law applicable to ships. Thus aircraft have normally a special relationship to a particular State which is entitled to make effective the privileges to which such aircraft may be entitled and such State is also reciprocally responsible for the international good conduct of such aircraft.[7]

The Chicago Convention lists 11 jurisdictional areas to which ICAO is instructed to devote itself, mostly focusing on safety and navigation.[8] Yet, since its creation, as air transport has grown and evolved, ICAO has focused on other areas not explicitly listed therein, including, for example, the promulgation of wholly new Annexes addressing environmental and security issues. Some authors assert that the involvement of ICAO in addressing aircraft emissions lacks "any sound textual basis in the Convention."[9] This author, however, takes the view that the Convention is sufficiently broad to permit such jurisdictional assertions, as it provides that in addition to those matters specifically

---

3 Chicago Convention Art. 38.
4 Chicago Convention Art. 12.
5 Paul Stephen Dempsey, "Compliance & Enforcement in International Law: Achieving Global Uniformity in Aviation Safety" 30 *N.C. J. Int'l L. & Com. Reg.* 1, 18–19 (2004).
6 See generally, Anthony Sampson, *Empires of The Sky: The Politics, Contests, and Cartels of World Airlines* 38 (Random House 1984).
7 John Cobb Cooper, "Backgrounds of International Public Air Law" 1 *Yearbook of Air and Space L.* 3 (1967).
8 Chicago Convention Art. 37.
9 Brian F. Havel and Gabriel S. Sanchez, *The Principles and Practice of International Aviation Law* 57 (Cambridge University Press 2014).

enumerated, ICAO may promulgate SARPs addressing "such other matters concerned with the safety, regularity, and efficiency of air navigation as may from time to time appear appropriate."[10]

ICAO began operations in 1947. The international Air Law legal regime governing air transport on issues such as safety, security, navigation, and air traffic management are now well developed, and set forth in the Chicago Convention and the 19 Annexes thereto.[11] By convening diplomatic conferences, ICAO also has been a major source of multilateral Conventions addressing aviation.[12]

---

10 Chicago Convention Art. 37.
11 The promulgation of SARPs has resulted in the following Annexes to the Chicago Convention:

- Annex 1 – Personnel Licensing

Licensing of flight crews, air traffic controllers, and aircraft maintenance personnel;

- Annex 2 – Rules of the Air;
- Annex 3 – Meteorological Service for International Air Navigation

Vol. I – Core SARPs
Vol. II – Appendices and Attachments;

- Annex 4 – Aeronautical Charts;
- Annex 5 – Units of Measurement to be used in Air and Ground Operations;
- Annex 6 – Operation of Aircraft

Part I – International Commercial Air Transport – Aeroplanes
Part II – International General Aviation – Aeroplanes
Part III – International Operations – Helicopters;

- Annex 7 – Aircraft Nationality and Registration Marks;
- Annex 8 – Airworthiness of Aircraft;
- Annex 9 – Facilitation;
- Annex 10 – Aeronautical Telecommunications

Vol. I – Radio Navigation Aids
Vol. II – Communication Procedures including those with PANS status
Vol. III – Communication Systems
Part I – Digital Data Communication Systems
Part II – Voice Communication Systems
Vol. IV – Surveillance Radar and Collision Avoidance Systems
Vol. V – Aeronautical Radio Frequency Spectrum Utilization;

- Annex 11 – Air Traffic Services – Air Traffic Control Service, Flight Information Service, and Alerting Service;
- Annex 12 – Search and Rescue;
- Annex 13 – Aircraft Accident and Incident Investigation;
- Annex 14 – Aerodromes

Vol. I – Aerodrome Design and Operations
Vol. II – Heliports;

- Annex 15 – Aeronautical Information Services;
- Annex 16 – Environmental Protection

Vol. I – Aircraft Noise
Vol. II – Aircraft Engine Emissions;

- Annex 17 – Security: Safeguarding International Civil Aviation Against Acts of Unlawful Interference;
- Annex 18 – The Safe Transport of Dangerous Goods by Air;
- Annex 19 – Safety Management (promulgated on 14 November 2013).

Adopted in 2013 Annex 19 was the first new Annex adopted by ICAO in four decades.
12 Public and Private International Air Law agreements are compiled in XXX(1) *Annals Air & Space L.* (2005).

The success of ICAO is reflected in the nearly universal ratification of both the Chicago Convention, and many of the multilateral Conventions it has generated.[13]

1.3 The Aviation Security Conventions

More than 190 States have ratified the Chicago Convention. Annex 17 reflects considerable work on the security front, particularly since September 11, 2001. Additionally, an impressive array of international aviation security agreements has been created under ICAO auspices. State ratifications have been widespread:

- the Tokyo Convention of 1963 – 185 States;
- the Hague Convention 1970 for the unlawful seizure of aircraft – 185 States;
- the Montreal Convention 1971 for the suppression of unlawful acts against the safety of aviation – 188 States;
- the Montreal Protocol of 1988 for the suppression of acts of violence at airports – 173 States;
- the MEX Convention of 1991 on the marking of explosives – 150 States.

In addition, ICAO convened diplomatic conferences in Beijing in 2010 and Montreal in 2014 that drafted additional aviation conventions and protocols, which have yet to enter into force. ICAO also has had impressive success in drafting a number of Private International Air Law Conventions addressing airline and air carrier liability.[14] ICAO has been a major catalyst for the unification of law globally. One source observed, "very positive results … have been obtained in the technical committees and commissions of ICAO, especially in the field of air law."[15]

---

13 Paul Stephen Dempsey, "Aviation Security: The Role of Law in the War against Terrorism" 41 *Columbia J. of Transnat'l Law* 649 (2003).
14 Air carrier liability for international delay, passenger injury or death, and cargo loss and damage is governed by several multilateral Conventions and amending Protocols, the first being the Warsaw Convention of 1929, and the most recent being the Montreal Convention of 1999. Professor Michael Milde has described Warsaw as "justly hailed as the most successful unification of private law." Professor Milde points out the major areas in which Warsaw has achieved uniformity: (1) the definition of international carriage; (2) the documents of carriage; (3) the regime of liability; and (4) jurisdiction. Michael Milde, "'Warsaw' System and Limits of Liability: Yet Another Crossroad?" 18 *Annals Air & Space L.* 201, 204–7 (1993).
  As for the liability conventions promulgated under ICAO auspices, ratification rates also are impressive:
  - the Hague Protocol – 137 States;
  - the Guadalajara Convention – 86 States;
  - the Montreal Protocol No. 4 – 58 States;
  - the Montreal Convention of 1999 – 107 States.

  Ratification rates for surface damage conventions have been less successful. The Rome Convention of 1952 received relatively few ratifications, and neither of the two Montreal Conventions of 2009, addressing air operator liability for surface damage, has received a sufficient number of ratifications to enter into force. Paul Stephen Dempsey, *Aviation Liability Law* 238–47 (LexisNexis 2nd ed. 2013).
15 Nicolas Mateesco Matte, "The Chicago Convention: Where From and Where To, ICAO?" XIX(1) *Annals Air & Space L.* 371, 379 (1994).

1.4 Air transport agreements

The Chicago Convention recognizes the customary international air law principle that every State has complete and exclusive sovereignty in the airspace above its territory.[16] It prohibits scheduled operations except with the permission or authorization of the State in whose territory an aircraft wishes to fly, and only in accordance with the terms established by that State.[17] This has led to a proliferation of bilateral air transport agreements, whereby States negotiate traffic rights, rates, capacity, frequency, and other commercial issues on behalf of their flag carriers. This, too, has created a large body of Public International Air Law.

Some misread the Chicago Convention to address ownership and control of *airlines*. It does not. It addresses nationality and registration of *aircraft*. The Chicago Convention provides that, "Aircraft shall have the nationality of the State in which they are registered."[18] Aircraft may not be registered in more than one State, though registration may be changed from one State to another.[19] Registration, and transfers thereof, as well as the nationality of aircraft owners are determined by the domestic laws of the registering State.[20]

The issue of whether aircraft or airline ownership was tied to nationality was left to national law. But since cabotage rights normally were conferred only to airlines owned by nationals of the State, and often nationality was a domestic law prerequisite of air carrier certification, the result would be the same in much of the world. So, the practice of most States has long been to restrict aircraft registration and the issuance of airline operating certificates to its citizens. That tradition began to be assaulted with the European Union's promulgation of rules prohibiting Member States from imposing such requirements on EU community air carriers.[21]

Airline nationality is nowhere addressed in the Chicago Convention.[22] The "substantial ownership and effective control" requirement (i.e., the requirement that an airline designated by a State to fly routes negotiated in an Air Services Agreement is owned and controlled by the designating State or its national citizens)[23] was included both in the multilateral Transit and Transport Agreements adopted at Chicago, and in most of the bilateral air transport agreements concluded since.[24] The existence of "substantial ownership and effective control" requirements have circumscribed adoption of the Maritime Law notion of "flags of convenience" – and the myriad of safety problems it has produced[25] – into international aviation. But, importantly,

---

16 Chicago Convention, Art. 1.
17 Chicago Convention, Art. 6.
18 Chicago Convention, Art. 17.
19 Chicago Convention, Art. 18.
20 Chicago Convention, Art. 19.
21 Under its governing treaties and regulations, an EU citizen enjoys the "right of establishment" anywhere within the EU.
22 Paul Stephen Dempsey, "Nationality Requirements and Cabotage Restrictions in International Aviation: Sovereignty Won and Sovereignty Lost" 20 *Studies in Air & Space Law* 129 (2006).
23 Brian F. Havel and Gabriel S. Sanchez, *The Principles and Practice of International Aviation Law* 69 (Cambridge University Press 2014).
24 Almost all bilateral air transport agreements, as well as the multilateral Transit and Transport Agreements, require that carriers designated thereunder "be substantially owned and effectively controlled" by citizens of the State that issues them an operating certificate.
25 Flags of convenience have created enormous problems in the maritime trade. See e.g., Paul Dempsey, "Compliance and Enforcement in International Law: Oil Pollution of the Marine Environment by Ocean Vessels" 6 *N.W. J. Int'l L. & Bus.* 459 (1984); and Paul Dempsey and Lisa Helling, "Oil Pollution by Ocean Vessels: An Environmental Tragedy: The Legal Regime of Flags of Convenience, Multilateral Conventions and Coastal States" 10 *Den. J. Int'l L. & Pol'y* 37 (1980).

although each State has the right to exercise this prohibition, it may also waive the right to exercise this discretion. Increasingly, the requirement is waived.

Some States also recognize the "public utility" attributes of commercial aviation – that frequent and economical air service creates wealth in many sectors of the overall economy beyond air transport, and that its preservation is essential to economic growth. Thus, the economic well being of their airline(s) may need some protection from the ravages of destructive competition.

Of late, the ownership and control requirement has been criticized by advocates of liberalization of governmental restrictions, who argue that the "open skies" bilateral approach of opening markets does not go far enough.[26] It continues to restrict the creation of global megacarriers. It prohibits cross-border mergers, acquisitions, and consolidations.[27] But, actually, three virtual megacarriers have emerged – the Star, Skyteam, and Star Alliances.

1.5 State sovereignty vs. global governance

As noted, Article 1 of the Chicago Convention essentially repeats Article 1 of its predecessor, the Paris Convention of 1919: every State enjoys "complete and exclusive sovereignty" in the airspace above its territory. The remaining provisions of those Conventions then limited that "complete and exclusive sovereignty" in a variety of ways, identifying what States must, and must not, do. The Annexes limit that sovereignty still further.[28] States have been willing to relinquish sovereignty in order to facilitate their common interest of ensuring safety and security in commercial aviation.[29]

In the twentieth and twenty-first centuries, State sovereignty has been eroded in a multitude of ways.[30] For example, it was once possible for a monarch to slaughter his people with impunity. Now, he can be dragged before an international criminal court for prosecution.[31] While a criminal court with adequate jurisdiction may prosecute one who violates human rights, most international organizations lack any power of prosecution. Some authors lament the fact that ICAO "possesses no *direct* powers ... to punish or demand compliance from recalcitrant States."[32] This reflects a confusion of domestic and international law. Under domestic law, the sovereign has enforcement power by corps of police, jails, courts, and prisons to coerce and punish those who violate his edicts; usually, the sovereign has the monopoly on the use of force. Yet, in

---

26 Professor Brian Havel, for example, calls for elimination of what he describes as

> the central legal pillars of the prevailing Chicago system of protective bilaterals – the principles of cabotage ... and the nationality principle.... Until these pillars crumble, in the US and among its aviation trading partners, no authentic globalization of the international aviation system will be possible.

Brian Havel, *In Search of Open Skies* 5–6 (Kluwer 1997). See also, Brian F. Havel and Gabriel S. Sanchez, *The Principles and Practice of International Aviation Law* 123 (Cambridge University Press 2014).

27 Brian F. Havel and Gabriel S. Sanchez, *The Principles and Practice of International Aviation Law* 89 (Cambridge University Press 2014).

28 Thomas Buergenthal, *Law-Making in the International Civil Aviation Organization* (University of Virginia Press 1969).

29 See Assad Kotaite, *My Memoirs 210–11* (ICAO 2014).

30 José E. Alvarez, "Governing the World: International Organizations as Lawmakers" 31 *Suffolk Transnat'l L. Rev.* 591 (2008).

31 Emmanuelle Jouannet, "What is the Use of International Law? International Law as a 21st Century Guardian of Welfare" 28 *Mich. J. Int'l L.* 815 (2007).

32 Brian F. Havel and Gabriel S. Sanchez, *The Principles and Practice of International Aviation Law* 61 (Cambridge University Press 2014).

international law, there are no equivalent institutions. Outside the powers held by the UN Security Council to bring sanctions against States that violate international law, no UN body has unrestricted power to punish an errant State. Global governance instead works in a system of compliance, and softer levels of enforcement.[33]

One of the most ingenious, and effective, is the audit program created by ICAO to ascertain State compliance with SARPs. In 1999, ICAO established a Universal Safety Oversight Audit Programme (USOAP) in order to assess State compliance with SARPs. In 2004, the ICAO General Assembly passed a resolution requiring the Secretary General to make the results of the audit available to all Member States, and to post them on the secure portions of the ICAO website.[34] In 2005, the ICAO Council approved a procedure for disclosing information about a State having significant SARPs deficiencies in its aviation safety obligations.[35] A more significant action was taken in 2006, when aviation directors general from 153 of 190 Member States agreed that by March 23, 2008, the names of those States that fail to agree to full transparency of their USOAP audits would be posted on the ICAO website. By 2006, more than 100 States agreed to transparency.[36]

It is unprecedented for an international organization to be given the authority to assess State compliance with international obligations, and to "name and shame" States that are delinquent. Also, in the area of aviation security, ICAO SARPs are to be applied to domestic, as well as international, airports. It is unprecedented for an international organization to apply its standards domestically.

The law-making competence of ICAO was also recognized by the UN when it delegated to ICAO the responsibility to promulgate a Convention addressing the issue of marking plastic explosives,[37] and was recognized by the international community in the Kyoto Protocol requiring States working through ICAO to address the environmental impact of emissions by aircraft.

Clearly, ICAO has had less success in overcoming State sovereignty on the issue of aircraft emissions.[38] The EU's rather reckless effort unilaterally to impose an Emissions Trading System (ETS) on all airlines serving EU airports in a way that impinged on the territorial sovereignty of their flag States was met with vigorous opposition, forcing the EU to retreat in 2012. Ultimately, ICAO can do nothing that the States do not want. If the heads of State are unable to agree as to how to arrest global warming, air transport ministers or foreign service diplomats on the Council or in the Assembly of ICAO can do no better.

Yet, a global solution must be found to the problem of aviation emissions. Aircraft contribute only between 2 and 3 percent of carbon pollution globally, but commercial aviation is growing at a faster pace than the ability of technology to reduce emissions, and aviation is the only polluter at high altitude. The ICAO General Assembly has commissioned the Council to develop a global Market Based Measures (MBM) scheme by 2016. The legally clumsy and coercive EU ETS may be the wrong approach, but a better way must be found.

33 Paul Stephen Dempsey, "Compliance & Enforcement in International Law: Achieving Global Uniformity in Aviation Safety" 30 *N.C. J. Int'l L. & Com. Reg.* 1 (2004).
34 ICAO G.A. Res. 16.2/1 (superseding Assembly Res. 33-8).
35 ICAO, Annual Report of the Council, Doc. 9862 (2005).
36 "The Net Tightens" *Flight Int'l* (July 18, 2006).
37 The 1991 Montreal Convention on the Marking of Plastic Explosives for the Purpose of Detection.
38 See Rachel F. Rosenfeld, "The European Union Aviation Directive and U.S. Resistance: A Deadlock on Aviation Emissions Control" 25 *Geo. Int'l Envtl. L. Rev.* 589 (2013).

1.6 Conclusion

The twenty-first century likely will see accelerated and robust technological, economic, environmental, and political change.[39] Air Law will be required to evolve at a pace adequate to address that change. The challenges and opportunities for global aviation are many, and will evolve in ways that cannot yet be perceived.

Aviation contributes much to our culture and our global economy. It shrinks the planet, and integrates people of vastly different backgrounds. Commercial aviation is, by far, the safest form of transportation, and likely will remain so throughout this century.[40]

The remainder of this century will be at least as challenging as its first decade-and-a-half. Since the non-event of Y2K, already we have seen fuel price spikes and collapses, major airline bankruptcies,[41] liquidations,[42] acquisitions and consolidations,[43] shifting alliances,[44] breathtaking advances in technology including aircraft made of composites flying longer distances and burning less fuel, aerospace vehicles,[45] drones landing on the White House lawn, catastrophic kamikaze terrorism,[46] surface-to-air missiles downing commercial aircraft, mysteriously disappearing aircraft swallowed by oceans, and growing concerns over carbon emissions, global warming, and climate change.[47] The ancient Chinese curse was, "May you live in interesting times." We live in such times.

39 Nicolas Mateesco Matte, "The Chicago Convention: Where From and Where To, ICAO?" XIX(1) *Annals Air & Space L.* 371, 394 (1994).
40 Paul Stephen Dempsey, "Compliance & Enforcement in International Law: Achieving Global Uniformity in Aviation Safety", 30 *N.C. J. Int'l L. & Com. Reg.* 1–74 (2004).
41 Paul Stephen Dempsey, "The Financial Performance of the Airline Industry Post-Deregulation" 45 *Houston L. Rev.* 421–85 (2008).
42 Paul Stephen Dempsey, "Airlines in Turbulence: Strategies for Survival" 23 *Transportation Law Journal* 15–98 (1995).
43 Paul Stephen Dempsey, "The Cyclical Crisis in Commercial Aviation: Causes and Potential Cures" XXVIII *Annals Air & Space L.* 1–17 (2003).
44 Paul Stephen Dempsey, "Carving the World into Fiefdoms: The Anticompetitive Future of Commercial Aviation", XXVII *Annals Air & Space L.* 247–304 (2002).
45 Paul Stephen Dempsey and Michael Mineiro, "The Regulation of Aerospace Vehicles", in *Space Safety Regulations and Standards* (J. Pelton and R. Jakhu eds. Elsevier 2010).
46 Paul Stephen Dempsey, "Aviation Security: The Role of Law in the War against Terrorism" 41 *Columbia J. of Transnat'l Law* 649 (2003).
47 Paul Stephen Dempsey, "Trade & Transport Policy in Inclement Skies: The Conflict between Sustainable Air Transportation and Neo-Classical Economics" 65 *J. Air L. & Com.* 639–93 (2000).

2

The Chicago Convention

Ludwig Weber

2.1 Overview and historical background

The Convention on International Civil Aviation, signed on 7 December 1944 at Chicago,[1] is the fundamental legal instrument governing rights and obligations of States with respect to international civil aviation. It provides the legal framework for international civil aviation activities of which numerous aspects are regulated in more detail by other multilateral and bilateral agreements. In its Part II, the Convention sets out the charter of the International Civil Aviation Organization (ICAO),[2] which is the UN Specialized Agency for international civil aviation.[3]

The predecessor of the Chicago Convention was the Convention on the Regulation of Air Navigation, signed on 13 October 1919 at Paris[4] as part of the Paris Peace Conference Agreements. Its main purpose was to ensure better control over international civil aviation through an international framework based on the principle of air sovereignty, so that aviation relations could be developed peacefully. The United States was not present at the Paris Conference. It supported the principle of air sovereignty and other Convention principles, but took the view that the Paris Convention did not sufficiently allow for the concept of freedom of air commerce and therefore never adhered to that Convention. This position was taken up in the Atlantic Charter of 1941 where the Allied Powers subscribed to the freedom of international exchange based on the freedoms of commerce and transport. By 1944, commercial international air transport had largely collapsed due to the hostilities of World War II. The United States therefore took the initiative to convene a conference aimed at establishing a new legal framework for the post-war period in which the principle of freedom of air commerce would be better realized.

The International Civil Aviation Conference[5] was held from 1 November to 7 December, 1944 in Chicago, Illinois, and was attended by 52 States plus observers from two occupied States. The Conference resulted in the adoption of the following instruments: (1) the Interim Agreement on International Civil Aviation, setting up the Provisional International Civil Aviation Organization

---

1 UNTS Vol. 15, 295; ICAO Doc. 7300/9.
2 Arts. 43–66 of the Convention; L. Weber, *International Civil Aviation Organization*, 2nd ed. (Kluwer: Alphen aan den Rijn 2012) with further references.
3 Agreement between the United Nations and the International Civil Aviation Organization, signed 13 May 1947, UNTS Vol. 8 (1947), 324; ICAO Doc. 7970.
4 Convention Portant Réglementation de la Navigation Aérienne, 13 October 1919, Conférence de la paix, Recueil des actes de la conférence, partie VII A – Conventions générales entre alliés, 1933.
5 US Department of State Printing Office (ed.), *Proceedings of the International Civil Aviation Conference, Chicago, Illinois, November 1–December 7, 1944* (ICAO: Washington 1948), 2 Vols.

(PICAO)[6] to bridge the time until the entry into force of the main Convention;[7] (2) the Convention on International Civil Aviation, the main Convention; (3) the International Air Services Transit Agreement[8] ("Two Freedoms Agreement"); (4) the International Air Transport Agreement[9] ("Five Freedoms Agreement"); (5) the Drafts of 12 Technical Annexes to the main Convention, to set standards and recommended practices for technical and operational aspects of international civil aviation, such as airworthiness of aircraft, licensing of personnel, air traffic control, telecommunications and others; and (6) a recommended standard Bilateral Agreement for the exchange of traffic rights for international scheduled air services, which was included in the Final Act.

The Convention on International Civil Aviation clearly reflects a compromise between the position of several States aiming at close international regulation of civil aviation on the one hand and the position of the United States favoring freedom of air commerce, on the other.[10] The "International Civil Aviation Organization" was set up with mainly technical standard-setting responsibilities[11] relating to aviation safety, while economic regulation of air transport was mainly left to bilateral agreements between States.[12] As from 1946, when the first post-war bilateral agreement on international air services was concluded,[13] issues of international routes, designation of air carriers, capacity, frequency of service and other air commerce matters were regulated bilaterally. The regulation of fares, rates and tariffs was left to self-regulation by airline industry conferences, subject to governmental approval.[14] The option to establish Regional Air Transport Commissions at a later stage was provided in Article 55(a) of the Convention.

2.2 The Two Freedoms and Five Freedoms agreements of 1944

This compromise was embodied not only in the Convention on International Civil Aviation, but also in the International Air Services Transit Agreement,[15] which was signed on the same day as the Convention. It provides for the multilateral exchange of air transit rights, i.e., the right of overflight (the first freedom of the air) and the right to land for technical purposes, in particular, for refueling (the second freedom of the air). The adoption of this Agreement became necessary since the principle of innocent passage through national airspace for aircraft of other contracting States, as contained in the Paris Convention, was no longer recognized in the Chicago Convention. To date, 130 out of 191 Member States of ICAO have ratified this Agreement. A number of large surface States, such as Brazil, Canada, China and the Russian Federation have refrained from ratifying or have denounced the Agreement after initially ratifying.

---

6 Interim Agreement on International Civil Aviation, 171 UNTS 345.
7 PICAO was provisionally entrusted with the tasks of ICAO and became operational on 6 June 1945. It operated until 4 April 1947, when the main Convention entered into force and the tasks, powers, institutions and assets were transferred from PICAO to ICAO.
8 International Air Services Transit Agreement, 84 UNTS 389.
9 171 UNTS 387.
10 See on this aspect Weber, op. cit. (note 2), pp. 15–16; *Proceedings*, op. cit. (note 5).
11 See in particular Arts. 37, 38, 54(l), 90 Chicago Convention. On the standard-setting functions, see L. Weber in: R. Bernhardt (ed.), *Encyclopedia of Public International Law* (Elsevier: Amsterdam 1992), Vol. I, 571 *et seq.* with further references.
12 The provisions on economic regulation in the Convention are framework provisions only, see in particular Art. 67 and Chapter XV of the Convention, which have not been frequently used. Other examples are Arts. 15, 21, 55(c), (d), (e) of the Convention.
13 Bermuda Agreement between the UK and the US, see note 18 below.
14 Fare- and ratemaking for international routes was entrusted to the IATA Conference machinery, see P.P.C. Haanappel, *Pricing and Capacity Determination in International Air Transport* (Kluwer: Deventer 1984), ch. 2.
15 International Air Services Transit Agreement, 84 UNTS 389.

Furthermore, the International Air Transport Agreement[16] was also adopted on 7 December, 1944. It was intended to provide for the multilateral exchange of traffic rights (landing rights for commercial purposes, also referred to as "five freedoms of the air"), but did not succeed, since it was signed and accepted by only a few States (some with reservations) and the Agreement has largely remained a dead letter.[17]

This situation led to the conclusion of the first post-war bilateral air services agreement between the United Kingdom and the United States during the bilateral Conference of Bermuda in 1946.[18] The so-called Bermuda Agreement came to play a special role in the reconstruction of aviation relations during the post-war period, because it established a template for hundreds of other bilateral air services agreements concluded between States over the next three decades.[19]

2.3 Sovereignty over national airspace

Under Article 1 of the Chicago Convention, the contracting States "recognize that every State has complete and exclusive sovereignty over the airspace above its territory." This fundamental principle, generally regarded as a principle of customary international law and first laid down in the Paris Convention of 1919, was reaffirmed with respect to all States, including non-contracting States. The principle of innocent passage through national airspace for aircraft of other contracting States, as contained in the Paris Convention, was no longer recognized in the Chicago Convention, largely due to the experience of World War II. As mentioned above, air transit rights were multilaterally exchanged in the International Air Services Transit Agreement, but only among its States parties.

Under Article 2 of the Convention, the principle of sovereignty extends to the airspace above a State's land areas and territorial waters adjacent thereto under the sovereignty, suzerainty, protection or mandate of the State. The limits of the territorial waters of a coastal State are determined by the provisions of Article 3 of the UN Convention on the Law of the Sea (12 sea miles). Similarly, under Article 49 of the same Convention, the sovereignty of an archipelagic State extends to the airspace above its archipelagic waters enclosed by the baselines drawn in accordance with Article 47. However, the principle of airspace sovereignty does not extend to the airspace above a State's Contiguous Zone or Exclusive Economic Zone.

As a result of airspace sovereignty, the territorial State may refuse permission of cabotage[20] (Article 7 of the Convention), declare prohibited areas (Article 9) and require application of its

---

16 171 UNTS 387.

17 The US, which had initially signed the Agreement, subsequently gave notice of termination on 25 July 1947.

18 Air Services Agreement between the UK and the US, signed on 11 December 1946, UKTS No. 3 (1946), 3 UNTS 253; see J.C. Cooper, "Air Transport and World Organization," in: I.A. Vlasic (ed.), *Explorations in Aerospace Law* (McGill University Press: Montreal 1968), 357 *et seq.*; G. Cribbett, "The Influence of Bilateral Agreements, Tariffs and Subsidies in International Air Transport," 3 *Journal of Aeronautical Science of India* (1951), 1 *et seq.*; M. Gillilland, "Bilateral Agreements," in: E. McWhinney and M.A. Bradley (eds.), *The Freedom of the Air* (A.W. Sijthoff: Leiden/Dobbs Ferry 1968), 159 *et seq.*

19 B. Cheng, *The Law of International Air Transport* (Stevens & Sons: London 1962) 422 *et seq.*; B. Cheng, "Beyond Bermuda," in: N.M. Matte (ed.), *International Air Transport: Law, Organization and Policies for the Future* (Carswell: Toronto/Paris 1976), 81; N.M. Matte, *Treatise on Air-Aeronautical Law* (McGill University Press: Montreal/Toronto 1981), 144 *et seq.*

20 *Cabotage* is defined as the privilege of a foreign aircraft to carry passengers, mail and cargo for remuneration or hire between two points in the territory of the same State. This privilege is rarely granted and it must not be granted on an exclusive basis. See Art. 7 Chicago Convention.

laws and regulation by foreign civil aircraft in its territory, subject to the provisions of the Convention (Articles 11 to 13). Foreign civil aircraft which have entered sovereign airspace without permission or which fail to follow essential rules or fail to identify themselves upon request may be intercepted by military aircraft (Article 3 *bis* (b) and (c)), in strict observance of the international interception procedures set out in Annex 2 to the Convention – "Rules of the Air".[21] Interception usually involves instructions from the intercepting to the intercepted aircraft to identify itself and if necessary land at a designated airport, or to follow the intercepting aircraft to such airport, or leave a prohibited zone, after establishing radio-communications contact.

It is important to note that these interception procedures applied to civil aircraft do not authorize or permit the use of weapons. Under Article 3 *bis* (a) of the Convention, States must refrain from the use of weapons against aircraft in flight and, in case of interception, the lives of persons on board and the safety of aircraft must not be endangered. The provisions of the UN Charter, in particular the right to self-defense under Article 51, remain, however, unaffected regarding the very exceptional circumstance of self-defense against an armed attack committed by means of civil aircraft.

2.4 Scheduled and non-scheduled air services

Article 6 of the Convention provides that "no scheduled international air service may be operated over or into the territory of a contracting State, except with the special permission or other authorization of that State, and in accordance with the terms of such permission or authorization." This provision, firmly based on the sovereignty principle, was a compromise given the fact that the Chicago Conference of 1944 could not agree on the multilateral exchange of commercial rights for scheduled international air services. In 1946, the United States and the United Kingdom concluded the first post-war bilateral air services agreement which became to be known as the "Bermuda Agreement."[22] It served as a model for an extensive network of bilateral agreements on international scheduled air services which developed during the post-war period when the route networks of international carriers expanded.

International non-scheduled air services (including in particular air charter, air taxi and non-commercial flights), on the other hand, are governed by Article 5 of the Convention. Aircraft engaged in such services have the right, "subject to the observance of the terms of this Convention, to make flights into or in transit non-stop across its territory and to make stops for non-traffic purposes without the necessity of obtaining prior permission." However, when such flights are performed for commercial purposes, the last sentence of Article 5 is restrictive in providing that the territorial State may impose "regulations, conditions or limitations as it may consider desirable." On this basis, many States have issued national regulations governing the conditions for commercial charter services and other commercial non-scheduled flights to and from their territory. A number of States have also addressed commercial charter services in bilateral air services agreements.

2.5 Nationality of aircraft: registration and certification

Article 17 of the Convention establishes the principle that aircraft have the nationality of the State in which they are registered. Under Article 18, an aircraft cannot be validly registered in more than one State, but its registration may be changed from one State to another. Article 19

21 ICAO Doc. AN 2, Section 3.8, Appendix 2 and Attachment A. On the coordination of civil and military aircraft operations, see ICAO Assembly Resolution A38-12, Appendix I, ICAO Doc. 10022.
22 3 UNTS 253.

provides that such registration shall be made in accordance with the laws and regulations of the registering State. For this purpose, each State maintains a registry for civil aircraft. In most States, there is a separate registry for State aircraft, which are defined as aircraft used in military, customs and police services in Article 3(b) of the Convention.

Section 5 of the International Air Services Transit Agreement as well as most bilateral air transport agreements prevent "flags of convenience" in international civil aviation by requiring that substantial ownership and effective control of the respective air transport enterprise and/or of the operating aircraft be vested in nationals of the respective State of registration.

All aircraft engaged in international air navigation, whether commercial, non-commercial or general aviation, must bear nationality and registration marks so as to permit identification.[23] Annex 7 to the Convention, "Aircraft Nationality and Registration,"[24] which is based on Articles 17 to 20 of the Convention, sets out standards and procedures for the use of letters, numbers and other graphic symbols to be used for the purposes of nationality and registration marks of aircraft. It also specifies where these will be located on different types of aircraft.[25] The Annex sets out procedures for selection by ICAO contracting States of nationality marks from the nationality symbols used in the radio call signs allocated by the International Telecommunications Union (ITU).[26]

Article 7 of the Convention permits joint operating organizations. The Annex therefore defines the terms *common mark*, *common mark registering authority* and *international operating agency*, so as to allow aircraft operated by joint operating organizations or agencies to be registered on other than a national basis.[27] Each international operating agency may be assigned a distinctive common mark, selected from symbols allocated by the ITU. In practice, these facilities have only been used in a few cases. The Annex also sets forth a *model registration certificate* for use by contracting States.[28] Under Article 29 of the Convention, each aircraft must carry its registration certificate on board at all times.

In accordance with Article 31 of the Convention, every aircraft engaged in international navigation shall be provided with a certificate of airworthiness issued or rendered valid by the State in which it is registered. This rule engages the international responsibility of the State of registry having issued such a certificate for the airworthiness of the aircraft wherever it may operate. The State of registry is therefore internationally responsible for the continuing safety of the aircraft and must comply with the safety oversight responsibilities regarding regular maintenance and overhaul of the aircraft. In case of lease, charter and interchange arrangements, the safety oversight functions can be transferred from the State of registry to the State of the operator of the leased aircraft in accordance with a transfer agreement between the two States, in line with Article 83 *bis* of the Convention.

Article 33 provides that certificates of airworthiness issued or rendered valid by the contracting State in which the aircraft is registered shall be recognized as valid by the other contracting States, provided that the requirements under which such certificates were issued or rendered valid are equal to or above the minimum standards which may be established from time to time pursuant to the Convention.

---

23 Art. 20 of the Convention; under Art. 19, the registration or transfer of registration of aircraft in any contracting State shall be made in accordance with its laws and regulations.
24 Doc. AN 7, 5th edn., incorporating Amendments 1–5, Corrigendum 1 (14 August 2007).
25 Doc. AN 7, section 3: Location of Nationality, Common and Registration Marks.
26 See sections 2, 4 and 5 of Annex 7; for the ITU.
27 Annex 7, see Definitions and subsections 2.1, 2.2, 2.4, note after 2.4.
28 Annex 7, section 7, Figure 1.

2.6 Aviation personnel licensing

In accordance with Article 32 of the Convention, the pilots and the other members of the oper-ating crew of every aircraft engaged in international navigation shall be provided with certifi-cates of competency and licenses issued or rendered valid by the State in which the aircraft is registered. However, each State reserves the right to refuse to recognize, for the purposes of flight above its own territory, certificates of competency and licenses granted to any of its nationals by another contracting State. Licensing entails the international responsibility of the State having issued a license pursuant to Article 32 for the competency and medical fitness of the holder of the license.

Annex 1, "Personnel Licensing" contains detailed standards and recommended practices (SARPs) for the licensing of flight crew members (pilots, flight engineers), air traffic controllers, maintenance engineers/technicians and other aviation personnel. Licenses are not required under Annex 1 for cabin crew (cabin attendants, purser etc.), who are therefore subject to national rules. The SARPs describe the skills necessary to ensure proficiency, the medical stand-ards required, periodic medical examinations and other exigencies for the different types of personnel licenses set out in the Annex. Licensing is the act of authorizing defined activities, which are otherwise prohibited in the absence of such license, because of the inherent risk of such activities being improperly performed without proper training, proficiency and fitness. Licensing is performed at the level of contracting States under national legislation that is in line with the SARPs of Annex 1.

Related training manuals issued by ICAO provide guidance to States for the establishment and management of a State personnel licensing system and the scope and depth of training cur-ricula. They also provide guidance for the training of other aviation personnel such as aero-drome emergency crews, flight operations officers, radio operators and related functions.

2.7 Rights of overflight and traffic rights

As a result of the requirement of prior permission for scheduled air services in Article 6, rights of scheduled aircraft for overflight and traffic rights need to be granted multilaterally or bilater-ally outside the Convention. As noted above, rights of overflight were conferred multilaterally in the International Air Services Transit Agreement[29] (also called "Two Freedoms Agreement"), which provides for the mutual exchange of air transit rights among the 130 States Parties to it. Air transit rights comprise the right to overfly the territory of another State without stop (so-called first freedom of the air), as well as the right of overflight with a stop for technical pur-poses, i.e., for purposes other than taking on board passengers, cargo or mail (so-called second freedom). Among States which are not parties to the Agreement, air transit rights for scheduled services need to be agreed bilaterally or to be obtained by special permission.

Traffic rights are commercial rights, namely rights to fly into the territory of another State in order to take on board and/or drop off passengers, cargo or mail for commercial purposes. They comprise the third, fourth and fifth freedom rights, namely the right to carry passengers, cargo or mail to a point in another State, the right to take on board passengers, cargo or mail at a point in another State for carriage to the home State of the air carrier and the right to carry passengers, cargo or mail from a point in another State to a beyond point in the territory of a third State, respectively. Sometimes, sixth, seventh, eighth and ninth freedom rights or privileges are also

---

29 International Air Services Transit Agreement signed on 7 December 1944 at Chicago, 84 UNTS 389. As of 15 December 2014, there were 130 States Parties to this Agreement.

referred to as traffic rights.[30] As noted above, the International Air Transport Agreement (also called "Five Freedoms Agreement") was an attempt to provide for the mutual exchange of traffic rights which did however not succeed.[31] Therefore, since the conclusion of the bilateral Bermuda Agreement between the US and the UK in 1946, traffic rights have been negotiated and exchanged principally on a bilateral basis between States.

These bilateral agreements, following the Bermuda model, defined the terms of operation of the designated air carriers in terms of frequency, capacity, tariffs, routes and other conditions. After 1992, with the gradual introduction of Open Skies agreements,[32] the terms of operation were liberalized so that frequency, capacity, tariffs and routes were largely left to the commercial judgment of the designated carriers, while maintaining the requirement of prior permission, designation, substantial ownership and effective control of designated carriers, and other requirements set out in the respective bilateral Agreement.

2.8 The Convention as the constitution of ICAO

2.8.1 General

Part II of the Convention sets out the constitution of the ICAO, including its establishment, name and composition (Article 43), its objectives (Article 44), its permanent seat (Article 45), its legal capacity (Article 47), the Assembly (Articles 48 and 49), the Council (Articles 50–55), the Air Navigation Commission (Articles 56–57), personnel (Articles 58–60), finance (Articles 61–63) and other international arrangements (Articles 64–66).

2.8.2 Objectives and mandate

The objectives of the Organization are set out in Article 44 of the Convention on International Civil Aviation, which provides that

> [t]he aims and objectives of the Organization are to develop the principles and techniques of international air navigation and to foster the planning and development of international

---

30 *Sixth Freedom* is the right or privilege, in respect of scheduled international air services, of transporting, via the home State of the carrier, traffic moving between two other States. The so-called Sixth Freedom of the Air, unlike the first five freedoms, is not incorporated as such into any widely recognized air service agreements such as the "Five Freedoms Agreement." *Seventh Freedom* is the right or privilege, in respect of scheduled international air services, granted by one State to another State, of transporting traffic between the territory of the granting State and any third State with no requirement to include on such operation any point in the territory of the recipient State, i.e., the service need not connect to or be an extension of any service to/from the home State of the carrier, i.e., the right to carry traffic between two points in two foreign States by a carrier operating outside its home State. *Eighth Freedom* is the right or privilege, in respect of scheduled international air services, of transporting cabotage traffic between two points in the territory of the granting State on a service which originates or terminates in the home country of the foreign carrier, or (in connection with the so-called Seventh Freedom of the Air) outside the territory of the granting State the right to carry cabotage, i.e., traffic between two points of a foreign territory. *Ninth Freedom* is the right or privilege of transporting cabotage traffic of the granting State on a service performed entirely within the territory of the granting State (also known as "stand alone" cabotage). See on this matter the ICAO "Manual on the Regulation of International Air Transport," Doc. 9626, Part 4.
31 The "Five Freedoms Agreement" of 7 December 1944, 171 UNTS 387 had been signed by only a few States. The US, which had initially signed the Agreement, subsequently gave notice of termination on 25 July 1947.
32 See L. Weber, "Current Developments in Aviation Law: Open Skies Policy," in: *Liber Amicorum A.M. Donato* (ALADA: Buenos Aires 2014), 327.

air transport so as to: (a) insure the safe and orderly growth of international civil aviation throughout the world; (b) encourage the arts of aircraft design and operation for peaceful purposes; (c) encourage the development of airways, airports, and air navigation facilities for international civil aviation; (d) meet the needs of the peoples of the world for safe, regular, efficient and economical air transport.

The overall mandate of ICAO comprised, from a historical perspective, the rebuilding of international civil aviation after World War II, and its orderly growth.[33] In so doing, the promotion of aviation safety and later the promotion of aviation security became central elements. The term aviation safety relates to technical and operational safety of flight, while the term aviation security relates to the safeguarding of civil aviation against acts of unlawful interference. Aviation safety is mentioned in paragraphs (a), (d) and (h) of Article 44 as well as in the preamble, while aviation security is not mentioned since it was not a known problem in 1944. In the course of the almost 70 years of operation of the Organization, the objective of safety has been recognized as having highest overall priority,[34] while aviation security has been added in the course of the 1960s and 1970s. Safety of flight is the basis, the *conditio sine qua non*, for all aviation activities, be they commercial, non-commercial, general aviation or other flying activities.[35]

The promotion of aviation safety and security has mainly been carried out through development and continuous updating of a comprehensive set of technical SARPs set out in the Annexes to the Convention. In recent years, the standard-setting activities of the Organization have been supplemented by a comprehensive audit system to monitor implementation of the technical safety standards by ICAO Member States (Universal Safety Oversight Audit Programme),[36] as well as by an integrated Global Aviation Safety Plan (GASP).[37]

2.8.3 Assembly

The Assembly is the main policy-setting body of ICAO. Each of the 191 Member States of ICAO has a seat in the Assembly and one vote.[38] It meets in ordinary session once every three years, and may meet in extraordinary session at any time upon call of the Council, or at the

---

33 A.D. Groenewege, *Compendium of International Civil Aviation*, 2nd ed. (International Aviation Development Corporation: Montreal 1998/99), 18 *et seq.*

34 See Assembly Resolution A37-5, Universal Safety Oversight Audit Programme (USOAP) continuous monitoring approach, first Whereas clause; A32-11, Establishment of an ICAO Universal Safety Oversight Audit Programme, first Whereas clause, ICAO Doc. 9790 (Assembly Resolutions in Force), I-53; see also Assembly Resolution A37-4, ICAO Global Planning for Safety; and previous resolutions A32-15 and A33-16, ICAO Global Aviation Safety Plan (GASP), first Whereas clause.

35 Assembly Resolutions A37-2 and A37-3, first Whereas clause; Resolution A33-16, ibid. (note 34); see also: Global Aviation Safety Plan (GASP), ed. by ICAO (2001); D. Olson, "Striving for Aviation Safety," in: ICAO (ed.), *100 Years of Civil Aviation* (ICAO and ICS Ltd.: Montreal and London 2003), 114 *et seq.*

36 ICAO Assembly Resolutions A37-5 and previous Resolutions A36-4, A35-6, A32-11, A33-8 and A33-9; see also the "Report of the DGCA Conference on a Global Strategy for Safety Oversight," ICAO Doc. 9707; ICAO "Oversight Audit Manual," ICAO Doc. 9735; ICAO "Safety Oversight Manual," Doc. 9734.

37 See *supra* note 34.

38 Art. 48(b) of the Convention; Rule 3 of the Standing Rules of Procedure of the Assembly of the International Civil Aviation Organization, 6th ed., 2008, Doc. 7600/6.

request of at least one-fifth of the membership.[39] A majority of the contracting States constitutes a quorum for the meetings of the Assembly. Decisions require a simple majority of votes cast;[40] in practice, however, most decisions of the Assembly are taken by consensus. The taking of formal votes is rare. Most decisions on substantive matters are taken in the form of a resolution.

2.8.4 Council

The Council is a "permanent body responsible to the Assembly"; Article 50(a) of the Convention. It is composed of 36 contracting States elected by the Assembly,[41] each of which has one vote. Decisions are taken by simple majority, except that decisions to adopt or amend or modify Annexes are taken by a two-thirds majority (Article 90 of the Convention). In practice, most decisions are taken by consensus. The Council is the executive governing body of the Organization. In accordance with Articles 54 and 55 of the Convention, the Council has legislative, administrative and judicial functions.

Among the legislative functions[42] are the adoption of international SARPs in the form of Annexes to the Convention, and amendments thereto (Articles 90, 54(l), 37 and 38); the Council has up to now adopted 19 Annexes and one of its major functions in practice is to keep these 19 Annexes up to date by adopting appropriate amendments.[43]

Among the administrative functions of the Council are[44]:

1   the administration of the finances of the Organization in accordance with Chapters XII and XV;
2   the appointment of the Secretary General and making provision for other personnel of the Secretariat, as required (Article 55(h));
3   the collection and dissemination of information on air navigation and air transport services;
4   the reporting of infractions of the Convention (Article 54(j) and (k));
5   the submission of annual reports to the Assembly and the carrying out of directions of the Assembly (Article 54(a) and (b)).

Regarding the last point, the Council fulfills the important function of administering and supervising the Universal Safety Oversight Audit Programme (USOAP)[45] as well as the Universal

---

39 Art. 48(a) of the Convention; Rules 1 and 2 of the Standing Rules of Procedure of the Assembly, ibid. (note 38).
40 Art. 48(c) of the Convention; Rule 28 of the Standing Rules of Procedure of the Assembly, ibid. (note 38).
41 The Council was enlarged in 2003 from 33 to 36 States when the Protocol of Amendment signed on 26 October 1990 entered into force; 34th Session (Extraordinary) of the Assembly, 31 March to 1 April 2003.
42 See on this matter T. Buergenthal, *Law-making in the International Civil Aviation Organization* (Syracuse University Press: New York 1969).
43 Arts. 54(l) and 90 of the Convention; see *infra*, section 2.9 "International Standards and Recommended Practices: Principles and Procedures."
44 "Repertory-Guide to the Convention on International Civil Aviation," 2nd ed., ICAO Doc. 8900/2, Arts. 54(a), (b), (f), (h)–(k).
45 H. Belai, "Expanding Programme to Adopt Systems Approach to Future Audits," 58(9) *ICAO Journal* (2003), 4 *et seq.*; Weber, op. cit. (note 2), pp. 103–105 with further references.

Security Audit Programme (USAP).[46] The gradual introduction of these programmes as mandatory programmes since 2001 have taken up an important part of the Council's time and efforts, and can be regarded as successful.[47]

Among the judicial functions of the Council[48] are:

1 the adjudication of disputes between contracting States relating to the interpretation or application of the Convention or its Annexes (Articles 84 and 54(b));
2 the adjudication of disputes between contracting States relating to the interpretation or application of the International Air Services Transit Agreement (Article 66 of the Convention, Article II International Air Services Transit Agreement and Article 1 of the ICAO "Rules for the Settlement of Differences").

2.8.5 Air Navigation Commission

The Air Navigation Commission, established by the Council under Article 54(e) and Chapter X of the Convention, is the main technical body of the Organization.[49] In accordance with Article 57(a) of the Convention, its principal function is to consider amendments or modifications to the Annexes to the Convention and to recommend them to the Council. It shall also advise the Council on the collection and dissemination of information it considers necessary and useful for the advancement of air navigation (Article 57(c) of the Convention).[50]

The Air Navigation Commission is composed of 19 members appointed by the Council in their personal capacity as experts (not as representatives) from among persons nominated by contracting States.[51]

2.8.6 Secretariat

The Secretariat is headed by a Secretary General who is appointed by the Council pursuant to Article 54(h) of the Convention. The staff of the Secretariat have the status of international civil servants. The conditions of service of the Secretariat are determined by the Council. Since ICAO is a Specialized Agency of the United Nations, the Council regularly adopts the recommendations of the International Civil Service Commission (ICSC) of the UN regarding the conditions of service as part of the UN Common System.

---

46 ICAO Secretariat, "Historic Conference Agrees on Strategy for Strengthening Aviation Security," 57(2) *ICAO Journal* (2002), 5 *et seq.*; A. Kotaite, "Civil Aviation Security is an Integral Part of our Global Security," 57(5) *ICAO Journal* (2002), 4 *et seq.*; D. Antonini, "Annex 17 Standards will be Primary Focus of Forthcoming Security System Audits," 57(5) *ICAO Journal* (2002), 11 *et seq.* On the USAP programme as it evolved since 2002, see Weber, op. cit. (note 2), pp. 105–106; A37-WP/32 EX/12: Implementation and Evolution of the ICAO Universal Security Audit Programme (26 July 2010); Assembly Resolution A37-5, Whereas clauses; see also *infra* Chapter 3.J.
47 See Assembly Resolution A37-5, eighth Whereas clause; A35-6, operating clause 1; and Assembly Resolution A35-9, Appendix E, ninth Whereas clause, ICAO Doc. 9848.
48 On the judicial functions of the Council, see: J. Erler, *Rechtsfragen der ICAO: Die Internationale Zivilluftfahrtorganisation und ihre Mitgliedstaaten* (Heymanns Verlag: Köln 1967), pp. 185–196; Cheng, *The Law of International Air Transport* (note 19), 100–105; R. Mankiewicz, "Organisation Internationale de l'Aviation Civile," III *Annuaire Français de droit international* (1957), 383 *et seq.*; Buergenthal, op. cit. (note 42), 123 *et seq.*; "Repertory-Guide to the Convention on International Civil Aviation," op. cit. (note 44), Art. 84 *et seq.*
49 See "Rules of Procedure for the Air Navigation Commission," Doc. 8229, Arts. 1–3; Buergenthal, op. cit. (note 42), 9 *et seq.*
50 See also the "Rules of Procedure for the Air Navigation Commission," ICAO Doc. 8229.
51 Art. 56, first sentence, of the Convention; Rule 16(a) of the "Rules of Procedure for the Council," ICAO Doc. 7559/7.

2.9 International standards and recommended practices: principles and procedures

2.9.1 International standards and recommended practices under Articles 37 and 38 of the Convention

Under Article 54(l), the Council is vested with competence to adopt, in accordance with the provision of Chapter VI of the Convention, *international SARPs*, to designate them, for convenience, as *Annexes* to the Convention, and to notify in each such case all contracting States of the action taken. An "international standard" in the sense of Articles 37, 38 and 54 is defined as:

> any specification for physical characteristics, configuration, material, performance, personnel or procedure, the uniform application of which is recognized as necessary for the safety or regularity of international air navigation and to which contracting States will conform in accordance with the Convention; in the event of impossibility of compliance, notification to the Council is compulsory under Art. 38 of the Convention.

A "recommended practice" in the sense of Articles 37 and 54 is defined as:

> any specification for physical characteristics, configuration, material, performance, personnel or procedure, the uniform application of which is recognized as desirable in the interest of safety, regularity or efficiency of international air navigation and to which contracting States will endeavor to conform in accordance with the Convention.

Under Article 54(m), the Council is empowered to consider recommendations of the Air Navigation Commission for amendment of the Annexes and to adopt such amendments in accordance with Article 90 of the Convention. In accordance with Article 54(l) and (m) and Chapter VI of the Convention, the Council has over the years since 1947 adopted *19 Annexes to the Convention* and updated them from time to time by adopting *amendments to the Annexes*.[52] Article 90(a) and (b) provide that the adoption by the Council of such Annexes and amendments thereto shall require the vote of two-thirds of the Council at a meeting called for that purpose and shall then be submitted by the Council to each contracting State.[53] Any such Annex or any amendment of an Annex shall become effective within three months after its submission to the contracting States or at the end of such longer period of time as the Council may prescribe, unless in the meantime a majority of the contracting States registers their disapproval with the Council.[54] Furthermore, the Council shall immediately notify all contracting States of the coming into force of any Annex or amendment thereto.[55]

---

52 The Annexes are published in loose-leaf format and electronically; amendments and revisions are published as and when adopted, and supplements (which set out differences officially notified) as and when filed. The 19 Annexes contain more than 10,000 Standards and Recommended Practices.

53 See Buergenthal, op. cit. (note 42), 57 *et seq.*

54 Art. 90(a) of the Convention. This provision has been characterized by Hailbronner as a "special veto right" of Member States, see K. Hailbronner in: Bernhardt (ed.), *Encyclopedia of Public International Law* (Elsevier: Amsterdam 1992), Vol. II, 1072. See also Cheng, *The Law of International Air Transport* (note 19), 64 *et seq.*

55 Member States are officially notified about amendments and revisions as and when adopted, including the respective date of effectiveness, Art. 90(b) Chicago Convention. The large number and frequency of amendments present a significant problem for a number of Member States with respect to their timely implementation. See Resolution A37-15, Appendix A, clause 8.

The basic procedure set forth in Article 90 of the Convention has been refined over the years in order to improve chances of acceptance by Member States.[56] A practice has developed whereby after the first discussion of a draft amendment by the Air Navigation Commission, the Secretariat will submit the draft to all Member States for comment before either discussing it further in the Commission or transmitting it to the Council. If necessary, this consultation round can be repeated until a consensus or near-consensus is reached. Although sometimes time-consuming, this approach has contributed to the successful adoption of many amendments and reduced the risk of rejection or modification at the end of the procedure.[57]

The *status of the Annexes* to the Convention is governed by Articles 37 and 38 of the Convention. These provisions clarify that the Annexes do not have the same legally binding force as the articles of the main body of the Convention. One reason is that they are not subject to ratification, and that they are a form of "technical international legislation." Article 37 provides that each contracting State undertakes to collaborate in securing the highest practicable degree of uniformity in regulations, standards, procedures and organization in relation to aircraft, personnel airways and auxiliary services in all matters in which such uniformity will facilitate and improve air navigation. For this purpose, ICAO shall adopt and amend from time to time, as may be necessary, international standards and recommended practices and procedures dealing with matters concerned with the safety, regularity and efficiency of air navigation as may from time to time appear appropriate.[58]

Article 38 deals with *departures from international standards and procedures* and provides that any State which finds it impracticable to comply in all respects with any such international standard or procedure shall give *immediate notification* to ICAO.[59] The same applies if any State finds it impracticable to bring its own regulations or practices into full accord with any international standard or procedure after amendment of the latter, or where it deems it necessary to adopt regulations or practices differing in any particular respect from those established by an international standard. Any notification to ICAO under Article 38 shall set out the differences between the State's own practice and that established by the international standard.

In the case of amendments to international standards, any State that does not make the appropriate amendments to its own regulations or practices shall *give notice* to the Council within 60 days of the adoption of the amendment to the international standard, or indicate the action it proposes to take.[60] In any such case, the Council shall make immediate notification to all other States of the difference which exists between one or more features of an international standard and the corresponding national practice of that State.

---

56 The procedure developed by the Air Navigation Commission and the Secretariat is set forth in Resolution A37-15, Appendix A and Associated Practices. See also previously A36-13, "Consolidated Statement of Continuing ICAO Policies and Associated Practices related Specifically to Air Navigation," ICAO Doc. 9902, II-2 *et seq.*; and A35-14, "Consolidated Statement of Continuing ICAO Policies and Associated Practices related Specifically to Air Navigation," ICAO Doc. 9848, II-2.
57 See Resolution A37-15, Appendix A; previously A36-13, Appendix A, clause 6, ICAO Doc. 9902.
58 Regarding Arts. 37 and 38 Chicago Convention, see Erler, op. cit. (note 48), 112 *et seq.*; Matte, *Treatise on Air-Aeronautical Law* (note 19), 210 *et seq.*; Hailbronner, op. cit. (note 54), 1072; M. Le Geoff, "Les Annexes Techniques à la Convention de Chicago," 19 *Revue Générale. de l'Air* (1956), 146 *et seq.*
59 This applies with the exception of Art. 12 Chicago Convention, which provides that in the airspace above the High Seas the rules in force are those established under the Convention, i.e., the SARPs adopted by ICAO. See also Matte, *Treatise on Air-Aeronautical Law* (note 19), 212 with further references; Buergenthal, op. cit. (note 42), 80 *et seq.* with further references.
60 Art. 38, first sentence, Chicago Convention sets out the strict wording "shall give immediate notification." This does not permit tacit non-implementation or non-application of an Annex or Standard, or an amendment thereto.

Under Article 38, *obligations to notify* relate to departures from international Standards or Procedures, but not to departures from Recommended Practices, which are only "recommended" and therefore their non-observance has no legal effect. International Standards and Procedures, by contrast, must be followed, unless a given State has notified a departure, or "filed a difference." Therefore, Articles 37 and 38 leave only two alternatives to States once an international Standard or Procedure has been notified by the Council as adopted; to implement them or immediately to file a difference. Other courses of action, e.g., tacit non-implementation or tacit partial implementation of a new Annex or Amendment to an Annex, are not compatible with Articles 37 and 38 and therefore not permissible because they constitute a breach of the provisions of Part II of the Convention.[61]

In the *practice of ICAO*, therefore, international standards have been clearly distinguished from recommended practices.[62] While the main body of each of the 19 Annexes typically consists of international standards, any paragraphs of text which have the status of a recommended practice will be clearly and visibly set out as such through appropriate print image (usually in italics).[63]

2.9.2 Procedures under Articles 37 and 38 of the Convention

SARPs should be distinguished from *Procedures*, which are a specific form of Technical Legislation. They are not published in Annexes 1–19, but rather in the Procedures for Air Navigation Services (PANS).[64] While set apart from SARPs, they are in practice treated on the same footing in most respects. The PANS which have global applicability are supplemented, as necessary, by Regional Supplementary Procedures (SUPPs),[65] which apply on a regional basis. The respective scope of implementation is defined in each SUPP. Both PANS and SUPPs are adopted by the Council upon recommendation by the Air Navigation Commission pursuant to the provisions of Articles 37 and 38.[66]

---

61 B. Cheng, "Centrifugal Tendencies in Air Law," 10 *Current Legal Problems* (1957), 200 *et seq.*; L. Weber, "Convention on International Civil Aviation: 60 Years," 53 *ZLW* (2004), 289, 305; in the same vein also the recent practice of the Council, which now applies the infraction procedure of Art. 54(j) Chicago Convention with regard to States that practice tacit non-implementation and thereby create significant safety risks while not cooperating with the ICAO Audit team for the removal of such risks, see C–WP 11186 and C–DEC 156/7, C–DEC 158/1. See on this problem also Hailbronner, op. cit. (note 54), 1072.
62 Art. 38 Chicago Convention does not mention Recommended Practices whereas Art. 37 sent. 2 Chicago Convention mentions them. See also Buergenthal, op. cit. (note 42), 78.
63 See e.g., Annex 1: Personnel Licensing, Doc. AN 1; Matte, *Treatise on Air-Aeronautical Law* (note 19), 210 *et seq.*
64 PANS – ATM, ICAO Doc. 4444, 14th edn., Amendment 3; PANS – OPS, ICAO Doc. 8168, vol. I "Flight Procedures," 4th edn. Amendment 13; Vol. II "Construction of Visual and Instrument Flight Procedures," 4th edn. Amendment 13 (effective 25 November 2004); PANS – ABC, ICAO Abbreviations and Codes, ICAO Doc. 8400, 6th edn. Amendment 27.
65 "Regional Supplementary Procedures," ICAO Doc. 7030, Amendments 1–197; ICAO Doc. 7030/E/17 to 7030/E/28, Amendments 198–208; Resolution A36-13, Appendix J, "Formulation of Regional Plans, including Regional Supplementary Procedures," ICAO Doc. 9902 II-8; the latter was not reproduced in Resolution A37-15 (Provisional Edition, November 2010).
66 Rule 2.2.1, "Rules of Procedure for the Conduct of Air Navigation Meetings and Directives to Divisional-Type Air Navigation Meetings," ICAO Doc. 8143 (AN/873); "Preface to the *SUPPS*," ICAO Doc. 7030. PANS und SUPP are adopted by the Council by way of approval, which means that Art. 90 of the Convention is not applied. As regards the SUPP, the Preface to Doc. 7030 refers only to recommendations to the Member States.

SARPs, PANS and SUPPs have become essential tools for ICAO's planning processes, both on a global and regional basis, as well as for the planning processes of contracting States. They are amended as necessary to reflect changing requirements and techniques and thus, *inter alia*, to provide a sound basis for regional planning and the provision of facilities and services. ICAO seeks to provide a high degree of stability in order to enable contracting States to maintain stability in their national regulations. According to the respective provisions of ICAO Resolution A37-15, Appendix A, "amendments shall be limited to those significant to safety, regularity and efficiency, and editorial amendments shall be made only if essential."

2.9.3 Regional Plans under Article 69 of the Convention

Technical Legislation also includes *Regional Plans*, which define and delineate the tasks of Member States on a regional basis regarding flight information services, air navigation services, air traffic control and management, search and rescue and other services.[67] Regional Plans apply on a geographic basis, e.g., by establishing the geographic boundaries of so-called Flight Information Regions (FIRs) and defining the respective services to be provided therein, as well as the geographic position, width and height of international air routes. The maps used for the geographic definition are supplemented by extensive textual materials which further define, explain or clarify the extent and conditions of the provisions of the Regional Plan.

Regional Plans are prepared by Regional Conferences of ICAO Member States which belong to the respective Region and, upon unanimous adoption by the Regional Conference, are submitted to the ICAO Council.[68] If the Council approves a Regional Plan under Article 69 of the Convention, it may enter into force. Although such Council approval under Article 69 is technically only a recommendation, in practice it has prime importance, for several reasons. First, the Regional Plans of the various regions of the world require coordination. Second, the discussions and negotiations among Member States regarding the terms of Regional Plans give rise to differences and disputes from time to time, which can best be settled by the Council during discussions leading up to the approval of Regional Plans under Articles 69 and 54(n) of the Chicago Convention.[69] This serves to ensure that differences or disputes relating to Regional Plans will not escalate into formal legal disputes under Article 84 of the Convention. Third, over the last 50 years, there has developed a continuous and uniform practice among contracting States of seeking Council approval before giving effect to Regional Plans.

---

67 Resolution A36-13, Appendix J, "Formulation of Regional Plans, including Regional Supplementary Procedures," ICAO Doc. 9902 II-8; Appendix K, "Regional Air Navigation (RAN) Meetings"; Appendix L, "Implementation of Regional Plans." See the "Regional Plans: Africa-Indian Ocean Region," Doc. 7474; "Asia and Pacific Regions," Doc. 9673; "Caribbean and South American Regions," Doc. 8733; "European Region," Doc. 7754; "Middle East Region," Doc. 9708; "North Atlantic, North American and Pacific Regions," Doc. 8755; "North Atlantic Region," Doc. 9634. See also the "Facilities and Services Implementation Document (FASID): North Atlantic Region," Doc. 9635.

68 "Rules of Procedure for the Conduct of Air Navigation Meetings and Directives to Regional Air Navigation Meetings," ICAO Doc. 8144; Resolution A36-13 Appendix J, "Formulation of Regional Plans including Regional Supplementary Procedures," ICAO Doc. 9902 II-8, first Whereas and operative clause 3; see Buergenthal, op. cit. (note 42), 118.

69 Such differences or disputes arise particularly with respect to establishing FIRs and of air traffic services (ATS), e.g., in the case "Amendment to the common Nadi/Auckland oceanic FIR boundary," C-WP/11723, C-WP/11427, C-DEC 161/11, C-DEC 163/2 and 6, C-DEC 164/5. With respect to the procedure under Art. 54(n) Chicago Convention, see *infra* 2.12 and note 110; for the procedure under Art. 84 Chicago Convention, see *infra* 2.12 and note 104.

Due to Article 69 of the Convention, Regional Plans should be legally regarded as international executive agreements or administrative agreements among States[70] rather than Council decisions. In practice, this distinction may not be of great relevance because Council approval is generally regarded as a prerequisite for entry into force of a Regional Plan. The same applies with regard to amendments or modifications of Regional Plans.

2.10 Aviation safety and security audits

The continuous enhancement of *aviation safety*, which is the main purpose for which ICAO was established, remains the principal driver of the activities of the Organization. During the past 60 years, accident rates per aircraft movement and per passenger have continuously decreased, not least due to the work of ICAO. Taking into account accident rate statistics, civil aviation has become the safest mode of transport. Nevertheless, according to ICAO calculations, the continuous increase of air traffic and the resulting higher number of aircraft movements would, if accident rates remain constant, result in 2020 in one aircraft crash per week. It is therefore a matter of utmost importance to work towards further enhancements of aviation safety.

For this purpose, ICAO has developed a strategy making use of several elements, including the GASP[71] and the USOAP.[72] An important component is also the promotion and application of the Safety Management System (SMS)[73] concept with regard to national civil aviation administrations, commercial aircraft operators, airport operators and other entities. The SMS concept is intended to ensure that safety-relevant measures and procedures are systematically applied, implemented and documented at all levels by national civil aviation administrations, airlines and airports and that the responsibility for doing so is clearly defined and mandated from the top level down. The SMS concept has been incorporated into a new Annex 19, "Safety Management," setting forth SARPs for the application of the SMS concept.[74] Furthermore, in order to apply its aviation safety strategy also in the developing world which often lacks sufficient resources, ICAO makes use of technical cooperation projects to assist States.

Article 33 of the Convention requires contracting States to recognize as valid certificates of airworthiness and personnel licenses issued by another contracting State, provided that the requirements under which such documents were issued are equal to or above the minimum standards established under the Convention.[75] Article 37 requires each contracting State to

---

70 Resolution A36-13, Appendix M, "Delimitation of Air Traffic Services (ATS) Airspaces" speaks in clause 7 correctly of "regional air navigation agreements"; the delimitations covered by Appendix M are normally included in the applicable Regional Plans.

71 Resolution A33-16, "Global Aviation Safety Plan (GASP)," ICAO Doc. 9848, II-19. See Resolution A37-4, "ICAO Global Planning for Safety," Provisional Edition of the Final Resolutions of the 37th ICAO Assembly (November 2010); Resolution A36-7, "ICAO Global Planning for Safety and Efficiency," Doc. 9902.

72 See www.icao.int/safety/cmaforum/Pages/default.aspx, www.icao.int/safety/cmaforum/Pages/default.aspx and www.icao.int/safety/cmaforum/documents/flyer_us-letter_anb-usoap_2013- 08-30.pdf (accessed 9 June 2016), and Paul Stephen Dempsey, Public International Air Law, Chapter 3 (Montreal: McGill University, Institute and Centre for Research in Air & Space Law 2008).

73 See ICAO "Safety Management Manual," Doc. 9859, 3rd ed. 2013.

74 Annex 19, "Safety Management" was adopted by the ICAO Council during its 198th session in February 2013 and became applicable on 14 November 2013; see A38-WP/82; ICAO Doc. AN 19. The SMS concept had previously been made part of Annex 14, "Aerodromes" with effect from 2003 as a Standard for the Certification of aerodromes, see Annex 14, vol. I, "Aerodrome Design and Operations," Amendment 9, Doc. AN14-1/A/13.

75 See the wording of Art. 33 of the Convention. On Art. 33, see M.B. Jennison, "The Chicago Convention and Safety after 50 Years," XX *Ann ASL* (1995), Part I, 283 *et seq.*

collaborate in securing the highest practicable degree of uniformity in regulations and practices in all matters in which such uniformity will facilitate and improve air navigation. Article 38 requires contracting States which find it impracticable to comply in all respects with such standards or procedures to give immediate notification to ICAO of the differences.

In practice, however, these provisions were not always followed by contracting States. In those cases where States refrained from timely filing of differences under Article 38, neither the Organization nor other contracting States had any clear and objective information on the degree of implementation of the technical Annexes in the field. It was realized in the mid-1990s that this situation started to present a major safety issue.[76]

At its thirty-second Session in 1998, the Assembly established the USOAP,[77] as from January 1, 1999.

The USOAP comprises the following elements:[78]

- regular, mandatory, systematic and harmonized safety audits carried out by ICAO;
- is applied to all contracting States;
- transparency and disclosure of audit results to all Member States;
- a systematic reporting and monitoring mechanism on the implementation of safety-related standards and recommended practices.

In its *first phase* from 1999–2001, the scope of the programme was limited to audits relating to *Personnel Licensing, Operation of Aircraft* and *Airworthiness of Aircraft*.[79] The audits were performed on site by audit teams of ICAO, composed of experts from the Secretariat and from contracting States, in accordance with an administrative framework including a standard Memorandum of Understanding (MOU) and the ICAO *Safety Oversight Manual*.[80] In this phase, nearly 180 States were visited and audited.[81]

In the *second phase* from 2001–2004, follow-up audits were performed, and the focus shifted to the issue of how to resolve deficiencies identified by the USOAP and to encourage quality assurance for related technical cooperation projects.[82]

In the *third phase* from 2004–2007, the scope of audits was widened to all safety-related Annexes.[83] It was also decided to increase transparency, by making the essence of all final audit

---

76 See the DGCA Conference Report (1997), Doc. 9707; Assembly Resolution A29-13, "Improvement of Safety Oversight," ICAO Doc. 9790.
77 Assembly Resolution A32-11, "Establishment of an ICAO Universal Safety Oversight Audit Programme"; on this subject, see M. Milde, "Aviation Safety Oversight Audits and the Law," XXVI *AnnASL* (2001), 165 *et seq.*
78 DGCA Conference Report (1997), Doc. 9707; "ICAO Safety Oversight Audit Manual," ICAO Doc. 9735, AN/960.
79 The main purpose of limiting audits to these three Annexes was to provide a focused starting point. See DGCA Conference Report (1997) Doc. 9707; 2279th Report to Council by the President of the Air Navigation Commission, C-WP/10898 (16/06/98), p. 2.
80 ICAO Doc. 9734; on the Standard MOU, see: "Sample Memorandum of Understanding between (State) and ICAO Regarding Safety Oversight Audit," in: "ICAO Safety Oversight Audit Manual," ICAO Doc. 9735, AN/960.
81 See "Annual Report of the Council for 2001," Doc 9786; "Annual Report of the Council for 2002," Doc. 9814; "Annual Report of the Council for 2003," Doc. 9826, and Supplement.
82 Resolution A33-9, Clauses 1–9; the Assembly adopted at its 35th Session Resolution A35-7, "Unified Strategy to Resolve Safety-Related Deficiencies," supplementing A33-9.
83 Resolution A35-6, "Transition to a Comprehensive Systems Approach for Audits in the ICAO Universal Safety Oversight Audit Programme (USOAP)"; ICAO Doc. 9848, "Assembly Resolutions in Force (as of 8 October 2004)"; A35-6 superseded A33-8.

reports available to all contracting States, including audit findings and recommendations, the audited States' Corrective Action Plan and its comments.[84] Furthermore, access is provided for all contracting States to the Audit Findings and Differences Database (AFDD) maintained by ICAO.[85]

In the *fourth phase* from 2010–present, the programme transited to the "continuous monitoring approach" (CMA), replacing on-site audits and visits to the largest degree by a continuous data exchange between the Member States and ICAO relating to the implementation of safety-related SARPs.[86]

2.10.1 Universal Aviation Security Audit Programme

Following the events of September 11, 2001, a High-level, Ministerial Conference on Aviation Security held in February 2002 recommended adopting an ICAO Aviation Security Plan of Action[87] including *inter alia* the establishment of an Aviation Security Audit Programme. It called for the establishment of a comprehensive programme of regular, mandatory, systematic and harmonized aviation security audits to be carried out by ICAO in all contracting States.[88]

The ICAO Aviation Security Plan of Action was adopted accordingly by the Council in June 2002, including the ICAO USAP.[89] The USAP was launched in November 2002.

The audit programme comprises the following elements:[90]

- regular, mandatory, systematic and harmonized aviation security audits of all ICAO contracting States;
- audits conducted at both national and airport levels;
- evaluation of States' aviation security oversight capabilities;
- evaluation of the actual security measures in place at selected key airports;
- audits to be carried out on the basis of a bilateral MOU signed between each contracting State and ICAO; and
- coordination with security-related audit programmes at regional and sub-regional level.

The methodology for the USAP is similar to that used for the USOAP, including the audit visit, the drafting of a preliminary report and the drafting of a final report, including the Action Plan formulated by the audited State.[91] The USAP, initially financed from voluntary contributions

---

84 See Clause 7 of A35-6.
85 Ibid. (note 83).
86 Assembly Resolution A37-5, "The Universal Safety Oversight Audit Programme (USOAP) Continuous Monitoring Approach" in: "Resolutions adopted at the 37th session of the Assembly," (Provisional Edition), November 2010.
87 "High-level, Ministerial Conference on Aviation Security, 19–20 February 2002, Report." For the Declaration issued, XXVI *Ann ASL* (2001), 441.
88 Assembly Resolution A35-9, Appendix E, "The ICAO Universal Security Audit Programme," Operative Clause 1.
89 Council 166th Session (June 2002). See A. Kotaite, "Aviation Safety and Security: Two Sides of the Same Coin," Keynote Address to the Aviation Study Group at Linacre College, Oxford University, 27 June 2003, pp. 2–3.
90 Assembly Resolution A35-9 Appendix E, Operative Clauses 1–4.
91 Kotaite, op. cit. (note 89), 2 *et seq.* However, it was considered not sufficient to audit only the security oversight arrangements in Member States, but also to include installations and equipment *in situ*, namely at the major airports in each Member State. See L. Weber, "Convention on International Civil Aviation: 60 Years," 53 *ZLW* (2004), 289 *et seq.*, 307.

from States[92] following the High-level, Ministerial Conference, was later progressively integrated into the Regular Programme budget of ICAO. An *ICAO Security Audit Reference Manual*[93] was issued in April 2004, setting forth the elements, methodology and procedures for the conduct of the programme. On the basis of the audits, ICAO has developed a comprehensive database of findings, which assists in addressing deficiencies.

Combating *acts of unlawful interference*, and in particular terrorist acts, is another important challenge. In response to the events of September 11, 2001, the ICAO Council adopted an ICAO Aviation Security Plan of Action[94] in 2002, including *inter alia*, the establishment of the USAP.[95] Launched in November 2002, it provides for a comprehensive programme of regular, mandatory, systematic and harmonized aviation security audits to be carried out by ICAO in all contracting States. The audit programme comprises audits conducted both at national and at airports levels, an evaluation of compliance with Annex 17, "Security," and in particular States' aviation security oversight capabilities, and an evaluation of the actual security measures in place at selected key airports. In addition, the Organization, on the advice of its Aviation Security Panel, has repeatedly adjusted security screening procedures in light of changes in threat assessments. All of these measures contribute to a further reduction in the number of acts of unlawful interference and in particular of terrorist attacks on civil aviation. The continuous enhancement of aviation security by applying systematic and strict measures of protection, in particular screening and access restrictions, to passengers, crew, baggage, cargo and also in relation to aircraft operators, is proving effective but inevitably results in delays and inconvenience. It will therefore be a challenge for ICAO to find ways to reduce the delays and inconvenience to the extent possible without compromising the effectiveness of security measures.

2.11 Law-making functions under the Convention: the role of diplomatic conferences in the creation of conventional air law

Like other UN Specialized Agencies, ICAO is responsible for the development and modernization of the rules of public international law applicable to its field. Under Article 49(k), in conjunction with Article 44 and the preamble of the Convention, the ICAO Assembly is primarily responsible to undertake this task.[96] Thus, the Assembly, during its first session in 1947, provided for the creation of the ICAO Legal Committee as a "permanent body of the Organization constituted by the Assembly."[97] The Legal Committee was tasked with giving legal advice to the Organization and its bodies as well as with the *development of international air law*. For purposes of this latter function, the Legal Committee submits its proposals and drafts to the Council.[98] The Council also submits

---

92 See Assembly Resolution A35-10, sixth Whereas clause, ICAO Doc. 9848.
93 ICAO Doc. 9807.
94 ICAO Council, 166th Session (June 2002), C-MIN 166/5.
95 Resolution A35-9. Appendix E, "The ICAO Universal Security Audit Program," ICAO Doc. 9848, VII-6. See now Resolution A37-17, "Consolidated Statement of Continuing ICAO Policies related to the Safeguarding of International Civil Aviation against Acts of Unlawful Interference," Appendix E, "The ICAO Universal Security Audit Program," in: "Provisional Edition of the Final Resolutions of the 37th ICAO Assembly" (November 2010).
96 See the "Repertory-Guide to the Convention on International Civil Aviation," 2nd ed. 1977, ICAO Doc. 8900/2; Art. 49 of the Convention.
97 Resolution A1-46, "Resolutions adopted by the First Assembly," ICAO Doc. 4411.
98 Legal Committee, "Constitution, Procedure for Approval of Draft Conventions, Rules of Procedure," Doc. 7669-LC/139/5.

proposals for the amendment of the Chicago Convention to the Assembly, which must approve them by two-thirds majority.[99]

In the case of other proposals and drafts, the Council may convene a Diplomatic Conference. According to the Rules of Procedure of Diplomatic Conferences convened under the auspices of ICAO,[100] the Conference will decide by a two-thirds majority on the proposals and drafts, including all proposals for textual amendments made before or during the Conference. After such approval, the Conference will formally adopt the text and open it for signature by Member States participating in the Conference. For its entry into force, the text will require ratification by at least the number of States stipulated in the Final Clauses of the adopted instrument. In this manner, since 1944 19 Protocols for the amendment of the Chicago Convention have been developed, of which four are not yet in force. 32 multilateral Conventions or Protocols for the modernization of international air law have been developed, of which six have not yet entered into force,[101] including four recently adopted Conventions and Protocols which are awaiting ratification. In most cases, the Conventions and Protocols developed under the auspices of ICAO have been ratified by a majority of the 191 ICAO Member States.

2.12 Judicial functions under the Convention

Under Chapter XVIII of the Convention, the Council is entrusted with certain *judicial functions* regarding disputes between contracting States;[102] such judicial functions of the Council are also foreseen in certain multilateral and bilateral agreements, in particular the International Air Services Transit Agreement, where the Council is entrusted with the judicial settlement of disputes between contracting States.[103]

Article 84 of the Convention provides that if any disagreement between two or more contracting States relating to the interpretation or application of the Convention and its Annexes cannot be settled by negotiation, the dispute shall, on the application of any State concerned, be decided by the Council. The *procedure* to be applied in hearing the dispute is established in the Rules of

---

99 See Art. 94(a) Chicago Convention; according to the practice in ICAO, the Assembly decides on a draft Protocol for the amendment of the Convention and after its adoption by the Assembly, the President of the Assembly and the Secretary General, in his capacity as Assembly Secretary, will sign it. The Protocol will then be certified, and certified copies will be sent to all Member States for ratification. It will enter into force once at least two-thirds of all Member States have ratified it, Art. 94(a) sent. 2 Chicago Convention, of the Convention. As regards the issue of Art. 94(a) Chicago Convention with regard to non-ratifying States, see Hailbronner, op. cit. (note 54), 1072; Buergenthal, op. cit. (note 42), 206 *et seq.* with further references.

100 See "Provisional Rules of Procedure for International Conferences on Air Law" (Model draft text used for Diplomatic Conferences convened under the auspices of ICAO, unnumbered). The Provisional Rules are submitted to a Diplomatic Conference at its first session for approval, along with the Provisional Agenda, and are usually approved and adopted without change, e.g., the Montreal Diplomatic Conference of May 1999, ICAO Doc. 9775, vol. II, DCW Doc. No. 2.

101 For the complete list of instruments in the Treaty Collection, see www.icao.int last accessed 22 February 2015.

102 See "Repertory-Guide to the Convention on International Civil Aviation," 2nd ed. 1977, ICAO Doc. 8900/2 concerning Art. 84; Buergenthal, op. cit. (note 42), 124 *et seq.*; Cheng, *The Law of International Air Transport*, op. cit. (note 19), 100 *et seq.*; Erler, op. cit. (note 48), 185 *et seq.*; Matte, *Treatise on Air-Aeronautical Law* (note 19), 205 *et seq.* with further references.

103 See Art. 66 Chicago Convention in conjunction with the "International Air Services Transit Agreement," 84 UNTS 389.

Procedure for the Settlement of Differences (ICAO Doc. 7782/2).[104] Under these Rules of Procedure, the Council functions as a judicial body; it may decide on the basis of written submissions of the parties (memorials and counter-memorials), and hold oral hearings. Before rendering a decision, it shall attempt to effect a settlement between the Parties through direct negotiations or conciliation. For this purpose, the Council may appoint a Conciliator. Only if these attempts fail, shall the Council follow through with the procedure and render a judgment.

In accordance with Article 84 of the Convention, any such decision of the Council may be *appealed*, either to the International Court of Justice (ICJ) or, if one of the parties does not recognize the jurisdiction of the ICJ, to an adhoc Arbitral Tribunal.[105] In case of lack of agreement on an adhoc Arbitral Tribunal, a special arbitral tribunal set up under Article 85 of the Convention will hear the appeal. The decision given on appeal shall be final and binding.

Applying these provisions, the Council to date has handled five *disputes* under Chapter XVIII[106] three of which were settled by direct negotiations between the Parties induced by the Council and two others were resolved through conciliation by the good offices of the President of the Council. In none of these cases was a formal Council decision on the merits necessary. However, in one case (*U.S.* v. *15 Member States of the EU*) a formal Council decision involving a vote was taken on procedural objections of one of the Parties. The five disputes were the following:

1 *India* v. *Pakistan* (1952), regarding the legality of a prohibited zone established by Pakistan under Articles 5, 6 and 9 of the Convention. The dispute was settled through direct negotiations between the parties induced by the Council.[107]

2 *UK* v. *Spain* (1967), regarding the legality of a prohibited zone established by Spain in the vicinity of Gibraltar airport under Article 9(a) of the Convention. The dispute was deferred *sine die* and subsequently settled by direct negotiation.[108]

3 *Pakistan* v. *India* (1971), regarding the suspension of flights of Pakistani aircraft over Indian territory, based on Article 5 of the Convention. India submitted preliminary objections against the jurisdiction of the Council, which were rejected by the Council.[109] India then

---

104 ICAO Doc. 7782, 2nd ed. 1975 (reprint 2000).

105 As confirmed by the ICJ in its decision in *Pakistan* v. *India, Appeal Relating to the Jurisdiction of the ICAO Council, Order of 19 January 1972*, ICJ Rep 1972, 3 (1971), appeal may be lodged in Art. 84 Chicago Convention disputes not only against decisions of the Council in the main matter, but also against decisions on preliminary objections.

106 *India* v. *Pakistan* (1952), ICAO Doc. 7367 and 7361 (C/858), 15 *et seq.*; *UK* v. *Spain* (1967), ICAO Doc. 8724, 116 *et seq.*, A16-P/3; *Pakistan* v. *India* (1971), ICAO Doc. 8985 C/1002, 47 ff.; Docs. 8986 and 8987; *Cuba* v. *United States* (1996), C-WP/10864 (Restricted); C-DEC 154/16; 149/7, 150/17, 152/14 and 153/14; *United States* v. *Fifteen Member States of the European Union* (2000), C-WP/12075, C-DEC 170/16; C-DEC 161/6, 166/12, 169/11.

107 The "Rules for the Settlement of Differences," ICAO Doc. 7782 provide *inter alia* that the Council may propose to the parties to the dispute further direct negotiations before it will hear the matter. It may for this purpose appoint a conciliator who shall facilitate the direct negotiations to the extent possible, see Arts. 14 *et seq.* of the "Rules for the Settlement of Differences." In the practice of the Council, a conciliator has been appointed in a number of cases, in particular in *Cuba* v. *United States* (1996) and in *United States* v. *Fifteen Member States of the European Union* (2000).

108 See *UK* v. *Spain* (1967), ICAO Doc. 8724, 116 *et seq.*, A16–P/3.

109 In the case *Pakistan* v. *India (1971)* a decision was made by the Council on the Preliminary Objections of India. Similarly, in *United States* v. *Fifteen Member States of the European Union* (2000) a decision was made by the Council on the Preliminary Objections of the 15 Member States of the EU, see the references *supra* note 106, *in fine*.

appealed to the ICJ, which confirmed the Council's decision. The Parties thereafter jointly suspended the proceedings before the Council and settled the dispute through direct negotiations.

4   *Cuba* v. *United States* (1996), regarding the denial by the US of overflight rights for Cuban aircraft for scheduled flights between Cuba and Canada. The Council, after hearing the parties' submissions, appointed its President as Conciliator. As a result of the conciliation, the parties reached a settlement which was formally registered with the Council, and provided for overflight rights for Cuban aircraft over US territory, subject to certain restrictions.

5   *United States* v. *15 Member States of the European Union* (2000), regarding the legality of the so-called "hushkit" Regulation of the European Union (EU) under the Convention and related provisions. The 15 EU Member States submitted preliminary objections to the jurisdiction of the Council, which were rejected by the Council. After hearing the parties on the substance, the Council appointed its President as Conciliator. As a result of the conciliation process, the EU repealed the "hushkit" Regulation and replaced it with an EC Council Directive acceptable to all the parties, including the United States. The case was thereupon settled between the parties and the settlement was formally registered with the Council.

The *judicial functions* should be distinguished from *quasi-judicial functions* under Article 54(n) of the Convention. Under this Article, the Council "shall consider any matter relating to the Convention which any Contracting State refers to it." From time to time, Member States make written submissions to the Council, in which they complain about one or more other Member State(s), and request the Council to settle the dispute or difference. Unless such complaints are made expressly under Article 84 and follow the formalities of the "Rules for the Settlement of Differences," such complaints are usually handled as referrals under Article 54(n).[110] This means, *inter alia*, that the Rules of Procedure for the Council instead of the Rules for the Settlement of Differences apply.[111] Consequently, the Council will hear such cases in a *quasi-judicial capacity*, but without the procedures and legal formalities foreseen in the Rules for the Settlement of Differences. The Council will invite the parties to the complaint to be present in the Council and to make written and/or oral statements, and will then discuss the matter in the presence of the parties to the complaint. The Council may, as a result of the discussion, express views, make statements, issue recommendations or take decisions in the form of a Council Resolution as may be appropriate, under the Rules of Procedure for the Council. In this quasi-judicial capacity, the Council has handled *numerous complaints*, e.g., the *Republic of the Congo* v. *Rwanda and Uganda* (State hijacking of civil aircraft and other matters), *PLO* v. *Israel* (destruction of Gaza Airport), *Cuba* v. *U.S.* (violation of Cuban airspace), *Samoa and Tonga* v. *Fiji* (amendment to the common Nadi/Auckland oceanic FIR boundary) and other cases. The settlement of disputes under Article 54(n) will often have the advantage of greater flexibility as well as lesser publicity for the parties to the dispute.

---

110 See "Repertory-Guide to the Convention on International Civil Aviation," 2nd ed. 1977, ICAO Doc. 8900/2 concerning Art. 54(n); for a practical example, see the case *Republic of the Congo* v. *Rwanda and Uganda*, Council – 155th Session, C-DEC 155/1; 156th Session, C-DEC 156/10; C-MIN 156/10; Memorandum AK/639; Council Declaration adopted on 10 March 1999.

111 "Rules of Procedure for the Council," ICAO Doc. 7559/7.

2.13 The role of supranational organizations and non-governmental organizations in ICAO

In accordance with Articles 92–94 of the Convention, only sovereign States may become parties to the Convention and members of ICAO. International organizations may be invited as observers to the Assembly, the Council and other bodies of ICAO, but are excluded from membership.

This subject came up as a result of the desire of the European Community (EC, since 2009 the EU) to become a member of ICAO in 2003. As the EU Member States have transferred part of their sovereign functions and powers in civil aviation matters to the EU,[112] the question arose whether the EU may become a member alongside the EU Member States and participate in the work and decision-making of ICAO with respect to those subject matters for which the EU has responsibility. In view of Articles 92 to 94 and the structure of the Convention, this is not possible *de lege lata*.[113] An amendment to the Convention to permit such membership of "Regional Economic Integration Organizations" (REIOs)[114] would be theoretically possible under Article 94 of the Convention; however, as such an amendment could not enter into force unless ratified by two-thirds of all members (Article 94(a)), i.e., 128 out of 191 States, such amendment and ratification process may take 15 to 20 years. As a result, it has been regarded as preferable on the part of the EU not to seek membership in ICAO for the time being, but to participate in ICAO's work through a resident observer.[115]

ICAO maintains a close working relationship with a number of non-governmental organizations on the basis of Assembly Resolution A1-11.[116] The following should be mentioned:

- International Air Transport Association (IATA),[117] the trade association of more than 280 scheduled international airlines, headquartered at Montreal;
- Airports Council International (ACI),[118] the international body of national airport associations, headquartered at Montreal;
- Civil Air Navigation Services Organisation (CANSO), the international body of national air navigation services providers with more than 165 full and associated members, headquartered at Hoofddorp near Amsterdam, the Netherlands;
- International Federation of Airline Pilots' Associations (IFALPA),[119] the world federation of national pilots' associations, headquartered at Chertsey (Surrey, UK), with an observer delegation office at Montreal;

---

112 L. Weber, "Convention on International Civil Aviation: 60 Years," 53 *ZLW* Vol. 53 (2004), 289 *et seq.*, 308; W. Schwenk and E. Giemulla, *Handbuch des Luftverkehrsrechts*, 3rd ed. (Heymanns Verlag: Köln 2005), 100.

113 Weber, op. cit. (note 112), 308, with further references.

114 The term "Regional Economic Integration Organization" was used in the Montreal Convention of 1999 (ICAO Doc. 9740), Art. 53 paragraph 2 and in the Capetown Convention of 2001 (Convention on International Interests in Mobile Equipment), ICAO Doc. 9793, Art. 48, in order to allow the EC to sign and ratify these international instruments.

115 Weber, op. cit. (note 112), 309.

116 ICAO Doc. 9848, Assembly Resolutions in force (as of 8 October 2004).

117 See A.D. Groenewege, *Compendium of International Civil Aviation*, 3rd ed. (IADC: Montreal 2003), 219 *et seq.*; L. Weber, "International Organizations, Section 2: International Air Transport Association," in: E.M. Giemulla and L. Weber (eds.), *International and EU Aviation Law* (Kluwer: Alphen aan den Rijn 2011), 75 *et seq.*, 112 *et seq.*

118 Groenewege, ibid. (note 117), 251 *et seq.*

119 Ibid., 324 *et seq.*

- International Federation of Airline Traffic Controllers' Associations (IFATCA),[120] the world federation of national air traffic controllers' associations, headquartered at Montreal;
- International Council of Aircraft Owner and Pilot Associations (IAOPA),[121] the world federation of national aircraft owner and pilot associations, headquartered near Washington, DC;
- International Chamber of Commerce (ICC),[122] the world body of the national chambers of commerce, headquartered at Paris;
- International Business Aviation Council (IBAC),[123] the federation of national business aviation associations, headquartered at Montreal.

Many of these organizations participate in ICAO meetings as observers, receive relevant ICAO documentation and exchange information with ICAO. In some cases, such as IATA and IFALPA, they participate in ICAO's work on a day-to day basis, in line with ICAO's policies in Assembly Resolution A1-11.

2.14 Special legal problems under the Convention

Under Article 3(a) of the Convention, the Convention shall be applicable only to civil aircraft. The question whether and to what extent the Convention and its Annexes may in certain cases also apply to State aircraft (in particular to military aircraft) is unresolved. Some States prefer a restrictive interpretation of Article 3(a) and take the view that the Convention and its Annexes do not apply at all to State aircraft, in particular military aircraft. Other States agree to the view based on Article 3(d) that it may apply to the extent that this is imperative to ensure the safety of civil aircraft and their passengers and crew.

In line with the latter view, it was decided in 1984 by the Assembly to insert Article 3 *bis* into the Convention, providing that States must refrain from the use of force against civil aircraft in flight, and that in case of interception the lives of persons on board and the safety of aircraft must not be endangered. The provision entered into force in October 1998. Furthermore, more precise rules were inserted into Annex 2, "Rules of the Air," Chapter 3, regarding interception of aircraft in order to avoid inadvertent errors during such interception procedures.[124]

As the shoot-down of Malaysian Airlines flight MH017 over eastern Ukraine on 17 July 2014 with the loss of 283 passengers and 15 crew demonstrated,[125] these new rules have not been sufficient to prevent the use of force against civil aircraft in a conflict zone. Preliminary findings pointed towards a shoot-down by a ground-to-air missile. While it is for the territorial State to declare a prohibited zone for reasons of military necessity or public safety under Article 9(a) of the Chicago Convention, or temporarily to restrict or prohibit flying over part or the whole of its territory in exceptional circumstances or a period of emergency or in the interest of public safety under Article 9(b) of the Convention, experience has shown that the airspace over many conflict zones remains open as usual. It has in these cases been left to the risk assessment of each air carrier flying on the route to decide whether to maintain the service.

---

120 Ibid., 325 *et seq.*
121 Ibid., 321 *et seq.*
122 Ibid., 318 *et seq.*
123 Ibid., 315 *et seq.*
124 See above, paragraph 2.3 with further references.
125 See UN Security Council Resolution 2166 (2014); Final Report of the Dutch Safety Board (DSB) dated 13 October 2015.

In response, ICAO established a Task Force on Risks to Civil Aviation arising from Conflict Zones (TF-RCZ) in coordination with IATA, ACI and CANSO[126] which developed recommendations and procedures for guidance to both airlines and States, including development and use of a centralized information sharing system.[127] Centralized information sharing is considered to be critical to improved conflict zone risk mitigation moving forward.

2.15 Summary and conclusions

The Chicago Convention has played a major role as "Magna Carta" for the development of international civil aviation since 1944. It has provided an international legal framework which has supported the exponential growth of the international air transport system in the last seven decades. The Annexes to the Convention, their continuous enhancement and updating by the ICAO Council with the support of the ICAO Air Navigation Commission and the Secretariat, and the audit of their implementation through ICAO USOAP audits have been essential elements for the safety, security, continuity and economic viability of the entire air transport system. While questions of economic regulation, often connected to political and commercial considerations, have been largely left to bilateral agreements, the multilateral focus on aviation safety, aviation security, environmental sustainability and related action have contributed to the successful role of the Convention.

---

126 ICAO News Release dated 28 October 2014, "ICAO Council Adopts Unanimous Resolution Condemning MH17 Downing"; for the Resolution adopted by the ICAO Council, see C-DEC 203/1, Attachment.
127 Report of the Task Force on Risks to Civil Aviation Arising from Conflict Zones (TF RCZ), Appendix A of C-WP/14220; see also C-WP/14223 (Draft Resolution of the Council), C-WP/14220 and C-WP/14227; C-DEC 203/1; ICAO News Release, Montréal, 19 October 2015, "ICAO Clarifies International Conflict Zone Guidance," www.icao.int/Newsroom/Pages/ICAO-Clarifies-International-Conflict-Zone-Guidance.aspx, accessed 4 November 2015.

3

International safety requirements

Jimena Blumenkron

Introduction

Article 37 of the Convention empowers the International Civil Aviation Organization (ICAO) to adopt international Standards and Recommended Practices (SARPs) which are contained in 19 Annexes to the Chicago Convention. While they are not specifically defined in the Convention, the First ICAO Assembly provided definitions for both terms in each Annex, which are as follows (emphasis added):

> "Standard" means any specification for physical characteristics, configuration, materiel, performance, personnel, or procedure, the uniform application of *which is recognized as necessary* for the safety or regularity of international air navigation and to which Member States will conform in accordance with the Convention; in the event of impossibility of compliance, notification to the Council is compulsory under Article 38 of the Convention.

> "Recommended practices" means any specification for physical characteristics, configuration, materiel, performance, personnel, or procedure, the uniform application of *which is recognized as desirable* in the interest of safety, regularity, or efficiency of international air navigation, and to which Member States will endeavour to conform in accordance with the Convention.

Because of the technical complexity, SARPs are formulated in broad terms and restricted to essential requirements. Detailed technical specifications are expanded in manuals called Procedures for Air Navigation Services (PANs), Regional Supplementary Procedures (SUPPs), Guidance Material and Circulars. These documents are amended periodically to reflect current practices and procedures. Differences to SARPs notified by Member States are also part of the Annexes and are published in Supplements and in the Aeronautical Information Service.

This international soft-law system facilitates the effective conduct of international air transportation, as supported by workforces of experts nominated by ICAO Member States to ensure that air transportation continues to be safe, secure, efficient and sustainable.

This chapter will analyse the following provisions related to the safe operation of aircraft engaged in international air transport: licensing of aeronautical personnel (Annex 1); aircraft operations (Annex 6) including the carriage of dangerous goods by air (Annex 18); aircraft design, manufacture, maintenance (Annex 8) and identification (Annex 7); aircraft search and rescue (Annex 12); the investigation of aircraft accidents and incidents (Annex 13) as well as safety management (Annex 19).

3.1 Personnel licensing

Although human beings are vital to the chain of aircraft operations, they are also the most flexible and variable link. Proper training is key to minimize human error and provide able, skilful, proficient and competent technical personnel. Medical standards of Annex 1, such as periodic health examinations, serve as an early warning for possible incapacitating medical conditions, and contribute to the general health of this type of aviation-related personnel. Annex 1 and associated training manuals describe the skills necessary to build proficiency at various technical personnel jobs, thereby contributing to occupational competency. Personnel training and licensing compliant with international requirements also inspire confidence among States, leading to international recognition and acceptance of technical personnel qualifications and licences.

These requirements are applicable to all applicants for and, on renewal, to all holders of the licences and ratings specified therein. In the case of amendments affecting existing licensing specifications, Member States have the discretion to re-examine licence holders' knowledge, experience and proficiency.[1]

Related training manuals provide guidance as to the scope and depth of training curricula to ensure Annex 1 requirements are maintained, while also providing training guidance for other aviation personnel to whom the provisions of Annex 1 do not apply, such as aerodrome emergency crews, flight operations officers, radio operators and individuals involved in other related disciplines.

3.1.1 Definitions and general rules concerning licences: validity, approved training, language requirements and specifications

Training and licensing are together critical for the achievement of overall competency. Annex 1 stipulates that a person can only act as a flight crew member of an aircraft if that individual holds a *valid licence* in compliance with the relevant specifications of Annex 1 and appropriate to the duties to be performed.[2]

For harmonization purposes, licences must be in English or include an English translation and contain minimum detailed requirements to determine easily the privileges and validity of ratings.[3] Licences are usually issued by the State of Registry of an aircraft, or by any other State and rendered valid by the State of Registry of that aircraft.[4] In the case when a State renders valid a licence issued by another State, the validity of such licence must be established by suitable authorizations carried out by the licence holder equivalent to those established by the original licensing State or the licence must be limited to specific privileges. When issuing licences, States must ensure that other States are enabled to be satisfied as to the validity of the licence.[5] This objective is achieved through various means of demonstrating pilot proficiency and skill, such

---

1 Application of the PEL Standards, Annex 1, at (vii).

2 See Annex 1, Standard 1.2.1.

3 For a complete list of licence requirements see ibid., *supra* note 2§ Standards 5.1.1 and 5.1.2.

4 Although the Chicago Convention allocates to the State of Registry certain functions, including the issuance of licences, there are circumstances in which the State of Registry may be unable to fulfil its responsibilities adequately in instances where aircraft are leased, chartered or interchanged by an operator of another State. Article 83 *bis* of the Chicago Convention establishes agreements for the transfer of certain oversight responsibilities from the State of Registry to the State of the Operator, subject to acceptance by the latter State. Guidance of the Implementation of Article 83 *bis* is provided in ICAO Cir. 295.

5 Annex 1, *supra* note 2§ Standard 1.2.5.1.2.

as flight checks or simulation training of flight crew members engaged in commercial air transport operations.

The validity of the authorization should not extend beyond the period of validity of the licence and ceases if the licence is revoked or suspended.[6] For licences used in commercial air transport operations, the Licensing Authority is required to confirm the validity of other licences before authorization is issued.[7]

To ensure effective communication skills of operational personnel, language proficiency requirements mandate aircraft pilots, air traffic controllers, aeronautical station operators and flight navigators to demonstrate proficiency in either the language normally used for radiotelephony communications by the station on the ground or in English,[8] as established by certain holistic descriptors[9] in Level 4 of the ICAO Language Proficiency Rating Scale.[10] Unless operational personnel demonstrate competencies at an Expert Level 6, they must be re-evaluated every three (Operational Level 4) or six years (Extended Level 5).[11]

3.1.2 Licences and ratings for pilots

Any person acting as a pilot-in-command or as co-pilot of an aircraft, i.e. aeroplane, airship, free balloon, glider, helicopter or powered-lift, must hold a pilot licence issued in accordance with Annex 1. Each licence specifies the category of aircraft or endorses the ratings its holder can operate, among other requirements.[12] Licences also specify different classes or type ratings.[13] For the issuance of type ratings, applicants are expected to gain supervised experience in the applicable type of aircraft and/or flight simulator in normal, abnormal and emergency flight procedures and manoeuvres during all phases of flight; instrument procedures and, for an aeroplane category type rating, upset prevention and recovery training.[14] Pilots-in-command or co-pilots may also acquire an instrument flight rules (IFR) rating as well.[15] Likewise, an individual may only provide flight training or instruction if authorized to do so through a "flight instructor rating".[16]

There are nine specific types of aviator licences subject to the requirements specified in Annex 1: Student Pilot Licence, Private Pilot Licence, Commercial Pilot Licence, Multi-crew Pilot Licence appropriate to the aeroplane category, Airline Transport Pilot Licence, instrument rating, flight instructor rating appropriate to aeroplanes, airships, helicopters and powered-lifts, Glider Pilot Licence and Free Balloon Pilot Licence.

---

6 Ibid., *supra* note 2§ Standard 1.2.2.1.
7 Ibid., *supra* note 2§ Standard 1.2.2.2.
8 Ibid., *supra* note 2§ Standards 1.2.9.1, 1.2.9.3 and 1.2.9.4.
9 The holistic descriptor contained in Annex 1, Attachment 1, calls for operational personnel to communicate effectively in voice-only and in face-to-face situations on common, concrete and work-related topics; appropriately exchange messages as well as recognize and resolve communication misunderstandings; and handle linguistic challenges presented by an unexpected turn of events in a routine work situation.
10 Annex 1, Attachment A includes details on the six expert, extended and operational ICAO language proficiency levels.
11 Annex 1, *supra* note 2§ Standard 1.2.9.5 and Recommended Practice 1.2.9.6.
12 Ibid., *supra* note 2§ Standards 2.1.1.1, 2.1.1.2, 2.1.1.2.1 and 2.1.1.3.
13 Ibid., *supra* note 2§ Standards 2.1.3.1 and 2.1.3.2.
14 Ibid., *supra* note 2§ Standard 2.1.5.2.
15 Ibid., *supra* note 2§ Standard 2.1.7.
16 Ibid., *supra* note 2§ Standards 2.1.8.1 and 2.1.8.2.

3.1.2.1 Student pilot

A person willing to become a pilot cannot constitute a hazard to air navigation. Thus, student pilots usually may not be less than 16 years old[17] and are precluded from flying solo unless under the supervision of a flight instructor. Student pilots are also prohibited from flying solo on an international flight. Student pilots are required to hold a Class 2 Medical Assessment.[18]

3.1.2.2 Private Pilot Licence (PPL)

Potential holders of a PPL must be not less than 17 years old.[19] A PPL holder is prohibited from earning revenue when acting as pilot-in-command or co-pilot of aircraft.[20] PPL holders must also demonstrate a number of skills and acquired knowledge for the Licensing Authority to issue a licence for the relevant aircraft category.[21]

Besides knowledge requirements, applicants are also expected to demonstrate the ability to perform specific procedures and manoeuvres with the degree of competency appropriate for a PPL holder for the relevant category of aircraft.[22]

Annex 1 details the experience and flight instructions requirements for the issuance of aeroplane, helicopter, powered-lift and airship category ratings:[23]

- For an *aeroplane* category rating, experience includes flight at critically slow/high airspeeds, recognition and recovery stalls/spiral dives, normal and crosswind take-offs and landings, flight by reference, emergency operations and operations in transiting controlled aerodromes.
- Flight skills for a *helicopter* category rating include helicopter inspection and servicing, aerodrome and traffic pattern operations, control of the helicopter by external visual reference, recovery techniques, ground manoeuvring, hovering, take-offs and landings in normal, out of wind, sloping ground, with minimum necessary power and maximum performance, quick stops, simulated helicopter equipment malfunctions and autorotative approach.
- *Powered-lift* operational requirements include experience in ground manoeuvring and run-ups, hover and rolling take-offs, climb-out, approach and landings in normal, out of wind and sloping ground, take-offs and landings with minimum necessary power and maximum performance, restricted site operations, quick stops, flight by reference solely to instruments, completion of a level 180° turn, recovery techniques and emergency operations.[24]
- For *airships*, applicants must receive dual instruction, including airship inspection and servicing, ground reference manoeuvres, aerodrome and traffic pattern operations, techniques

---

17 Although ICAO does not usually prescribe an age limit for student pilots, restrictions may vary from State to State and tend to coincide to 16 years old as the minimum age for aeroplane, airship, helicopter and powered-lift categories.
18 See Section 1.6 *infra* (citing Annex 1, *supra* note 2§ Standard 2.2.3).
19 Annex 1, *supra* note 2§ Standards 2.3.1 and 2.3.1.1.
20 Ibid., *supra* note 2§ Standard 2.3.2.1.
21 For a complete list of requisite information and acquired skills to obtain a PPL see Annex 1, *supra* note 2§ Standard 2.3.1.2.
22 For a complete list of minimum experience hours required to obtain a license for specific aircraft category holdings, see Annex 1, *supra* note 2§ Standards 2.3.3.1.1 and 2.3.3.1.2 (aeroplanes); Annex 1, *supra* note 2§ Standards 2.3.3.1.1 and 2.3.3.1.2 (helicopters); Annex 1, *supra* note 2§ Standards 2.3.4.1.1 and 2.3.3.1.2 (powered-lifts); Annex 1, *supra* note 2§ Standards 2.3.4.1.1, 2.3.4.1.2 and 2.3.4.2.1 (airships).
23 For details about the flight instruction in the mentioned aircraft, see Annex 1, *supra* note 2§ Standards and Recommended Practices 2.3.3.2, 2.3.4.2.1, 2.3.5.2 and 2.3.6.2.
24 Ibid., *supra* note 2§ Standard 2.3.5.2.

and procedures for take-off with obstacle clearance, landings and go-arounds, instrument-only flight, navigation, cross-country flying using visual reference, recognition of leaks and equipment malfunctions.[25]

3.1.2.3 Commercial Pilot Licence (CPL)

CPL applicants can only act as pilot-in-command or co-pilot of the appropriate aircraft category engaged in commercial air transport operations and must be at least 18 years old.[26] CPL candidates may only exercise IFR privileges after receiving relevant and specialized instruction,[27] and must demonstrate the requisite level of knowledge in several specific subjects in order to obtain a CPL.[28] CPL applicants can also demonstrate specific skills for the aircraft intended by pursuing dual flight instruction in additional category ratings.[29]

3.1.2.4 Multi-crew Pilot Licence (MPL)

Applicants to an MPL to aeroplane category must be at least 18 years old and capable of exercising the privileges of an instrument rating in a multi-crew operation while acting as co-pilot in an aeroplane operated as such.[30] MPL applicants are expected to demonstrate a level of knowledge equivalent to an applicant for an Airline Transport Pilot Licence (ATPL) appropriate to the aeroplane category,[31] and operate in a multi-crewed piloted environment, in addition to demonstrating knowledge and proficiency in several other advanced airmanship skills.[32]

3.1.2.5 Airline Transport Pilot Licence

Holders of an ATPL must be at least 21 years old and may perform as pilot-in-command of an aircraft in commercial air transportation operations with more than one pilot.[33] ATPL applicants are expected to demonstrate extensive knowledge appropriate to the category of aircraft to be operated and acquire the minimum flight hour requirement for that category.[34]

ATPL holders may also meet requirements for dual flight instruction in other categories of aircraft, and are expected to demonstrate skills as pilot-in-command of a multi-engine aeroplane.[35]

---

25 Ibid., *supra* note 2§ Standard 2.3.6.2.
26 Ibid., *supra* note 2§ Standards 2.4.1 and 2.4.1.1
27 Ibid., *supra* note 2§ Standard 2.4.2.1.
28 For a complete list of information and minimum experience hours required to acquire a CPL licence, see Annex 1, *supra* note 2§ Standard 2.4.1.2 and Annex 1, *supra* note 2§ Standards 2.4.3.1.1, 2.4.3.1.1.1 (aeroplanes); Annex 1, *supra* note 2§ Standards 2.4.4.1.1 and 2.4.4.1.1.1 (helicopters); Annex 1, *supra* note 2§ Recommend Practices 2.4.5.1.1 and 2.4.5.1.2. (powered-lifts); Annex 1, *supra* note 2§ Standards 2.4.6.1.1 and 2.4.6.1.1.1 (airships).
29 For additional information on dual flight instruction category ratings see Annex 1, *supra* note 2§ Standard 2.4.
30 Ibid., *supra* note 2§ Standard 2.5.2.1.
31 Ibid., *supra* note 2§ Standard 2.5.1.2.
32 For a complete list of information and minimum experience hours required to acquire an MPL licence see ibid., *supra* note 2§ Standards 2.5.2.3 and 2.5.3.1.
33 Ibid., *supra* note 2§ Standards 2.6.1.1 and 2.6.2.1.
34 For a complete list of information and minimum experience hours required to acquire an ATPL licence, see Annex 1, *supra* note 2§ Standard 2.6.1.2.1 and Annex 1, *supra* note 2§ Standards 2.6.3.1.1 and 2.6.3.1.1.1 (aeroplanes); Annex 1, *supra* note 2§ Standards 2.6.4.1.1 and 2.6.4.1.1.1 (helicopters); Annex 1, *supra* note 2§ Recommend Practices 2.6.5.1.1 and 2.6.5.1.2 (power-lifts).
35 Ibid., *supra* note 2§ Standards 2.6.1.3.1 and 2.6.1.3.1.1.

3.1.2.6 Instrument rating

An instrument flight rating is pursued by licence holders who intend to pilot a category of aircraft solely by reference to instruments and without external reference points, and may be obtained for aeroplane, airship, helicopter and powered-lift categories.[36] In order to qualify for an instrument rating, applicants should possess specific operational experience[37] and at least 40 total hours with 20 hours of ground time or 30 hours of ground time in the simulator.[38]

3.1.2.7 Flight instructor

A flight instructor rating allows its holder to supervise solo flights by student pilots and to carry out flight instruction to issue PPLs, CPLs, instruments and flight instructor ratings.[39]

Flight instructors must meet the CPL knowledge and must meet a number of teaching and operational requirements,[40] and must practise instruction in flight instructional techniques.[41]

3.1.2.8 Glider Pilot Licence (GPL)

GPL applicants must be at least 16 years old to act as pilot-in-command of a glider, provided the pilot has experience in the launching method being used.[42] A glider pilot must also possess the requisite operational knowledge required to fly a glider and have at least six hours of total flight time (ten hours if passengers are to be carried), two of which must be flying solo, with at least 20 launches and landings.[43]

3.1.2.9 Free Balloon Pilot Licence (FBPL)

FBPL applicants may act as pilot-in-command of free balloons using hot air or gas if they are at least 16 years old, demonstrate specific operational knowledge in a non-commercial free balloon operation and acquire 16 hours of flight time, which must include eight launches and landings, one of which must be done solo.[44]

3.1.3 Licences for other flight crew members

A flight crew member is a licensed person responsible for duties essential to the operation of an aircraft during a flight duty period, including flight navigators and flight engineers.[45]

Before the implementation of radio navigation aids, such as GPS, flight navigators were responsible for air navigation, although their function has been either downsized or replaced in

---

36 Ibid., *supra* note 2§, see definition of *Instrument Flight Time*, Standards 2.7.1 and 2.7.2.1.
37 For specific operation experience required to obtain an Instrument Rating, see ibid., *supra* note 2§ Standard 2.7.1.1.
38 Ibid., *supra* note 2§ Standards 2.7.3.1, 2.7.3.2, 2.7.4.1 and 2.7.4.2.
39 Ibid., *supra* note 2§ Standard 2.8.2.
40 For a complete list of requirements for certification as a Flight Instructor, see ibid., *supra* note 2§ Standard 2.8.1.1.
41 Ibid., *supra* note 2§ Standards 2.8.1.2 and 2.8.1.4.
42 Ibid., *supra* note 2§ Standards 2.9.1.1 and 2.9.2.1.
43 For a complete list of operational and flight time requirements for certification as a Glider Pilot, see ibid., *supra* note 2§ Standard 2.9.1.2.1 and Recommended Practice 2.9.1.2.2.
44 For a complete list of operational and flight time requirements for certification as a FBPL, see ibid., *supra* note 2§ Standard 2.10.1.2.1 and Recommended Practice 2.10.1.2.2.
45 Ibid., *supra* note 2§ definition of *Flight crew member*.

commercial operations by contemporary navigation aids and dual-licensed pilot-navigators. All requirements necessary to obtain a Flight Navigation Licence (FNL) are contained in Annex 1.[46]

Similar to flight navigators, the flight engineer position, designated to monitor and operate aircraft systems, vanishes upon the advent of technology onboard modern aircraft whereby complex systems monitored and adjusted by electronic microprocessors and computers. The requirements contained in Annex 1 includes the requirements that holders of a Flight Engineer Licence (FEL) must meet.

3.1.4 Licences and ratings for other operational personnel

Operational personnel other than flight crew members, such as aircraft maintenance technicians, engineers, mechanics, student air traffic controllers, air traffic controllers, flight operations officers, flight dispatchers and aeronautical station operators are also required to hold specific licences or ratings issued by the Licensing Authority to perform their functions.

3.1.4.1 Aircraft maintenance technician/engineer/mechanic (terms used interchangeably)

Aircraft maintenance mechanics should be not less than 18 years of age to apply for an Aircraft Maintenance Licence (AML). This licence allows its holders to certify aircraft or its parts as airworthy after an authorized repair, modification or installation of an engine, accessory, instrument and/or item of equipment as well as to sign the maintenance release.[47] AML applicants must demonstrate specific adequate knowledge with regards to aircraft maintenance,[48] and have a minimum of four years' experience.[49]

3.1.4.2 Air Traffic Controller Licence (ATCL)

Applicants for an ATCL should be at least 21 years old and not less than three months of service engaged in the control of air traffic under supervision to pursue an approved training course.[50] ATCL applicants must demonstrate specific knowledge with regards to the principles, rules and regulations related to air traffic management services.[51] An ATCL may acquire six different ratings,[52] each providing a specific privilege to be exercised. If they cease to exercise their ratings privileges for six months, the rating becomes invalid.[53] A complete listing of privileges associated with each type of air traffic controller rating and the experience needed for each is established in Annex 1.[54]

---

46 Ibid., *supra* note 2§ Standards 3.2.1.1 and 3.2.2.
47 Ibid., *supra* note 2§ Note and Standards 4.2.1.1 and 4.2.2.1.
48 For a complete list of licensing requirements for certification as an AML, see ibid., *supra* note 2§ Note and Standard 4.2.1.2.
49 For the complete AML experience time requirements, see ibid., *supra* note 2§ Standards 4.2.1.4, 4.2.1.5 and 4.2.1.3.
50 Ibid., *supra* note 2§ Standards 4.4.1.1, 4.4.1.3 and 4.3.1.
51 For a complete list of licensing requirements for ATCL certification, see ibid., *supra* note 2§ Standard 4.4.1.2.
52 Ibid., *supra* note 2§ Standard 4.5.1.
53 See ibid., *supra* note 2§ Standard 4.5.3.4.
54 Ibid., *supra* note 2§ Standards 4.5.2.1, 4.5.2.2.1, 4.5.2.3 and 4.5.3.1.

3.1.4.3 Flight operations officer/flight dispatcher and aeronautical station operator licences

Similarly, an individual must be at least 21 years old to apply for a Flight Dispatcher Licence (FDL). Flight dispatchers control and supervise flight operations by providing support, briefings or assistance to the pilot-in-command so as to ensure the safe conduct of the flight.[55] Alternatively, any person 18 years of age or older may apply for an Aeronautical Station Operator Licence (ASOL) to act as an operator in an aeronautical station with which he/she is familiar.[56]

3.1.5 Medical provisions for licensing

In order to determine whether licence applicants are fit to perform their proposed duties,[57] medical assessments are performed on each candidate and subject to various temporal limitations for validity.[58]

The validity of the medical assessments starts from the date of the examination and may be extended by the Licensing Authority or deferred if the holder operates in an area distant from examination facilities.[59] Validity periods may be reduced for medical reasons, such as in cases of crew members who are either over 40 years old and engaged in single-crew commercial operations, or those who are above 60 years old and engaged in multi-crew-pilot commercial operations.[60] Pilots who attain their sixtieth birthday cannot act as a pilot in international commercial air transport operations for operations with more than two pilots; and licence holders cannot act as pilots if they have attained their sixty-fifth birthday,[61] subject to specific rules on medical assessments.

Applicants must meet all medical requirements and are certified in three distinct classes. The general physical and mental examination is intended to test that the applicant is free from any abnormality, disability, disease, wound, injury or sequelae from operation, or effect or side-effect of medication taken that entails an incapacity likely to interfere with the safe performance of duties.[62] Operational personnel are prevented from performing their duties should there be a decrease in their physical fitness or if they are found to be under the influence of psychoactive substances that can hamper their abilities.[63] Detailed requirements to undergo Class 1, 2 and 3 medical assessments are contained in Annex 1.

3.2 Aircraft operations

The purpose of Annex 6 is to provide criteria for safe operating practices and to encourage States to facilitate passage of international aircraft over their territories by operating in conformity with these specific criteria in conformance to the safety, efficiency and regularity of international air navigation. In all phases of aircraft operations, ICAO SARPs are the minimum acceptable

---

55 Ibid., *supra* note 2§ Standards 4.6.1.1 and 4.6.2, and Annex 6 to the Chicago Convention "Aircraft Operations", 9th ed., Montréal, ICAO, July 2010 (Annex 6), SARPs in Section 4.6.
56 Annex 1, *supra* note 2§ Standards 4.7.1.1, 4.7.1.2 and 4.7.2.
57 Ibid., *supra* note 2§ Standard 1.2.5.1.
58 Ibid., *supra* note 2§ Standard 1.2.5.2.
59 Ibid., *supra* note 2§ Standards 1.2.4.3.1 and 1.2.5.2.6.
60 Ibid., *supra* note 2§ Standards 1.2.5.2.1, 1.2.5.2.2 and 1.2.5.2.3.
61 Ibid., *supra* note 2§ Standard 2.1.10.
62 Ibid., *supra* note 2§ Standard 6.2.2.
63 Ibid., *supra* note 2§ Standards 1.2.6.1 and 1.2.7.

compromise as they make commercial and general aviation viable without prejudicing safety. However, the implementation of ICAO standards does not preclude the development of national standards, which may be more stringent. These requirements cover aircraft operations and limitations, performance, communications and navigation equipment, maintenance, flight documents, responsibilities of flight personnel, security, flight instruments, navigation equipment, fuel consumption, environmental factors, operations of twin-engine aeroplanes operating over extended ranges (ETOPS), human factors, flight time limitations, flight duty and rest periods, among others.

In three parts, Annex 6 is applicable to: international commercial air transport operations (Part I), including scheduled and non-scheduled operations for remuneration or hire; international general aviation (Part II); and international commercial air transport operations and general aviation operations in helicopters (Part III).

3.2.1 Definitions, applicability and general considerations

Annex 6, Part I (hereafter Annex 6) is regularly updated and contains a number of functions States are expected to discharge. In cases where the State of Registry is unable to fulfil these responsibilities, Article 83 *bis* of the Chicago Convention allows the State of Registry to transfer its duties to the State of the Operator subject to acceptance by the State of Transfer.[64]

The Annex specifies that States, through the enactment of laws, regulations and procedures, are expected to ensure operators and operational personnel comply with the legal framework enacted, including requirements pertinent to the performance of operational personnel duties, those related to the airspace to be navigated, and to the aerodromes where the aircraft may take off or land. State operators are responsible for the operational control of their aircraft in all circumstances, until such responsibility is transferred to pilots-in-command and flight dispatchers upon aircraft operation.[65]

3.2.2 Flight operations

3.2.2.1 Operational certification and surveillance

An air operator requires a valid "Air Operator Certificate" (AOC) issued by the State of the Operator[66] to engage in commercial air transport.[67] The AOC indicates the authorized operations specifications (OPS Specs) and contains specific information as to the authorized operator. A true copy of the AOC and OPS Specs must be carried onboard each aircraft of the operator, along with an English translation if the documents are produced in another language.[68]

To obtain an AOC, an aircraft operator must demonstrate to the relevant aviation authority that it has adequate organization, method of control and supervision of its flight operations, and executes viable training programmes, ground handling and maintenance arrangements through

---

64 Registered States may be unable to fulfil their responsibilities under Annex 6 for a number of reasons, most usually if the aircraft is leased, chartered or interchanged by an operator of another State. See Chicago Convention, *supra* note 7§ Article 83 *bis*.

65 See Annex 6, *supra* note 96§ Standards 3.1.1, 3.1.2, 3.1.3 and 3.1.4.

66 The "State of Operator" is that in which the operator's principal place of business or permanent residence is located.

67 See Annex 6, *supra* note 96§ definition of *State of the Operator* and *Standards*, 4.2.1.1.

68 Ibid., *supra* note 96§ Standards 4.2.1.2, 4.2.1.5, 4.2.1.6 and 6.1.2 and Appendix 6.

a certification process. The validity of the AOC depends upon the operators' ability to maintain these requirements, which are supervised regularly.[69]

Because States usually recognize valid AOCs from foreign operators that meet the minimum safety-related standards adopted by ICAO, State surveille operators certified by its aviation authority and also foreign aircraft operators. Thus, foreign operators should meet the requirements of States where they conduct operations in addition to those requirements established by the aviation authority that issues its AOC.[70]

To obtain its AOC, the operator is required to provide an up-to-date *Operations Personnel Manual* to the aviation authority for review, acceptance and approval. The operations manual must contain four parts: (1) general, (2) aircraft operating information, (3) areas, routes and aerodromes and (4) training.[71]

3.2.2.2 Flight preparation

Ground facilities in aerodromes have the responsibility of safeguarding both aircraft operations and aircraft passengers, and may be reported to the authority responsible for such facilities should they fail to do so.[72]

Aircraft operators must ensure that passengers are familiarized with the location and use of seat belts, emergency exits, life jackets, oxygen dispensing equipment, emergency briefing cards and other emergency equipment. Passengers onboard are also required to use seat belts or harnesses during take-off, landing, turbulence or any emergency occurring during flight.[73] The pilot-in-command must complete flight preparation forms certifying the aircraft is airworthy.[74] These forms are kept for three months.[75] The operational flight plan includes alternate aerodromes for take-off while en route and destination alternate aerodromes are contained in air traffic services (ATS) flight plans.[76] An operational flight plan is completed for every flight which is approved and signed by the pilot-in-command and flight dispatcher – a copy of which is left with the operator or aerodrome authority.[77]

The flight crew is also responsible for verifying that the meteorological conditions are appropriate for the type of flight to be conducted (visual flight rules (VFR) vs instrument flight rules (IFR)),[78] and that the aircraft carries sufficient fuel to complete the planned flight safely and to allow for deviations.[79]

---

69 Ibid., *supra* note 96§ Standards 4.2.1.3 and 4.2.1.4.
70 Ibid., *supra* note 96§ Standards 4.2.2.1, 4.2.2.2 and 4.2.2.3.
71 Ibid., *supra* note 96§ Appendix 2. Detailed information on the content of each part of the personnel manual is also included in Annex 6.
72 Ibid., *supra* note 96§ Standard 4.2.11.1.
73 Ibid., *supra* note 96§ Standards 4.2.12.1, 4.2.12.2 and 4.2.12.4.
74 Airworthiness considerations include certification that the appropriate certificates are on board, relevant instruments and equipment are installed, a maintenance release has been issued, the aircraft mass and centre of gravity location are such that the flight can be conducted safely, the load carried is distributed and secured, and complete flight plans have been filed with the appropriate authorities.
75 See Annex 6, *supra* note 96§ Standards 4.3.1 and 4.3.2.
76 Ibid., *supra* note 96§ Standards 4.3.4.1, 4.3.4.2 and 4.3.4.3.1.
77 Ibid., *supra* note 96§ Standard 4.3.3.1.
78 Ibid., *supra* note 96§ Standards 4.3.5 and 4.3.9.1.
79 Ibid., *supra* note 96§ Standard 4.3.6.1. Fuel planning and fuel management are very sophisticated procedures at which aircraft operators look closely due to their economic impact. Safety and business considerations must be carefully balanced to ensure safety while promoting a lean cost for the airline. Specific and more detailed requirements on this topic are available in the Flight Planning and Fuel Management (FPFM) Manual (Doc. 9976).

3.2.2.3 In-flight procedures

During take-off and landing, all flight crew members are required to be at their stations with their safety harness/belts fastened. While en route, flight crew members must remain at their stations except when performing duties in connection with the operation of the aircraft or for physiological needs.

Each aircraft operating an international commercial flight has a pilot-in-command designated by the operator,[80] who is responsible for the safety of all crew members, passengers and cargo onboard from the time the doors of the aircraft are closed and it is ready to move for the purpose of taking-off until the moment it finally comes to rest at the end of the flight and the engine(s) are shut down.[81]

In certain operations, a flight dispatcher may be designated by the operator to brief and assist the pilot-in-command by providing relevant information assisting with the preparation and filing of ATS flight plans, and by offering support in emergencies.[82]

Aircraft are expected to abide by the instrument approach procedures approved and promulgated by States for instrument runways or aerodromes utilized for instrument flight operations.[83] The flight crew must ensure that the intended landing can be effected at the destination or alternate aerodrome using either VFR or IFR and that any diversion time to an en route alternate aerodrome can be operated safely.[84]

Annex 6 contains a section on fatigue management intended to ensure that flight and cabin crew members perform at an adequate level of alertness.[85] Hazardous flight conditions are also addressed regularly during in-flight operations. With the exception of meteorological conditions, such hazards are reported to appropriate authorities to ensure safety of other aircraft.[86]

3.2.3 Instruments, equipment and flight documents

Annex 8 contains minimum equipment requirements necessary for the issuance of a certificate of airworthiness. Annex 6 lists additional instruments, equipment and flight documents needed on aircraft engaged in international operations approved by the State of Registry.[87] Such items include the *operations manual*, the *flight manual* and charts to cover the route of the proposed or diverted flight.[88] The aircraft operating manual contains normal, abnormal and emergency procedures, and

---

80 Ibid., *supra* note 96§ Standards 4.2.6, 4.2.7.1, 4.2.7.2, 4.2.8.1 and 4.2.8.2.
81 The definitions of accident, serious incident and incident is contained in Annex 13 to the Chicago Convention and is part of Chapter X that specifies the requirements for aircraft accident and incident investigation.
82 Ibid., *supra* note 96§ Standards 4.6.1 and 4.6.2.
83 Ibid., *supra* note 96§ Standards 4.4.8.1 and 4.4.8.2.
84 Ibid., *supra* note 96§ SARPs 4.4.1.1 and all those contained in section 4.7.2 Requirements for extended diversion time operations (EDTO).
85 Such regulations enacted by the aviation authority should include flight time, flight duty period, duty period and rest period limitations which should be followed by operators, and may also include authorization of a Fatigue Risk Management System (FRMS) to introduce prescriptive fatigue management regulations based on approved risk assessments. See Annex 6, *supra* note 96§ Standards 4.10.1, 4.10.2, 4.10.3 and 4.10.4.
86 Ibid., *supra* note 96§ Standard 4.4.3.
87 Ibid., *supra* note 96§ Standard 6.1.1. For a complete list of mandatory manuals, logs and records kept by the operator pursuant to Annex 6, see ibid., *supra* note 96§ Standards 4.2.10, 8.4, 4.10.8, 4.3, 4.3.3.1, 8.7, 9.4.3.4, 11.1, 11.2, 11.3, 11.3.2, 11.4, 11.5 and 11.6.
88 Ibid., *supra* note 96§ Standard 6.2.3.

contains aircraft systems and checklists to be used,[89] including a minimum equipment list (MEL) which enables the pilot-in-command to determine whether a flight may be commenced or continued should any instrument, equipment or system become inoperative during the flight. A master minimum equipment list (MMEL) is also included and identifies items which individually may be unserviceable at the commencement of a flight.[90] Aeroplanes must also carry noise certification standards documents in English or a translated version.[91]

All aircraft are furnished with *instruments* that enable the flight crew to control its flight path, carry out procedural manoeuvres and observe its operating limitations, navigation and anti-collision lights, medical supplies, portable fire extinguishers, a seat with seatbelt for each person onboard, oxygen equipment, life jackets or flotation devices and spare electrical fuses.[92]

Flight recorders subject to strict crashworthiness and fire protection specifications are installed within an aircraft to provide maximum protection for flight recordings to ensure the recorded information is preserved and accessible should an accident occur. These recorders are subject to regular checks and evaluations.[93]

Aeroplanes should also carry a pressure-altitude reporting transponder and an *automatic emergency locator transmitter* (ELT) which is activated in the event of an accident or with a manual switch.[94] Most aeroplanes over 5,700 kg are equipped with a ground proximity *warning system* (GPWS) to provide a warning for the flight crew should the aeroplane become hazardously close to the ground.[95] Aeroplanes over 5,700 kg are also equipped with an *airborne collision avoidance system* (ACAS).[96]

When operating *over water*, landplanes must carry one life jacket or flotation device for each passenger, life-saving rafts in sufficient numbers to carry all persons on board, equipment for pyrotechnical distress signals and an underwater locating device able to operate for 30 days.[97] Seaplanes carry one life jacket or flotation device for each person on board, equipment for making the sound signals and one sea anchor. Aeroplanes travelling *over land areas designated as difficult for search and rescue activities* carry signalling devices and appropriate life-saving equipment,[98] which may include oxygen storage for aeroplanes conducting *high altitude flights*. Aeroplanes are also equipped with oxygen storage and a dangerous loss of pressurization warning device.[99] In *icy conditions*, aeroplanes are equipped with de-icing and/or anti-icing devices. *Pressurized aeroplanes* benefit from installation of weather radar to detect hazards, such as thunderstorms,[100] as well as a radiation indicator for those operating above 49,000 ft.[101] *Turbo-jet aeroplanes* may also be equipped with forward-looking wind shear warning systems and indications if automatic landing equipment limits are being reached.[102]

---

89 Ibid., *supra* note 96§ Standard 6.1.4.
90 Ibid., *supra* note 96§ Standard 6.1.3 Definitions of MEL and MMEL.
91 Ibid., *supra* note 96§ Standard 6.13.
92 Ibid., *supra* note 96§ Standards 6.1.3, 6.2.1 and 6.2.2.
93 Ibid., *supra* note 96§ Standards 6.3.4.1, 6.3.4.2 and 6.3.4.3.
94 Ibid., *supra* note 96§ SARPs 6.17.1, 6.17.2, 6.17.3 and 6.19.1.
95 Ibid., *supra* note 96§ Standards 6.15 and 6.15.7. For specific types of aircraft subject to this equipment, see SARPs 6.15.1–6.15.6.
96 Ibid., *supra* note 96§ Standard 6.18.1 and Recommended Practice 6.18.2.
97 Ibid., *supra* note 96§ Standards 6.5.2.1 and 6.5.3.1.
98 Ibid., *supra* note 96§ Standard 6.7.1.
99 Ibid., *supra* note 96§ Standards 6.5.1, 6.6 and 6.7.3.
100 Ibid., *supra* note 96§ Standards 6.8 and 6.11.
101 Ibid., *supra* note 96§ Standard 6.12.
102 Ibid., *supra* note 96§ Standard 6.21.1.

Aeroplanes are also provided with *radio communication equipment* capable of conducting two-way communication for aerodrome control purposes, receiving meteorological information and conducting two-way communication with aeronautical stations. *Navigation equipment* is also onboard to enable execution of operational flight plans and to follow the requirements of air traffic services. For *reduced vertical separation minimum* (RVSM) operations of 1,000 ft, approved by the State responsible for that airspace, aeroplanes must have equipment to indicate the flight level being flown, maintain a selected flight level and report any deviation from the selected flight level.[103] All operators should also maintain the *manuals, logs and records* required in Annex 6.[104]

3.2.4 Airworthiness and maintenance

The safe operation of aircraft and their level of airworthiness are intrinsically related. While Annex 8 to the Chicago Convention contains the SARPs applicable to the certification of aircraft, Annex 6 contains requirements in the complementary chapter "Aeroplane Performance Operating Limitations", which stipulates a comprehensive and detailed code of aeroplane performance established by the State of Registry.[105]

Aeroplanes over 5,700 kg are expected to be operated in compliance with the terms of its certificate of airworthiness and within the approved operating limitations contained in its flight manual. Further, the following factors affecting the aircraft performance should be taken into consideration for the implementation of airworthiness provisions intrinsically related to the operation of aircraft: mass of the aeroplane as well as its limitations at the start of take-off and at the expected time of landing, operating procedures, pressure-altitude appropriate to the elevation of the aerodrome, ambient temperature, wind, runway slope and its surface condition, and noise limitations.[106]

Aircraft maintenance is also intrinsically related to airworthiness. Annex 6 requires that each aeroplane operated by a service provider engaged in international commercial operations be airworthy, in that its operational and emergency equipment is serviceable, and that all certificates of airworthiness remain valid. Further, the operator's fleet must be maintained in accordance with an up-to-date operator's maintenance control manual and the maintenance programme must be accepted by the State of Registry and released to service by a maintenance organization approved by the State in the operator's place of business. Any aircraft modification or repair should also comply with airworthiness requirements acceptable to the State of Registry.[107]

It must be noted that an operator is responsible for ensuring every aircraft in its fleet is airworthy, regardless of whether it is registered in the same State of the Operator or in a State other than that of the operator.

3.2.5 Crew

3.2.5.1 Flight crew

The number and composition of each flight crew is determined by the provisions specified in the operations manual, flight manual and documents associated with the certificate of airworthiness.

---

103 Ibid., *supra* note 96§ Standards 7.1.1, 7.2.1, 7.2.4 and 7.2.8.
104 Ibid., *supra* note 96§ Standards 4.2.10, 8.4, 4.10.8, 4.3, 4.3.3.1, 8.7, 9.4.3.4, 11.1, 11.2, 11.3, 11.3.2, 11.4, 11.5 and 11.6.
105 Ibid., *supra* note 96§ Standard 5.1.2.
106 Ibid., *supra* note 96§ Standards 5.2.1, 5.2.3, 5.2.6 and 5.2.7.
107 Ibid., *supra* note 96§ Standards 8.1.1, 8.1.2, 8.1.4, 8.1.5, 8.2.1, 8.2.2, 8.3.1, 8.6, 8.7 and 8.8.

A crew includes at least one member licensed to operate radio transmitting equipment, a flight engineer if a station is incorporated into the design of the aeroplane, a licensed flight navigator and all members necessary to perform emergency evacuations. The crew must be adequately trained in conformance with the flight training programme,[108] and approved by the State of the Operator.[109]

Key personnel in the operation of aircraft are the pilot-in-command and co-pilot who are required to conduct at least three take-offs and landings 90 days before flying. Likewise, a cruise relief pilot needs 90 days of recent experience as a pilot-in-command, co-pilot or cruise relief pilot, or a flying skill refresher training programme including normal, abnormal, emergency, approach and landing procedures.[110]

The pilot-in-command needs to demonstrate knowledge of the area, route and aerodrome to be used. Practical and recent experience on approach and landing on a specific route is also required along with initial and recurrent flight training.[111] Proficiency checks on emergency procedures must also be conducted twice a year.[112]

With regard to single pilot operations under IFR or at night, it is recommended that the State of the Operator prescribes the experience and training requirements needed by the flight crew, which is recommended for pilots to include 50 hours of flight time, and ten hours listed as pilot-in-command. For IFR operations, 25 hours of experience are required with 15 hours of flight time at night.[113]

3.2.5.2 Flight dispatcher and cabin crew

Certain States require a flight operations officer or flight dispatcher to control and supervise specific flight operations. In addition to the requirements contained in Annex 1 for obtaining his/her licence, flight dispatchers must also complete a one-way qualification flight of the area over which he/she is authorized to supervise, and demonstrate knowledge of the operations manual, radio equipment, navigation equipment, meteorological information, conditions and their effects on human performance relevant to dispatch duties.[114]

The number of cabin crew required for each aeroplane type is determined upon seating capacity or the actual number of passengers carried, so as to effectuate a safe and expeditious evacuation of the aircraft or to carry out other emergency functions and duties. Cabin crew occupy a specific seat during take-off, landing and when the pilot-in-command so directs, which is secured with a seat belt or safety harness. Cabin crew also serve passengers in the cabin and ensure that baggage carried into the passenger cabin is adequately and securely stowed.[115] Cabin crew undergo initial and recurrent training programmes approved by the State of the Operator to ensure their competency to safely execute duties and functions in emergency situations, such as evacuations, drills using life-saving equipment and procedures for lack of oxygen in pressurized aeroplanes. Cabin crew must also acquire knowledge on dangerous goods and human performance.[116]

108 For details about the training programme, see Annex 6, Standard 9.
109 See Annex 6, *supra* note 96§ Standards 9.1.1, 9.1.2, 9.1.3, 9.1.4, 9.2 and 9.3.
110 Ibid., *supra* note 96§ Standards 9.4.1.1, 9.4.2.1, 9.4.3.2 and 9.4.3.2.
111 Ibid., *supra* note 96§ Standards 9.4.3.2, 9.4.3.3, 9.4.3.5 and 9.4.5.3.
112 Ibid., *supra* note 96§ Standards 9.4.4.1 and 9.4.4.1.
113 Ibid., *supra* note 96§ Standards 9.4.5.1.
114 Ibid., *supra* note 96§ Standard 10.3.
115 Ibid., *supra* note 96§ Standards 4.8, 12.1, 12.2 and 12.3.
116 Ibid., *supra* note 96§ Standard 12.4.

3.2.6 Security

Following the terrorist attacks of September 11, 2001, a set of security requirements was established to mitigate the recurrence of similar actions. Although most of these requirements are contained in Annex 17, Annex 6 contains provisions requiring the installation of cockpit doors capable of protecting the flight crew in the event of suspicious activity or security breaches from within the cabin. For aeroplanes over 45,500 kg, or passenger seating capacity greater than 60, such compartment doors must be able to resist penetration by small fire arms, grenade shrapnel and forcible intrusions by unauthorized persons. The compartment door is normally closed and locked from the time all external doors are closed following embarkation until any such door is opened for disembarkation, except when necessary to permit access/egress by authorized persons.[117]

A search procedure checklist and guidance on the appropriate course of action for searching for or identifying bombs in the case of suspected sabotage or concealed weapons, explosives or other unlawful interference is also required. A security training programme aimed at minimizing or preventing unlawful interference should also be established and maintained by the operator. The pilot-in-command must submit a report to the designated local authority in the case of a security-related event.[118]

3.3 Dangerous goods

More than half of all cargo carried by all modes of transport is dangerous. Because of the advantages of air transport, however, a great deal of this type of cargo is carried by air. ICAO recognized the importance of dangerous cargo and took steps to ensure it is carried safely by adopting Annex 18, together with the Technical Instructions for the Safe Transport of Dangerous Goods by Air (Doc. 9284) (hereafter referred to as the "Technical Instructions"). The Technical Instructions contain numerous detailed instructions necessary for the correct handling of dangerous cargo – which require frequent updating as developments occur in the chemical, manufacturing and packaging industries. A special procedure has been established by the ICAO Council to allow the Technical Instructions to be revised and reissued to keep up with new products and advances in technology.

3.3.1 Definitions, applicability and classification

Annex 18 defines *Dangerous Goods* as, "articles or substances which are capable of posing a risk to health, safety, property or the environment, which are either shown in the list of dangerous goods in the Technical Instructions or are classified according to those Instructions".[119]

The ICAO requirements for the safe handling of dangerous goods identify a limited list of substances which are unsafe to carry in any circumstances, and how other potentially dangerous articles or substances that can be transported safely can be so transported without issue. These requirements are based on the determination made by the United Nations Committee of Experts on nine hazard classes that are used for all modes of transport.[120]

---

117 Ibid., *supra* note 96§ Standards 13.1, 13.2.1, 13.2.2 and 13.2.3.
118 Ibid., *supra* note 96§ Standards 13.3, 13.4.1, 13.4.2 and 13.5.
119 See Definitions, Annex 18, *supra* note 186 at 1-1 and 1-2.
120 "Recommendations on the Transport of Dangerous Goods", 17th ed., New York and Geneva, UN, 2009 (RTDG), Classification.

The transport of dangerous goods by air is forbidden unless specifically accepted or allowed under an approval granted by the State of Origin.[121]

3.3.2 Packing, labelling and marking

Dangerous goods transported by air must be contained in packaging of good quality, constructed and securely closed to prevent leakage. The packaging must be suitable for its contents, and resistant to chemical or other actions of such goods. Inner packaging or linings must also be packed, secured or cushioned to prevent breakage or leakage, and to control any movement within the outer packaging. Packaging may be reused after it is inspected and found to be free from corrosion or any other damage, and if it is not contaminated by its contents.[122]

Each package must be appropriately labelled and marked with the proper shipping name of its contents and its UN number, which is a four-digit identification code for hazardous substances and other dangerous goods such as explosives, flammable liquids or other toxic substances within the framework of international transport. Markings related to such dangerous goods should be inserted in the languages required by the State of Origin and in English. All packaging's material, construction, testing, labelling and marking specifications are contained in the Technical Instructions.[123]

3.3.3 Air operators' and shippers' responsibilities

Annexes 6 and 18 also allow States to extend such dangerous goods requirements to domestic commercial operations. The policies and procedures of operators authorized to carry dangerous goods must provide for the identification or rejection of undeclared or misdeclared dangerous goods, report violations, dangerous goods accidents and incidents to appropriate authorities, and provide the pilot-in-command necessary information concerning dangerous goods to be carried as cargo. All personnel involved in the acceptance, handling, loading and unloading of cargo, should be familiar with these policies.[124]

Aircraft operators can only transport such cargo if accompanied by a completed dangerous goods transport document, following an inspection of the package, overpack or freight container containing the dangerous goods. Leaking or damaged packages or unit load devices should either not be loaded or removed from the aircraft – in the latter case, the aircraft is inspected for damage or contamination.[125] Packages containing dangerous goods capable of reacting with other dangerous goods must be stowed in such a way as to render the interaction impossible in the event of leakage. Toxic, infectious or radioactive materials are stowed separately from persons, live animals and undeveloped film. Dangerous goods cargo loads are also secured to prevent movement in flight should changes occur to the orientation of the packages.[126]

The pilot-in-command is informed by the operator in the case of carrying dangerous goods onboard, which is normally included in the Operations Manual. Passengers should also be informed about dangerous goods forbidden onboard an aircraft. In the case of an in-flight emergency, the pilot-in-command must inform air traffic services for onward notification of the dangerous goods onboard to aerodrome authorities.[127]

---

121 Ibid., *supra* note 186§ Standards 2.4.1, 4.1 and 4.2.
122 Ibid., *supra* note 186§ Standards 5.2.1, 5.2.2, 5.2.6 and 5.2.7.
123 Ibid., *supra* note 186§ Standards 6.1, 6.2.1, 6.3 and 5.2.3.
124 Ibid., *supra* note 96§ Standards 14.2, 14.3 and 14.5, and Annex 18, *supra* note 186§ Standard 2.3.
125 Ibid., *supra* note 186§ Standards 8.1, 8.4.1, 8.4.2, 8.4.3, 8.4.4 and 8.6.2.
126 Ibid., *supra* note 186§ Standards 8.7.1, 8.7.2, 8.7.3 and 8.8.
127 Ibid., *supra* note 186§ Standards 9.1, 9.2, 9.3 and 9.5.

Any packager of dangerous goods for transport by air must ensure that such goods are not forbidden for transport by air and that they are in proper condition and adequately classified, packed, marked, labelled and accompanied by a transport document dully completed and signed.[128]

3.4 Airworthiness of aircraft

In accordance with Article 33 of the Chicago Convention, each State of Registry must recognize and render valid any airworthiness certificate issued by another State, subject to confirmation that the airworthiness requirements under which the certificate was issued and or rendered valid are equal to or above the minimum standards adopted by ICAO in Annex 8.

ICAO airworthiness requirements are not intended to replace national regulations and codes of airworthiness containing the full scope and extent of detail required for the certification of individual aircraft. Each State develops its own code of airworthiness or adopts one established by another State.[129]

Through Articles 31 and 33 of the Chicago Convention and Annex 8, the State of Registry receives certain functions that it is entitled or obligated to discharge in relation to the airworthiness of aircraft. Article 83 *bis* to the Chicago Convention stipulates that in cases of leased, chartered or interchanged aircraft, the State of Registry may transfer to the State of the Operator by agreement, those functions of the State of Registry that can more adequately be discharged by the State of the Operator. The transfer of functions is further detailed in Circular 295 – Guidance on the Implementation of Article 83 *bis* of the Convention on International Civil Aviation.

The requirements in Annex 8 include those for performance, flying qualities, structural design and construction, engine and propeller design and installation, systems and equipment design and installation, and operating limitations such as procedures and general information to be provided in the aeroplane flight manual, crashworthiness of aircraft and cabin safety, operating environment, human factors and security in aircraft design.

The broad standards contained in Annex 8 define the minimum basis for the recognition by States of Certificates of Airworthiness (CoA) for the purpose of flight of aircraft of other States into and over their territories, thereby achieving protection of other aircraft, third parties and property. Annex 8 is supplemented by guidance material provided in the Airworthiness Technical Manual (Doc. 9760) and other related documents.[130]

3.4.1 Procedures for certification and continuing airworthiness

3.4.1.1 Type Certification and production

Type Certification standards are applicable to all aircraft and cover the design aspects of the appropriate airworthiness requirements for a class of aircraft or for any change prior to certification. Production requirements apply to all aircraft and their parts.[131]

A Type Certificate is "a document issued by a State to define the design of an aircraft type and to certify that this design meets the appropriate airworthiness requirements of that State".[132]

---

128 Ibid., *supra* note 186§ Standards 7.1, 7.2.1 and 7.2.2.
129 Annex 8 to the Chicago Convention, "Aircraft Operations", 9th ed., Montréal, ICAO, July 2010 (Annex 8), Historical Background at p. xv.
130 For a list of related manuals and guidance material related to airworthiness of aircraft, see Annex 8.
131 See Annex 8, *supra* note 200§ Standards 1.1 and 2.1.
132 Ibid., *supra* note 200§ definition of *Type Certificate*.

A request for a Type Certificate is submitted by the manufacturer when an aircraft is intended for serial production.[133] Each design subject to type certification must avoid unsafe features or characteristics under the anticipated operating conditions or to ensure that their features give at least an acceptable level of safety.[134]

For an aircraft to obtain a Type Certificate, an approved design of the aircraft consisting of drawings, specifications, reports and documentary evidence needs to demonstrate compliance with relevant airworthiness requirements. The approved design will be then be used for production purposes. The aircraft is then subject to inspections, ground and flight tests. The approval of the design is withheld if the aircraft may have dangerous features. In the case of an approval for a design modification, repair or replacement part, States must require evidence that such modification, repair or replacement is in compliance with the airworthiness requirements used for the issuance of the original Type Certificate.[135] Once the State of Design is satisfied with the evidence presented by the manufacturer that the aircraft type is in compliance with the design aspects of the appropriate airworthiness requirements, the Type Certificate is issued defining and approving the design of the aircraft type.[136]

The State of Manufacture has the responsibility of ensuring that each aircraft and its parts are airworthy, even if manufactured by sub-contractors and/or suppliers. To approve the production of aircraft or their parts, States need to examine supporting data and inspect the production facilities and processes so as to maintain a quality system or a production inspection system to guarantee the airworthiness of each aircraft or its parts (e.g. manufacturer, date of manufacture and serial number).[137]

3.4.1.2 Certificate of Airworthiness

Article 31 of the Chicago Convention mandates that every aircraft engaged in international navigation be provided with a CoA issued or rendered valid by the State where it is registered. A CoA is issued or rendered valid by a State upon the rendition of evidence demonstrating aircraft compliance with the design aspects of the appropriate airworthiness requirements. Its renewal is subject to the laws of the State of Registry and requires a periodic inspection to determine the continuing airworthiness of the aircraft.[138]

When an aircraft with a valid CoA issued by one State is entered on to the register of another, the new State of Registry may take into consideration the prior CoA as evidence the aircraft complies with the applicable airworthiness requirements when issuing the new CoA. Certain States transfer aircraft within their Registries through an "Export Certificate of Airworthiness". A State of Registry may also render valid CoAs issued by another State through an authorization, as an alternative to issuance of its own CoA. However, such authorization cannot extend the validity of a previously valid CoA.[139] Article 29 of the Chicago Convention requires an aircraft engaged in international air navigation to carry a CoA. An English translation must be issued if the document is produced in another language.[140]

---

133 Ibid., *supra* note 200§ Standards 1.1, 1.2.1 and 1.2.2.
134 Ibid., *supra* note 200§ Standards 1.2.2, 1.2.3 and 2.4.2.
135 Ibid., *supra* note 200§ Standards 1.3.1, 1.3.2 and 1.3.3.
136 Ibid., *supra* note 200§ Standards 1.3.1, 1.3.2, 1.3.3 and 1.4.1.
137 Ibid., *supra* note 200§ Standards 2.2, 2.3, 2.4.1 and 2.4.3.
138 Ibid., *supra* note 200§ Standards 3.2.1, 3.2.2 and 3.2.3.
139 Ibid., *supra* note 200§ Standards 3.2.4 and 3.2.5.
140 Ibid., *supra* note 200§ Standards 3.3.1 and 3.3.2.

As indicated in the CoA, aircraft airworthiness may be subject to limitations which are contained in the flight manual, placards or other related documents. The failure to maintain an aircraft in an airworthy condition results in aircraft ineligibility to operate until airworthiness is restored. Similarly, any damage assessed by the State of Registry will affect the airworthiness of the aircraft. Aircraft may be prohibited from resuming flight if the damage is sustained in the territory of another State until such damage is repaired.[141]

Annex 8 contains two sets of international requirements for airworthiness certification of aeroplanes over 5,700 kg intended for international transport of passengers, cargo or mail: Part IIIA, applicable to aircraft for which the application for certification was submitted before 2 March 2004, and Part IIIB, applicable to aircraft for which an application for issuance of a Type Certificate was submitted after 2 March 2004.[142] Annex 8 also contains airworthy requirements for small aeroplanes and helicopters, as well.

3.4.2 Continuing airworthiness

Under the provisions related to continuing airworthiness of aircraft, the *State of Registry* must inform the State of Design when it first enters an aircraft into its register of the type certified by the latter. This is to enable the State of Design to transmit to the State of Registry any generally applicable information it has found necessary for the continuing airworthiness and safe operation of the aircraft. The State of Registry must also transmit to the State of Design all continuing airworthiness information originated by it for transmission, as necessary, to other States known to have the same type of aircraft on their registers.

The *State of Design* has the responsibility of transmitting to all States operating that particular type of aircraft on their registers the information necessary for the continuing airworthiness of that aircraft (also known as "mandatory continuing airworthiness information"). It also must notify other States of the suspension or revocation of a Type Certificate, transmit any relevant information necessary to decide on airworthiness actions needed, develop airworthiness actions, establish a continuing structural integrity programme and ensure that the manufacturing organization cooperates with the organization responsible for the type design in assessing information received on experience with operating the aircraft. The State of Design of the modification also transmits mandatory continuing airworthiness information to all States that have the modified aircraft on their registries.[143]

In turn, the *State of Manufacture must* ensure that the manufacturing organization works with the organization responsible for the Type Design in assessing information received on experience with operating the aircraft. The *State of Registry* is expected to advise the State of Design about entries of aircraft into its register, determine the continuing airworthiness of those aircraft, develop/adopt requirements to ensure the continuing airworthiness of the aircraft during their service life and after modifications or repairs, take action upon receipt of mandatory continuing airworthiness information, and establish a reporting system on faults, malfunctions, defects and other occurrences that might cause adverse effects on the continuing airworthiness of aircraft.[144]

---

141 Ibid., *supra* note 200§ Standards 3.4, 3.5, 3.6.1, 3.6.2 and 3.6.3.
142 Ibid., *supra* note 200§ Part IIIA, Standards 1.1.1 and 1.1.3; and Part IIIB, Standards 1.1.1 and 1.1.2.
143 Ibid., *supra* note 200§ Standards 4.2.1.1 and 4.2.1.3.
144 Ibid., *supra* note 200§ Standards 4.2.2 and 4.2.3.

3.5 Aircraft nationality and registration marks

Article 17 of the Chicago Convention requires aircraft to assume the nationality of the State in which they are registered.[145] Article 18 prohibits an aircraft from being registered in more than one State, however, its registration may be changed from one State to another.[146] Article 19 mandates that the registration or transfer of registration of aircraft in any contracting State shall be made in accordance with the laws and regulations of that State,[147] and any aircraft engaged in international air navigation shall bear its appropriate nationality and registration marks.[148]

The first amendment to Annex 7 of the Chicago Convention, entitled "Aircraft Nationality and Registration Marks", introduced the definition of a "rotorcraft" into the Convention and modified the required location of nationality and registration marks on wings. The second amendment further refined the definition of "aircraft" to exclude all air-cushion-type vehicles, such as hovercraft and other ground-effect machines.[149]

Article 77 of the Chicago Convention permits joint operating organizations to pool "air services on any routes or in any regions"[150] with a third amendment introducing the concepts of "Common Mark", "Common Mark Registering Authority" and "International Operating Agency". Under such schemes, each international operating agency must be assigned a distinctive common mark by ICAO selected from a series of symbols included in the radio call signs allocated by the International Telecommunication Union (ITU).[151]

The fourth amendment introduced provisions related to registration and nationality marks for unmanned free balloons. The fifth amendment required the Certificate of Registration to carry an English translation if issued in another language. And the sixth amendment introduced registration and nationality marks provisions for remotely piloted aircraft (RPAs).[152]

3.5.1 Definitions and classification of aircraft

Annex 7 has 17 definitions and contains the classification of aircraft[153] shown in Figure 3.1.

3.5.2 Nationality and registration marks

Each aircraft has a nationality mark comprising a group of characters followed by the registration mark. Nationality marks are selected from a series of nationality symbols included in the radio call signs allocated to the State of Registry by the ITU, which, in turn, are then reported to ICAO. The registration marks consist of letters, numbers or a combination of both, which are assigned by the State of Registry.

The nationality and registration marks are usually painted on the aircraft and should be kept clean and visible at all times. All additional formatting, size and typeface requirements for registration marks, including appropriate placement and nationality marks can be found in Annex 8.[154]

---

145 Chicago Convention, *supra* note 7§ Article 17.
146 Ibid., *supra* note 7§ Article 18.
147 Ibid., *supra* note 7§ Article 19.
148 Ibid., *supra* note 7§ Article 20.
149 See Annex 8, *supra* note 221§ Table A; Amendments to Annex 7 at p. ix.
150 Chicago Convention, *supra* note 7§ Article 77.
151 See Annex 8, *supra* note 221§ Table A; Amendments to Annex 7 at p. ix and Standard 3.4.
152 Ibid., *supra* note 221§ Table A; Amendments to Annex 7 at p. ix.
153 Ibid., *supra* note 221§ Definitions pp. 1 and 2 and Standards 2.1 and 2.2.
154 Ibid., *supra* note 221§ Standards 4.1, 4.2, 4.2.1, 4.2.2, 4.2.3, 4.2.4, 4.2.5, 4.3, 4.3.1 and 4.3.2.

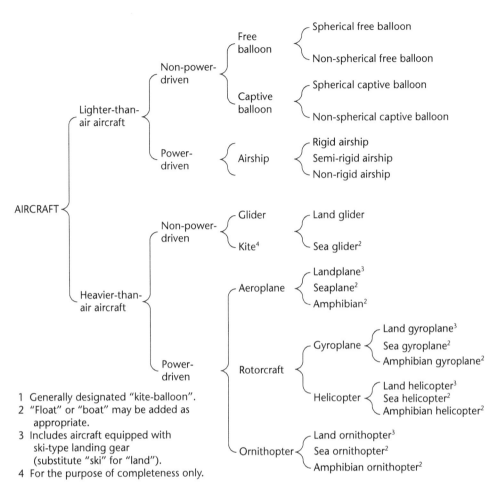

1 Generally designated "kite-balloon".
2 "Float" or "boat" may be added as
   appropriate.
3 Includes aircraft equipped with
   ski-type landing gear
   (substitute "ski" for "land").
4 For the purpose of completeness only.

Figure 3.1 Aircraft types

Each State is expected to maintain a register for each aircraft. This register contains information recorded in the certificate of registration. This certificate should be issued in English or include an English translation, and should be carried on board the aircraft.[155] Finally, a fireproof identification plate should also secured to every aircraft in a prominent position by the registration mark near the main entrance. This plate should be inscribed with the aircraft's nationality and registration marks.[156]

3.6 Search, rescue and accident investigation

Search and rescue (SAR) services are defined in Annex 12 and are organized to respond to the need to rapidly locate and rescue survivors of aircraft accidents.[157] In accordance with Article 25

155 Ibid., *supra* note 221§ Standards 5.1, 5.1.1, 5.2.1, 5.2.2, 6.1, 6.3, 6.4, 7, 8.1 and 8.2.
156 Ibid., *supra* note 221§ Standards 9.1 and 9.2.
157 Annex 12 to the Chicago Convention, "Search and Rescue", 8th ed., Montréal, ICAO, July 2004
     (Annex 12), Historical Background at p. v.

of the Chicago Convention, States are required to provide assistance measures in their territory to aircraft in distress and to permit the owners of the aircraft or authorities of the State in which the aircraft is registered to provide assistance. States should also collaborate in undertaking searches for missing aircraft.[158] Annex 12 details the organization and cooperative principles for effective SAR operations, and outlines preparatory measures and operating procedures for SAR services in actual emergencies along with the relevant signals. This Annex is complemented by the three-part International Aeronautical and Maritime Search and Rescue Manual (IAMSAR).[159]

Annex 13 sets forth the requirements for the investigation of aircraft accidents and incidents. First adopted in April 1951, Annex 13 requirements are directed to all participants in an investigation of an aircraft accident or serious incident.[160] Article 26 of the Chicago Convention stipulates that

> in the event of an accident to an aircraft … involving death or serious injury, or indicating serious technical defect in the aircraft or air navigation facilities, the State in which the accident occurs will institute an inquiry into the circumstances of the accident. … The State in which the aircraft is registered shall be given the opportunity to appoint observers to be present at the inquiry and the State holding the inquiry shall communicate the report and findings in the matter to that State.[161]

Annex 13 outlines the protection of evidence and the responsibility of the State of Occurrence for the custody and removal of the aircraft, and requests for participation in the investigation from other States. This Annex is complemented by a Manual of Aircraft Accident and Incident (Doc. 9756) that covers the organization and planning of an investigation, relevant procedures and checklists, the investigation itself and reporting.

3.6.1 SAR

The first element addressed in Annex 12 is the *organizational aspects* required for States to arrange for prompt provision of SAR services within their territories and over portions of the high seas or areas of undetermined sovereignty. States delineate non-overlapping and contiguous SAR regions based on technical and operational considerations, not the delineation of boundaries between States. This obligation is discharged individually or in cooperation with other States, and is intended to ensure 24-hour assistance is rendered to persons in need, regardless of their nationality or the circumstances in which they are found.[162]

States must establish a legal framework and a responsible authority, organize available resources and communication facilities, and provide a workforce skilled in coordination, operational functions and processes on SAR services provision, including planning domestic and international cooperative arrangements and training.

A rescue coordination centre must be established in each SAR region. These centres are staffed 24 hours a day by personnel proficient in English and the appropriate language for radiotelephony communications. These centres must be adequately equipped to communicate and

---

158 Chicago Convention, *supra* note 7§ Article 25.
159 See Annex 12, *supra* note 231§ Table of Contents and Chapter 1 Note.
160 Annex 13 to the Chicago Convention, "Aircraft Accident and Incident Investigation", 10th ed., Montréal, ICAO, July 2010 (Annex 13), Historical Background at pp. xi and xii.
161 Chicago Convention, *supra* note 7§ Article 26.
162 See Annex 12, *supra* note 231§ SARPs 2.1.1, 2.1.1.1, 2.1.2, 2.2.1, 2.2.1.1.

coordinate with SAR units and entities serving the SAR region.[163] Mobile SAR units also assist aircraft or its occupants in case of an emergency. Such SAR units are public or private services suitably located and equipped for search and rescue operations.[164] Equipment of rescue units must give adequate assistance to victims at the scene of accidents, and due regard is given to the number of passengers involved. Appropriate aerodromes should also have survival equipment suitably packed for dropping by air.[165]

Coordination between the SAR services of neighbouring States is essential to the efficient conduct of operations. Upon request and subject to the conditions prescribed by local authorities, States should permit the entry into its territory of SAR units of other States to search for aircraft accident sites and to rescue survivors. This can be expedited and strengthened through SAR agreements. The States are further encouraged to coordinate SAR operations, especially when conducted in adjacent regions. This can be facilitated through the development of common SAR plans and procedures, authorization of rescue coordination centres to request or provide assistance, including to aircraft, vessels, persons or equipment and facilitation of entry, as well as to promote joint SAR training exercises.[166]

With regard to *cooperation*, States should arrange for facilities outside the SAR organization, such as aircraft, vessels and local services, to cooperate fully and extend any possible assistance to the survivors of aircraft accidents. It is also recommended for States to ensure a close coordination between aeronautical, maritime and accident investigation authorities. States are also required to publish and disseminate information needed for the expeditious entry of rescue units of other States into their territories to assure accident investigators accompany those rescue units.[167]

An SAR operation is dynamic and requires comprehensive operating procedures that are flexible to meet extraordinary needs. The first step is to identify and categorize the emergency situation, which is normally triggered by communication from the aircraft to an air traffic control (ATC) unit. Three distinct phases categorize emergency situations. The first is the "Uncertainty Phase", which is commonly declared when radio contact has been lost with an aircraft and cannot be re-established, or when an aircraft fails to arrive at its destination. During this phase, the Rescue Coordination Centre (RCC) concerned may be activated to cooperate with the ATC unit in the collection and evaluation of reports and data pertaining to the subject aircraft. Depending on the situation, the uncertainty phase may develop into an "Alert Phase", at which time the RCC alerts appropriate SAR units and initiates further action.[168]

The "Distress Phase" is declared when there is reasonable certainty that an aircraft is in distress. The RCC is responsible for taking immediate action to assist the aircraft and to determine its location as rapidly as possible. The RCC then informs the aircraft operator, adjacent RCCs, ATC units, State of Registry and appropriate accident investigation authorities about the situation. The RCC draws and amends a detailed plan for the conduct of the SAR operation and

---

163 International Cospas-Sarsat Programme is a satellite-based SAR distress alert detection and information distribution system, established by Canada, France, the US and the former Soviet Union. It detects and locates emergency beacons activated by aircraft, ships and backcountry hikers in distress. As of 2014, 43 States and organizations have joined the project, either as providers of ground segments or as user States.

164 Ibid., *supra* note 231§ SARPs 2.5.1.

165 See Annex 12, *supra* note 231§ SARPs 2.6.1, 2.6.2, 2.6.3, 2.6.4 and 2.6.8.

166 Ibid., *supra* note 231§ SARPs 3.1.1, 3.1.2, 3.1.2.1, 3.1.3, 3.1.4, 3.1.5, 3.1.6, 3.1.7 and 3.1.8.

167 Ibid., *supra* note 231§ SARPs 3.2.1, 3.2.2, 3.2.3 and 3.2.4.

168 Ibid., *supra* note 231§ Standards 5.2.1 and 5.2.2.

coordinates its execution. It also requests any aircraft, vessels, coastal stations and other services to assist in the operation.[169]

Annex 12 contemplates the initiation and execution of SAR actions if an aircraft position is unknown as well as procedures involving two or more RCCs, both for authorities in the field and for termination or suspension of SAR operations, which normally occurs when all survivors are delivered to a place of safety or until all reasonable hope of rescuing survivors has passed. Annex 6 requires operators to ensure that pilots-in-command have essential SAR services information in the area over which the aeroplane will be flown.[170] Finally, provisions on SAR include specific SAR signals, including air-to-surface and surface-to-air visual, which are contained in an Appendix to the Annex and the need to maintain records and prepare SAR appraisals by RCCs.[171]

3.6.2 Aircraft accident and incident investigation

Annex 13 includes the definition of an accident that is key for liability and safety purposes. It is defined as:[172]

> **Accident.** An occurrence associated with the operation of an aircraft which, in the case of a manned aircraft, takes place between the time any person boards the aircraft with the intention of flight until such time as all such persons have disembarked, or in the case of an unmanned aircraft, takes place between the time the aircraft is ready to move with the purpose of flight until such time as it comes to rest at the end of the flight and the primary propulsion system is shut down, in which:
>
> a) a person is fatally or seriously injured as a result of: being in the aircraft, or direct contact with any part of the aircraft, including parts which have become detached from the aircraft, or direct exposure to jet blast, except when the injuries are from natural causes, self-inflicted or inflicted by other persons, or when the injuries are to stowaways hiding outside the areas normally available to the passengers and crew; or
> b) the aircraft sustains damage or structural failure which: adversely affects the structural strength, performance or flight characteristics of the aircraft, and would normally require major repair or replacement of the affected component, except for engine failure or damage, when the damage is limited to a single engine (including its cowlings or accessories), to propellers, wing tips, antennas, probes, vanes, tires, brakes, wheels, fairings, panels, landing gear doors, windscreens, the aircraft skin (such as small dents or puncture holes), or for minor damages to main rotor blades, tail rotor blades, landing gear, and those resulting from hail or bird strike (including holes in the radome); or
> c) the aircraft is missing or is completely inaccessible.

Annex 13 defines incidents as "occurrences, other than an accident, associated with the operation of an aircraft which affects or could affect safety".[173] Further, Annex 13-type investigations

---

169 Ibid., *supra* note 231§ Standard 5.2.3.
170 See Annex 6, *supra* note 96§ Standard 3.1.7.
171 See Annex 12, *supra* note 231§ SARPs 5.8.1, Appendix and 5.9.1 and 5.9.2.
172 See Annex 13, *supra* note 234§ definition of *Accident*.
173 Ibid., *supra* 234§ definition of *Incident*.

are also expected to be performed for serious incidents, which are defined as "incidents involving circumstances indicating that there was a high probability of an accident and associated with the operation of an aircraft".[174] ICAO has developed a list of serious incidents which are of interest for accident prevention studies, contained in Attachment C.

The provisions of Annex 13 apply to activities following accidents wherever they occurred. In case of events occurring in the territory of non-contracting States which do not intend to conduct an investigation, the State of Registry or, failing that, the State of the Operator, the State of Design or the State of Manufacture should institute an investigation. In the event of an accident occurring outside the territory of any State, the State of Registry or, failing that, the State of the Operator, the State of Design or the State of Manufacture, is responsible for instituting the investigation.[175] This responsibility for instituting an investigation can be delegated in whole or in part to another State or a regional accident investigation organization by mutual arrangement.[176]

The sole objective of an aircraft accident investigation is to identify probable causes and/or contributing factors of the accident to prevent repeated occurrences. It is not to apportion blame or liability; thus, the investigation should be conducted separate from any judicial or administrative proceedings and ensure that evidence, such as the examination and identification of victims and read-outs of flight recorder recordings, is not impeded by such proceedings. Given the nature of aircraft accidents, it is also recognized that there is a need for coordination between the investigator-in-charge and the judicial authorities. If an act of unlawful interference is suspected, aviation security authorities of the State(s) concerned should be immediately informed.[177]

The State of Occurrence has specific responsibilities, including the protection of evidence, custody and the removal of aircraft after the investigation is finalized. The protection of evidence includes the preservation, by photographic or other means, of any evidence, including the flight recorders, which might be removed, effaced, lost or destroyed, while custody is intended to protect the wreckage against further damage, access by unauthorized persons, pilfering and deterioration. Once the aircraft, or its contents or any parts thereof are no longer needed for the investigation, the State of Occurrence should release custody of those items to persons designated by the State of Registry or the State of the Operator.[178]

The State of Registry, State of the Operator, State of Design, State of Manufacture and ICAO States must be notified of the accident by the State of Occurrence. In turn, the notified States should acknowledge receipt of the notification and provide the State of Occurrence with relevant information available on the aircraft and flight crew involved.[179] In the event of an accident involving dangerous goods, the operator must provide details to inform emergency services. This information is transmitted to the State of the Operator and the State of Occurrence.[180]

The investigation process is based on the gathering, recording and analysis of all relevant information with the aim of determining probable causes and/or contributing factors to aviation accidents to prevent their recurrence. Safeguarding accident investigation authorities' continued access to essential information during the course of an investigation relies on States' ability to implement appropriate protection to accident and incident records obtained.[181]

174 Ibid., *supra* note 234§ definition of *Serious incident* at Attachment C to Annex 13.
175 Ibid., *supra* note 234§ Standards 2.1, 2.2, 5.2 and 5.3.
176 Ibid., *supra* note 234§ SARPs 5.1, 5.4, 5.5 and 5.6.
177 Ibid., *supra* note 234§ Standards 3.1, 5.4.1, 5.4.3, 5.10 and 5.11.
178 Ibid., *supra* note 234§ Standards 3.2 and 3.4.
179 Ibid., *supra* note 234§ SARPs 4.5, 4.7 and 4.9.
180 See Annex 18, *supra* note 186§ Standard 9.6.1.
181 See Annex 13, *supra* note 234§ Standards 5.7, 5.8, 5.9, 5.9.1, 5.12, 5.12.1 and 5.12.2.

States are required to provide relevant information to the State conducting the investigation. States of Registry, Operator, Design and Manufacture can, and sometimes are called to, participate in an investigation by appointing an accredited representative. Advisers may also be appointed. The State conducting the investigation may call on the best technical expertise available from any source to assist. Further, States having suffered fatalities or serious injuries to its citizens can visit the scene of the accident, access relevant factual information and receive a copy of the Final Report.[182]

The Final Report of an investigation is the foundation for initiating the safety actions necessary to prevent further accidents from similar causes. It establishes a record and analysis of relevant facts, conclusions in the form of findings, causes and/or contributing factors as well as safety recommendations. Before being issued, distributed and made available to the public, the draft Final Report is transmitted for consultation to the States that participated in the investigation. Safety recommendations proposed are expected to be considered, taken on board and monitored by receiving States.[183]

Computerized databases greatly facilitate the storing and analysing of information on accidents and incidents. The sharing of such safety information is vital to accident prevention. To facilitate this sharing of information, ICAO operates a database known as the Accident/Incident Data Reporting (ADREP) system. States should also establish and maintain a database to facilitate the analysis of safety deficiencies and to determine preventive actions required.[184]

3.7 Safety management

Given the increasing complexity of the global air transportation system and its interrelated aviation activities required to assure the safe operation of aircraft, there is a need to transition from reactive safety practices into a proactive strategy to improve safety performance. This is achieved through provisions aimed at assisting States and aviation service providers in managing aviation safety risks. Proactive safety management practices are subject to factors that affect their implementation, including the complexity of the air transportation system as well as the maturity of the aviation safety oversight capabilities of States.

Annex 19 to the Chicago Convention was adopted in 2013, and consolidated existing material from Annexes 1, 6, 8, 11, 13 and 14 regarding the State Safety Programme (SSP),[185] safety management systems (SMS)[186] and State safety oversight activities. A number of manuals assist States in implementing safety management provisions.[187]

3.7.1 State safety management responsibilities

Safety management responsibilities consist of activities aiming at improving aviation safety by establishing an SSP and an acceptable level of safety performance (ALoSP), which is the minimum level of safety performance of civil aviation in a State expressed in terms of safety performance targets and safety performance indicators. The SSP requires coordination among

---

182 Ibid., *supra* note 234§ Standards 5.18, 5.19, 5.20, 5.23, 5.24 and 5.27.
183 Ibid., *supra* note 234§ Standards 6.1, 6.2, 6.3, 6.4, 6.5, 6.10, 6.11, 6.12, 8.3 and Appendix.
184 Ibid., *supra* note 234§ Standards 7.1–7.7 and 8.1.
185 An SSP is defined as "an integrated set of regulations and activities aimed at improving safety".
186 An SMS is defined as "a systematic approach to managing safety, including the necessary organizational structures, accountabilities, policies and procedures".
187 For a comprehensive list of manuals and guidance material related to safety management, see Annex 19.

authorities responsible for individual elements of civil aviation functions.[188] The SSP contemplates the surveillance of SMS implementation by product and service providers.[189]

The SSP and SMS are proactive mechanisms designed to manage aviation safety that rely on the collection, analysis and exchange of safety information for the timely identification and subsequent mitigation of risks and hazards that may result in an accident or an incident. To achieve this objective, States establish and maintain incident reporting systems, both mandatory and voluntary, analyse the safety data contained in safety databases and determine preventive actions required. The success of this proactive approach depends on the appropriate protection of safety information and related sources.[190] States also establish safety information networks to facilitate the free sharing/exchange of information on actual and potential safety deficiencies with the aim of reducing the number of accidents and serious incidents worldwide.[191]

3.7.1.1 Relationship between safety management and safety oversight

The first set of safety management provisions were adopted in 2006 with the introduction of SMS in different Annexes while the concept of a safety oversight system was introduced in 1994 when the Safety Oversight Assessment Programme (SOAP) was established by the ICAO Council.[192] The difference in time for the adoption and implementation of both methodologies, enabled ICAO to provide a solid foundation for the establishment and implementation of a safety oversight system.[193]

Safety oversight is a function by which a State ensures the effective implementation of SARPs and associate procedures contained in the Annexes of the Chicago Convention through the enactment of a legislative framework comprising the primary aviation legislation and the establishment of an oversight agency (typically a Civil Aviation Authority (CAA)). With appropriate safety oversight, the State ensures that its national aviation industry is at or above the safety levels established by the SARPs.[194]

3.7.1.1.1 ASSESSMENT OF SAFETY-RELATED REQUIREMENTS

ICAO's Universal Safety Oversight Audit Programme (USOAP)
In order to assess the level of implementation of safety-related SARPs through the safety oversight system, ICAO established the USOAP,[195] which has evolved into a Continuous Monitoring Approach (CMA) that incorporates the analysis of safety risk factors.[196] Through this mechanism, ICAO collects and analyses safety information from States and other stakeholders to identify and prioritize appropriate oversight and monitoring activities. The outcomes of these

---

188 See Annex 19, *supra* note 270§ Standards 3.1.1, 3.1.2, 3.1.3 and 3.1.4.
189 Product and service providers include approved training organizations, international commercial operators of aeroplanes or helicopters and general aviation operators of large/turbojet aeroplanes, approved maintenance organizations, type design or manufacturing organizations, ATS providers and aerodromes operators.
190 See Annex 19, *supra* note 270§ SARPs 5.1.1, 5.1.2, 5.2.1, 5.3.1 and 5.3.2.
191 See Annex 19, *supra* note 270§ Recommended Practices 5.4.1. and 5.4.2.
192 See Michael Milde, "Aviation Safety Oversight: Audits and the Law" (2001) XXVI *Ann. Air & Sp. L.* 165 at 173.
193 See Annex 19, *supra* note 270§ Standard 3.2 and Appendix 1.
194 "Safety Oversight Manual", ICAO Doc. 9734 AN/959 (2006) § 2.1.1 and 2.1.2.
195 See "Assembly Resolutions in Force", Res. A32-11: "Establishment of an ICAO Universal Safety Oversight Audit Programme", ICAO Doc. 9730 (1998) at I-48 (Doc. 9739).
196 See "Universal Safety Oversight Audit Programme Manual", ICAO Doc. 9735 AN/960 (2014) at 2-1, 2-2 and 2-3 (USOAP Manual).

activities result in an Effective Implementation (EI) score made available to ICAO Member States and the general public through ICAO's websites.[197]

USOAP-CMA allows ICAO to use a risk-based approach for measuring and monitoring the safety oversight capabilities and improving safety performance of States and global aviation on a continuous basis through the use of "States safety risk profiles" to prioritize activities. These profiles assess the existence of Significant Safety Concerns (SSC),[198] level of aviation activities in the State, projected traffic growth, corrective actions informed and implemented by States addressing prior deficiencies, significant changes in the organizational structure of the State, air navigation deficiencies and other factors to determine a State's EI.[199]

US International Aviation Safety Assessments (IASA) Program
The IASA program was established to address the concern that some States were not implementing the safety standards required by ICAO. The basis for this assessment programme is the "safety clauses" contained in air transport agreements in which parties reserve the right to withhold, revoke, suspend, limit or impose conditions on the operating authorization or permissions of airline(s) if minimum safety-related standards are not maintained.[200]

Under IASA, the Federal Aviation Administration (FAA) sends teams to assess different States to determine whether the oversight of such air carriers from those States operating into the US or codesharing with a US air carrier, comply with relevant international safety standards established by ICAO. The IASA program focuses on Annexes 1, 6 and 8 requirements. Once data is collected and assessed, the FAA assigns a rating (Category 1 – in compliance; Category 2 – not in compliance) to the CAA. Carriers from Category 1 States are permitted to operate and/or codeshare without limitation with carriers operating in the US; whereas carriers from Category 2 States operating/codesharing within the US have such services limited to levels that existed at the time of the assessment; while carriers from Category 2 States that seek to initiate commercial service are prohibited from initiating such services. A State-by-State category summary listing of IASA determinations is published on the FAA website and is updated regularly.[201]

EU aviation safety list
In 2005, the European Parliament and the Council of the European Union promulgated Regulation (EC) No. 2111/2005 on the establishment of a Community list of air carriers subject to an operating ban within the Community and on informing passengers of the identity of air carriers operating within the EU. This regulation established a "list of air carriers subject to an operating ban in the Community".[202]

197 See USOAP Manual, *supra* note 283§ 3.1, 3.2 and 3.7.
198 An SSC

> occurs when the State allows the holder of an authorization or approval to exercise the privileges attached to it, although the minimum requirements established by the State and by the Standards set forth in the Annexes to the Convention are not met, resulting in an immediate safety risk to international civil aviation.

199 See USOAP Manual, *supra* note 283§ 3.5.1.
200 See Session of the ICAO Council. "Summary of Decisions", Subject No. 14.3.4 Report of the ANC – Model Clause on Aviation Safety, 163rd Sess., ICAO Doc. C-DEC 163/8 (2001) § 9.
201 See IASA Program, www.faa.gov/about/initiatives/iasa/media/FAA_Initiatives_IASA.pdf.
202 EC, Council Regulation 2004/36/CE of 14 December 2005 on the establishment of a Community list of air carriers subject to an operating ban within the Community and on informing air transport passengers of the identity of the operating air carrier, and repealing Article 9 of Directive 2004/36/EC [2005] OJ L344/15 § Article 3.

Decisions imposing a partial or total operating ban on an air carrier are based on common criteria set out in an Annex to the EU Safety List Regulations, and are grouped into three areas: (a) verified (objective) evidence of serious safety deficiencies on the part of an air carrier; (b) lack of ability and/or willingness of an air carrier to address safety deficiencies; and (c) lack of ability and/or willingness of the authorities responsible for the oversight of an air carrier to address safety deficiencies.[203]

3.7.2 SMS

Annex 19 requires service providers to implement an SMS to identify safety hazards and risks and assist with the implementation of mitigating actions. As part of the SMS, service providers are expected to monitor and improve safety performance.[204]

The SMS of service providers such as approved training organizations, international commercial air operators, approved maintenance organizations, type design organizations and manufactures, ATS providers and certified aerodromes should also be commensurate with the size and complexity of their products or services.[205] Whereas general aviation operators of large or turbojet aeroplanes are also expected to implement an SMS including processes to identify safety hazards and risks, implement remedial actions, and monitor the appropriateness and effectiveness of its safety management activities.

3.8 Emerging areas

Similar to the recent evolution of safety management where proactive and predictive methodologies are being put in place to improve further the safety record of the safest mode of transportation, new areas are starting to interrelate with international air transportation: remote piloted aircraft systems (RPAS) and the integration of commercial space activities with international civil aviation. Consideration of these topics has become fundamental due to the recurrence of their activities and the potential they have in affecting international civil aviation.

3.8.1 RPAS

Article 8 of the Chicago Convention states that "no aircraft capable of being flown without a pilot shall be flown without a pilot over the territory of a contracting State without special authorization by that State and in accordance with the terms of such authorization".[206] ICAO issued the Circular on Unmanned Aircraft Systems (Cir. 328) in 2011 and the Manual on Remotely Piloted Aircraft Systems (Doc. 10019) 2015. The aim of this material is to provide guidance on technical and operational issues related to the integration of RPAS in non-segregated airspace and at aerodromes.[207]

Due to this integration, States should be able to grant the necessary authorizations in accordance with minimum requirements with the object of assuring safe operations alongside manned aircraft.[208] Operations of RPAS started to be conducted in segregated airspace to minimize

---

203 European Commission, Commission Staff Working Document on the report from the Commission regarding the application of the EU Safety List, SEC(2009) 1735 final, p. 2.
204 See Annex 19, *supra* note 270§ Standard 4.1.1, (a) and Appendix 2.
205 Ibid., *supra* note 270§ Standards 4.1.1, (b), 4.1.2, 4.1.3, 4.1.4, 4.1.5, 4.1.6, 4.1.7 and 4.1.8.
206 See Chicago Convention, *supra* note 7§ Article 8.
207 See "Unmanned Aircraft Systems (UAS)", ICAO Cir. 328 (2011) § 1.2.
208 Ibid., § 2.2, 2.3, 2.4, 2.5 and 2.8.

dangers to other aircraft. However, the integration of their operations with manned aircraft in non-segregated airspace is inevitable as their operations evolve. To this end, these systems should be able to act and respond as manned aircraft, including in communications with ATC, in licensing requirements, in how safety management principles are applied to them and to the aircraft flying in their environment, in their operation.[209]

One of the items that has been defined by ICAO is the concept of RPAS that is

> an aircraft piloted by a licensed "remote pilot" situated at a "remote pilot station" located external to the aircraft (i.e. ground, ship, another aircraft, space) who monitors the aircraft at all times and can respond to instructions issued by ATC, communicates via voice or data link as appropriate to the airspace or operation, and has direct responsibility for the safe conduct of the aircraft throughout its flight.[210]

Likewise, RPAS comprises "a set of configurable elements including an RPA, its associated remote pilot station(s), the required C2 links and any other system elements as may be required, at any point during flight operation".[211] The evolution of their operational capabilities, potential for civil operations, expected growth and environmental impacts are not yet fully known; thus, the standardization of rules is still under development.[212]

As indicated above, RPAS are subject to the framework established by the Chicago Convention and related provisions. Therefore, certain provisions have been introduced in different Annexes and will be further developed in the years to come.

3.8.2 Commercial space

The recent developments in the civil space transportation industry, specifically the potential increased frequency of suborbital flights, have focused attention on how these activities can be integrated into non-segregated airspace in the upcoming years. After recognizing the imminent growth of this industry, ICAO established a Learning Group with those actively engaged in civil space transportation, and to develop a plan for a safe, efficient and more routine space activities. The members of this learning forum are States that started the development and implementation of regulatory activities for commercial space operators, including the US, the UK, France and Switzerland.

While it is uncertain at this stage whether an existing international organization will be mandated with the development of an international framework for these activities, no one can deny that these craft intended to go to outer space will necessarily cross airspace that is already very congested and where traffic is forecasted to grow exponentially in the next decades. If these operations are to be conducted on a regular basis, their safe integration would need to be addressed to ensure that the safest mode of transportation, air transportation, can coexist with the riskiest mode of transportation, space travel, without affecting aviation safety and third parties on the ground.

---

209 Ibid., § 2.12, 2.13, 2.14, 2.17 and 3.1.
210 Ibid., § 3.2.
211 Ibid., § 3.8.
212 Ibid., § 3.12, 3.13, 3.14, 3.15, 3.16, 3.17 and 3.18.

3.9 Summary and conclusions

This chapter studied the safety-related requirements related to operation of aircraft engaged in international air transport contained in Annexes 1, 6, 18, 8, 7, 12, 13 and 19.

Annex 1 to the Chicago Convention deals with the licensing of operational personnel, including pilots and other air and ground personnel such as air traffic controllers. This Annex aims to standardize their competence, skills, training and health requirements that remain essential to guarantee efficient and safe operations.

Annex 6 aims to ensure the harmonization of aircraft operations of aircraft engaged in international air transport to ensure the highest levels of safety and efficiency. Annex 6 has three parts; Part I covers provisions for the operation of aircraft engaged in international commercial air transport, while Parts II and III establish international general aviation and helicopter operations. Annex 18 to the Chicago Convention sets the minimum requirements for the safe transportation of dangerous goods by air.

Article 33 of the Chicago Convention calls upon States to recognize and render valid airworthiness certificates issued by other Contracting States, subject to the condition that the requirements under which such certificates are issued are equal to or above the minimum standards established by ICAO pursuant to the Chicago Convention. Such requirements are contained in Annex 8 and facilitate operations of aircraft in international air navigation, as well as their import and export or their exchange for lease, charter or interchange.

Annex 7 establishes provisions for the classification and identification of aircraft, including rules for nationality and registration marks.

The SARPs in Annex 12 provide direction in the provision of SAR services to locate promptly and respond to persons in need of assistance aboard distressed aircraft or to rescue survivors of aircraft accidents.

Annex 13 stipulates the international requirements for the investigation of aircraft accidents and incidents. These investigations are intended to identify the causes and causal factors of these unfortunate events to prevent repeated occurrences and not to apportion blame of liability.

Annex 19, adopted in April 2013, includes safety management provisions extracted from SARPs gradually introduced into Annexes 1, 6, 8, 11, 13 and 14. These provisions are intended to facilitate safety management functions related to, or in direct support of, the safe operation of aircraft.

This chapter further tapped into the emerging areas where international requirements may be introduced in the future along with those assessment/audit mechanisms established at the international, regional and national level to determine effective implementation of SARPs.

4

Safety regulation and oversight

Christopher M. Petras and Mathieu Vaugeois

4.1 Overview of US FAA and EASA: origins, organization, jurisdiction

4.1.1 FAA

4.1.1.1 Origins

The US Federal Aviation Administration (FAA) was originally established as the Federal Aviation Agency pursuant to the Federal Aviation Act of 1958.[1] However, the FAA's origins date back to the earliest days of powered flight and are rooted in the efforts of what was then known as the Post Office Department to improve navigational tools for the pioneer airmail pilots of the early 1920s.[2] Indeed, the debt owed by commercial aviation as a whole to the extraordinary role the US Postal Service played in the early development of air transport can hardly be overstated.[3] As a further case in point, the Air Mail Act of 1925 (the Kelly Act),[4] which first authorized the Postmaster General to use private contractors to carry the mail by air, is widely viewed as the genesis for the birth of the US airline industry.[5]

It was notably on the heels of the enactment of the Kelly Act in 1925 that President Calvin Coolidge selected Dwight Morrow[6] and eight "leaders of the fledgling aviation industry" to plot

---

1 Pub. L. No. 85-726, 72 Stat. 731 (1958); see generally Theresa L. Kraus, Fed. Aviation Admin., U.S. Dept. of Trans., "The Federal Aviation Administration: A Historical Perspective, 1903–2008" (2008), available at www.faa.gov/about/history/historical_perspective/.

2 See Kraus, *supra* note 1, at 1; see also Postal Service, Publication 100, "The United States Postal Service: An American History" 31 (2012), available at https://about.usps.com/publications/pub100.pdf.

3 See Henry R. Lehrer, *Flying the Beam: Navigating the Early US Airmail Airways, 1917–1941* at 76 (Perdue University Press 2014):

> [Between 1923 and 1926,] ... the Post Office Department ... established a series of rules for the type of equipment required for carrying mail.... Included in these regulations were detailed sections on airplane airworthiness, pilot certificates, the location and suitability of any landings fields, and the type of radio and navigational equipment required.

4 Pub. L. No. 68-359, ch. 128, 43 Stat. 805 (1925). The Air Mail Act of 1925 is commonly referred to as the Kelly Act after its chief sponsor, Rep. Clyde Kelly of Pennsylvania, who chaired the House Committee on Post Offices and Post Roads.

5 See Kraus, *supra* note 1, at 1; see also Robert M. Kane, *Air Transportation 101–104* (14th ed., Kendall/Hunt Publishing Company 2003); generally Lehrer, *supra* note 3, at 76–79.

6 Amherst College classmate and friend of President Coolidge, and a partner in J.P. Morgan & Co., Morrow would later gain notoriety as father-in-law to American aviation pioneer and legend Charles Lindbergh.

a course for the future of air transportation.[7] And, after hearing the testimony of nearly 100 witnesses, the "Morrow Board," as it became known, issued its report on November 30, 1925, which, among other things, called for federal oversight and standards to maintain and improve civil aviation safety.[8] "Approved by Coolidge and backed by the prestige of the members of the board, the report was to become perhaps the principal influence on the passage of legislation ... forming a basic air policy for the nation"[9] – namely, the Air Commerce Act of 1926.[10]

The Air Commerce Act of 1926 became the "cornerstone" of federal regulation of civil aviation.[11] It charged the Department of Commerce with the dual responsibilities of promoting air commerce, while at the same time maintaining regulatory oversight over the safety of commercial flight operations.[12] To carry out the safety regulation function, Congress created the Aeronautics Branch of the Department of Commerce,[13] and aviation law visionary and pioneer William P. MacCracken became its head, as the first Assistant Secretary of Commerce for Aeronautics.[14]

Still, "[a]s Senator Hiram Bingham, who introduced the Air Commerce Act into the Senate, explained, the purpose of the act was 'not so much to regulate as to promote civil aviation.'"[15] Thus, although the Department initially concentrated on such functions as safety rulemaking and the certification of pilots and aircraft, and incontrovertibly worked to improve the nation's system of lighted airways, aeronautical radio communications, and radio beacons as an aid to navigation,[16] a number of high profile accidents in the 1930s called into question the effectiveness of its safety oversight. So much so that members of Congress ultimately came to see the Department's aviation regulatory arm as working too closely with the airlines and aircraft manufacturers to be objective.[17]

"To ensure a focus on aviation safety,"[18] President Roosevelt signed into law the Civil Aeronautics Act of 1938,[19] which transferred responsibility for federal oversight of civil aviation from the Department of Commerce to a new newly created independent agency, the Civil Aeronautics Authority (CAA).[20] The act thusly replaced the pre-existing patchwork of statutes that provided sanction for the federal government's regulation of the aviation industry and consolidated all air transportation oversight and regulatory functions under a single authority.[21]

---

7 Kraus, *supra* note 1, at 1; see also James P. Tate, *The Army and its Air Corps: Army Policy toward Aviation, 1919–1941* at 40–41 (Air University Press 1988).
8 S. Doc. No. 18, 69th Cong., 1st Sess. (1925).
9 Tate, *supra* note 7, at 41.
10 Pub. L. No. 69-254, ch. 344, 44 Stat. 568 (1926), *repealed by* Act of August 23, 1958, § 1401, 72 Stat. 731, 806.
11 Kane, *supra* note 5, at 195.
12 See Harry Lawrence, *Aviation and the Role of Government* at 88 (Kendall/Hunt Publishing Company 2004); see also Kane, *supra* note 5, at 104.
13 Renamed Bureau of Air Commerce by Secretary's administrative order of July 1, 1934.
14 See F. Robert van der Linden, *Airlines and Air Mail: The Post Office and the Birth of the Commercial Aviation Industry* at 15–16 (University Press of Kentucky 2015).
15 Michael Nolan, *Fundamentals of Air Traffic Control* at 3 (Cengage 2011).
16 Kane, *supra* note 5, at 195.
17 Kraus, *supra* note 1, at 4; see Staff of Senate Comm. on Interstate and Foreign Commerce, Aviation Study, S. Doc. No. 163, 83d Cong., 2d Sess. (1955).
18 Kraus, *supra* note 1, at 4.
19 Pub. L. No. 75-706, 52 Stat. 973 (1938); see also Exec. Order No. 7959, 3 Fed. Reg. 2071 (August 24, 1938).
20 Kane, *supra* note 5, at 195.
21 See Airmail (Kelly) Act of 1925, *supra* note 4; Airmail Act of 1930, Pub. L. No. 71–178, ch. 223, 46 Stat. 259 (1930); Airmail Act of 1934, Pub. L. No. 74-270, ch. 530, 49 Stat. 614 (1934); Air Commerce Act of 1926, *supra* note 10.

"[It] also expanded the government's role by giving the CAA the power to regulate airline fares and to determine the routes that air carriers would serve."[22]

As prescribed by the act, the CAA would comprise three separate bodies: a five-person quasi-judicial policy-making board (the "Civil Aeronautics Authority") principally concerned with economic regulation of air carriers; an Administrator of Operations responsible for carrying out Authority safety policies and overseeing the construction, operation, and maintenance of the airway system; and a three-person semi-autonomous Air Safety Board that would conduct accident investigations and make recommendations for improving safety to the policy-making Authority.[23] However, the arrangement quickly proved unworkable;[24] thus, the independent status of the CAA proved to be "extremely short lived."[25]

For less than two years later, in 1940, acting under the authority conferred by the Reorganization Act of 1939,[26] President Roosevelt split the CAA into separate rule-making and operational agencies, respectively.[27] To wit, "the functions of the Air Safety Board and the five-person Authority were combined into a new organization known as the Civil Aeronautics Board (CAB),"[28] which was entrusted with aviation safety rule-making, accident investigation, and economic regulation of airlines; while the Office of the Administrator was renamed the Civil Aeronautics Administration (CAA) and assigned responsibility for air traffic control (ATC), airman and aircraft certification, safety enforcement, and airway development.[29] Both organizations were made part of the Department of Commerce, but the CAB was placed in the Department only for administrative purposes and functioned independently of the Secretary's influence; not so for the new CAA.[30]

While the CAA certainly enjoyed some successes,[31] "[a]s a subordinate bureau in a huge department, the CAA found its requirements for expansion and modernization of aviation facilities largely ignored and neglected in the annual battles of the budget."[32] For example, with the postwar advent of the jet age, "[m]any experts recognized the need to institute a form of positive control [over air traffic]" in order to segregate slower-moving piston engine aircraft from the new faster jet airliners.[33] "Yet, year after year, CAA's requests for funds to buy long range radar and other equipment necessary to permit a higher degree of positive traffic control were denied by the Department of Commerce."[34] It should thus perhaps have

---

22 Kane, *supra* note 5, at 195.
23 See Vern Haugland, "The FAA: The Creation of our New Federal Aviation Agency should ease the Introduction of the Air Transport Industry to Jets," *Flying* 26 (January 1959).
24 Richard H. K. Vietor, *Contrived Competition: Regulation and Deregulation in America* at 29 n.30 (Belknap Press of Harvard University Press 1994).
25 Nolan, *supra* note 15, at 16.
26 Pub. L. 76-19, 53 Stat. 561 (1939) (codified at 5 U.S.C. § 133).
27 Haugland, *supra* note 23, at 26.
28 Nolan, *supra* note 15, at 16; see Reorganization Plan No. III of 1940 (Eff. June 30, 1940), 5 F.R. 2107, 54 Stat. 1231, by act June 4, 1940, ch. 231, §4, 54 Stat. 231; and Reorganization Plan No. IV of 1940 (Eff. June 30, 1940), 5 Fed. Reg. 2421, 54 Stat. 1234, by act June 4, 1940, ch. 231, §4, 54 Stat. 231; see also Reorganization Act of 1940, 54 Stat. 735 (1940), 49 U.S.C.A. §401 (Supp. 1944), cited in Vietor, *supra* note 24, at 29 n.30.
29 Kane, *supra* note 5, at 195; see also Kraus, *supra* note 1, at 4–5.
30 Nolan, *supra* note 15, at 16; Kane, *supra* note 5, at 195.
31 Kraus, *supra* note 1, at 5–6.
32 Haugland, *supra* note 23, at 26.
33 Kraus, *supra* note 1, at 7.
34 Haugland, *supra* note 23, at 26; see also "Study of Operation of Civil Aeronautics Administration: Hearings on S. 2818 before the Aviation Subcomm. of the Senate Comm. on Interstate and Foreign Commerce," 84th Cong., 2d Sess. (1956).

come as no surprise when the dramatic rise in air traffic and the ushering in of the age of commercial jets that followed the end of World War II were met with an alarming increase in the number midair collisions attributable, in significant part, to the inadequacy of the ATC system.[35]

So it was in 1956 that the Congressional spotlight became fixed on the CAA, as its effectiveness and the problems of airspace and ATC management became the focus of hearings and investigations in both the House and the Senate.[36] Then, in the midst of this turmoil, a Trans World Airlines Super Constellation and a United Airlines DC-7 collided in spectacular fashion over the Grand Canyon on June 30, 1956, killing all 128 souls onboard the two airplanes.[37] Although the CAB blamed the disaster on pilot error,[38] it nevertheless raised public concern and served as a flashpoint for debate about the failure of the existing system to keep pace with the demands of increased capacity and high-speed air traffic.[39] Hence, the high-profile crash effectively spelled the end of the CAA and, with it, the Department of Commerce's role regulating aviation safety.[40]

On August 14, 1957, Congress approved the Airways Modernization Act,[41] which was signed by President Eisenhower that same day. The law created the Airways Modernization Board (AMB) to oversee provisionally "development and modernization of the national system of navigation and traffic control facilities to serve present and future needs of civil and military aviation[,]"[42] until a new independent aviation authority was established.[43] Then, just over a year later, on August 23, 1958, the Federal Aviation Act[44] passed Congress and was signed into law. It formally abolished the CAA and transferred its functions and authorities to the newly

---

35 "In fact, sixty-five such collisions had occurred in the United States between 1950 and 1955." Kraus, *supra* note 1, at 7.

36 See sources cited *supra* 34; and House Comm. on Government Operations, "Federal Role in Aviation," H.R. Rep. No. 294, 84th Cong., 2d Sess. (1956); see also "Aviation Hearings," in *CQ Almanac 1956*, 10-720-10-725 (12th ed., 1957), available at http://library.cqpress.com/cqalmana c/ cqal56-1347714.

37 The Grand Canyon crash was characterized as "the worst disaster in the history of civil aviation" to that point. "Federal Role in Aviation," *supra* note 36, at 2.

38 See "Aviation Hearings," *supra* note 36.

39 Ibid.; "Federal Role in Aviation," *supra* note 36, at 2.

40 See Kraus, *supra* note 1, at 6–7; see also Emmette S. Redford, *The Regulatory Process: With Illustrations from Commercial Aviation* (University of Texas Press 1969):

> [Senator Monroney, the chairman of the Aviation Subcommittee of the Senate Committee on Interstate and Foreign Commerce, who wrote and sponsored the Federal Aviation Act of 1958] … came to have a deep conviction that the Department of Commerce restrained the development of the CAA's services and that no real solution to the problems of air space use and air traffic management could be effected without placing control of these in an agency which was free of departmental control.

41 Pub. L. 85-133, 71 Stat. 349 (1957); see also "Airways Modernization Board: Hearings on S. 1856 before the Senate Comm. on Interstate and Foreign Commerce," 85th Cong., 1st Sess. (1957).

42 The Airways Modernization Act contained a "sunset" clause that provided for the automatic termination of the law, and hence the dissolution of the AMB, on June 30, 1960. Congress was initially divided on the question of whether the temporary board could meet the long-term demands of aviation safety regulation, but support for deferring the establishment of a new independent aviation authority so as to give more time to evaluate the AMB evaporated in the wake of another midair collision over Brunswick, Maryland, on May 20, 1958. See Emmette S. Redford, *Congress Passes the Federal Aviation Act of 1958* (University of Alabama Press 1961).

43 Pub. L. 85-133, § 7, 71 Stat. 349, 351 (1957).

44 Pub. L. 85-726, 72 Stat. 731 (1958).

created rule and standard setting body for civil aviation safety, the Federal Aviation Agency,[45] which commenced operations on December 31, 1958 – 60 days after the appointment of retired Air Force General Elwood "Pete" Quesada as the agency's first Administrator.[46]

Although the Federal Aviation Act similarly transferred the CAB's responsibility for making and enforcing aviation safety rules to the new agency, it nevertheless reestablished the CAB as a statutory entity, with the Board retaining its existing structure, as well as its authority over aviation accident investigation and economic regulation.[47] In hindsight, however, opponents of the Act who feared it was but a first step toward the elimination of the CAB altogether appear to have been prescient.[48] For in 1967, the Federal Aviation Agency was incorporated into the newly created Department of Transportation (DOT) and renamed the Federal Aviation Administration (FAA), while the CAB's accident investigation duties were reassigned to DOT's new National Transportation Safety Board (NTSB).[49] Later, the Airline Deregulation Act of 1978 was enacted, eliminating government control over fares, routes, and market entry,[50] thereby stripping the Board of its primary purpose.[51] Ultimately, the CAB was shut down, and its remaining functions were assumed by DOT, on January 1, 1985, pursuant to the Civil Aeronautics Board Sunset Act of 1984.[52]

4.1.1.2 Organization

When the FAA began operations on December 31, 1958, it inherited its initial organizational structure from the defunct Civil Aeronautics Authority.[53] However, Administrator Quesada's first priority was to reconfigure the agency to handle better the safety issues and gaps between

---

45 "Federal Aviation Agency Act: Hearings on S. 3880 before the Aviation Subcomm. of the Senate Comm. on Interstate and Foreign Commerce," 85th Cong., 2d Sess., 2 (1957).

46 Section 1505(2) of Pub. L. 85-726, title XV, August 23, 1958, 72 Stat. 810, provided that the amendment made by Pub. L. 85-726 shall be effective on the 60th day following the date on which the Administrator of the Federal Aviation Agency first appointed under Pub. L. 85-726 qualifies and takes office.

47 Ibid.; the CAB retained

> its authority with regard to airline certificates and permits, rates and fares, mail payments, loans and financial aid, accounts and reports, merger proceedings, methods of competition, and inquiry into airline management and similar activities … [and] full responsibility for investigating aviation accidents.

Haugland, *supra* note 23, at 27

48 To allay concerns over the power of the FAA and the loss of CAB authority, proponents of the act made clear that legislative language encouraging "promotion" of civil aviation was not intended to connote economic promotion of the airline industry. House Comm. on Interstate and Foreign Commerce, Federal Aviation Act of 1958, H.R. Rep. No. 2360, 85th Cong., 2d Sess., 89–90 (1958).

49 Department of Transportation Act, Pub. L. 89-670, 80 Stat. 931 (1966). It was not until November 22, 1963, that the Federal Aviation Agency's Washington headquarters staff began moving into the newly completed Federal Office Building 10A, at 800 Independence Avenue, S.W., where its successor, the Federal Aviation Administration (FAA), still currently resides. Fed. Aviation Admin., U.S. Dept. of Trans., "A Brief History of the FAA" (2015), available at www.faa.gov/about/history/brief_history/.

50 Pub. L. 95-504, 92 Stat. 1705 (1978).

51 See Kraus, *supra* note 1, at 52; see also Paul Stephen Dempsey and Andrew R. Goetz, *Airline Deregulation and Laissez-faire Mythology* at 193, 199 (Quorum Books 1992).

52 Pub. L. 98-443, 98 Stat. 1703 *et seq.*; see Dempsey, *supra* note 51, at 196.

53 Kraus, *supra* note 1, at 9.

the needs of civil and military aviation that predicated its creation. So, on January 15, 1959, he issued Agency Order 1, prescribing a new organizational structure for the fledgling agency.[54]

The configuring and reconfiguring of the agency would resume in 1961, as Quesada's successor, Najeeb Halaby, began a process of decentralization, whereby much authority was delegated to regional organizations.[55] The decentralization of the FAA would more or less continue until 1988, when an organizational "straightlining" consolidated authority over field operations in four new executive director positions in the Washington headquarters.[56] Yet, after a major FAA reorganization in 1990 increased the number of executive directorships to five, subsequent reorganizations in 1991 and 1994, respectively, would see the executive director positions reduced to three and then abolished altogether.[57]

Besides eliminating the executive director "layer of management," the 1994 reorganization created an FAA headquarters organizational structure featuring 11 Associate and Assistant Administrators' offices, which along with the Office of the Chief Counsel, all reported to the Administrator and Deputy Administrator – i.e., the Office of the Administrator (AOA).[58] Though some of the names of these offices would change over time, the addition in 2003 of the Office of the Chief Operating Officer (COO), Air Traffic Organization (ATO), as the thirteenth office in the FAA's operating core, brought the headquarters' organizational structure to its present composition.[59]

The 13 positions currently reporting directly to the Office of the Administrator include the:

- Chief Counsel (AGC)
- Chief Operating Officer, Air Traffic Organization (AJO)
- Assistant Administrator for Civil Rights (ACR)
- Assistant Administrator for Communications (AOC)
- Assistant Administrator for Finance and Management (AFN)
- Assistant Administrator for Government and Industry Affairs (AGI)
- Assistant Administrator for Human Resources Management (AHR)

54 Ibid.

> Three staff offices headed by assistant administrators for management services, personnel and training, and plans and requirements … assisted the administrator and his deputy. Other staff officials reporting to the administrator included the general counsel, the civil air surgeon, and the heads of the offices of public affairs, congressional liaison, and international coordination. Four bureau directors ran the agency's major programs: research and development (testing and development of new equipment); flight standards (certification of airmen, aircraft, and air carriers); air traffic management (planning and operation of the airspace system); and facilities (acquisition and maintenance of air navigation facilities and related equipment).

> See also Filippo De Florio, *Airworthiness: An Introduction to Aircraft Certification: A Guide to Understanding JAA, EASA, and FAA Standards* at 21 (Elsevier 2006) ("The agency's first Administrator favored a management system under which officials in Washington exercised direct control over programs in the field.").

55 Ibid.; see also Kraus, *supra* note 1, at 17 ("Administrator Halaby centralized the development of programs, policies, and standards in Washington and delegated broad operational responsibilities to the regional offices.").

56 De Florio, *supra* note 54, at 21.

57 Kraus, *supra* note 1, at 83, 115.

58 Ibid.

59 Ibid., at 115, 130–131; see also Fed. Aviation Admin., U.S. Dept. of Trans., "FAA Organizational Chart" (2014), available at www.faa.gov/about/office_org/.

- Assistant Administrator for NextGen (ANG)
- Assistant Administrator for Policy, International Affairs and Environment (APL)
- Assistant Administrator for Security and Hazardous Materials Safety (ASH)
- Associate Administrator for Airports (ARP)
- Associate Administrator for Aviation Safety (AVS)
- Associate Administrator for Commercial Space Transportation (AST).

Notably, Agency Order 1 had retained the field structure of the Civil Aeronautics Administration, with its system of six numbered regions headed by regional directors reporting to the agency administrator, together with its three major field facilities;[60] however, like the headquarters' organizational structure, the field structure would be the subject of repeated reorganization. For starters, Administrator Halaby would expand the number of regional offices to seven, which were then to be identified by geographic rather than numerical designations.[61] The number of regional offices would later balloon to 11 under a 1971 regional

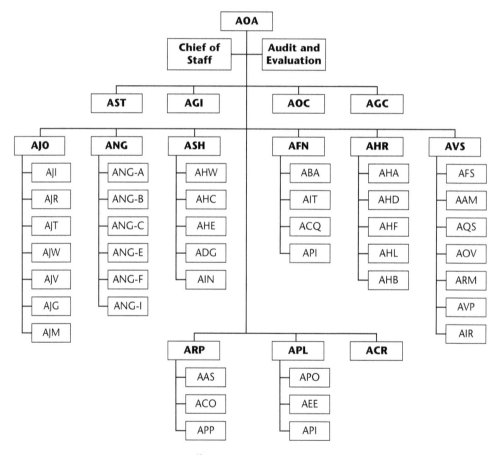

Figure 4.1   Organization of the FAA.[62]

60 Kraus, *supra* note 1, at 10.
61 Ibid., at 16–17.
62 Ibid.

realignment, before a 1981 consolidation would subsequently reduce the number of regions from 11 to the current nine.[63]

Today, the FAA has more than 45,000 people employed at its headquarters in Washington, DC, and in offices and facilities throughout the United States and around the world.[64] Many of these employees are air traffic controllers, as the FAA provides air navigation services throughout the United States. Due to the scope and variety of the FAA's responsibilities both nationally and globally, and the economic importance of the US aviation industry and its prominence on the world stage, as well as the sheer size of the United States itself, the FAA is an expansive and complex organization. Beyond the nine Regional Offices,[65] the FAA field structure comprises:

- nine Security and Hazardous Materials Offices (co-located with the Regional Offices);
- more than 23 Airports Regional and District Development Offices (ADO) distributed throughout the nine FAA regions;
- 24 Certificate Management Offices (CMO) in 16 US states;
- 19 geographically dispersed Manufacturing and Inspection District Offices (MIDO);
- ten geographically dispersed Aircraft Certification Offices (ACOs);
- five Aircraft Evaluation Group (AEG) Offices in five different US states;
- five International Field Offices and Units (IFO/IFU) located in and outside the United States;
- 50 Flight Standards District Offices (FSDO) (one in each US state); and
- two major centers: the Mike Monroney Aeronautical Center, Oklahoma City, Oklahoma; and the William J. Hughes Technical Center, Atlantic City, New Jersey.[66]

4.1.1.3 Jurisdiction

The US Federal Government first assumed jurisdiction over the safety of civil aviation with the enactment of the Air Commerce Act of 1926,[67] which gave the Department of Commerce's Aeronautics Branch (later renamed the Bureau of Air Commerce) authority over such matters as "examination and licensing of pilots and mechanics, registration and licensing of airplanes, issuance of aircraft certificates of airworthiness, inspection of aircraft, issuance of air traffic rules, and rating of airports."[68]

Although the Civil Aeronautics Act of 1938 substantially repealed the Air Commerce Act, in adopting the new law, Congress utilized its authority under the "Commerce Clause" of the

---

63 Ibid., at 32–33, 79; Arnold E. Briddon, Ellmore A. Champie, and Peter A. Marraine, *FAA Historical Fact Book: A Chronology, 1926–1971*, at 232 (Department of Transportation, Federal Aviation Administration, Office of Information Services 1974).

64 Fed. Aviation Admin., U.S. Dept. of Trans., "Fiscal Year 2014 Performance and Accountability Report" at 2 (2014), available at www.faa.gov/about/plans_reports/.

65 The FAA's nine geographically designated Regional Offices include the Alaskan (Anchorage, AK), Central (Kansas City, MO), Eastern (Jamaica, NY), Great Lakes (Des Plaines, IL), New England (Burlington, MA), Northwest Mountain (Renton, WA), Southern (Atlanta, GA), Southwest (Fort Worth, TX), and Western-Pacific (Los Angeles, CA).

66 Available at www.faa.gov/about/office_org/.

67 *Supra* note 10. Prior to adoption of the Air Commerce Act of 1926, "Federal legislation in the aviation field took the form of appropriations for air mail service." Charles S. Rhyne, "Federal, State and Local Jurisdiction Over Civil Aviation," in 11 *Law & Contemp. Probs.* 459, 460 (Spring 1946); see also the Air Mail Act of 1925, *supra* note 4.

68 See Rhyne, *supra* note 67, at 460 (citing 1928 United States Aviation Reports (1928 U.S. Av. R.) 365–431).

US Constitution to broaden significantly Federal jurisdiction over civil aviation.[69] First, Federal regulation of aviation safety was expanded, so it not only encompassed such matters as aircraft airworthiness and airman competency as before, but also, for example, airport safety and control over aircraft in-flight.[70] The Act further gave the Federal Government sweeping powers over "the business activities of air transportation," including "the issuance of certificates of public convenience and necessity, the supervision of rates, consolidations of air services, and interlocking relationships."[71] Finally, the Act made international aviation the exclusive province of the Federal Government, as well.[72]

With the passage of the Federal Aviation Act of 1958, the various entities statutorily designated to exercise Federal regulatory authority over the business and safety aspects of aviation changed – the Act abolished the CAA, divested the CAB of promulgation authority for aviation safety regulations and transferred it to the newly established FAA, and granted the FAA sole responsibility for the nation's civil–military system of air navigation and ATC, while leaving only aviation accident investigation and economic regulation within the purview of the CAB.[73] However, after the Department of Transportation Act of 1966 gave responsibility for aircraft accident investigation to the NTSB,[74] and economic regulation of aviation was later abandoned, the CAB would be dissolved.[75] Thus, the Federal Government's complete, all-encompassing jurisdiction over the regulation of aviation safety came to rest almost exclusively in the hands of the FAA.[76]

As a part of the DOT, however, the role of the FAA has evolved and expanded over time, to include additional responsibilities not originally contemplated by the Federal Aviation Act. For example, the hijacking epidemic of the 1960s brought the agency into the field of aviation security,[77] and, in 1968, the Aircraft Noise Abatement Act vested in the FAA Administrator, in consultation with the Secretary of Transportation, the power to prescribe aircraft noise standards.[78] FAA involvement in the regulation of aviation's environmental impacts would subsequently extend to aviation emissions, as well.[79] And, more recently, in November 1995, the Office of Commercial Space Transportation, which was originally established in 1984 as part of the Office of the Secretary of Transportation within the DOT, was transferred to the FAA.[80]

---

69 U.S. Const. art. I, § 8, cl. 3 ("The Congress shall have the power to … regulate commerce with foreign nations, and among the several states, and with Indian tribes"); see also Rhyne, *supra* note 67, at 461.

70 Rhyne, *supra* note 67, at 460 (citing 49 U.S.C. §§ 551–560 (1940)).

71 Rhyne, *supra* note 67, at 460 (citing 49 U.S.C. §§ 481–495 (1940)).

72 Ibid., at 461; see also Charles S. Rhyne, "Legal Rules for International Aviation," 31 *Va. L. Rev.* 267, 286 (1945).

73 See *supra* text accompanying notes 44–52.

74 See *supra* note 49 and accompanying text.

75 See *supra* notes 50–52 and accompanying text.

76 Kane, *supra* note 5, at 233.

77 See Kraus, *supra* note 1, at 39–45; see generally Airport Security, 14 C.F.R. pt. 107 (2002), available at www.gpo.gov/fdsys/granule/CFR-2002-title14-vol2/CFR-2002-title14-vol2-part107.

78 Pub. L. No. 90-411, 82 Stat. 395 (1968). "On December 1, 1969, FAA added a new Part 36 to the Federal Aviation Regulations that established allowable engine noise levels as part of the criteria for transport aircraft." Kraus, *supra* note 1, at 32; see generally "Noise Standards: Aircraft Type and Airworthiness Certification," 14 C.F.R. pt. 36 (2015).

79 See Kraus, *supra* note 1, at 54–45; see also Fed. Aviation Admin., U.S. Dept. of Trans., "Emissions Certification," available at www.faa.gov/about/office_org/headquarters_offices/apl/noise_emissions/certifications/; see generally Clean Air Act of 1970 § 232, 42 U.S.C. § 7572 (2012); and "Fuel Venting and Exhaust Emission Requirements for Turbine Engine Powered Airplanes," 14 C.F.R. pt. 34 (2015).

80 Department of Transportation and Related Agencies Appropriations Act, Pub. L. No. 104-50, 109 Stat. 436 (1995); see also Fed. Aviation Admin., U.S. Dept. of Trans., Office of Commercial Space Transportation, "About the Office," available at www.faa.gov/about/office_org/headquarters_offices/ast/about/.

Notably, however, in the shadow of the terrorist attacks of September 11, 2001, the Aviation and Transportation Security Act[81] created a new DOT organization to oversee federal security responsibilities in all modes of transportation, the Transportation Security Administration (TSA),[82] and transferred all aviation security functions formerly assigned to the FAA to the TSA.[83] In November 2002, the TSA then became one of the 22 federal agencies that were consolidated to form the new cabinet-level Department of Homeland Security, pursuant to the Homeland Security Act.[84]

Today, the major roles of the FAA include:

- regulating civil aviation to promote safety;
- encouraging and developing civil aeronautics, including new aviation technology;
- developing and operating a system of ATC and navigation for both civil and military aircraft;
- researching and developing the National Airspace System and civil aeronautics;
- developing and carrying out programs to control aircraft noise and other environmental effects of civil aviation; and
- regulating US commercial space transportation.[85]

Activities carried out by the FAA in support of the foregoing roles, include:

- *Safety Regulation*: issuing and enforcing regulations and minimum standards covering the manufacture, operation, and maintenance of aircraft; and certifying the airmen and airports that serve air carriers.
- *Airspace and Air Traffic Management*: operating a national network of airport towers, air route traffic control centers, and flight service stations, for the safe and efficient use of navigable airspace; and developing air traffic rules, assigning the use of airspace, and controlling air traffic.
- *Air Navigation Facilities*: building and installing visual and electronic aids to air navigation; maintaining, operating, and assuring the quality of these facilities; and sustaining other systems to support air navigation and ATC, including voice and data communications equipment, radar facilities, computer systems, and visual display equipment at flight service stations.
- *Civil Aviation Abroad*: promoting aviation safety and encouraging civil aviation abroad by exchanging aeronautical information with foreign authorities; certifying foreign repair shops, airmen, and mechanics; providing technical aid and training; negotiating bilateral airworthiness agreements with other countries; and taking part in international conferences.
- *Commercial Space Transportation*: regulating and encouraging the US commercial space transportation industry; and licensing commercial space launch facilities and private launches of space payloads on expendable launch vehicles.
- *Research, Engineering, and Development*: conducting research on and developing systems and procedures needed for a safe and efficient system of air navigation and ATC; assisting the development of better aircraft, engines, and equipment and testing or evaluating aviation systems, devices, materials, and procedures; and conducting aeromedical research.

81 Pub. L. No. 107-71, 115 Stat. 597 (2001).
82 49 U.S.C. § 114 (2012).
83 See "Airport Security," 67 Fed. Reg. 8355 (Feb. 22, 2002) (codified at 49 C.F.R. pt. 1542).
84 Pub. L. No. 107-296, 116 Stat. 2135 (2002).
85 Fed. Aviation Admin., U.S. Dept. of Trans., "What We Do," available at www.faa.gov/about/mission/activities/.

- *Other Programs*: registering aircraft and recording documents reflecting title or interest in aircraft and their parts; administering an aviation insurance program; developing specifications for aeronautical charts; and publishing information on airways, airport services, and other technical subjects in aeronautics.[86]

There is periodically renewed debate within aviation and governmental circles over separating the FAA from the DOT and making it an independent agency reporting directly to the President, as it was when originally established in 1958, and until 1966.[87] Some in the industry see the movement for an independent FAA as arising from perceived failings of the FAA and DOT to address adequately concerns of the public, airlines, airports, and users of the system,[88] while others see it as a way to address FAA funding and managerial problems.[89] It is expected Congress will continue to struggle with the issue in the twenty-first century.[90]

4.1.2 EASA

4.1.2.1 Origins

Early attempts in harmonizing safety regulations in Europe started in 1970 with the creation of the *Joint Airworthiness Authorities* (JAA).[91] Initially, its aim was to produce common standard certification for large aircraft and engines and its primary objective was to meet the needs of the European industry, especially for products manufactured by international consortia such as Airbus.[92] As a result of these activities, the "Arrangement concerning the development and the acceptance of Joint Airworthiness Requirements" was signed in 1979 by the aeronautical authorities of 13 EU Member States.[93] This "Arrangement" aimed at setting common European airworthiness standards for civil aircraft, engines, propellers, controls, and other aircraft components.[94] During this initial phase, common certification in respect of large transport aircraft, engines, and auxiliary power units were established.[95] In 1987, the cooperation was further expanded, in order to cover other areas of aviation, namely operations, maintenance, licensing, and certification for all types of aircraft.[96]

---

86 Ibid.
87 Kane, *supra* note 5, at 197.
88 Am. Ass'n of Airport Execs., "History, the Regulation of Air Transportation, Airports, and the Federal Aviation Administration" at 7 (2005) (hereinafter Airport Execs.); see Jake Kirchner, "FAA Executive Lauds Agency's Safety Record," *Computerworld*, September 1, 1980, at 13, 15.
89 Trans. Research Bd., Nat'l Research Council, "Winds of Change: Domestic Air Transport Since Deregulation" at 345–365 (1991).
90 Airport Execs., *supra* note 88, at 7.
91 Frank Manuhutu, "Aviation Safety Regulation in Europe," 25(6) *Air & Space L.* 264, 267 (2000).
92 I.H.P. Diederiks-Verschoor, *An Introduction to Air Law* 85 (8th ed., Kluwer Law International 2006).
93 Arrangement Concerning the Development and the Acceptance of Joint Airworthiness Requirements, signed on March 21, 1979, by 13 European Civil Aviation Authorities (Austria, Belgium, Denmark, Finland, France, FRG, Italy, Netherlands, Norway, Spain, Sweden, Switzerland, UK). See Eileen Denza, "From Aerostats to DC-10s: Recognition of Certificates of Airworthiness," in *Essays in Air Law* at 39, 48–49 (Arnold Kean ed., Martinus Nijhoff 1982).
94 "Report of the Committee of Transport and Tourism on the Commission Proposal for a Council Directive on the Harmonization of Technical Requirements and Procedures Applicable to Civil Aircraft" (COM(90) 0442 final – C3-0367/90), Sess. Doc. 1991, Doc. A3-0153/91, May 30, 1991.
95 Ibid.
96 "Memorandum of Understanding on Future Airworthiness Procedures," signed on June 19, 1987, by 12 European National Aviation Authorities (NAA); see De Florio, *supra* note 54, at 15.

Also, in 1989, the JAA joined the European Civil Aviation Conference (ECAC)[97] with the status of associated body.[98]

These early attempts in safety harmonisation led to the signature by the civil aviation authorities of 16 European countries,[99] on September 11, 1990, of the "Cyprus Arrangements" which established the JAA, a body without legal personality.[100] The main objectives of the JAA were to:

- achieve the standardization of aviation regulation in the field of aviation safety among the JAA members;
- internationally promote, JAA standards in order to improve the safety of aviation worldwide;
- ensure, through the application of unified standards, a fair and equal competition among JAA members; and
- achieve a cost-effective system in order to contribute to the efficiency of the aviation industry.[101]

The standards created by the JAA were referred to as the Joint Aviation Requirements (JARs). The JARs were designed to be used by the National Civil Aviation Authorities (NCAA) of JAA Members. They were intended to cover all fields related to aircraft safety and safe operation of aircraft, in particular the design and manufacture of products and components, the maintenance and operation of those products, as well as the competence of persons and organizations responsible for such design, manufacture, and maintenance.[102] However, the JARs were not legally binding norms, they were proposals for regulations intended to be transferred in national law by the EU Member States.[103] Therefore, the lack of direct application of the JARs was viewed by certain observers as a weakness.[104] Nevertheless, in order to solve this poor enforcement problem, the EU took the initiative in 1991 to transfer certain JARs into binding EU Regulations.[105]

---

97 ECAC was founded in 1955 and is currently composed of 44 EU Member States. ECAC's mission is the promotion of continued development of a safe, efficient, and sustainable European air transport system. See www.ecac-ceac.org.
98 Manuhutu, *supra* note 91, at 267.
99 At the end of the operation of the JAA, it was composed of 37 State members (Austria, Belgium, Bosnia and Herzegovina, Bulgaria, Croatia, Cyprus, Denmark, Estonia, Finland, France, Germany, Greece, Hungary, Ireland, Iceland, Italy, Latvia, Lithuania, Luxembourg, Malta, Former Yugoslav Republic of Macedonia, Moldova, Monaco, Netherlands, Norway, Poland, Portugal, Romania, Sweden, Switzerland, Serbia, Slovakia, Slovenia, Spain, Czech Republic, Turkey, United Kingdom) as well as six so-called State member candidates (Albania, Armenia, Azerbaijan, Georgia, Montenegro, and Ukraine).
100 "Arrangements Concerning the Development, the Acceptance and the Implementation of Joint Aviation Requirements," signed on September 11, 1990, at Cyprus, available at http://easa.europa.eu/system/files/dfu/cyprus.pdf (hereafter Cyprus Arrangements).
101 See Manuhutu, *supra* note 91, at 267; Elmar M. Giemulla and Heiko Van Schyndel, "The European Organization of Aviation," in *International and EU Aviation Law* at 309, 319 (E. M. Giemulla and L. Weber eds., Kluwer Law International 2011).
102 See Cyprus Arrangements, Appendix 1, para. (b).
103 Ibid., para. 3; see also Giemulla and Van Schyndel, *supra* note 101, at 319.
104 See e.g., Diederiks-Verschoor, *supra* note 92, at 86; and Peter Malanik, "Recent EU Initiatives in Aviation Safety," 22(3) *Air & Space L.* 122, 123 (1977).
105 Regulation (EEC) No. 3922/91 of 16 December 1991 on the harmonization of technical requirements and administrative procedures in the field of civil aviation, OJ L 373, 31 December 1991; see Jacques Naveau, Marc Godfroid, and Pierre Frühling, *Précis de Droit Aérien* 147 (Bruylant 2006); Nicola Arrigoni, "Joint Aviation Authorities Development of an International Standard for Safety Regulation : The First Steps are being taken by the JAA," 17(3) *Air & Space L.* 130, 131 (1992); and Malanik, *supra* note 104, at 123.

The JAA was controlled by the JAA Committee (JAAC), which was working under the authority of the Plenary Conference of ECAC and was reporting to the JAA Board (JAAB).[106] Thus, the JAAC was responsible for the administrative and technical implementation of the Cyprus Arrangements,[107] as well as for making arrangements for the preparation of JARs.[108] It was composed of a member from each NCAA.[109] As one of the other JAA institutions, the JAAB, composed by the Directors General of the NCAA, considered and reviewed the general policies and long-term objectives of the JAA.[110]

Over the years, the JAA reached its limits for various reasons, including the use of the consensus-based approach in its decision-making process, the lack of binding mechanism for resolving conflicts, as well as the inconsistency of certain proposals with the EU's obligations and policies.[111] There was therefore the need for the creation of a strong organization with extended powers in every aspect of safety, an organization which would be somewhat similar to the FAA.[112] June 30, 2009, marked the end of JAA's operations. Its mandate was to be pursued by the European Aviation Safety Agency (EASA). During the transition from JAA to EASA, it was decided to assign the mandate of training activities to the JAA-Training Organization (JAA-TO) with headquarters in Hoofddorp (Netherlands).[113] JAA-TO is still in operation and is an associate body of ECAC.[114]

4.1.2.2 Organization

EASA was established in 2002 pursuant to the adoption of Council Regulation 1592/2002 of July 15, 2002,[115] revised by EU Regulation 216/2008 (Basic Regulation).[116] It is an independent body of the EU with legal personality.[117] EASA is not strictly speaking a civil aviation authority. In fact, the Agency is established as a Regional Safety Oversight Organization (RSOO).[118] To this end, it is recognized by ICAO that RSOOs are a viable solution for States to pool their resources for the establishment of a regional system that can conduct

---

106 Cyprus Arrangements, para. 1.
107 Ibid., para. 4 (c).
108 See ibid., Appendix 3, para. 3.
109 Ibid., para. 4 (c).
110 Ibid., para. 4 (b).
111 Thaddée Sulocki and Axelle Cartier, "Continuing Airworthiness in the Framework of the Transition from the Joint Aviation Authorities to the European Aviation Safety Agency," 18(6) *Air & Space L.* 311, 313 (2003); and Manuhutu, *supra* note 91, at 269.
112 Ibid., at 270.
113 JAA-Training Organization, "Background," available at https://jaato.com/page/101.
114 Ibid.
115 Regulation (EC) No. 1592/2002 of the European Parliament and of the Council of 15 July 2002 on common rules in the field of civil aviation and establishing a European Aviation Safety Agency, OJ L 240/1, 7.9.2002, amended by Regulation (EC) No. 1701/2003 of 24 September 2003 adapting Art. 6 of Regulation (EC) No. 1592/2002 of the European Parliament and of the Council on common rules in the field of civil aviation and establishing a European Aviation Safety Agency, OJ L 243/5, 27 September 2003.
116 Regulation (EC) No. 216/2008 of the European Parliament and of the Council of 20 February 2008 on common rules in the field of civil aviation and establishing a European Aviation Safety Agency, and repealing Council Directive 91/670/EEC, Regulation (EC) No. 1592/2002 and Directive 2004/36/EC, OJ L 79/1, 19 March 2008 (hereinafter Regulation (EC) No. 216/2008).
117 Ibid., art. 28.
118 See ICAO, "Safety Manual Oversight Part B The Establishment and Management of a Regional Safety Oversight Organization," at 2–2, para. 2.1.7, ICAO Doc. 9734 (2nd ed., 2011).

safety oversight tasks and functions on their behalf.[119] Nevertheless, States must still retain the minimum capability required to carry out their responsibilities under the Chicago Convention.[120]

The Agency took up work on September 28, 2008. EASA's headquarters are located in Cologne (Germany) and it also has an office in Brussels (Belgium) as well as three permanent international representations located in Washington (USA), Montreal (Canada) and Beijing (China).[121] According to its Basic Regulation, EASA's objectives are to:

- establish and maintain a high uniform level of civil aviation safety in Europe;
- ensure a high uniform level of environmental protection;
- facilitate the free movement of goods, persons, and services;
- promote cost-efficiency in the regulatory and certification processes and avoid duplication at national and European levels;
- assist its Member States in fulfilling their obligations under the Chicago Convention by providing a basis for a common interpretation and uniform implementation of its provisions, and by ensuring that its provisions are duly taken into account in this Regulation and in the rules drawn up for its implementation;
- promote Community views regarding civil aviation safety standards and rules throughout the world by establishing appropriate cooperation with third countries and international organizations; and
- provide a level playing field for all actors in the internal aviation market.[122]

EASA's main functions consist of:

- assisting the Commission to develop common rules in the field of civil aviation and providing technical, scientific, and administrative support;
- conducting standardisation inspections to ensure that these rules are correctly applied within the Member States; and
- issuing certificates to European companies involved in aircraft design, certifying aircraft used in Europe, and certifying air carriers, maintenance organisations, and training organisations located in third countries.[123]

The Agency is led by an Executive Director[124] and by a Management Board composed of one representative of each EU Member States and one representative from the EU Commission.[125]

---

119 Ibid., at 2.1, para. 2.1.4.
120 Ibid., at 2–2, para. 2.1.8.
121 EASA, "The Agency," available at www.easa.europa.eu/the-agency.
122 See Regulation (EC) No. 216/2008, art. 2.
123 See European Union, "Civil Aviation and the European Aviation Safety Agency," available at http:// eur-lex.europa.eu/legal-content/EN/TXT/?qid=1426628541302&uri=URISERV:l24492; see also Regulation (EC) No. 216/2008, arts. 20–23; Regulation (EC) No. 1108/2009 of the European Parliament and of the Council of 21 October 2009 amending Regulation (EC) No. 216/2008 in the field of aerodromes, air traffic management and air navigation services and repealing Directive 2006/23/ EC, OJ L 309/51, 24 November 2009, arts. 22a, 22b, 54 and 55 (hereinafter Regulation (EC) No. 216/2008, as amended by Regulation (EC) No. 1108/2009).
124 Regulation (EC) No. 216/2008, art. 38.
125 Ibid., art. 34.

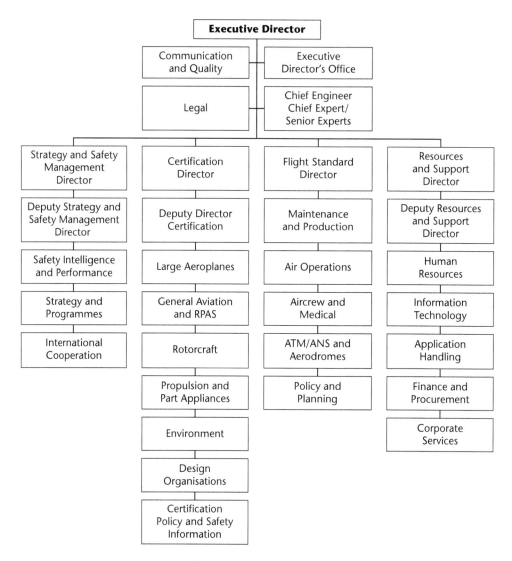

Figure 4.2 Organization of EASA.[126]

Also, a Board of Appeal is responsible for settling disputes between EASA and NCAA.[127] EASA's personnel consist of officials assigned or seconded by the European Commission or Member States, as well as of other employees recruited by the Agency. The membership of EASA is composed of the 28 EU Member States and the Members States of the European Free Trade Association (EFTA).[128] EASA is required to design an annual program of work aimed at promoting continuous improvement of European aviation safety and complying with the

126 See EASA, "Agency Organisation Structure," available at www.easa.europa.eu/the-agency/agency-organisation-structure.
127 See Regulation (EC) No. 216/2008, arts. 40–49.
128 EFTA members are entitled to participate to EASA pursuant to art. 66 of Regulation (EC) No. 216/2008. There are also members of EASA Management Board without voting rights.

objectives, mandates, and tasks of the Agency, as set out in its Basic Regulation.[129] In order to guarantee its full autonomy and independence, EASA's revenues mainly come from fees (paid for certificates issued) and charges (for publications, training, and other services), as well as from contributions from the EU, its Member States, and third countries.[130]

4.1.2.3 Jurisdiction

Pursuant to its Basic Regulation, EASA has jurisdiction over airworthiness and environmental certification, pilot certification, air operation certification as well as third-country operators.[131] Moreover, following the adoption of Regulation (CE) 1108/2009, EASA has also jurisdiction over certification of certain air traffic management organization as well as air traffic controller certification.[132] To this end, EASA can issue two types of regulations, one that can be categorized as hard law and the other as soft law.

The provision regarding EASA's contribution to hard law is mentioned at Article 17 2(b) of the Basic Regulation. To this end, EASA shall assist the Commission by preparing measures to be taken for the implementation of the said Regulation (Implementing Rules). When these measures comprise technical rules and in particular rules related to construction, design, and operational aspects, the Commission may not change their content without prior coordination with the Agency.[133] In practice, EASA drafts proposals and consults with various stakeholders, before submitting an "Opinion" to the Commission. The Commission then turns the Opinion into a formal legislative proposal, either to the Parliament and the Council in the case of the Basic regulation or to a Committee of Member States in the case of Implementing Rules. For example, EASA's contribution to hard law covers *inter alia* its Basic Regulation, initial airworthiness, continuing airworthiness, aircrew, air operations, as well as third countries' operators.

In addition, EASA's contribution to soft law is set out at Article 18 (c), which provides that the Agency shall issue, where appropriate, certification specifications, including airworthiness codes and Acceptable Means of Compliance (AMC), as well as any guidance material for the application of its Basic Regulation and its Implementing Rules. It should be noted that AMC[134] issued by EASA are non-binding standards.[135] They are not creating any additional obligations on the regulated persons, who may decide to show compliance with the applicable requirements using other means.[136] Also, as the legislator wanted such material to present legal certainty and to contribute to uniform implementation, it provided the AMC adopted by EASA with a

---

129 Regulation (EC) No. 216/2008, art. 56, para. 1.
130 Ibid., art. 59.
131 See ibid., arts. 20–22.
132 See Regulation (EC) No. 216/2008, as amended by Regulation (EC) No. 1108/2009, art. 22 (a) and 22 (b).
133 Regulation (EC) No. 216/2008, art. 17, para. 2 (b).
134 AMC are modeled on FAA guidance and are divided into Parts *inter alia*: Part 21 (Initial Airworthiness); Part M (Continuing Airworthiness); Part 145 (Maintenance Organization Approvals); Part 66 (Aircraft Maintenance Licence for Certifying Staff); Part 147 (Approved Training Organization of Maintenance License for Certifying Staff); Part FCL (Flight Crew Licensing); Part MED (Aero-Medical); Part CC (Cabin Crew); Part ARA (Authority Requirements for Aircrew); Part ORA (Organization Requirements for Aircrew).
135 EASA, "Acceptable Means of Compliance (AMC) and Alternative Means of Compliance (AltMOC)," available at https://easa.europa.eu/document-library/acceptable-means-compliance-amcs-and-alternative-means-compliance-altmocs.
136 Ibid.

presumption of compliance with the rules; therefore, national authorities must recognize regulated persons' compliance with an EASA AMC as complying with the law.[137]

In March 2015, EASA presented an Opinion to the European Commission, in order to provide its vision for the future of aviation regulatory system.[138] The said Opinion proposes a revision and possible amendments to EASA's Basic Regulation. Among others, it proposes that when national authorities lack resources or expertise, they should be able to delegate some of their oversight functions to other authorities or to the Agency. Moreover, it proposes that, on a voluntary basis, Member States can decide that their State aircraft (excluding military) can be regulated by EASA. Also, it suggests to include the extension of EASA's scope of intervention in new domains, such as airport ground handling, remotely piloted aircraft systems, and security.

4.2 Safety audits by US FAA (category 2) and EU (blacklisting)

4.2.1 FAA International Aviation Safety Assessment (IASA) Program

The 1944 Convention on International Civil Aviation (Chicago Convention) established the International Civil Aviation Organization (ICAO) – a specialized agency of the United Nations that develops standards and recommended practices (or SARPs) for aviation safety and security, and prescribes the duties and responsibilities of its Member States' civil aviation authorities.[139] ICAO's internationally agreed-upon SARPs are delineated in one of the 19 Annexes to the Chicago Convention produced by the Organization, and State signatories are treaty-bound to comply with them to the fullest extent practicable.[140] The primary sources for aviation safety standards are Annex 1 (personnel licensing), Annex 6 (aircraft operations), and Annex 8 (aircraft airworthiness).

Prior to 1999, however, ICAO lacked a mandate to monitor States' compliance with their safety oversight obligations.[141] So, in 1992 the United States established its International Aviation Safety Assessment (IASA) program to ensure that all foreign air carriers operating to or from the United States, or in code-sharing arrangements with US carriers, were properly certificated and subject to safety oversight by a competent Civil Aviation Authority (CAA) in accordance with ICAO standards.[142] The focus of the program is thus the ability of *the State* – not the ability of individual air carriers – to adhere to international aviation safety standards.[143] Accordingly, each country with carriers serving, or wishing to serve, the United States in their own right or as part of a code-sharing arrangement with a US airline must first undergo an IASA assessment.[144]

Authority for the IASA program is derived from federal regulatory provisions mandating that aircraft operations within the United States be in compliance with Annex 6 of the Chicago

137 Ibid.
138 European Commission policy initiative on aviation safety and a possible revision of Regulation (EC) No. 216/2008, EASA Opinion No. 01/2015, available at http://easa.europa.eu/system/files/dfu/Opinion%20No%2001-2015.pdf; see Frank Manuhutu and Michael Gerhard, "Perspectives of the European Aviation Safety Agency," 64 *ZLW* 310 (2015).
139 Convention on International Civil Aviation, December 7, 1944, 61 Stat. 1180, 15 U.N.T.S. 295 (hereinafter Chicago Convention).
140 Ibid., art 38.
141 See "Establishment of an ICAO Universal Safety Oversight Program," ICAO Assembly Res. A32-11, 32d Sess., ICAO Doc. 9958, Assembly Resolutions in Force (as of October 8, 2010), at I-88 (1999).
142 "Information Concerning FAA Procedures for Examining and Monitoring Foreign Carriers," 57 Fed. Reg. 38,342 (August 24, 1992); see also 14 C.F.R. § 129.11(a) (2006).
143 Fed. Aviation Admin., U.S. Dept. of Trans., "IASA Program and Process 1," available at www.faa.gov/about/initiatives/iasa/.
144 Ibid., at 3.

Convention, and is imposed on other countries through bilateral air transport agreements. Under the program, the FAA reviews the capabilities of a foreign country's CAA by checking their compliance with ICAO standards (Annexes 1, 6, and 8) and assigns them either a category 1 rating – meets ICAO standards – or a category 2 rating – does not meet ICAO standards – using the same ICAO standards as evaluation criteria.[145] Specifically, FAA personnel carrying out the IASA evaluation process conduct on-site assessments of CAAs for compliance with ICAO standards in eight critical areas: (1) primary aviation legislation; (2) aviation regulations; (3) organization of the CAA; (4) adequacy of the technical personnel; (5) technical guidance; (6) licensing and certification; (7) records of continuing inspection and surveillance; and (8) resolution of safety issues.[146]

Beginning in 1994, results of the IASA program assessments were made public.[147] This gave the IASA program added "teeth," since the stigma of a noncompliant rating was unto itself sufficient to cause a deleterious economic impact on a State's air carriers and tourism industry, "thereby encouraging, albeit grudgingly, increased compliance with their legal obligations under the SARPs."[148] However, these developments notwithstanding, the FAA's need to "go it alone" with the IASA program would soon diminish, as would its capacity to do so.

With the launch of ICAO's Universal Safety Oversight Audit Program (USOAP) in 1999, the FAA announced plans to increase its reliance on ICAO audit reports, necessitating fewer on-site visits by FAA teams.[149] And, in 2004, the FAA recognized the safety audit accreditation program developed by the International Air Transport Association (IATA) for use by US carriers in meeting their obligation to conduct safety audits of code-share partners from countries with category 1 ratings.[150] At the same time, a larger than anticipated workload and resource constraints served to undermine the robustness of the IASA program. For example, although the FAA's intent under the program was to reassess the category for each CAA every two years, FAA data indicates 67 of the 100 foreign CAAs in the program, or about two-thirds, were not assessed between 2000 and 2005.[151]

As a further sign of the IASA program's limitations, in 2013, the FAA announced a policy change to the program, whereby the FAA would henceforth simply remove a country from the IASA summary listing when that country's air carriers no longer provided air service to the United States or participated in code-share arrangements with US air carriers, *and* its CAA had ceased interacting with the FAA for a period of four years.[152] Nevertheless, IASA results, along with the safety audits that US airlines conduct of their foreign code-share partners, remain the FAA's principle measures of the safety of foreign carriers.[153]

Current IASA category determinations for countries included in the IASA categorization system are shown in Table 4.1.

---

145 Ibid., at 3–4.
146 Ibid., at 1.
147 59 Fed. Reg. 46,332 (September 8, 1994).
148 Paul S. Dempsey, *Public International Air Law* at 92–93 (McGill University, Institute and Centre for Research in Air & Space Law 2008).
149 Carole A. Shiffrin, "FAA Plans Safety Change," *Airline Business* (June 1, 1999), available at www.flightglobal.com/news/articles/faa-plans-safety-change-51703/.
150 Fed. Aviation Admin., U.S. Dept. of Trans., Press Release "FAA Recognizes International Safety Audit Program," Release No. 26–04 (2004), available at www.faa.gov/news/press_releases/news_story.cfm?newsId=5703.
151 U.S. Gov't Accountability Office, GAO-05-930, "Aviation Safety: Oversight of Foreign Code-Share Safety Program should be Strengthened" at 15 (2005) (hereinafter Aviation Safety: Oversight), available at www.gao.gov/products/GAO-05-930.
152 78 Fed. Reg. 14,912 (March 8, 2013).
153 Aviation Safety: Oversight, *supra* note 151, at 16.

Table 4.1 IASA Program Summary Listing (as of April 8, 2015)[154]

Country	Category	Country	Category
Argentina	1	Jamaica	1
Aruba	1	Japan	1
Australia	1	Jordon	1
Austria	1	Kuwait	1
Azerbaijan	1	Luxembourg	1
Bahamas	1	Malaysia	1
Bangladesh	2*	Malta	1
Barbados	2	Mexico	1
Belgium	1	Morocco	1
Bermuda	1	Netherlands	1
Bolivia	1	New Zealand	1
Brazil	1	Nicaragua	2*
Bulgaria	1	Nigeria	1
Canada	1	Norway	1
Cape Verde	1	Org. of Eastern Caribbean States	1
Cayman Islands	1	Pakistan	1
Chile	1	Panama	1
China	1	Peru	1
Colombia	1	Philippines	1
Costa Rica	1	Poland	1
Croatia	1	Portugal	1
Curacao	2	Qatar	1
Czech Republic	1	Republic of Korea	1
Denmark	1	Romania	1
Dominican Republic	1	Russia	1
Ecuador	1	Samoa	1
Egypt	1	Saudi Arabia	1
El Salvador	1	Serbia	1
Ethiopia	1	Singapore	1
Fiji	1	Sint Maarten	2
Finland	1	South Africa	1
France	1	Suriname	1
Germany	1	Sweden	1
Ghana	2	Switzerland	1
Greece	1	Taiwan	1
Guatemala	1	Thailand	1
Hong Kong	1	Trinidad and Tobago	1
Hungary	1	Turkey	1
Iceland	1	Ukraine	1
India	1	United Arab Emirates	1
Indonesia	2	United Kingdom	1
Ireland	1	Uruguay	2*
Israel	1	Uzbekistan	1
Italy	1	Venezuela	1

Category 1: meets ICAO Standards – Category 2: does not meet ICAO Standards

Notes
1 Those countries not serving the United States at the time of the assessment are indicated with an asterisk (*) added to their Category 2 determination.
2 As of March 8, 2013, countries are removed from the list after four years if they do not provide air transport service to the United States, have no code-share arrangements with US air carriers, and have no significant interaction with the FAA.

154 Available at www.faa.gov/about/initiatives/iasa/. The FAA also issues a public release when any change of IASA Category for a country occurs.

4.2.2 EU safety list (air carriers operating ban)

Following a number airplane crashes that occurred during 2004–2005 and resulted in many European deaths,[155] the European Commission decided in 2005 to subject unsafe air carriers to a Community-wide ban on operations within the European Union, which became commonly known as the "EU blacklist."[156] The end result is that aircraft operators, as well as specific aircraft identified in the list are prohibited to operate within the European airspace.[157] The list is prepared by EASA and updated every four months. It contains two parts: the first part comprises the carriers of named States for which all operations within the EU are prohibited; and the second covers individual carriers that are subject to certain operational restrictions within the EU.[158]

Operational bans on specific carriers are imposed on a case-by-case basis relying on established common criteria.[159] According to Regulation (EC) No. 2111/2005, these criteria are based on "relevant safety standards,"[160] consisting of the international safety standards contained in the Chicago Convention and its Annexes, as well as, where applicable, those contained in relevant Community law.[161] The decision to include a carrier or aircraft on the blacklist is mainly based on data derived from the Safety Assessment of Foreign Aircraft (SAFA)[162] inspections carried out at Community airports, which may be augmented by ICAO Safety Audit Reports.[163]

It has been argued that the European practice with respect to airline blacklisting is inconsistent with the provisions of Article 33 of the Chicago Convention, which requires States to recognize as valid certificates of airworthiness issued by another States.[164] Indeed, an airline complying with the ICAO SARPs can be banned from European skies if it does not comply with the relevant "Community law."[165] Thus, the fact that the EU, which itself is not a party to

---

155 Ronald Schnitker and Dick van het Kaar, *Safety Assessment of Foreign Aircraft Programme* at 145 (Eleven International Publishing 2013).

156 See Regulation (EC) No. 2111/2005 of the European Parliament and of the Council of 14 December 2005 on the establishment of a Community list of air carriers subject to an operating ban within the Community and on informing air transport passengers of the identity of the operating air carrier, and repealing Article 9 of Directive 2004/36/EC, OJ L 344/15, 27 December 2005; see also Regulation (EC) No. 473/2006 of 22 March 2006, OJ L 84/8, 23 March 2006; and Regulation (EC) No. 474/2006 of 22 March 2006, OJ L 84/14 23 March 2006.

157 Prior to the establishment of such list, several EU Member States had already blacklisted certain airlines from their skies. See Paul S. Dempsey, "Blacklisting: Banning the Unfit from the Heavens," 32 *Annals of Air & Space L.* 29, 50 (2007).

158 For a complete list of air carriers see Appendix I, *infra*.

159 See Regulation (EC) No. 2111/2005, Annex.

160 Ibid.

161 Regulation (EC) No. 2111/2005, art. 2 (j).

162 Directive 2004/36/CE of the European Parliament and of the Council of 21 April 2004 on the safety of third-country aircraft using Community airports, OJ L 143/76, 30 April 2004, imposes a legal obligation upon EU Member States to perform ramp inspections upon third country aircraft landing at their airports. For the application of the said Directive, "third country aircraft" implied an aircraft which is not used or operated under control of a competent authority of an EU Member State. See European Comm'n, "The EC SAFA Programme: Past, Present and Future," available at http://ec. europa.eu/transport/modes/air/safety/doc/2009_12_04_info_fiche_safa_programme.pdf.

163 Schnitker and Kaar, *supra* note 155, at 146–147.

164 See Vincent Correia, *L'Union Européenne et le Droit International de l'Aviation Civile* at 755 (Bruylant 2014); Alan D. Reitzfeld and Cheryl S. Mpande, "EU Regulations on Banning of Airlines for Safety Concerns," 33(2) *Air & Space L.* 132, 150 (2008); Dempsey, *supra* note 157, at 51.

165 Dempsey, *supra* note 157, at 51.

the Chicago Convention, is unilaterally imposing safety requirements on foreign carriers beyond those contained in the treaty and its Annexes is a matter of controversy,[166] though challenges to the legality of the "blacklist" are less fervent than in the past.[167]

While aiming to achieve the same results, the European approach regarding blacklisting of airlines differs from the US approach of State safety assessments in certain significant respects. For example, whereas the US approach places an operational prohibition on the State of registration based on the FAA's assessment of the State's compliance with ICAO SARPs, the European method imposes constraints on individual airlines based mainly on the results of ramp inspections done at EU airports.[168] A notable consequence of the EU's blacklisting is that airlines from less developed countries are encouraged to operate their newest and safest planes within the EU, leaving the aging, unsafe and less maintained aircraft operating in States that potentially lack a robust inspection program.[169] Nevertheless, the EU blacklisting can be viewed as inevitably giving a commercial advantage to EU carriers, since the banning of airlines from operating in the EU, leaves less competition for EU carriers on certain routes.[170] However, it should also be mentioned that most of the carriers under an EU ban have never operated within the EU.[171]

Table 4.2 List of countries that have air carriers subject to an operational ban or restrictions within the EU (as of June 26, 2015)[172]

Countries' air carriers "blacklisted" by EU Member States

Afghanistan	Gabon*	Madagascar**
Angola*	Gabon; South Africa**	Mozambique
Aruba**	Ghana**	Nepal
Benin	Indonesia	Sao Tome
Comoros*	Iran**	Sierra Leone
Congo	Kazakhstan	Suriname (see Note 4)
Democratic Republic of Congo	Korea (Republic of)**	Sudan
Djibouti	Kyrgyz Republic	Zambia
Equatorial Guinea	Liberia	
Eritrea	Libya	

Notes
1 Unless otherwise specified, all air carriers certified by authorities of the listed countries are banned from operating within the EU.
2 Those countries which also have certain of their air carriers subject to operational restrictions within the EU are indicated with an asterisk (*).
3 Those countries which only have air carriers subject to operational restrictions within the EU are indicated with a double asterisk (**).
4 Only one Suriname air carrier (Blue Wing Airlines) is currently subject to an operating ban within the EU.

166 Dempsey, *supra* note 148, at 97.
167 Correia, *supra* note 164, at 757.
168 Dempsey, *supra* note 157, at 53.
169 Ibid.
170 Ibid.; see also Schnitker and Kaar, *supra* note 155, at 162.
171 Schnitker and Kaar, *supra* note 155, at 160.
172 Available at http://ec.europa.eu/transport/modes/air/safety/air-ban/doc/list_en.pdf. Air carriers of the countries listed in Table 4.2 could be permitted to exercise traffic rights by using wet-leased aircraft of an air carrier which is not subject to an operating ban, provided that the carrier complies with relevant safety standards.

4.3 Summary and conclusions

In the field of air transport safety, it might be argued that the United States and the EU have taken different approaches to the same end. However, unlike the FAA, EASA does not have a full mandate with respect to aviation at this time, and so does not benefit from as broad a scope of jurisdiction within Europe as the FAA does in the United States. Consequently, EASA may perhaps for now remain more limited in its activities when compared to the FAA. Nevertheless, due to the European specificity, it is however foreseeable that EASA's mandate will gradually expand over the coming years in parallel with the development of the EU jurisdiction within the aviation sector.

The implementation of the IASA program by the FAA as well as the "blacklisting" of airlines by EASA are eloquent examples of national/regional initiatives having extra-territorial impact. Although the objectives of these initiatives are to provide the highest level of safety in air transport, the answer to the question of whether they actually achieve their intended objectives is not entirely clear.

With the anticipated continual increase in air transport over the coming years, the role played by both the FAA and EASA in advancing aviation safety will no doubt remain crucial, as safety has and will always be the most critical facet of the aviation industry.

Appendix I[173]

Part A – List of air carriers subject to a ban within the EU[174]

- Afghanistan: Ariana Afghan Airlines, Kam Air, Pamir Airlines, Safi Airways
- Angola: Aerojet, Air Gicango, Air Jet, Air Nave, Air26, Angola Air Services, Diexim, Fly540, Gira Globo, Heliang, Helimalongo, Mavewa, Sonair
- Benin: Aero Benin, Africa Airways, Alafia Jet, Benin Golf Air, Benin Littoral Airways, Cotair, Royal Air, Trans Air Benin
- Congo: Aero Service, Canadian Airways Congo, Emeraude, Equaflight Services, Equajet, Equatorial Congo Airlines SA, Mistral Aviation, Trans Air Congo
- Democratic Republic of Congo: Air Fast Congo, Air Kasai, Air Katanga, Air Tropiques, Blue Airlines, Blue Sky, Busy Bee Congo, Compagnie Africaine D'aviation (Caa), Congo Airways, Dakota Sprl, Doren Air Congo, Gomair, Kin Avia, Korongo Airlines, Malu Aviation, Mango Airlines, Serve Air, Services Air, Swala Aviation, Transair Cargo Services, Will Airlift
- Djibouti: Daallo Airlines
- Equatorial Guinea: Ceiba Intercontinental, Cronos Airlines, Punto Azul, Tango Airways
- Eritrea: Eritrean Airlines, Nasair Eritrea
- Gabon: Afric Aviation, Allegiance Air Tourist, Nationale Regionale Transport (NRT), Sky Gabon, Solenta Aviation Gabon, Tropical Air-Gabon

173 "List of Air Carriers which are Banned from Operating within the EU and Air Carriers which are Subject to Operational Restrictions within the EU," available at http://ec.europa.eu/transport/modes/air/safety/air-ban/doc/list_en.pdf. The air carriers listed could be permitted to exercise traffic rights by using wet-leased aircraft of an air carrier which is not subject to an operating ban, provided that the relevant safety standards are complied with.
174 All air carriers certified by the authorities with responsibility for regulatory oversights of the countries listed in Part A are banned from operating within the EU except for Suriname in which only one air carrier is banned as well as for certain countries having a number of air carriers subject to restriction (see air carriers listed in Part B of this Appendix).

- Indonesia: Air Born Indonesia, Air Pacific Utama, Alfa Trans Dirgantata, Angkasa Super Services, Asco Nusa Air, Asi Pudjiastuti, Aviastar Mandiri, Aviastar Mandiri, Batik Air, Citilink Indonesia, Dabi Air Nusantara, Deraya Air Taxi, Derazona Air Service, Dirgantara Air Service, Eastindo, Elang Lintas Indonesia, Elang Nusantara Air, Enggang Air Service, Ersa Eastern Aviation, Gatari Air Service, Heavy Lift, Indonesia Air Asia Extra, Indonesia Air Transport, Intan Angkasa Air Service, Jayawijaya Dirgantara, Johnlin Air Transport, Kal Star, Kartika Airlines, Komala Indonesia, Kura-Kura Aviation, Lion Mentari Airlines, Manunggal Air Service, Martabuana Abadion, Matthew Air Nusantara, Mimika Air, My Indo Airlines, Nam Air, National Utility Helicopter, Nusantara Air Charter, Nusantara Buana Air, Pacific Royale Airways, Pegasus Air Services, Pelita Air Service, Penerbangan Angkasa Semesta, Pura Wisata Baruna, Riau Airlines, Sayap Garuda Indah, Smac, Sriwijaya Air, Survei Udara Penas, Surya Air, Transnusa Aviation Mandiri, Transwisata Prima Aviation, Travel Express Aviation Service, Travira Utama, Tri Mg Intra Asia Airlines, Trigana Air Service, Unindo, Wing Abadi Airlines
- Kazakhstan: Air Almaty, Atma Airlines, Avia-Jaynar/Aviazhaynar, Bek Air, Beybars Aircompany, Burundayavia Airlines, Comlux-Kz, East Wing, Euro-Asia, Fly Jet Kz, Investavia, Irtysh Air, Jet Airlines, Kazair Jet, Kazairtrans Airline, Kazaviaspas, Prime Aviation, Scat, Zhetysu Aircompany
- Kyrgyz Republic: Air Bishkek (formerly Eastok Avia), Air Manas, Avia Traffic Company, Central Asian Aviation Services (Caas), Heli Sky, Air Kyrgyzstan, Manas Airways, S Group International (formerly S Group Aviation), Sky Bishkek, Sky Kg Airlines, Sky Way Air, Tez Jet, Valor Air
- Liberia: all air carriers certified by the authorities with responsibility for regulatory oversight of Liberia
- Libya: Afriqiyah Airways, Air Libya, Buraq Air, Ghadames Air Transport, Global Aviation and Services, Libyan Airlines, Petro Air
- Mozambique: Aero-Serviços SARL, CFM – Trabalhos E Transportes Aéreos LDA, COA – Coastal Aviation, CPY – Cropsprayers, CRA – CR Aviation LDA, Emílio Air Charter LDA, ETA – Empresa de Transportes Aéreos LDA, HCP – Helicópteros Capital LDA, KAY – Kaya Airlines LDA, LAM – Linhas Aéreas De Moçambique SA, Makond LDA, MEX – Moçambique Expresso SARL, OHI – Omni Helicópteros International LDA, SAF – Safari Air LDA, SAM – Solenta Aviation Mozambique SA, TTA – Trabalhos e Transportes Aéreos LDA, Unique Air Charter LDA
- Nepal: Air Dynasty Heli. S., Air Kasthamandap, Buddha Air, Fishtail Air, Goma Air, Makalu Air, Manang Air Pvt Ltd, Mountain Helicopters, Muktinath Airlines, Nepal Airlines Corporation, Shree Airlines, Simrik Air, Simrik Airlines, Sita Air, Tara Air, Yeti Airlines Domestic
- Sao Tome and Principe: Africa's Connection, STP Airways
- Sierra Leone: Air Rum Ltd, Destiny Air Services Ltd, Heavylift Cargo, Orange Air Sierra Leone Ltd, Paramount Airlines Ltd, Seven Four Eight Air Services Ltd, Teebah Airways
- Sudan: Alfa Airlines, Almajal Aviation Service, Bader Airlines, Bentiu Air Transport, Blue Bird Aviation, Dove Airlines, Elidiner Aviation, Fourty Eight Aviation, Green Flag Aviation, Helejetic Air, Kata Air Transport, Kush Aviation, Marsland Company, Mid Airlines, Nova Airlines, Sudan Airways, Sun Air Company, Tarco Airlines
- Suriname: Blue Wing Airlines
- Zambia: Zambezi Airlines

Part B – List of air carriers subject to operational restrictions within the EU

- Angola: Taag Angola Airlines
- Aruba (Netherlands): Air Astana
- Comoros: Air Service Comores
- Gabon: Afrijet, Gabon Airlines
- Gabon; South Africa: Nouvelle Air Affaires Gabon (SN2AG)
- Ghana: Airlift International (GH) Ltd
- Iran: Iran Air
- Democratic People's Republic of Korea: Air Koryo
- Madagascar: Air Madagascar

5

Air navigation

Francis Schubert

5.1 Introduction

The development of an efficient global air transportation system requires a seamless, safe and efficient infrastructure to support international air navigation. Whereas the generic concept of air navigation facilities covers a wide range of services and systems, the core air navigation functions were historically based on Air Traffic Services (ATS). These served their intended purpose until the late 1980s, at which time they became increasingly unable to cope with growing traffic demand. Airspace congestion, traffic delays and flight cancellations soared as the legacy ATS system was stretched to its limits. The cause of the failing performance was found primarily in outdated technology. In September 1991, the International Civil Aviation Organization (ICAO) Assembly endorsed a new ambitious programme under the name of CNS/ATM[1] with a view of optimising the use of the airspace. That programme promoted the use of advanced digital and satellite based technologies. In addition, an Air Traffic Flow Management (ATFM) function was put in place to protect the system against a traffic overload. But major institutional issues were also identified as limiting factors, including the well-established tendency of States to establish segregated civil and military ATS systems. An Airspace Management (ASM) function was put in place to optimise the allocation of airspace among the different categories of users. The modern concept of Air Traffic Management (ATM) resulted from the combination of the historical ATS and the newly created ATFM and ASM functions.

The last two decades were characterised by two main trends that have fundamentally modified the Air Navigation Services (ANS) landscape worldwide. First, many States have entrusted their Air Navigation Service Providers (ANSPs) with some degree of institutional, financial and managerial autonomy, separating service provision from the regulatory responsibilities. Autonomous ANS authorities have been established in various legal forms, ranging from public companies to outright privatised corporations. Second, the need for more intensive cross-border service provision wherever such practices are likely to improve the safety and flight efficiency of air navigation is challenging the historical preference of States for national ANS systems heavily determined by political boundaries.

---

1 The CNS/ATM (Communication, Navigation, Surveillance/Air Traffic Management) programme was agreed by the ICAO Tenth Air Navigation Conference based on a report submitted by the Council's Future Air Navigation Systems (FANS) Committee (Phase II).

5.2 Article 28 of the Chicago Convention

Article 28 of the Chicago Convention addresses the need for an efficient and seamless network of ANS facilities. It prescribes to that end that:

> Each contracting State undertakes, so far as it may find practicable, to:
>
> (a) Provide, in its territory, airports, radio services, meteorological services and other air navigation facilities to facilitate international air navigation, in accordance with the standards and practices recommended or established from time to time, pursuant to this Convention;
> (b) Adopt and put into operation the appropriate standard systems of communications procedure, codes, markings, signals, lighting and other operational practices and rules which may be recommended or established from time to time, pursuant to this Convention;
> (c) Collaborate in international measures to secure the publication of aeronautical maps and charts in accordance with standards which may be recommended or established from time to time, pursuant to this Convention.[2]

The obligations on States under Article 28 of the Chicago Convention are not defined in any detail. Whereas ANS facilities must be adequate to serve the needs of international aviation, States retain considerable discretion regarding the level of infrastructure and service they intend to make available to international aviation. Contracting States are required to ensure that the ANS facilities provided over their territory comply with ICAO standards and recommended practices (SARPs).[3] This commitment is however not absolute and is only given by a contracting State "so far as it may find practicable". In effect, Article 38, by allowing a State to notify differences between their national rules and those enacted by ICAO, offers some discretion to contracting States, where a State finds it impracticable to ensure full compliance.

Contracting States may bring complaints regarding an alleged breach by another State of its obligations under Article 28 to the ICAO Council, in accordance with Article 84 of the Chicago Convention. Article 69 of the Chicago Convention states that

> [i]f the Council is of the opinion that the airports or other air navigation facilities ... of a contracting State are not reasonably adequate for the safe, regular, efficient, and economical operation of international air services, present or contemplated, the Council shall consult with the State directly concerned, and other States affected, with a view to finding means by which the situation may be remedied, and may make recommendations for that purpose.

However it insists that "[n]o contracting State shall be guilty of an infraction of this Convention if it fails to carry out these recommendations".

ANS constitute a system which relies on two core functions: a regulatory function and a service provision function. The regulatory function is meant to define the general framework

---

2 Chicago Convention, Article 28 (Air navigation facilities and standard systems).
3 "Article 28 of the Convention places on each Contracting States the responsibility for the provision of ANS in its territory in accordance with the Standards and Recommended Practices established pursuant to the Convention" (Privatisation in the Provision of Airports and Air Navigation Services, ICAO Circular 284 AT/120, March 2002 (ICAO Circular 284)).

within which ANSPs will be required to perform their activities, and then to supervise compliance of the ANSPs' activities with that framework. The service provision function is for the designated provider to execute relevant operational tasks and to deploy and operate the necessary infrastructure. States responsibilities under Article 28 relate primarily to the policy and regulatory aspects of ANS. They are limited to "setting and maintaining the standards of the services provided and for the quality of services provided".[4] Whereas Article 28 requires contracting States to "provide, in its territory, . . . air navigation facilities" it is commonly agreed that nothing in the Convention or in the Annexes thereto obliges States to provide the facilities and services themselves.

States are required to provide air navigation facilities over their territory, as defined under Article 2 of the Chicago Convention. However they are not required to establish air navigation facilities over their entire territory and can limit their availability to those parts where there is an operational justification for such services.[5] In order to establish a global seamless ANS network, arrangements need to be taken to provide air navigation facilities also over territories which escape any sovereign jurisdiction, in particular over the high seas. Annex 11 foresees that "[t]hose portions of the airspace over the high seas or in airspace of undetermined sovereignty where air traffic services will be provided shall be determined on the basis of regional air navigation agreements".[6] Such arrangements are approved by the ICAO Council, normally on the advice of a Regional Air Navigation Meeting. States that have accepted the responsibility to provide ATS over the high seas or over areas of undetermined sovereignty are required to do so in accordance with the provisions of Annex 11.[7] However, Annex 11 also specifies that

> a Contracting State accepting the responsibility for providing air traffic services over the high seas or in airspace of undetermined sovereignty may apply the Standards and Recommended Practices in a manner consistent with that adopted for airspace under its jurisdiction.[8]

Consequently, States that have notified differences between their domestic ATS regulations and the SARPS adopted by ICAO, are entitled to extend these differences to those parts of the high seas under their responsibility.[9]

5.3 Air Navigation Services

The term "Air navigation facilities and standard systems", as used in Article 28 of the Chicago Convention covers a broad range of various services and equipment, known in common aviation terminology as ANS. The overwhelming majority of ANS regulations are dedicated to

---

4 ICAO, Air Navigation Services Economic Panel, "Report on Financial and Related Organisational and Managerial Aspects of Global Navigation Satellite System (GNSS) Provision and Operation", Montreal, May 1996, ICAO Doc. 9660, §2.6.1.
5 In respect specifically of Air Traffic Services (ATS) "Contracting States shall determine . . . for the territories over which they have jurisdiction, those portions of the airspace and those aerodromes where air traffic services will be provided", "Air Traffic Services", Annex 11 to the Chicago Convention, 13th edition, July 2001 (Annex 11)), § 2.1.1.
6 Annex 11, § 2.1.2.
7 Annex 11, § 2.1.2.
8 Annex 11, § 2.1.2 Note 2. A similar statement appears in the foreword of Annex 11.
9 The regime applicable to ANS procedures thus differs from that applicable to the Rules of the Air, in the sense that Article 12 of the Chicago Convention does not allow any deviation to the latter.

ATS which form the core of the broader ANS term. In most cases, the legal principles that have specifically been developed for ATS will also apply by analogy to other ANS components.

ICAO offers a formal definition neither of the term "air navigation facility" nor for the commonly used term "Air Navigation Services". An unofficial definition can however be derived from ICAO's Policies on Charges for Airports and ANS, which contain an enumeration of services covered by the words "air navigation services" that includes "air traffic management (ATM), communication, navigation and surveillance systems (CNS), meteorological services for air navigation (MET), search and rescue (SAR) and aeronautical information services (AIS)".[10]

5.3.1 Air Traffic Services

"Air Traffic Services" are governed by Annex 11 to the Chicago Convention and are defined as: "[F]light information service, alerting service, air traffic advisory service, air traffic control service (area control service, approach control service or aerodrome control service)."[11] Annex 11 also prescribes that "air traffic services shall comprise three services identified as follows: the air traffic control service, ... the flight information service, ... the alerting service".[12]

The Air Traffic Control (ATC) service itself is subdivided in three separate services, serving different phases of flight.[13] The objectives of ATC are to "prevent collisions between aircraft" and "collisions between aircraft on the manoeuvring area and obstructions on that area" and to "expedite and maintain an orderly flow of air traffic".[14] Any controlled flight is subject to a binding ATC clearance.[15] However, "[i]f an air traffic control clearance is not satisfactory to a pilot-in-command of an aircraft, the pilot-in command may request and, if practicable, will be issued an amended clearance".[16] In addition, in accordance with the principle of the final authority of the pilot in command, pilots are allowed and required to deviate from the terms of their clearance if so dictated by an emergency situation[17] and it is widely accepted that an ATC clearance is not a substitute for the pilots' own duty of care.[18]

The objective of Flight Information Service (FIS) is to "provide advice and information useful for the safe and efficient conduct of flights".[19] FIS must be provided to "[a]ll aircraft which are likely to be affected by the information and which are provided with air traffic control service or otherwise known to the relevant air traffic services units".[20] Annex 11 insists

---

10 "ICAO's Policies on Charges for Airports and Air Navigation Services", ICAO Doc. 9082/7, 7th edition, 2004. Also see "International Civil Aviation Vocabulary", ICAO Doc. 9713, 2nd edition, 2001. It is accepted that the aeronautical obstacle service and the calibration service also form part of the ANS catalogue.
11 Annex 11, "Definitions".
12 Annex 11, § 2.3.
13 The area control service, the approach control service and the aerodrome control service (Annex 11, § 2.3.1 in conjunction with § 2.2).
14 Annex 11, § 2.2.
15 Defined as an "authorization for an aircraft to proceed under conditions specified by an air traffic control unit", "Procedures for Air Navigation Services: Air Traffic Management", ICAO Doc. 4444 ATM/501, 15th edition, 2007 (ICAO Doc. 4444), "Definitions".
16 "Rules of the Air", Annex 2 to the Chicago Convention, 10th edition, July 2005 (Annex 2), § 3.6.1.1 note 2.
17 Ibid. § 3.6.2.1.
18 Ibid. § 3.2 "Avoidance of Collisions".
19 Annex 11, § 2.2.
20 Annex 11, § 4.1.1.

on the fact that "Flight information service does not relieve the pilot-in-command of an aircraft of any responsibilities and the pilot-in-command has to make the final decision regarding any suggested alteration of flight plan."[21] The scope of the information falling under the remits of FIS is very broad and covers various subjects such as meteorological situations, volcanic activity, the release into the atmosphere of radioactive materials or toxic chemicals, and changes in the serviceability of navigation aids and aerodromes conditions. It also includes information regarding collision hazards.

The Alerting Service (ALRS) is established to "notify appropriate organisations regarding aircraft in need of search and rescue (SAR) aid, and assist such organisations as required".[22] The ALRS is provided when ATS operators are made aware that a particular aircraft is or may be in need of SAR assistance. Annex 11 requires ALRS to be maintained

> for all aircraft provided with air traffic control service, in so far as practicable, to all other aircraft having filed a flight plan or otherwise known to the air traffic services and to any aircraft known or believed to be the subject of unlawful interference.[23]

The Flight Information Centre or the Area Control Centre in charge of the airspace concerned[24] shall forward all relevant information to the competent SAR unit.

In addition to the ATC, FIS and ALRS, the definition of ATS also refers to an "air traffic advisory service", the scope and objectives of which are not detailed in Annex 11. The air traffic advisory service is defined as "[a] service provided within advisory airspace to ensure separation, in so far as practical, between aircraft which are operating on IFR flight plans".[25] Historically, the air traffic advisory service was established as a temporary measure to be deployed in parts of the airspace where FIS was not sufficient to ensure the safety and efficiency of air navigation, but where the concerned State lacked the financial or practical means to deploy a fully fledged ATC service.[26]

5.3.2 Air Traffic Flow Management

ATFM is a capacity management function defined as

> a service established with the objective of contributing to a safe, orderly and expeditious flow of air traffic by ensuring that ATC capacity is utilized to the maximum extent possible, and that the traffic volume is compatible with the capacities declared by the appropriate ATS authority.[27]

Annex 11 requires that ATFM "shall be implemented for airspace where air traffic demand at times exceeds, or is expected to exceed, the declared capacity of the air traffic control services concerned".[28] ATFM measures normally take the form of a slot related to an aircraft departure time or to the time of flying over a significant point.

---

21 Annex 11, § 4.1.1 Note.
22 Annex 11, § 2.2.
23 Annex 11, § 5.1.1.
24 Annex 11, § 5.1.2.
25 Annex 11, "Definitions".
26 Annex 11, § 2.6.1 Note. See also ICAO Doc. 4444, ch. 9.
27 ICAO Doc. 4444, "Definitions".
28 Annex 11, § 3.7.5.1.

5.3.3 Airspace Management

The purpose of ASM is to manage the airspace in such a manner that the available airspace can be allocated among all civil and military airspace users in an equitable manner. The objective of ASM "is to maximize, within a given airspace structure, the utilization of available airspace by dynamic time-sharing and, at times, segregation of airspace among various categories of users based on short-term needs".[29] The most common method used for airspace management is based on the Flexible Use of Airspace (FUA) concept, defined as "an airspace management concept which determines that airspace should not be designated as either pure civil or military airspace, but rather considered as one continuum in which all users' requirements have to be accommodated to the maximum extent possible".[30]

5.3.4 Air Traffic Management

ATM is a generic term combining ATS, ATFM and ASM. It is defined by ICAO as

> The dynamic, integrated management of air traffic and airspace including air traffic services, airspace management and air traffic flow management – safely, economically and efficiently – through the provision of facilities and seamless services in collaboration with all parties and involving airborne and ground-based functions.[31]

5.3.5 Communications, Navigation and Surveillance

The provision of ANS relies on the availability of a technical infrastructure governed by Annex 10 to the Chicago Convention and the main functions of which are known as Communications, Navigation and Surveillance (CNS). Under the CNS/ATM initiative of ICAO, ground-based analogical facilities are gradually being replaced by digital technologies supported by satellite-based infrastructures. According to ICAO, "[p]lanning and implementation is the responsibility of a State within the flight information regions (FIRs) where it provides air traffic services".[32] Before introducing new CNS services, States are required to evaluate the related technical systems against accuracy, integrity, continuity of service and availability of service.

5.3.6 Global Navigation Satellite System

The Global Navigation Satellite System (GNSS) is defined as "a worldwide position and time determination system that includes one or more satellite constellations, aircraft receivers and system integrity monitoring, augmented as necessary to support the required navigation performance for

---

29 Basic APAC-ANP, p. V-2. A definition can be found in the SES Framework Regulation, according to which "Airspace Management means a planning function with the primary objective of maximising the utilisation of available airspace by dynamic time-sharing and, at times, the segregation of airspace among various categories of users based on short term needs." (Regulation (EC) No. 549/2004 of the European Parliament and of the Council of 10 March 2004 laying down the Framework for the Creation of the single European sky, as amended by EC Regulation 1070/2009 (the Framework Regulation).

30 European Commission Directive (EC) No. 2150/2005 of 23 December 2005 laying down the implementation rules for the Flexible Use of Airspace.

31 ICAO Doc. 4444, "Definitions".

32 "Global Navigation Satellite System (GNSS) Manual", ICAO Doc. 9849 AN/457, 1st edition, 2005 (ICAO Doc. 9849) § 5.2.1.2.

F. Schubert

the intended operation".[33] The GNSS presently consists of two primary constellations.[34] The primary satellite network is complemented by a number of augmentation systems which increase the accuracy of the signals.[35] The ICAO Thirty-second General Assembly recognised "the need for an appropriate long-term legal framework to govern the implementation of GNSS"[36] which currently comprises

> the Chicago Convention, its Annexes, Assembly Resolutions (especially including the Charter of GNSS Rights and Obligations),[37] associated ICAO guidance (especially including the Statement of ICAO Policy on CNS/ATM Systems Implementation and Operation), regional navigation plans, and exchanges of letters between ICAO and the States operating satellite navigation constellations.[38]

These were complemented in 2005 by the GNSS Manual. The Charter on the Rights and Obligations of States Relating to GNSS Services expresses fundamental principles such as the right for every State and aircraft of all States to "have access, on a non-discriminatory basis under uniform conditions, to the use of GNSS services". It reiterates the principle of the States' complete and exclusive sovereignty by insisting on the fact that "the implementation and operation of GNSS shall neither infringe nor impose restrictions upon States' sovereignty". Although ICAO makes it clear that "[i]t is a State's responsibility to authorize GNSS operations in its airspace", the Charter also puts an obligation on States providing GNSS services and signals to guarantee the continuity, availability, integrity, accuracy and reliability of such services and signals, as well as their compliance with applicable ICAO SARPs. Finally the document requires any charge levied in respect of GNSS services comply with Article 15 of the Chicago Convention.

5.3.7 Aeronautical Information Service

The Aeronautical Information Service[39] (AIS) is governed by Annex 15 to the Chicago Convention. Its objective is to "ensure the flow of information/data necessary for the safety, regularity and efficiency of international air navigation".[40] The AIS is meant to deliver several products, the most important of which are the Aeronautical Information Publication (AIP), Notice to Airmen (NOTAM), Aeronautical Information Regulation and Control (AIRAC) and Aeronautical Information Circulars (AIC).

---

33 "Aeronautical Communications", Annex 10 to the Chicago Convention, 6th edition 2006 (Annex 10), "Definitions".
34 The American Global Positioning System (GPS) and the Russian GLObal NAvigation Satellite System (GLONASS). Once mature, future developments will include the European GALILEO and Chinese Beidou systems.
35 "The total system, including core satellite constellations (i.e. GPS and GLONASS), and all augmentation systems, is referred to as GNSS", ICAO Doc. 9849, § 3.1.1.
36 ICAO Resolution of the General Assembly A32-20, "Development and Elaboration of an Appropriate Long-term Legal Framework to Govern the Implementation of GNSS".
37 "Charter on the Rights and Obligations of States Relating to GNSS Services", ICAO Resolution of the General Assembly A32-19.
38 Resolution A37-22.
39 Defined as "[a] service established within the defined area of coverage responsible for the provision of aeronautical information/data necessary for the safety, regularity and efficiency of air navigation", "Aeronautical Information Service", Annex 15 to the Chicago Convention, 12th edition, July 2004 (Annex 15), "Definitions".
40 Annex 15, p. 1-1.

The AIP constitutes the basic source for information of a lasting character which is essential to air navigation. Annex 15 includes an important requirement for States to include in their AIP a list of the most significant differences between their national regulations and practices and related ICAO provisions. NOTAM are issued for information of temporary and short duration which must be brought promptly to the users' attention and for significant short notice permanent or long duration changes.[41] AIRAC are issued in paper form for information regarding planned changes that will significantly impact air navigation. AIC are issued in printed form for information which does not qualify for any other category, but which is nevertheless deemed important for the purpose of safe and efficient air navigation. Such information pertains in particular to forecasted changes in legislation, regulations, procedures or facilities and material of advisory and explanatory nature.[42]

Another important function of the AIS is to provide material regarding pre-flight and post-flight information at aerodromes used for international air navigation.[43] Information for pre-flight briefing includes relevant elements of the Integrated Aeronautical Information Package, maps and charts, and information concerning the conditions at the aerodrome of departure. Post-flight briefing is primarily intended to collect observations from aircrews regarding the state and operations of air navigation facilities.

5.3.8 Aeronautical Meteorological Service

Meteorological conditions play an essential role for the safety and efficiency of air navigation. It is important that appropriate processes are in place in order to collect and disseminate all relevant information, in a consistent and harmonised manner. This is the purpose of the Aeronautical Meteorological Service (MET). The provisions governing the provision of the MET service are included in Annex 3 to the Chicago Convention. The MET serves the needs of a wide range of actors, including operators, flight crew members, air traffic services units, SAR services units and airport management.[44]

5.3.9 Search and Rescue

The SAR service is defined as "[t]he performance of distress monitoring, communication, coordination and search and rescue functions, initial medical assistance or medical evacuation, through the use of public and private resources, including cooperating aircraft, vessels and other craft and installations". The SAR service itself is generally provided by organisations which are formally independent from ANSPs and whose activities extend to occurrences related to all modes of transportation.[45]

5.4 The regulation of ANS

The safety and efficiency of air navigation requires a highly standardised and robust regulatory framework where the main common principles are defined globally, but implemented regionally and locally. At the international level, ICAO performs the central regulatory function by

41 Annex 15, § 5.1.1.
42 Annex 15, § 7.1.1.1.
43 Annex 15, ch. 8.
44 Annex 3, § 2.1.2.
45 The rules governing the organisation and provision of the SAR service are detailed in Annex 12 of the Chicago Convention.

promulgating SARPs. In some parts of the world, regional regulatory authorities support the implementation of ICAO provisions. The responsibilities of national regulatory authorities consist essentially in regulating the local application of air navigation rules, certifying the service provider(s) and supervising compliance of the latter's activities with applicable standards.

Historically, the regulatory intervention of ICAO has focused on safety regulation. The production by SARPs and Procedures for Air Navigation Services (PANS) has remained ICAO's main activity and still constitutes the bulk of the existing regulatory material.

Large segments of the ANS activity are still provided under monopoly conditions. In particular, the ATS activities, most often qualify as both a natural monopoly "in the market" and a legal monopoly "for the market". Whereas competition in the market[46] is presently impracticable for economic and practical reasons,[47] competition for the market[48] is often excluded for domestic political reasons. Except for an increasing number of aerodrome control operations, which have already been deregulated to some extent in a number of countries,[49] national laws usually reserve the exclusive right to provide ANS within their airspace to a single designated national provider. The purpose of economic regulation is to protect ANS users from any abuse of monopoly position. The regulatory protection put in place by States has however remained very light to this date. The only mandatory principle, established under Article 15 of the Chicago Convention, is the prohibition of user charges that discriminate against foreign aircraft. ICAO has issued policies in order to establish a common framework for the financing of ANS worldwide.[50] But these policies retain a nonbinding status and are much less authoritative than formal SARPS. At the domestic level, in most countries, the State itself will establish a process to ensure the fairness of the user charges. But with few exceptions, these processes, the main component of which is a users' consultation procedure, fall short of any sort of genuine economic regulation.

As a consequence of traffic growth and competing needs of various users' groups, the airspace itself has gradually become a scarce resource, leading to the need to put in place airspace regulation measures. Traffic restrictions (ATC slots) and other regulatory measures falling within the remits of the ATFM function have been put in place. In addition, ASM processes also are implemented in order to establish clear priority rules and to ensure a fair allocation of the airspace available between the various categories of users.

5.5 Standards and recommended practices

5.5.1 Annex 2: Rules of the Air, 10th edition, July 2005

Annex 2 constitutes the "Rules of the Air" as referred to in Article 12 of the Chicago Convention. Annex 2 has two unique features. First it contains only Standards as opposed to Recommended Practices. Second, Annex 2 applies without derogation over the high seas.[51] Annex 2 is closely connected to Annex 11 (Air Traffic Services). Both instruments address air navigation from a pilot perspective (Annex 2) and, respectively, from an ATS perspective (Annex 11).

---

46 That is, several providers operating within the same airspace block. Competition in the market is however feasible for all support functions, such as technical services and training of air traffic controllers.
47 Annex 11, § 3.5.2.
48 Several providers competing to obtain an exclusive mandate for service provision within a given block of airspace.
49 For example, Germany, UK, Spain, Sweden, UK, USA.
50 See *infra* Section 5.9 *et seq*.
51 Annex 2, foreword and § 2.1.1, note.

According to Annex 2, aircraft in flight over the territory of a State other than their State of registration must comply with the rules of State overflown.[52] Elsewhere, aircraft must comply with the rules of their State of registration.

Annex 2 establishes two categories of flight rules[53] (Visual Flight Rules (VFR) and Instrument Flight Rules (IFR)) and details the requirements and procedures applicable to each of these. It prescribes general rules such as rules for the avoidance of collisions by pilots as well as requirements for minimum levels for aircraft in flight.

Annex 2 defines the responsibility of the pilot in command. In accordance with § 2.3.1

> [t]he pilot-in-command of an aircraft shall, whether manipulating the controls or not, be responsible for the operation of the aircraft in accordance with the rules of the air, except that the pilot-in-command may depart from these rules in circumstances that render such departure absolutely necessary in the interests of safety.[54]

Section 2.4 provides that "[t]he pilot-in-command of an aircraft shall have final authority as to the disposition of the aircraft while in command".[55]

Annex 2 prescribes provisions relating to the relationship between aircrews and ATS. It defines in particular the requirements applicable to flight plans to be filed for ATS purposes.

An important chapter in Annex 2 includes procedures for interception of civil aircraft[56] which emphasise that such interventions shall be undertaken only as a last resort, and practise interceptions are not allowed.[57]

5.5.2 Annex 3: meteorological service for international air navigation

Annex 3 governs the MET which covers the forecasting, observation and reporting of weather data (including those pertaining to volcanic ash contamination).[58] State obligations under Annex 3 consist essentially in determining the meteorological service required to meet the needs of international air navigation within their airspace.[59] States are required to designate an aeronautical meteorological authority which will be in charge of providing the MET or arrange for its provision on its behalf.[60] The arrangement for the provision of the MET must comply also with relevant requirements of the World Meteorological Organization.[61]

5.5.3 Annex 4: aeronautical charts

Annex 4 requires States to ensure the availability of reliable and precise navigation charts, presented in a harmonised manner, for navigation over their territory.[62] States can produce the

---

52 Annex 2, § 2.1.1.
53 Annex 2, § 2.2.
54 Annex 2, § 2.3.1, in conjunction with § 4.5 of Annex 6.
55 Annex 2, § 2.4.
56 Annex 2, § 3.8.
57 Annex 2, Appendix 2, § 1.1 lit. (a).
58 See Annex 3, ch. 8.
59 Annex 3, § 2.1.3.
60 Annex 3, § 2.1.4.
61 WMO Publication No. 49 "Technical Regulations", vol. I "General Meteorological Standards and Recommended Practices", ch. B.4 "Education and Training".
62 Annex 4 is complemented by guidance material contained in the ICAO "Aeronautical Chart Manual" (ICAO Doc. 8697).

charts themselves or arrange for their production by another State or an appropriate agency.[63] States are required to ensure that charts published under their authority are adequate, accurate and up to date, presenting information in a form which is "free from distortion and clutter, unambiguous, and be readable under all normal operating conditions".[64] In order to achieve the necessary level of accuracy, contracting States are required to introduce an appropriate data quality management system, in accordance with the provisions of Annex 15.[65]

5.5.4 Annex 5: units of measurement to be used in air and ground operations

The standardised system of Units of Measurement adopted under Annex 5 is based on the International System of Units (SI).[66] The SI relies on the metric system, but Annex 5 also recognises some non-SI units which are deemed necessary to meet the specific needs of international civil aviation. Some of these are to be used on a definitive basis but others, such as the Nautical Mile (NM) and the knot (kt) are accepted for temporary use. The system of units of measurement is also coordinated with the International Organisation for Standardisation (ISO), with which ICAO maintains liaison regarding the standardised application of SI units in aviation.

5.5.5 Annex 6: operation of aircraft

Under Annex 6,[67] States hold the responsibility to implement a safe operational environment over their territory. They must establish a safety programme "in order to achieve an acceptable level of safety in the operation of aircraft".[68] This requirement is cascaded down upon aircraft operators who are required to implement a safety management system acceptable to the authorities of the State of registration.[69]

Annex 6 defines the responsibilities of aircraft operators, which focus on the safety of the aircraft and its occupants. Operators must ensure that aircraft crews are familiar with the rules, regulations and procedures pertaining to air navigation through the airspace of all countries in which the aircraft will be operated[70] and aircrews are required to comply with these rules. As under Annex 2, however, Annex 6 recognises that in emergency situations, pilots may be compelled to take an action which involves a violation of local procedures.[71]

The responsibility for operational control of an aircraft rests with the aircraft operator. When the aircraft operator is not at the same time the pilot-in-command, it must designate one pilot to act as the pilot-in-command,[72] to whom the operator's responsibility can be delegated.[73] In accordance with Annex 6, "[t]he pilot-in-command shall be responsible for the safety of all crew

---

63 Annex 4, § 1.3.2.1.
64 Annex 4, § 2.1.2.
65 Annex 4, § 2.17.1.
66 Système International d'Unité (SI).
67 Annex 6, 8th edition, July 2001. Annex 6, is divided into three parts: aeroplanes, general aviation and helicopters. The basic structure of all three parts of Annex 6 is the same and each addresses the same items in the light of their respective specific focus. The summary presented in this chapter focuses on Part I.
68 Annex 6-1, § 3.2.1.
69 Annex 6-1, § 3.2.4.
70 Annex 6-1, § 3.1.1 and 3.1.2.
71 Annex 6-1, § 3.1.6.
72 Annex 6-1, § 4.2.10.1.
73 Annex 6-1, § 3.1.4.

members, passengers and cargo on board when the doors are closed".[74] Aircraft operators must ensure that aircrews are proficient in the language used for radiotelephony telecommunication purposes,[75] and that all operations personnel are properly instructed in their respective duties and responsibilities.[76]

Individual operators are required to define their operating minima, for instance regarding minimum flight altitudes and aerodrome operating minima, which cannot be below any minimum established by the State holding jurisdiction for the airspace within which the aircraft is to be operated.[77] The competent State authorities are responsible to approve the method used by aircraft operators to define their own minima.

5.5.6 Annex 10: aeronautical telecommunications

Annex 10 is the most voluminous of all Annexes and is divided into five volumes. Its content is largely dictated by the "Radio Regulations" published by the International Telecommunications Union (ITU) which carries the overall responsibility to ensure the consistency of telecommunication provisions across all domains. It is for each State to determine the needs for specific radio navigation aids over its territory, in order to satisfy the needs of international air navigation. These needs are to be coordinated within the frame of Regional Air Navigation Meetings which will carry out periodic reviews of the infrastructure available.

Annex 10 volume 1 (Radio Navigation Aids) establishes a list of standard non-visual aids for precision approach and landing (Instrument Landing System, Microwave Landing System and GNSS) as well as of additional permissible aids. It defines the specifications and requirements associated with each of these navigational aids, detailing aspects such as performance tolerances and siting requirements, in order to ensure the integrity, continuity and availability of the radio navigation services.

Annex 10 volume 2 (Communication Procedures including those with PANS status) contains communication procedures for worldwide use meant to support the international aeronautical telecommunication service.[78]

The provisions covering digital communications systems are detailed in Annex 10, volume 3 (Communication Systems). The state of development of this volume reflects a technical environment in fast evolution. Various parts are still to be developed or are currently very embryonic. Others prepare for future developments such as the global dissemination of information. Annex 10, volume 3 addresses the aeronautical telecommunication network, an important component of which is the VHF Air–Ground Digital Link (VDL), which supports emerging surveillance equipment such as the Automatic Dependent Surveillance-Broadcast (ADS-B).

Annex 10 volume 4 (Surveillance and Collision Avoidance Systems) establishes requirements which apply to surveillance systems such as the Secondary Surveillance Radar (SSR) and provisions applicable to the technical requirements for Airborne Collision Avoidance Systems (ACAS).

Annex 10, volume 5 (Aeronautical Radio Frequency Spectrum Utilization) governs the utilisation of the aeronautical radio frequency including the allocation of radio frequencies for the various purposes of the aeronautical telecommunication service. The allocation within the band reserved by ITU for aviation is performed on the basis of regional air navigation agreements.

---

74 Annex 6-1, § 4.5.
75 Annex 6-1, § 3.1.8.
76 Annex 6-1, § 4.3.2.1.
77 Annex 6-1, § 4.2.6.1.
78 Defined as "a telecommunication service provided for any aeronautical purpose" (Annex 10, vol. 2).

Annex 10 volume 5 finally includes provisions to prevent unauthorised interference with frequencies used for air navigation purposes and rules for the use of the specific radio frequencies dedicated to distress communications.[79]

5.5.7 Annex 11: air traffic services

Annex 11 is complementary to Annex 2 (Rules of the Air) and their joint purpose is "to ensure that flying on international air routes is carried out under uniform conditions designed to improve the safety and efficiency of air operation".[80] The States' obligations in respect of ATS consist primarily in determining those parts of the airspace where ATS shall be provided, as well as designating a service provider. Annex 11 lays down rules for the organisation of airspace for air navigation purposes. States must also prescribe required navigation performance criteria for the airspace under their responsibility and determine and promulgate minimum flight altitudes for each ATS route and control area over their territory.[81]

Fundamental rules are established with respect to coordination between civil and military authorities, including provisions applicable to the interception of civil aircraft. Coordination with organisations providing other services, such as meteorological services or AIS, is also covered.

The safety of air navigation is at the core of Annex 11, which requires that States "establish a safety programme, in order to achieve an acceptable level of safety in the provision of ATS".[82] In addition to general operational procedures, Annex 11 covers a broad range of topics such as assistance to aircraft in emergency (including aircraft subject to unlawful interference) or strayed aircraft as well as requirements with respect to contingency planning to guarantee the continuity of services.[83]

Annex 11 finally lays down requirements regarding communications in ATS based on radiotelephony or datalink procedures, as well as their recording for use in accidents and incidents investigations.

5.5.8 Annex 15: aeronautical information services

Annex 15[84] outlines States' responsibilities with respect to AIS. States can either provide the service themselves, agree on arrangements with one or more States for the provision of a joint service or delegate the responsibility for service provision to a third party.[85] Contracting States remain responsible for the information published and must ensure that AIS performed on their behalf remains consistent with applicable SARPs, regardless of the effective provider. The purpose of Annex 15 is to ensure utmost uniformity and consistency in the management and dissemination of aeronautical information. Annex 15 establishes requirements with respect to data quality, measured in terms of accuracy, resolution and integrity. Data integrity must be ensured through the data process from origin to the next intended user. The target integrity level will vary depending on the data criticality.[86] Annex 15 allows States to recover the costs of

---

79 Annex 10, vol. 5, ch. 2.
80 Annex 11, foreword.
81 Annex 11, § 2.22.
82 Annex 11, § 2.27.1.
83 Annex 11, § 2.30 "Contingency Arrangements". Also see Annex 11, Attachment D, "Material Relating to Contingency Planning".
84 Annex 15 is complemented by the "Aeronautical Information Services Manual" (ICAO Doc. 8126).
85 Annex 15, § 3.1.1.
86 Annex 15 establishes three categories of data: critical, essential and routine (§ 3.2.8).

collecting and compiling aeronautical information as a part of non-discriminatory airport and air navigation charges levied in accordance with Article 15 of the Chicago Convention.[87]

5.6 Procedures for ANS and Regional Supplementary Procedures

The implementation of ICAO Annexes requires provisions of a more detailed granularity, which also take into account specific features encountered at regional level. For that reason, these documents are complemented by PANS and Regional Supplementary Procedures (SUPPS).

PANS are divided in five separate documents:

1 Procedures for Air Navigation Services – Air Traffic Management (PANS-ATM);[88]
2 Procedures for Air Navigation Services – Aircraft Operations (PANS-OPS);[89]
3 Procedures for Air Navigation Services – Training (PANS-TRG);[90]
4 Procedures for Air Navigation Services – ICAO Abbreviations and Codes (PANS-ABC);[91]
5 Procedures for Air Navigation Services – Aerodromes.[92]

PANS enjoy a lower regulatory status than SARPs and are subject to a lighter approval procedure. Whereas SARPs are adopted by the ICAO Council in accordance with Article 37 of the Chicago Convention and following the full procedure prescribed under Article 90, PANS are approved by the Council and recommended to contracting States for implementation. PANS are not subject to an obligation of notification of differences under Article 38 of the Chicago Convention. States are nevertheless required to publish a list of significant differences between their national procedures and the related ICAO PANS.[93]

SUPPS address specific regional needs arising from the implementation of regional Air Navigation Plans (ANPs). SUPPS have a lower regulatory status compared to SARPs and PANS. SUPPS are approved by the Council and recommended to contracting States for implementation in those FIRs to which they are relevant. All SUPPS must comply with existing SARPs or PANS. SUPPS are published in ICAO Doc. 7030, which is divided into several chapters, each of which lists the SUPPS relevant to a particular ICAO region.

5.7 Air Navigation Plans

5.7.1 Global Air Navigation Plan

The harmonised and coordinated development of air navigation facilities is managed under the ICAO Global Air Navigation Plan (GANP).[94] The GANP is a "high-level policy document

87 ICAO, "Policies on Charges for Airports and Air Navigation Services" (ICAO Doc. 9082), 9th edition, 2012 (ICAO Doc. 9082).
88 ICAO Doc. 4444.
89 "Procedures for Air Navigation Services: Aircraft Operations", ICAO Doc. 8168 OPS/611, 5th edition, 2006.
90 ICAO Doc. 9868, 1st edition, 2006.
91 ICAO Doc. 8400, 10th edition, 2010.
92 ICAO Doc. 9981, 1st edition, not yet in force.
93 Annex 15, § 4.1.2.
94 "Global Air Navigation Plan 2013–2028", ICAO Doc. 9750-AN/963, 4th edition, 2013 (GANP), which succeeded the ICAO "Global Air Navigation Plan for CNS/ATM Systems" (ICAO Doc. 9750) published in 1998.

guiding complementary and sector-wide air transport progress"[95] under the authority of the ICAO Council. The purpose of the GANP is to "to assist ICAO Regions, subregions and States with the preparation of their Regional and State Air Navigation Plans".[96] The elements agreed at the global level are detailed at regional level in the form of regional ANPs, the contents of which are managed by Planning and Implementation Regional Groups (PIRGs).

5.7.2 Regional Air Navigation Plans

The purpose of regional ANPs is to facilitate the implementation of the GANP at regional level by specifying the facilities, services and procedures that are required for international air navigation in a particular region. ANPs are amended upon an initiative from one or more States, submitted to the ICAO Secretariat through the appropriate regional office. Proposals which do not raise any objection during the consultation procedures are forwarded to the President of the Council for approval on behalf of the Council.

5.8 The provision of Air Navigation Services

5.8.1 States' responsibilities in respect of service provision

By ratifying the Chicago Convention, States commit to provide ATS over their territory. To fulfil their obligations States are required to "designate the authority responsible for providing such services".[97] The provider may be the State itself, through a governmental body or "a suitable agency".[98] States may also decide to delegate the responsibility for service provision to a foreign State.[99] When the responsibility for providing the service is entrusted to an autonomous or foreign body, States however remain ultimately responsible for the ANS facilities and services in place over their territory. Regardless of the status and identity of the provider "the relevant States continue to be responsible under Article 28 of the Chicago Convention".[100] After having designated an ANSP the State still must "arrange for such services to be established and provided in accordance with the provisions of this Annex".[101] ICAO documents refer to a historical context where States have designated one organisation as the sole provider of ANS over their territory. In the modern era, and in particular in the wake of the liberalisation of ANS activities at aerodromes, many States have designated several providers. This is not in contradiction with ICAO provisions under the condition that each ANSP operates on an exclusive basis within the airspace allocated to it.

---

95 GANP, p. 32.
96 GANP, p. 15.
97 Annex 11, § 2.1.3.
98 Annex 11, § 2.1.3, Note 1.
99 Annex 11, § 2.1, "Establishment of Authority".
100 ICAO, "Report of the Secretariat Study Group on Legal Aspects of CNS/ATM Systems", 1st Meeting, Montreal, 7–8 April 1999, SSG-CNS/I-Report, 9 April 1999 (Report of the Secretariat Study Group), § 3.8.1. The Thirty-eighth General Assembly of ICAO also reminded Member States that "with regard to airports and air navigation services they alone remain responsible for the commitments they have assumed under Article 28 of the Convention regardless of what entity or entities operate the airports or air navigation services concerned" (Resolution A38-14: "Consolidated Statement of Continuing ICAO Policies in the Air Transport Field").
101 Annex 11, § 2.1.1.

5.8.2 Organisational models

For practical and political reasons, States have traditionally elected to perform operational ATS functions themselves through government agencies which ICAO refers to as "the appropriate ATS authority".[102] However, nothing in the Chicago Convention prevents a State from designating another entity, whether a national, foreign, public or private organisation.

5.8.2.1 State agencies

Historically, States have favoured a national State agency, forming part of the governmental structure often financed by public taxation. State agencies were initially self-regulated organisations. This structure was seen as the most effective model to provide the service while meeting the State responsibilities in respect of national sovereignty, commitment under Article 28 of the Chicago Convention and general public service obligations. The State agency model prevailed until the late 1980s and remains in place in many regions of the world, in particular in those countries where the management of civil air traffic is entrusted to a military organisation.

The organisational structures in place in many States were ill-fitted to cope with the massive investments necessary to upgrade existing facilities to meet the needs of the CNS/ATM programme. The financing of State-run ANSPs was subject to State budgetary mechanisms. The experience made in numerous countries was that these processes were lengthy, cumbersome and uncertain as to their outcome. National ANSPs consequently received too little money too late and were doomed to lag behind increasing traffic demand. Then, the State's procurement requirements and bureaucratic culture showed to be particularly inadequate to take the urgent decisions required for the updating of the technical infrastructures.[103] Considering the challenges raised by the necessity to adapt to a quickly developing environment, States began to investigate alternative organisational forms which would reconcile two essential requirements. On the one hand, the ANS organisation must achieve financial autonomy. On the other hand, the State needs to retain a sufficient level of control to guarantee its capability to fulfil its international obligations under the Chicago Convention as well as its domestic public service obligations.

5.8.2.2 Autonomous entities

The key feature of most institutional initiatives undertaken by States to reform their ANS system is the establishment of an "autonomous ANS authority". An autonomous authority is defined by ICAO as "an independent entity established for the purpose of operating and managing one or more ANS, and empowered to manage and use the revenues it generates to cover its costs".[104] ICAO emphasises that the word "autonomous authority" "does not normally imply regulatory authority when used in this context".[105] Autonomy endows ANSPs with the freedom to manage their resources, to access capital market to finance their investments and to decide on all matters within the remits of their statutory mandate. Financial autonomy also requires the

---

102 Defined as "the relevant authority designated by the State responsible for providing air traffic services in the airspace concerned", Annex 11, "Definitions".
103 See "ATS Planning Manual", ICAO Doc. 9426-AN/924, 1st (provisional) edition, 1984 (ICAO Doc. 9426) part 1, Section 2, ch. 1, § 1.3.5.
104 ICAO Circular 284.
105 ICAO Circular 284.

ANSP to finance all its activities independently from any State funding. ICAO openly supports the principle of autonomy,[106] without expressing any preference for any specific formal organisational structure.

The establishment of autonomous service providers requires the separation of the regulatory and service provision functions. Separation allows States to retain within the governmental structure those functions which belong to the core prerogatives of the State and to externalise those activities which can be performed better outside the administrative structure. It also acknowledges the fact that self-regulated organisations are inadequate in the ANS domain, because of the risks of internal conflicts of interests that can arise within such organisational models. In practice, separation can be organisational, when the service provider is taken out of the governmental structure and established as a new independent entity with its own legal personality. Separation can also be functional, when independent divisions are established within the administrative structure to perform the regulatory and services provision functions.[107] ICAO notes that "Autonomy can take many forms and does not necessarily mean privatisation (although privatisation is one form of autonomy) since ownership can rest in public or private hands or a mixture of both."[108]

5.8.2.2.1 CORPORATISED AGENCIES

Corporatisation is defined by ICAO as the "creation of a legal entity outside government to manage certain facilities and services, either through a specific statute or under an existing statute such as company law".[109] The term "corporatisation" thus refers to the legal status of the ANSP. In itself, however, it does not imply that ownership is transferred to private investors.

Corporatised ANSPs are usually established as share capital corporations. In the overwhelming majority of cases, the State will retain full ownership, or at least a majority stake in the company. These companies are normally created, structured and governed by the law that applies to ordinary private corporations. Special provisions however often reserve specific exceptions that account for the particular status of ANS as a public service. Such exceptions may pertain to the business orientation of the company (not-for-profit), the applicable liability regime or specific provisions intended to safeguard the sovereign interests of the State (requirement for State approval of particular decision items).

5.8.2.2.2 PRIVATISATION

The term privatisation refers to the ownership of a corporatised ANSP. It is defined by ICAO as the "transfer of full or majority ownership of facilities and services from the public sector to the private sector".[110] The main objective of the few existing cases of ANS privatisation is related to the need to raise external capital to finance the development of infrastructures. While there is no requirement under ICAO provisions for States to retain full or majority ownership of their ANSPs, cases of genuine privatisation of national ANSPs have remained

---

106 ICAO "encourages the establishment by States of autonomous authorities to operate their airports and air navigation services or both" ICAO, "World-wide CNS/ATM Systems", Implementation Conference, Rio de Janeiro, 11–15 May 1998, WW/IMP WP/4, 4/2/98 (Rio Conference WP/4).
107 For example, USA, France.
108 Rio Conference WP/4.
109 ICAO Circular 284.
110 ICAO Circular 284.

very rare to this date.[111] ICAO advises in this respect that "[w]hen considering privatisation or private participation in the provision of ANS, a more cautious approach is required because of cross-border and other implications".[112] In addition, privatisation raises a risk of conflicts between core objectives within the organisation. Moreover, many governments are concerned that a privatised ANSP may be tempted to lower the safety standards under pressure from the shareholders to improve the financial performance of the company.

5.8.2.3 International agencies

A number of States have preferred to create a multinational organisation jointly with other countries that provides services over the territories of the participating States instead of establishing a national infrastructure of their own. These include EUROCONTROL,[113] ASECNA[114] and COCESNA.[115] Such ventures are motivated by the challenge of managing small size and complex airspaces and the search of economies of scale.

5.9 Air navigation fees and charges

Article 15 of the Chicago Convention deals with "airport and similar charges", which stipulates that:

> Any charges that may be imposed or permitted to be imposed by a contracting State for the use of … air navigation facilities by the aircraft of any other contracting State shall not be higher,
>
> (a) As to aircraft not engaged in scheduled international air services, than those that would be paid by its national aircraft of the same class engaged in similar operations, and
>
> (b) As to aircraft engaged in scheduled international air services, than those that would be paid by its national aircraft engaged in similar international air services. All such charges shall be published and communicated to the International Civil Aviation Organisation.… No fees, dues or other charges shall be imposed by any contracting State in respect solely of the right of transit over or entry into or exit from its territory of any aircraft of a contracting State or persons or property thereon.

111 These include NATS, the UK service provider, and to some extent NavCanada although that company does not meet the ICAO definition of a privatised ANSP, since it was established as a "non-share capital company".
112 ICAO Circular 284.
113 EUROCONTROL is an international governmental organisation established in 1960 by the International Convention relating to Cooperation for the Safety of Air Navigation of 13 December 1960 (EUROCONTROL), modified by three protocols (1970, 1978 and 1981). EUROCONTROL operates an air traffic control centre in Maastricht, Netherlands, which manages air traffic in the upper airspace of Belgium, Luxembourg, Netherlands and part of Germany.
114 The Agence pour la Sécurité Aérienne en Afrique et à Madagascar, with headquarters in Dakar, succeeded in 1974 the organisation created by the Convention Relative à la Création d'une Agence Chargée de Gérer les Installations et Services Destinés à Assurer la Sécurité de la Navigation Aérienne en Afrique et Madagascar signed in Saint-Louis du Sénégal on 12 December 1959. ASECNA is entrusted with the responsibility to provide ANS over the territory of its Member States (Burkina Faso, Cameroon, Central African Republic, Congo, Ivory Coast, Dahomey, Gabon, Madagascar, Mali, Mauritania, Niger, Senegal, Sudan, Chad and Togo).
115 The Corporacion Centroamericana des Servicios de Navigacion Aerea is an international organisation in charge of providing ANS within the airspace of its five Member States (Costa Rica, El Salvador, Guatemala, Honduras and Nicaragua). It was created by the Convention on the Central American Air Navigation Corporation signed in Tegucigalpa on 26 February 1960.

Article 15 does not impose any obligation on States to charge airspace users for ANS, but lays down the conditions that are to be respected by States or designated ANSPs that elect to do so. Article 15 lays down the principle of non-discrimination which requires States to apply the same charges to aircraft registered in other States as those applied to its own national aircraft. Finally, the charges must relate to the effective provision of a service and airspace users cannot be charged for the sole right of entering or overflying the territory of a contracting State.

Article 15 of the Chicago Convention is supplemented by ICAO's Policies on Charges for Airports and Air Navigation Services[116] and by the "Manual on Air Navigation Services Economics".[117] The ICAO policies are of non-binding nature and do not qualify either as SARPs and PANS.[118] States and ANSPs are entitled to recover the full cost of providing the service,[119] but where services cannot be reasonably charged at full cost, for instance at remote facilities with low traffic figures "[g]overnments may choose to recover less than full costs in recognition of local, regional or national benefits".[120] In accordance with ICAO Policies, ANS are normally provided on a not-for-profit basis but ANSPs are allowed to "produce sufficient revenues to exceed all direct and indirect operating costs and so provide for a return on assets ... to contribute towards necessary capital improvements".[121] The full cost recovery system has been increasingly criticised mainly because it imposes the entire financial risk on the airspace users.

Not all States however have introduced a formal user charge. The financing of the US ANS system, for instance, relies on the Airport and Airway Trust Fund (AATF)[122] which complements the General Fund which finances the Federal Aviation Administration's activities. The AATF combines a variety of sources, such as taxes on domestic airline passenger tickets and flight segments, taxes on international passenger arrivals and departures, and taxes on aviation fuel, which are not directly correlated to the provision of ANS.

5.10 Airspace

In accordance with Article 1 of the Chicago Convention, States are free to determine those parts of their sovereign airspace which will be open to international civil aviation. In those parts of the airspace which are open to civil aviation, aircraft are constrained to the route structure established by the concerned State.[123]

5.10.1 Flight Information Regions

States are required to establish FIRs[124] in those portions of their airspace where FIS and ALRS will be provided.[125] The delineation of FIRs' limits is a relatively rigid process, conducted in

---

116 ICAO Doc. 9082.
117 ICAO, "Manual on Air Navigation Services Economics", ICAO Doc. 9161/3, Montreal, 3rd edition, 1997.
118 A binding common charging system based directly on the ICAO Policies was implemented in Europe by the "Multilateral Agreement relating to Route Charges", signed at Brussels, 12 February 1981 ("Multilateral Agreement").
119 ICAO Doc. 9082, § 38 (i).
120 ICAO Doc. 9082, § 39, lit. i.
121 ICAO Doc. 9082, § 38 (iv) A.
122 Established by the Airport and Airway Revenue Act of 1970 (26 U.S. Code § 9502).
123 According to Article 68 of the Chicago Convention, each State retains the freedom to "designate the route to be followed within its territory by any international air service and the airports which any such service may use".
124 Defined as "an airspace of defined dimensions within which flight information service and alerting service are provided", Annex 11, "Definitions".
125 Annex 11, § 2.5.2.1.

accordance with ICAO guidelines; but States are free to delineate the FIRs over their territory. Annex 11 foresees that FIRs should be delineated to meet operational and technical needs rather than to reflect national boundaries.

5.10.2 Control areas and control zones

Annex 11 prescribes that "those portions of the airspace where it is determined that air traffic control service will be provided to IFR flights shall be designated as control areas or control zones".[126] A control area is defined as "a controlled airspace extending upwards from a specified limit above the earth". Control areas will contain "airways"[127] or ATS routes.[128] Control zones are established to support ATC at controlled aerodromes[129] with IFR traffic and are defined as "a controlled airspace extending upwards from the surface of the earth to a specified upper limit".

5.10.3 Airspace classification

ICAO has established different classes of airspace to account for the diversity of ATS needs, depending on traffic density, complexity and mix.[130] The classification of a given block of airspace will determine the type of flights allowed (VFR/IFR), the type of services offered (ATC, FIS, ALRS), the requirements in respect of maintaining bilateral communications with ATS, the requirements to carry a radar transponder and the means to maintain traffic separation (ATC separation and/or traffic information).

5.10.4 Airspace restrictions

Article 9 of the Chicago Convention prescribes that "each contracting State may, for reasons of military necessity or public safety, restrict or prohibit ... aircraft ... from flying over certain areas of its territory" under the condition of non-discrimination between its own nationally registered aircraft and foreign registered aircraft. Article 9(b) also states that

> Each contracting State reserves also the right, in exceptional circumstances or during a period of emergency, or in the interest of public safety, and with immediate effect, temporarily to restrict or prohibit flying over the whole or any part of its territory.[131]

The purpose of Article 9 is chiefly to protect civil aircraft in flight from human activities that could endanger air navigation (in particular military operations), to protect the interests of third parties on the ground from risks caused by aircraft in flight, for instance in respect of large gathering of people, and to prevent aircraft from over-flying sensitive ground-based equipment and installations.[132]

---

126 Annex 11, § 2.5.2.2.
127 Defined as "a control area or portion thereof established in the form of a corridor", Annex 11, "Definitions".
128 Defined as "A specified route designed for channelling the flow of traffic as necessary for the provision of air traffic services", ibid.
129 Defined as "those aerodromes where it is determined that air traffic control service will be provided to aerodrome traffic", Annex 11, § 2.5.2.3.
130 The classification includes seven classes (A to G) as prescribed in Annex 11, § 2.6.
131 Chicago Convention, Article 9.
132 See "Manual Concerning Safety Measures Relating to Military Activities Potentially Hazardous to Civil Aircraft Operations", ICAO Doc. 9554-AN/932, 1st edition, 1990.

Article 9 is not meant to protect aircraft against natural phenomena such as adverse weather or volcanic ashes, the exact location of which often remains uncertain, upon which man can exercise no control and are prone to develop in unpredictable ways. While States and ANSPs will take measures to assist airspace users to avoid natural hazards, the general ICAO regulatory philosophy in this respect, and more specifically the provisions of Annex 6, put the responsibility for the avoidance of such phenomena on the aircraft operators themselves.

The detailed rules applicable to airspace restrictions, and the typology of restricted airspace are prescribed in Annex 2 to the Chicago Convention.

5.10.4.1 Danger areas

A "Danger area" is defined as "an airspace of defined dimensions within which activities dangerous to the flight of aircraft may exist at specified times".[133] Danger areas are often established to delineate the perimeter of military activities. There are no restrictions imposed on pilots regarding the penetration of a danger area and the purpose declaring such airspace sectors is exclusively to create awareness on the aircrews' side as to the existence of a specific risk. The decision to enter a danger area belongs to the pilot alone.

5.10.4.2 Restricted areas

A "Restricted area" is defined as "an airspace of defined dimensions, above the land areas or territorial waters of a State, within which the flight of aircraft is restricted in accordance with certain specified conditions".[134] States will generally declare a restricted area "when the risk level involved in the activities conducted within the area is such that it can no longer be left to the discretion of individual pilots whether or not they want to expose themselves to such risk".[135] The declaration of a restricted area is accompanied by the publication of specific conditions (e.g. VFR only, below or above a certain altitude, at certain times of the day) governing the penetration of the airspace sector.

5.10.4.3 Prohibited areas

Prohibited areas are subject to the most severe restrictions. A prohibited airspace is defined as "an airspace of defined dimensions, above the land areas or territorial waters of a State, within which the flight of aircraft is prohibited".[136] Prohibited areas are often established for security purposes, to protect sensitive or critical human activities or installations on the ground (e.g. facilities used for a high profile political summit, nuclear facility) from the risk of a falling aircraft, and not to protect aircraft and their occupants themselves from the potential consequences of a dangerous situation.

5.11 Civil–military cooperation

Historically, most States have established segregated systems, where the airspace structure comprises sectors assigned to civil traffic and others allocated to military users. The responsibility for

133 ICAO Annex 2, "Definitions".
134 ICAO Annex 2, "Definitions".
135 ICAO Doc. 9426, § 3.3.2.5.
136 Annex 2, "Definitions".

managing civil and military sectors is entrusted to different organisations using their own equipment. The shared usage of the airspace requires a close cooperation between civil and military actors. For that reason Annex 11 requires that "[a]ir traffic services authorities shall establish and maintain close cooperation with military authorities responsible for activities that may affect flights of civil aircraft".[137] Annex 11 recommends in particular that States should implement arrangements for the flexible use of airspace, under which all aircraft, civil and military, should have safe access to sectors reserved for military activities.[138]

Annex 11 also requires that special procedures shall be established to notify ATS units, if a (potentially) civil aircraft is approaching or has entered an airspace sector in which interception might become necessary. All assistance measures must be taken to avoid the need for interception.[139]

Finally, ICAO offers some guidance regarding the organisational models which can be put in place at the national level to optimise the joint utilisation of the airspace by civil and military users. These include the total integration of civil and military operations into a single organisation, a partial integration where a single service is offered jointly by military and civil ANS personnel, and a colocation model, where military and civil ANS personnel operate side by side from a common facility.[140]

5.12 Cross-border service provision

The boundaries of the air traffic control sectors tend to follow political boundaries, which often imposes unnecessary constraints on the provision of services. Annex 11 recognises that "[t]he delineation of airspace, wherein air traffic services are to be provided, should be related to the nature of the route structure and the need for efficient service rather than to national boundaries".[141] Further, Annex 11 states that "conclusion of agreements to permit the delineation of airspace lying across national boundaries is advisable when such action will facilitate the provision of air traffic services".[142] Arrangements which result in a situation where a service provider located on the territory of one State provides services within the sovereign airspace of another State are known as cross-border service provision.[143] There is no compelling technical obstacle against such practices. From an institutional perspective, however cross-border service provision raises legal questions associated with State sovereignty, the designation of service providers, liability, the financing of services and the regulation and supervision of ANS activities.

The early examples of cross-border service provision have been based on so-called "ATS delegations", by which "a State may delegate to another State the responsibility for establishing and providing air traffic services".[144] Whereas ATS delegation is the only model explicitly

---

137 Annex 11, § 2.17.1. See also ICAO Assembly Resolution A32-14, ICAO Doc. 9554, "Manual Concerning Interception of Civil Aircraft", Doc. 9433 and Doc. 9426.
138 Annex 11, § 2.18.6.
139 Annex 11, § 2.17.3.2.
140 Annex 11, Part II, ch. 11, § 2.2.4.
141 Annex 11, § 2.10.1.
142 Ibid. § 2.9.1, Note 1.
143 According to SES Framework Regulation "'cross-border services' means any situation where air navigation services are provided in one Member State by a service provider certified in another Member State".
144 Annex 11, § 2.11.

described in the ICAO framework to support cross-border service provision, it is not the only possible legal arrangement. Other approaches can be followed, in particular those foreseen under the Single European Sky (SES) Regulations.

ATS delegations do not challenge the sovereignty of the delegating State. Annex 11 insists that "if one State delegates to another State the responsibility for the provision of air traffic services over its territory, it does so without derogation of its sovereignty".[145] It further makes it clear that the delegation remains strictly functional and that "the providing State's responsibility is limited to technical and operational considerations and does not extend beyond those pertaining to the safety and expedition of aircraft using the concerned airspace".[146] Finally "The providing State in providing air traffic services within the territory of the delegating State will do so in accordance with the requirements of the latter."[147]

ATS delegations are firmly anchored in a State-to-State relationship and formalised by a State agreement. This has given strong confidence to the States concerned that the sovereignty aspects involved will be addressed adequately. The drawback of classical ATS delegation agreements is that these arrangements are often heavy and rigid. The delegation agreement normally covers the main legal principles of the arrangements, such as the scope of the ATS delegation, the delineation of the concerned airspace, applicable rules and procedures, and liability arrangements. The operational details are covered in separate Letters of Agreement between the individual ATS providers involved.

ICAO Annex 11 is silent, as far as the legal liability aspects of ATS delegations are concerned. The rules governing this matter are to be included in the delegation agreement. The application of the predominant "territorial State" doctrine results in a regime where liability for damages caused by a failure of the providing State must be compensated by the delegating State. The latter will then recover the expenses paid by the means of a recourse action. The alternative and little applied "provider State" doctrine puts on the latter the obligation to compensate any damage it causes to third parties.

5.13 The Single European Sky

The SES is an initiative launched by the European Commission (EC) in the late 1990s in response to the failing performance of the European air navigation system. Its objective is to defragment the patchwork of ill-coordinated national infrastructures and to replace it by a continuous and seamless network.

The SES legislation is based on Regulation (EC) No. 549/2004 of the European Parliament and of the Council laying down the framework for the creation of the Single European Sky (Framework Regulation) and three additional technical regulations:

- Regulation (EC) No. 550/2004 of the European Parliament and of the Council of 10 March 2004 on the provision of air navigation services in the single European sky (the Service Provision Regulation – SPR);
- Regulation (EC) No. 551/2004 of the European Parliament and of the Council of 10 March 2004 on the organisation and use of the airspace in the single European sky (the airspace Regulation);
- Regulation (EC) No. 552/2004 of the European Parliament and of the Council of 10

145 Annex 11, § 2.1.1, Note.
146 Annex 11, § 2.1.1, Note.
147 Annex 11.

March 2004 on the interoperability of the European Air Traffic Management network (the interoperability Regulation).

These instruments are complemented by a large number of implementing rules.

The first package of SES entered in force on 20 April 2004 with the objective of establishing the SES by the end of that year. Following a review conducted in 2008, a second legislative package (SES II) was enacted in 2009 to strengthen the contents of the programme. While the first package established an institutional framework, the second focuses on four specific pillars: performance, safety,[148] new technologies and airport capacity. In June 2013, a third impulsion (SES II+) was given by the EC, the ambition of which is limited to adjustments to some of features of the SES. This package has not yet been adopted.

The organisation of the airspace under the SES legislation is primarily based on the concept of Functional Airspace Blocks (FABs)[149] which may cover the airspace of more than one country and within which ANSPs and National Supervisory Authority (NSA) cooperate for the management of air traffic, regardless of national boundaries. The SES legislation imposes a separation of function by requiring States to designate, jointly or individually, one or more NSA(s), which must be independent from ANSPs. States are allowed to delegate the performance of supervisory tasks to a recognised organisation which fulfil defined conditions.

The provision of ANS within the airspace of the EU requires the service providers to be certified. The common certification requirements relate, among other things, to the ANSPs' technical and operational competence, the adequacy of their systems and processes for safety and quality management, quality of services, financial solidity, liability and insurance protection, ownership and organisational structure, security and human resources aspects. States are required to designate a service provider to operate on an exclusive basis within airspace blocks over their territory.[150] They are free to designate any service provider under the condition that it holds a valid certificate.

The SES has introduced innovative models for cross-border service provision. Article 8 SPR allows a State to designate a foreign service provider, an option which is not explicitly stated in ICAO documents and which is not formalised by the means of a State agreement. Contrary to a classical ATS delegation model, except for supervisory matters, the direct designation process does not involve the State of the foreign designated provider and neither do the SES regulations require the approval of the State of the latter. Another innovation takes the form of arrangements between designated providers. Under such arrangements the ATS provider designated by a State can sub-delegate by the means of a written contract the responsibility to provide services within a part of the airspace entrusted to it to another service provider. The agreement must be notified to the national authority or authorities concerned. When the provision of ATS is involved, the States' approval will be required.

---

148 The safety pillar extends the competences of the European Aviation Safety Agency (EASA) to include also safety rules applicable to ATM and aerodromes.

149 A FAB is defined as

> an airspace block based on operational requirements and established regardless of State boundaries, where the provision of air navigation services and related functions are performance-driven and optimised with a view to introducing, in each functional airspace block, enhanced cooperation among air navigation service providers or, where appropriate, an integrated provider.

Framework Regulation, "Definitions"

150 The mandatory certification and designation scheme applies only to ATS. These features are discretionary for meteorological services and not required for other services.

While the EU authorities hold no competence to regulate military activities, the SES legislation establishes a framework to optimise the coordination of civil and military air navigation activities[151] and more specifically to allow the application of Flexible Use of Airspace (FUA) arrangements and the allocation of airspace sectors based on clear priority rules. Article 13 of the Framework Regulation allows EU countries to suspend the application of arrangements deployed under the SES regulations, in case of conflict with national military requirements.

The second package of SES legislation establishes a European performance scheme[152] based on the setting of European-wide performance targets in the key areas of safety, capacity, cost-efficiency and environment for reference periods of five years. States are required to define national performance plans that are consistent with the achievement of the objectives set at European level. States may also coordinate their efforts within the frame of Functional Airspace Blocks initiatives. The performance of the ANS system is reviewed by an independent body (i.e. the Performance Review Board) and this role is entrusted to EUROCONTROL.

A Network Manager function was also created as a centralised function at EU level by the second SES legislative package. The consistent management of the European network should, among other objectives, allow for the optimum use of airspace and for aircraft to follow their preferred trajectories. This function covers the airspace design, flow management (slot coordination and allocation), allocation of scarce resources such as radar transponder codes and radio frequencies. EUROCONTROL has been designated as Network Manager until 2019.

The second SES legislative package has also established a new binding framework for the setting of en-route navigation charges as well as for the financing by the means of the charging scheme, of the Common Projects adopted within the deployment phase of the Single European Sky Air Traffic Management Research (SESAR) programme.

Finally, the European ANS infrastructure has been criticised for its obsolescence and fragmentation. One of the goals of the SES initiative is consequently to harmonise the ANS technical infrastructure. The interoperability Regulation plays a key role in this respect. It defines common requirements and Community specifications in order to ensure the interoperability between the different ATM systems used by ANSPs. All technical constituents must be accompanied by a declaration of conformity or suitability for use, attesting that they comply with the applicable requirements. ANSPs must establish a declaration of verification of compliance, which must be submitted to the competent NSA. The Regulation also aims to promote the synchronised implementation of agreed and validated concepts of operation and technologies in the SES under the SESAR programme.[153]

5.14 Summary and conclusions

International air navigation relies on a complex and comprehensive network of ANS. Since it was established on the basis of the Chicago Convention and related Annexes, its development reflects a tension between political considerations related to State sovereignty and the galloping evolution of technology. The most significant changes to the historical ANS model were brought by the ICAO CNS/ATM programme in 1991, which has resulted in the implementation

---

151 Statement by the Member States on military issues related to the Single European Sky, Official Journal of the European Union, 31 March 2004, L 96/9.
152 Commission Implementing Regulation (EU) No. 390/2013 of 3 May 2013 laying down a performance scheme for ANS and network functions.
153 The SESAR programme aims at the same goal as the US NextGen Program. Both are closely coordinated.

of important new operational, technical and institutional solutions. Yet ANS stand once again on the threshold of a fundamental reform driven by disrupting technologies which are likely to challenge many of the legal assumptions underlying the provision of these services. The virtualisation of infrastructures and the offer for shared services observable in most network activities will extend to the ANS domain, putting into question the legacy of national monolithic systems and creating new cross-border dependencies as ANSPs increasingly rely on data provided by third parties. The introduction of Remote Piloted Aircraft in non-segregated airspace will modify the relationship between pilots and air traffic controllers and introduce new operational challenges. The deployment of "Remote Towers" will require regulators and ANSPs to reconsider the assumption that ATC at an aerodrome can only be safely provided by the means of a physical control tower on the site. Finally, from a general perspective, technological developments have made the location of the service provider irrelevant, which opens the door to innovative operational and business models for ANS. A successful answer to these emerging opportunities will require both a strong political will and major adjustments to the regulatory framework for ANS.

6

Airport business and regulation

Isabelle Lelieur and Charles E. Schlumberger

Introduction

The history of airports is as old as aviation, which commenced 100 years ago.[1] The first airports, however, were grassy fields with little infrastructure; operations were limited to daytime flights in good weather. During the First World War, military infrastructure, mainly buildings and hangars, were added to airfields. After the war, some of these military airfields added facilities for the handling of civilian passenger traffic, and, as such, created the concept of a civilian airport. One of the first military airfields to become a civilian airport after the First World War was Paris – Le Bourget airport, which served as the French capital's main airport for decades. Before the end of the Second World War airport regulation, and civil aviation regulation in general, was still in its infancy. Aviation had some international rules agreed to in the Paris Convention of 1919, which primarily focused on sovereignty of air space, and overflight and landing rights.[2] However, airport regulation, if any, was purely derived from local law covering primarily property rights and early building standards.

Today's regulation of airports for international air services was born out of the Chicago Convention, which in Article 15 embraced the principle of nondiscrimination for airport charges.[3] However, the bulk of airport relevant regulation was developed and published in the International Civil Aviation Organization (ICAO) Standards and Recommended Practices (SARPs) years after the signing of the Chicago Convention.[4] The first set of SARPs specifically addressing airports was Annex 14, "Aerodromes", which was only adopted in 1953.[5] Today, however, airports are complex and large infrastructure systems, which are covered by a multitude of international regulations, national laws, and local rules which cover a landscape of legal and regulatory aspects of which only the main ones are covered in this chapter.

6.1 Airport legal statute

"Public or Private?" A simple question, but the answer is not so easy when it comes to airports. Matters are not helped by the ambiguity and even the confusion sometimes between the ownership

---

1 College Park Airport in Maryland, US, established in 1909 by Wilbur Wright, is generally agreed to be the world's oldest continually operating airfield.
2 Convention Relating to the Regulation of Aerial Navigation, signed 13 October 1919, 11 L.N.T.S. 173.
3 Convention on International Civil Aviation, done 7 December 1944, 61 Stat. 1180, T.I.A.S. No. 1591, U.N.T.S. 295 (hereinafter Chicago Convention), ICAO Doc. 7300/8.
4 At the Chicago Conference in 1944, drafts of 12 technical Annexes were prepared, which addressed various topics, such as airways systems, communications, rules of the air, airworthiness, and aircraft registration. However, no annex dealt with airports. Online: www.icao.int/secretariat/PostalHistory/standards_and_recommended_practices.htm, accessed 17 October 2014.
5 Ibid.

and the management of airports. One of the reasons of that confusion could stem from the fact that many airports are now operated by private concession companies, still most of the time majority owned by public shareholdings, alongside private shareholders, with the assets being held by a public authority. In reality, as it will be addressed below, airports around the globe are managed by various types of operators, through various types of contracts, depending on the culture of the State, its political will for its strategic public infrastructures, and its need of cash inflow.

6.1.1 Airport ownership

When it comes to airport ownership, most airports are owned by a public authority, whether the federal/national government, the local authority such as the region or the city or even a public entity (airport authority or multipurpose (air)port authority). Thus, in Canada, in the US, in Central and South America, and in Australia, the federal government or the municipal authorities own most of the airports. In the Association of Southeast Asian Nations (ASEAN) countries, most of the airports are owned by the State (e.g. the royal Government of the Kingdom of Cambodia owns the two international airports of Phnom Penh and Siem Reap; the Republic of the Philippines owns Cebu airport) or by a public entity (e.g. in Indonesia, the two public airport companies PT Angkasa Pura I and PT Angkasa Pura II own, fully or partly, the land of the airports). In Europe, public ownership of airports prevails as well. The powerful *Länder* own most of the airports in Germany. In France, 150 medium- and small-size airports were decentralized in 2007 from the State to the public local authorities (the Regions, the Departments or the municipalities), while the French State has kept the ownership of the 12 biggest regional airports.[6]

Despite the dominance of public ownership, several international and regional airports are owned by a private company. In Europe, two States transferred the airport asset and land ownership to the private airport operator. In Great Britain, the company Heathrow Airport Holdings Limited (HAH),[7] operates several British airports (Heathrow, Southampton, Glasgow, Aberdeen), and in France, the company Aéroports de Paris, a listed private company, operates all airports in the Parisian region. Having two hats, the ownership and the operation, the airport operator becomes in such a case an integrated airport authority, operating to a certain extent a public service activity with more freedom and action capacity.

---

6 The French law 2004/809 of 13 August 2004, *relative aux libertés et responsabilités locales*, article 28, foresaw the decentralization of 150 airports with regional and local vocation, to public local authorities, by 1 January 2007. This important reform was encouraged by the fact that the French State was still responsible for local infrastructures, without any will or means to realize the necessary investments, whereas local authorities were involved for decades in the development and maintenance of these infrastructures, without being liable. Thus, this French reform just allowed alignment of the law with the reality.

7 HAH is the former British Airport Authority (BAA). BAA was created in 1966 by the Airport Authority Act. It was first a public entity, and then became in 1986 a private company publicly owned. This evolution of the statute was the occasion for the British Government to transfer the airport ownership to the company. In 2006, BAA was sold to the private sector, for US$2.5 billion offering. In 1987, BAA became a listed company on the London stock market. Since 2009, Ferrovial has been asked by the British Competition Authority to sell London Gatwick, London Stansted, and Edinburgh airports. In August 2014, Aberdeen and Glasgow airports were put up for sale. The current shareholdings of HAH are owned by FGP Topco Limited, a consortium owned and led by the infrastructure specialist Ferrovial S.A. (25 percent), Qatar Holding LLC (20 percent), Caisse de dépôt et placement du Québec (13.29 percent), the Government of Singapore Investment Corporation (11.88 percent), Alinda Capital Partners (11.18 percent), China Investment Corporation (10 percent), and Universities Superannuation Scheme (USS) (8.65 percent).

6.1.2 Airport management

Airport operation and management is a more heterogeneous picture than the airport ownership one, which is rather uniform.

6.1.2.1 State control airport operator

At first, most airports in the world were directly controlled and managed by the public owner: the government itself or through a civil aviation administration, or the public local authorities, such as the Region or the Municipality. Still today, several airports remain operated directly by public owner, even in "liberalized" States. A significant example is the US where most airports are owned and operated by federal or municipal governments.[8] In Mexico, 20 airports, including Mexico City International Airport, are operated by a government agency created in 1965, called Aeropuertos y Servicios Auxiliares (ASA). In Ireland, Dublin Airport Authority plc (DAA) is the state-owned airport authority, running Dublin Airport and controlling the Cork Airport Authority.[9] In Thailand, 26 airports, representing 8.1 million passengers in 2013, are still operated directly by the civil aviation administration. For these situations where a government plays both the role of regulator (i.e. performing its technical and economic oversight function) and of service provider, ICAO recommends that States consider a clear separation of the regulatory and operational functions, in order to avoid conflicts of interest. Separation enhances transparency in the decision making process and makes clear the lines between accountability and the authority to monitor the activities of the other.[10]

When it comes to airport operators indirectly controlled by the State, there are two categories. The first category is the administrative body benefiting from a certain degree of autonomy. Administrative bodies can be either a *sui generis* body, as Aéroports de Paris was until 2005, before it was transformed into a private limited liability company,[11] or a Chamber of Commerce and Industry (CCI). In fact, airports in many countries have been operated from their creation by a CCI that was considered as a "natural" airport operator. For example, since the 1930s France has granted the operation of all regional airports, including the largest ones (Nice, Lyon, Toulouse, Marseille, etc.) to the local CCI. They were very powerful bodies, locally, and, until recently, have remained in France a key player in the sector. The second category of airport operators indirectly State controlled are the corporatized public airport operator, which is defined as an independent acting economic entity, structured according to and complying with commercial law, whose shares are wholly owned by public authorities. Today, more than half of the operator companies are fully publicly owned. In 2016, they represent 53 percent of the European airports and 73 percent of the non-European airports.[12] Spain has chosen this option with the AENA Group, 100 percent public shareholdings, managing 46 airports in Spain.[13] In France, the 12 biggest airports, initially operated

---

8 Very few exceptions in the US where airports have been privatized. One example is Stewart International Airport, NY, privatized under a 99 year lease.

9 The DAA used to control Shannon Airport but Shannon Airport became a publicly owned commercial airport on 31 December 2012.

10 ICAO Doc. 9082, Section 1, para. 12; ICAO Doc. 9562, Chapter 2, Section B.

11 In France, in 2014, only one airport remains operated by a public undertaking (in French: *établissement public*), Bâle-Mulhouse airport, because it is a bi-national airport (Swiss and French).

12 "The ownership of Europe's airports", ACI-Europe 2016 Report.

13 The AENA Group, 100 percent State-owned, is a group of companies devoted to airport management and the provision of air navigation services. Through AENA Aeropuertos S.A., AENA operates in addition to the 46 airports, two heliports in Spain and participates directly and indirectly in the management of 15 more airports around the world. It is the world's leading airport operator in terms of passenger numbers, handling more than 200 million.

by the CCI as mentioned above, have been corporatized within the last six years, owned by the State (60 percent), the local CCI (25 percent), and the public local authorities (15 percent).[14] Likewise, in Asia, the Indonesia airport market is shared between two State-owned limited liability companies, PT Angkasa Pura I and PT Angkasa Pura II,[15] while Vietnam operates 22 airports through a public owned company, called Airports Corporation of Vietnam (ACV). In Canada, the four biggest airports (Toronto, Vancouver, Montreal, and Calgary) are operated by non-profit, non-share capital corporations. Thus, these numerous examples show the creation of entities, autonomous and independent vis-à-vis the owner, in all regions for the past two decades, generating several advantages: the revenues generated through the use of airport resources are transparently reinvested in operating and developing the facilities and the airport users contribute directly to the upkeep and development of the facilities that they use.

When airports remain under the overall ownership and control of governments or local authorities, the organizations operating them are expected to act with public interest in mind rather than primarily governed by profit considerations, although this should not preclude the setting of clear objectives and adoption of best commercial practices.[16] In fact, this form of management fitted the airports' needs for decades, as airports used to be mere infrastructure providers, dependent on public finances and focused on the interests of their State's flag carriers.

6.1.2.2 Toward a more privatized airport world

In the past two decades, public authorities around the globe have progressively withdrawn from the airport business, most of the time partly, sometimes fully, implementing various privatization legal models.

6.1.2.2.1 THE REASONS FOR THE SHIFT

In recent years, airports have undergone a process of business transformation. From a mere infrastructure provider, operating public service as a monopoly, airports have become complex businesses with diversified activities, self-financed (for the biggest airports), and responding to the needs of diversified customers. Subsequently, private investors have stepped into the airport business around the globe, to respond to the new need. There are a number of reasons for this transformation.

A first reason is that aviation deregulation and liberalization, commencing first in the US in 1978, then in the EU in the 1990s, has exposed airports to ever increasing competitive pressures. The gradual completion of the internal markets have led to the removal of all commercial restrictions for airlines flying within the US and the EU, such as restrictions on routes, number of flights, or the setting of fares. This liberalization movement is currently ongoing within the ten Member States[17] of the ASEAN, who have identified a 2015 deadline to establish an ASEAN

14 The French law 2005–357 of 20 April 2005 allowed the local CCI to give its concession contract to a private company, fully publicly owned for the following airports: Strasbourg, Lyon, Nice, Marseille, Montpellier, Toulouse, Bordeaux, Nantes, Pointe-à-Pitre, Fort-de-France, La Réunion, Cayenne. In 2015, the French State sold 49.9 percent of its shares in Toulouse airport company to a Chinese consortium called Symbiose, and, in March 2016, the French State launched the tender procedure to sell 60 percent of its shares in Nice and Lyon airport companies.
15 Indonesian secondary airports are still directly operated by the civil aviation administration.
16 R. Abeyratne R., *Law and Regulation of Aerodromes*, Springer, 2014; ICAO Doc. 9562, Chapter 2.
17 The ten ASEAN Member States are: Indonesia, Malaysia, Philippines, Singapore, Thailand, Brunei, Vietnam, Laos, Myanmar, and Cambodia.

single aviation market. Liberalization has paved the way for the emergence of low-cost carriers and has enabled the industry to expand as never before. This development has generated a tremendous increase in traffic. Faced with the traffic growth, there was, and still is, a crucial lack of infrastructure capacity: States have to build new airports, as well as invest substantially in order to expand airport runway and terminal capacity of existing airports. This situation requires significant financial capacity. Thus, airport financing has become a focus for many governments, and several factors have led to the need of private financing, the necessity to enhance access to capital markets, and to the need to achieve a financial return on investment. First, States do not always have financial liquidity, and they are usually restricted in their ability to borrow money in capital markets to finance infrastructure improvements. Second, the world has faced an ongoing global economic crisis for several years. Nevertheless, the demand for air services continues to grow.

The second reason is that airports have had to become more attractive vis-à-vis the airlines, whether low-cost carriers or traditional carriers, and develop a wide variety of commercial practices. These practices have led to a step-change in the nature of airport competition, airports increasingly competing not just for additional traffic, but also for airlines to base aircraft and form route networks at their airports.[18] Consequently, a strong marketing policy, improved efficiency, and maximized profitability are prerequisites for an airport to be attractive and competitive. Public authorities have been more and more conscious of the need to attract private investors to fit these requirements, and stimulate innovation and responsiveness to market. On their side, public entities are focusing more on public service, stimulating tourism (which implies route development with little profitability consideration), and job creation.

The third reason that explains the evolution of the airport sector is that States have been increasingly eager to transfer the legal and financial responsibility, and thus the risk, of the entire airport activities, from the design, construction, and the operation (including sometimes airport safety and security missions), to an independent operator, with States retaining the role of regulator. Indeed, privatization does not mean abandonment of a State's prerogatives and goals. Airports remain a strategic public asset and when a private operator manages the airport, it does it though an authorization (a license) or a Public–Private Partnership (PPP) agreement that defines the rights and obligations of the two partners with the State wearing the owner and regulator hat and the private investor wearing the operations hat. Thus, the State, usually through its civil aviation administration, continues to provide oversight of airline access, safety, security, and environmental protection, as well as a veto power over airport investment and divestiture, and airport charges. ICAO's position on airport privatization is that governments be "guardians" of security and safety at the airports; ICAO recommends the institutional strengthening of the aeronautical authority prior to privatization.[19]

To sum-up on the privatization advantages, increase of the private sector involvement has significant benefits. On one side, while benefiting from a high-level private investor with airport expertise for a strategic infrastructure asset, governments have an obvious financial interest. Privatization relieves States of the responsibility for financing infrastructure developments. Governments also expect to gain a one-time cash windfall from the sale of the airport company shares, as well as periodic tax revenue from privatized airports. On the other side, the private investor will be incentivized to provide a high return on investment.

---

18 ACI Europe Position Paper, "Competition in the European Aviation Sector", March 2014.
19 ICAO Doc. 9562, ch. 2; ICAO Doc. AT Conf.6.WP6, 10 December 2012.

6.1.2.2.2 HOW DO THE PUBLIC AUTHORITIES LEAVE MORE SPACE TO THE PRIVATE MARKET?

a Through the airport company shareholdings

Since the 1990s, the private sector has been more involved in the operation of airports, whether in a mixed public–private ownership structure or in a fully privatized company. The predominant scheme is the private company, with a mixed public–private shareholding.[20] Given the important role of airports as engines of economic growth and employment, public authorities have a strong incentive to work closely together with the private sector on the efficient operation and management of the airports. There are numerous examples: the French State still owns 50.6 percent of Aéroports de Paris shares;[21] the Russian Federal Government owns 83 percent of Sheremetyevo airport; the three major Brazilian airports were privatized in 2012, the private investor having 51 percent alongside the public entity Infraero keeping 49 percent of the shares;[22] the Dutch Government has kept 69.77 percent of the Schiphol Airport shares;[23] while the Hungarian State has 25 percent of the shares (plus one vote) of Budapest airport.

Some governments make the choice of full privatization of their airport operation, while retaining ownership.[24] All continents are concerned. Cambodia is one of the "pioneer" countries that has privatized its airports, in 1995 granting a private company[25] a concession contract to operate Phnom Penh and Siem Reap airports. Cambodia was followed by Argentina, where Aeropuertos Argentina 2000 S.A. (AA2000) created in 1998, manages the 33 major airports in the country.[26] Australia engaged a vast airport privatization wave from the late 1990s,[27] followed by the UK privatizing BAA in 2006.[28] In 2007, the Jordanian State granted Aman Queen Alia International airport to a fully privately owned operation company with several shareholders including Abu Dhabi Investment Company (UAE), Noor Financial Investment Company (Kuwait), and Aéroports de Paris Management (France). Two European States recently privatized their airports: in 2013, Portugal sold 100 percent of its stakes in ANA, operating ten airports in Portugal, to a French airport operator; and Slovenia sold Ljubljana airport to a German

---

20 See *supra* note 12.

21 Aéroports de Paris S.A. was fully owned by the French State when it was created in 2005. Since then, the State opened its capital to private shareholders. Thus, from 31 December 2014, the shareholders are: French State (50.6 percent), Schiphol Group (8 percent), VINCI (8 percent), institutional investors (20.9 percent), Predica (4.8 percent), employees (1.7 percent), individual shareholders (6 percent).

22 The three Brazilian airports are the two airports of Sao Paulo (Guarulhos and Campinas) and Brasilia airport, all three representing about 30 of the total passenger number in Brazil. After an auction procedure, the price of the three airports reached US$14 billion. The French company, Egis, in consortium with Triunfo Participações, UTC Participações won Campinas airport, the companies Invepar, OAS, and the South-African ACSA won Guarulhos airport, and Brasilia airport has been won by the consortium Engevix and the Argentinian Corporacion America.

23 Schiphol Airport shareholders: the Dutch government (69.77 percent), City of Amsterdam (20.3 percent), City of Rotterdam (2.20 percent), and Aéroports de Paris (8 percent).

24 According to the ACI Europe 2016 report "The Ownership of Europe's Airports", only 17 percent of airport operators in Europe are fully privately owned.

25 The concession company is owned at 70 percent by VINCI Airports (French) and at 30 percent by Muhibbah (Malaysian).

26 Grupo Corporacion America owns 89 percent of AA2000. It is the world's largest private airport operator handling more than 98 percent of Argentine commercial air traffic. It also operates many airports in the world.

27 Sydney airport company is owned by McQuarie (85 percent), Hochtief (12 percent), and an Australian Fund (3 percent).

28 See *supra* note 4.

airport group.[29] In these different examples of airport companies, it is interesting to identify the various types of shareholders. In many cases, when forming a consortium, an airport operating company becomes "engaged" with a complementary business corporation, such as a construction company (when a new airport has to be built) or a financial fund (when a substantial amount of equity is required).

When the airport operator is corporatized, in other words when a company is created, whether in a mixed public–private ownership structure or in a fully privatized one, the governing bodies have to be defined very carefully by the shareholders, in the company charter. Aside from the General Shareholders' Assembly, a board of directors is usually the key governance body, entitled to make certain strategic decisions. While ordinarily the number of shares of each shareholder is linked to the voting rights in the company, it is sometimes voluntarily misbalanced, and a minority shareholder may have as many rights as a majority shareholder, if strategic decisions are taken unanimously. The charter also defines which shareholder designates the top management positions, such as the Chief Executive Officer (CEO), the Chief Operating Officer (COO) as well as the Chief Financial Officer (CFO). The charter's usual provisions include tag-along and drag-along rights, a pre-emption right, as well as call and put options.

b By implementing contractual schemes between the public authorities and the airport company
Apart from airports directly operated by the public owner, most airports are now operated by an autonomous entity: either indirectly by the public owner, through a CCI or through a corporatized public airport operator, or by a private entity (with public, private, or public/private shareholdings). These autonomous entities obtain their right to operate the airport from a license, a long-term lease, or from a contract granted by the public owner. Lease agreements are commonly granted in Anglo-Saxon countries, such as in Canada, Australia, or Great Britain.[30] As regards contracts, they are generally granted through a transparent public bid process. The contractual framework depends on the public owner's will, on the extent of services and facilities it wants to transfer to the autonomous entity, and on the financial structure it wants to define.

With respect to services and facilities, when the public owner wants to hand over specific services or facilities to a third party, it concludes a service contract. Thus, by operating a specific service or facility, the entity is compensated by a price, generally a lump sum, pre-defined in the contract. Implementing this rather simple contractual scheme is not considered airport privatization.[31] A service contract is a common type of contract used in US airports. Also, in general, large airports outsource non-core operations to private firms specialized in those functions, such as airport security services or shuttle bus airport operations.

29 The ten airports in Portugal operated by ANA are Lisbon, Porto, Faro, and Beja on the mainland; Ponta Delgada, Horta, Flores, and Santa Maria in the Azores; and Funchal and Porto Santo in Madeira. ANA, holding a 50 year contract, was acquired by the French airport group, VINCI Airports, on 21 February 2013, for more than EUR 3 billion. On 5 February 2014, the Republic of Slovenia sold the listed public company Aerodrom Ljubljana, holding a 40 year lease contract, to the German airport group, Fraport, for EUR 177.1 million.
30 The Canadian federal government has granted long-term lease (60 years + an 80 year option) to non-profit corporations to operate the main Canadian airports, such as Montreal, Vancouver, or Calgary. Australia has granted long-term leases (50 years + 49 extension period) to private companies to operate Sydney and Melbourne airports. In Great Britain, BAA benefits from a 99 year lease. In the US, the State of New York granted in 2000 a 99 year lease to the UK-based company, National Express Group Plc, to operate Stewart International Airport in Newburgh.
31 As airport privatization involves a full or majority ownership of the entity managing the whole airport infrastructure.

Where the public owner wants to transfer the entire airport operation, which gathers all facilities and services, it enters into a PPP with an autonomous entity. By this scheme, this latter assumes a great role in the airport management and operation as a whole, and is paid, not by the public owner, but directly by the airport users (airlines and passengers). The type of PPP contract depends mainly on the financial structure defined by the owner. There are two main alternatives. When the public owner wants to keep financing capital expenditures, it will grant a management contract to a third entity, according to which the responsibilities of all airport operations and infrastructures are transferred to the entity for a certain period of time (usually less than ten years), except for the airport infrastructure development, which remains financed by the owner. Alternatively, the owner may be willing to transfer a "full package" to the entity (usually a private one) including the financing, construction, development, operation, and maintenance of the airports. This is commonly known as the Design–Build–Finance–Operate–Maintain (DBFOM) model or Build–Operate–Transfer (BOT) model.[32] BOT schemes are more and more chosen by airport public owners, especially when an airport project requires substantial capital expenditures, such as in case of the construction of a new airport infrastructure or in case of the extension of an existing airport. Indeed, the BOT option allows a State, without financial liquidity, to pursue ambitious infrastructure projects, financed by a third party. The duration of BOT contracts depends mainly on the amortization duration of the capital expenditures.[33] At the end of the contract, the entity transfers the airport facility to the State. The type of PPP contract most chosen by airport owners around the globe is the concession contract:[34] from Portugal to Peru and from Cambodia to Croatia.[35] In most cases, a concession contract consists of the design, construction, financing, management, operation, maintenance, and exploitation of one or several airport(s).

The aim of the concession contract is to define the rights and obligations of the owner (the grantor) and the operator as regards the design, construction, financing, operation and maintenance of the airport. The airport operator gets the right to use the land and to exploit it commercially, in exchange for a number of obligations and objectives. Usual obligations and objectives are the payment of an up-front concession fee to the grantor, establishing a revenue-sharing mechanism, reporting on the airport's activities (aeronautical and non-aeronautical) and figures, through the annual report and regular meetings with the grantor, respecting the transparency and equal-treatment principles vis-à-vis the users, keeping the quality and adequacy of the infrastructures at all times, fitting with the traffic needs (ICAO, Annex 14). In fact, the concession model allows for a wide range of contractual considerations. However, in case of the recourse by the operator of debt financing, a number of must-have provisions has to be

---

32 Abeyratne, *Law and Regulation of Aerodromes*, p. 156, describes the various form of BOT.
33 BOT contract duration usually varies from 20 to 55 years, i.e., Athens airport's concession is 25 years, Lisbon airport's concession is 50 years, Nantes airport's concession is 55 years. In fact, the ten biggest airports in Portugal, including Lisbon, are operated by one concessionaire company, ANA, that benefits from one 50 year concession Agreement.
34 See the definition of the term "concession" in EU Directive 2014/23, 26 February 2014, Article 5.
35 Portugal signed a 50 year concession contract with VINCI Airports, in 2013, to operate ten Portuguese airports; Peru signed in April 2014 a 40 year concession contract to operate Chinchero-Cusco airport, with the consortium Kuntar Wasi formed by Corporación América S.A. companies and Andino Investment Holding S.A.; Cambodia signed in 1995 a 45 year concession contract with a company owned by VINCI (70 percent) and Muhhibah (30 percent) to operate Phnom-Penh, Siem Reap, and Sihanoukville airports; and Croatia signed in 2013 a 30 year concession contract to operate Zagreb airport, with MZLZ, a private company owned by Aéroports de Paris Management (20.77 percent) (a wholly owned subsidiary of Aéroports de Paris), Bouygues Bâtiment International (20.77 percent), Marguerite Fund (20.77 percent), IFC (17.58 percent), TAV Airports (15.0 percent), and Viadukt (5.11 percent).

guaranteed in the contract, in order to protect the operator's interests. These include a clear and predictable economic regulation framework (parameters determining the tariff evolution must be set *ab initio*), hardship clauses, and set forth mechanisms to reestablish the economic and financial balance of the concession agreement (change of law, *force majeure*), competition clause protecting the asset against a similar infrastructure project in the same area, dispute resolution (arbitrage procedure), concessionaire/grantor variations, etc.

When a substantial investment is at stake, the airport company needs to secure its investment within the concession contract, as mentioned above, as well as through other legal instruments such as Bilateral foreign Investment Treaties (BITs). When setting up the investment structure, BITs are a crucial tool for investors. Such treaties prohibits the host State from expropriating investors except for a public purpose, in a non-discriminatory manner, and upon payment of prompt and adequate compensation.

6.2 Legal relationship between the airport operator and the stakeholders

An airport is a city where numerous entities live together. Since they are interlinked, they all have to work together hand in hand to make the airport work. The main entities are airlines, retailers, ground-handlers, public authorities, and other contractors. The airport operator, whose role is to coordinate all these activities, has a specific legal/contractual relationship with each of them.

6.2.1 Airlines

Airlines, as the airport main clients, are obviously the main stakeholder present at the airport. The airline/airport relationship is rather simple: no contract needs to be signed between them, the sole rule is the payment of the airport charges by the airline in counterpart of the services rendered by the airport. This basic rule still prevails today, although the airport/airline relationship has become more and more complex over the past 15 years. The air transport liberalization wave, in the US and in the EU, has paved the way for the rapid growth of the sector and the development of low-cost carriers. And these newcomers now exceed the market share of incumbent air carriers in many regions.[36] This phenomenon was a factor of substantial development for all airports and even a stake of survival for many small airports. But this fantastic growth opportunity has had a price for airports. The balance of powers has changed: whereas for decades airlines used to pay airport charges "easily", they are much more demanding today vis-à-vis the airports. Indeed, before deciding to land/take-off from an airport, they now more often require the airport to conclude a tailor-made agreement with various financial arrangements, airport charges reduction, sometimes substantial amounts of incentives, and marketing support. This bargaining practice initially started with low-cost carriers flying to small regional airports. It is today generalized to all carrier and airport categories around the globe.

The incentive practice has tremendously increased competition in the sector and has led many airlines and airports, feeling prejudiced by the financial arrangements of their competitors, to react formally by sending complaints to the European Commission or by suing their competitors before national courts, alleging unlawful State aid. In Europe, it started with the Charleroi airport case in

---

36 For the EU: see EU Commission, DG Competition discussion paper, "New State Aid Rules for a Competitive Aviation Industry", February 2014; Commission Communication, "Guidelines on State Aid to Airports and Airlines", 4 April 2014, 2014/C 99/03, ch. 1. Same trend in Asia: see Network ASEAN Forum 2013, "Aviation: Lifting the Barriers Report".

2004, concerning the commercial incentives granted by both the Walloon Region and Brussels South Charleroi Airport to the Irish low-cost airline, Ryanair.[37] Since then, the European Commission and national courts have had to render decisions on several cases every year, as to whether the financial incentives granted to an airline are illegal State aid on the ground of the EU Treaty (Article 107(1)).[38] When this struggle started in 2004, the Commission decided to settle a clear legal framework drawing the borders of the authorized incentives, in order to stop these tensions among aviation stakeholders. In 2005, the EU Commission adopted guidelines on "the financing of airports and start-up aid to airlines departing from regional airports", with the intent to formalize the new practices and to adopt general rules which ought to be respected by the whole industry.[39] The 2005 framework was revised in 2014 with the adoption of the guidelines on "State aid to airports and airlines".[40] Thus, as regards airlines specifically,[41] since 2005, the EU Commission has analyzed the incentive schemes granted to airlines on the grounds of these two major documents, which are based on EU State aid rules and distortion of competition. The Commission considers that arrangements between airports and airlines are free of State aid when, by granting the aid, the airport has acted as a private investor, operating under normal market conditions. The most relevant criterion to assess the private investor test is the *ex ante* profitability prospects over the expected duration of the arrangements. The airport manager should demonstrate that through the revenue stemming from the airline's activity at the airport (e.g. airport charges, non-aeronautical revenues) it is capable of covering the costs stemming from the arrangement with an airline (e.g. an individual contract or an overall scheme of airport charges) with a reasonable profit margin on the basis of sound prospects when setting up the arrangement.[42] The new guidelines also allow start-up aid to airlines for operating new schedules, with increased flight frequencies. The 2014 guidelines simplify the conditions for start-up aid, initially defined in 2005. In the future, airlines will be able to receive aid covering 50 percent of airport charges for new destinations during a three-year period.

6.2.2 Retail

The other primary activity at the airports is the retail and other non-aeronautical activities, inside and outside terminals.[43] As addressed above, the airport landscape has evolved considerably these

---

37 EU Commission decision OJ L 137, 30 April 2004, p. 1. In 2008, the Tribunal of the European Union annulled the 2004 decision: see ECJ, Case T-196/04, 17 December 2008.

38 Examples of EU Commission decisions on State aid in the aviation sector: C 12/2008, "Slovakia Agreement between Bratislava Airport and Ryanair", 27 January 2010; seven decisions on 23 July 2014 on public financing of airports and airlines in Germany, France, and Austria (EU Commission Memorandum 14/498); seven decisions on 1 October 2014 on public support to airports and airlines in Belgium, Germany, Italy, and Sweden (EU Commission Press Release, IP/14/1065). On the French level: see *Conseil d'Etat*, Strasbourg airport, 27 February 2006.

39 Commission Communication, "Community Guidelines on Financing of Airports and Start-up Aid to Airlines departing from Regional Airports", OJ C 312, 9 December 2005.

40 Commission Communication, "Guidelines on State aid to Airports and Airlines", 2014/C 99/03, 4 April 2014.

41 The airport financing issue will be addressed below, in the section entitled "Airport finance".

42 Ibid., paras 46 to 52; EU Commission Memorandum, "Commission adopts New Guidelines on State Aid to Airports and Airlines (Aviation Guidelines): Frequently asked Questions", Memo 14/121, 20 February 2014; Annabelle Lepièce "Les Nouvelles Lignes Directrices de la Commission Européenne sur les Aides d'Etat aux Aéroports et aux Compagnies Aériennes: Sursis de Dix Ans pour les Aéroports Régionaux", *Revue du Droit des Industries de Réseau*, 2014/3, pp. 321–337.

43 The main non-aeronautical activities are aviation fuel suppliers, food and beverage activities (incl. restaurants, bars, and vending machines), duty-free shops, car rental, car parking, airport advertising hotels, souvenir shops, offices occupied by airlines or governmental agencies, etc.

past 20 years: airports being more and more managed as private business companies and private investors having high expectation on financial return on investment. Financial returns require high revenues. Considering that aeronautical revenues (airport charges) are highly regulated and based on the cost-related principle, higher margins can be expected by airport operators on their other source of revenues: the non-aeronautical revenues. Thus, non-aeronautical revenues have become a key source to the financial success of the airports. While many international airports around the globe have actively developed non-aeronautical activities these past years, others still need to improve retail and commercial areas to fit their needs.[44] As mentioned by ICAO, "as airport traffic increases, not only do revenues from non-aeronautical activities tend to increase in absolute terms, but their share of total airport revenues also tends to increase compared to revenues from charges on air traffic".[45]

As regards the legal regime of these activities, it is first important to recall that airports, no matter how they are operated, generally belong to public authorities (the State or local authorities). Therefore, they are located on the public domain, which responds, in many countries, to a specific legal regime that grants specific rights to the public domain owner, such as the right for the airport to terminate existing agreements for a reason of general/public interest (i.e. the need to use the retail area for air traffic operation).[46]

When the airport is not operated directly by the State or the local authority, but is operated by a separate company, benefitting from a license or a concession contract, it is the company's responsibility to protect the public domain, on behalf of the public owner, and to develop commercial activities on it. The airport operator concludes a contract with the occupier of the public domain, generally named a "sub-concession contract" or a "license". The contract defines in particular the designation of the occupied premises, the duration of the occupation, the fees paid by the occupier and their annual review, the guarantee deposit requirement, the insurance requirement, and the termination conditions. As for the duration, it generally depends on the amount of investments the occupier has to do. The contract can be few decades long if the investment amortization requires it. As regards the fee, it is usually composed of two parts. First, a rental charge, based on the costs of the premises or land occupied. This charge shall respect the equal treatment principle, which means that the same charge amount shall be paid for the same type/quality of land/premises occupied at the airport.[47] The second part is the concession fee, based on the occupier turnover. Thus, the contract should address the necessary accounting, auditing, and control procedures to monitor turnover levels.

6.2.3 Ground-handling

Ground-handling is a crucial activity for airports. Without such services, aircraft cannot be handled and airports cannot function. States must ensure that airports are equipped to provide services such as ground-handling to all aircraft which land in such airports.[48] The term "ground-handling" has no formal definition on the international level, but it is generally defined as

---

44 The need is substantial because, in addition to travelers and their accompanying relations, increasing attention is paid to the market composed of people working at the airport and people living in nearby communities.

45 ICAO Doc. 9562, "Airport Economics Manual, 2013", ch. 5, section A.

46 In France, the legal regime of the public domain is detailed in the "Code Général de la Propriété des Personnes Publiques".

47 For more details on the definition of market value for charges, see ICAO Doc. 9562, "Airport Economics Manual", ch. 5, section D.

48 Articles 28 and 37 of the Chicago Convention.

"services necessary for an aircraft's arrival at, and departure from, an airport".[49] The EU ground-handling Directive provides that "ground-handling means the services provided to airport users at airports as described in the Annex".[50] In this Annex, 11 categories of ground-handling (GH) services are listed.[51]

Initially, GH was provided by national carriers and/or by the airport itself. In the 1980s, the air transport liberalization wave as well as the fact that GH activity was considered a commercial activity, spurred increasing pressure from airlines, which questioned the wisdom of the monopolistic context. Consequently, while the US has encouraged the development of independent GH providers and promoted more competition, in the "Airport and Airway Improvement Act" in 1982, Europe liberalized the EU GH market in 1996 with the EU ground-handling Directive.[52] Since then, the EU Commission and the European Court of Justice (ECJ) keep a close eye on each EU Member State, assessing whether the EU Directive is properly applied.[53] In Asia, in the framework of air transport liberalization among ASEAN States,[54] guidelines have been produced by the ASEAN Air Transport Working group to implement liberalization of Air Transport Ancillary services by the end of 2015. As a result, GH liberalization has led to an open and competitive market, where market access for third-party service providers is now well established. The two largest markets have liberal regulatory regimes and there are only few regions where GH monopolies prevail.[55]

Today, GH services are provided either by the airport operator, by airlines, and/or by independent ground-handlers. In any case, to be entitled to provide GH services, GH providers have to receive formal approval from a public authority, independent from the airport operator. The approval procedure is usually an administrative process to control in particular the financial

49 ICAO Doc. ANSConf-WP/10, 9 February 2000.
50 OJ L 272/39, 25 October 1996.
51 The Annex of the EU Ground-handling Directive provides a list of 11 services: (1) ground administration and supervision; (2) passenger handling; (3) baggage handling; (4) freight and mail handling; (5) ramp handling; (6) aircraft services; (7) fuel and oil handling; (8) aircraft maintenance; (9) flight operations and crew administration; (10) surface transport; (11) catering services.
52 R. Abeyratne, "Ground Handling Services at Airports as a Trade Barrier", *Journal of World Trade* 2008/42(2), pp. 261–277; the EU Directive allows (1) self-handling for airport terminal services (e.g. passenger check-in) at all EU airports, and for ramp services (e.g. baggage loading, fueling) at airports with at least one million passengers per year from 1 January 1998; and (2) third party handling at airports with annual traffic exceeding three million passengers from 1 January 1999, and of at least two million passengers from 1 January 2001. Service providers are to be limited to two for certain service categories (e.g. baggage handling, fueling), and from 1 January 2001, at least one service provider must be independent from both dominant air carrier and airport authority. Member States may grant exemptions on the basis of space or capacity constraints for a renewable three year period.
53 The EU Commission has rendered several decisions on the issue: see *inter alia* Case 98/387/EC – Flughafen Frankfurt/Main AG, OJ L 173, 18 June 1998, pp. 32–44. Case 98/630/EC, Flughafen Stuttgart GmbH, OJ L 300, 11 November 1998, pp. 25–32. More recently, the ECJ considered that Republic of Portugal has failed to fulfill its obligations under Article 11 of the EU Directive at Lisbon, Porto, and Faro airports: see Case 277/13, 11 September 2013.
54 ASEAN Air Transport Liberalization has been formalized by the signature on 12 November 2010 of the Multilateral Agreement on the full liberalization of passenger air services. The concept of progressive liberalization of air transport services had been laid out by an Action Plan for ASEAN Air Transport Integration and Liberalization 2005–2015. This Action Plan, together with an accompanying document known as the Roadmap for Integration of Air Travel Sector (RIATS), had identified the target date of 2015 for achieving an effective "open skies" regime for the region.
55 In addition to national or regional liberalization regulation, one further consideration in GH services is whether the functions of GH should be brought under the purview of the General Agreement on Trade in Services Air Transport Annex of the World Trade Organization.

situation of the provider, its sufficient insurance cover, and its compliance with the relevant safety and social legislation.[56]

As regards the contractual link with the airport on this field, it depends on who provides the service. When the airport operator provides GH services directly to airlines,[57] it concludes a contract with each airline, defining the GH services to be provided, the operation modalities, liability of each party, and the GH fee. The contract is usually based on the Standard Ground-Handling Agreement (SGHA), provided by International Air Transport Association (IATA).[58] As regards the GH fees, they are collected from the aircraft operators for the use of facilities and services provided by the airport. They must be relevant and non-discriminatory.[59] As recalled by the ECJ in 2003, a GH fee should only cover the use of airport installations as well as the services related to the use of such installations.[60] When the GH service is not provided by the airport itself but by airlines and/or independent ground-handlers, they become occupiers of the public domain vis-à-vis the airport operator, as they need space to store their GH equipment. Thus, the contractual link between the airport and the provider is a license or a sub-concession contract, and the fee paid to the airport is a rental fee, as part of the non-aeronautical revenues.

6.2.4 Public services

Public services, such as security, safety, immigration, health, customs, meteorology, and air navigation, are required at the airport,[61] and often are provided by the State. Sometimes, security and safety are provided by the airport, or by the airport subcontractor, but, in any case, the State remains liable for security and safety, as they are deemed to be State/public missions.[62] They should work in full cooperation with the airport operator. To exercise their missions, each public service occupies offices at the airport, benefitting from a license or a concession contract.

6.2.5 Airport contractors

Airport contractors enter into contracts of works, supplies, and services with the airport operator. Typically, a major service contract is concluded when the airport operator subcontracts to a third-operator, e.g. the airport security service. The main issue here is whether there is a specific award procedure the airport operator shall comply with in selection of its contractors.

---

56 See *supra* note 51, EU Ground-handling Directive, Article 14. The EU Ground-handling Directive shall be transposed in national laws to be applicable. Thus, all EU Member States transposed it within the following years after the Directive publication, sometimes with additional requirements to the ones defined in the Directive. More than ten years after, the EU Commission is thinking of defining a more harmonized approval procedure between the Member States for less discrimination between them.

57 When the airport operator provides the GH service, the EU Directive (Article 4) requires that the airport operator "rigorously separates the accounts of the GH activities from the accounts of their other activities".

58 IATA regularly provides a revised SGHA. Thus, different versions exist today: 1998, 2004, 2008, and 2013. One of the differences between the different versions is related to the provider's liability (Article 8 of the SGHA).

59 See Article 16.3 of the EU Ground-handling Directive. In addition, competition law (see Article 86 of the EU Treaty and the US antitrust law) applies to GH services and fees: it forbids predatory pricing, which means prices set below their marginal costs in order to through other competitors out of the market.

60 ECJ Case C-363/01, October 2003, Flughafen Hannover-Langenhagen GmbH against Deutche Lufthansa AG.

61 Article 15 of the Chicago Convention.

62 See *supra* note 34, p. 46.

In the EU, the airport management is considered an economic activity,[63] and, as such, is subject to competition law. Thus, in any case, and regardless of the nature of the airport operator shareholding, airport operators are called upon to comply with competitive bidding requirements for the award of its work/supply/service contract. Now, the question is whether they also need to comply with public procurement rules, as defined by the EU Directive of 26 February 2014 on procurement by entities operating in the water, energy, transport, and postal service sectors. The answer is affirmative if the airport company is qualified as a "Contracting entity" fulfilling one of these two following criteria. First, if the company is owned or controlled by the State or a public body, and is under direct or indirect dominant influence of a body governed by public law, qualified as "contracting authorities".[64] Second, if the airport company is not under dominant influence of contracting authorities, which means that it is owned or controlled in majority by private shareholders, but has a "special and exclusive right" to operate the airport (which means that the concession contract was awarded directly by the State and not in the framework of a transparent, objective, and non-discriminatory procedure).[65]

6.3 Airport regulation

6.3.1 Operational regulation (safety oversight, airport certification, Annex 17)

Since its creation, safety has been the main focus in the technical work and guidance of ICAO. Most SARPs incorporate and address safety from various aspects of civil aviation. Airports in particular are covered in Annex 14 of the Chicago Convention, which include a large set of technical standards and definitions, such as minimum runway width, lighting and signing installations.[66] Compliance with these technical specifications establishes a sort of minimum safety standard on which international air traffic can rely on unless they are notified otherwise.[67] These standards are then adopted as such or further enhanced to be enacted in national aviation regulation.

Compliance with aviation regulation, including those that cover airport operations, is the responsibility of each Contracting State of the Chicago Convention, which must adhere to a set of rules and practices of the SARPs. Monitoring compliance is done by a national entity, usually the Civil Aviation Authority (CAA), according to a State's national legislation. Airport design, its infrastructure, and installation, as well as airport operations in general must be overseen. Any departure from these rules and standards must be sanctioned in order to restore safe operations. The oversight of a State's compliance with its own oversight responsibility is done, since 1999, by ICAO through its Universal Safety Oversight Audit Programme (USOAP).[68]

---

63 ECJ Case T-128/98, Aéroports de Paris/Commission, confirmed by ECJ Case C-82/01 and T-455/08 *Flughafen Leipzig-Halle GmbH and Mitteldeutsche Flughafen AG* v. *Commission*: in its decision "Aéroports de Paris v. Commission", the Court stated clearly that the management and running of airports comprise economic activities. And in its "Leipzig-Halle airport" case, the Court made it clear that the construction of the infrastructure – and its financing – is an integral part of this economic activity. Airports should thus be considered as undertakings subject to the EU Treaty rules, including aspects relating to competition and State aid.
64 Directive 2014/25/EU, OJ L 94/243, 26 February 2014, Article 4.2.
65 Ibid., Article 4.3.
66 See generally Annex 14, Chicago Convention.
67 Article 38 of the Chicago Convention provides that any State finding it impracticable to comply with a SARP, or which has or adopts regulations different therefrom, shall give immediate notification to ICAO of the differences.
68 See ICAO, "Establishment of an ICAO Universal Safety Audit Programme, Assem. Res. A32-11, compiled in Assembly Resolutions in Force", ICAO Doc. 9790, 5 October 2001.

In the wake of privatization of major airports in the late 1980s, agreed standards for airport design and operation standards by ICAO were no longer considered sufficient to ensure airport safety.[69] ICAO subsequently amended Annex 14, Volume 1, "Aerodrome Design and Operations", and introduced new airport licensing and certification requirements, which were adopted by the ICAO Council in March 2001. ICAO further called for the implementation of safety management systems for airports.[70] To facilitate the certification by Contracting States of their aerodromes, ICAO issued a specific manual, which covers all aspects of airport certification.[71] To help Contracting States implementing safety management systems for airports, in 2006 ICAO published the "Safety Management Manual", in which Chapter 18 describes airport operations.[72]

Another area of international standards, which shapes national regulation of airports, is security, defined as the safeguard against acts of unlawful interference. In the wake of several hijackings of aircraft in the 1970s, ICAO developed specific standards and practices to address security. This subsequently yielded in Annex 17 of the Chicago Convention, which was first published in 1971.[73] ICAO further published a technical manual, which gives guidance on security measures.[74] Many of these recommendations are integrated into national regulations on airports.[75] The so-called Universal Security Audit Programme (USAP) audit inspects aviation security oversight capabilities and audits security measures at selected airports.

6.3.2 Economic regulation

Economic regulation of aviation is as old as commercial air transportation. Early initiatives of economic regulation focused primarily on competition, and the urge of operators to have the government protect them from the evils of destructive competition. Economic regulation of airports has its roots in government funded airport development programs, where airport infrastructure to be funded had to be economically justified. In the US, federal funding for airport projects began as early as 1933. Under two such programs, the Development of Landing Areas Program and the Development of Civil Landing Areas Program, 584 airports were built.[76]

Today, economic regulation of commercial airports by a national regulatory body is a fairly complex matter. On one side, the user needs to be protected against excessive charges and practices by airports which abuse their monopoly based powers; on the other hand free, market forces are the proven fundamentals to foster growth and to attract private investments in major infrastructure projects, such as an airport expansion. A good example of economic regulation of large airports is provided by the UK's CAA, which, based on the UK Civil Aviation Act of 2012, has the power

---

69 Safety Management Systems for Airports, Airport Cooperative Research Program, Transportation Research Board, Washington DC, 2007, at 19.
70 Annex 14, "Aerodromes", vol. I, "Aerodrome Design and Operations", July 2004, Section 1.4, "Certification of Aerodromes"; Section 1.5, "Safety Management".
71 "Manual on Certification of Aerodromes", ICAO Doc. 9774, first edition, 2001.
72 "Safety Management Manual", ICAO Doc. 9859, first edition, 2006.
73 ICAO, Annex 17, "Security: Safeguarding International Civil Aviation Against Acts of Unlawful Interference", 2006.
74 "Security Manual for Safeguarding Civil Aviation Against Acts of Unlawful Interference", ICAO Doc. 8973, eighth edition, 2011.
75 Similar to ICAO's safety audit program USAP, in 2006 it introduced the Universal Security Audit Programme (USAP), which is a regular, mandatory, systematic, and harmonized review of security oversight.
76 See generally, "FAA Historical Chronology 1926–1996", online: www.faa.gov/about/media/b-chron. pdf, accessed 20 October 2014.

of economic regulation of operators of airports.[77] The airport market power assessments, a precondition for granting an airport operator, consist of a competition analysis that evaluates whether an airport operator has or could acquire a substantial power in a market, and whether national competition law provides sufficient protection against an airport operator's abuse of its market power. If the assessment confirms the need for regulation, which is expected to provide effective protection to the customer, then an airport is to be licensed and regulated by the CAA.

The major element of economic airport regulation concerns airport charges. The UK, being a member of the EU, bases its airport charges on the common principles for the levying of airport charges at airports of the EU.[78] These principles were enacted into UK law in 2011 with the Airport Charges Regulations 2011.[79] The EU Directive covers airports that handle more than five million passengers per annum, and (i) introduces common principles of transparency and consultation for airports in determining charges levied on airlines; (ii) stipulates that airport charges should be non-discriminatory; (iii) allows differentiated charges based on relevant, objective, transparent, and non-discriminatory criteria; (iv) requires Member States to appoint an independent supervisory authority (ISA) to ensure the correct application of the Directive; and (v) sets up mechanisms for resolving disputes about the level of airport charges, unless satisfactory procedures already exist under national law to assess whether airports are subject to effective competition. The Regulations further require the CAA, as the UK ISA, to publish an annual report concerning the exercise of its functions.[80]

In general, the airline industry endorses the above stated principles. IATA, for example, calls for strong, robust, and independent economic regulation to protect airlines and their passengers from monopoly abuse. It sees regulation as required to give sufficient protection to users against potential monopoly abuse of dominant position, especially for privatized or profit-maximizing providers, such as airports or air navigation service providers (ANSPs). In a memo to the EU Commission, IATA identifies ten key elements for a strong, robust, and politically independent economic regulation.[81] IATA's position reflects the airline industry's concern about worldwide rising user charges for airports.

On the other side, airports often defend their charges by stating that they must invest in infrastructure enhancement and expansion projects in order to meet future demand. In addition, airports advocate the need for less regulation on charges. The market requires less and less legal regulatory constraints, due to the increasing competition between airports. Indeed, competition has led to a shift of the bargaining power between airports and airlines.[82] Nevertheless, despite clear general principles about general charges at airports, there are great concerns in the airline industry about certain user charges. In the UK, for example, the air passenger duty (APD), introduced in

---

77 Civil Aviation Authority of the UK, "Airport Regulation", online: www.caa.co.uk/default.aspx?catid =78&pagetype=90&pageid=67, accessed 20 October 2014.

78 EC Directive 2009/12/EC of the European Parliament and of the Council of 11 March 2009 on airport charges, OJ L 70/11, 14 March 2009. The EU Directive had to be transposed into national law of all EU Member States by March 2011.

79 The Airport Charges Regulations 2011, SI 2011/2491.

80 Ibid., Article 32.

81 IATA, "Economic Regulation of Airports and Air Navigation Service Providers", online: www.iata. org/policy/Documents/economic-regulation.pdf, accessed 20 October 2014; IATA memo to EC (DG Move) "Need for a Strong Regulatory Framework", June 2014. See also ICAO Doc. 9082/7, paras 13 and 15.

82 The European Commission confirmed this statement in its communication of 19 June 2014 on the application of the airport charges Directive. See COM(2014) 278 "Report from the Commission to the European Parliament and the Council on the Application of the Airport Charges Directive".

1994, is currently set at GBP 71.00 per passenger. According to IATA, this tax is costing the UK economy about GBP 300 million per year in lost GDP and around 7,000 lost jobs, and calls for a reduction.[83] Several other States have introduced or are planning to enact new passenger taxes. The most prominent examples include France, which in 2005 instated an international solidarity levy on air tickets, ranging from EUR 1.13 to 45.07 to help finance international development work. Germany followed in 2011 when it introduced an air passenger duty ranging from EUR 7.50 to EUR 42.18 depending on destination. Sweden, finally, plans to introduce a "Green Passenger" tax, which is estimated to put 10,000 jobs at risk and reduce the air transport sector's contribution to the Swedish GDP by SEK 6 billion.[84] Some States, however, have recognized the adverse effect of additional charges on air transportation can have. The Northern Ireland Assembly, for example, set its rate of APD to zero for all flights from Northern Ireland to protect the only direct flight from Belfast to the US. The Netherlands had to abolish a 2008 air ticket tax, after Amsterdam's Schiphol Airport lost 18 percent of its passengers to neighboring airports.[85]

6.3.3 Tariff regulation

Tariff regulation applies to aeronautical revenues of airports. These revenues from air traffic operations, paid by the airlines, include the landing charge, passenger service charge, and aircraft parking charge.[86] In Switzerland, airport tariffs typically include about eight specific charges, which are levied at the nation's two main airports, Geneva and Zurich.[87]

The regulation of airport related charges and tariffs are generally a national matter, regulated under domestic law. For international air services, the Chicago Convention provides two principles for setting tariffs: Article 15 III 2 of the Convention opposes charging the right for overflights or entry and exit of a territory and Article 24 prohibits levying customs duties. Even though these two principles only address a rather narrow aspect of imposing tariffs, namely taxing traffic rights and equipment on board of international flights, their subsequent application implied the basic principle that charges should only be levied in international air traffic for actual costs occurred. For

---

83 IATA Economic Briefing, "Impact of UK APD Reduction", March 2014, online: www.iata.org/whatwedo/Documents/economics/APD-reduction-mar14.pdf, accessed 22 October 2014.
84 Antony Tyler, Letter to the Swedish Prime Minister, 15 September 2014, online: www.iata.org/policy/Documents/Swedish%20Departure%20Tax%20-%20Fredrik%20Reinfeldt%20Prime%20Minister.pdf, accessed 22 October 2014.
85 Brian F. Havel and Niels van Antwerpen, "Dutch Ticket Tax and Article 15 of the Chicago Convention", 2009/34(2) *Air and Space Law*, pp. 141–146.
86 ICAO Doc. 9562, "Airports Economic Manual", ch. 4; French law: Article R.224-2 "Code de l'Aviation Civile".
87 For Zurich Airport, these include: (i) landing charge per landing based on the maximum take-off weight, (ii) noise charge per landing during the day and per landing and take-off at night according to the noise level measured at Zurich Airport, (iii) emission charge per landing according to the amount of nitrogen oxide emissions, (iv) aircraft parking charge per parking procedure based on the maximum take-off weight and duration of time on the ground, (v) passenger charge per outbound passenger with distinction made between local and transfer passengers, (vi) security charge per outbound passenger with distinction between local and transfer passengers, (vii) charge to assist passengers with restricted mobility per departing passenger, and (viii) freight charge per kilo of air freight. "Airport Charges at Zurich Airport", Zurich Airport, 1 October 2014, online: www.zurich-airport.com/~/media/FlughafenZH/Dokumente/Business_und_Partner/Flugbetrieb/20140801_Gebuehrenreglement_en.pdf, accessed 21 October 2014. The economic basis and the procedure for setting airport related tariffs are regulated in detail in a specific regulation: see generally "Swiss Airport Charges Regulation", SR 748.131.3, online: www.admin.ch/opc/de/classified-compilation/20110517/index.html, accessed 21 October 2014.

international airport users, ICAO states the general principle that users shall *bear their full and fair share* of the cost of providing the airport.[88] This implies that airport operators establish a transparent cost allocation system, revealing the actual cost for services rendered.

Given the above-mentioned principles on airport charges, most countries regulate tariffs for usage of their major airports. Tariff regulation is based on three main principles, enshrined in most national law: cost adequacy, non-discrimination, and transparency. First, charges are cost related, which means that the airport invoices the airline the full cost of the service, as well as essential ancillary services. It shall not include in the cost calculation costs not attributable to the services and shall not make a profit out of the charge.[89] Today, the cost-related principle is interpreted largely, and the airport operator is thus allowed to take several factors into consideration in the costing of the airport service, which includes cost of capital, cost inflation, depreciation, anticipated future investments,[90] but it must also compensate for past excess income.

The general objective behind these principles is to strike a balance between maximizing the airport operators' income against the airport's obligation of rendering a *public service*. In Switzerland, airport concessions are therefore granted with the explicit policy that their operational income should not exceed air transport-related operational airport cost.[91] Second, airport charges must not be discriminatory; they shall be applicable equally to airlines, foreign and domestic. However, this principle does not prevent the modulation of airport charges for issues of public and general interest, including environmental issues. The criteria used for such a modulation shall be relevant, objective, and transparent.[92] The non-discrimination principle does not prevent an airport from defining a different tariff among its terminals. The level of airport charges may be differentiated according to the quality and scope of such services and their costs or any other objective and transparent justification.[93] The third principle is the transparency obligation of the airport operator vis-à-vis the airlines. The prescribed procedure for setting tariffs includes consultations and formal negotiations with users every year, which typically concerns major air carriers.[94] Should users not agree with new tariffs, an appeal can be filed which suspends their application.[95] Without prejudice to the obligation of annual user consultation, tariff evolution may be set in a multiannual contract (maximum five years).[96]

88 "ICAO's Policies on Charges for Airports and Air Navigation Services", ICAO Doc. 9082, ninth edition, 2012, at II-1.
89 ICAO Doc. 9082, Section II, para. 2 i; ICAO Doc. 9562, ch. 4, at 4.60.
90 In 2005, the French law added into the airport charges regulation all the factors to consider in the costing of the airport service: Article L.6325-1, "Code des Transports" and Article R.224-2-1, "Code de l'Aviation Civile".
91 Swiss Aviation Act, SR 748.0, Article 39, para. 5.
92 EC Directive 2009/12/EC of 11 March 2009 on airport charges, OJ L 70/11, 2009, Article 3; French law: Article R.224-2-2 "Code de l'Aviation Civile".
93 EC Directive 2009/12/EC of 11 March 2009 on airport charges, OJ L 70/11, 2009, Article 10.
94 Swiss Airport Charges Regulation, SR 748.131.3, Article 24; in France, tariffs are discussed every year in an Assembly called *Commission Consultative Economique*, as foreseen in Article R.224-3 "Code de l'Aviation Civile".
95 In Switzerland, an appeal can be filed against tariffs enacted by the Swiss Federal Office of Civil Aviation (FOCA). Thus, in 2014, airport users at Zurich airport filed an appeal against all increases of airport charges. "Notice to Airport Users", Zurich Airport, 13 January 2014, online: www.zurich-airport.com/~/media/FlughafenZH/Dokumente/Business_und_Partner/Flugbetrieb/20131121-Info-Verfügung_EN.pdf, accessed 22 October 2014. In Europe, the EC 2009 Directive, Article 11, states that each Member State shall establish a national independent supervisory authority, in order to ensure the correct application of the measures taken to comply with the Directive.
96 In France, see Article 6325-2 "Code des Transports".

Consistent with the three above-mentioned principles, airport tariffs are enacted by the public authority, on the basis of the airport operator proposal. In Switzerland, for example, airport tariffs are enacted by the Swiss Federal Office of Civil Aviation (FOCA), after being prepared by the airport operator.[97]

6.3.4 Airport access

"Public airports need to provide indiscriminate access to all users" is a frequent policy principle found in concession legislation and agreements. The right to use an airport, generally referred to as airport access, is not a major concern at most airports. However, many large public use airports in major aviation markets face saturation at least during certain peak hours, and access needs to be regulated to a certain extent. Airports are victims of their own success and, due to traffic growth, many of Europe's most important airports are now facing a capacity crunch. Seventy percent of all flight delays are caused by problems on the ground not in the air. Air traffic in Europe will nearly double by 2030, and, as a consequence, 19 key European airports will be at saturation and unable to accommodate any more flights by that date.[98] And, over the next few years, air transport growth will be driven by other regions such as Asia Pacific, the Middle East, and Latin America. Thus, in ASEAN countries, due in particular to the low-cost carrier boom, major airports will face capacity saturation, as in Europe.[99] Airport capacity (considered as a combination of runway, terminal, apron, airspace, and surface access capacity) has become one of the main challenges for the sector around the globe. One of the reasons for this looming airport capacity crunch is the fact that airports have considerably reduced their capacity expansion plans and related investments in the wake of the economic crisis,[100] as well as the fact of the lack of public support for the construction of new large infrastructure.[101] Under such circumstances, the priority is thus ensuring the use of existing capacity to the best extent possible. In other words, at congested airports, slots (that is to say the permission to land and take-off at a specific date and time) are essential and their allocation shall be maximized. In the US, access to airports declared High Density Traffic Airports, such as New York JFK Airport, LaGuardia Airport, and Washington Reagan National Airport, is limited by the requirement of obtaining slots or reservations.[102] Access to all other airports for domestic flights in the US has generally not been regulated by law. If saturation at an airport was only of a temporary nature during certain periods and did not impose the allocation of landing slots, access traditionally is given on a "first come, first served" basis.[103] This has proven to be the most efficient method of allocating runway or tarmac access, even if it implied certain traffic delays.[104]

---

97 Swiss Aviation Act, SR 748.0, Article 39, online: www.admin.ch/opc/de/classified-compilation/ 19480335/index.html, accessed 21 October 2014.
98 EU Commission, MEMO/11/857, 1 December 2011, "Europe's Airports 2030: Challenges Ahead"; EU Commission, COM(2011) 823 final, 1 December 2011, "Airport Policy in the EU: Addressing Capacity and Quality to Promote Growth, Connectivity and Sustainable Mobility".
99 "Aviation: Lifting the Barriers Report", Network ASEAN Forum 2013.
100 In addition to the global economic crisis, regulation does not help to increase the level of capital expenditure in the sector; see *supra* note 36, the 2014 EU "Guidelines on State aid to Airports and airlines".
101 "European airports were planning for a 38% capacity increase by 2030. Now, they are just planning for a 17% capacity increase by 2035": see ACI Europe Position Paper on Airport Capacity, October 2014.
102 *Federal Aviation Regulations*, Title 14 of the Code of Federal Regulations, Part 93, Subpart K.
103 Achim I. Czerny, Peter Forsyth, David Gillen and Hans-Martin Niemeier, *Airport Slot Allocation: International Experiences and Options for Reform*, Ashgate Publishing Ltd, 2008, at 272.
104 Ibid., at 274; Katja Brecke, "Airport Slot Allocation: Quo Vadis, EU?" 2011/36(3) *Air and Space Law*, p. 183.

In Australia, acquiring landing slots is generally a formality (for domestic and foreign operators) at most international airports in Australia, particularly outside peak times. [105] In the EU, the aim of the 1993 legal framework, revised in 2004, is to ensure that where airport capacity is scarce, the available landing and take-off slots are used efficiently and distributed in an equitable, non-discriminatory, and transparent way.[106] The regulation lays down the objective criteria on the basis of which an airport can be designated "coordinated" or "schedules facilitated" on the grounds that its capacity is insufficient. The general principle regarding slot allocation in the EU is that an air carrier having operated its particular slots for at least 80 percent during the summer/winter scheduling period is entitled to use the same slots in the equivalent scheduling period of the following year (the so-called "grandfather rights"). Consequently, slots which are not sufficiently used by air carriers are reallocated (the so-called "use it or lose it" rule). In 2007, the EU Commission report on the application of slot Regulation concluded that a number of provisions of the Regulation are still not fully implemented. Consequently, in its 2008 Communication on slot allocation, the Commission recommended improving local guidelines, the independency of coordinators, and the practice of exchange of slots.[107] In 2011, the EU Commission submitted to the EU Parliament a revised slot Regulation that introduces the following key measures: secondary trading of slots, clear conditions for the transparent trading of slots, and the increase of the slot utilization threshold from 80 to 85 percent.[108] The aim is to ensure that airlines willing to keep slots for the coming season, effectively use the capacity.[109]

6.3.5 Airport finance

There are a variety of commercial airports, which range from small rural airports with a few flights a week to major intercontinental hubs with thousands of movements a day. However, all airports share in common that they are generally quite capital intensive requiring substantial funds for land acquisition or lease, airport landscape development, and terminal construction, as well as for the installation of required air and land transport infrastructure.

6.3.5.1 Airport revenues and the coverage of operating costs

There are basically three methods for determining the required coverage of operational costs of airports by revenue and other income. The first and the most widely used and advocated method aggregates all airport revenues from operational and non-operational sources to offset against an airport operational cost. This methodology is generally referred to as the *single-till* or *Residual Cost* method and has the advantage that non-airline commercial revenues, such as income from duty-free

---

105 OECD, Directorate for Financial and Enterprise Affairs – Competition Committee, "Airline Competition: Note by Australia", DAF/COMP/WD(2014)24 (2014) at 3.

106 Council Regulation (EEC) No. 95/93 of 18 January 1993 on common rules for the allocation of slots at Community airports, OJ L 14, 22 January 1993, p. 1, as revised by Regulation (EC) No. 793/2004 of the European parliament and of the Council of 21 April 2004, OJ L 138, 30 April 2004, p. 50.

107 "Communication from the Commission on the application of Regulation No. 95/93 on common rules for the allocation of slots at Community airports, as amended", COM(2008) 227 final, 30 April 2008.

108 "Proposal for a Regulation on common rules for the allocation of slots at European Union airports", COM(2011) 827 final, 1 December 2011.

109 Christoph Naumann, "New Proposal to Amend the System of Airport Slot Allocation in the European Union", 2012/37(3) *Air and Space Law*, p. 185.

sales, lower residual airport operational cost.[110] The residual cost of operations is generally used for setting operational airport user charges, which include landing and parking fees, passenger fees, and in some cases security fees if an airport can claim security-related costs it must cover.

The second method is the *dual-till* or *Cost of Service* (sometimes "multiple cost center") methodology, which consists of dividing an airport into multiple cost centers. For each cost center, the appropriate costs and revenues need to be determined and accounted for to determine the respective fees for usage, such as landing charges for aircraft movements or rent and lease amounts for commercial tenants. Some argue that this methodology is more transparent, as it eliminates cross-subsidies.[111] However, when UK airport regulators considered regulating tariffs by single or dual-till method in 2000/2001, the UK Competition Commission questioned whether dual-till arrangements would lead to improved efficiency and stated that a switch to dual-till would lead to "a substantial transfer of income to airports from airlines and/or their passengers, potentially undermining regulatory credibility and creating regulatory uncertainty".[112]

The third method is called the "hybrid system". It exists when part of the non-aeronautical revenues are removed from the single-till.

In recent years there have been continuous debates about the application of the single or dual-till method for the cost basis on which user fees are determined. The airline industry, represented at large by IATA, strongly advocates that the single-till method is the fairest mechanism of charging airline users.[113] In contrast, airports represented by Airports Council International (ACI) generally oppose the single-till methodology. ACI contends that including non-aeronautical revenues in the cost base for airport charge calculations creates an artificial constraint on airports, as they must focus heavily on non-aeronautical revenue in order to obtain reasonable returns.[114] ACI supports the dual-till structure, as it allows the so-called "monopolistic" part of an airport's business – the provision of core aeronautical activities – to be regulated, while allowing the other parts of the airport business to compete in a normal market environment.[115]

Today, most airports use the single-till system, although more and more airports are moving toward the hybrid system or a pure dual-till system. This trend is consistent with the airport privatization move, since a dual-till system encourages investors to enter into the airport business so as to enjoy higher revenues. Access to private debt or equity requires profitability; private investors will not invest without profit. In Europe, while French regional airports and British airports are under a single-till, Copenhagen, Frankfurt and Schiphol airports are under a dual-till system. Aéroports de Paris moved from a single-till to a hybrid-till in 2011, six years after it became a private limited company, by removing from the till some non-aeronautical

110 Peter C. Stettler, "Airport Financing in the United States", *Shared Horizons – A Biannual Publication of the US-India Aviation Development Program* (2010), p. 34, online: www.ricondo.com/articles/Airport-Financing-in-the-United-States.pdf, accessed 9 November 2014.

111 "BAA Ltd: A Report on the Economic Regulation of the London Airports Companies (Heathrow Airport Ltd and Gatwick Airport Ltd)", Report presented to the Civil Aviation Authority, Competition Commission (2007), 28 September 2007, p. 104.

112 See generally, "Economic Regulation of BAA London Airports (Heathrow, Gatwick and Stansted) 2003–2008 – CAA Decision", Civil Aviation Authority, CAA House, February 2003, online: www.caa.co.uk/docs/5/ergdocs/baadecision200308.pdf, accessed 9 November 2014.

113 IATA Policy Paper, "Single Till", online: www.iata.org/policy/Documents/single-till.pdf, accessed 10 November 2014.

114 ACI, "The Airport Business", ACI Position Brief (October 2007), p. 2, online: www.aci.aero/Media/aci/file/Position%20Briefs/position%20brief_AIRPORT%20BUSINESS.pdf, accessed 10 November 2014.

115 Ibid.

activities such as the real-estate revenues.[116] Outside Europe, the dual-till system is also implemented at Australian and New Zealand airports.

In terms of airport finance, best practices in financial management require transparent accounts, which are published on a regular basis. For this, a financial accounting system must be in place, which clearly identifies costs, revenues, and, if applicable, subsidies and cross-subsidies between operating entities. However, at airports applying the so-called single-till principle, where all non-aeronautical revenues are taken into account when calculating aeronautical charges, there should be no differentiation between the income and costs from the various sources.[117] Further elements in good financial management are detailed budgeting, good bank and cash management, regular presentation of financial statements, measuring performance and productivity and benchmarking, service level agreements, economic pricing, and the collection of charges and concessions and rentals.[118]

6.3.5.2 Funding for airport infrastructure

Air transport grows robustly; last year, more than three billion passengers flew globally. Air transport liberalization and the fantastic expansion of low-cost carriers around the globe, whether in Europe,[119] in America, in Asia,[120] have required international and national authorities to face the need of additional airport infrastructure, through the construction of new airports or new terminals at existing airports. Governments should pay more attention to airport capacity investments, as a significant gap increases between traffic demand and infrastructure capacity. Construction of new infrastructure requires large financial investment; public authorities, organizations, funds, whether international, regional, national, or local, often contribute financially to improve or expand airport infrastructure. The World Bank Group is supporting emerging and developing countries in the development of a sustainable air transport sector, mainly in Africa, but as well in Asia and in Latin America.[121] In Europe, EU-funded investments in airport infrastructures is very active as well. Tens of airports have been EU funded and, among them, 20 airports in five Member States (Estonia, Greece, Spain, Italy, and Poland) received a total of

---

116 The hybrid-till is implemented in the multiannual (2011–2015) regulation contract signed by Aéroports de Paris. See L. Vidal, "Contrat de Régulation ADP/Etat: Les Redevances Aéroportuaires face à la Comptabilité Analytique", Contrats Publics n°112 Juillet–Août 2011.

117 "Airport Economics Manual", ICAO Doc. 9562, third edition, 2013, para. 3.4.

118 Ibid., para. 3.7.

119 See note 36: the EU Guidelines, paras 1 and 2 (822 million passengers transported to and from Union airports in 2011); World Bank Air Transport Annual Report 2013 mentions that "strong growth of over 12% was maintained in the Middle East and China, as well as 7.4% in Latin America, while traffic in Africa and the Asia-Pacific Region grew at 5.2%".

120 See note 36, Network ASEAN Forum 2013:

> Major airports like Jakarta Soekarno-Hatta, Manila Ninoy Aquino and Bangkok Suvarnabhumi have reached saturation point and even exceeded their intended capacity. This has naturally resulted in increasing congestion and ever longer delays. The re-opening of Bangkok Don Mueang to cater to LCC operations is a reminder of the infrastructural constraints posed by the LCCs' spectacular continuing growth.

121 World Bank Air Transport Annual Report 2015, p. 8:

> The fiscal year 2015 portfolio includes approximately 26 projects in five World Bank regions through the operations of the International Bank for Reconstruction and Development (IBRD) and International Development Association (IDA), as well as the International Finance Corporation (IFC)'s portfolio of lending and investment advisories in the aviation sector.

EU-funding of EUR 666 million during the 2000–2006 and 2007–2013 program periods through the European Regional Development Fund (ERDF) and the Cohesion Fund (CF).[122]

The main issue related to airport public subsidies is the question of the compatibility of airport State aid with competition law. It has been a major legal issue in Europe for the last ten years. Indeed, despite their positive effects on regional development and accessibility, regional airports present a dilemma. First, public funding of airport infrastructure often has resulted in duplication of (unprofitable) airports in the same catchment area, creating overcapacity at regional airports, while leaving the congestion problem of main airports unresolved. Second, the vast majority of regional airports do not generate sufficient revenue to even cover their costs.[123] Subsidies are then used to pay for investments and to cover operating losses. At the end, the granting of State aid to some airports leads to distortion of competition vis-à-vis their competitors that do not benefit from subsidies. Although State aid to airports has always existed, it has become a major issue as airports now face increased competition and many of them have therefore been sued these past years on the ground of illegal State aid. In this context, the EU Commission had to define a clear legal framework on airport State aid, and it did so in its 2005 Guidelines, reviewed in 2014, as it did for airline State aid.[124] The Guidelines address to what extent operating aid and investment to airports are allowed. The Commission has based the new rules on the principle settled by the ECJ – that the construction and the management of an airport is an economic activity, subject to competition regulation.[125] And, the other related ground of the EU guidelines is the principle of the Market Economy Investor, as detailed above about State aid to airlines. The EU Commission has taken a number of decisions on the issue, and especially since the publication of the 2014 Guidelines. For instance, the Commission issued three decisions on French airports and three on German airports, on 23 July 2014.[126] On 1 October 2014, the Commission issued seven additional decisions concerning German, Belgium, Italian, and Sweden airports.[127] The Commission considered, in some of the cases, the State aid received by the airport as illegal on the basis of the private investor principle.

---

122 The 2014 Special Report of the European Court of Auditors "EU-funded Airport Infrastructures: Poor Value for Money": the Court analyzed EU-funded investments in airport infrastructures and examined whether there was a demonstrated need for these investments, constructions were completed on time and on budget and the newly built (or upgraded) infrastructures were fully used. The conclusion of the report is that

> the EU-funded investments in airports produced poor value for money: too many airports were funded and in many cases the EU-funded infrastructures were oversized. Only half of the audited airports succeeded in increasing their passenger numbers and improvements in customer service were either not measured or not evidenced.

123 "42% of European airports remain loss-making": see EU Commission "Competition Policy Brief", February 2014.
124 See notes 36 and 39.
125 See note 63.
126 EU Commission, "State Aid: Further Details on Commission Decisions regarding Public Financing of Airports and Airlines in Germany, France and Austria", Memo/14/498, 23 July 2014.
127 EU Commission, "State Aid: Commission Decisions on Public Financing of Airports and Airlines in Germany, Belgium, Italy and Sweden – Further Details", Memo/15/544, 1 October 2014.

7

Security regulations
International requirements

Jiefang Huang

The Chicago Convention does not specifically refer to "aviation security". As time went by, it was realized that in addition to the inherent and natural risk associated with flights, civil aviation had also encountered extrinsic threats and dangers, such as the man-made threats of terrorists or other actors of unlawful interference. The concept of "security" in the context of civil aviation was developed and defined as "a combination of measures and human and material resources intended to safeguard civil aviation against acts of unlawful interference".[1] Consequently, the International Civil Aviation Organization (ICAO) has developed a number of treaties and other instruments to combat terrorism and other acts of unlawful interference. The treaties under the auspices of ICAO are as follows:

- Convention on Offences and Certain Other Acts Committed on Board Aircraft, signed at Tokyo on 14 September 1963 (Tokyo Convention) (ICAO Doc. 8364);
- Convention for the Suppression of Unlawful Seizure of Aircraft, signed at The Hague on 16 December 1970 (The Hague Convention) (ICAO Doc. 8920);
- Convention for the Suppression of Unlawful Acts against the Safety of Civil Aviation, signed at Montreal on 23 September 1971 (Montreal Convention) (ICAO Doc. 8966);
- Protocol for the Suppression of Unlawful Acts of Violence at Airports Serving International Civil Aviation, Supplementary to the Convention for the Suppression of Unlawful Acts against the Safety of Civil Aviation, at Montreal on 23 September 1971, signed at Montreal on 24 February 1988 (Airport Protocol, 1988) (ICAO Doc. 9518);
- Convention on the Marking of Plastic Explosives for the Purpose of Detection, done at Montreal on 1 March 1991 (MEX Convention) (ICAO Doc. 9571);
- Convention on the Suppression of Unlawful Acts Relating to International Civil Aviation, done at Beijing on 10 September 2010 (Beijing Convention);
- Protocol Supplementary to the Convention for the Suppression of Unlawful Seizure of Aircraft, done at Beijing on 10 September 2010 (Beijing Protocol);
- Protocol to Amend the Convention on Offences and Certain Other Acts Committed on Board Aircraft, done at Montreal on 4 April 2014 (Montreal Protocol of 2014).

---

1 Annex 17 to the Convention on International Civil Aviation, "Security: Safeguarding International Civil Aviation from the Acts of Unlawful Interference", Chapter 1, "Definitions".

These multilateral air law treaties form part of 19 global treaties against terrorism adopted by the United Nations (UN) system.[2] Some of them have been almost universally accepted by States.[3] The contents of these treaties have been discussed in widely circulated legal literature.[4]

In addition, ICAO has also developed Annex 17 to the Convention on International Civil Aviation, "Security: Safeguarding International Civil Aviation from the Acts of Unlawful Interference", which has been amended from time to time.

7.1 The Tokyo Convention

The Tokyo Convention is generally regarded as the first worldwide treaty on counter-terrorism,[5] but it has gone far beyond counter-terrorism and established the basic framework for law and public order on board civil aircraft engaged in international flights. It not only applies to "offences against

2 Other 11 treaties are as follows:

  - 1973 Convention on the Prevention and Punishment of Crimes Against Internationally Protected Persons (Diplomatic Agents Convention);
  - 1979 International Convention against the Taking of Hostages (Hostages Convention);
  - 1980 Convention on the Physical Protection of Nuclear Material (Nuclear Materials Convention);
  - 1988 Convention for the Suppression of Unlawful Acts against the Safety of Maritime Navigation (1988 SUA Convention);
  - 1988 Protocol for the Suppression of Unlawful Acts Against the Safety of Fixed Platforms Located on the Continental Shelf (Fixed Platform Protocol);
  - 1997 International Convention for the Suppression of Terrorist Bombings (Terrorist Bombing Convention);
  - 1999 International Convention for the Suppression of the Financing of Terrorism (Terrorist Financing Convention);
  - 2005 International Convention for the Suppression of Acts of Nuclear Terrorism (Nuclear Terrorism Convention);
  - 2005 Protocol to the Convention for the Suppression of Unlawful Acts against the Safety of Maritime Navigation;
  - 2005 Protocol to the Protocol for the Suppression of Unlawful Acts against the Safety of Fixed Platforms Located on the Continental Shelf;
  - 2005 Amendments to the Convention on the Physical Protection of Nuclear Material.

3 As of 28 January 2016, the numbers of states parties to the nine aviation security conventions and protocols are as follows: the Tokyo Convention: 186; The Hague Convention: 185; the Montreal Convention: 188; the Montreal Airport Protocol: 173; the MEX Convention: 153; the Beijing Convention: 13 (not yet in force); the Beijing Protocol: 14 (not yet in force); the Montreal Protocol of 2014: 2 (not yet in force). The present chapter focuses on the last three recently adopted treaties, whereas the material on other five treaties are based on the previous work done by the same writer in J. Huang, *Aviation Safety through the Rule of Law: ICAO's Mechanisms and Practices* (Alphen aan den Rijn: Kluwer, 2009).

4 See, for example, R.P. Boyle and R. Pulsifer, "The Tokyo Convention on Offences and Certain Other Acts Committed on Board Aircraft" (1964) 30 *JALC* 305; B. Cheng, "International Legal Instruments to Safeguard International Air Transport: The Conventions of Tokyo, The Hague, Montreal, and a New Instrument Concerning Unlawful Violence at International Airports", in *Conference Proceedings, Aviation Security*, January 1987, Peace Palace, The Hague, published by International Institute of Air and Space Law, University of Leiden; E. McWhinney, *Aerial Piracy and International Terrorism*, 2nd revised ed. (Dordrecht/Boston/Lancaster: Martinus Nijhoff Publishers,1987); G. Guillaume, "Terrorisme et Droit International" (1989:III) 215 *RdC* 287; R.I.R. Abeyratne, *Aviation Security: Legal and Regulatory Aspects* (Aldershot: Ashgate, 1998); W. Zhao, *International Air Law* (Beijing: Publications for Treatises of Social Sciences, 2000, in Chinese) at 419–482; J. Huang, *supra* note 3; United Nations Office of Drugs and Crime (UNODC): Counter-Terrorism Legal Training Curriculum, MODULE 5, *Transport-related (civil aviation and maritime) Terrorism Offences* (New York: United Nations, 2014).

5 Cf. www.un.org/en/terrorism/instruments.shtml; see, also, Guillaume, *supra* note 4 at 311–312. The Convention on the Prevention and Suppression of Terrorism, signed in Geneva on 16 November 1937, never came into force.

penal law", but also to "acts which, whether or not they are offences, may or do jeopardize the safety of the aircraft or of persons or property therein or which jeopardize good order and discipline on board".[6] The terms "safety", "good order" and "discipline" are clearly not just aimed at terrorism, but are also broadly designed to maintain law and public order on board civil aircraft.

Before the Tokyo Convention, there were some cases in which the courts of the States of registration of aircraft could not exercise criminal jurisdiction because the alleged offences took place outside their respective territory.[7] Article 3, paragraph 1 of the Tokyo Convention addresses this issue by providing that the State of registration of the aircraft is competent to exercise jurisdiction over offences and acts committed on board. This clause was regarded as "probably the most important aspect of the Convention" by Boyle, who had been the Chief of the US Delegation to the Tokyo Conference adopting the treaty.[8] Moreover, Article 3, paragraph 2 the Tokyo Convention requires States Parties to establish such jurisdiction.[9] It is this provision that has sealed the loophole and ensured that aircraft flying over the high seas are not to become "oases of lawlessness".[10]

When an aircraft is flying above the territory of a State other than that of its registry, the offences on board are subject to the concurrent jurisdiction of the flag State and the subjacent State. According to the study of Cheng, in many cases, the jurisdiction of the State of registry to enforce must give way to the same jurisdiction of the State in which the aircraft is found.[11] In the Tokyo Convention, the enforcement power of the subjacent State is restricted by Article 4. The article provides that a "Contracting State which is not the State of registration may not interfere with an aircraft in flight in order to exercise its criminal jurisdiction over an offence committed on board", except in the cases where the offence has effect on its territory, is committed by or against its national or permanent resident, is against its security, is a breach of the rules of the air or is an offence over which the exercise of jurisdiction is necessary to ensure the observance of any obligation of such State under a multilateral international agreement. The reason for such a restriction, according to FitzGerald, who was one of the secretaries of the Tokyo Conference, is "to preserve the safety of air navigation".[12]

---

6 Art. 1, para. 1.
7 In *US* v. *Cordova*, two drunken passengers started a fight on board an aircraft during a flight from Puerto Rico to New York, with other passengers crowding aft to watch them, causing the plane to become tail heavy and to lose balance. When one of the passengers, Cordova, was prosecuted, a US Federal Court declared that it had no jurisdiction over the offence alleged to have been committed on board a US registered aircraft flying over the high seas. See, 3 CCH *Aviation Case* 3 (1950–1953) at 17,306. See also, *R* v. *Martin* [1956] 2 Queen's Bench 272.
8 Boyle and Pulsifer, *supra* note 4 at 329.
9 The exact provision of Art. 3, para. 2 is as follows: "Each Contracting State shall take such measures as may be necessary to establish its jurisdiction", which might leave some ambiguity regarding the strictness of the obligation. However, it is clear from the records of the Conference that the Drafting Committee was instructed to "reflect the principle that, while each State is obliged to establish jurisdiction over offences committed on board aircraft registered in that State, each State has power to define the precise offences over which jurisdiction is to be asserted and to decide whether to enforce its jurisdiction". See, ICAO Doc. 8565-LC/152-1, "International Conference on Air Law", Tokyo, August to September 1963, Vol. 1, Minutes (1966) at 97. See also Boyle and Pulsifer, *supra* note 4 at 355.
10 Cheng, *supra* note 4 at 25.
11 B. Cheng, "Air Law", in *Encyclopedia of Public International Law*, published under the auspices of the Max Planck Institute for Comparative Public Law and International Law under the Direction of Rudolf Bernhardt, Vol. II (Amsterdam-Lausanne-New York-Oxford-Shannon-Tokyo: Elsevier Science B.V., 1995) at 69.
12 G.F. FitzGerald, "Offences and Certain Other Acts Committed on Board Aircraft: The Tokyo Convention of 1963" (1964) 2 *CYIL* 191 at 195. See also Art. 17 which provides that in exercising their jurisdiction, the Contracting States shall pay due regard to the safety and other interests of air navigation.

J. Huang

The Tokyo Convention has also established the authority of the aircraft commander over flights which contain international elements as defined in Article 5, paragraph 1.[13] For the first time in history, the aircraft commander is expressly granted certain police power on board aircraft by a worldwide treaty:

> The aircraft commander may, when he has reasonable grounds to believe that a person has committed, or is about to commit, on board the aircraft, an offence or act contemplated in Article 1, paragraph 1, impose upon such person reasonable measures including restraint which are necessary:
>
> a   to protect the safety of the aircraft, or of persons or property therein; or
> b   to maintain good order and discipline on board; or
> c   to enable him to deliver such person to competent authorities or to disembark him in accordance with the provisions of this Chapter.[14]

The terms "disembark" and "deliver" represent two different concepts, leading to two different consequences. The aircraft commander may disembark a person in the territory of any State in which the aircraft lands, if he has reasonable grounds to believe that such a person *has committed or is about to commit*, on board the aircraft an *act* which, whether or not it is an offence, may or does jeopardize the safety of the aircraft or of persons or property therein or which jeopardize good order and discipline on board.[15] Once the person is disembarked, no further action by the authorities of the place of disembarkation is contemplated. In the case of delivery, the aircraft commander must have reasonable grounds to believe that the person so delivered *has committed* on board the aircraft an act which, in his or her opinion, is a *serious offence* according to the penal law of the State of registry of the aircraft.[16] Obviously, the threshold required for delivery is much higher and the person so delivered would be subject to further legal process of the State taking delivery. Article 13 of the Tokyo Convention not only obligates each contracting State to take the delivery of such a person, but also requires the State immediately to make a preliminary inquiry, and, if the circumstances so warrant, take custody or other measures to ensure the presence of such a person for any criminal or extradition proceedings.

The power granted to the aircraft commander is very broad. For instance, the aircraft commander may impose certain measures, including restraint, if he or she has reasonable grounds to believe that a person is about to commit an act contemplated in Article 1, paragraph 1.[17] The term "reasonable grounds" gives the aircraft commander a certain amount of discretion and does not require that his or her judgement be proven as correct. Moreover, it would be irrelevant if the person did not actually commit the act, or if the act did not actually jeopardize safety. To ensure that the aircraft commander would not be blamed for his or her possible mistake, Article 10 provides a blanket immunity for the aircraft commander and for other persons who have

---

13 Under Art. 5, the provisions concerning the power of the aircraft commander do not apply to offences and acts committed or about to be committed by a person on board an aircraft in flight in the airspace of the State of registration or over the high seas or any other area outside the territory of any State unless the last point of take-off or the next point of intended landing is situated in a State other than that of registration, or the aircraft subsequently flies in the airspace of a State other than that of registration with such person still on board.
14 Art. 6, Tokyo Convention.
15 Arts 8 and 12, ibid.
16 Art. 9, ibid.
17 Art. 6, ibid.

taken action, from any responsibility in any proceeding on account of the treatment undergone by the person against whom the actions were taken. This presumption is in favour of safety and of the persons who have acted to preserve the safety of the aircraft. Accordingly, in one US case, a court held that the action taken by the aircraft commander to disembark a passenger was completely justified when the passenger made the statement that he planned to hijack the aircraft. The court went on to state that the aircraft commander "did not have to tempt fate so that the prospect of hijacking became reality".[18]

The broad power and extraordinary protection granted to the aircraft commander had been a subject of intense debate during the Tokyo Conference. It had been said that the aircraft commander was neither a lawyer nor a police officer, that he or she could not determine if there had been an offence and that the immunity clause conflicted with the principle that no one can be wholly freed from responsibility for his actions. In the end, the paramount consideration of safety prevailed. States not only recognized the power of the aircraft commander but also demonstrated a spirit of cooperation in facilitating his or her functions by allowing the aircraft commander to disembark any person in accordance with the provisions of the Convention,[19] by taking any person delivered by the aircraft commander[20] and by taking all appropriate measures to restore control of the aircraft to its lawful commander in the event of hijacking or other acts of unlawful interference.[21]

In addition to the power of the aircraft commander to impose certain measures, any crew member or passenger may also take reasonable preventive measures when he or she has reasonable grounds to believe that such action is immediately necessary to protect the safety of aircraft or of persons or property therein.[22] These crew members and passengers are also protected by Article 10 and shall not be held responsible for actions taken.[23] Again, safety was the central concern.

As the first worldwide convention on aviation security, the Tokyo Convention was not expected to be perfect by its authors.[24] The Convention has focused on the State of registration, without addressing the jurisdiction of the State of the operator, which became an issue subsequently.[25] It neither specifically criminalizes any act endangering the safety of civil aviation, nor does it create an obligation for extradition.[26] Overall, the Convention covers offences against penal law, and acts which may or do jeopardize the safety of the aircraft or of persons or property therein or which jeopardize good order and discipline on board. While this is a wide coverage, the enforcement measure is minimal and non-obligatory. The net is wide, but the hole is big; the mouth is large, but there are no teeth.[27]

18 *Zervignon* v. *Piedmont Aviation, Inc.,* 558 F. Supp. 1305 (S.D.N.Y.), cited by S.R. Ginger, "Violence in the Skies: The Rights and Liabilities of Air Carriers when Dealing with Disruptive Passengers" (1998) XXIII *Air and Space Law* 106 at 116.
19 Art. 12, ibid.
20 Art. 13, ibid.
21 Art. 11, ibid.
22 Art. 6, para. 2, ibid.
23 Art. 10, however, is not intended to take away the right of an innocent third party to institute legal proceedings. Such a party could be a passenger on board the aircraft whose camera might have been damaged in a scuffle between a crew member and a person who was endangering the safety of the aircraft. See FitzGerald, *supra* note 12 at 198.
24 FitzGerald wrote: "None of its authors would pretend that it is a perfect instrument; but, whether perfect or not, it does represent yet another stone added to the edifice of international law that has been so long abuilding." *Supra* note 12 at 204.
25 See Huang, *supra* note 3, at 117 and 118. See *infra* note 84 and accompanying text.
26 Cheng, *supra* note 4 at 147; Zhao, *supra* note 4 at 446; Abeyratne, *supra* note 4 at 154–155.
27 See Huang, *supra* note 3, at 119.

7.2 The Hague Convention

The incompleteness of the Tokyo Convention was soon noticed by the ICAO Assembly.[28] In 1969, the year that the Convention entered into force, the total number of incidents of hijacking of aircraft in the world was 82, of which 70 were successful.[29] In the first nine months of 1970, 86 aircraft had been hijacked and more than 8,000 passengers were affected,[30] the most notorious event being the hijacking of four aircraft at the same time in September 1970.[31] It was against this backdrop that the International Conference on Air Law was held from 1 to 16 December 1970 in The Hague. The Minister of Justice of the Kingdom of the Netherlands, Dr Karl Polak stated in his opening speech:

> The safety and smooth running of international civil aviation is a matter of prime and common concern to countries and peoples throughout the world. All States, however different their interests may be, share the same basic interest in the preservation and promotion of international air transport. Modern society cannot function properly without it. Yet today, no airline, no air passenger, no country, can feel secure against the unlawful seizure of an airplane.[32]

The Conference successfully adopted The Hague Convention. Unlike the Tokyo Convention which casts a wide net but leaves big loopholes, The Hague Convention criminalizes only one act, namely, the act of hijacking, but at the same time provides an undertaking to make the offence punishable by severe penalties.[33] Article 1 of The Hague Convention reads:

> Any person who on board an aircraft in flight:
>
> a   unlawfully, by force or threat thereof, or by any other form of intimidation, seizes, or exercises control of, that aircraft, or attempts to perform any such act, or
> b   is an accomplice of a person who performs or attempts to perform any such act commits an offence (hereinafter referred to as "the offence").

The most significant contribution of The Hague Convention is the establishment of the legal principle of *aut dedere aut judicare*, which is widely, *albeit* imprecisely, understood as "extradition or prosecution". This principle is expressed in Article 7 as follows:

> The Contracting State in the territory of which the alleged offender is found shall, if it does not extradite him, be obliged, without exception whatsoever and whether or not the

28 ICAO Assembly Resolution A16-37 noted that Art. 11 of the Tokyo Convention provides certain remedies for the unlawful seizure of civil aircraft, but was of the opinion "that this Article does not provide a complete remedy". ICAO Doc. 8779 A16-RES, "Resolution Adopted by the Assembly and Index to Documentation", Sixteenth Session (1968) at 92. See also Abeyratne, *supra* note 4 at 157.
29 Cheng, *supra* note 4 at 27. Cheng mentioned that between 1930 and 1967, the highest number of hijackings in any given year was six. In 1968, the number jumped to 38, 33 of which were successful.
30 Statement of His Excellency, the Minister of Justice of the Kingdom of the Netherlands, Dr Karl Polak, on 1 December 1971, at the opening of the International Conference on Air Law in The Hague, recorded in ICAO Doc. 8979-LC/165-1, "International Conference on Air Law", The Hague, December 1970, Vol. 1, Minutes (1972) at 1.
31 As cited by Cheng from 17 *Keesing's Contemporary Archives* (1969–70) at 24,203–9, the four aircraft were a VC-10 of BOAC, a DC-8 of Swissair, a Boeing 747 of Pan American and a Boeing 707 of TWA. Although hundreds of passengers were released as part of the deal, all four aircraft were destroyed. See Cheng, *supra* note 4 at 33.
32 *Supra* note 30 at 1.
33 Art. 2, The Hague Convention.

offence was committed in its territory, to submit the case to its competent authorities for the purpose of prosecution.

These authorities shall take their decision in the same manner as in the case of any ordinary offence of a serious nature under the law of that State.

According to Zhao, prior to The Hague Convention, there was only one global convention, namely, the Single Convention on Narcotic Drugs, which had genuinely incorporated the concept and imposed the obligation of extradition or prosecution.[34] However, he pointed out that the Narcotics Convention is much less politically sensitive than The Hague Convention. Accordingly, The Hague Convention is the first global treaty in aviation which incorporated this principle. Its formula of the principle since has been followed by a number of multilateral treaties.[35]

Extradition means "the official surrender of a fugitive from justice, regardless of his consent, by the authorities of the State of residence to the authorities of another State for the purpose of criminal prosecution or the execution of a sentence".[36]

With respect to "prosecution", while many States pressed for the strengthening of the obligation to prosecute, the key phrase in Article 7 remains the same as it was originally drafted: "to submit the case to its competent authorities". Most writers acknowledge that a certain discretion exists for a State not to prosecute. The reasons are numerous. For example, Boyle said that the State having the hijacker may not have available to it proof of a crime, since the act was committed in a distant State;[37] Cheng noted that sometimes a State has to negotiate with the hijacker in order to secure the freedom of hundreds of passengers.[38] On the other hand, the discretionary power of the competent authorities of a State is not unlimited. The last sentence of Article 7 provides that "[t]hose authorities shall take their decision in the same manner as in the case of any ordinary offence of a serious nature under the law of that State". While the term "under the law of that State" may allow certain flexibility, good faith still requires that a State maintain a consistent standard.[39] Moreover, as subsequently illustrated in the Lockerbie case, the prerogative of a State may still be challenged under certain circumstances.[40]

34 Art. 36 of the Convention, 520 *UNTS* 204 [1964]. See also Zhao, *supra* note 4 at 451. Moreover, the four Geneva Conventions on international humanitarian law come close in this respect. For instance, Art. 146 of the Convention (IV) relative to the Protection of Civilian Persons in Time of War (Geneva, 12 August 1949) provides that each High Contracting Party shall be under the obligation to search for persons alleged to have committed, or to have ordered to be committed, such grave breaches, and shall bring such persons, regardless of their nationality, before its own courts. It may also, if it prefers, and in accordance with the provisions of its own legislation, hand such persons over for trial to another High Contracting Party concerned, provided such High Contracting Party has made out a *prima facie* case. There might be different views and interpretations as to whether Art. 7 of The Hague Convention imposes a stricter obligation than this provision. In the view of this writer, at least in the matter of extradition, The Hague Convention does impose a stricter obligation. In the Geneva Conventions, extradition is an option but not an obligation. Even if a State party does not bring the alleged offenders before its own courts, there are no grounds for other States to request extradition.
35 See, for example, some UN treaties referred to in *infra* notes 68 and 69: Terrorist Bombing Convention, and Financing Terrorism Convention. See also, *supra* note 4, Guillaume at 313, Cheng at 28, Zhao at 420; van den Wyngaert, "Aviation Terrorism, Jurisdiction and its Implications", in *Conference Proceedings, Aviation Security, supra* note 4 at 137.
36 T. Stern, "Extradition", in *Encyclopedia of Public International Law, supra* note 11 at 327.
37 Boyle, cited by Abeyratne, *supra* note 4 at 161.
38 Cheng, *supra* note 4 at 32.
39 See Huang, *supra* note 3 at 124.
40 See *infra* note 44 and accompanying text for the discussion of the case.

In addition to traditional grounds of jurisdiction, such as the jurisdiction of the State of registration, The Hague Convention also includes the jurisdiction of the State of the operator and that of the State of landing when the alleged offender is still on board.[41] More significantly, the Convention obligates each Contracting State to establish its jurisdiction when the alleged offender is present in its territory and it does not extradite him. As van den Wyngaert observes: The Hague Convention has "developed rules that aim at being comprehensive, in order to ensure that 'aviation terrorists' do not go unpunished. The system is probably as comprehensive as it can possibly be in the political circumstances of the present international scene."[42]

Another provision of The Hague Convention, which is not often mentioned in academic circles, but is important to the mandate of ICAO, is Article 11, which requires each Contracting State to provide, in accordance with its national law, a report to the ICAO Council any relevant information in its possession concerning the circumstances of the offence, the action taken to restore the authority of the aircraft commander and to facilitate the continuation of the journey, and the measures taken in relation to the offender or the alleged offender, and, in particular, the results of any extradition proceedings or other legal proceedings.

The remarkable achievements of The Hague Convention do not mean that there is no room for improvement. The Convention only covers one offence; it does not cover other crimes, such as sabotage of aircraft. This explains why the Montreal Convention was needed nine months later.

7.3 The Montreal Convention

At the time when The Hague Convention was negotiated, parallel work had been initiated to deal with other crimes against civil aviation, such as sabotage, which is done very often through detonation of explosives on board aircraft. Consequently, the Montreal Convention was adopted in 1971.

The Montreal Convention moved one more step further than The Hague Convention by internationally criminalizing a number of acts against the safety of civil aviation. The offences listed under the Montreal Convention include, *inter alia*, acts of violence against a person on board an aircraft in flight, destruction of an aircraft in service, causing damage to an aircraft rendering it incapable of flight, placing or causing to be placed on an aircraft in service, by any means whatsoever, a device or substance which is likely to destroy that aircraft, destruction of or damage to air navigation facilities or interference with their operation, and communication of information which is knowingly false. In most cases, these acts would be considered as offences only when they are "likely to endanger the safety of aircraft in flight".[43]

Article 1, paragraph 1(a) of the Montreal Convention provides that any person commits an offence if he unlawfully and intentionally "performs an act of violence against a person on board

---

41 Art. 4, The Hague Convention.

42 *Supra* note 35 at 138.

43 See the preparatory work in support of this point, in ICAO Doc. 9081-LC/170-1, "International Conference on Air Law", Montreal, September 1971, Vol. 1, Minutes (1973) at 27–30. In particular, the Delegate of the People's Republic of the Congo stated that the protection of human life would have to be related to the safety of air navigation. If there was no relationship to aviation, then he would question whether the Conference was acting competently. Supporting this view, the Delegate of Spain mentioned that the purpose of the provision was not the individual protection of the person on board but the safety of the flight. After the discussion, the President of the Conference indicated that all had been in agreement on the principle to include acts of violence likely to endanger the safety of aircraft in flight.

an aircraft in flight if that act is likely to endanger the safety of that aircraft". According to this provision, the likelihood of endangering the safety of an aircraft in flight forms an integral part of the *actus reus*, the physical part of the offence, in the absence of which the act of violence itself does not constitute the offence. In other words, the Convention does not punish a simple act of violence, but imposes liability upon an act of violence which is likely to endanger the safety of flight. The legislative intent is to protect aviation safety. In the case of communication of information which is known to be false, the mere likelihood of endangering safety would not in and of itself constitute an offence; Article 1, paragraph 1(e) requires that the act must endanger "the safety of an aircraft in flight". Consequently, the act of communicating a hoax that an aircraft will be bombed would not constitute an offence unless it actually endangered the aircraft in flight.

Subparagraphs (b) and (c) of Article 1, paragraph 1 in the Montreal Convention contemplate certain situations in which the offences do not contain the element of "endangering the safety of an aircraft in flight" in the *actus reus*. This is the case when the aircraft subject to the offences is in service but not in flight. Under Article 2, paragraph (b) of the Convention, an aircraft is considered to be in service from the beginning of the preflight preparation of the aircraft by ground personnel or by the crew for a specific flight until 24 hours after any landing. Since this notion of "in service" is broader than the notion of "in flight", destroying or damaging an aircraft in service does not necessarily endanger the safety of flight of such an aircraft, because the flight may not have yet started or may have terminated. Nevertheless, even in the cases of destruction or damage to aircraft which are not in flight, these offences still present serious threats to the safety of aviation in general, although they may not necessarily endanger the specific flights.

Aside from enlarging the scope of offences against the safety of civil aviation, the Montreal Convention basically mirrors The Hague Convention, including the famous principle of *aut dedere aut judicare*. The Lockerbie case is related to the application of this provision.[44]

On 21 December 1988, a Boeing 747 of Pan American Airlines (Pan Am Flight 103) exploded over Lockerbie, Scotland, killing all 256 persons on board and 11 persons on the ground. In November 1991, the Lord Advocate of Scotland charged two Libyan nationals alleging, *inter alia*, that they had caused a bomb to be placed aboard that flight, which bomb had exploded causing the aeroplane to crash. Following on the charges, the UK and the US declared on 27 November 1991 that Libya must:

> surrender for trial all those charged with the crime; and accept responsibility for the actions of Libyan officials; disclose all it knows of this crime, including the names of all those responsible, and allow full access to all witnesses, documents and other material evidence, including all the remaining timers; pay appropriate compensation.[45]

The subject of the declaration by the UK and the US was subsequently considered by the UN Security Council, which on 21 January 1992 adopted Resolution 731 (1992), strongly deploring the fact that the Libyan Government had not yet responded effectively to the above requests

---

44 *Questions of Interpretation and Application of the 1971 Montreal Convention arising from the Aerial Incident at Lockerbie (Libyan Arab Jamahiriya v. United States) Provisional Measures, Order of 14 April 1992*, [1992] *ICJ Reports* 114. On 31 October 2008, BBC reported that Libya paid 1.5 billion US dollars to compensate the victims of Lockerbie and UTA 772, http://news.bbc.co.uk/1/hi/world/americas/7703110.stm. For UTA 772, see ICAO Cir. 262-AN/156, "Aircraft Accident Digest", No. 36 (1989), and UTA 772, "The Forgotten Flight" in the BBC website, above.

45 Ibid. at 122.

contained in the declaration and urging the Libyan Government immediately to provide a full and effective response to those requests so as to contribute to the elimination of international terrorism.[46]

Libya took the position that it had fully complied with the 1971 Montreal Convention by submitting the case to its competent authorities for the purpose of prosecution, and therefore was not obliged to extradite the alleged offenders. Furthermore, Libyan law prohibits the extradition of Libyan nationals. On 3 March 1992, Libya instituted proceedings in the International Court of Justice (ICJ) against the UK, seeking, *inter alia*, the declaration that it had fully complied with the Montreal Convention, and provisional measures to enjoin the UK from taking any action against Libya calculated to coerce or to compel Libya to surrender the accused individuals to any jurisdiction outside Libya.

On 31 March 1992, three days after the close of the hearing of the case and before the Court rendered its decision, the Security Council adopted Resolution 748 (1992) expressing deep concern that the Libyan Government had still not provided a full and effective response to the requests in its Resolution 731 (1992) of 21 January 1992, and imposing sanctions on Libya under Chapter VII of the UN Charter.

On 14 April 1992, the Court, by 11 votes to five, found that the circumstances of the case were not such as to require the exercise of its power under Article 41 of its Statute to indicate provisional measures. The Court cited Security Council Resolution 748 (1992) as the sole ground for its order: "both Libya and the United Kingdom, as Members of the United Nations, are obliged to accept and carry out the decisions of the Security Council in accordance with Article 25 of the Charter".

> [T]he Court, which is at the stage of proceedings on provisional measures, considers that *prima facie* this obligation extends to the decision contained in resolution 748 (1992).... [I]n accordance with Article 103 of the Charter, the obligations of the Parties in that respect prevail over their obligations under any other international agreement, including the Montreal Convention.[47]

The Court stated, at the same time, that this decision in no way prejudged any other questions raised by the parties, and left unaffected the rights of the parties to submit arguments in respect of any of the questions. Thus, despite the rejection of provisional measures, the proceedings continued. Subsequently, the Court, in two judgments rendered on 27 February 1998, dismissed the preliminary objections of the UK and the US, which challenged the jurisdiction of the Court. It found, *inter alia*, that the objection raised by them on the ground that the Security Council resolutions would have rendered the claim of Libya without object did not, in the circumstances of the case, have an exclusive preliminary character.[48]

In the meantime, negotiations were taking place between the parties. In April 1999, Libya agreed that the two suspects be delivered to the Netherlands for a trial before a Scottish court composed solely for this purpose at Camp Zeist in Utrecht, the Netherlands. On 31 January 2001, the special court found one suspect guilty and sentenced him to life imprisonment, with

46 Ibid. at 123–124.
47 Ibid. para. 42.
48 *Questions of Interpretation and Application of the 1971 Montreal Convention arising from the Aerial Incident at Lockerbie (Libyan Arab Jamahiriya* v. *United States of America), Preliminary Objections, Judgment* [1998] *ICJ Reports* at 115, as well as the corresponding judgment in *Libyan Arab Jamahiriya* v. *United Kingdom.*

a minimum of 20 years in jail. The other suspect was acquitted.[49] On 9 September 2003, all parties discontinued the proceedings before the ICJ.[50]

From the order of 14 April 1992 of the ICJ, it may be concluded that the Security Council may override the treaty rights and obligations of States, including the applicability of the principle *aut dedere aut judicare* in The Hague–Montreal system, when the Security Council decides to take action under Chapter VII of the UN Charter.

7.4 The Airport Protocol

The Hague and Montreal Conventions mainly focused on the safety of aircraft in flight. Although the Montreal Convention criminalizes the act of destroying or damaging air navigation facilities, and the act of communicating false information, the purpose of such criminalization, as already discussed above, is to protect "the safety of aircraft in flight". Subsequently, the terrorist groups changed their tactics and focused not on seizing or destroying aircraft but upon inflicting death and serious injury in airport terminals. This phenomenon was a tactic of fanatical groups which attacked crowded airports with the intent of causing maximum loss of life.[51] An early example of this violent tactic was carried out in May 1972 by members of the Japanese Red Army revolutionary group. Using automatic weapons and hand grenades, the attackers killed or wounded over 100 victims at Lod Airport in Tel Aviv with automatic weapons and hand grenades. A similar attack was carried out in August 1973 at the Athens airport by members of the Black September organization. Three persons were killed and over 50 wounded, and hostages were held for several hours before the two attackers surrendered. In August 1982, a bomb and firearms attack was carried out by an Armenian terrorist organization at the Ankara airport with multiple deaths and injuries. In July 1983 another bomb was placed by members of the same organization near the Turkish Airlines area at Orly Airport, Paris, killing or wounding some 150 persons. In December 1985, coordinated attacks were carried out at Rome and Vienna airports by the Abu Nidal organization. Most of the attackers were killed by police, but they had succeeded in killing 20 persons and wounding 140.[52]

In response to these attacks, the ICAO Assembly, upon the initiative of Canada, adopted a resolution on 8 October 1986 during its twenty-sixth Session calling for a new instrument for the "suppression of unlawful acts of violence at airports serving international civil aviation". Consequently, a diplomatic conference was held in February 1988, which adopted the Airport Protocol. The Protocol, designed to be read as one single legal instrument with the Montreal Convention, extends the application of the latter Convention to cover two additional offences, namely, an act of violence against a person at an airport, and an act of destroying or seriously damaging the facilities of an airport or aircraft not in service or disrupting the services of the airport. To constitute an offence, it is a prerequisite that the act in question "endangers or is likely to endanger safety at that airport".[53]

The Airport Protocol introduced the concept of "an airport serving international civil aviation". The instrument is applicable only to international airports. Domestic airports which

---

49 "Secretary-General Expresses Hope that Healing Process Can Begin Following Lockerbie Verdict", UN: SG/SM/7694, 31 January 2001. See also CNN report "Lockerbie Trial: Quotes of the Day", 31 January 2001, http://archives.cnn.com/2001/WORLD/europe/01/31/lockerbie.quotes/index.html.
50 See Order of 10 September 2003, ICJ, www.icj-cij.org/docket/files/89/7247.pdf.
51 UNODC, *supra* note 4 at 39.
52 UNODC, ibid.
53 Art. II, Airport Protocol.

do not have any international element are within the exclusive domain of the State where the airports are located, and are not governed by the Protocol. There were discussions as to whether the term "an airport serving international civil aviation" should be further defined when the draft protocol was tabled at the ICAO Legal Committee. Most delegations were of the view that any definition or qualification would be to the detriment of the necessary flexibility in the application of the instrument. They emphasized that it should be a matter of fact to be determined by the State concerned or by the judge in the proceedings whether an airport in fact served international civil aviation, and that the answer may be different at different times.[54] The Diplomatic Conference subsequently decided to keep the term as it was. From the discussion, it transpired that "an airport serving international civil aviation" would at least include the following: (1) an airport designated as a customs airport under Article 10 of the Chicago Convention; (2) an airport designated under Article 68 of the Chicago Convention for the use by any international air service; and (3) an airport not designated under (1) or (2) but which is in fact used as an alternate airport by an international flight. It remains to be seen to what extent flexibility will be applied in the interpretation of the term by the competent authorities. For instance, if a group of international passengers are attacked at a feeder or "spoke" airport, while they intended to fly to a "hub" airport for a connection of a long-haul international fight, would the feeder airport be considered as "serving international civil aviation"? One may argue that in this case the feeder airport contains sufficient international elements for the purpose of the application of the Protocol, while another may argue that the feeder airport is merely a domestic airport and the flight of those passengers is a domestic flight. Although interpretations may differ, it is arguable that the safety of these passengers forms an integral part of the safety of international civil aviation. The confidence of the travelling public would be affected if they are not protected by uniform international rules when they are on feeder flights. From this perspective, an airport where feeder flights for an international hub are provided might under certain conditions be considered as "an airport serving international civil aviation".

In the application of the Montreal Convention and the Airport Protocol, an issue has been raised whether these treaties are applicable to acts by States. It is submitted that they only apply to the acts of individuals but not those of States.[55]

7.5 The MEX Convention

The catastrophe in Lockerbie again highlighted the need to take preventive measures through modern technology, since it was determined that the destruction of the Pan Am aircraft was caused by a small amount of Semtex, a hard-to-detect, high performance explosive.[56] In response to that event, the MEX Convention was adopted in 1991 and its objective is to establish a uniform international system, under which certain explosives will be marked by one of the detection agents specified in the Convention, in order to enhance their detectability by certain equipment.

The mandate to develop the Convention was given to ICAO by the UN Security Council, which, in its Resolution 635, urged ICAO "to intensify its work … on devising an international régime for the marking of plastic or sheet explosives for the purpose of detection". The Convention

---

54 ICAO Doc. 9823-DC/5, "International Conference on Air Law (Protocol for the Suppression of Unlawful Acts of Violence at Airports Serving International Civil Aviation, Supplementary to the Convention for the Suppression of Unlawful Acts Against the Safety of Civil Aviation)", Montreal, 9–24 February 1988, Minutes and Documents (2003) at 161.

55 For more detailed discussion, see Huang, *supra* note 3 at 135 *et seq.*

56 J. Augustin, "The Role of ICAO in Relation to the Convention on the Marking of Plastic Explosives for the Purpose of Detection" (1992) XVII *AASL* 33 at 33.

is not an arms control or disarmament treaty and does not restrict or prohibit the manufacture of plastic explosives per se. It merely prohibits the manufacture of unmarked plastic explosives.

The regime of the Convention only applies to certain explosives as defined in the Technical Annex. The list of detection agents to be used to enhance the detectability of explosives is also provided in the Annex. The amendment of the Annex does not require the express consent of any State party. Instead, the ICAO Council may, upon the recommendation of an expert body called the International Explosives Technical Commission, propose an amendment to States parties for adoption. If the amendment has not been objected to by five or more States parties within 90 days from the date of notification of the amendment by the Council, it shall be deemed to have been adopted and becomes binding on all States parties which do not object to it.[57] This procedure has been designed to cope with the requirements of rapid technical changes which need to be incorporated into the Technical Annex promptly, without going through the lengthy process of ratifications of a treaty amendment.

The MEX Convention has contributed to aviation security by establishing an international regime for the detection of plastic explosives. Since its adoption, various other technological solutions for the detection of explosives have also been developed.

7.6 The Beijing Convention

As an immediate response to the terrorist attacks in the US on 11 September 2001, the thirty-third Session of the ICAO Assembly adopted Resolution A33-1 and directed the Council and the Secretary General to address the new and emerging threats to civil aviation, and, among other things, to review the adequacy of the existing aviation security conventions.[58]

After several years of work consecutively done by the ICAO Secretariat, the Secretariat Study Group, a Rapporteur, a special Sub-Committee and the thirty-fourth Session of the Legal Committee, the ICAO Council convinced a diplomatic conference in Beijing, which adopted on 10 September 2010 the Beijing Convention and the Beijing Protocol.

7.6.1 Criminalization of certain acts under the Beijing Convention

The Beijing Convention is designed to consolidate the provisions of the Montreal Convention of 1971, the provisions of the Airport Protocol of 1988 and the new provisions adopted at the Beijing Conference.

The salient features of the Beijing Convention include the criminalization of an act of using civil aircraft in service as a weapon, an act of using certain dangerous substances to attack aircraft or other targets, an act for the unlawful air transport of biological, chemical and nuclear (BCN) weapons, and an act of cyber attack on air navigation facilities.

7.6.1.1 Using civil aircraft in service for the purpose of causing death, injury or damage

One of the unforgettable facts on 11 September 2001 is that civil aircraft, which have become one of the essential means of transportation in modern society, were used and diverted by

---

57 Arts VI and VII.
58 ICAO Assembly Resolution A33-1 "Declaration on Misuse of Civil Aircraft as Weapons of Destruction and other Terrorist Acts involving Civil Aviation", ICAO Doc. 9958 "Assembly Resolutions in Force (as of 8 October 2010)" at VII-1.

terrorists to become powerful weapons of destruction. The attacks on 11 September were the aggregation of various offences, such as the unlawful seizure of an aircraft in flight, the intentional destruction of an aircraft in service, acts of violence on board aircraft, murders, and other criminal acts causing injuries and damage. While the provisions of the existing aviation security instruments cover various components of these offences,[59] they do not specifically address the aggravated aspects of diverting civil aircraft in service into weapons of destruction. Deliberately using a hijacked aircraft to murder innocent people in the air or on the ground or to cause serious damage constitutes a criminal act of immense gravity which is utterly different from a simple hijacking for such purposes as smuggling or immigration, without causing death or serious injury. Accordingly, the Beijing Convention provides in paragraph 1(f) of Article 1 that any person commits an offence if that person unlawfully and intentionally "uses an aircraft in service for the purpose of causing death, serious bodily injury, or serious damage to property or the environment".

The term "for the purpose of" is inserted to make clear that this provision is designed to cover the deliberate use of a civil aircraft as a weapon, and not intended to capture certain unlawful operational behaviour of a crew member which inadvertently causes death, injury or damage. The term further signifies that the act does not necessarily lead to the result of actual death, injury or damage. It would be considered sufficient if the actor had the intention to cause such a result.[60]

In the earlier discussions in the Legal Committee, different views were expressed whether the damage to the environment should be covered by this provision. Some delegates were of the view that the term "environment" was vague. After some debate, there was general agreement in the Legal Committee that reference to the environment should be retained in order to encompass any possible environmental catastrophe.[61] The Diplomatic Conference accepted the text of the Legal Committee.

7.6.1.2 Using dangerous substances to attack aircraft or other targets

In addition to the use of civil aircraft as weapons, the use of BCN weapons or similar substances against civil aircraft or other targets has also been perceived as one of the new and emerging threats. For this reason, subparagraphs (g) and (h) have been included in Article 1, paragraph 1 of the Beijing Convention, to criminalize the act of using BCN weapons and similar substances to attack civil aircraft or other targets. The difference between the subparagraphs (g) and (h) is that the latter addresses the attacks against or on board civil aircraft, whereas the former covers the attacks from civil aircraft against other targets.

From the preparatory work of the treaty, it appears clear that these provisions are aimed at terrorist attacks or other acts of sabotage. They should not be applied to an act with no intention to attack, such as an act of a pilot who forgot to renew his or her licence when he or she sprayed pesticides on crops and subsequently caused death, injury or damage. While these

---

59 For example, the unlawful seizure of aircraft is listed as an offence under Art. 1 of The Hague Convention; destruction of aircraft is covered by Art. 1, para. 1(b) of the Montreal Convention; an act of violence on board may be covered by Art. 1, para. 1(a) of the Montreal Convention.

60 Cf. ICAO Doc. LC/SC-NET, "Report of the Special Sub-Committee on the Preparation of One or More Instruments Addressing New and Emerging Threats", Montreal, 3–6 July 2007, "Rapporteur's Report" at A3-13, para. 44.

61 "Report of the Special Sub-Committee", ibid. at 2-4, para. 10.2.12. See also ICAO Doc. 9926-LC/194, "Report of the 34th Session of the Legal Committee" at 2-2, para. 2:10.

types of acts may be punishable, they do not need to be subject to the international regime of "extradite or prosecute".[62]

7.6.1.3 Unlawful transport of BCN weapons and related material

The issue concerning unlawful transport of BCN weapons and related material, which is conveniently referred to as the transport offence, has been extensively discussed in the ICAO fora. The issue was first considered during the second meeting of the Sub-Committee of the Legal Committee and the opinions were divided. The group in favour of the inclusion of this offence in the new treaty relied upon the precedent of the Convention for the Suppression of Unlawful Acts against the Safety of Maritime Navigation of 2005 (the SUA Convention). It was forcefully argued that since the SUA Convention has prohibited the unlawful transport of BCN weapons by sea, the same should be done for the unlawful transport by air. Otherwise there would be a gap in the legal system. Another group was not in favour of the inclusion. They believed that there was no connection between the criminalization of mere transport of these materials and the safety of civil aviation. They preferred that this matter, which was related to non-proliferation of nuclear weapons, be dealt with by the UN bodies other than ICAO.[63] After long deliberation, the Legal Committee managed to narrow down the difference to the following text of the chapeau of draft Article 1, paragraph 1(i):

> transports, causes to be transported or facilitates the transport on board an aircraft of the following items, knowing that it is to be used to facilitate an act intended to cause [with or without a condition] death or serious bodily injury to a civilian [or to any person not taking an active part in the hostilities in a situation of armed conflict], when the purpose of such act, by its nature or context, is to intimidate a population or to compel a government or an international organization to do or to abstain from doing any act.

There was an emerging consensus that the unlawful transport of BCN weapons needs to be addressed by the treaty, but one group preferred to criminalize the act of transport only when the transporter knows that BCN material will be used for terrorist purposes, while another group believed that any unlawful and intentional transport of BCN weapons, whether for terrorist purposes or not, should be punishable. The Diplomatic Conference considered this issue at length, and consequently the view of the second group prevailed, and the adopted text of Article 1, paragraph 1(i) is as follows:

> transports, causes to be transported, or facilitates the transport of, on board an aircraft:
>
> 1   any explosive or radioactive material, knowing that it is intended to be used to cause, or in a threat to cause, with or without a condition, as is provided for under national law, death or serious injury or damage for the purpose of intimidating a population, or compelling a government or an international organization to do or to abstain from doing any act; or
>
> 2   any BCN weapon, knowing it to be a BCN weapon as defined in Article 2; or

---

62 ICAO Doc. LC/SC-NET-2, "Report of the Second Meeting of the Special Sub-Committee on the Preparation of One or More Instruments Addressing New and Emerging Threats", Montreal, 19–21 February 2008 at 3-1, para. 3.3.

63 "Report of the Second Meeting the Special Committee", ibid. at 2-1.

3   any source material, special fissionable material, or equipment or material especially designed or prepared for the processing, use or production of special fissionable material, knowing that it is intended to be used in a nuclear explosive activity or in any other nuclear activity not under safeguards pursuant to a safeguards agreement with the International Atomic Energy Agency; or

4   any equipment, materials or software or related technology that significantly contributes to the design, manufacture or delivery of a BCN weapon without lawful authorization and with the intention that it will be used for such purpose provided that for activities involving a State Party, including those undertaken by a person or legal entity authorized by a State Party, it shall not be an offence under subparagraphs (3) and (4) if the transport of such items or materials is consistent with or is for a use or activity that is consistent with its rights, responsibilities and obligations under the applicable multilateral non-proliferation treaty to which it is a party including those referred to in Article 7.

In the adopted text, the terms "to intimidate a population or to compel a government or an international organization to do or to abstain from doing any act" have been deleted from the chapeau but they are still retained in subparagraph (1). As a result, the "terrorist motive" is one of the constitutive elements of the offence of unlawful transport of explosive or radioactive material, but is not a required element for the offence of unlawful transport of BCN weapons. Moreover, the proviso at the end of paragraph 1(i) was added during the Diplomatic Conference to mention specifically that subparagraphs (3) and (4) do not apply to certain acts of a State Party which are consistent with the applicable multilateral treaties. It is also clear from the context of paragraph (i) as well as the history of negotiation that *mens rea*, i.e. guilty mind, is required to constitute this offence. If an air carrier unintentionally transported BCN weapons, it does not commit such an offence.

7.6.1.4 Cyber attacks on air navigation facilities

Article 1, paragraph 1(c) of the Montreal Convention of 1971 already provides that any person commits an offence if that person unlawfully and intentionally destroys or damages air navigation facilities or interferes with their operation, if any such act is likely to endanger the safety of aircraft in flight. This provision remains unchanged in the Beijing Convention, but the following provision has been added to Article 2, paragraph (c): "(c) 'Air navigation facilities' include signals, data, information or systems necessary for the navigation of the aircraft." Consequently, Article 1, paragraph 1(c) not only covers attacks on the hardware, but also the software of the air navigation facilities.

7.6.1.5 Threats to commit an offence

In the earlier discussion of the draft treaty, it was realized that under certain circumstances, "a threat to commit an act, without the actual commission of the act contemplated, may cause grave adverse consequences to civil aviation".[64] For instance, a threat to use chemical or biological substances and other lethal devices on board an aircraft or at an airport may

---

64 ICAO Council Working Paper C-WP/12851, "Final Report Relating to the Secretariat Study Group on Aviation Security Conventions" (20 February 2007) at para. 2.1.2.7.

seriously shake the public confidence and seriously disrupt international air transport, without the actual commission of such an offence. However, the existing aviation security conventions mainly criminalize commission of certain acts, but generally do not deal with the threat to commit such acts. In view of this, it was considered necessary to criminalize certain threats to commit offences. Thus, Article 1, paragraph 3 of the Beijing Convention reflects this legislative intent:

> Any person also commits an offence if that person:
>
> a   makes a threat to commit any of the offences in subparagraphs (a), (b), (c), (d), (f), (g) and (h) of paragraph 1 or in paragraph 2 of this Article; or
> b   unlawfully and intentionally causes any person to receive such a threat,
>
> under circumstances which indicate that the threat is credible.

The offences under Article 1, paragraph 1, subparagraphs (e) and (i) are deliberately excluded from the above provision concerning the threat to commit an offence. As a result, a threat to communicate false information or a threat to transport BCN weapons and related material is not an offence under the Convention.

The element of the credibility of a threat is essential in constituting the offence. The term "credible" is not defined and will be left to the competent courts to interpret, taking into account the specific circumstances of each case.

7.6.1.6 Assisting an offender

A new provision has been incorporated into the treaty to provide that any person also commits an offence if that person unlawfully and intentionally assists another person to evade investigation, prosecution or punishment, knowing that the person has committed an act that constitutes an offence under the Convention or the Protocol, or that the person is wanted for criminal prosecution by law enforcement authorities for such an offence or has been sentenced for such an offence.[65]

During the discussion at the Legal Committee, some States intended to include the "transport of fugitive" as one of the principal offences in the new instruments. Other States and the industry were uncomfortable with this proposal. As a compromise, an informal working group proposed to merge this concept into an accessory offence as described in the preceding paragraph. This compromise proposal was endorsed by the Legal Committee and subsequently by the Diplomatic Conference. The resulted text criminalizes not only the transport but also other kinds of assistance provided to a person having committed an offence under the Convention or the Protocol and trying to evade investigation, prosecution or punishment. Again, in this provision, the "intention" is the built-in constitutive element for the offence. Moreover, depending on the provisions under the domestic law, Article 21, subparagraph 4(b) of the Convention and Article XXII of the Protocol envisage certain situations in which family exemptions from liability are possible.

---

65 Art. 1, para. 4(c) of the Beijing Convention and Art. II of the Beijing Protocol which added Art. 1, para. 3(d) to The Hague Convention.

J. Huang

7.6.1.7 Agreement or contribution to an offence

Article 1, paragraph 5 of the Beijing Convention may be considered as introducing an innovative element into aviation security conventions by the following text:

> 5. Each State Party shall also establish as offences, when committed intentionally, whether or not any of the offences set forth in paragraph 1, 2 or 3 of this Article is actually committed or attempted, either or both of the following:
>
>   a agreeing with one or more other persons to commit an offence set forth in paragraph 1, 2 or 3 of this Article and, where required by national law, involving an act undertaken by one of the participants in furtherance of the agreement; or
>
>   b contributing in any other way to the commission of one or more offences set forth in paragraph 1, 2 or 3 of this Article by a group of persons acting with a common purpose, and such contribution shall either: (i) be made with the aim of furthering the general criminal activity or purpose of the group, where such activity or purpose involves the commission of an offence set forth in paragraph 1, 2 or 3 of this Article; or (ii) be made in the knowledge of the intention of the group to commit an offence set forth in paragraph 1, 2 or 3 of this Article.

The aim of this new clause is to criminalize preparatory behaviour for an offence without the requirement of an accomplished act. This is of particular significance in the context of preventive efforts in civil aviation with a view to foiling as many attempted attacks as possible. The text was first developed at the phase of the Legal Sub-Committee, taking into account the precedent in Article 5, paragraph 1, subparagraph (a)(i) and (ii) of the 2000 UN Convention Against Transnational Organized Crime. The drafting intention was to create an optional regime compatible with virtually all national legal systems, including the concept of the crime of conspiracy in common law jurisdictions, and the concept of "association de malfaiteurs" in civil law jurisdiction.[66] The text developed by the Legal Subcommittee was approved by the Legal Committee, and subsequently accepted by the Diplomatic Conference only with minor changes. As can be seen, the optional regime was carefully crafted in several subparagraphs with different alternatives within alternatives, endeavouring to accommodate various concepts in domestic laws.

7.6.1.8 Liability of a legal entity involved with an offence

During the Diplomatic Conference, an issue was raised concerning the liability of a legal entity when a person responsible for management or control of that entity has, in that capacity, committed an offence set forth in the Convention or the Protocol. Upon further deliberation, it was considered that the maritime precedent as provided in Article 5*bis* of the 2005 SUA Convention may be transplanted into the aviation counterpart. Consequently, Article 4 of the Beijing Convention and Article IV of the Protocol explicitly allow its respective State Party to hold such an entity liable in accordance with its national legal principles. Such liability may be criminal, civil or administrative. Such liability is incurred without prejudice to the criminal liability of individuals having committed the offence. The Convention and the Protocol further provide that the relevant State Party shall endeavour to ensure that the applicable criminal, civil or administrative sanctions are effective, proportionate and dissuasive. Such sanctions may include monetary sanctions.

---

66 "Report of the Special Sub-Committee", *supra* note 60 at 2-7.

154

7.6.2 Incorporation of provisions commonly found in the more recent counter-terrorism conventions

There are certain provisions commonly found in the more recent counter-terrorism treaties within the UN system, which did not occur in the previous aviation security conventions. The Diplomatic Conference in Beijing decided to include these provisions in the two new instruments adopted by it, in order to keep ICAO instruments fully consistent with other UN treaties.

7.6.2.1 Organizing or directing an offence

The existing aviation security conventions focus on the persons actually committing the punishable acts, mainly on board an aircraft or at an airport, without specific provisions addressing the persons organizing and directing the commission of the offences. In the case of suicide attacks similar to those on 11 September, the attackers on board the aircraft perished during the attacks and could no longer be held accountable under criminal law.[67] It has become much more important to pursue the directors and organizers behind the scene. While the culprits on board aircraft may perish after their suicide attacks, their masterminds on the ground should not be allowed to have any safe haven. In this connection, it should be mentioned that the more recent UN conventions, such as the International Convention for the Suppression of Terrorist Bombings[68] and the International Convention for the Suppression of the Financing of Terrorism,[69] specifically extend the offence provisions to a person who organizes or directs others to commit an offence. The Beijing Convention and the Beijing Protocol follow the same, respectively, in Article 1, paragraph 4(b) and in the amended Article 1, paragraph 3(b) of The Hague Convention.

7.6.2.2 Exclusion of military activities

Article 6 of the Beijing Convention and Article VI of the Protocol contain the following provisions:

1　Nothing in this Convention shall affect other rights, obligations and responsibilities of States and individuals under international law, in particular the purposes and principles of the Charter of the United Nations, the Convention on International Civil Aviation and international humanitarian law.

2　The activities of armed forces during an armed conflict, as those terms are understood under international humanitarian law, which are governed by that law are not governed by this Convention, and the activities undertaken by military forces of a State in the exercise of their official duties, inasmuch as they are governed by other rules of international law, are not governed by this Convention.

67　The same result occurred when suicide bombers destroyed two Russian civil aircraft on 24 August 2004. See Assembly Resolution A35-1, "Acts of Terrorism and Destruction of Russian Civil Aircraft resulting in the Deaths of 90 People – Passengers and Crew Members", in ICAO Doc. 9848, "Assembly Resolutions in Force (as of 8 October 2004)" at I-30.

68　Adopted by the General Assembly of the United Nations on 15 December 1997, http://untreaty.un.org.

69　Adopted by the General Assembly of the United Nations on 9 December 1999, http://untreaty.un.org.

3   The provisions of paragraph 2 of this Article shall not be interpreted as condoning or making lawful otherwise unlawful acts, or precluding prosecution under other law.

These provisions had been subject to intensive debates since the phase of the Legal Sub-Committee. General consensus has been achieved with respect to the text of paragraphs 1 and 3. The divided views focused on paragraph 2, or more precisely the clause regarding "the activities undertaken by military forces of a State in the exercise of their official duties, inasmuch as they are governed by other rules of international law, are not governed by this Convention". A strong majority preferred to maintain this clause and exclude these activities from the scope of applicability of the instruments, while a minority disagreed.

It should be noted that the text of this article does not originate from the ICAO fora. It has been incorporated, in one form or another, into various conventions within the UN system which are already in force, such as the Terrorist Bombing Convention, the Terrorist Financing Convention, the Nuclear Terrorism Convention and the 2005 SUA Convention. ICAO legal bodies only added the reference to the Convention on International Civil Aviation in its paragraph 1, which has not given rise to any objection. As for the rest of the provisions, they were taken virtually word for word from other conventions within the UN system.

7.6.2.3 Exclusion of political offence exception

As most of the ICAO aviation security conventions were concluded decades ago, they did not and could not possibly include the provisions which reflect the more recent developments in international law. For instance, in The Hague Convention, there is no express provision to exclude hijacking from the scope of political offence.[70] As the campaign against international terrorism developed, the international community gradually became more receptive to the concept that terrorist acts should be treated as ordinary rather than as political offences. A number of the more recent international treaties specifically exclude the political offence exception. For instance, Article 11 of the Terrorist Bombings Convention reads:

> None of the offences set forth in article 2 shall be regarded, for the purposes of extradition or mutual legal assistance, as a political offence or as an offence connected with a political offence or as an offence inspired by political motives. Accordingly, a request for extradition or for mutual legal assistance based on such an offence may not be refused on the sole ground that it concerns a political offence or an offence connected with a political offence or an offence inspired by political motives.[71]

This provision, representing the progressive development of international law, has now been incorporated into Article 13 of the Beijing Convention. It may provide additional deterrence to unlawful interference against civil aviation.

7.6.2.4 Jurisdictional clauses

The Hague Convention of 1970 and the Montreal Convention of 1971 already contain wide jurisdictional provisions, but the more recent counter-terrorism conventions within the UN

---

70 For more background information, see J. Huang, *Aviation Safety through the Rule of Law: ICAO's Mechanisms and Practices* (Alphen aan den Rijn: Kluwer, 2009) at 123 *et seq.*
71 *Supra* note 68.

system have further expanded jurisdictional grounds.[72] To be consistent with this trend, paragraph 1 article 8 of the Beijing Convention, as a new mandatory jurisdictional clause, reads as follows:

> 1   Each State Party shall take such measures as may be necessary to establish its jurisdiction over the offences set forth in Article 1 … in the following cases:
> [...]
> e   when the offence is committed by a national of that State.

The Diplomatic Conference considered it necessary to add this mandatory jurisdiction. In addition, certain optional jurisdictions were also considered. As a result, Article 8, paragraph 2 of the Beijing Convention contains the following provisions:

> 2   Each State Party may also establish its jurisdiction over any such offence in the following cases:
> a   when the offence is committed against a national of that State;
> b   when the offence is committed by a stateless person whose habitual residence is in the territory of that State.

7.6.2.5 Fair treatment and non-discrimination clauses

The relevant UN conventions include clauses with respect to fair treatment and non-discrimination. These provisions are aimed at the protection of basic human rights. These provisions have now been incorporated into the Beijing instruments. The fair treatment clause reads as follows:

> Any person who is taken into custody, or regarding whom any other measures are taken or proceedings are being carried out pursuant to this Convention, shall be guaranteed fair treatment, including enjoyment of all rights and guarantees in conformity with the law of the State in the territory of which that person is present and applicable provisions of international law, including international human rights law.[73]

The following clause of non-discrimination has also been included in Article 14 of the Beijing Convention:

> Nothing in this Convention shall be interpreted as imposing an obligation to extradite or to afford mutual legal assistance if the requested State Party has substantial grounds for believing that the request for extradition for offences set forth in Article 1 or for mutual legal assistance with respect to such offences has been made for the purpose of prosecuting or punishing a person on account of that person's race, religion, nationality, ethnic origin, political opinion or gender, or that compliance with the request would cause prejudice to that person's position for any of these reasons.

---

72 See, for examples, Art. 6 of the Terrorist Bombing Convention, Art. 7 of the Terrorist Financing Convention and Art. 9 of the Nuclear Terrorism Convention.
73 Art. XI, Beijing Convention.

7.7 The Beijing Protocol

The Beijing Protocol is designed to update the Convention for the Suppression of Unlawful Seizure of Aircraft (The Hague Convention of 1970). One of the salient amendments introduced in Beijing may be illustrated by the comparison of the following provisions of The Hague Convention and the Beijing Protocol. Article 1, paragraph (a) of The Hague Convention provides that "Any person who on board an aircraft in flight: (a) Unlawfully, by force or threat thereof, or by any other form of intimidation, seizes, or exercises control of, that aircraft,… commits an offence."

This provision has been amended by Article II of the Beijing Protocol to read as follows:

> Any person commits an offence if that person unlawfully and intentionally seizes or exercises control of an aircraft in service by force or threat thereof, or by coercion, or by any other form of intimidation, or by any technological means.

The new amendment has deleted the term "on board", thereby expanding the scope of the applicability of the new provision to certain acts which take place outside the aircraft in question. The additional reference to "any technological means" further envisages the future possibility of unlawful control of aircraft by technical means, such as by remote controlled electronic devices, instead of by the presence of an individual on board the aircraft.[74] For example, "control" could be obtained by a person on the ground jamming the signals without seizing the aircraft physically.[75] The term "aircraft in flight" has been replaced by "aircraft in service", in order to align it with the Montreal Convention of 1971. The latter term covers a period "from the beginning of the pre-flight preparation of the aircraft by ground personnel or by the crew for a specific flight until twenty-four hours after any landing".[76]

The term "coercion" is also a new addition. The term originally came from the proposal of "constrainte" in the French language. The intention was to address all possible situations where perpetrators try to gain control of an aircraft, even in the absence of physical violence or the use of firearms on board the aircraft. At the 34th Session of the Legal Committee, it was decided to replace the English word "constraint" with "coercion".[77]

The Beijing Protocol has also included the provisions in the Beijing Convention relating to threats to commit an offence, assisting an offender, agreement or contribution to an offence, liability of a legal entity involved with an offence, as well as all the provisions mentioned in 7.6.2 above.

7.8 The Montreal Protocol of 2014

The Diplomatic Conference convened by ICAO in 2014 adopted on 4 April a protocol to amend the Tokyo Convention to address the concern about the escalation of the severity and frequency of unruly behaviour on board aircraft. The ICAO legal work addressing the issue of unruly behaviour started in 1996 and resulted in a resolution of the ICAO Assembly in 2001, urging States to adopt domestic legislation following the model provided by ICAO.[78] Due to

---

74 "Report of the Special Sub-Committee", *supra* note 60 at 2-13.
75 "Report of the Legal Committee", *supra* note 61 at 2-15, para. 2:99.
76 Art. V, Beijing Protocol.
77 *Supra* note 61, paragraph 2:100.
78 Resolution A33-4, ICAO Doc. 9790, "Assembly Resolution in Force (as of 5 October 2001)" at V-5. See also ICAO Cir. 288 LE/1, "Guidance Material on the Legal Aspects of Unruly/Disruptive Passengers" (June 2002).

the events on 11 September 2011, this item became somewhat inactive, as the priority was given to the work which eventually led to the adoption of the Beijing Convention and Protocol. Upon the proposal by the International Air Transport Association, the work was reactivated through a study group in 2011, followed by a Legal Sub-Committee and the Legal Committee, culminating in the Diplomatic Conference.[79] The focus of the Protocol is to modernize the Tokyo Convention by, *inter alia*, introducing additional jurisdictional bases for criminal jurisdiction and expressly extending legal recognition and protections to in-flight security officers (IFSOs), commonly known as air marshals.[80]

7.8.1 Jurisdiction

The provisions relating to jurisdiction in the Protocol of 2014 are considered a "centerpiece" of the modernization of the Tokyo Convention.[81] The main feature of these provisions relates to the jurisdiction of the State of landing.

One of the frustrations experienced by airlines in dealing with unruly behaviour is that the State of landing, which has custody of an alleged offender delivered by an aircraft commander, does not have jurisdiction on this matter. For instance, an offence may take place on board a foreign aircraft when such aircraft is outside the territorial airspace of the State where it subsequently lands. When the State of landing is requested to prosecute the alleged offender who is not its national, it often finds itself having no jurisdiction, since the offence has taken place neither in its territory nor on board its aircraft, and it is neither directed against it or its national nor involving a crime of sufficient gravity to establish universal or quasi-universal jurisdiction.[82] To remedy this undesirable situation, the Protocol of 2014 has added Article 3.1*bis* to the Tokyo Convention to provide that the State of landing "is also competent to exercise jurisdiction over offences and acts committed on board", "when the aircraft on board which the offence or act is committed lands in its territory with the alleged offender still on board".

While there was a unanimous recognition of the competency of the State of landing to exercise such jurisdiction, the Diplomatic Conference was more cautious when the issue was whether the establishment of such a jurisdiction should become mandatory. The text added to the Tokyo Convention as Article 2*bis* (a) is as follows:

> Each Contacting State shall take measures to establish jurisdiction as may be necessary to establish its jurisdiction over offences committed on board aircraft in the following cases:
>
> a   as the State of landing, when
>
> > i   the aircraft on board which the offence is committed has its last point of departure or next point of intended landing within its territory, and the aircraft subsequently lands in its territory with the alleged offender still on board; and
> >
> > ii the safety of the aircraft or of persons or property therein, or good order and discipline on board, is jeopardised.

---

79 ICAO Doc. 10014-LC/35, "Report of Legal Committee 35th Session" (2013).
80 UNODC, *supra* note 4 at 59.
81 M. Jennison, "The Montreal Protocol of 2014 is intended to Modernize the Tokyo Convention of 1963: Can it Succeed?" XXXIX *Annals of Air and Space Law* (2014). Mr Jennison was the Chairman of the thirty-fifth Session of the ICAO Legal Committee, at which the text of the draft protocol was prepared.
82 ICAO Cir. 288, *supra* note 78 at 7.

Additionally, Article 3.2*ter* requires that in exercising its jurisdiction as State of landing, the State shall consider whether the offence in question is an offence in the State of the operator.

Accordingly, mandatory jurisdiction does not apply to an aircraft diverted to an unintended destination.[83] Moreover, it only applies to offences but not "acts". Finally, it does not apply unless the offence in fact endangered the safety of the aircraft or persons or property therein, or jeopardized the good order and discipline.

The Protocol of 2014 has also resolved the issue left over by the Tokyo Convention concerning the jurisdiction of the State of the operator, which has been outstanding for decades.[84] Under Article 3.1*bis* the State of the operator is competent to exercise jurisdiction over offences and acts committed on board when the offence or act is committed on board an aircraft leased without crew to a lessee whose principal place of business or, if the lessee has no such place of business, whose permanent residence, is in that State. In the same situation, Article 3.2*bis* further mandates the State of the operator to establish its jurisdiction in this situation over the offences but not act on board. In addition, Article 1.3(b) clarifies that when the State of the operator is not the same as the State of registration, the term "the State of registration" used in certain provisions shall be deemed to be the State of the operator. This amendment will facilitate the resolution of certain issues arising from the relationship between the State of registration and the State of the operator. For example, Article 4 of the Tokyo Convention restricts the criminal jurisdiction of States which are not the State of registration. If the amendment in the form of Article 1.3(b) had not been adopted, the literal meaning of Article 4 would have unduly restricted the jurisdiction of the State of the operator.

7.8.2 The status of IFSOs

IFSOs did not exist when the Tokyo Convention was adopted, but today they are being increasingly deployed on international flights. There were reportedly 40 countries which have established IFSO programmes.[85] During the Diplomatic Conference, some delegations preferred not to include any reference to IFSOs in the Tokyo Convention, others believed that they should be given at least some of the powers of the aircraft commander. After a long debate, the broad consensus reached was that IFSOs should be referred to in the amendments to the Tokyo Convention in order to identify them as a specific category of travellers, enjoying the same level of protection as crew members.

The text adopted therefore mentions that the aircraft commander may request or authorize, but not require, the assistance of IFSOs, that IFSOs may take reasonable preventive measures to protect the safety of the aircraft or persons therein from an act of unlawful interference and that IFSOs shall not be held responsible for the actions taken in accordance with the Convention.[86]

7.9 Annex 17 to the Chicago Convention and other regulatory tools

The importance of preventive measures has long been recognized. The system of criminal law may bring the perpetrators to justice, but will not cure/remedy the damage caused by their

83 Jennison, *supra* note 81.
84 See *supra* note 25 and its accompanying text.
85 ICAO DCTC Doc. No. 7 "Draft Protocol to Amend the Tokyo Convention of 1963: Authority and Protections of In-Flight Security Officers", presented by the US (23 January 2014). See also DCTC Doc. No. 4, "Notes of the Secretariat" (22 January 2014) at 2 and 3; "Report of the 35th Session of Legal Committee", *supra* note 79.
86 For precise wording, see amended Arts 6 and 10 in the Protocol of 2014.

criminal activities. In view of this, since its early days ICAO has undertaken a proactive approach towards prevention. In 1974, ICAO initiated the adoption of Annex 17 to the Chicago Convention, which contains specific technical measures to prevent terrorists and other offenders from taking weapons, explosives and any other harmful devices and substances on board aircraft or into airports. As a matter of fact, the experience of ICAO has shown that it would be much more convenient to deal with the matter of prevention in Standards and Recommended Practices (SARPs) or other less binding material. An instrument in the form of a treaty is more cumbersome to adopt and could not promptly address the rapidly changing modes of terrorist and other threats. For example, following the attempted attack using man-portable air defence systems (MANPADS) against a civil aircraft taking off from Mombasa, Kenya, in November 2002, there was a debate whether a treaty for controlling MANPADS should be developed within the auspices of ICAO.[87] It was subsequently decided that ICAO would not develop such a treaty but would participate in the work of the UN to negotiate an international instrument to enable States to identify and trace illicit small arms and light weapons.[88] At the same time ICAO had developed SARPs and procedures that incorporated preventive measures on the ground, which were accessible on the secure ICAO AVSEC website.[89] All these were developed within two years, which would be considered too short for the adoption of a treaty.[90]

87 See ICAO Council Working Paper C-WP/12238, "International Legal Instrument Dealing with Man-Portable Air Defence Systems (MANPADS)" (13 April 2004).
88 See "Statement of ICAO at the United Nations Second Biennial Meeting of States to Consider the Implementation of the Programme of Action to Prevent, Combat and Eradicate the Illicit Trade in Small Arms and Light Weapons in All its Aspects" (11–15 July 2005), www.un.org/events/small arms2005/regional-intlorg-pdf/ICAO.pdf. Eventually, the UN itself did not adopt a treaty but "an international instrument of a political character". See UNGA A/60/88 "Report of the Open-ended Working Group to Negotiate an International Instrument to Enable States to Identify and Trace, in a Timely and Reliable Manner, Illicit Small Arms and Light Weapons" (27 June 2005) at para. 26.
89 See UN Press Release DC/2977, "Statement of Jiefang Huang on behalf of ICAO" (12 July 2005), www.un.org/News/Press/docs/2005/dc2977.doc.htm.
90 There are numerous other instances in which ICAO resorted to non-treaty material to address the issue of prevention. The issue of unruly passengers was dealt with by a resolution of the Assembly, despite the earlier call to conclude a treaty. The establishment of the Public Key Directory, a computer system facilitating the identification of travel documents, is wholly based on a memorandum of understanding which is not a treaty; see ICAO Assembly Working Paper A36-WP/18, "Progress Made in Implementing Resolution A35-18, Appendix D, Section III: International Cooperation in Protecting the Security and Integrity of Passports" (28 June 2007).

8

Domestic regulation of security

The example of the European Union

George Leloudas

8.1 Terrorism risk events and risk perceptions

The motives behind terrorist attacks against civil aviation have been thoroughly analysed in the literature.[1] The bottom line is that terrorists are attracted by the potential of civil aviation to amplify risks socially. The impact of terrorism risk events transcends the harm that victims experience and the financial consequences that air carriers witness; both are a means to an end for terrorists. More importantly, terrorist risk events give rise to a crisis of trust. They result in a betrayal of faith in "fellow citizens, foreigners and governments all over the world",[2] as well as in "institutions and individuals charged with managing risks".[3]

The end result is what Ulrich Beck describes as the "self-multiplication of risks by the de-bounding of risk perceptions and fantasies".[4] Under the influence of a ubiquitous media-driven dramatic construction of risk events, the public believes that his everyday life has become more hazardous. Hence, the line between real and perceived risks is blurred with the public demanding proactive risk management action even when probabilistic risk analysis suggests that no threat exists.

Concurrently, any errors of aviation professionals are attributed by the media to their personal traits and mental processes, such as forgetfulness, inattention, poor motivation, carelessness, and recklessness.[5] Risk events "happen because people make them happen, and what things people make happen depends on the kind of people they are".[6] Inevitably, this portrayal impacts on the way people perceive the aviation industry that suddenly is considered to be "morally irresponsible" in managing its risks.[7] For how long this perception lasts depends on the gravity of the risk event in question and the reaction of the industry and the targeted State.

---

1 P. Dempsey, "Aviation security: The role of law in the war against terrorism" (2002–2003) *Colum. J. Transnat'l L.* 649; M. Milde, *International air law and ICAO* (Eleven Publishing 2012), Ch. 8; R. Abeyratne, "Hijacking and the Tehran incident: A world in crisis?" (1985) *Air L.* 120; J. Harrison, *International aviation and terrorism: Evolving threats, evolving security* (Routledge 2009), Ch. 2.
2 U. Beck, *World risk society* (Polity Press 1999), p. 44.
3 T. Horlick-Jones, "Modern disasters as outrage and betrayal" (1995) *International Journal of Mass Emergencies and Disasters* 305, 311.
4 Beck, p. 44.
5 J. Reason, "Human error: Models and management" (2000) *West. J. Med.* 393–396.
6 N. Feigenson, "Accidents as melodrama" (1999) *N.Y.L. Sch. L. Rev.* 741, 745.
7 J. Wolff, "Policy and risk: Railway safety and the ethics of the tolerability of risk", Study commissioned by Railway Safety, published in October 2002 and found at www.rssb.co.uk/research-develop ment-and-innovation/research-and-development/research-reports-catalogue/pb009473 (last accessed, 28 February 2015).

The said reactions of the public suggest that the management of terrorism risk events has a strong qualitative dimension that looks past probabilistic risk analysis. Therefore, one of the aims of any security-related reform is to manage social perceptions, as much as real threats. Achieving this aim is not an easy task. As has been demonstrated by Paul Slovic, trust is easier to destroy than to create, since "[t]rust-building events, while sometimes visible, more often are fuzzy or indistinct".[8]

Rebuilding trust in the aftermath of a major terrorism risk event faces this very problem, since security reforms usually proceed by incremental (and quite often confidential) advances that attract little attention from the popular press.[9] Yet, the aviation industry does not have the luxury to disregard it. It is not sufficient to take security measures that will eventually deter future terrorism risk events. The measures are also required to attenuate, within a short period of time, the fears of the public and re-establish the trust in the risk management capabilities of the targeted State and the aviation industry. To achieve this aim, they are required to be impressionistic, so that they attract the public's attention and influence the dramatic version of reality constructed by the media.[10]

The response of the USA to the risk events of 9/11 had strong elements of impressionism in two respects. First, sweeping security reforms were implemented at a level where the (travelling) public could easily identify.[11] They attracted extensive publicity and persuaded even their critics to admit that they have contributed to the restoration of public trust to the risk management capabilities of the aviation industry:

> [c]ertainly anyone who has travelled by air lately, and seen what is being done in the name of reducing risks of terrorism may well have had the thought: obviously not much better than useless, but nevertheless somehow strangely reassuring, at least for some people.[12]

Second, the "war on terror" was a way of making sense of the new risk reality that satisfied the US public's demand for immediate corrective action. Controversial a decision as it was, it was a means for the US government of rebuilding the protective cocoon over the American public. At the same time, it provided a diversion from what happened on American soil by giving the media a dramatic development that had all the elements of a successful story: "death, destruction, mystery, conflict, human interest, and tragedy".[13]

These two developments overshadowed the change that came as the result of the single most important failure in the pre-9/11 environment, namely the "misdirection, poor coordination, bureaucratic inefficiency and overconfidence" of the numerous (at the time) US intelligence agencies.[14] In the immediate aftermath of 9/11 a revamp of the structure and form of the US intelligence community took place:

> [t]he centralization of upwards of twenty law enforcement and public safety agencies within the D[epartment of]H[omeland]S[ecurity] enables the coordination of the vast array of intelligence available to the government.... The [FBI] would have the ability to produce

---

8 P. Slovic, *The perception of risk* (Routledge 2000), p. 317.
9 G. Leloudas, *Risk and liability in air law* (Informa 2009), p. 22.
10 Ibid., pp. 24–26.
11 For a detailed description of the measures see Dempsey, p. 712ff.
12 J. Wolff, "Risk, fear, blame, shame and the regulation of public safety" (2006) *Economics and Philosophy* 409, 416.
13 R. Cobb and D. Primo, *The plane truth* (Brookings Institution Press 2003), p. 9.
14 Harrison, p. 86.

its own information, but it could also consume new information developed and maintained by the DHS. This is critical: the DHS has to be able to receive raw intelligence from the CIA and FBI as well as information for its databases, in order to produce the analysis that is required. Failure to share new information will lead to weak analysis and poor advice to policy makers.... The new TSA will house the intelligence function of the FAA and other agencies and hence will be producing at least some of its own intelligence, the quality of which should increase.[15]

Intelligence is arguably the most important element of counter-terrorism. Yet, this restructuring played a secondary role (at least in the short term) in restoring the public's faith in the risk management capabilities of the US. This is so, because it does not have the visible or dramatic attributes that airport security measures or war have, courtesy of its sensitive nature; unless, of course, it is seen in the context of spy movies.

Having said that, the implementation of security measures creates problems of its own. The most prevalent problem is the impact of such measures on fundamental human rights, most prominent among them the right to privacy, the right to data protection and the protection of human dignity. Striking a balance between societal security and the said fundamental human rights has always been a delicate act. The more intrusive and/or secretive aviation security measures become, the more questions are asked about their legitimacy. With the questions multiplied when the ripple effects of terrorism risk events are perceived as having been managed and the protective cocoon restored.

At such times, legislative responses to "mass panics" do not enjoy a carte blanche any more. Instead, a balancing act is required between the need to protect national security and to retain the integrity of fundamental human rights that requires a fuller appreciation of the risk environment and does not always work in favour of security. This balancing of interest is to what the Advocate General E. Sharpston referred in the *Gottfried Heinrich* case when recommending that Regulation No. 622/2003[16] shall be treated as legally non-existent, because it imposed a number of secret aviation security measures:[17]

> it may perhaps be suggested that the public interest in preserving rules enhancing airport security requires that the Court should either turn a Nelsonian blind eye to the clear breach of a mandatory publication requirement, or make use of the exceptional power to maintain, definitively, the effects of a defective measure.... Similar arguments ... have no place in a European Union that is governed by the rule of law and whose Court is under the Treaty obligation to ensure that "the law is observed".[18]

There is no doubt that an image-conscious industry, such as aviation, is required to manage social perceptions vis-à-vis security risks. The use of civil aircraft as terrorist weapons (even through no fault of the industry) has already contributed to the demystification of air carriers with significant liability and insurance implications;[19] the tension between security measures and fundamental human rights plays well in the hands of the critics of the industry. As a result, there

---

15 Ibid., p. 113.
16 Commission Regulation (EC) No. 622/2003 of 4 April 2003 laying down measures for the implementation of the common basic standards on aviation security.
17 Opinion of AG E. Sharpston in the Gottfried Heinrich case (C-345/06) delivered on 10 April 2008. The judgment of the Court of Justice (Grand Chambers) was delivered on 10 March 2009. For both, see [2009] ECR 1659.
18 Sharpston, para. 100.
19 See Leloudas, pp. 41–45.

is little room for oversight. The industry is and will remain a target of terrorists. As such, it is imperative that aviation security measures are constantly renewed in order to prevent future terrorist attacks and to give the public a reassuring sense of security.

The aim of this chapter is to provide a bird's eye view of aviation security measures in Europe. The analysis is limited to selected, "visible" measures, namely those that have the potential to influence the perceptions of the (travelling) public, as well as to cargo-related ones. When required, special reference will be made to security measures taken by the UK, considering that it is the European country with the heaviest exposure to terrorist threats. The chapter will also touch upon the interaction between human rights and security measures, uneasy bedfellows in the quest for balance between protecting societal security and civil liberties.

8.2 Managing the new risk reality after 9/11

The implementation of aviation security measures in the post-9/11 European Union can be divided into two main periods. The first one lasted from the immediate aftermath of 9/11 until the "underwear bomber" incident on Christmas Day of 2009, and the second one is currently taking place. Both periods are characterised by legislative changes in response to major terrorism risk events.

In the first one, the terrorist attacks of 9/11 questioned the philosophy behind aviation security measures worldwide. Such was their impact that the Member States of the EU for the first time authorised the Union to create mandatory, pan-European rules on aviation security. The fact that it took such a major risk event to have a legally binding aviation security framework is an indication of (i) the secondary role that aviation security was playing in the agenda of the Union, and (ii) the (un)willingness of Member States to be tied down in a field that was still considered part and parcel of their sovereign powers:

> [a]viation security policy proposed after the Lockerbie bombing in 1988 was not mandatory, and on 11 September 2001 most States had not implemented many of the proposals put forward to improve the security situation (e.g. 100% passenger and hold baggage screening and positive baggage reconciliation). Whilst the European States were members of ECAC and were, in theory, implementing the requirements contained in ECAC's Document 30, the speed of implementation varied across the European States. It was generally considered unlikely that the ECAC deadline of 31 December 2002 would have been voluntarily met by all of the States. Some States, including the UK had been moving ahead with the introduction of 100% passenger and hold baggage screening during the 1990s following the Lockerbie bombing in 1988.[20]

The result of this authorisation was Regulation No. 2320/2002 that came into force on 19 January 2003.[21] Understandably, the objective of the Regulation reflected the new political and risk reality vis-à-vis aviation security:

> to establish and implement appropriate Community measures, in order to prevent acts of unlawful interference against civil aviation … [by] (a) the setting of common basic standards on aviation security measures; [and] (b) the setting up of appropriate compliance monitoring mechanisms.[22]

---

20 European Commission, "Study on civil aviation security financing" (September 2004, No. TREN/F3/51-2002), p. 7 of the summary of the final report (EC Study on financing).
21 Regulation (EC) No. 2320/2002 of the European Parliament and of the Council of 16 December 2002 establishing common rules in the field of civil aviation security (Regulation No. 2320/2002).
22 Art. 1(1) and (3) Regulation No. 2320/2002.

G. Leloudas

In a nutshell, Regulation No. 2320/2002 made the fundamental (yet recommended), security measures of the ECAC Document mandatory to "any airport located in the territories of the Member States".[23] It also gave authority to the European Commission to adopt detailed measures by means of implementing regulations in consultation with a "committee composed of representatives of the Member States and chaired by the representative of the Commission".[24] These measures became part of the national civil aviation security programme that each Member State, via its dedicated national aviation security authority, was required to establish.[25] The monitoring of their implementation was left to the said authority of each Member State and it was performed on the basis of a national quality control programme that followed European-wide criteria.[26] More importantly, the Regulation enabled the European Commission to monitor the compliance of the national security programmes by means of mandatory, "on-site" inspections of community airports and the national aviation security authorities.[27] As with any effective audit, the Regulation provided that the inspection of airports (but not of aviation authorities) would be unannounced.[28] The audit reports were "secret and not to be published" and they were only made available to the national aviation security authorities.[29] Further dissemination was permitted on a need-to-know basis and only if in accordance with domestic laws on disclosing sensitive information.[30]

The Regulation and its implementing rules enjoyed high approval rates. This is so because they remedied what was Europe's main deficiency in the fight against aviation terrorism risk events, namely the absence of a unified security front that would use best operational practices, share terrorism-related information, and provide for a system of assessment:

> [t]he level and quality of aviation security in Europe is widely considered to have improved significantly since the introduction of Regulation (EC) No 2320/2002 together with a system of legally-binding inspections.... This has followed years of inertia in the implementation of common security standards.... The Commission inspections programme is also ensuring that the legislative standards do apply not only in theory but in practice in the European Union.[31]

It is submitted that Europe experienced a security reform equal to that of the US in the aftermath of 9/11. Achieving security integration was not an easy (political and operational) task. At the time of the attacks, Europe was lagging behind the US, which already had a security network. The events of 9/11 demonstrated that this network required adjustments to deal with the new risk reality. In Europe, such a comprehensive network was not available and 9/11 triggered its creation. Admittedly, this reform was not as impressionistic as its American counterpart, but it did not need to be. Europe was not at the epicentre of the 9/11 events, and the risk management expectations were different. They focused mostly on deterring a future terrorism risk event on European soil and, at a second level, on managing the immediate aftermath of 9/11.

---

23 Arts 3 and 4(1) Regulation No. 2320/2002. The measures were laid out in the Annex to the Regulation.
24 Arts 4(2) and 9(2) of Regulation No. 2320/2002 and Art. 5(1) of Council Decision 1999/468/EC (that was applicable at the time).
25 Art. 5 of Regulation No. 2320/2002. Prior to the implementation of the Regulation "[t]he majority of States already had a National Aviation Security Programme (NASP) ... [The i]ntroduction of the Regulation caused the Member States to review their NASPs to reflect any new requirements within the Regulation" in EC Study on financing, p. 8 of the summary of the final report.
26 Art. 5(2) and (3) and Art. 7(1) Regulation No. 2320/2002.
27 Art. 7 Regulation No. 2320/2002.
28 Art. 7(3) Regulation No. 2320/2002.
29 Art. 8(1) Regulation No. 2320/2002.
30 Ibid.
31 EC Study on financing, p. 29, s. 2.

166

This different philosophy explains the reason that Regulation No. 2320/2002 came into force almost a year-and-a-half after the events of 9/11.

The Regulation did not come as a hurried response to a risk event that demands a rebuilding of the failed norms. Instead, it was the result of what Cass Sunstein described as the "cooling effect" on the passions of the legislators in the immediate aftermath of risk events: long-term policy decisions are driven by a full appreciation of the effects of their relevant risks and their control rather than by hysteria.[32]

The absence of a major terrorism risk event involving aviation in Europe during the years of the Regulation's operation did contribute to its popularity. To what extent this terrorism-free period can be attributed to the Regulation and its implementing measures cannot be quantified. Yet, the perception is that it was a successful legal instrument that carried Europe during a period of international turmoil.

8.3 A legislative philosophy that fits the management of terrorism risk events

Regulation No. 2320/2002 was replaced by Regulation No. 300/2008 that is currently the operative legal instrument in Europe in the field of aviation security.[33] Its replacement was not dictated by a particular security failure, but instead it was the result of the proactive application of "the experience gained" during its operation.[34]

Regulation No. 300/2008 has a three-layered philosophy that gives "more flexibility in adopting security measures and procedures in order to meet evolving risk assessments and to allow new technologies to be introduced".[35] In the upper layer, Regulation No. 300/2008 provides the "common basic standards for safeguarding civil aviation against acts of unlawful interference", as well as the basic rules on inspecting the implementation of the basic security standards by the Member States.[36] In the second layer, the Regulation delegates authority to the European Commission to adopt measures that supplement the security standards of the Regulation:[37] "[f]or instance, the introduction of 'body scanners' as an additional method of screening passengers falls into this category of measure" (supplementing legislation).[38] In the third layer, the Regulation authorises the European Commission to issue "detailed measures for the implementation of the common basic standards [of the Regulation] and the general measures

---

32 C. Sunstein, *Risk and reason: Safety, law and the environment* (Cambridge University Press 2002), p. 46.

33 Regulation (EC) No. 300/2008 of the European Parliament and of the Council of 11 March 2008 on common rules in the field of civil aviation security and repealing Regulation (EC) No. 2320/2002. Regulation (EC) No. 300/2008 came into force on 29 April 2008, but it was not until 29 April 2010 that it applied.

34 Preamble of Regulation No. 300/2008, para. 4.

35 Ibid., para. 5.

36 Arts 1, 15 and Annex 1 to Regulation 300/2008.

37 Art. 4(2) Regulation 300/2008. The procedure to adopt these measures is found in Art. 5a of Council Decision 1999/468/EC (regulatory procedure with scrutiny); see Art. 19(3) Regulation No. 300/2008. Art. 5a has survived the repeal (for acts existing at the time of repeal) of Council Decision 1999/468/EC by Regulation (EU) No. 182/2011 of the European Parliament and of the Council of 16 February 2011 laying down the rules and general principles concerning mechanisms for control by Member States of the Commission's exercise of implementing powers; see Art. 12. As its name suggests, the procedure gives extensive rights of scrutiny and veto of the measures proposed by the Committee that consists of representatives of Member States and the Commission to the European Parliament and the European Council.

38 DG for Internal Policies, "The EU regulatory framework applicable to civil aviation security" (May 2013), p. 7 (EU Report on civil aviation security).

[of the Commission in the second layer]",[39] e.g. "[m]inimum performance standards of 'body scanners' … pertain to this category" (implementing legislation).[40]

The flexible (and substantially quicker) legislative process contemplated in the second and third layer has the following two major benefits for aviation security. First, intelligence information on terrorist threats can be acted upon quickly by implementing appropriate measures to avert them (proactive risk management). Second, security measures to attenuate the fears of the (travelling) public in the immediate aftermath of terrorist events can also be implemented rapidly (reactive risk management).

These two benefits were evident during the second period of aviation security in Europe that started with the "underwear bomber" incident in late 2009. The first period was relatively calm. The main event was the failed plot to blow up several aircraft taking off from London Heathrow Airport by using liquid explosives carried in hand bags. However, the period between late 2009 and 2012 witnessed an upsurge in terrorism risk events:

> [t]he underwear-bomber incident during Christmas 2009, the Yemen cargo bomb incident in late 2010, several laser pointer threats in early 2012 and potential cyber attacks as well as a remaining high vulnerability for liquid explosives all served as reminders that civil aviation continues to be targeted in new and innovative ways, which should be addressed with adequate and risk based protection measures.[41]

The legislative response to the new risk reality was swift. Within a year (2012), three new Supplementing Regulations and three (confidential due to security concerns) Implementing Decisions of the Commission were adopted to manage the new threats.[42] Furthermore, from the end of 2012 until early 2015 the legislative process continues at a rapid pace with one Supplementing Regulation and eight Implementing Regulations having been issued.[43]

8.4 The legislative backbone of security risk management in the field of aviation

The scope of application of Regulation No. 300/2008 is comprehensive.[44] It applies to airports situated in Member States and a few ones beyond,[45] to operators, including air carriers

---

39 Art. 4(3) Regulation 300/2008. The procedure to adopt these measures is now found in Art. 5 (examination procedure) of Regulation (EU) No. 182/2011 of the European Parliament and of the Council of 16 February 2011 laying down the rules and general principles concerning mechanisms for control by Member States of the Commission's exercise of implementing powers. In that respect, Art. 19(2) of Regulation No. 300/2008 has been amended.
40 EU Report on civil aviation security, p. 8.
41 European Commission, "2012 Annual Report from the Commission to the European Parliament and the Council on the Implementations of Regulation (EC) No. 300/2008 on Common Rules in the Field of Civil Aviation Security", COM(2013) 523, p. 5.
42 For a list refer to ibid., pp. 5–6.
43 For a list refer to http://ec.europa.eu/transport/modes/air/security/legislation_en.htm (last accessed, 28 February 2015).
44 What follows is a synopsis of the framework established by Regulation No. 300/2008.
45 Art. 2(1)(a) Regulation 300/2008. Art. 4(2) permits Member States to derogate from the standards imposed by the Regulation: Commission Regulation (EU) No. 1254/2009 of 18 December 2009 setting criteria to allow Member States to derogate from the common basic standards on civil aviation security and to adopt alternative security measures. Apart from the airports located in the 28 Member States of the EU, the Regulation also applies to airports located in Switzerland, Norway, and Iceland.

(irrespective of nationality), providing services (i.e. engaged or offering to engage in air trans-port operations) at the said airports,[46] as well as to entities "that operate from premises located inside or outside [the said] airport premises and provide goods and/or services to or through [the said] airports".[47]

The establishment of national civil aviation security and quality control programmes by the Member States to implement the standards of the Regulation remains at the forefront of the security framework.[48] The national security programme, or parts thereof, is to be made available to the regulatees, i.e. airport operators, air carriers, and other entities, on a "need to know" basis.[49] In contrast to its predecessor, Regulation No. 300/2008 imposes a direct obli-gation on airport operators, air carriers, as well as aviation entities, to implement such pro-grammes.[50] Airports are under an obligation to submit their programmes to the designated civil aviation security authority;[51] air carriers and other entities are only required to submit them upon request from the authority.[52] If a European air carrier's security programme has been validated by the national security authority of the Member State that granted its operat-ing licence, such programme is automatically recognised by all Member States, unless the Member States have imposed more stringent security measures or there are local procedures to be followed.[53]

Regulation No. 300/2008 has also expanded the scope of the Commission's mandatory inspections. Inspections of the regulatees (i.e. airports, operators, and other entities)[54] are taking place unannounced, although the Commission gives advance, confidential notice to the rel-evant Member State.[55] The Commission produces an inspection report at the end of each audit, identifying the security deficiencies, communicated to the relevant Member State; upon receiv-ing the reply of the Member State, that shall contain the remedial measures taken in response to the report, the findings are communicated to the other Member States.[56] The Commission's inspections are complementary to the national ones:[57] Member States are required to monitor (via their national quality control programme) the regulatees located in their territory to allow for "the swift detection and correction of deficiencies".[58] Detailed procedures for conducting

---

46 Arts 2(1)(b) and 3(3) Regulation 300/2008.
47 Art. 2(1)(c) Regulation 300/2008.
48 Arts 10 and 11 Regulation 300/2008.
49 Art. 10(2) Regulation 300/2008.
50 Arts 12, 13, and 14 Regulation 300/2008, respectively.
51 Art. 12(2) Regulation 300/2008.
52 Arts 13(2) and 14(2) Regulation 300/2008, respectively.
53 Art. 13(3) Regulation 300/2008.
54 Art. 15(1) Regulation 300/2008.
55 Art. 15(2) Regulation 300/2008.
56 Art. 15(3) Regulation 300/2008.
57 The Commission is required under Art. 16 Regulation No. 300/2008 to produce an annual report on the application of the Regulation. At the time of writing (February 2015), the latest report (publicly available) was the following: European Commission, "2013 Annual Report from the Commission to the European Parliament and the Council on the Implementations of Regulation (EC) No. 300/2008 on Common Rules in the Field of Civil Aviation Security", COM(2014) 399.
58 Art. 11(2) Regulation 300/2008. Detailed provisions for conducting national audits, training national auditors, and reporting deficiencies are found in Commission Regulation (EU) No. 18/2010 of 8 January 2010 amending Regulation (EC) No. 300/2008 of the European Parliament and of the Council as far as specifications for national quality control programmes in the field of civil aviation security are concerned. Art. 18.1 of the Annex to the Regulation requires Member States to submit an annual security report to the Commission.

Commission's inspections and reporting their findings can be found in Regulation No. 72/2010 (Implementing Regulation);[59] Article 13 of the Regulation permits the Commission to conduct follow-up inspections to verify the rectification of serious deficiencies. Interestingly, the auditors undertaking the Commission's inspections are a mix of Commission inspectors and national auditors;[60] national auditors are not permitted to "participate in Commission inspections in the Member State where [they are] employed".[61]

Annex I to Regulation No. 300/2008 contains the common aviation standards. In essence, it provides the European interpretation of Chapter 4 of Annex 17 to the Chicago Convention.[62] It is divided into 12 sections that reflect Annex 17, ranging from airport and aircraft security, to passengers, cabin, and hold baggage, cargo and mail, in-flight and airport supplies, as well as in-flight security measures, staff recruitment and training, and security equipment.

To those familiar with Annex 17 of the Chicago Convention, the Annex to Regulation No. 300/2008 does not contain groundbreaking provisions. Yet, a few of them are worth mentioning in this context, because they aim to streamline the European security network. The basic rule imposed by the Annex is that all passengers and their cabin baggage, as well as hold baggage originating from, transferring, or transiting through European airports, shall be screened.[63] However, it provides for one notable exception to the "100% screening" rule: transfer/transit passengers, as well as their cabin and hold baggage are exempted from screening if they arrive from a Member State or a third country that applies equivalent to the European standards.[64] This exemption has been a long-standing aim of air carriers, as it allows the establishment of a "one-stop security" regime. Thus, passengers and their cabin and hold baggage are screened at their airport of departure and not at intermediate transfer/transit points, hence "allowing for faster connection times, lower costs and greater convenience for travellers".[65]

The implementation of such a regime indicates that the regulation of aviation security is entering a period of maturity, where facilitation makes inroads on security. This change is particularly important for air carriers which are the first to be blamed for security-related delays and the ensuing inconvenience experienced by passengers at airports, although most are not of their own making. Still, it is submitted that this is a fragile balancing act that will tilt in favour of security whenever a major terrorism risk event takes place. Opting for security also seems to be the preferred option of the Union:

> [t]he legislation contains no specific provision about "the one-stop security" which is referred to as a "goal" (Reg. 300/2008, Whereas 20). In fact, "the one-stop security" ensues from the proper and comprehensive implementation of the common standards and the resulting mutual trust.[66]

---

59 Commission Regulation (EU) No. 72/2010 of 26 January 2010 laying down procedures for conducting Commission inspections in the field of aviation security.

60 Art. 6 Regulation No. 72/2010.

61 Art. 6(4) Regulation No. 72/2010.

62 Annex 17 to the Convention on International Civil Aviation, "Security: Safeguarding civil aviation against acts of unlawful interference".

63 Sections 4.1.1 and 5.1.1. The Regulation treats as transfer passengers, baggage, or cargo those "departing on an aircraft other than that on which they arrived" in Art. 3(16); transit passengers, baggage, or cargo are those departing on the same aircraft as that on which they arrived in Art. 3(17).

64 Sections 4.1.2 and 5.1.2. The Annex also provides for a number of other exemptions from screening of lesser operational importance in sections 4.1.3 and 5.1.3.

65 IP/10/479, 29 April 2010.

66 EU Report on civil aviation security, p. 10, fn. 24.

Considering that terrorism risk events have the potential to impact inter-governmental trust (even among allied countries), this statement gives a clear indication that facilitation will settle for second best, if need be. Not surprisingly, then, Europe has not seen a proliferation of agreements with third countries recognising their security standards and enabling beyond the EU "one-stop security" schemes.[67]

With respect to cargo, the Annex imposes a rule of 100 per cent screening: "[a]ll cargo … shall be subjected to security controls prior to being loaded on an aircraft".[68] The Annex does not contain detailed provisions for screening transfer cargo, leaving their determination to Implementing Regulations;[69] it provides that "[t]ransit cargo … may be exempted from security controls if it remains on board the aircraft".[70] Securing cargo operations is an equally complex activity (if not more complex) to securing the carriage of passengers, albeit a less publicised one. In most instances, the cargo would reach the air carrier by road transport that would be organised by the original shipper, by a freight forwarder acting as a consolidator or on behalf of the shipper, or by the air carrier via subcontracted road carriers. With the exception of the third alternative, the air carrier has little control of the cargo and the security standards used by the intermediate movers.

One might argue that this operational complexity shall not cause concerns, since the air carrier can always screen the cargo once it comes into its possession prior to loading. Considering that speed is the main reason for transporting cargo by air, such a strict approach would cause considerable delays. To facilitate the carriage of cargo, the Annex provides an alternative: security controls may be applied at an earlier stage in the supply chain by (i) a regulated agent which can be another air carrier, a freight forwarder, or a cargo handling agent, (ii) a known consignor, i.e. the original shipper of the goods whose security procedures permit the carriage of its cargo in any aircraft, including combined passenger/cargo aircraft, or (iii) an account consignor, i.e. the original shipper of the goods whose security procedures permit the carriage of its cargo only in all-cargo aircraft.[71] The conditions for qualifying in any of the said categories is left for determination to the Implementing Regulations.

This provision opens the door for the establishment of a "one-stop" security regime in the carriage of cargo, since it enables the carrier to transfer cargo within the EU without additional security controls so long as the cargo has been protected from unauthorised interference from its screening until it leaves the possession of the carrier or its subcontractors at the destination.[72] Having said that, the Annex does not regulate the security checks of cargo located at a non-EU airport, although destined for an EU airport. Can entities located outside the Union perform security checks prior to the cargo reaching the air carrier at a non-EU airport to expedite the transportation? The Regulation leaves the Implementing Regulations to deal with them.

---

67 The EU has had such an agreement with the US since 1 April 2011 that is applicable to aircraft, passengers, cabin, and hold baggage, see Commission Regulation (EU) No. 983/2010 of 3 November 2010 amending Regulation (EU) No. 185/2010 laying down detailed measures for the implementation of the common basic standards on aviation security (Implementing Regulation). The European Commission is currently in the process of concluding a similar agreement with Canada.
68 Section 6.1.1.
69 Section 6.1.2.
70 Section 6.1.3.
71 Section 5.1.1, second sentence.
72 See section 6.1.1. Commission Regulation (EU) No. 185/2010 of 4 March 2010 laying down detailed measures for the implementation of the common basic standards on aviation security (Implementing Regulation).

Manifestly, Regulation No. 300/2008 is the backbone of aviation security in the EU. Yet, the practical details of this framework are left to (i) the Supplementing Regulations which make provision for additional security measures, and (ii) the Implementing Regulations that give detailed guidance as to how to implement the security measures envisaged in Regulation No. 300/2008, as well as in the Supplementing Regulations.

8.5 Supplementing and implementing risk management measures[73]

8.5.1 Supplementing Regulations

Prominent among the Supplementing Regulations applicable in the EU is Regulation No 272/2009 as amended.[74] It provides for a wide array of measures supplementing Regulation No. 300/2008.[75] This is not the place to go through the Regulation, yet, two issues are worth mentioning in this context.

First, the EU is not lagging behind the US any more in terms of screening methods. The introduction of body scanners and liquid explosive detection equipment has brought it on a par with the US (although their actual deployment portrays a different picture). The current list is as follows: (i) hand search;[76] (b) walk-through metal detection (WTMD) equipment;[77] (iii) hand-held metal detection (HHMD) equipment;[78] (iv) explosive detection dogs;[79] (v) explosive trace detection (ETD) equipment;[80] (vi) security scanners which do not use ionising radiation;[81] (vii) visual check and X-ray equipment;[82] (viii) explosive detection systems (EDS) equipment;[83]

---

73 See E. Giemulla, "Aviation security in the European Union" in E. Giemulla and L. Weber, *International and EU aviation law: Selected issues* (Kluwer 2011), p. 357ff.
74 Commission Regulation (EC) No. 272/2009 supplementing the common basic standards on civil aviation security, as amended. Regulation No. 272/2009 has been amended four times since its entry into force by Commission Regulation (EU) No. 297/2010 of 9 April 2010 amending Regulation (EC) No. 272/2009 supplementing the common basic standards on civil aviation security, Commission Regulation (EU) No. 720/2011 of 22 July 2011 amending Regulation (EC) No. 272/2009 supplementing the common basic standards on civil aviation security as regards the phasing-in of the screening of liquids, aerosols and gels at EU airports, Commission Regulation (EU) No. 1141/2011 of 10 November 2011 amending Regulation (EC) No. 272/2009 supplementing the common basic standards on civil aviation security as regards the use of security scanners at EU airports, Commission Regulation (EU) No. 245/2013 of 19 March 2013 amending Regulation (EC) No. 272/2009 as regards the screening of liquids, aerosols and gels at EU airports. For a list of the applicable Supplementing Regulations in the EU see http://ec.europa.eu/transport/modes/air/security/legislation_en.htm (last accessed, 28 February 2015).
75 See Art. 1 Regulation No. 272/2009 for a list of measures.
76 For the screening of persons, cabin baggage, hold baggage, and cargo, Part A, sections 1(a), 2(a), and 3(a) of Annex to Regulation No. 272/2009.
77 For the screening of persons. Part A, section 1(b) of Annex to Regulation No. 272/2009.
78 For the screening of persons. Part A, section 1(c) of Annex to Regulation No. 272/2009.
79 For the screening of persons, cabin baggage, hold baggage, and cargo. Part A, sections 1(d), 2(e), 3(e) of Annex to Regulation No. 272/2009.
80 For the screening of persons, cabin baggage, hold baggage, and cargo. Part A, sections 1(e), 2(f), 3(f) of Annex to Regulation No. 272/2009 as amended by Regulation No. 297/2010.
81 For the screening of persons, Part A, section 1(f) of Annex to Regulation No. 272/2009 as amended by Regulation No. 1141/2011.
82 For the screening of cabin baggage, hold baggage, and cargo. Part A, sections 2(b) and (c), 3(b) and (c) of Annex to Regulation No. 272/2009.
83 For the screening of cabin baggage, hold baggage, and cargo. Part A, sections 2(d) and 3(d) of Annex to Regulation No. 272/2009.

(ix) liquid explosive detection systems (LEDS) equipment;[84] and (x) simulation chambers and metal detection equipment.[85]

Second, Regulation No. 272/2009 provides that regulated agents and known consignors shall be approved by the relevant national security authority once it is satisfied that their security measures comply with European standards; such approval to be provided following an on-site verification of the security controls implemented.[86] The Regulation, though, distinguishes account consignors: they are to be audited and designated as such by a regulated agent, rather than the relevant national authority.[87] The looser procedure for approval explains the reason that consignments of account consignors can only be carried on all-cargo aircraft. This restriction is justified in terms of passenger protection. Still, it is debatable whether the damage potential of all-cargo aircraft justifies such treatment.

8.5.2 Implementing Regulations

The Supplementary Regulations, more detailed as they are compared to Regulation 300/2008, do not contain comprehensive security rules. These are found in the Implementing Regulations.[88]

The following two Implementing Regulations are currently in force in the EU: (i) Commission Regulation (EU) No. 72/2010 of 26 January 2010 laying down procedures for conducting Commission inspections in the field of aviation security; and (ii) Commission Regulation (EU) No. 185/2010 of 4 March 2010 laying down detailed measures for the implementation of the common basic standards on aviation security as amended.[89]

Regulation No. 185/2010 is the compendium of aviation security in the EU. In essence, it puts flesh on the bones of Regulation No. 300/2008 and Regulation No. 272/2009.[90] The fact that it has been amended 19 times, since it came into force, demonstrates that this is the powerhouse of aviation security in Europe.

8.5.2.1 The controversial use of security scanners

A full analysis of the Regulation is beyond the scope of this work, yet two issues are worth mentioning in this context. Until 2011, security scanners were not included in EU legislation.[91] Yet, individual Member States could use them either

---

84 For the screening of cabin baggage. Part A, sections 2(d) and 3(d) of Annex to Regulation No. 272/2009 as amended by Regulation No. 245/2013.
85 For the screening of hold baggage and cargo. Part A, sections 3(g) and 3(h) of Annex to Regulation No. 272/2009 as amended by Regulation No. 297/2010.
86 Part F, sections 2(1) and 2(2) of Annex to Regulation No. 272/2009.
87 Part F, sections 2(3) of Annex to Regulation No. 272/2009.
88 Detailed rules are also to be found in Decisions of the European Commission. Yet, most of them are confidentially addressed to Member States due to their sensitivity. For an analysis of the rationale behind issuing confidential Decisions see J. McClean (ed.), *Shawcross and Beaumont: Air law*, issue 144 (Lexis Nexis Butterworths 2015), Division III, [230].
89 For a list of the applicable Implementing Regulations in the EU and the amendments to Regulation No. 185/2010 see http://ec.europa.eu/transport/modes/air/security/legislation_en.htm (last accessed, 28 February 2015).
90 The Regulation "lays down detailed measures for the implementation of common basic standards for safeguarding civil aviation against acts of unlawful interference that jeopardise the security of civil aviation", Art. 1.
91 As to what constitutes security scanner for the purposes of EU law, see Chapter 12.11 of Regulation No. 185/2010 as amended by Commission Implementing Regulation (EU) No. 1147/2011 of 11 November 2011 amending Regulation (EU) No. 185/2010 implementing the common basic standards on civil aviation security as regards the use of security scanners at EU airports.

i) by exercising their right to apply security measures that are more stringent than existing EU requirements [under Article 6 of Regulation No. 300/2008] or ii) temporarily, by exercising their right to conduct trials of new technical process or methods for a maximum period of 30 months [under section 12.8 of Regulation No. 185/2010];[92]

and quite a few did so.[93] Following extensive consultations, their deployment was permitted on a regular basis.[94]

The EU consultation focused on three pillars of concerns: (i) operational effectiveness; (ii) health issues; and (iii) protection of fundamental human rights. Their operational effectiveness was confirmed on the basis of the positive international experience with their use, especially in the US and Canada. They demonstrated "an enhanced detection probability for non-metallic items and liquids compared to walk-through metal detectors".[95] At the same time, the consultation concluded that they have the potential to reduce security check times: "[they] permit a rigorous screening for a great number of passengers in a short amount of time while providing a reliable detection capability".[96] Establishing that they add real value to the fight against terrorism was an issue of major importance, so that the limitations on the fundamental human right they entail could have been justified. Without this evidence any discussion would have been moot.

Which were the said limitations?

[s]ome security scanners have raised privacy and human dignity concerns since they reveal a detailed display of the human body and medical details and have the capability to capture and process the image of a person without his/her consent. The deployment of some security scanners has also been seen critically … from the perspective of reconciling religious beliefs with the review of detailed body images by a human screener and also from the perspective of the protection of the children…. With reference to health, the type of radiation emitted by security scanners, and especially ionising radiation, has been a matter of concern for the European Parliament and the civil society.[97]

This debate was particularly fierce in the UK which was one of the first Member States to use security scanners in 2010. They were initially deployed at London Heathrow and Manchester airports and then gradually introduced to a number of airports around the country, with an interim code of practice initially governing their operation. Their initial deployment raised a number of questions that fuelled the EU debate that was also taking place at the time:

•   Is the use of "full body" images necessary or can they be replaced by less intimate images? If there are no such technologies available, how do we protect the right to privacy of the screened passengers?

92 European Commission, "Communication from the Commission to the European Parliament and the Council on the Use of Security Scanners at EU Airports", COM(2010) 311, para. 9 (EC Communication on scanners).
93 Ibid., para. 10 for a list of EU countries that took advantage of the said provision on trials.
94 They were introduced by Regulation No. 1141/2011 that amended Regulation No. 272/2009 (Supplementing Regulations).
95 EC Communication on scanners, para. 45.
96 Ibid., 47.
97 European Commission, "Impact assessment on the possible use of security scanners at EU airports" (2011), paras 45–46 (EC Impact assessment on use of scanners).

- How do we treat the images of the screened passengers? Shall they be retained or destroyed as soon as the passenger is cleared? Do we treat the images of passengers who raise security concerns differently?
- Shall passengers be provided with an alternative to full body scans? And if so, what that might be? How do passengers make an informed decision about the method to be screened?
- What are the criteria for selecting passengers to undergo a full body scan?
- Shall we permit the use of scanners with ionising X-ray radiation or shall we deploy alternative technologies?

At their initial deployment the UK government followed a strict approach: ionising X-ray radiation scanners that produce full body images without any blurring were used and no alternative screening methods were given to the passengers who were selected to undergo the full scan ("no scan, no fly" policy). Some good practices were adopted, i.e. separating the reviewer of the images from the screened passengers; permitting the passengers to request that a person of the same sex reviews their images; not retaining the images of screened passengers.[98] This strict (and rather muddled approach) is explained by the fact that their deployment at UK airports came as a kneejerk reaction to the December 2009 incident of the underwear bomber; its main aim was to attenuate the fears of the public and prevent any epidemics of similar incidents.[99]

At an EU level, no such hurried response was given; at the end of the day individual Member States were at liberty to take more stringent measures or deploy body scanners on a trial basis to deal with the immediate aftermath of the said incident. Instead, the consultation process lasted longer with the scanners made part of the EU aviation framework in 2011 under the following strict conditions:

1   Only non-ionising security scanners are permitted to be deployed.[100] It was realised that the radiation levels of X-ray backscatter security systems are low, yet still they may have long-term effects. Since there are scanners available that do not emit ionising radiation, the

---

98   For a review of the debate that took place in the UK see Department for Transport, *Code of practice for the acceptable use of advanced imaging technology (body scanners) in an aviation security environment*. A consultation paper is available at www.gov.uk/government/consultations/code-of-practice-for-the-acceptable-use-of-advanced-imaging-technology-security-scanners-in-an-aviation-security-environment (last accessed, 28 February 2015).

99   The then Prime Minister, Mr Gordon Brown, made a strong policy statement on the BBC *The Andrew Marr Show* only a few days (3 January 2010) following the incident:

> This is a new threat, a new type of threat, and it's from a new source which is obviously Yemen, but there are many other potential sources like Somalia as well as Afghanistan and Pakistan. First of all, in airports people will see gradually being brought in the use of full body scanners. They will see checks for explosive traces. That will be done on hand luggage. Transit passengers will also be checked, as well as transfer passengers. And we will do everything in our power to tighten up on the security that is essential. We've recognised that there are new forms of weapon that are being used by al-Qaeda, so we've got to respond accordingly.

The transcript of the interview is available at http://news.bbc.co.uk/1/hi/programmes/andrew_marr_show/8438431.stm (last accessed, 28 February 2015).

100   Regulation No. 1141/2011 that amended Regulation No. 272/2009 (Supplementing Regulations). See also section 4.1.1.2(e) of Regulation No. 185/2010 as amended by Commission Implementing Regulation (EU) No. 687/2014 of 20 June 2014 amending Regulation (EU) No. 185/2010 as regards clarification, harmonisation and simplification of aviation security measures, equivalence of security standards and cargo and mail security measures.

Regulation opted for their use.[101] This restriction has not proved to be a problem for Member States which are moving towards millimetre wave technology:

> it poses no known health and safety risks. Millimetre wave scanners utilise a very low power, non-ionising form of electromagnetic technology.... The amount of electromagnetic radiation emitted by [them] is many times lower than that emitted by a mobile phone.[102]

2   If the scanner creates an image of the screened passengers' bodies,[103] the reviewer of the image shall observe a number of conditions to avoid issues of interference with the protection of personal data. The most important are as follows:

a   the image shall be deleted as soon as the passenger is cleared and it shall not be retained in any way, shape, or form;[104]

b   the reviewer shall not have visual access to the screened passenger and shall be based in a separate location;[105]

c   the images shall not be linked to any data of the screened passengers who shall remain anonymous;[106]

d   the screened passenger shall have the option to choose the gender of the reviewer;[107]

e   the images shall be blurred or obscured to prevent the identification of the face of the passenger.[108]

---

101 For a detailed discussion on the health impacts of the various technologies, see EC Impact assessment on use of scanners.

102 Department for Transport, "Code of practice for the acceptable use of security scanners in an aviation security environment" (January 2015), p. 2 (DfT Code of practice).

103 See section 12.1.1. Regulation No. 185/2010 as amended by Commission Implementing Regulation (EU) No. 1147/2011 of 11 November 2011 amending Regulation (EU) No. 185/2010 implementing the common basic standards on civil aviation security as regards the use of security scanners at EU airports.

104 Section 4.1.1.10.(a) Regulation No. 185/2010 as amended by Commission Implementing Regulation (EU) No. 1147/2011 of 11 November 2011 amending Regulation (EU) No. 185/2010 implementing the common basic standards on civil aviation security as regards the use of security scanners at EU airports.

105 Section 4.1.10.(b) Regulation No. 185/2010 as amended by Commission Implementing Regulation (EU) No. 1147/2011 of 11 November 2011 amending Regulation (EU) No. 185/2010 implementing the common basic standards on civil aviation security as regards the use of security scanners at EU airports.

106 Section 4.1.10.(d) Regulation No. 185/2010 as amended by Commission Implementing Regulation (EU) No. 1147/2011 of 11 November 2011 amending Regulation (EU) No. 185/2010 implementing the common basic standards on civil aviation security as regards the use of security scanners at EU airports.

107 Section 4.1.10.(e) Regulation No. 185/2010 as amended by Commission Implementing Regulation (EU) No. 1147/2011 of 11 November 2011 amending Regulation (EU) No. 185/2010 implementing the common basic standards on civil aviation security as regards the use of security scanners at EU airports.

108 Section 4.1.10.(f) Regulation No. 185/2010 as amended by Commission Implementing Regulation (EU) No. 1147/2011 of 11 November 2011 amending Regulation (EU) No. 185/2010 implementing the common basic standards on civil aviation security as regards the use of security scanners at EU airports.

3   If the scanner reduces the image of the screened passenger to a stick outline and indicates the location of the object on the stick there are certainly less concerns regarding the breach of fundamental rights.[109] There is no human reviewer and no sensitive images of the screened passengers are displayed.[110] As such, the Regulation imposes only the first two requirements above (2.a and 2.b).[111]

The Regulation provides that information as to the technology used, the conditions associated to its use, and the possibility to opt out from a security scanner shall also be given to the screened passengers.[112] Furthermore, the passengers shall be given the option to be screened by alternative methods which includes at least a hand search.[113]

Interestingly, the UK government has now abandoned the "no scan, no fly" policy on the basis that "the number of passengers refusing to be scanned is very low".[114] Yet, the alternative is not a basic "hand search" as the Regulation provides, but an enhanced one that shall be conducted in non-public areas of the airport as it can "require the loosening or removal of clothing and a detailed physical search of the person".[115]

8.5.2.2 Carriage of cargo and terrorism risk events: ignore at your own peril

In the post-9/11 risk environment the security of cargo operations was not the focus of regulatory attention worldwide. This attitude was not surprising considering that cargo-related security measures were not at the forefront of the media's attention. Still, in terms of damage potential there was (and still is) very little to differentiate passengers from cargo. This attitude changed in October 2010 following the failed plots of Al-Qaeda to detonate explosives on board two cargo planes. Suddenly, the security of air cargo operations attracted the attention of popular media. At the same time it triggered a wealth of new regulations in Europe with respect to cargo being flown into EU airports from non-EU countries. Speaking a few days after the incident, the then Home Secretary of the British government, Mrs Theresa May, set the tone for what was expected to happen:

> we will review all aspects of air freight security and work with international partners to make sure that our defences are as robust as possible. We will update the guidance given to airport security personnel based on what we have learned to enable them to identify similar

---

109 See section 12.1.1. Regulation No. 185/2010 as amended by Commission Implementing Regulation (EU) No. 1147/2011 of 11 November 2011 amending Regulation (EU) No. 185/2010 implementing the common basic standards on civil aviation security as regards the use of security scanners at EU airports.

110 The Automatic Threat Recognition (ATR) software provides such benefits as:

> interprets the scan data [on the basis of algorithms], instead of creating an image, and identifies areas where items may be concealed on the body. These areas are flagged on a standardised stick-figure on a screen, to indicate to the security officer areas of the individual's body which should receive a targeted hand-search.

(DfT Code of practice, p. 2).

111 Section 4.1.1.10. Regulation No. 185/2010 as amended by Commission Implementing Regulation (EU) No. 1147/2011 of 11 November 2011 amending Regulation (EU) No. 185/2010 implementing the common basic standards on civil aviation security as regards the use of security scanners at EU airports.

112 Ibid.

113 Ibid.

114 Department for Transport, "Equality impact assessment on the use of security scanners at UK airports" (November 2013), p. 2.

115 DfT Code of practice, p. 2.

packages in future. From midnight tonight, we will extend the suspension of unaccompanied air freight to this country from not just Yemen but Somalia.... From midnight
tonight, we will suspend the carriage of toner cartridges larger than 500 grams in passengers'
hand baggage on flights departing from UK airports. Also from midnight tonight, we will
prohibit the carriage of these items by air cargo into, via or from the UK unless they
originate from a known consignor – a regular shipper with security arrangements approved
by the Department for Transport.... During that time, we will work closely with the aviation industry, screening equipment manufacturers and others, to devise a sustainable, proportionate, long-term security regime to address the threat.[116]

Not surprisingly, the EU followed with a comprehensive programme for screening cargo being
carried into its airports from third countries. The philosophy behind the programme is to expand
the security standard of the European community to the cargo supply chain outside the EU,
creating as such a seamless security network that starts with an original shipper outside the EU
and ends at a consignee located in the EU or even beyond.

Any air carrier (irrespective of nationality) that carries cargo from a non-EU airport to an EU
airport, shall be designated as "Air Cargo or Mail Carrier operating into the Union from a Third
Country Airport" (ACC3).[117] Granting such status depends on the security authority of the EU
Member State auditing the carrier's security programme;[118] such audit includes "on-site" inspections of its operations at the third country airport, and the issuance of an EU aviation security
validation report confirming the implementation of the security measures.[119] The basic rule is
that the authorisation is airport-specific.[120] Yet, the Regulation provides for a blanket permission upon auditing a representative number of non-EU airports from which the air carrier operates and agreeing a roadmap of further audits for each year of the designation as ACC3.[121]

Under the Regulation, the ACC3 shall ensure that all cargo carried for transfer, transit, or
unloading at a Union airport is screened.[122] The screening can be undertaken by the ACC3 or
by an EU-validated third country regulated agent (RA3),[123] a third country known consignor
(KC3),[124] or a third country account consignor (AC3) that is under the responsibility of an EU
validated regulated agent;[125] in this last case the cargo will only be transported by an all-cargo
aircraft.[126] The Regulation gives two options to non-EU entities to become RA3s or KC3s.
They can be part of an ACC3's security validation and be valid only for the ACC3's supply
chain or be audited by an EU aviation security validator independently of any ACC3 and as
such gain independent status.[127]

---

116 Mrs Theresa May, Secretary of State for the Home Department, HC Deb 1 November 2010, col. 633.
117 Section 6.8.1.1. Regulation No. 185/2010 as amended by Commission Implementing Regulation
   (EU) No. 1082/2012 of 9 November 2012 amending Regulation (EU) No. 185/2010 in respect of
   EU aviation security validation.
118 The allocation of air carriers to the Member State is found in section 6.8.1.1.
119 Section 6.8.2.
120 Section 6.8.2.1.
121 Section 6.8.2.2. The criteria for granting the ACC3 status are found in Attachments 6-G; the Regulation also provides a validation checklist for ACC3s in Attachment 6-C3.
122 Section 6.8.3.1.
123 Section 6.8.3.1.(a).
124 Section 6.8.3.1.(b).
125 Section 6.8.3.1.(c).
126 Ibid.
127 For the conditions of each programme, see section 6.8.4.

There is no doubt that the ACC3 programme of the EU has far-reaching repercussions, forcing third countries' entities to upgrade aviation security in order to comply with EU standards. The agreement with the US mutually to recognise their security standards in the field of cargo and provide for a "one-stop" security scheme in their carriage of cargo is a further testament to its success.[128]

Having said that, the 2010 incidents demonstrated that security shall be treated as an undivided concept. There is a perception that the management of terrorism risk events involving passenger aircraft deserves more attention, as such events have the potential for a heavier death toll. Yet, this is a misconception, as all-cargo aircraft may inflict considerable damage, especially when carrying the type of dangerous goods that are prohibited from passenger aircraft or when heavy-lift aircraft are involved. The ripple effects of such events will not be any different from the ones involving passenger aircraft. The public would demand action because it would feel vulnerable, the regulators would react to attenuate its fears, and the industry would be blamed for its sloppy security (and not only) standards: a failure is a failure, no matter what.

At the same time, the 2010 incidents demonstrated the importance of the cliché that the security chain is as strong as its weakest link. The pre-2012 Regulations were treating cargo security in a vacuum, putting also a lot of strain on screenings at EU airports that had to deal with transfer cargo from third countries that might have been inadequately checked, if at all. By ignoring the security realities of supply chains outside its borders, the EU and the Member States were burying their heads in the sand.

8.6 Conclusion

The attacks of 9/11 put security at the forefront of the aviation agenda. The security measures taken on both sides of the Atlantic aimed to prevent future terrorist events and at the same time to restore the public's trust in the risk management capabilities of the industry. The EU was not under the same pressure as the US to act. Still, the European aviation security system was unified and revamped and since then it has been continuously evolving to meet the new risk realities, learning its lessons from near misses rather than full-blown disasters.

Having said that, its future evolution, assuming that no major terrorism risk event will take place, is gradually becoming more difficult, not so much because terrorists have evolved their weapons of choice and methods of attacks. Instead, in a period of relative calmness, as the one we currently experience, the concerns and criticism that delay its evolution come from within the system, namely as a result of the concerns for the (arguably unjustified) limitations of fundamental human rights and the travelling public's demands for less hassle during travelling. As such, the industry and the regulators are now required to find a balance among three (sometimes conflicting) aims: facilitate the passengers' experience at airports, avoid infringing their privacy and dignity, and protect them from future terrorist attacks. One might correctly argue that this trilemma is an indication of prosperity: security does not preoccupy the minds of the (travelling) public, the protective cocoon has been restored, and facilitation becomes, yet again, the focus of the industry.

Yet, if the attacks of 9/11 taught us a lesson, it is that the threat of terrorism cannot be ignored. Any solutions to the trilemma need to factor this lesson in, rather than dismiss it on the basis of the current risk reality. Unfortunately, this preoccupation with uncertainty and risk is the curse of proactive risk management and the price we pay for keeping aviation terrorism free.

128 Memo/12/400, 1 June 2012.

9

Aircraft and airport noise

Local issues with global implications

Yaw Nyampong

9.1 Introduction

Aviation noise is a complex subject matter that has been studied and regulated for decades, and still remains the focus of many ongoing research and regulatory efforts. Today, aviation noise continues to be a critical issue for local communities living in the vicinity of airports and policy makers alike. It is reported that, as a result of technological improvements, the noise footprint of new aircraft is at least 15 percent smaller than that of the aircraft they replace,[1] and that modern aircraft are 75 percent quieter today than their predecessors were 50 years ago.[2] Despite the development of newer and quieter aircraft over the years, the concurrent growth in air transport operations around the world over the same period of time has meant that the problem of aviation noise cannot be resolved exclusively through technological advancements. As one commentator put it:

> [w]hen combined with [the air transport industry's] forecast growth rates of 5.4% per annum until 2017 and headline-grabbing infrastructure developments, balancing the benefits of enhanced global connectivity with the needs of people living under continues to be of high importance.[3]

As a result of concerns emanating from aviation noise, airport expansion has become a major issue around the world as the interests of airlines and airport operators trying to meet growing demand for travel are pitted against those of people who live near airports and see their property values diminished by planes roaring overhead. At Munich Airport for instance, the planned construction of a third runway, which would increase airport capacity by 30 flights a day, brought the noise issue to the forefront, despite the fact that it was a greenfield site specially selected to limit its noise impact.[4] A planning application was made for the construction of the third runway in 2007 and, on 26 July 2011, the local government of Upper Bavaria approved the application and issued the required zoning approval for the commencement of construction.

---

1 IATA, "Fact Sheet: Night Flights", online: www.iata.org/policy/environment/Documents/iata-factsheet-nightflights.pdf.
2 Ibid.
3 Martin Rivers, "Reducing Noise", *Airlines International*, 22 May 2014.
4 Ibid.

In June 2012, in a city referendum held on the matter, residents of Munich voted by a narrow margin to oppose construction of the runway. The matter eventually ended up in court. After five on-site meetings, 41 days of proceedings and an extremely intensive examination of the 2,800 pages of the planning application submitted to the local government of Upper Bavaria, the Bavarian Higher Administrative Court dismissed 16 objections raised against the approval granted by the local government of Upper Bavaria and gave express permission for the construction of the third runway to proceed.[5] This notwithstanding, Munich Airport has deployed 16 stationary and three mobile noise measuring facilities within 20 kilometers of the two existing runways in pursuit of better long-term land-use management. The airport has also calculated which homes the third runway in its proposed location would worst affect. Owners of these homes are guaranteed the right to sell their property if they so wish. Above all, Munich Airport maintains open dialogue with local residents and publishes all of its noise data online.[6] The political and environmental debate about aircraft and airport noise pollution rages on both domestically and internationally.

This chapter discusses aviation noise as a local issue with global repercussions. It focuses on the efforts that have been made to regulate it at the international level over the years.

9.2 Aircraft and airport noise: the issue

Noise can be defined as any unwanted sound. There are many variables that may influence people's perception of noise. However, since the level of annoyance changes from person to person, it is difficult to determine what is too noisy or annoying for an entire community.[7] There are many sources of noise in the commercial aviation sector. As an aircraft flies, the air around it is compressed and rarefied, causing movement of air molecules. The movement is propagated through the air as pressure waves. If these pressure waves are strong enough and within the audible frequency spectrum, they create a sensation of hearing – noise. Different aircraft types have different noise levels and frequencies associated with them.

The most commonly known source of aviation noise is the aircraft engine. Most of the noise generated from aircraft engines typically occurs from the high velocity exhaust gases and the airflow in the fan system.[8] "The noise is a mixture of sources originating within the aircraft engines and those produced by the jet exhausts, where high-velocity gases are propelled into the atmospheric air ('jet noise')".[9] Airframes also generate a significant amount of noise, as do various ground operations at airports. The noise generated within the engine is mainly high frequency whereas the jet noise and the airframe noise are low frequency. Low frequency noise sources travel large distances from the aircraft and are noticed most by people living in airport surroundings.[10] In general, during take-off, the exhaust (jet) and the fan are the dominant noise contributors. During landing, the fan and airframe are the dominant sources of aircraft noise.[11]

---

5 See Munich Airport, "Development and Growth: Third Runway", online: www.munich-airport.de/en/company/konzern/ausbau/bahn3/index.jsp.

6 Rivers, "Reducing Noise", *supra* note 3.

7 NoiseQuest, Aviation Noise Information and Resources, "Sources of Aviation Noise", www.essc.psu.edu/~bjh18/download/www.noisequest.psu.edu/SourcesAviation.Overview.html.

8 Ibid.

9 Benedicte A. Claes, "Aircraft Noise Regulation in the European Union: The Hushkit Problem" (2000) 65 *Journal of Air Law and Commerce* 329.

10 Ibid.

11 NoiseQuest, "Sources of Aviation Noise", *supra* note 7.

9.2.1 Mechanisms of noise production in aviation

9.2.1.1 Aircraft engine noise

The two main types of aircraft engines used in commercial aviation today are propeller aircraft engines and jet engines. A propeller is attached to the end of the crankshaft of a propeller aircraft engine effectively to pull it through the air. Large propeller aircraft are powered by turbo shaft engines, which are very similar to jet engines. The source of noise in a propeller aircraft emanates from the turning of the propeller itself as well as the engine exhaust.[12]

Jet engines, on the other hand, are equipped with a set of large fan blades in the front, which pull air into the engine. After this initial set of blades, there are several stages of rotating (rotors) and stationary (stator) blades that make up the compressor section of the engine.[13] In the compressor, each consecutive stage of blades gets smaller and smaller in order to compress the air as it is drawn further into the engine. At this point, the air has been compressed by up to 40 times its original density, and its temperature has dramatically increased. The reason for compressing the air is because compressed air is very flammable. Once the air has been compressed, it enters the combustion chamber where it is mixed with some jet fuel and ignited.[14] The resulting combustion causes the compressed air to expand rapidly, forcing it to escape through the rear of the engine, as it cannot go through the front of the engine due to the force of the incoming air. The escaping air produces thrust that moves the aircraft in the opposite direction – forward. Just before the exhaust gases exit the engine, they pass through another set of turbines – the exhaust turbines. The gases spin the exhaust turbines, which are connected to the fan and the compressor blades in the front of the engine through a shaft. This, in turn, draws new air into the front of the engine and starts the cycle over again. Each jet engine component contributes to the total level of noise generated by the engine.[15]

9.2.1.2 Airframe noise

Another aspect of an aircraft that generates noise is the airframe. Airframe noise is the non-propulsive noise made by an aircraft in flight. Parts of the airframe such as wings, flaps and landing gear also produce a lot of noise when deployed. These airframe components tend to modify the aerodynamic profile of the aircraft when deployed, causing further compression and rarefication of the air passing around the airframe and thereby generating noise. As such, during landing, most of the noise heard from the ground is caused by the deployment of these airframe components. Airframe noise is thus particularly noticeable on approach, when propulsion and throttle-related noise sources are relatively low.[16]

9.2.1.3 Airport noise

A proportion of aviation noise is generated on the ground at the airport – both from aircraft and other sources. Aircraft need to be maintained and inspected. Fully loaded aircraft, ready for take-off, will perform an engine "run-up". This is done to check that the engine is working properly

12 Ibid.
13 Ibid.
14 Ibid.
15 Ibid.
16 Ibid.

and that certain instrumentation is reading correctly. In some instances, the engines need to run for an extended period of time while inspections are performed. This is called a full power run-up and its goal is not to take off from the airport. Another source of airport noise emanates from auxiliary power units (APU) mounted on aircraft. The APU is a relatively small self-contained turbo shaft engine used in aircraft to start the main engines, usually with compressed air, and to provide electrical power and air conditioning while the aircraft is on the ground. In many aircraft, the APU can also provide electrical power in the air. Use of APUs on stationary aircraft contributes to the level of noise created at airports.[17]

General airport operations also involve heavy movement of vehicular traffic to perform services such as refueling, luggage and cargo delivery, aircraft catering and servicing etc. All these vehicular movements contribute to the level of ambient noise generated in and around airports.[18]

9.2.2 The impact of aviation noise

Aviation operations create considerable noise and this becomes a problem particularly for people living in the vicinity of airports or under flight paths. Noise from aircraft and airport operations directly affects the daily lives of people exposed to it in many different ways. Aircraft noise remains one of the principal grounds for launching objections to airport construction or expansion projects. Thus, the noise issue is not only environmental but also political, and numerous attempts to regulate noise have been made both at the domestic and international levels.[19]

A community's "health" refers to the total psychological and physiological well being of its members. Short-term community reaction to aviation noise can be different from the long-term community reaction. As such, when looking at how noise might affect people, we must consider the long-term, cumulative effects on the whole population, not just individuals. The scientific-medical community has divided the effects of noise on people into two general categories:

9.2.2.1 Psychological impacts

These are people's psychological reaction to their noise environment and its interference with their daily activities. For example, noise can make it hard to hear, concentrate and sleep. This may affect work and school performance. One of the main effects of aircraft noise on communities surrounding airports is long-term annoyance. The scientific community has adopted the use of long-term annoyance as its primary gauge of community response because it attempts to account for all negative aspects of effects from noise. Two examples are: increased annoyance due to being awakened the previous night by aircraft; and, interference with everyday conversation.[20]

Speech interference from aircraft noise is a major cause of annoyance for communities. Examples include: the disruption of routine activities such as listening to the radio or watching television, telephone use, family conversation and the disruption of speech communication in classrooms, offices and industrial settings. The disturbance of sleep is also a major concern for communities exposed to night-time aircraft noise. Currently, there is no research that links permanent, long-term health effects to night-time aircraft noise. However, sleep disturbance is

17 Ibid.
18 Ibid.
19 NoiseQuest, Aviation Noise Information and Resources, "Effects of Noise on People", www.essc.psu.edu/~bjh18/download/www.noisequest.psu.edu/NoiseAffect.People.html.
20 Ibid.

still a major cause of annoyance. Consequently, numerous research studies have attempted to measure the complex effects of noise on sleep.[21]

Generally, aircraft noise seems to produce a stronger annoyance response than noise from other forms of transportation (e.g. road traffic or railway noise). This notwithstanding, the World Health Organization (WHO) has recommended that the following five major factors should be considered in interpreting data from different studies on the psychological impact of noise:

- personal factors
- demographic factors
- lifestyle factors
- the duration of noise exposure
- the population experience with noise.

9.2.2.2 Physiological impacts

These are the effects on the systems of the human body, for example, noise-induced hearing loss. It has also been suggested that cardiovascular disease might be affected by environmental noise. Residents in communities surrounding airports often have real concerns regarding the effects of aircraft noise on hearing. It is a well-established fact that continuous exposure to high levels of noise over an extended period of time will damage human hearing. Hearing loss is generally identified as a decrease in the ear's sensitivity or ability to perceive sound.[22]

Studies have been conducted to examine the non-auditory health effects of aircraft noise exposure, focusing mainly on stress response, blood pressure, birth weight, mortality rates and cardiovascular health. It is an established finding that exposure to very loud noise can elevate blood pressure and also stress hormone levels. However, this response is typically seen for much higher noise levels than those produced by aircraft in the community. The response to such loud noise is typically short in duration. After the noise stops, the physiological effects reverse and levels return back to normal. In the case of repeated exposure to aircraft noise, the connection is not as clear. The results of most studies are uncertain and are often contradictory. As such a definite link between aircraft noise exposure and the various types of non-auditory health effects has not been found.[23]

9.2.2.3 Other impacts of aircraft noise

Normally, the most sensitive parts of a structure to airborne noise are the windows, though plastered walls and ceilings can also be sensitive. In general, structural parts are affected when peak sound levels are above 130 dB. Certain frequencies may cause more concern than others. For example, window breakage can occur at 30 hertz. However, only sounds lasting more than one second above 130 dB are potentially damaging to structural parts. Noise-induced structural vibration may annoy occupants because they may in turn cause secondary vibrations leading to rattling of objects within the dwelling such as hanging pictures, dishes, plaques and bric-a-brac. Windowpanes may also vibrate when exposed to high levels of airborne noise. In general, such

21 Ibid.
22 Ibid.
23 Ibid.

noise-induced vibrations occur at peak sound levels of 110 dB or greater. Thus, assessments of noise exposure levels for compatible land use should take into account aircraft noise-induced secondary vibrations.[24]

9.2.3 The trade-off between noise and emissions

Aircraft noise and aircraft engine emissions are closely related. Changing the design or operation of an aircraft can significantly change its engine emissions and noise profile. This close relationship between noise and emissions warrants the use of sophisticated environmental models such as the Aviation Environmental Design Tool (AEDT) developed by the Federal Aviation Administration (FAA) in the United States. These models include variables such as aviation noise exposure, local air quality emissions and climate issues. The interdependent relationship between noise and emissions is exemplified as follows: aircraft can make operational changes during take-off, in flight or landing. A reduced thrust take-off for instance reduces the throttle setting (and the noise levels generated by an aircraft) during the take-off and climb-out. However, reduced thrust procedures also produce increases in emissions of carbon dioxide (CO_2) and oxides of sulphur (SO_x).[25]

Another aircraft operation that has an effect on both noise and emissions is the Continuous Descent Approach (CDA). This is a flight technique that involves the continuous, gradual descent of aircraft on a constant slope at idle or minimal low power settings. Airframe noise is reduced by the delayed deployment of flaps and landing gear until the aircraft is established on final approach. Instead of using the normal step down arrival procedure, with a CDA the pilot flies a constant descent angle to the runway with engines at idle power as long as possible. This can conserve fuel, limit emissions and reduce noise during the descent when the airplane is closer to the ground. However, there are many challenges associated with this technique, which limit its use at many airports. In some situations, the required separation distances between airplanes would not be maintained if the aircraft were allowed to continue on their flight paths toward the airport. Therefore, an air traffic controller may switch an aircraft from a continuous descent approach to a standard landing or command the aircraft to perform a go-around. These correction techniques increase the noise reaching the community, thereby effectively negating the intended benefits of the continuous descent approach.[26]

9.3 International regulation of aviation noise

Toward the end of the Second World War, at the invitation of the government of the United States, representatives from nations around the world gathered in Chicago to discuss the future of the then burgeoning international aviation industry.[27] Ultimately, the conference adopted the Convention on International Civil Aviation (Chicago Convention),[28] which is the constitutive instrument of the International Civil Aviation Organization (ICAO), a specialized agency of the United Nations. The goal of the Chicago Convention was "to achieve a system of uniform

---

24 Ibid.
25 Ibid.
26 Ibid.
27 Michael Gerard Green, "Control of Air Pollutant Emissions from Aircraft Engines: Local Impacts of National Concern" (1999) 5:2 *Envtl. Law.* 513 at 530.
28 Convention on International Civil Aviation, 7 December 1944, 15 U.N.T.S. 295, Article 37 (entered into force 4 April 1947) (Chicago Convention).

regulation of matters affecting international aviation".[29] Currently, there are 191 state parties to the Chicago Convention who are also Member States of ICAO.

Article 37 of the Chicago Convention enjoins contracting states to "collaborate in securing the highest practicable degree of uniformity in regulations, standards, procedures, and organization in relation to aircraft, personnel, airways and auxiliary services in all matters in which such uniformity will facilitate and improve air navigation".[30] It also vests ICAO with the authority to adopt and amend international Standards and Recommended Practices (SARPs) dealing with, among other things, communications systems and air navigation aids, including ground marking,[31] rules of the air and air traffic control practices,[32] aircraft in distress and investigation of accidents,[33] and "*such other matters concerned with the safety, regularity, and efficiency of air navigation as may from time to time appear appropriate*".[34] All the international SARPs adopted by ICAO under Article 37 are, *for convenience*,[35] designated as Annexes to the Chicago Convention.[36] Between 1948 and 1953, 15 Annexes were adopted.[37] Presently, there are 19 Annexes to the Chicago Convention and they address matters ranging from the licensing of personnel to the safe carriage of dangerous goods by air.

The Chicago Convention does not define the terms "international standard" and "recommended practice". The ICAO Assembly formulated the requisite definitions as far back as 1947 in Assembly Resolution A1-31.[38] A "Standard" is defined in the Resolution as follows:

> Any specification for physical characteristics, configuration, materiel, performance, personnel, or procedure, the uniform application of which is recognized as necessary for the safety or regularity of international air navigation and to which Member States will conform in accordance with the Convention; in the event of impossibility of compliance, notification to the Council is compulsory under article 38 of the Convention.[39]

---

29 Heather L. Miller, "Civil Aircraft Emissions and International Treaty Law" (1998) 63 *J. Air Law & Com.* 697 at 706.
30 Chicago Convention, *supra* note 28, Article 37.
31 Ibid., Article 37(a).
32 Ibid., Article 37(c).
33 Ibid., Article 37(k).
34 Ibid., Article 37 final paragraph (emphasis added). This provision was an omnibus residuary clause intended to cater for the adoption of SARPs to meet the growing needs of civil aviation. It is however limited to matters concerning the safety, regularity and efficiency of air navigation.
35 The opinion is widely held among authors that the use of the term "for convenience" means that Annexes do not form an integral part of, and possess the same legal force as, the Convention. See ibid., Article 54(l); Bin Cheng, *The Law of International Air Transport* (New York: Oceana, 1962) at 64; Roderick D. van Dam, "Regulating International Civil Aviation: An ICAO Perspective" in Tanja L. Masson-Zwaan and Pablo M.J. Mendes-de-Leon, eds, *Air and Space Law: De Lege Ferenda* (Dordrecht: Martinus Nijhoff, 1992) 11 at 13; Ingrid Detter, *Law Making by International Organizations* (Stockholm: P.A. Norstedt & Söners Förlag, 1965) at 248, where the author notes that unlike the Technical Annexes to the Paris Convention of 1919, which formed part of, and had the same force as, the Convention, the Annexes to the Chicago Convention do not have the same compulsory force as the Convention. They are placed on a more voluntary basis, being subject to a number of safeguards.
36 Ibid., Article 54(l).
37 Thomas Buergenthal, *Law-making in the International Civil Aviation Organization* (New York: Syracuse University Press, 1969) at 60.
38 ICAO, "Definition of 'International Standards' and 'Recommended Practices'", Assembly Resolution A1-31, ICAO Doc. 4411; see Buergenthal, *supra* note 37 at 60.
39 Assembly Resolution A1-31, ibid.

On the other hand, a "Recommended Practice" is defined as follows:

> Any specification for physical characteristics, configuration, materiel, performance, personnel, or procedure the uniform application of which is recognized as desirable in the interest of safety, regularity, or efficiency of international air navigation, and to which Member States will endeavour to conform in accordance with the Convention.[40]

In line with the foregoing, ICAO regulates aviation noise internationally through the international SARPs contained in Annex 16 Volume I to the Chicago Convention. To date, ICAO's international regulatory efforts in connection with aviation noise have focused almost exclusively on the reduction of aircraft noise at source (i.e. quieter aircraft).[41] Once noise standards are promulgated by ICAO, all contracting states of the Chicago Convention are obliged either to implement them domestically or to notify the ICAO Council of differences existing between their national regulations and practices and the international standards prescribed in the Annex.[42]

Concerns about aircraft noise grew in the mid to late 1960s as air traffic expanded rapidly, as jet aircraft and first generation turbofans were introduced and the first jumbo jets were in their late stages of development. The ICAO Assembly adopted Resolution 16-3 in September 1968 acknowledging that noise levels around many major airports represented a very serious problem, and this would only intensify with the introduction of new aircraft types. Many meetings and conferences were held following the adoption of this Resolution, and all these efforts culminated in the adoption in April 1971 of Annex 16 – Aircraft Noise – to the Chicago Convention.[43]

Part I of Annex 16 Volume I contains definitions and Part II contains international standards, recommended practices and guidelines for noise certification of aircraft specified in individual chapters of that part, where such aircraft are engaged in international air navigation. Parts III, IV and V of Annex 16 Volume I contain SARPs and guidance materials for use by states with a view to promoting uniformity in measurement of noise for monitoring purposes, assessing noise around airports and regarding the balanced approach to noise management.[44] Since ICAO adopted the first set of international SARPs for aircraft noise in 1971, certification standards have periodically been made more stringent as will be demonstrated below.

9.3.1 Noise certification of aircraft under Annex 16 Volume I – Aircraft Noise

Annex 16 Volume I establishes a noise certification regime for aircraft. It provides that noise certification shall be granted or validated by the State of Registry of an aircraft on the basis of

---

40 Ibid.
41 In 2001, ICAO adopted a balanced approach to aircraft noise management and thereby recommended three other approaches for the management of aircraft noise (i.e. in addition to reduction at source – quieter aircraft). These are: land-use planning and management, noise abatement operational procedures and operating restrictions. The balanced approach is discussed in detail below.
42 Article 38 of the Chicago Convention obliges Contracting States to notify the ICAO Council of any differences between their national regulations and practices and the international standards contained in the Annexes. Under Annex 15, States are encouraged to publish such differences through the Aeronautical Information Service.
43 In its original form, Annex 16 only addressed aircraft noise. In 1981, the scope of the Annex was broadened to cover all environmental issues relating to aviation. Thus, it was split into two volumes. Volume I addresses "Aircraft Noise" whereas Volume II addresses "Aircraft Emissions".
44 See ICAO, Annex 16 Volume I "Aircraft Noise", xii–xiii.

satisfactory evidence that the aircraft complies with requirements that are at least equal to the applicable standards specified in the Annex.[45] It provides further that documents attesting the noise certification of an aircraft shall be approved by the State of Registry and shall be required by the State to be carried on the aircraft.[46]

Thus, under Annex 16 Volume I, the State of Registry of an aircraft is the entity authorized to issue noise certification for the aircraft. Such noise certification must be issued on the basis of a standardized procedure in which the aircraft noise emissions are measured at three fixed measuring points during flyby as well as flyover prior to landing and after take-off. The aircraft then receives a noise certificate based on the measuring results, the maximum take-off weight and the number of engines.

Contracting States to the Chicago Convention are obliged to recognize the validity of a noise certificate granted by another Contracting State provided that the requirements under which such certification was granted are at least equal to the applicable standards specified in the Annex.[47] Contracting States are also required to suspend or revoke the noise certification of any aircraft on their respective registers if the aircraft ceases to comply with the applicable noise standards.[48] In determining the applicability to aircraft of the standards contained in Annex 16 Volume I, Contracting States are required to use the date on which the application for a Type Certificate[49] for the aircraft was submitted to the State of Design, or the date of submission under an equivalent application procedure prescribed by the certificating authority of the State of Design.[50]

For purposes of noise certification of aircraft, Part II of Annex 16 Volume I classifies aircraft under 12 chapters[51] according to their year of design, type and weight. For each aircraft type and for each corresponding weight, a maximum noise emission level is set – expressed in units of Effective Perceived Noise Decibels (EPNdB). These noise emission levels are calculated on the basis of the following criteria: level, frequency, distribution and variation over time of aircraft noise.[52] When it was initially promulgated in 1971, Annex 16 Volume I did not cover the first generation of jet-powered aircraft and these are consequently referred to as non-noise certificated (NNC) aircraft.[53] Chapter 2 of the original Annex 16 contains the first set of noise standards that

---

45 ICAO, Annex 16 Volume I, "Aircraft Noise", paragraph 1.2.
46 Ibid., paragraph 1.4.
47 Ibid., paragraph 1.8.
48 Ibid., paragraph 1.9.
49 A Type Certificate is defined in Annex 16 Volume I as: "a document issued by a State to define the design of an aircraft type and to certify that this design meets the appropriate airworthiness requirements of that State". It is issued to signify the airworthiness of an aircraft manufacturing design. A regulating body issues the certificate, and, once issued, the design cannot be changed. A Type Certificate reflects a determination made by the regulating body that the aircraft is manufactured according to an approved design, and that the design ensures compliance with airworthiness requirements. The regulating body compares design documents and processes to determine if the design meets requirements established for the type of equipment. The Type Certificate implies that aircraft manufactured according to the approved design can be issued an Airworthiness Certificate – a certificate that is issued for each aircraft that is properly registered if it conforms to its type design. With a valid airworthiness certificate, an aircraft may be operated as long as it is maintained in accordance with the rules issued by the regulatory authority.
50 ICAO, Annex 16 Volume I, "Aircraft Noise", paragraph 1.11.
51 Chapters 2–13 of Part II of Annex 16 Volume I.
52 See ICAO, Annex 16 Volume I, "Aircraft Noise", Appendix 2 (Measurement of Aircraft Noise Received on the Ground). See also Éric Vallières, "Aircraft Noise: A Legal Perspective", *ABA Forum on Air and Space Law 2014 Annual Meeting*, September 2014.
53 See www.icao.int/environmental-protection/Pages/noise.aspx. These included the Boeing 707 and Douglas DC-8.

were promulgated in 1971. It covers subsonic jet aircraft in respect of which the application for Type Certificate was submitted before 6 October 1977.[54]

In January 1975, ICAO's then Committee on Aircraft Noise agreed that a second wave of standards should be promulgated to regulate aircraft for which the application for Type Certificate was submitted after 6 October 1977. The resulting set of SARPs, which were stricter in terms of the maximum noise levels permitted and the mode of calculating them, was promulgated in Chapter 3 of Annex 16 Volume I. Aircraft certificated as conforming to those standards are referred to as Chapter 3 Aircraft, and they include subsonic jet aircraft in respect of which the application for Type Certificate was submitted on or after 6 October 1977 but before 1 January 2006, as well as propeller-driven aircraft weighing over 8,618 kg for which the application for Type Certificate was submitted on or after 1 January 1985 and before 1 January 2006.[55]

Between 1975 and 2001, although commercial air traffic continued to grow steadily, concurrent advancements in technology allowed net aircraft noise levels to decrease. Thus, no new chapters were added to Annex 16 Volume I. In 2001, however, ICAO's Committee on Aviation Environmental Protection (CAEP) concluded that growth in traffic would soon outstrip the gains made possible by advancements in technology. At its fifth meeting (CAEP/5), the Committee recommended new standards for noise certification of aircraft for which the application for Type Certificate would be submitted after 1 January 2006. These recommendations were ultimately approved by the ICAO Council and promulgated as Chapter 4 of Annex 16 Volume I. Chapter 4 therefore covers subsonic jet aircraft and propeller-driven aircraft weighing over 8,618 kg for which the application for Type Certificate was submitted on or after 1 January 2006.[56]

On 7 February 2013, at the ninth meeting of CAEP, new even more stringent standards were agreed upon, which are set to become the new Chapter 14 of Annex 16 Volume 1. Also,

---

54 The standards promulgated in Chapter 2 Part II of Annex 16 Volume I were prospective in scope and applied to aircraft for which the Type Certificate was submitted before 6 October 1977. Aircraft granted noise certification under these standards are typically referred to as Chapter 2 Aircraft. The Boeing 727 and the Douglas DC-9 are examples of Chapter 2 aircraft. Today, with the exception of smaller jets, Chapter 2 Aircraft are only permitted to operate in certain developing countries. See Irina Gabriela Ionescu, "Aircraft Noise Regulation" (2004) (LL.M Thesis, McGill University).

55 Chapter 3 was adopted in 1977 and it contained more stringent noise standards. Boeing 737–300/400, Boeing 767 and Airbus A319 are examples of Chapter 3 aircraft types. See Vallières, *ABA Forum on Air and Space Law 2014 Annual Meeting, supra* note 52.

56 Chapter 4 covers modern aircraft such as the Boeing 777 and 787, as well as the Airbus A380 and A350. The remainder of the chapters of Annex 16 Volume I and the aircraft types they cover respectively are set out below:

Chapter 5:   Propeller-driven aircraft weighing over 8,618 kg for which the application for type certificate was submitted before 1 January 1985.

Chapter 6:   Propeller-driven aircraft not exceeding 8,618 kg for which the application for type certificate was submitted before 17 November 1988.

Chapter 7:   Propeller-driven STOL (Short Take-Off and Landing) aircraft.

Chapter 8:   Helicopters.

Chapter 9:   Installed Auxiliary Power Units (APUs) and Associated Aircraft Systems during Ground Operations.

Chapter 10:   Propeller-driven aircraft not exceeding 8,618 kg for which the application for type certificate or certification of Derived Version was submitted on or after 17 November 1988.

Chapter 11:   Helicopters not exceeding 3,175 kg Maximum Certificated Take-Off Mass.

Chapter 12:   Supersonic Aircraft.

Chapter 13:   Tilt-Rotor Aircraft.

in 2014, ICAO adopted a new standard that will result in a noise reduction of 7 EPNdB compared to the current Chapter 4 standard. The new standard, which will replace the current Chapter 4, will apply from 2018 onwards.[57]

9.3.2 ICAO Doc. 9501: Environmental Technical Manual – procedures for the noise certification of aircraft

In 2010, in an effort to promote uniformity of implementation of the technical procedures of Annex 16 Volume I among its Member States, ICAO published the "Environmental Technical Manual on the use of Procedures in the Noise Certification of Aircraft".[58] The Manual provides guidance to certificating authorities and applicants regarding the intended meaning and stringency of the standards in Annex 16 Volume I as well as the specific procedures that are deemed acceptable in demonstrating compliance with those standards. The Manual contains three types of information, namely, explanatory information, equivalent procedures and technical procedures.

The explanatory information contained in the Manual consists of *guidance material* – which helps to illustrate the meaning of a specification or requirement – or *acceptable means of compliance* – which illustrates a means by which a requirement specified in Annex 16 Volume I can be met. The purpose of explanatory information is threefold: it explains the language of the noise standards appearing in the various chapters of Annex 16 Volume I, it states the current policies of regulatory authorities regarding compliance with the Annex, and it provides information on critical issues concerning approval of an applicant's compliance methodology proposals.[59]

An equivalent procedure is a test or analysis procedure, which while differing from the one specified in the Annex, yields effectively the same noise levels as the specified procedure in the technical judgment of the certificating authority. A technical procedure, on the other hand, is a test or analysis procedure not defined in the Annex but which certificating authorities have approved as being acceptable for compliance with the general provisions of the Annex. In granting or validating noise certification to aircraft, the procedures described in the Annex must be used unless the certificating authority has approved an equivalent procedure or alternative technical procedure.[60]

In 2006, the French Directorate General of Civil Aviation developed a Noise database under the aegis of ICAO. The database is intended to be a general source of information to the public on noise certification levels for each aircraft type as provided by certification authorities.[61]

9.4 The balanced approach to noise management

In 2001, the ICAO Assembly adopted a balanced approach to aircraft noise management, in an attempt to "achieve a balance between the benefits accruing to the world community through civil aviation and the harm caused to the environment in certain areas through the progressive advancement of civil aviation". Under the balanced approach, each airport is encouraged to

---

57 See www.iata.org/policy/environment/pages/aircraft-noise.aspx.
58 ICAO, "Environmental Technical Manual on the use of Procedures in the Noise Certification of Aircraft", ICAO Doc. 9501.
59 ICAO, "Environmental Technical Manual on the use of Procedures in the Noise Certification of Aircraft", ICAO Doc. 9501 p. 1-1.
60 ICAO, "Environmental Technical Manual on the use of Procedures in the Noise Certification of Aircraft", ICAO Doc. 9501 p. 1-2.
61 For access to the noise certification database, see http://noisedb.stac.aviation-civile.gouv.fr.

identify a noise problem based on objective data, to consider all available alternatives for addressing the noise issue and to select the most cost-effective approach. ICAO's guidance on the balanced approach is contained in "Guidance on the Balanced Approach to Aircraft Noise Management" – Doc. 9829. Four approaches are recommended:

1   reduction at source (quieter aircraft);
2   land-use planning and management;
3   noise abatement operational procedures;
4   operating restrictions.

9.4.1 Land-use planning and management

Land-use planning and management is an effective means to ensure that the activities nearby airports are compatible with aviation. The main goal is to minimize the population affected by aircraft noise by introducing land-use zoning around airports. Compatible land-use planning and management is also a vital instrument in ensuring that the gains achieved by the reduced noise of the latest generation of aircraft are not offset by further residential development around airports. ICAO guidance on this subject is contained in Annex 16, Volume I, Part IV and in the "Airport Planning Manual", Part 2 – "Land Use and Environmental Control" (Doc. 9184). The Manual provides guidance on the use of various tools for the minimization, control or prevention of the impact of aircraft noise in the vicinity of airports and describes the practices adopted for land-use planning and management by some States. In addition, with a view to promoting a uniform method of assessing noise around airports, ICAO recommends the use of the methodology contained in "Recommended Method for Computing Noise Contours around Airports" (Circular 205).

9.4.2 Noise abatement operational procedures

Noise abatement procedures enable reduction of noise during aircraft operations to be achieved at comparatively low cost. There are several methods, including preferential runways and routes, as well as noise abatement procedures for take-off, approach and landing. The appropriateness of any of these measures depends on the physical layout of the airport and its surroundings, but in all cases the procedure must give priority to safety considerations. ICAO's noise abatement procedures are contained in Annex 16, Volume I, Part V and "Procedures for Air Navigation Services: Aircraft Operations" (PANS-OPS, Doc. 8168), Volume I – "Flight Procedures", Part V. On the basis of recommendations made by CAEP/5, new noise abatement take-off procedures became applicable in November 2001. Doc. 9888 "Review of Noise Abatement Research and Development and Implementation Projects" contains a summary of two surveys of key aviation stakeholders conducted in 2006 and 2009.

9.4.3 Operating restrictions and noisy disputes

Although the noise certification standards contained in the various chapters of Annex 16 Volume I were initially driven by a prospective philosophy and were thus not designed to result in the removal from service of aircraft previously certificated as "noiseworthy", technological progress and public pressure ultimately elevated the need to address the continued operation of older noisy aircraft in international air navigation. Noise concerns have led some States, mostly developed countries, to consider banning the operation of certain noisy aircraft at noise-sensitive airports. In the 1980s, the focus was on NNC aircraft; in the 1990s, it moved to Chapter 2 aircraft. However, operating restrictions of this kind can have significant economic implications for the airlines concerned, both those based in the States taking action and those based in other States (particularly developing countries) that operate to and from the affected airports.

On each occasion, the ICAO Assembly succeeded in reaching an agreement – contained in an Assembly resolution – that represented a careful balance between the interests of developing and developed States and took into account the concerns of the airline industry, airports and environmental interests. In the case of Chapter 2 aircraft, the ICAO Assembly in 1990 urged States not to restrict aircraft operations without considering other possibilities first. It then provided a basis upon which States wishing to restrict operations of Chapter 2 aircraft may proceed to do so. States could start phasing out operations of Chapter 2 aircraft from 1 April 1995 and have all of them withdrawn from service by 31 March 2002. However, prior to the latter date, Chapter 2 aircraft were guaranteed 25 years of service after the issue of their first certificate of airworthiness. Thus Chapter 2 aircraft, which had completed less than 25 years of service on 1 April 1995, were not immediately affected by this requirement. Similarly, widebody Chapter 2 aircraft and those fitted with quieter (high by-pass ratio) engines were not immediately affected after 1 April 1995.

A large number of aircraft certificated as noiseworthy under the Chapter 2 standard were in use in international air navigation in 1977 when the stricter Chapter 3 noise certification standard was adopted. However, aircraft initially certificated to Chapter 2 or equivalent standards, or initially not noise-certificated could be recertificated to meet the baseline Chapter 3 noise standard through technical modifications such as hushkits,[62] engine modifications or other technical measures, or through operational restrictions, such as weight restrictions and reduced flap settings. In response, most operators in the United States, who kept the bulk of such aircraft within their existing fleets, hushkitted them in order to meet the new Chapter 3 standard. Hushkitted Chapter 2 aircraft could be, and indeed were, recertificated as Chapter 3 compliant aircraft.

In 1999, the EU passed Regulation 925 seeking to ban the addition of hushkitted aircraft that had been recertificated as Chapter 3 compliant to the registries of European Member States with effect from 1 April 1999 (i.e. three years before the ICAO deadline of 1 April 2002), and completely to prohibit their operation within European airspace after 1 April 2002.[63] Although such aircraft were technically compliant with the then prevailing ICAO standards, the Europeans saw

---

62 A hushkit is a device for reducing noise from an engine. It is typically used on a low-bypass turbofan engine in older commercial aircraft. In modern high-bypass turbofan engines, the fan mounted at the front of the jet engine core is very large. The bigger the fan in comparison to the jet core, the more effective the bypass air is in enveloping the jet exhaust at the rear of the engine, reducing noise. The larger turbines needed to spin the large fan slow the jet exhaust, which also reduces noise. A hushkit produces a similar effect, using several modifications to the existing engine. Primarily, a device called a multilobe exhaust mixer on the rear of the engine mixes the exhaust gases of the jet core with the surrounding air and the small amount of bypass air available. Similar systems are also employed on many modern turbofan engines as standard equipment to reduce noise further. Most kits also make further modifications to the exhaust via acoustically treated tailpipes, revised inlet nacelles and guide vanes, all of which reduce forward propagating high-pitched noise caused by the small, high-speed fan.

63 Council Regulation (EC) No. 925/1999 of 29 April 1999 on the registration and operation within the Community of certain types of civil subsonic jet aeroplanes which have been modified and recertificated as meeting the standards of volume I, Part II, Chapter 3 of Annex 16 to the Convention on International Civil Aviation, third edition (July 1993) OJ L115/1 (Regulation 925/1999).

them as violating the spirit of the law – the promotion of positive technological progress. The United States (then in possession of the largest number of hushkitted aircraft and the home of a significant number of companies producing them) first passed House Resolution 661 in March 1999 in a retaliatory effort to suspend landing rights for Concorde in the United States – Concorde being only Chapter 2 compliant.[64] The EU Council decided to delay the entry into force of the Regulation by one year (i.e. until 4 May 2000).

Ultimately, the United States filed a complaint before the ICAO Council against the then 15 Member States of the EU under the provisions of Article 84 of the Chicago Convention, alleging, among other things, that the standards adopted by the EU would be in clear breach of the Chicago Convention if implemented. The EU challenged the admissibility of the complaint, arguing that the Convention requires parties to negotiate the legal aspects of the dispute prior to any complaint being brought. The ICAO Council rejected the EU's challenge on 16 November 2001. Although there was no definitive pronouncement on the legality of the EU Regulation, it was eventually repealed in 2002 after a lengthy legal and political battle. The regulation was replaced with a Directive[65] drafted along the lines of ICAO's balanced approach to aircraft noise management.

In the case of Chapter 3 aircraft, the ICAO Assembly in 2001 urged States not to introduce any operating restrictions at any airport on such aircraft before fully assessing available measures to address the noise problem at the airport concerned in accordance with the balanced approach. The Assembly also listed a number of safeguards that would need to be put in place if restrictions are imposed on Chapter 3 aircraft. For example, restrictions should be based on the noise performance of the aircraft and should be tailored to the noise problem of the airport concerned, and the special circumstances of operators from developing countries should be taken into account.

9.4.4 Noise charges

ICAO's policy with regard to noise charges was first developed in 1981 and is contained in "ICAO's Policies on Charges for Airports and Air Navigation Services" (Doc. 9082). The ICAO Council recognizes that, although reductions are being achieved in aircraft noise at source, many airports still need to apply noise alleviation or prevention measures. The Council considers that the costs incurred may, at the discretion of States, be attributed to airports and recovered from the users. In the event that noise-related charges are levied, the Council recommends that they should be levied only at airports experiencing noise problems and should be designed to recover no more than the costs applied to their alleviation or prevention; and that they should be non-discriminatory between users and not be established at such levels as to be prohibitively high for the operation of certain aircraft.

Practical advice on determining the cost basis for noise-related charges and their collection is provided in the ICAO "Airport Economics Manual" (Doc. 9562), and information on noise-related charges actually levied is provided in the ICAO "Manual of Airport and Air Navigation Facility Tariffs" (Doc. 7100).

---

64 Andreas Knorr and Andreas Arndt, "Noise Wars: The EU's Hushkit Regulation – Environmental Protection or Eco-protectionism" (Andreas Knorr, Alfons Lemper, Axel Sell and Karl Wohlmuth, eds, Bremen, IWIM, 2002).

65 Directive 2002/30/EC of the European Parliament and of the Council of 26 March 2002 on the establishment of rules and procedures with regard to the introduction of noise-related operating restrictions at Community airports, OJ L 85, 28 March 2002, pp. 40–46.

9.5 Summary and conclusions

Aviation operations create considerable noise and this becomes a problem particularly for people living in the vicinity of airports or under flight paths. As an overarching issue that affects the commercial viability of international air transportation, clearly, the problem of aviation noise cannot be discounted. Past efforts at regulating aviation noise have been limited to certification of aircraft with the aim of promoting technological progress. Unfortunately, the reality is that noisy aircraft that are withdrawn from service in developed countries end up being sold to developing and third world countries where they are put back into international air navigation for many years. Rules are then enacted which prohibit such aircraft from operating within or into the airspace of the developed countries. Given the localized nature and impact of aircraft noise, the balanced approach advocated by ICAO should provide an optimal way forward in addressing aircraft noise issues in a sustainable fashion.

10

Environmental law

Emissions

Tanveer Ahmad

10.1 Introduction

At present, the protection of the environment is one of the pressing issues throughout the globe. Anthropogenic emissions of various substances, including greenhouse gases, are polluting the environment to such an extent that the survival of all living species is in jeopardy. Such emissions are significantly responsible for, among others, ozone depletion, climate change, and global warming. Such emissions are increasing: in a quest to maintain and expand their economic development, States continue their industrialization, and are reluctant to lessen the speed of such developments. The Intergovernmental Panel on Climate Change (IPCC) Fifth Assessment Report states that "[a]bout half of cumulative anthropogenic [carbon dioxide] emissions between 1750 and 2010 have occurred in the last 40 years."[1]

Emissions know no border; emissions occurring anywhere in the planet contribute to the global environmental problems. Due to its transboundary nature, emissions have drawn much attention from States, intergovernmental organizations, non-governmental organizations, municipalities, civil society, etc. Ways to reduce emissions frequently appear in multilateral, bilateral, and domestic negotiations. States are currently negotiating a Paris Convention addressing greenhouse gas emissions, which is due to be concluded at the end of 2015.

Transportation is a significant source of emissions that contaminate the environment. Currently, direct emissions from transportation account for 14 percent of global greenhouse gas emission.[2] Aviation is responsible for approximately 2 percent of total global carbon dioxide (CO_2) emissions,[3] and 12 percent of total CO_2 emissions from the transportation sector.[4] Concern over

---

1 IPCC, "Summary for Policymakers" in Ottmar Edenhofer, Ramón Pichs-Madruga, Youba Sokona, Jan C. Minx, Ellie Farahani, Susanne Kadner, Kristin Seyboth, Anna Adler, Ina Baum, and Steffen Brunner, eds., *Climate Change 2014: Mitigation of Climate Change: Contribution of Working Group III to the Fifth Assessment Report of the Intergovernmental Panel on Climate Change* (New York: Cambridge University Press, 2014) 1 at 7.

2 See ibid., at 8.

3 See Air Transport Action Group (ATAG), "Facts & Figures," online: www.atag.org/facts-and-figures. html (ATAG "Facts & Figures"); ICAO Secretariat, "Climate Change Outlook" in ICAO, *ICAO Environmental Report 2010: Aviation and Climate Change* (Montreal: ICAO, 2010) 31 at 31 (ICAO Secretariat, "Climate Change Outlook").

4 See ATAG, "Facts & Figures," *supra* note 3.

aviation's contribution is rising mainly due to rapid growth of this transportation sector. The International Civil Aviation Organization (ICAO) has forecast that, at the global level, the revenue passenger-kilometers will "increase at an average annual rate of 4.7 percent between 2010 and 2030."[5] The average annual fleet growth rate for passenger aircraft is 3.1 percent, and 2.7 percent for cargo aircraft.[6] To rescue our planet, anthropogenic emissions have to be significantly reduced. All sectors must contribute to this effort to successfully curb emissions.

10.2 Emissions from aviation

Aviation entails many activities in addition to aircraft and their operation. Hence, there exists a variety of sources of emissions in aviation. Sources of emissions in aviation include: aircraft engines, aircraft auxiliary power units (APUs),[7] airports, and airport-associated activities, e.g., ground support equipment, motor vehicles (including fleet vehicles,[8] landside road traffic, ground access vehicles, and airside vehicle traffic), construction and airport maintenance, airport-owned power plants for heat, cooling, and electricity production, emergency electricity generation, off-site electricity generation, airport fire training facility, waste disposed of both on-site and off-site, food preparation, aircraft and engine maintenance, de-icing, and fuel storage facilities.[9] This chapter focuses on the international civil aviation regulatory regime and not on the domestic regulatory regime. Emissions from airports and airport-associated activities are more local than international; hence, emissions from aircraft engines and APUs, which are the only sources that fall within the jurisdiction of ICAO,[10] are addressed here. Hence, the term "aviation emissions" used in this chapter refers to aircraft engine emissions and APUs.

Like an automobile engine, an aircraft engine or jet engine or gas turbine is an internal combustion engine wherein "the fuel and an oxidizer combust (or burn) and the products of that combustion are exhausted through a narrow opening at high speed."[11] Kerosene, a fossil fuel, is

---

5 ICAO, "Global and Regional 20-Year Forecasts: Pilots • Maintenance Personnel • Air Traffic Controllers," ICAO Doc. 9956 (2011) at 18.

6 See ibid., at 22.

7 Aircraft APU, a component of a large aircraft, is "essentially a small turbine engine" which "generates electricity and compressed air to operate the aircraft's instruments, lights, ventilation, and other equipment and for starting the aircraft main engines." In the absence of a ground-based power or air source, "the APU may be operated for extended periods when the aircraft is on the ground with its engines shut down." Like larger engines, APUs burn jet fuel and, hence, create the same exhaust emissions. See Energy and Environmental Analysis, Inc., "Technical Data to Support FAA's Advisory Circular on Reducing Emissions from Commercial Aviation," prepared for the US Environmental Protection Agency (EPA) in cooperation with Federal Aviation Administration, US Department of Transportation (29 September 1995) at 29, online: www.epa.gov/otaq/regs/nonroad/aviation/faa-ac.pdf.

8 "Airport-owned (or leased) vehicles for passenger transport, maintenance vehicles and machinery operating both airside and landside." Airports Council International, "Guidance Manual: Airport Greenhouse Gas Emissions Management," 1st ed. (ACI World Environment Standing Committee, November 2009) at 16 (ACI, "Guidance").

9 See ICAO, "Airport Air Quality Manual," 1st ed., ICAO Doc. 9889 (2011) at 3-4–3-5, online: ICAO www.icao.int/publications/Documents/9889_cons_en.pdf (ICAO, "Airport Manual"); ICAO, "Contaminants," online: www.icao.int/environmental-protection/Pages/Contaminants. aspx [ICAO, "Contaminants"); ACI, "Guidance," *supra* note 8 at 16–17.

10 See ICAO, "Contaminants," *supra* note 9.

11 NASA Glenn Research Center, NASA Facts, "Safeguarding Our Atmosphere: Glenn Research Reduces Harmful Aircraft Emissions," FS-2000-04-010-GRC (March 2000), online: www.nasa.gov/centers/glenn/pdf/84797main_fs10grc.pdf (NASA Glenn Research Center).

the primary energy source for international civil aviation.[12] Aircraft engines burn kerosene thus producing the same gases, e.g., CO_2 and water vapor, produced by burning of other fossil fuels.[13] Below is a list of major gases and other elements that are emitted by aircraft during different phases of operation:

- CO_2;
- carbon monoxide (CO);
- nitric oxide (NO);
- nitrogen dioxide (NO_2);[14]
- water vapor (H_2O);
- sulfur oxides (SO_xO);
- unburned hydrocarbons (HC);
- volatile organic compounds (VOCS), e.g., benzene (C_6H_6) and acrolein (C_3H_4O);
- semi-volatile organic compounds (SVOCS);
- ozone (O_3) – this is formed from the emitted nitrogen oxides (NO and NO_2 together) and VOCS;
- particulate matter (PM) – this leaves the exhaust as carbon black soot;
- metals;
- odor; and
- noise.[15]

Aircraft emitted gases and elements listed above have deleterious impacts on both human health and the environment.[16] However, this chapter chiefly focuses on environmental impacts of

---

12 See Md Tanveer Ahmad, "Environmental Effectiveness of ICAO's Basket of Mitigation Measures to Arrest Emissions from International Civil Aviation" (2014) 39 *Ann. Air & Sp. L.* 75 at 88 (Ahmad, "Environmental"). In domestic civil aviation, aircraft powered by piston engines are used as well as jet engine aircraft. Unlike jet engines, gasoline (100 octane low-leaded fuel) is used for piston engines. See US EPA, "Toxic Emissions from Aircraft Engines: A Search of Available Literature," EPA-453/R-93-028, prepared for Air Risk Information Support Center (Air RISC), US Environmental Protection Agency, co-sponsored by Office of Air Quality Planning & Standards, Office of Air & Radiation, Environmental Criteria & Assessment Office, Office of Health & Environmental Assessment, and Office of Research & Development (July 1993) at 1, online: www.areco.org/airemiss.pdf (US EPA, "Toxic"); National Business Aviation Association (NBAA), "Piston Engine Aircraft," online: www.nbaa.org/business-aviation/aircraft/pistons/.
13 See NASA Glenn Research Center, *supra* note 11. However, it should be noted that jet fuel is "a complex chemical mixture and only 200 of its 2000+ chemicals have been formally identified." CloseTheAirport.com, "Jet Pollution," online: www.closetheairport.com/jet-pollution/.
14 Nitric oxide and nitrogen dioxide are jointly termed nitrogen oxides (NO_x).
15 See ICAO, "Contaminants," *supra* note 9; IPCC, "Summary for Policymakers: Aviation and the Global Atmosphere" in Joyce E. Penner, David H. Lister, David J. Griggs, David J. Dokken and Mack McFarland, eds., *Aviation and the Global Atmosphere: A Special Report of IPCC Working Groups I and III in collaboration with the Scientific Assessment Panel to the Montreal Protocol on Substances that Deplete the Ozone Layer* (Cambridge: Cambridge University Press, 1999) 1 at 3 (IPCC, "Summary for Policymakers"; Penner, *Aviation*); World Bank, "Air Transport and Energy Efficiency," Transport Papers, TP–38 (February 2012) at 31, online: siteresources.worldbank.org/INTAIRTRANSPORT/Resources/TP38.pdf (World Bank, "Air Transport").
16 To learn about health impacts of aviation emissions, see US EPA, "Toxic," *supra* note 12; Wolfram Schlenker and W. Reed Walker, "Airports, Air Pollution, and Contemporary Health," Working Paper 17684, National Bureau of Economic Research (NBER) (December 2011), online: www.nber.org/papers/w17684.pdf; Mason Inman, "Plane Exhaust Kills more People than Plane Crashes," *National Geographic News* (10 October 2010), online: news.nationalgeographic.com/news/2010/10/101005-planes-pollution-deaths-science-environment/; ICAO, "Contaminants," *supra* note 9; CloseTheAirport.com, *supra* note 13; Christopher J. Sequeira, "An Assessment of the Health Implications of Aviation Emissions Regulations" (MSc Thesis, Massachusetts Institute of Technology Department of Aeronautics and Astronautics and the Engineering Systems Division, 2008) (unpublished).

aviation emissions. Since environmental impacts of aircraft noise have been addressed in the previous chapter, noise emissions are not discussed here.

10.3 Environmental impacts of aviation emissions

Aviation emissions have "the potential to have an impact on air quality in the local, regional and global environments."[17] Aircraft emitted nitrogen oxides (NO_X), CO, unburned HC, and PM contribute to the degradation of air quality that can affect human health.[18] Aviation is a small but significant contributor to climate change and global warming.[19] Emissions from aviation can drive ozone depletion as well.[20] Concern over aviation is mounting due to the fact that the aviation industry and related activities are growing rapidly outpacing technological innovation in this field toward reducing emissions.[21] It is expected that passenger traffic will grow "at an average rate of 4.8% per year through the year 2036."[22]

Aircraft emissions alter at different flight stages.[23] While major emissions from aircraft occur at higher altitudes, approximately 10 percent of all aircraft emissions, except HC and CO, occur during airport ground level operations and at landing and takeoff (LTO).[24] For CO and HC,

17 ICAO, "Airport Manual," *supra* note 9 at 1-2.
18 See Ian Waitz, Jessica Townsend, Joel Cutcher-Gershenfeld, Edward Greitzer, and Jack Kerrebrock, "Report to the United States Congress: Aviation and the Environment: A National Vision Statement, Framework for Goals and Recommended Actions" (Massachusetts Institute of Technology (MIT), 2004) at 15, online: web.mit.edu/aeroastro/partner/reports/congrept_aviation_envirn.pdf; Steven R.H. Barrett, Rex E. Britter, and Ian A. Waitz, "Global Mortality Attributable to Aircraft Cruise Emissions" (2010) 44:19 *Environmental Science & Technology* 7736 at 7736. See also H. Lee, S.C. Olsen, D.J. Wuebbles, and D. Youn, "Impacts of Aircraft Emissions on the Air Quality near the Ground" (2013) 13:11 *Atmospheric Chemistry & Physics* 5505; Leonor Tarrasón, Jan Eiof Jonson, Terje K. Berntsen, and Kristin Rypdal, "Study on Air Quality Impacts of Non-LTO Emissions from Aviation," Report No. 3, Air Pollution Section, Norwegian Meteorological Institute (met.no), Final Report to the European Commission (2004), online: ec.europa.eu/environment/air/pdf/air_quality_impacts_finalreport.pdf; Scott C. Herndon, J.T. Jayne, P. Lobo, T.B. Onasch, G. Fleming, D.E. Hagen, P.D. Whitefield, and R.C. Miaki-Lye, "Commercial Aircraft Engine Emissions Characterization of In-use Aircraft at Hartsfield-Jackson Atlanta International Airport" (2008) 42:6 *Environmental Science & Technology* 1877; Gregor Schürmann, Klaus Schäfer, Carsten Jahn, Herbert Hoffmann, Martina Bauerfeind, Emanuel Fleuti, and Bernhard Rappenglück, "The Impact of NOx, CO and VOC Emissions on the Air Quality of Zurich Airport" (2007) 41:1 *Atmospheric Environment* 103.
19 See Ahmad, "Environmental," *supra* note 12 at 80; D.S. Lee, L.L. Lim, and B. Owen, "Mitigating Future Aviation CO_2 Emissions: 'Timing is Everything'" (27 August 2013) at 2, online: www.cate.mmu.ac.uk/docs/mitigating-future-aviation-co2-emissions.pdf (Lee, "Mitigating").
20 See D.S. Lee, G. Pitari, V. Grewe, K. Gierens, J.E. Penner, A. Petzold, M.J. Parther, U. Schumann, A. Bais, T. Berntsen, D. Iachetti, L.L. Lim, and R. Sausen, "Transport Impacts on Atmosphere and Climate: Aviation" (2010) 44:37 *Atmospheric Environment* 4678.
21 See e.g. "Consolidated Statement of Continuing ICAO Policies and Practices related to Environmental Protection: Climate Change," ICAO Assembly Res. A38-18, 38th Sess., ICAO Doc. 10022, I-68 at I-68, online: www.icao.int/publications/Documents/10022_en.pdf (ICAO Res. A38-18); "Consolidated Statement of Continuing ICAO Policies and Practices related to Environmental Protection : Climate Change," ICAO Assembly Res. A37-19, 37th Sess., ICAO Doc. 9958, I-67, online: www.icao.int/publications/Documents/9958_en.pdf (ICAO Res. A37-19); ICAO Secretariat, "Aviation Outlook Overview" in ICAO, *ICAO Environmental Report 2010: Aviation and Climate Change* (Montreal: ICAO, 2010) 18 at 18 (ICAO Secretariat, "Aviation Outlook"); IPCC, "Summary for Policymakers," *supra* note 15; World Bank, "Air Transport," *supra* note 15 at 31.
22 ICAO Secretariat, "Aviation Outlook," *supra* note 21 at 18.
23 World Bank, "Air Transport," *supra* note 15 at 32.
24 See ibid.; Travis M. Norton, "Aircraft Greenhouse Gas Emissions during the Landing and Takeoff Cycle at Bay Area Airports" (Master's Project, University of San Francisco, 2014) at 11 (unpublished).

LTO operations make up 30 percent of emissions.[25] ICAO has defined a specific reference LTO cycle below a height of 3,000 ft above ground level.[26] This is referred to as "mixing height," i.e., "the height of the vertical mixing of the lower troposphere"[27] which extends to a height of approximately 3,000 ft.[28] While emissions below the mixing height have the potential to affect "local air quality concentrations," emission occurring closer to the ground have "possibly greater effects on ground level concentrations."[29] Aircraft emit gases and particles directly into the upper troposphere, the only human enterprise to do so,[30] and lower stratosphere which affect atmospheric composition by, *inter alia*, altering the concentration of atmospheric greenhouse gases, prompting the formation of condensation trails, called contrails,[31] and increasing cirrus cloudiness.[32] Like thin high clouds, "contrails tend to warm the Earth's surface."[33] All these effects of emissions from aircraft contribute to climate change and global warming.[34]

Carbon dioxide and water vapor are greenhouse gases. As one of the long-lived greenhouse gases,[35] CO_2 is chemically stable, has a long atmospheric residence time, and, consequently, it admixes throughout the atmosphere much faster than it is removed.[36]

---

25 See ibid. at 11.
26 ICAO, "Airport Manual," *supra* note 9 at 3-A1-2.
27 Ibid. at 3-A1-2, n. 2.
28 Ibid. at 3-A1-2.
29 Ibid.
30 According to the IPCC, aviation emissions are *"the predominant anthropogenic emissions deposited directly into the upper troposphere and lower stratosphere."* IPCC, "Summary for Policymakers," *supra* note 15 at 3 (emphasis in original).
31 "Contrails are triggered from the water vapor emitted by aircraft," ibid. at 7.
32 See ibid. at 3.

> Atmospheric changes from aircraft result from three types of processes: direct emission of radiatively active substances (e.g., CO_2 or water vapor); emission of chemical species that produce or destroy radiatively active substances (e.g., NO_X, which modifies O_3 concentration); and emission of substances that trigger the generation of aerosol particles or lead to changes in natural clouds (e.g., contrails).

> Michael Prather and Robert Sausen, eds., "Potential Climate Change from Aviation" in Penner, *Aviation, supra* note 15 185 at 187.

33 IPCC, "Summary for Policymakers," *supra* note 15 at 7.
34 See ibid. at 3.
35 See Susan Solomon, Dahe Qin, Martin Manning, Richard B. Alley, Terje Berntsen, Nathaniel L. Bindoff, Zhenlin Chen, Amnat Chidthaisong, Jonathan M. Gregory, Gabriele C. Hegerl, Martin Heimann, Bruce Hewitson, Brian J. Hoskins, Fortunat Joos, Jean Jouzel, Vladimir Kattsov, Ulrike Lohmann, Taroh Matsuno, Mario Molina, Neville Nicholls, Jonathan Overpeck, Graciela Raga, Venkatachalam Ramaswamy, Jiawen Ren, Matilde Rusticucci, Richard Somerville, Thomas F. Stocker, Penny Whetton, Richard A. Wood, and David Wratt, "Technical Summary" in Susan Solomon, Dahe Qin, Martin Manning, Melinda Marquis, Kristen Averyt, Melinda M.B. Tignor, Henry LeRoy Miller, and Zhenlin Chen, eds., *Climate Change 2007: The Physical Science Basis: Working Group I Contribution to the Fourth Assessment Report of the Intergovernmental Panel on Climate Change* (New York: Cambridge University Press, 2007) 19 at 23–24 (Solomon, "Technical"; Solomon, *Climate*):

> Long-lived greenhouse gases (LLGHGs), for example, CO_2, methane (CH_4) and nitrous oxide (N_2O), are chemically stable and persist in the atmosphere over time scales of a decade to centuries or longer, so that their emission has a long-term influence on climate. Because these gases are long lived, they become well mixed throughout the atmosphere much faster than they are removed and their global concentrations can be accurately estimated from data at a few locations.

36 Ibid.; IPCC, "Summary for Policymakers," supra note 15 at 3; Drew Shindell, "Simultaneously Mitigating Near-Term Climate Change and Improving Human Health and Food Security" (2012) 335 Science 183 at 184.

Carbon dioxide is considered to be the most important anthropogenic greenhouse gas;[37] it does not have a specific lifetime due to the fact that "it is continuously cycled between the atmosphere, oceans and land biosphere and its net removal from the atmosphere involves a range of processes with different time scales."[38] At present, civil aviation accounts for less than 2 percent of total global CO_2 emissions,[39] which is projected to grow around 3–4 percent per year.[40] Aviation is responsible for 12 percent of total CO_2 emissions from the transportation sector, compared to 74 percent from road transport,[41] and the CO_2 emissions from aviation are projected to grow to 23 percent by 2050 unless effective measures to curb such emissions are initiated.[42] Aviation would be the seventeenth largest emitter of CO_2 in 2010 if international civil aviation were a "country."[43]

The other gases and particles emitted by aircraft have shorter atmospheric residence times and remain concentrated near flight routes.[44] Nevertheless, it is worth mentioning that "the overall climate impact of aviation is much greater than the impact of CO_2 alone."[45] The effects of aircraft emitted NO_X and other gases "are estimated to be about two to four times greater than those of aviation's CO_2 alone, even without considering the potential impact of cirrus cloud enhancement."[46] These emissions can lead to radiative forcing that is regionally located near the flight routes for some components, e.g., ozone and contrails,[47] contrary to emissions that are globally mixed, e.g., CO_2 and methane (CH_4).[48] Radiative forcing is defined as:

---

37 See e.g. IPCC, "Summary for Policymakers" in Solomon, *Climate, supra* note 35 at 2.
38 Solomon, "Technical," *supra* note 35 at 24.
39 See ICAO Res. A38-18, *supra* note 21 at I-68; ATAG, "Facts & Figures," *supra* note 3; ICAO Secretariat, "Climate Change Outlook," *supra* note 3 ("[t]otal aviation CO_2 emissions (domestic and international) are approximately 2% of the world's anthropogenic (human-made) CO_2 emissions" at 31).
40 ICAO Secretariat, "Climate Change Outlook," *supra* note 39 at 31.
41 See ATAG, "Facts & Figures," *supra* note 3.
42 See World Bank, "Air Transport," *supra* note 15 at 31.
43 See Lee, "Mitigating," *supra* note 19 at 2; International Coalition for Sustainable Aviation (ICSA), "Effective Market-based Measures to Address Greenhouse Gas Emissions from International Aviation," ICAO Assembly, 38th Sess., Agenda Item 17, Working Paper No. 288, Doc. A38-WP/288/Ex/100 (12 September 2013), online: www.icao.int/Meetings/a38/Documents/WP/wp288_en.pdf:

   [t]aking into account the non-CO_2 effects of aircraft emissions (a critical issue that has fallen outside of ICAO's current focus), aviation today accounts for around 5% of the total radiative forcing attributable to manmade activities. In fact, the aviation sector would be the 7th largest emitter of greenhouse gases if it were a country.

   (at 2) (ICSA, "Effective").
44 See IPCC, "Summary for Policymakers," *supra* note 15 at 3.
45 Terry Barker, Igor Bashmakov, Lenny Bernstein, Jean E. Bogner, Peter Bosch, Rutu Dave, Ogunlade Davidson, Brian S. Fisher, Sujata Gupta, Kirsten Halsnæs, BertJan Heij, Suzana Kahn Ribeiro, Shigeki Kobayashi, Mark D. Levine, Daniel L. Martino, Omar Masera, Bert Metz, Leo Meyer, Gert-Jan Nabuurs, Adil Najam, Nebojsa Nakicenovic, Hans-Holger Rogner, Joyashree Roy, Jayant Sathaye, Robert Schock, Priayadarshi Shukla, Ralph E.H. Sims, Pete Smith, Dennis A. Tirpak, Diana Urge-Vorsatz, and Dadi Zhou, "Technical Summary" in Bert Metz, Ogunlade Davidson, Peter Bosch, Rutu Dave, andLeo Meyer, eds., *Climate Change 2007: Mitigation: Contribution of Working Group III to the Fourth Assessment Report of the Intergovernmental Panel on Climate Change* (New York: Cambridge University Press, 2007) 25 at 49 (Metz, *Climate*).
46 Ibid.
47 See World Bank, "Air Transport," *supra* note 15 at 31–32.
48 See IPCC, "Summary for Policymakers," *supra* note 15 at 3.

[T]he change in net (down minus up) irradiance (solar plus longwave; in $W\,m^{-2}$) at the tropopause after allowing for stratospheric temperatures to readjust to radiative equilibrium, but with surface and tropospheric temperatures and state held fixed at the unperturbed values.[49]

Radiative forcing is "a simple measure for both quantifying and ranking the many different influences on climate change."[50] Radiative forcing provides "a limited measure of climate change as it does not attempt to represent the overall climate response."[51] Nonetheless, "as climate sensitivity and other aspects of the climate response to external forcings remain inadequately quantified," radiative forcing has "the advantage of being more readily calculable and comparable than estimates of the climate response."[52]

Aircraft emitted NO_X, i.e., NO and NO_2 jointly, participate in ozone chemistry expediting climate change and global warming.[53] Ozone is one of the greenhouse gases and one of the common air pollutants.[54] Ozone "is continually produced and destroyed in the atmosphere by chemical reactions."[55] Human activities have increased ozone in the troposphere "through the release of gases such as carbon monoxide, hydrocarbons and nitrogen oxide, which chemically react to produce ozone."[56] Nevertheless, ozone protects the Earth's surface from harmful ultraviolet radiation.[57] Aircraft emitted NO_X more effectively produces ozone in the upper troposphere than do an

---

49 Piers Forster, Venkatachalam Ramaswamy, Paulo Artaxo, Terje Berntsen, Richard Betts, David W. Fahey, James Haywood, Judith Lean, David C. Lowe, Gunnar Myhre, John Nganga, Ronald Prinn, Graciela Raga, Michael Schulz, and Robert Van Dorland, "Changes in Atmospheric Constituents and in Radiative Forcing" in Solomon, *Climate*, *supra* note 35 at 133 (Forster, "Changes"):

> Ramaswamy et al. (2001) define it as 'the change in net (down minus up) irradiance (solar plus longwave; in $W\,m^{-2}$) at the tropopause after allowing for stratospheric temperatures to readjust to radiative equilibrium, but with surface and tropospheric temperatures and state held fixed at the unperturbed values'. Radiative forcing is used to assess and compare the anthropogenic and natural drivers of climate change. The concept arose from early studies of the climate response to changes in solar insolation and CO_2, using simple radiative-convective models. However, it has proven to be particularly applicable for the assessment of the climate impact of [long-lived greenhouse gases] (Ramaswamy et al., 2001). Radiative forcing can be related through a linear relationship to the global mean equilibrium temperature change at the surface (ΔT_s): $\Delta T_s = \lambda RF$, where λ is the climate sensitivity parameter (e.g., Ramaswamy et al., 2001). This equation, developed from these early climate studies, represents a linear view of global mean climate change between two equilibrium climate states.

50 Ibid.
51 Ibid.
52 Ibid.
53 See IPCC, "Summary for Policymakers," *supra* note 15 at 3. See Solomon, "Technical," *supra* note 35 at 24:

> Ozone is a significant greenhouse gas that is formed and destroyed by chemical reactions involving other species in the atmosphere. In the troposphere, the human influence on ozone occurs primarily through changes in precursor gases that lead to its formation, whereas in the stratosphere, the human influence has been primarily through changes in ozone removal rates caused by chlorofluorocarbons (CFCs) and other ozone-depleting substances.

54 See Forster, "Changes," *supra* note 49 at 135.
55 Ibid.
56 Ibid.
57 Ozone "also shields the surface of the [E]arth from harmful ultraviolet (UV) radiation, and is a common air pollutant." IPCC, "Summary for Policymakers," *supra* note 15 at 3.

equivalent amount of emissions at the surface.[58] In response to NO_X increases, ozone in the upper troposphere and lower stratosphere – the flying zone of subsonic aircraft – is expected to increase, and CH_4,[59] one of the long-lived greenhouse gases,[60] is expected to decrease.[61] At higher altitudes, where the supersonic aircraft fly,[62] increases in NO_X lead to decreases in the stratospheric ozone layer.[63] In these regions, ozone precursor (NO_X) residence times "increase with altitude, and hence perturbations to ozone by aircraft depend on the altitude of NO_X injection and vary from regional in scale in the troposphere to global in scale in the stratosphere."[64]

Furthermore, aircraft emitted water vapor, SO_XO that form sulfate particles, and soot, play both direct and indirect roles in ozone chemistry.[65] Sulfur and water emissions from aircraft "in the stratosphere tend to deplete ozone, partially offsetting the NO_X-induced ozone increases."[66] Nevertheless, science has not developed an ability to quantify the degree of such increases and depletions of ozone and, hence, the impact of subsonic aircraft emissions on stratospheric ozone needs further evaluation.[67]

Water vapor is the most abundant and important greenhouse gas in the atmosphere.[68] Nevertheless, human activities have only a small direct influence on the amount of atmospheric water vapor; indirectly, humans have the potential to affect water vapor substantially by changing climate.[69] For example, a warmer atmosphere contains more water vapor.[70] Human activities also influence water vapor through CH_4 emissions, because CH_4 undergoes chemical destruction in the stratosphere, producing a small amount of water vapor.[71] Water vapor from subsonic aircraft is mostly emitted in the troposphere, and a small fraction of such emissions occur in

---

58 See ibid. at 6.
59 Forster, "Changes," *supra* note 49 at 135:

> Methane has increased as a result of human activities related to agriculture, natural gas distribution and landfills. Methane is also released from natural processes that occur, for example, in wetlands. Methane concentrations are not currently increasing in the atmosphere because growth rates decreased over the last two decades.

60 See Solomon, "Technical," *supra* note 35 at 23–24.
61 See IPCC, "Summary for Policymakers," *supra* note 15 at 3 ("[i]n addition to increasing tropospheric ozone concentrations, aircraft NO_X emissions are expected to decrease the concentration of methane, which is also a greenhouse gas. These reductions in methane tend to cool the surface of the Earth" at 6).
62 At present, there is no commercial supersonic aircraft. Concorde, which was withdrawn from service 24 October 2003, was a commercial supersonic aircraft. Currently, only military aviation uses supersonic aircraft. See e.g. Bryony Jones, "Paris Air Show: Race to be first with 'son of supersonic'," *CNN* (21 June 2011), online: articles.cnn.com/2011-06-21/tech/concorde.hyper.sonic_1_supersonic-aircraft-concorde-ramjets?_s=PM:TECH; Jerry S. Lewis and Richard W. Niedzwiecki, eds., "Aircraft Technology and Its Relation to Emissions" in Penner, *Aviation, supra* note 15 at 261–266; British Airways, "Celebrating Concorde: About Concorde," online: www.britishairways.com/en-gb/information/about-ba/history-and-heritage/celebrating-concorde#flying; "End of an Era for Concorde," *BBC News* (24 October 2003), online: news.bbc.co.uk/2/hi/uk_news/3211053.stm.
63 See IPCC, "Summary for Policymakers," *supra* note 15 at 3.
64 Ibid.
65 See ibid. at 4.
66 Ibid. at 6.
67 See ibid.
68 Forster, "Changes," *supra* note 49 at 135.
69 Ibid.
70 Ibid.
71 Ibid.

the lower stratosphere.[72] While such emissions in the troposphere are rapidly removed by precipitation within one to two weeks, the smaller fraction of such emissions in the lower stratosphere can build up to larger concentrations leading to warming the surface of the Earth.[73] Nevertheless, for subsonic aircraft, this effect of water vapor on global warming is minimal compared to other aircraft emissions, e.g., CO_2 and NO_X.[74]

The actual effects of aircraft emitted contrails and aerosol on climate change and global warming are still unknown to modern science.[75] Aircraft emitted water vapor triggers the formation of contrails; the optical properties of contrails "depend on the particles emitted or formed in the aircraft plume and on the ambient atmospheric conditions."[76] However, the radiative effect of contrails relies on "their optical properties and global cover, both of which are uncertain."[77] The contrails created by aircraft may also have an impact on the environment.[78] However, research is not conclusive about whether these have a net warming or cooling effect on the Earth.[79] Under some meteorological conditions, these can remain in the atmosphere and form cirrus clouds that may have an effect on climate change.[80] For example, some research suggests that cirrus clouds "may have different cooling and warming effects, depending on whether flights occur during the day or night."[81] Research of this type "can identify whether there are any potential benefits to altering operational behavior."[82] More work is being done in the area of aviation operations and the aviation industry is helping with "research into the effects of contrails on climate change, including putting high-altitude atmospheric testing equipment on some passenger aircraft."[83]

Aerosols are "microscopic particles suspended in air."[84] In aviation, examples of aerosols are airborne sulfate particles and soot particles.[85] While increases in soot tend to warm the Earth's surface, increases in sulfate tend to cool the surface.[86] However, the direct radiative forcing of these aerosols from aircraft is "small compared to those of other aircraft emissions."[87] Since aerosols shape "the formation of clouds, the accumulation of aerosols from aircraft *may* play a role in enhanced cloud formation and change the radiative properties of clouds."[88]

Though aviation is a small contributor to air quality degradation, ozone depletion, climate change, and global warming, several factors necessitate immediate and firm action from the air transport sector toward halting aviation emissions that contribute to such environmental degradation. Those factors include the rapid growth of the aviation industry and aviation-related activities outpacing technological reductions in emissions, the fact that aviation is the only

72 See IPCC, "Summary for Policymakers," *supra* note 15 at 7.
73 See ibid.
74 See ibid.
75 See Forster, "Changes," *supra* note 49 at 186–188.
76 IPCC, "Summary for Policymakers," *supra* note 15 at 7.
77 Ibid.
78 See World Bank, "Air Transport," *supra* note 15 at 31–32.
79 Ibid. at 31.
80 Ibid.
81 Ibid.
82 Ibid. at 31–32.
83 Ibid. at 32.
84 IPCC, "Summary for Policymakers," *supra* note 15 at 4, n. 5.
85 Ibid.
86 See ibid. at 8.
87 Ibid.
88 Ibid. (emphasis added).

human enterprise to emit pollutants directly into the upper troposphere and lower stratosphere,[89] disruption of air transport facilities due to natural disasters caused by climate change, the proverb "prevention is better than cure,"[90] and the need to combat global environmental problems globally, simultaneously, and collectively by all sectors.

10.4 The international framework for the reduction of emissions

International environmental law on the protection of the atmosphere focuses on three issues, namely, transboundary air pollution, ozone depletion, and climate change, all of which largely developed during the last development stage of international environmental law.[91] The development of international environmental law is commonly divided into three stages.[92] During the first stage that pre-dates the 1972 United Nations (UN) Conference on the Human Environment,[93] environmental benefits were viewed as incidental to largely economic concerns such as the exploitation of living natural resources.[94] During the second stage, a significant rise in the number of treaties directed to pollution abatement and to species and habitat conservation, yet largely reactive and piecemeal in nature, can be observed.[95] This stage commenced with the creation of

89 See ibid. at 3.
90 The fifth IPCC assessment report states:

> Substantial emissions reductions over the next few decades can reduce climate risks in the twenty-first century and beyond, increase prospects for effective adaptation, reduce the costs and challenges of mitigation in the longer term and contribute to climate-resilient pathways for sustainable development.

The Core Writing Team, Rajendra K. Pachauri and Leo Meyer, eds., *Climate Change 2014: Synthesis Report: Contribution of Working Groups I, II and III to the Fifth Assessment Report of the Intergovernmental Panel on Climate Change* (Geneva: IPCC, 2015) at 17. See also Paul Stephen Dempsey, *Public International Air Law* (Montreal: McGill University, Institute and Centre for Research in Air & Space Law, 2008) (Dempsey, *Public International Air Law*) ("[t]he long-term cost of inaction with regard to prevention of climate change will most probably be far surpassed by the cost of cure" at 411 (footnote omitted)); Nicholas Stern, *The Economics of Climate Change: The Stern Review* (Cambridge: Cambridge University Press, 2007); Ottmar Edenhofer, Christian Flachsland, Michael Jakob, and Kai Lessmann, "The Atmosphere as a Global Commons: Challenges for International Cooperation and Governance," Discussion Paper 13–58, Harvard Project on Climate Agreements, Belfer Center for Science and International Affairs, John F Kennedy School of Government, Harvard University (August 2013) at 20, online: belfercenter.ksg.harvard.edu/publication/23364/atmosphere_as_a_global_commtonschallenges_for_international_cooperation_and_governance.html?breadcrumb=%2Fproject%2F56%2Fharvard_project_on_climate_agreements%3Fgroupby%3D0%26parent_id%3D%26page_id%3D211%26filter%3D2013.
91 See Catherine Redgwell, "International Environmental Law" in Malcolm D. Evans, ed., *International Law*, 3rd ed. (New York: Oxford University Press, 2010) 687 at 687–692 ("[t]here are three principal areas of international regulatory activity in respect of protection of the atmosphere – transboundary air pollution, ozone depletion, and global warming [or climate change]" at 701) (Redgwell, "International Environmental Law"). See also Ian H. Rowlands, "Atmosphere and Outer Space" in Daniel Bodansky, Jutta Brunnée, and Ellen Hey, eds., *The Oxford Handbook of International Environmental Law* (New York: Oxford University Press, 2007) 315 at 316ff. (Rowlands, "Atmosphere"); Patricia Birnie, Alan Boyle, and Catherine Redgwell, *International Law and the Environment*, 3rd ed. (New York: Oxford University Press, 2009) at 335ff. (Birnie, *International Law*).
92 Redgwell, "International Environmental Law," *supra* note 91 at 687, 690.
93 This was the first global environmental conference. See Günther Handl, "Declaration of the United Nations Conference on the Human Environment (Stockholm Declaration), 1972 and the Rio Declaration on Environment and Development, 1992," United Nations Audiovisual Library of International Law (2012) at 1, online: legal.un.org/avl/pdf/ha/dunche/dunche_e.pdf (Handl, "Declaration").
94 Redgwell, "International Environmental Law," *supra* note 91 at 687, 690.
95 Ibid.

international institutions from 1945 and saw its culmination in the 1972 Stockholm Conference.[96] The third and final stage that characterizes existing international environmental law "demonstrates a precautionary approach to environmental problems of global magnitude such as biodiversity conservation and climate change."[97] This last stage "witnesses instruments adopting a holistic approach to environmental protection and seeks to marry such protection with economic development, embraced in the concept of sustainable development."[98] This was the theme of the 1992 UN Conference on Environment and Development that, in addition to producing the Rio Declaration and Agenda 21,[99] witnessed the conclusion of two major treaties, namely, the Convention on Biological Diversity,[100] and the United Nations Framework Convention on Climate Change (UNFCCC),[101] under the auspices of the UN.[102] The UNFCCC and the Kyoto Protocol to the UNFCCC,[103] the two international agreements, are the existing global measures to arrest climate change and global warming by reducing emissions of greenhouse gases. The following sections provide a brief overview of the international framework for reduction of emissions.

10.4.1 Stockholm Declaration

In 1968, on recommendation from the UN Economic and Social Council,[104] the UN General Assembly decided to convene a UN Conference on Human Environment (Stockholm Conference) in 1972.[105] The main purpose of the conference was:

> [T]o serve as a practical means to encourage, and to provide guidelines for, action by Governments and international organizations designed to protect and improve the human environment and to remedy and prevent its impairment, by means of international cooperation, bearing in mind the particular importance of enabling developing countries to forestall the occurrence of such problems.[106]

---

96 Ibid. at 690.
97 Ibid. at 687.
98 Ibid. at 691.
99 Rio Declaration on Environment and Development, UN Doc. A/CONF.151/5/Rev.1 (1992), 31 ILM 874, online: www.unep.org/Documents.Multilingual/Default.asp?documentid=78&articleid= 1163 (Rio Declaration); "Agenda 21" in "Report of the United Nations Conference on Environment and Development," vol. 1, Resolutions adopted by the Conference, Annex II, UN Doc. A/ CONF.151/26/Rev.1 (1993) 12, online: www.unep.org/Documents.Multilingual/Default.asp? documentid=52 (Agenda 21).
100 Convention on Biological Diversity, 5 June 1992, 1760 UNTS 79, Can. TS 1993 No. 24 (entered into force 29 December 1993).
101 United Nations Framework Convention on Climate Change, 9 May 1992, 1771 UNTS 107, Can. TS 1994 No. 7 (entered into force 21 March 1994) (UNFCCC).
102 Redgwell, "International Environmental Law," *supra* note 91 at 691.
103 Kyoto Protocol to the United Nations Framework Convention on Climate Change, 11 December 1997, 2303 UNTS 162 (entered into force 16 February 2005) (Kyoto Protocol).
104 See "Question of Convening an International Conference on the Problems of Human Environment," ESC Res. 1346 (XLV), UNESCOR, 1968, online: www.un.org/en/ga/search/view_doc. asp?symbol=e/res/1346(XLV).
105 See "Problems of the Human Environment," GA Res. 2398 (XXIII), UNGAOR, 23rd Sess. (1968), online:daccess-dds-ny.un.org/doc/RESOLUTION/GEN/NR0/243/58/IMG/NR024358.pdf?Open Element.
106 United Nations Conference on the Human Environment, GA Res. 2581 (XXIV), UNGAOR, 24th Sess. (1969), online: daccess-dds-ny.un.org/doc/RESOLUTION/GEN/NR0/257/15/IMG/NR02 5715.pdf?OpenElement.

Hence, one of the essential objectives of the conference was

> a declaration on the human environment, a "document of basic principles," whose basic idea originated with a proposal by the [UN] Educational, Scientific and Cultural Organization (UNESCO) that the conference draft a "Universal Declaration on the Protection and Preservation of the Human Environment."[107]

The Stockholm Conference was held in Stockholm from 5 to 16 June 1972, and produced the Stockholm Declaration and an Action Programme.[108] The declaration contains "a preamble featuring seven introductory proclamations"[109] and 26 principles "to inspire and guide the peoples of the world in the preservation and enhancement of the human environment."[110] Although a soft law instrument, the declaration included principles that at the time of its adoption were "either understood to already reflect customary international law or expected to shape future normative expectations."[111] Notably, Principle 21 of the declaration is an established customary international law principle and, arguably, forms the basis for the main three treaties on international environmental law on the protection of the atmosphere, namely, the Convention on Long-range Transboundary Air Pollution (LRTAP Convention),[112] the Vienna Convention for the Protection of the Ozone Layer (Vienna Convention),[113] and the UNFCCC.[114] Principle 21 provides:

> States have, in accordance with the Charter of the United Nations and the principles of international law, the sovereign right to exploit their own resources pursuant to their own environmental policies, and the responsibility to ensure that activities within their jurisdiction or control do not cause damage to the environment of other States or of areas beyond the limits of national jurisdiction.[115]

107 Handl, "Declaration," *supra* note 93 at 1.
108 "Declaration of the United Nations Conference on the Human Environment, 1972, in Report of the United Nations Conference on the Human Environment," UNESCOR, UN Doc. A/Conf.48/14/ Rev. 1 (1972), online: www.unep.org/Documents.multilingual/Default.asp?DocumentID=97&Arti cleID=1503 (Stockholm Declaration).
109 Handl, "Declaration," *supra* note 93 at 3.
110 See Stockholm Declaration, *supra* note 108.
111 Handl, "Declaration," *supra* note 93 at 3.
112 See Convention on Long-range Transboundary Air Pollution, 13 November 1979, 1302 UNTS 217, Can. TS 1983 No. 34 (entered into force 16 March 1983) (LRTAP Convention).
113 Vienna Convention for the Protection of the Ozone Layer, 22 March 1985, 1513 UNTS 293, Can. TS 1988 No. 23 (entered into force 22 September 1988) (Vienna Convention).
114 Birnie, *International Law*, *supra* note 91 at 339.
115 Stockholm Declaration, *supra* note 108, Principle 21. This principle "is related to the obligation of all states 'to protect within the territory the rights of other states, in particular their right to integrity and inviolability in peace and war'." Philippe Sands and Jacqueline Peel, *Principles of International Environmental Law*, 3rd ed. (New York: Cambridge University Press, 2012) at 196 (footnotes omitted); *The Island of Palmas Case (or Miangas) (United States v Netherlands)* (1928), 11 RIAA 829 at 839 (Permanent Court of Arbitration) (Arbitrator: M. Huber) (*Island of Palmas* case). This obligation of States was subsequently relied upon and elaborated in the famous *Trail Smelter* arbitration where it was held that the principles of international law do not grant any State "the right to use or permit the use of its territory in such a manner as to cause injury by fumes in or to the territory of another or the properties or persons therein, when the case is of serious consequence and the injury is established by clear and convincing evidence." *Trail Smelter Arbitration (United States v Canada)* (1938), 3 RIAA 1905 at 1965, reprinted in 33 AJIL 182 (Arbitrators: Charles Warren, Robert A.E. Greenshields, Jan Frans Hostie)

10.4.2 Convention on Long-range Transboundary Air Pollution

After the Stockholm Conference, new environmental issues on the protection of the atmosphere arose "that had not been perceived earlier, such as long-range air pollution and depletion of the ozone layer."[116] Hence, new legal instruments to address those issues became essential. The first international legally binding instrument to address the issue of air pollution is the LRTAP Convention concluded in 1979.[117] The Convention addresses long-range transboundary air pollution, and is regional, not global, in nature.[118] According to the Preamble, the Parties to the Convention considered the relevant provisions of the Stockholm Declaration, particularly Principle 21.[119] The Convention lays down "the general principles of international cooperation for air pollution abatement, [and] sets up an institutional framework bringing together research and policy."[120] Fundamental principles of the Convention include: protecting man and his environment against air pollution;[121] endeavoring to limit and, to the extent possible, progressively reduce and prevent air pollution;[122] developing policies and strategies to combat air pollution;[123] and, exchanging information on, and reviewing, their policies, scientific activities, and technical measures aimed at combating air pollution.[124]

Although not dubbed a framework treaty, the Convention mainly provides for a framework for future agreements to, among others, address specific pollutants and set strict reduction limits.[125]

(*Trail Smelter*). "Within international environmental law, apart from a specific breach of the Climate Change Convention regime, States are subject to the universal notion of State responsibility for transboundary environmental harm (*Trail Smelter Arbitration*, 1941)." David M. Ong, "International Legal Efforts to Address Human-induced Global Climate Change" in Malgosia Fitzmaurice, David M. Ong, and Panos Merkouris, eds., *Research Handbook on International Environmental Law* (Cheltenham, UK: Edward Elgar, 2010) 450 at 452 (emphasis in original). The International Court of Justice (ICJ), in the *Legality of the Threat or Use of Nuclear Weapons Case*, opined that "[t]he existence of the general obligation of States to ensure that activities within their jurisdiction and control respect the environment of other States or of areas beyond national control is now part of the corpus of international law relating to the environment." *Legality of the Threat or Use of Nuclear Weapons Case*, Advisory Opinion [1996] ICJ Rep 226 at 241–242 (*Nuclear Weapons* case). See also "Report of the Commission to the General Assembly on the Work of its Fifty-third Session" (UN Doc. A/56/10) in *Yearbook of the International Law Commission 2001*, vol 2, part 2 (New York: UN, 2007) at 148 (UNDOC A/CN.4/SER.A/2001/Add.1 (Part 2)) (*ILC Report of 53rd Session*); *Award in the Arbitration regarding the Iron Rhine Railway (Belgium v Netherlands)* (2005), ICGJ 373 at para. 222 (Permanent Court of Arbitration) (*Iron Rhine Arbitration*).

116 Alexandre Kiss and Dinah Shelton, *International Environmental Law*, 3rd ed. (Ardsley, NY: Transnational Publishers, 2004) at 50 (Kiss, *International*).
117 See UN Economic Commission for Europe (UNECE), "The Convention: The 1979 Geneva Convention on Long-range Transboundary Air Pollution," online: www.unece.org/fr/env/lrtap/lrtap_h1.html (UNECE, "The Convention").
118 Except Canada and the United States, all the Parties to the Convention are European States. The European Union is a Party as well. The Convention has 51 Parties. For more information regarding the status of the Convention, see online: treaties.un.org/Pages/ViewDetails.aspx?src=TREATY&mtdsg_no=XXVII-1&chapter=27&lang=en.
119 LRTAP Convention, *supra* note 112, Preamble.
120 UNECE, "The Convention," *supra* note 117.
121 LRTAP Convention, *supra* note 112, art. 2.
122 Ibid.
123 Ibid. art 3.
124 Ibid. art 4.
125 See e.g. David Hunter, James Salzman, and Durwood Zaelke, *International Environmental Law and Policy*, 4th ed. (New York: Thomson Reuters/Foundation Press, 2011) at 526.

To date, eight protocols have been concluded.[126] Among those, two protocols address sulfur dioxide (SO_2) emissions,[127] one addresses NO_X emissions,[128] one addresses VOC emissions,[129] one addresses emissions of persistent organic pollutants (POPs),[130] and one addresses acidification, eutrophication, and ground-level ozone.[131] However, this Convention along with its protocols do not address emissions from aviation.

10.4.3 Vienna Convention

In 1985, the Vienna Convention was adopted with the primary purpose "to protect human health and the environment against adverse effects resulting or likely to result from human activities which modify or are likely to modify the ozone layer."[132] The Vienna Convention is one of the first to perceive the necessity of "preventive action in advance of firm proof of actual harm, and in that sense it is indicative of the emergence of a more 'precautionary' approach than had been typical for earlier pollution conventions."[133] Instead of requiring the Parties to the Convention "to take concrete actions to control ozone depleting substances," the Convention "served as a framework for efforts to protect the globe's ozone layer."[134] Hence, the Convention is often referred to as a framework treaty.[135]

Similar to the LRTAP Convention, the Parties to the Vienna Convention recalled the Stockholm Declaration,[136] specifically Principle 21.[137] The Vienna Convention places an obligation on the Parties to "take appropriate measures in accordance with the provisions of this Convention and of those protocols in force to which they are party" to achieve the Convention's primary purpose mentioned above.[138] To this end, the Parties are required to take certain initiatives, in proportion to the means at their disposal and capabilities. Those initiatives are: to

---

126 See UNECE, "Protocols," online: www.unece.org/fr/env/lrtap/status/lrtap_s.html.
127 Those protocols are: Protocol to the 1979 Convention on Long-Range Transboundary Air Pollution on the Reduction of Sulphur Emissions or their Transboundary Fluxes by at least 30 percent, 8 July 1985, 1480 UNTS 215; Protocol to the 1979 Convention on Long-Range Transboundary Air Pollution on Further Reduction of Sulphur Emissions, 14 June 1994, 2030 UNTS 122.
128 That protocol is: Protocol to the 1979 Convention on Long-range Transboundary Air Pollution concerning the Control of Emissions of Nitrogen Oxides or their Transboundary Fluxes, 31 October 1988, 1593 UNTS 287.
129 That protocol is: Protocol to the 1979 Convention on Long-range Transboundary Air Pollution concerning the Control of Emissions of Volatile Organic Compounds or their Transboundary Fluxes, 18 November 1991, 2001 UNTS 187.
130 That protocol is: Protocol to the 1979 Convention on Long-range Transboundary Air Pollution on Persistent Organic Pollutants, 24 June 1998, 2230 UNTS 79.
131 That protocol is: Protocol to the 1979 Convention on Long-range Transboundary Air Pollution to Abate Acidification, Eutrophication and Ground-level Ozone, 30 November 1999, 2319 UNTS 81.
132 Vienna Convention, *supra* note 113, art. 2(1). The Convention was concluded with the determination to protect human health and the environment against adverse effects resulting from modifications of the ozone layer. Ibid. Preamble. For the latest version of the Convention, see UNEP, *Handbook for the Vienna Convention for the Protection of the Ozone Layer (1985)*, 9th ed. (Nairobi: UNEP Secretariat for the Vienna Convention for the Protection of the Ozone Layer & the Montreal Protocol on Substances that Deplete the Ozone Layer, 2012).
133 Birnie, *International Law, supra* note 91 at 351.
134 UNEP, Ozone Secretariat, "The Vienna Convention for the Protection of the Ozone Layer," online: ozone.unep.org/new_site/en/vienna_convention.php (UNEP, "Vienna Convention").
135 See ibid.
136 Stockholm Declaration, *supra* note 108.
137 See Vienna Convention, *supra* note 113, Preamble.
138 Ibid. art. 2(1).

cooperate by means of systemic observations, research, and information exchange; to adopt appropriate legislative or administrative measures; to cooperate in harmonizing appropriate policies to control, limit, reduce, or prevent human activities under their jurisdiction or control; to cooperate in the formulation of agreed measures, procedures, and standards for the implementation of this Convention; and to cooperate with competent international bodies to implement effectively this Convention and Protocols to which they are Party.[139] The following chemical substances of natural and anthropogenic origin are thought to have the potential to modify the chemical and physical properties of the ozone layer: carbon substances (CO, CO_2, CH_4, and non-methane HC species), nitrogen substances (nitrous oxide (N_2O), and NO_X), hydrogen substances (hydrogen (H_2), and water (H_2O)), chlorine substances, and bromine substances.[140] The Convention established a Conference of the Parties with the responsibility, *inter alia*, to "keep under continuous review the implementation of this Convention."[141] Annexes to the Vienna Convention or to any Protocol shall form an integral part of this Convention or of such Protocol,[142] and no reservation may be made to this Convention.[143] The Parties to the Convention meet triennially "in order to take decisions designed to administer the Convention."[144]

In 2009, the Convention "became the first Convention of any kind to achieve universal ratification."[145] The Convention has 197 Parties.[146] Since the Convention provides a framework for further action, it became necessary to adopt a Protocol to the Convention that would require the Parties to take solid action to regulate ozone-depleting substances. Article 8 of the Convention provides for the adoption of a Protocol to this Convention that gave birth to the Montreal Protocol.[147]

10.4.4 Montreal Protocol

The Montreal Protocol to the Vienna Convention was concluded in 1987.[148] The Parties to the Protocol are determined

> to protect the ozone layer by taking precautionary measures to control equitably total global emissions of substances that deplete it, with the ultimate objective of their elimination on the basis of developments in scientific knowledge, taking into account technical and economic considerations.[149]

139 Ibid. art. 2(2). However, the Convention does not define the nature of such measures. See Birnie, *International Law, supra* note 91 at 350.
140 Vienna Convention, *supra* note 113, Annex I(4).
141 See ibid. art. 6.
142 See ibid. art. 10(1).
143 Ibid. art. 18.
144 UNEP, "Vienna Convention," *supra* note 134.
145 Ibid.
146 To learn more about the status of this convention, see UN Treaty Collection, online: treaties.un.org/pages/ViewDetails.aspx?src=TREATY&mtdsg_no=XXVII-2&chapter=27&lang=en.
147 Vienna Convention, *supra* note 113, art. 8.
148 Montreal Protocol on Substances that Deplete the Ozone Layer, 16 September 1987, 1522 UNTS 3, Can. TS 1989 No. 42 (entered into force 1 January 1989) (Montreal Protocol). For the latest version of the Protocol, see UNEP, *Handbook for the Montreal Protocol on Substances that Deplete the Ozone Layer*, 9th ed. (Nairobi: UNEP Secretariat for the Vienna Convention for the Protection of the Ozone Layer & the Montreal Protocol on Substances that Deplete the Ozone Layer, 2012) (*Handbook for the Montreal Protocol*).
149 Montreal Protocol, *supra* note 148, Preamble.

The Protocol provides for control measures,[150] which have to be assessed and reviewed by the Parties on the basis of available scientific, environmental, technical, and economic information, commencing in 1990, and at least every four years thereafter.[151] Some authors consider this requirement – to assess and review control measures – as the most important innovation of the Montreal Protocol and the most impressive feature of the ozone-depletion regime.[152] Based on that assessment, "[c]ombined majorities of industrialized and developing states are empowered to amend standards set by the protocol for production and consumption of controlled ozone-depleting substances."[153] Once these adjustments have been adopted, they become automatically binding on all Parties to the Protocol.[154] If any State does not find such an amendment acceptable, "[w]ithdrawal from the protocol is then the only option left for" that State.[155] This precedent of the Montreal Protocol is unique among environmental agreements, Birnie, Boyle, and Redgwell argue.[156]

The Protocol imposes a reporting obligation on the Parties regarding statistical data on their production, imports, and exports of the controlled substances.[157] To ensure more effectiveness of the control measures and to ensure that non-Parties do not benefit from the control measures obligatory on the Parties to the Protocol, a restriction on export–import of controlled substances is imposed.[158] A later amendment introduces a new export–import licensing system for better implementation of the Protocol.[159] The Protocol contains a non-compliance procedure,[160] "the first multilateral environmental agreement to do so."[161] Concerning this procedure, it is argued that, "although the non-compliance procedure is an example of 'soft enforcement', it is not without teeth, and it has enabled the parties to give serious and sustained attention to their responsibility for reviewing implementation of the protocol."[162] The Parties to the Protocol are required to cooperate in promoting research, development, and exchange of information on best technologies for improving the containment, recovery, recycling, or destruction of controlled substances, on possible alternatives to controlled substances, to products containing such substances, and to products manufactured with them, and on costs and benefits of relevant control strategies.[163] Furthermore, cooperation in promoting public awareness of the environmental effects of the emissions of controlled substances and other substances that deplete the ozone layer is made obligatory under the Protocol.[164] Like the Vienna Convention,[165] no

---

150 See ibid. art. 2.
151 Ibid. art. 6.
152 See Rowlands, "Atmosphere," *supra* note 91 at 323.
153 Birnie, *International Law*, *supra* note 91 at 92 (footnote omitted). See Montreal Protocol, *supra* note 148, art. 2(9). See the amended art. 2(9) in *Handbook for the Montreal Protocol*, *supra* note 148 at 5.
154 Birnie, *International Law*, *supra* note 91 at 92.
155 Ibid.
156 Ibid.
157 Montreal Protocol, *supra* note 148, art. 7.
158 See ibid. art. 4.
159 See ibid. art. 4B in *Handbook for the Montreal Protocol*, *supra* note 148 at 14–15.
160 See Montreal Protocol, *supra* note 148, art. 8, which provides: "The Parties, at their first meeting, shall consider and approve procedures and institutional mechanisms for determining non-compliance with the provisions of this Protocol and for treatment of Parties found to be in non-compliance."
161 Birnie, *International Law*, *supra* note 91 at 353 (footnote omitted). See also Rowlands, "Atmosphere," *supra* note 91 at 324.
162 See Birnie, *International Law*, *supra* note 91 at 354.
163 Montreal Protocol, *supra* note 148, art. 9(1).
164 Ibid. arts. 9(2), 10(1).
165 See Vienna Convention, *supra* note 113, art. 18.

reservations may be made to the Montreal Protocol.[166] To date, four amendments to the Protocol have been made.[167]

The Protocol regulates 95 ozone-depleting substances grouped as chlorofluorocarbons (CFCs), halons, other fully halogenated CFCs, carbon tetrachloride, methyl chloroform, hydrochlorofluorocarbons (HCFCs), hydrobromofluorocarbons (HBFCs), bromochloromethane, and methyl bromide.[168] The Protocol requires a phased reduction of these substances.[169] The Protocol applies to aviation as far as these controlled substances are concerned, though aviation is not specifically mentioned in the Protocol.[170] Like the Vienna Convention, the Montreal Protocol and all its four amendments have 197 Parties and, hence, have achieved universal ratification.[171] The ozone-depletion regime, composed of the Vienna Convention and the Montreal Protocol, "continues to be celebrated as one of the most 'successful' multilateral environmental agreements of our time."[172] Particularly, the Montreal Protocol is "considered to be a very effective agreement."[173] However, the Protocol's "success is difficult to transfer to other environmental problems."[174] The Protocol's success can be attributable to the following factors: "CFCs were produced by a very small number of facilities, less damaging technology was available, and the industry supported the Protocol."[175]

10.4.5 Rio Declaration

The second global environmental conference, namely the UN Conference on Environment and Development (Rio Conference), took place in Rio de Janeiro from 3 to 14 June 1992.[176] The initial goal of the Rio Conference was "to proclaim an Earth Charter, i.e., principles containing general environmental obligations of states."[177] However, due to opposition from the Group of 77 developing States and China, the proposal for an Earth Charter was defeated.[178] Instead, a soft law instrument in the form of a declaration, called the Rio Declaration,[179] was adopted by more than 178 States.[180] In addition to the Declaration, the conference also adopted

---

166 Montreal Protocol, *supra* note 148, art. 18.
167 See *Handbook for the Montreal Protocol*, *supra* note 148 at 643.
168 See Montreal Protocol, *supra* note 148, Annexes A–C, E; *Handbook for the Montreal Protocol*, *supra* note 148, section 1.2.
169 See Montreal Protocol, *supra* note 148, art. 2; Arnold W. Reitze, "Air and Climate Change" in Roger R. Martella and J. Brett Grosko, eds., *International Environmental Law: The Practitioner's Guide to the Laws of the Planet* (Chicago, IL: American Bar Association, 2014) 61 at 68 (Reitze, "Air").
170 For more information, see *Handbook for the Montreal Protocol*, *supra* note 148 at 170–173, 268–269, 523.
171 See UNEP, Ozone Secretariat, "Treaties and Decisions," online: ozone.unep.org/en/treaties.php.
172 Feja Lesniewska, "Filling the Holes: The Montreal Protocol's Non-compliance Mechanism" in Malgosia Fitzmaurice, David M. Ong, and Panos Merkouris, eds., *Research Handbook on International Environmental Law* (Cheltenham, UK: Edward Elgar, 2010) 471 at 471.
173 Reitze, "Air," *supra* note 169 at 69.
174 Ibid.
175 Ibid.
176 See UN, "UNCED: United Nations Conference on Environment and Development," online: www.un.org/jsummit/html/basic_info/unced.html (UN, "UNCED"). See also Handl, "Declaration," *supra* note 93 at 1.
177 Kiss, *International*, *supra* note 116 at 54.
178 See Handl, "Declaration," *supra* note 93 at 3.
179 Rio Declaration, *supra* note 99.
180 See UN, "Sustainable Development Knowledge Platform: Agenda 21," online: sustainabledevelopment.un.org/index.php?page=view&nr=23&type=400 (UN, "Agenda 21"); UN, "UNCED," *supra* note 176; Handl, "Declaration," *supra* note 93 at 3.

Agenda 21,[181] and the Statement of Forest Principles.[182] Two major treaties, namely, the Convention on Biological Diversity[183] and the UNFCCC,[184] which had been drafted and adopted before the conference, were opened for signature at the Rio Conference.[185]

The Rio Declaration contains a Preamble and 27 Principles.[186] The goal of the Declaration is to establish "a new and equitable global partnership through the creation of new levels of cooperation among States, key sectors of societies and people."[187] The Declaration reaffirms and builds upon the Stockholm Declaration,[188] and this fact "reinforces the normative significance of those concepts common to both" the Rio Declaration and the Stockholm Declaration.[189] For example, the established customary international law principle contained in Principle 21 of the Stockholm Declaration is reproduced in Principle 2 of the Rio Declaration, though with slightly different wording.[190] Whereas the former is concerned with environmental policies of States,[191] the latter is concerned with both environmental and "developmental" policies.[192] Concern over developmental policies in the Rio Declaration is understandable, since the Rio Declaration's "approach and philosophy are very different" from the Stockholm Declaration.[193] Unlike the Stockholm Declaration, the central concept of the Rio Declaration is sustainable development that "integrates development and environmental protection."[194] Most Principles of the Rio Declaration concern sustainable development. Most importantly, Principle 4 provides that, "[i]n order to achieve sustainable development, environmental protection shall constitute an integral part of the development process and cannot be considered in isolation from it."[195] Apart from the principle of sustainable development, the Declaration includes some "then-emerging"[196] principles of international environmental law. These principles include: the principle of common but differentiated responsibility,[197] the precautionary principle,[198] and the polluter pays principle.[199]

---

181 Agenda 21, *supra* note 99.
182 "Non-Legally Binding Authoritative Statement of Principles for a Global Consensus on the Management, Conservation and Sustainable Development of All Types of Forests, 1992, in Report of the United Nations Conference on Environment and Development," UN Doc. A/CONF.151/26 (vol. III) (1992) ("Statement of Forest Principles"). The ("Statement of Forest Principles" is "a set of 15 non-legally binding Principles governing national and international policy-making for the protection and a more sustainable management and use of global forest resources." UN, "UNCED," *supra* note 176.
183 Convention on Biological Diversity, *supra* note 100.
184 UNFCCC, *supra* note 101.
185 See Kiss, *International*, *supra* note 116 at 55.
186 See Rio Declaration, *supra* note 99.
187 Ibid. Preamble.
188 Ibid.; Handl, "Declaration," *supra* note 93 at 3.
189 Handl, "Declaration," *supra* note 93 at 3.
190 Rio Declaration, *supra* note 99, Principle 2, provides:

> States have, in accordance with the Charter of the United Nations and the principles of international law, the sovereign right to exploit their own resources pursuant to their own environmental and developmental policies, and the responsibility to ensure that activities within their jurisdiction or control do not cause damage to the environment of other States or of areas beyond the limits of national jurisdiction.

191 See Stockholm Declaration, supra note 108, Principle 21.
192 See Rio Declaration, *supra* note 99, Principle 2.
193 Kiss, *International*, *supra* note 116 at 55.
194 Ibid.
195 Rio Declaration, *supra* note 99, Principle 4.
196 Kiss, *International*, *supra* note 116 at 56.
197 See Rio Declaration, *supra* note 99, Principle 7.
198 See ibid. Principle 15.
199 See ibid. Principle 16.

Agenda 21 is "a comprehensive plan of action to be taken globally, nationally and locally by organizations of the [UN] System, Governments, and Major Groups in every area in which human impacts on the environment."[200] Therefore, as one of the specialized organizations of the UN system, ICAO has the mandate to adopt this plan of action in international civil aviation, since emissions from aviation have impacts on the environment.[201] This program of action consists of 40 chapters with 115 particular topics.[202] Although not legally binding, Agenda 21 is "potentially relevant to interpretation of treaties and other instruments adopted in accordance with its provisions."[203] Agenda 21 demands "new ways of investing in our future to reach global sustainable development in the 21st century."[204] The recommendations of this program of action "ranged from new ways to educate, to new ways to care for natural resources, and new ways to participate in designing a sustainable economy."[205]

10.4.6 United Nations Framework Convention on Climate Change

The issue of climate change has been on "a number of different scientific agendas for over a century."[206] However, "substantial legal attention was not directed to the issue until the mid-1980s."[207] Eventually, the issue became rooted in the UN system at the end of 1990 when the UN General Assembly established the Intergovernmental Negotiating Committee for the UNFCCC. The Committee met and debated over a period of 15 months, and finally adopted the UNFCCC.[208] As mentioned earlier, the Convention was opened for signature at the Rio Conference.

In the Preamble to the UNFCCC,[209] a number of principles, most of which are considered "emerging principles,"[210] in the field of international environmental law are acknowledged, recalled, recognized, and reaffirmed. The Parties to the UNFCCC acknowledge climate change and its adverse effects as "common concern of humankind."[211] The Parties to the Convention recall the Stockholm Declaration,[212] the Vienna Convention,[213] the Montreal Protocol to the Vienna Convention,[214] and the customary international law principle recognized in Principle 21

---

200 UN, "Agenda 21," *supra* note 180.
201 See also Dempsey, *Public International Air Law*, *supra* note 90 at 448.
202 See Agenda 21, *supra* note 99; Kiss, *International*, *supra* note 116 at 57.
203 Birnie, *International Law*, *supra* note 91 at 52.
204 UN, "UNCED," *supra* note 176.
205 Ibid.
206 Rowlands, "Atmosphere," *supra* note 91 at 327.
207 Ibid.
208 Ibid. at 327–328.
209 UNFCCC, *supra* note 101, Preamble.
210 For a concise but good discussion on the principles, see Ian Brownlie, *Principles of Public International Law*, 7th ed. (New York: Oxford University Press, 2008) at 275–280. However, Birnie, *International Law*, *supra* note 91 at 28, argue that these principles "may lack the supposedly harder edge of a 'rule' or 'obligation', but they should not be confused with 'non-binding' or emerging law." They further argue, ibid. at 38, that

> [w]hile the status of all of these principles in customary law is doubtful or disputer, they have nevertheless become important modifiers of existing rules and treaties, or influenced the negotiation and elaboration of treaty regimes. They are too important for courts, governments, or international organizations and treaty bodies to ignore.

211 UNFCCC, *supra* note 101, Preamble.
212 Stockholm Declaration, *supra* note 108.
213 Vienna Convention, *supra* note 113.
214 Montreal Protocol, *supra* note 148.

of the Stockholm Declaration and Principle 2 of the Rio Declaration.[215] The Convention reaffirms the principle of sovereignty of States in international cooperation to address climate change, and determines to protect the climate system for present and future generations,[216] i.e., intergenerational equity. The Parties to the Convention recognize, *inter alia*:

- that States should enact effective environmental legislation;
- the need for developed States to take immediate action that takes into account all greenhouse gases and States, especially developing, who are vulnerable to the adverse effects of climate change and whose economies are dependent on fossil fuel production, use, and exportation and, as a consequence of action taken on limiting greenhouse gas emissions, who will face special difficulties; and
- the need of all States, especially developing, to have access to resources required to achieve sustainable social and economic development.[217]

The objective of the UNFCCC is to *stabilize* "greenhouse gas concentrations in the atmosphere at a level that would prevent dangerous anthropogenic interference with the climate system."[218] The objective "should be achieved within a time frame sufficient to allow ecosystems to adapt naturally to climate change, to ensure that food production is not threatened and to enable economic development to proceed in a sustainable manner."[219] It is apparent from the objective that the Parties envisage that some degree of climate change is inevitable.[220] The Parties to the UNFCCC have significant commitments to achieve the objective of the Convention.[221] However, not all States have the same obligation. The Convention has divided States mainly into two groups: Annex I developed States and non-Annex I developing States.[222]

---

215 UNFCCC, *supra* note 101, Preamble.
216 Ibid.
217 Ibid.
218 Ibid., art. 2. To achieve this objective, the Parties to the UNFCCC shall be guided by five principles:

    1 Protecting climate system for the benefit of present and future generations on the basis of equity and according to their common but differentiated responsibilities and respective capacities in which respect the developed country Parties should take the lead;
    2 Considering in full the specific needs and special circumstances of developing country Parties and of those Parties that would have to bear a disproportionate or abnormal burden under UNFCCC;
    3 Taking precautionary measures to anticipate, prevent or minimize the causes of climate change and mitigate its adverse effects. In this respect, efforts to address climate change may be carried out cooperatively by interested Parties;
    4 Promoting sustainable development;
    5 Cooperation to promote a supportive and open international economic system that would lead to sustainable economic growth and development in all Parties, particularly developing country Parties. Measures taken to combat climate change, including unilateral ones, should not constitute a means of arbitrary or unjustifiable discrimination or a disguised restriction on international trade.

    Ibid. art. 3.
219 Ibid. art. 2. "The Convention does not specify what that level might be, nor does Article 2 envisage that it should be achieved immediately," Birnie, *International Law*, *supra* note 91 at 358.
220 Birnie, *International Law*, *supra* note 91 at 358.
221 See UNFCCC, *supra* note 101, art. 4.
222 See UNFCCC, "Parties & Observers," online: unfccc.int/parties_and_observers/items/2704.php (UNFCCC, "Parties").

There is another group of developed States, namely Annex II developed States. All Annex I developed States except States with economies in transition are members of Annex II developed States.[223] Developed States have more obligations than the developing States. Those commitments reflect the principle of common but differentiated responsibility.[224] Additionally, it has been emphasized that the extent to which developing State Parties will effectively implement their commitments under the UNFCCC will depend on the effective implementation of their commitments under the Convention related to financial resources and transfer of technology.[225] Since, under the Convention, special consideration has been accorded to least developed countries (LDCs) of non-Annex I developing States, LDCs can be classified as another group of developing States.[226]

The Convention addresses the issue of emissions from aviation, though to a limited extent, by providing that all Parties to the Convention are committed to,[227] *inter alia*, promote and cooperate, in the development, application, and diffusion of technologies, practices, and processes that control, reduce, or prevent anthropogenic emissions of greenhouse gases not controlled by the Montreal Protocol[228] in the transport sector.[229] Although aviation does fall within the transport sector, aviation, whether domestic or international, is not explicitly mentioned, and the Convention does not define "transport." It appears that, with regard to transport, parties must concern themselves with technologies, practices, and processes and not with the enactment and implementation of legally binding measures, whether national or international. The Convention does not provide any guidance regarding how to promote and cooperate in those respects and does not provide for any concrete goal that must be achieved by the aviation sector, e.g., reduction of CO_2 emissions by 5 percent below 1990 levels within a certain time limit. In the absence of any guidance and any binding aim,[230] this commitment is manifestly weak and vague,[231] and States are left with the discretion of choosing how to meet this commitment. The application of this discretion can inevitably give rise to a number of fragmented procedures of promoting and cooperating in those three areas, namely, technologies, practices, and processes, to arrest aviation emissions that heighten climate change and global warming. However, since the commitment itself is weak and vague, and does not provide for any solid target that has to be achieved, how those procedures will be successful in curbing relevant aviation emissions is unclear.[232] Furthermore,

223 See ibid.
224 See Birnie, *International Law, supra* note 91 at 359.
225 UNFCCC, *supra* note 101, art. 4(7). The UNFCCC provides for a financial mechanism for the provision of financial resources on a grant or concessional basis. See ibid. art. 11.
226 Forty-nine Parties are classified as LDCs by the UN. See UNFCCC, "Parties," *supra* note 222.
227 UNFCCC, *supra* note 101, art. 4(1).
228 Montreal Protocol, *supra* note 148.
229 UNFCCC, *supra* note 101, art. 4(1)(c).
230 See e.g. Malte Petersen, "The Legality of the EU's Stand-alone Approach to the Climate Impact of Aviation: The Express Role given to the ICAO by the Kyoto Protocol" (2008) 17:2 *RECIEL* 196 (Academic Search Complete) ("the UNFCCC neither contains mandatory limits on greenhouse gas emissions nor enforcement provisions" at 199) (Petersen, "Legality"); International Law Commission (ILC), "First Report on the Protection of the Atmosphere," UNGAOR, 2014, UN Doc. A/CN.4/667 at 26, online: daccess-dds-ny.un.org/doc/UNDOC/GEN/N14/237/23/PDF/N1423723.pdf?OpenElement (ILC, "First Report").
231 See also Birnie, *International Law, supra* note 91 at 359–360; Kiss, *International, supra* note 116 at 584–585.
232 See also Petersen, "Legality," *supra* note 230 ("the provisions of the UNFCCC were not sufficient to reach the goals agreed upon in the UNFCCC" at 199).

areas in addition to technologies, practices, and processes (e.g., legislation) have to be covered to ensure the effectiveness of this provision under the UNFCCC in terms of arresting climate change and global warming.

The Convention has established the Conference of the Parties (COP) as the supreme body of the UNFCCC with the obligation to keep under regular review the implementation of the Convention and any related legal instruments that it may adopt and to make necessary decisions to promote effective implementation.[233] The UNFCCC has also established a Secretariat,[234] a Subsidiary Body for Scientific and Technological Advice,[235] and a Subsidiary Body for Implementation.[236] Like the Vienna Convention,[237] Annexes to the UNFCCC form an integral part of the Convention,[238] and Parties are not allowed to make any reservation to the Convention.[239] Currently, the Convention has 195 Parties: 194 States and one regional economic integration organization.[240]

10.4.7 Kyoto Protocol

As a framework convention, the UNFCCC did not establish any quantitative commitments to limit greenhouse gas emissions; it "ultimately established only an aspirational commitment from industrialized countries to control these emissions in the future."[241] Hence, it became imperative to adopt a Protocol that would strengthen the Convention. Article 17 of the UNFCCC, which facilitates adoption of Protocols to the Convention,[242] has paved the way for the adoption of the Kyoto Protocol adopted at the third session of the COP (COP 3).[243] Unlike the UNFCCC, the Kyoto Protocol established quantitative restrictions on emissions from industrialized economies,[244] which mended the weakness of the UNFCCC. In fact, notwithstanding the obligations of the Parties under the Convention, it was not until the negotiation of the Kyoto Protocol that developed State Parties committed themselves "to explicit, unambiguous targets and timetables for the reduction of the chief greenhouse gases and to the development of international mechanisms for ensuring the [fulfillment] of these commitments."[245]

The objective and principles of the Kyoto Protocol are the ultimate objective and the five principles of the UNFCCC, respectively.[246] Article 3 requires the Annex I Parties to ensure,

233 UNFCCC, *supra* note 101, art. 7.
234 See ibid. art. 8.
235 This Body will provide the COP and its other subsidiary bodies with timely information and advice on scientific and technological matters relating to the Convention. Ibid. art. 9.
236 This Body will assist the COP in the assessment and review of the effective implementation of the Convention. Ibid. art. 10.
237 See Vienna Convention, *supra* note 113, arts. 10(1), 18.
238 UNFCCC, *supra* note 101, art. 16(1).
239 Ibid. art. 24.
240 For a complete list of Parties, see UNFCCC, "Status of Ratification of the Convention," online: unfccc.int/essential_background/convention/status_of_ratification/items/2631.php.
241 Sean T. Fox, "Responding to Climate Change: The Case for Unilateral Trade Measures to Protect the Global Atmosphere" (1996) 84:7 *Geo L.J.* 2499 at 2499 (footnote omitted) (HeinOnline).
242 See UNFCCC, *supra* note 101, art. 17.
243 Kyoto Protocol, *supra* note 103. See also Ong, "International Legal Efforts," *supra* note 115 at 456.
244 Birnie, *International Law*, *supra* note 91 at 360–361, consider that the key feature of the Kyoto Protocol is its establishment of quantitative restrictions on emissions from industrialized economies.
245 Redgwell, "International Environmental Law," *supra* note 91 at 704.
246 Kyoto Protocol, *supra* note 103, Preamble.

individually or jointly,[247] that their aggregate anthropogenic CO_2 equivalent (CO_2e) emissions of the greenhouse gases listed in Annex A do not exceed their assigned amounts,[248] calculated according to their quantified emission limitation and reduction commitments inscribed in Annex B,[249] "with a view to reducing their overall emissions of such gases by at least 5% below 1990 levels in the [first] commitment period 2008 to 2012."[250] Additionally, Annex I developed State Parties are required, by 2005, to "have made demonstrable progress in achieving its commitments under this Protocol."[251] In achieving its quantified emission limitation and reduction commitments under Article 3,[252] and in order to promote sustainable development, the Protocol requires the Annex I developed State Parties:[253]

- to implement and/or further elaborate policies and measures in accordance with its national circumstances, such as, *inter alia*, measures to limit and/or reduce emissions of greenhouse gases not controlled by the Montreal Protocol in the transport sector;[254] and
- to cooperate with other such Parties to enhance the individual and combined effectiveness of their policies and measures adopted under Article 2, according to Article 4(2)(e)(i) of the UNFCCC.[255]

Therefore, similar to the UNFCCC, the transportation sector is identified as one where measures related to emissions reductions can be implemented.[256] However, unlike other environmental treaties discussed above, the Protocol specifically mentions aviation. Paragraph 2 of Article 2 provides that the Annex I developed State Parties shall pursue limitation or reduction of emissions of greenhouse gases not controlled by the Montreal Protocol[257] from aviation and marine bunker fuels, working through the ICAO and the International Maritime Organization, respectively.[258] Thus, ICAO has been provided with "a clear mandate … to be the authoritative body" in international civil aviation to deal with climate change issues, which the Organization welcomed.[259] However, it appears that emissions from international aviation are kept outside the

247 Joint activities must comply with the procedure set out in art. 4. See ibid. art. 4.
248 Annex A lists the following greenhouse gases: carbon dioxide (CO_2), methane (CH_4), nitrous oxide (N_2O), hydrofluorocarbons (HFCs), perfluorocarbons (PFCs), and sulphur hexafluoride (SF_6). See ibid. Annex A. In the 18th session of the Conference of the Parties to the UNFCCC held in Doha in 2012, this list has been amended applicable from the beginning of the second commitment period. According to the amendment to the Kyoto Protocol, a new greenhouse gas, namely, nitrogen trifluoride (NF_3), has been included in the list. See Doha Amendment to the Kyoto Protocol, 8 December 2012, C.N.718.2012.TREATIES-XXVII.7.c, art. 1(B), online: treaties.un.org/doc/Publication/CN/2012/CN.718.2012-Eng.pdf (Doha Amendment).
249 See Kyoto Protocol, *supra* note 103, Annex B. In the 18th session of the Conference of the Parties to the UNFCCC held in Doha in 2012, Annex B has been amended. See Doha Amendment, *supra* note 248, art. 1(A).
250 Kyoto Protocol, *supra* note 103, art. 3(1).
251 Ibid. art. 3(2).
252 See ibid. art. 3.
253 Ibid. art. 2(1).
254 See ibid. art. 2(1)(a)(vii).
255 Ibid. art. 2. See UNFCCC, *supra* note 101, art. 4(2)(e)(i).
256 See Kyoto Protocol, *supra* note 103, art. 2(1)(a)(vii); Dempsey, *Public International Air Law*, *supra* note 90 at 450.
257 Montreal Protocol, *supra* note 148.
258 Kyoto Protocol, *supra* note 103, art. 2(2).
259 Dempsey, *Public International Air Law*, *supra* note 90 at 450.

purview of the Kyoto Protocol,[260] since the provision refers to "aviation," not "international civil aviation" specifically.[261] Therefore, it is argued that the Kyoto Protocol includes emissions from domestic civil aviation requiring Annex I developed State Parties to regulate those, but excludes emissions from international civil aviation, leaving such responsibility to ICAO.[262] According to the Guidelines of the IPCC and of the UNFCCC,[263] emissions from both national and international aviation should be calculated as part of the national greenhouse gas inventories of Parties, but emissions from international aviation "should be excluded from national totals and reported separately."[264] Such exclusion has been made due to the disagreement among States on how emissions from international aviation can be allocated to a specific country or divided between States.[265]

It is apparent that the provision has been drafted ambiguously, and this ambiguity has given rise to much difficulty.[266] The provision does not define the phrase "working through" leaving the question whether ICAO has been granted exclusive jurisdiction to deal with emissions from international aviation unanswered. Moreover, the Kyoto Protocol does not provide for detailed regulation of the interaction between ICAO and Parties to the Protocol.[267] Other issues stem from the absence of further guidelines. For example, the provision does not define how ICAO and Parties to the Protocol will cooperate, how to deal with any conflict that arises between those regarding any proposed measure, and what would be the consequence of ICAO's failure to come up with any meaningful measure.[268] Although it has been argued that the phrase

---

260 See also ibid. Emissions from international aviation "are not subject to the limitation and reduction commitments of Annex I Parties under the [UNFCCC] and the Kyoto Protocol." UNFCCC, "Emissions from Fuel used for International Aviation and Maritime Transport (International Bunker Fuels)," online: unfccc.int/methods/emissions_from_intl_transport/items/1057.php (UNFCCC, "Emissions from Fuel Used").

261 See Dempsey, *Public International Air Law, supra* note 90 at 450.

262 See Michael Milde, "The EU Emissions Trading Scheme: Confrontation or Compromise? A Unilateral Action Outside the Framework of ICAO" (2012) 61:2 *ZLW* 173 at 175 (Milde, "The EU Emissions"); Jane Barton, "Including Aviation in the EU Emissions Trading Scheme: Prepare for Take-off" (2008) 5:2 *J. Eur. Envtl. & Plan. L.* 183 at 184 (HeinOnline) (Barton, "Including Aviation"); Matthew D. Kasper, "The Air Transport Association's Challenge to the European Union's Extension of its Emissions Trading Scheme to International Aviation: A Legal Analysis" (2010) 10:1 *Issues in Aviation L. & Policy* 145 at 153–154 (HeinOnline); Jane Barton, "Tackling Aviation Emissions: The Challenges Ahead" (2006) 3:4 *J. Eur. Envtl. & Plan. L.* 316 at 317 (HeinOnline) (Barton, "Tackling Aviation"); Daniel B. Reagan, "Putting International Aviation into the European Union Emissions Trading Scheme: Can Europe Do It Flying Solo?" (2008) 35:2 *Boston College Envtl. Aff. L. Rev.* 349 at 364 (HeinOnline) (Reagan, "Putting").

263 Simon Eggleston, Leandro Buendia, Kyoko Miwa, Todd Ngara, and Kiyoto Tanabe, eds., *2006 IPCC Guidelines for National Greenhouse Gas Inventories* (Hayama, Japan: Institute for Global Environmental Strategies, 2006) (Eggleston, *2006 IPCC Guidelines*).

264 UNFCCC, "Emissions from Fuel Used," *supra* note 260; Amit Garg and Tinus Pulles, "Volume 2: Energy" in Eggleston, *2006 IPCC Guidelines, supra* note 263 at 3.57 (Garg, "Volume 2: Energy"). See also Ahmad, "Environmental," *supra* note 12 at 80–81.

265 Milde, "The EU Emissions," *supra* note 262 at 175; Barton, "Including Aviation," *supra* note 262 at 184; Barton, "Tackling Aviation," *supra* note 262 at 317; Dempsey, *Public International Air Law, supra* note 90 at 450. A formula has been created by the IPCC "to determine when emissions are domestic and when they are international." Dempsey, ibid. at 450 (footnote omitted). See also Garg, "Volume 2: Energy," *supra* note 264 at 3.58–3.59.

266 See also Petersen, "Legality," *supra* note 230 at 202; Dempsey, *Public International Air Law, supra* note 90 at 450.

267 Petersen, "Legality," *supra* note 230 at 202.

268 See ibid.

"working through" does not confer exclusive jurisdiction to ICAO,[269] regard must be made to the term "shall" that makes the obligation of working through ICAO mandatory.[270] While proponents of the former argument are in favor of individual State action in the event of ICAO's failure in this regard,[271] those who advocate the latter oppose any such unilateral initiative.[272]

It should be underlined that since ICAO is not a Party to either the UNFCCC or the Kyoto Protocol, these two instruments cannot bind this international organization. Rather, the Kyoto Protocol binds Annex I developed State Parties (not all Parties, in recognition of the principle of common but differentiated responsibility) to pursue action for the limitation or reduction of greenhouse gas emissions from international aviation working through ICAO. The provision does not grant those States any authority to establish or implement, whether legal or economic, any measure to curb emissions from international aviation individually. Cooperation between ICAO and those States with regard to international aviation has been mandated. As mentioned earlier, at present, emissions from international aviation are reported under the UNFCCC and the Kyoto *Protocol*, but excluded from the national total emissions, and, hence, they are not counted toward Annex I Parties' emission targets under the Protocol.[273] Thus, only Annex I developed State Parties have an obligation to reduce emissions from their domestic aviation in meeting their emission targets under the Protocol.

All Parties to the Kyoto Protocol are required to discharge certain obligations "taking into account their common but differentiated responsibilities and their specific national and regional development priorities, objectives and circumstances, without introducing any new commitments" for non-Annex I Parties, "but reaffirming existing commitments" under Article 4(1) of the UNFCCC, and "continuing to advance the implementation of these commitments in order to achieve sustainable development, taking into account" Article 4(3), (5), and (7) of the UNFCCC.[274] While under the UNFCCC, countries must meet their targets primarily through national measures, the Kyoto Protocol "offers them an additional means of meeting their targets by way of three market-based mechanisms,"[275] namely, the joint

269 See *Air Transport Association of America and others v Secretary of State for Energy and Climate Change*, C-366/10, Advocate General's Opinion [2011] ECR I-13765 at I-13817–I-13820 (*Opinion*); Petersen, "Legality," *supra* note 230 at 202.

270 See Brian F. Havel and John Q. Mulligan, "The Triumph of Politics: Reflections on the Judgment of the Court of Justice of the European Union Validating the Inclusion of Non-EU Airlines in the Emissions Trading Scheme" (2012) 37:1 *Air & Space L.* 3 at 25 (Kluwer Law Online) (Havel, "Triumph").

271 See *Opinion, supra* note 269 at I-13817–I-13820; Petersen, "Legality," *supra* note 230 at 202–203.

272 Havel, "Triumph," *supra* note 270 at 24–25. Although Havel and Sanchez do not agree that ICAO has exclusive jurisdiction, they do not favor any unilateral or non-consensual agreement to reduce emissions from aircraft. Rather, they argue that "states remain free – within certain broad parameters – to work with or without the Organization to develop a consensual treaty-based approach to carbon emissions reduction." Brian F. Havel and Gabriel S. Sanchez, "Toward an International Aviation Emissions Agreement" (2012) 36 *Harv. Envtl. L. Rev.* 351 at 358 (HeinOnline).

273 See Kati Kulovesi, "Addressing Sectoral Emissions outside the United Nations Framework Convention on Climate Change: What Roles for Multilateralism, Minilateralism and Unilateralism?" (2012) 21:3 *RECIEL* 193 at 196 (Academic Search Complete); UNFCCC, "Emissions from Fuel Used," *supra* note 260; Garg, "Volume 2: Energy," *supra* note 264 at 3.57.

274 Kyoto Protocol, *supra* note 103, art. 10.

275 See UNFCCC, "Kyoto Protocol," online: unfccc.int/kyoto_protocol/items/2830.php. It should be noted that market-based mechanisms were "first used as environmental tools in the [United States] in the 1990s in the form of Title IV of the Clean Air (Amendment) Act 1990." Birnie, *International Law, supra* note 91 at 364.

implementation (JI),[276] clean development mechanism (CDM),[277] and emissions trading.[278] All these market-based measures are supplemental to, and not a replacement for, the national measures to reach the emissions target under the Protocol.[279] These mechanisms are often referred to as flexibility mechanisms.[280] Some authors regard these mechanisms as an innovative feature of the Protocol.[281] Rowlands considers that these mechanisms "represent a noteworthy development in international environmental law."[282]

Like the Montreal Protocol,[283] the Kyoto Protocol contains a non-compliance procedure. Article 18 provides for the adoption of appropriate and effective non-compliance procedures and mechanisms by the COP.[284] A compliance mechanism, designed to strengthen the Protocol's environmental integrity, support the carbon market's credibility, and ensure transparency of

276 Joint implementation allows a developed State

> with an emission reduction or limitation commitment under the Kyoto Protocol (Annex B Party) to earn emission reduction units (ERUs) from an emission-reduction or emission removal project in another Annex B Party, each equivalent to one tonne of CO_2, which can be counted towards meeting its Kyoto target.
>
> UNFCCC, "Joint Implementation (JI)," online: unfccc.int/kyoto_protocol/mechanisms/ joint_implementation/items/1674.php. For more on joint implementation, see Kyoto Protocol, *supra* note 103, art. 6.

277 The Clean Development Mechanism allows a State

> with an emission-reduction or emission-limitation commitment under the Kyoto Protocol (Annex B Party) to implement an emission-reduction project in developing [States]. Such projects can earn saleable certified emission reduction (CER) credits, each equivalent to one tonne of CO_2, which can be counted towards meeting Kyoto targets.
>
> UNFCCC, "Clean Development Mechanism (CDM)," online: unfccc.int/kyoto_protocol/ mechanisms/clean_development_mechanism/items/2718.php. For more on CDM, see Kyoto Protocol, *supra* note 103, art. 12.

278 Emissions trading allows States "that have emission units to spare – emissions permitted them but not 'used' – to sell this excess capacity to [States] that are over their targets." UNFCCC, "International Emissions Trading," online: unfccc.int/kyoto_protocol/mechanisms/emissions_trading/items/2731. php. For more on emissions trading, see Kyoto Protocol, *supra* note 103, art. 17.

279 Ong, "International Legal Efforts," *supra* note 115 at 457, states that the main policy and legal prescriptions adopted by the UNFCCC and confirmed by the Kyoto Protocol "were arguably primarily based upon the reduction of emissions through traditional 'command and control'-type regulations, with economic-based instruments . . . initially conceived mainly as a secondary tool in the fight against global warming."

280 See Rowlands, "Atmosphere," *supra* note 91 at 330ff.; Birnie, *International Law*, *supra* note 91 at 361ff; Ong, "International Legal Efforts," *supra* note 115 at 456.

281 See Rowlands, "Atmosphere," *supra* note 91 ("Ellen Hey calls these flexibility mechanisms, from a legal and institutional perspective, 'the most noteworthy and complicating innovation introduced by the Kyoto Protocol.' Philippe Sands, meanwhile, labels them 'by far the most innovative . . . aspect of the Kyoto Protocol negotiations.'" at 330 (footnotes omitted)); Birnie, *International Law*, *supra* note 91 ("[t]he Kyoto Protocol's use of market-based instruments to generate emission reductions is commonly described as innovative or radical" at 363 (footnote omitted)).

282 Rowlands, "Atmosphere," *supra* note 91 at 332. Rowlands, ibid. at 332, asserts that the introduction of market-based measures

> to meet an environmental goal is significant for it represents further commodification of the international environment. Moreover, with the potential for large sums of money to be exchanged in markets, it brings in domestic players to a much greater extent.

283 See Montreal Protocol, supra note 148, art. 8.

284 See Kyoto Protocol, *supra* note 103, art. 18.

accounting by Parties,[285] has already been adopted.[286] It has been claimed that "[i]t is among the most comprehensive and rigorous systems of compliance for a multilateral environmental agreement."[287] One of the objectives of the Protocol's compliance mechanism is enforcement that gives the Protocol "a distinctive character unique among environmental treaties."[288] Undoubtedly, a strong and effective compliance mechanism is key to the success of the implementation of the Kyoto Protocol.[289] The Protocol is a substantial advancement of the UNFCCC, "which it strengthens by providing means for remedial and precautionary action to address climate change."[290]

Like the UNFCCC, Annexes form an integral part of the Kyoto Protocol,[291] and no reservations can be made thereto.[292] The implementation of this Protocol shall be reviewed regularly, and decisions necessary to promote effective implementation shall be made by the UNFCCC supreme body, COP.[293] Under the Kyoto Protocol, the COP shall serve as the meeting of the Parties to the Protocol.[294]

The Protocol also contains provision for taking decisions regarding second and subsequent commitment periods, i.e., beyond 2012.[295] At the eighteenth session of the COP (COP 18), States made good use of this provision. States successfully launched the second commitment period from 1 January 2013 to 31 December 2020, agreed to a firm timetable to adopt a universal climate agreement by 2015, and agreed to a path to raise necessary ambition to respond to climate change.[296] Furthermore, the Kyoto Protocol has been amended so that it will continue as of 1 January 2013.[297] Those amendments have not become effective at this writing.[298] Among others, a new list of greenhouse gases will replace the existing list in Annex A to the Protocol,[299] and Annex I Parties shall have a new obligation to ensure, individually or jointly, that their aggregate anthropogenic CO_2 equivalent emissions of the greenhouse gases listed in

285 See UNFCCC, "Introduction: An Introduction to the Kyoto Protocol Compliance Mechanism," online: unfccc.int/kyoto_protocol/compliance/items/3024.php (UNFCCC, "Introduction: Compliance").
286 See "Decision 27/CMP.1: Procedures and Mechanisms relating to Compliance under the Kyoto Protocol," UNFCCC CMPOR, 1st Sess., Doc. FCCC/KP/CMP/2005/8/Add.3 (2006) 92, online: unfccc.int/resource/docs/2005/cmp1/eng/08a03.pdf.
287 UNFCCC, "Introduction: Compliance," *supra* note 285.
288 Birnie, *International Law*, *supra* note 91 at 249.
289 UNFCCC, "Introduction: Compliance," *supra* note 285.
290 Birnie, *International Law*, *supra* note 91 at 362.
291 Kyoto Protocol, *supra* note 103, art. 21(1).
292 Ibid. art. 26.
293 Ibid. art. 13(4).
294 Ibid. art. 13(1).
295 See ibid. art. 3(4), (9).
296 United Nations Climate Change Secretariat, Press Release, "At UN Climate Change Conference in Doha, Governments take Next Essential Step in Global Response to Climate Change" (8 December 2012), online: unfccc.int/files/press/press_releases_advisories/application/pdf/pr20120812_cop18_close.pdf ("At UN Climate Change Conference"). See also Conference of the Parties serving as the meeting of the Parties to the Kyoto Protocol, "Agenda Item 4: Report of the Ad Hoc Working Group on Further Commitments for Annex I Parties under the Kyoto Protocol," UNFCCC CMPOR, 8th Sess., Doc. FCCC/KP/CMP/2012/L.9 (2012), online: unfccc.int/resource/docs/2012/cmp8/eng/l09.pdf.
297 See "At UN Climate Change Conference," *supra* note 296.
298 For the amendments to become effective, a total of 144 instruments of acceptance are required. However, at the time of this writing, only 51 instruments of acceptance have been submitted. For updated information, see UN Treaty Collection, online: treaties.un.org/Pages/ViewDetails.aspx?src=TREATY&mtdsg_no=XXVII-7-c&chapter=27&lang=en.
299 See Doha Amendment, *supra* note 248, art. 1(B).

Annex A do not exceed their assigned amounts with a view to reducing their overall emissions of greenhouse gases by at least 18 percent below 1990 levels in the second commitment period from 2013 to 2020.[300]

At present, 191 States and one regional economic integration organization have ratified the Kyoto Protocol.[301] Unfortunately, the United States (US), one of the largest industrialized Annex I Parties, has not ratified the Protocol, and Canada, another industrialized Annex I State, has withdrawn from the Protocol.[302]

10.4.8 Paris Agreement 2015

The Paris Agreement was scheduled to be adopted in December 2015.

10.4.9 ICAO Regulation of Aviation Emissions

The Chicago Convention of 1944 governs the area of law in the field of international civil aviation.[303] The 1944 Convention established ICAO,[304] which is the global forum for cooperation among its 191 Member States in all fields of civil aviation.[305] The Convention is the primary source of public international air law,[306] and is often regarded as the "Constitution"[307] of international civil aviation. The Convention was signed on 7 December 1944, i.e., during the first stage of the development of international environmental law, when environmental costs and benefits were regarded as incidental to mainly economic concerns.[308] Emissions from aviation "emerged as a problem in the 1970s."[309] Therefore, it can be easily appreciated that the need to protect the environment was not envisaged at the time of negotiation and drafting of the Convention in 1944 and, hence, no explicit provisions on environmental protection were incorporated therein.[310]

However, the Convention tacitly confers responsibility on ICAO to address aviation environmental issues.[311] According to Article 44 of the Convention, one of the aims and objectives of ICAO is "to develop the principles and techniques of international air navigation and to foster

300 Ibid. art. 1(C).
301 See UNFCCC, "Status of Ratification of the Kyoto Protocol," online: unfccc.int/kyoto_protocol/status_of_ratification/items/2613.php.
302 See ibid.
303 Convention on International Civil Aviation, 7 December 1944, 15 UNTS 295, Can. TS 1944 No. 36, ICAO Doc. 7300/9 (Chicago Convention).
304 See ibid. art. 43.
305 See ICAO, "Vision & Mission," online: www.icao.int/about-icao/Pages/vision-and-mission.aspx.
306 See generally Michael Milde, "International Air Law and ICAO" in Marietta Benkö, ed., *Essential Air and Space Law*, vol. 4 (Utrecht: Eleven International Publishing, 2008) at 17 (Milde, "International"); Elmar M. Giemulla, "Chapter 1: Chicago System: Genesis and Main Characteristics" in Elmar M. Giemulla and Ludwig Weber, eds., *International and EU Aviation Law: Selected Issues* (AH Alphen aan den Rijn: Kluwer Law International, 2011) 3 at 5.
307 See Dempsey, *Public International Air Law*, *supra* note 90 at 69; Pablo Mendes de Leon, "Enforcement of the EU ETS: The EU's Convulsive Efforts to Export its Environmental Values" (2012) 37:4 *Air & Space L.* 287 at 289 (Kluwer Law Online) (de Leon, "Enforcement of the EU ETS").
308 Redgwell, "International Environmental Law," *supra* note 91 at 687, 690.
309 Dempsey, *Public International Air Law*, *supra* note 90 at 444.
310 See also ICAO, "The Convention on International Civil Aviation: Annexes 1 to 18," online: www.icao.int/safety/airnavigation/NationalityMarks/annexes_booklet_en.pdf (ICAO, "Annexes 1 to 18").
311 See Ahmad, "Environmental," *supra* note 12 at 82.

the planning and development of international air transport so as to ... promote generally the development of all aspects of international civil aeronautics."[312] Since reducing environmental impacts of aviation to ensure protection of the environment is one of the aspects of international civil aeronautics,[313] it follows that ICAO has a duty to regulate emissions from international civil aviation.[314]

The Chicago Convention facilitates adoption of international standards and recommended practices (SARPs) as Annexes to the Convention by the ICAO Council, in accordance with Article 90,[315] to address new issues to meet the current global need.[316] The ICAO Council is bound to adopt SARPs in accordance with the provisions of Chapter VI of the Convention,[317] i.e., Articles 37–42. Among these provisions, Article 37 provides guidelines regarding such adoption: each contracting State "undertakes to collaborate in securing the highest practicable degree of uniformity in regulations, standards, procedures, and organization in relation to aircraft, personnel, airways and auxiliary services in all matters in which such uniformity will facilitate and improve air navigation."[318] To this end, ICAO "shall adopt and amend from time to time, as may be necessary, international standards and recommended practices and procedures dealing with" communications systems, air navigation aids, characteristics of airports and landing areas, rules of the air and air traffic control practices, licensing of personnel, airworthiness of aircraft, registration and identification of aircraft, collection and exchange of meteorological information, log books, aeronautical maps and charts, customs and immigration procedures, aircraft in distress and investigation of accidents, and "such other matters concerned with the safety, regularity, and efficiency of air navigation as may from time to time appear appropriate."[319] The ICAO Council made good use of this authority by adopting Annex 16 to the Chicago Convention to address aviation environmental issues.[320] The SARPs are designated as Annexes to the Chicago Convention for convenience.[321] However, unlike the UNFCCC, the Kyoto Protocol, the Vienna Convention, and the Montreal Protocol, Annexes to the Chicago Convention do not actually become a *de jure* part of the Convention.[322]

---

312 Chicago Convention, *supra* note 303, art. 44(i).
313 In fact, environmental protection is one of the five strategic objectives of the ICAO for the 2014–2016 triennium. See ICAO, "ICAO Strategic Objectives 2014–2016," online: www.icao.int/about-icao/Pages/Strategic-Objectives.aspx.
314 See Armand de Mestral and Md Tanveer Ahmad, "A Pre-analysis of Canada–EU Aviation Relations post-ICAO Assembly Meeting Concerning Emissions Trading System" (April 2013) produced for the *Canada-Europe Transatlantic Dialogue* (Carleton University: Centre for European Studies, Ottawa) at 7, online: labs.carleton.ca/canadaeurope/2013/a-pre-analysis-of-canada-eu-aviation-relations-post-icao-assembly-meeting-concerning-emissions-trading-system/ (de Mestral, "A Pre-analysis").
315 Chicago Convention, *supra* note 303, art. 90. According to art. 90, the adoption of the Annexes requires the vote of two-thirds of the ICAO Council at a meeting called for that purpose and shall then be submitted by the ICAO Council to each contracting State and that Annex or any amendment thereto shall become effective within three months after its submission to the contracting States or at the end of such longer period of time as the ICAO Council may prescribe, unless in the meantime the majority of the contracting States register their disapproval with the ICAO Council.
316 See ibid. art. 37.
317 Ibid. art. 54(l).
318 Ibid. art. 37.
319 Ibid.
320 For a brief discussion on Annex 16, see ICAO, "Annexes 1 to 18," *supra* note 310.
321 Chicago Convention, *supra* note 303, art. 54(l).
322 See Dempsey, *Public International Air Law*, *supra* note 90 at 75; Michael Milde, "Aviation Safety Oversight: Audits and the Law" (2001) 26 *Ann. Air & Sp. L.* 165 at 168 (Milde, "Aviation").

Annex 16, divided into two volumes, addresses aviation environmental issues. While Volume I of Annex 16 deals exclusively with the protection of the environment from the effect of aircraft noise, Volume II is devoted to addressing the issue of aircraft engine emissions.[323]

Part II of Volume II contains standards relating to vented fuel with regard to all turbine engine powered aircraft intended for operation in international air navigation manufactured after 18 February 1982.[324] This Part requires that the design and construction of an aircraft shall be such as to prevent the intentional discharge into the atmosphere of liquid fuel from the fuel nozzle manifolds resulting from the process of engine shutdown following normal flight or ground operations.[325]

Part III contains standards relating to emissions certification applicable to the types of aircraft engines specified in the individual chapters of the Part, "where such engines are fitted to aircraft engaged in international civil aviation."[326] Standards are defined as

> [a]ny specification for physical characteristics, configuration, material, performance, personnel or procedure, the uniform application of which is recognized as necessary for the safety or regularity of international air navigation and to which Contracting States will conform in accordance with the [Chicago] Convention.[327]

Emissions certification shall be granted on the basis of satisfactory evidence that the engine complies with the minimum requirements set by the provisions of Volume II of Annex 16.[328]

Chapter 2 of Part III deals with turbojet and turbofan engines intended for propulsion only at subsonic speeds and Chapter 3 deals with turbojet and turbofan engines intended for propulsion at supersonic speeds. For the emissions certification for all types of engines, the following emissions shall be controlled: smoke and three gases, namely, unburned HC, CO, and NO_x.[329] Smoke emissions are measured and reported in terms of Smoke Number (SN),[330] and the mass (D_P) of the gaseous pollutant HC, CO, or NO_x emitted during the reference emissions LTO cycle are measured and reported in grams.[331] Regulatory SN and regulatory gaseous emission levels for different engines are specifically defined.[332] A certificate of compliance is issued if the mean of the values measured and corrected for all the engines tested does not exceed the regulatory level.[333]

However, Volume II of Annex 16 cannot effectively reduce environmental impacts of aviation emissions for various reasons. First and foremost, Annexes to the Chicago Convention are not mandatory like the provisions of the Convention since, as noted earlier, Annexes do not

---

323 ICAO (2014) 7 International Standards and Recommended Practices: Annex 16 to the Convention on International Civil Aviation: Volume 1, "Aircraft Noise"; ICAO (2008) 3 International Standards and Recommended Practices: Annex 16 to the Convention on International Civil Aviation: Volume 2, "Aircraft Engine Emissions" (Annex 16: Volume 2).
324 Annex 16: Volume 2, *supra* note 323 at ix, II-1-1.
325 Ibid. at II-2-1.
326 Ibid. at ix.
327 Ibid. at x.
328 Ibid. at III-1-1.
329 Ibid. at III-2-1, III-3-1.
330 Ibid. at III-2-1, III-3-1.
331 Ibid.
332 See ibid. at III-2-3ff., III-3-3.
333 See ibid. at App. 6-1.

become part of the Convention.[334] In fact, neither their adoption nor their legal force are "subject to the general international law of treaties."[335]

The contracting States to the Chicago Convention are required to adopt measures to insure that all aircraft flying over or maneuvering within its territory or carrying their nationality mark shall comply with the rules and regulations relating to the flight and maneuver of aircraft there in force.[336] In these respects, all the contracting States undertake to keep their own regulations "uniform, *to the greatest possible extent*, with those established from time to time under this Convention,"[337] i.e., with SARPs promulgated by ICAO. Nevertheless, two articles of the Convention, namely, Articles 37 and 38,[338] weaken the binding nature of the Annexes. Both articles allow any contracting State to the Convention to avoid implementing the Annexes.[339] Although Article 37 invites all the contracting States "to collaborate in securing the *highest practicable degree of uniformity* in regulations, standards, procedures, and organization,"[340] any State can refrain from doing everything possible by it since the phrase "highest practicable degree of uniformity"[341] has not been defined.[342] Article 38 allows deviation from any standard or procedure of any Annexes or any amendments thereto by any contracting State.[343] According to Article 38, if any State finds it "impracticable to comply in all respects" with any of those standards or procedures, it merely has to notify ICAO of the discrepancy between its own practice and the respective standard or procedure.[344] What is meant by the term "impracticable?"[345] The Convention provides no guidance.[346] Again, although the deviating contracting State must give "immediate notification"[347] to ICAO of such "differences between its own practice and that established by the international standard,"[348] the concerned State can avoid notifying since no defined time limit is set for that purpose.[349] The Convention is silent on the definition of the term "immediate."[350] In fact, "States have notified ICAO of impracticality of compliance with SARPs at any time, or indeed not at all, thereby violating the plain meaning of the phrase

---

334 See Milde, "Aviation," *supra* note 322 at 168. See also *New Zealand Airline Pilots' Association v Attorney General* [1997] 3 NZLR 269 (CA). Milde, "International," *supra* note 306 at 18 (footnote omitted), observes that

> [t]he provisions of [Chicago] Convention are mandatory since there is no provision permitting any reservations to the Convention. The mandatory nature of the Convention is underlined by Article 82 in which contracting states committed themselves to abrogate any inconsistent obligations and understandings and not to enter into any such obligations or understanding.

335 Milde, "Aviation," *supra* note 322 at 168. However, the ILC considers Volume II of Annex 16 as one of the multilateral agreements relating to air pollution. See ILC, "First Report," *supra* note 230 at 19.
336 Chicago Convention, *supra* note 303, art. 12.
337 Ibid. (emphasis added).
338 Ibid. arts. 37, 38.
339 See Md Tanveer Ahmad, "Achieving Global Safety in Civil Aviation: A Critical Analysis of Contemporary Safety Oversight Mechanisms" (2012) 37 *Ann. Air & Sp. L.* 81 at 86.
340 Chicago Convention, *supra* note 303, art. 37 (emphasis added).
341 Ibid.
342 See Ahmad, "Achieving," *supra* note 339 at 86; Milde, "Aviation," *supra* note 322 at 168–169.
343 See ibid.; Chicago Convention, *supra* note 303, art. 38.
344 See Chicago Convention, *supra* note 303, art. 38.
345 Ahmad, "Achieving," *supra* note 339 at 86.
346 Ibid.
347 Chicago Convention, *supra* note 303, art. 38.
348 See ibid.
349 See ibid.; Ahmad, "Achieving," *supra* note 339 at 86.
350 See Chicago Convention, *supra* note 303, art. 38.

'immediate notification'."[351] Interestingly, a 60-day notification requirement is established for filing of differences with regard to any amendment to the Annexes.[352]

Twelve States, including the US, already have notified ICAO of differences which exist between their national regulations and practices and the SARPs of Volume II of Annex 16 utilizing their authority under Article 38, while a large number of countries remains silent.[353] It cannot be stated with sufficient certainty that only those 12 States are not complying with Volume II of Annex 16. In fact, the overwhelming majority of States do not discharge their obligation to notify ICAO of differences between the SARPs set forth in the Annexes and their domestic legislation.[354] ICAO itself admitted this unexpected fact.[355] Most importantly, "[t]here is no explicit sanction in the Convention for failing to notify."[356]

Furthermore, Annex 16 suffers from lack of modern effective provisions dealing with the issues of climate change and global warming.[357] It appears that, although the Kyoto Protocol provides a clear mandate for ICAO to limit or reduce emissions of greenhouse gases not controlled by the Montreal Protocol from international civil aviation,[358] ICAO has yet discharged this duty by including all the greenhouse gases emitted by aircraft, which are required to be controlled under the Kyoto Protocol, in the list of controlled gases in Volume II of Annex 16.[359] Most importantly, two major greenhouse gases emitted by aircraft, namely, CO_2 and water vapor, are not regulated by Annex 16. In fact, Volume II of Annex 16 was "originally designed to respond to concerns regarding air quality in the vicinity of airports," and, hence, it established limits for emissions of unburned HC, CO, and NO_X, "for a reference landing and take-off . . . cycle below 915 [meters] of altitude (3000 ft)."[360]

Since the Chicago Convention and Annex 16 to the Convention do not sufficiently address the issue of climate change and global warming, ICAO has taken several initiatives to address the same. The Organization adopted the Programme of Action on International Aviation and Climate Change (PAIACC) in June 2009, which included the following admirable elements:[361]

351 Dempsey, *Public International Air Law*, *supra* note 90 at 77 (footnote omitted).

352 See Chicago Convention, *supra* note 303, art. 38:

> [i]n the case of amendments to international standards, any State which does not make the appropriate amendments to its own regulations or practices shall give notice to the Council within sixty days of the adoption of the amendment to the international standard, or indicate the action which it proposes to take.

353 See ICAO, "Supplement to Annex 16, Volume II (Second Edition)" in Annex 16: Volume 2, *supra* note 323.

354 See Dempsey, *Public International Air Law*, *supra* note 90 at 78.

355 See Milde, "Aviation," *supra* note 322 at 170 (footnote omitted):

> a Secretariat document in 1995 admitted that "it is at the present time impossible to indicate with any degree of accuracy or certainty what the state of implementation of regulatory Annex material really is, because a large number of States have not notified ICAO of their compliance with or differences to the Standards in the Annexes for some considerable time".

356 Dempsey, Public International Air Law, *supra* note 90 at 79 (footnote omitted).

357 See also ibid. at 455–458.

358 See Kyoto Protocol, *supra* note 103, art. 2(2).

359 For the list of gases, see above.

360 ICAO, "Technology Standards," online: www.icao.int/environmental-protection/Pages/technology-standards.aspx (ICAO, "Technology").

361 ICAO Secretariat, "ICAO Programme of Action on International Aviation and Climate Change" in ICAO, *ICAO Environmental Report 2010: Aviation and Climate Change* (Montreal: ICAO, 2010) 8 at 9 (ICAO Secretariat, "ICAO Programme of Action").

1   a 2 percent annual improvement target in fuel efficiency globally until the year 2050;
2   a decision to develop global CO_2 standards for aircraft;
3   a decision to develop a framework for market-based measures for international aviation;
4   measures to assist developing States and to facilitate access to financial resources, technology transfer, and capacity-building;
5   collection of international aviation emissions data by ICAO;
6   development and submissions to ICAO of States' voluntary action plans on emissions; and
7   continued work on alternative fuels for aviation.[362]

The ICAO Council fully accepted the PAIACC,[363] and this decision of the Council was welcomed by the High-level Meeting on International Aviation and Climate Change, held by ICAO in October 2009.[364] The High-level Meeting reaffirmed ICAO's leading role in international aviation matters, and approved a Declaration as well as Recommendations concerning further work for the Council on international civil aviation and climate change.[365] The High-level Meeting, in fact, agreed on the PAIACC elements, mentioned above.[366] ICAO claims that "[t]his is the first globally-harmonized agreement on a goal that addresses climate impacts from a specific sector."[367]

In 2010, ICAO Assembly adopted Resolution A37-19 to limit or reduce emissions from aviation that contribute to climate change.[368] Airline and airport groups applauded this event.[369] Resolution A37-19 included the following:

1   a global goal of 2 percent annual fuel efficiency improvement up to the year 2050;
2   a global framework for the development and deployment of sustainable alternative fuels for aviation;
3   a target of 2013 for a CO_2 standard for aircraft engines;
4   the development of a framework for market-based measures;
5   a feasibility study on the creation of a global market-based measure scheme and guiding principles for States to use when designing and implementing market-based measures for international aviation;
6   mechanisms for technology transfer to developing States;
7   a requirement for States to submit to ICAO their action plans for reaching goals set by the Organization;
8   assistance for States to meet their respective objectives; and
9   exemptions from market-based measures for States with very low emissions due to their small traffic base.[370]

---

362 See ibid. at 8.
363 See ibid.
364 See ibid.; "Declaration by the High-level Meeting on International Aviation and Climate Change (HLM-ENV/09) in October 2009," online: www.icao.int/environmental-protection/Pages/pro-gramme-of-action.aspx ("Declaration by the High-level Meeting").
365 See ICAO Secretariat, "ICAO Programme of Action," *supra* note 361 at 8. To view the whole Declaration, see "Declaration by the High-level Meeting," *supra* note 364.
366 See ICAO Secretariat, "ICAO Programme of Action," *supra* note 361 at 8; "Declaration by the High-level Meeting," *supra* note 364.
367 ICAO Secretariat, "ICAO Programme of Action," *supra* note 361 at 8.
368 See ICAO Res. A37-19, *supra* note 21.
369 Adrian Schofield, "Industry Groups Welcome ICAO Climate Agreement," *Aviation Week – Commercial Aviation Bulletin (McGraw-Hill Companies)* (11 October 2010).
370 See ICAO, Press Release, PIO 14/10, "ICAO Member States Agree to Historic Agreement on Aviation and Climate Change" (8 October 2010), online: www.icao.int/Newsroom/Pages/icao-member-states-agree-to-historic-agreement-on-aviation-and-climate-change.aspx.

At its eighth meeting in February 2010, the Committee on Aviation Environmental Protection (CAEP) agreed on a new NO_X standard that "improves on the current Standard by up to 15% with an effective date of 31 December 2013, as well as a production cut-off engines according to the current Standard with an effective date of 31 December 2012."[371] ICAO adopted more stringent NO_X standards in 2010.[372] The CAEP also agreed at the same meeting in 2010 to establish a certification requirement for non-volatile PM emissions by 2013 and a certification standard by 2016.[373]

On 10 July 2012, ICAO's CAEP unanimously agreed on a CO_2 metric system which characterizes the CO_2 emissions for aircraft types with varying technologies.[374] The development of a CO_2 certification requirement, including a CO_2 metric system and procedures, has been accomplished.[375] The CAEP already delivered agreement on the certification procedures.[376] The new CO_2 aircraft standard will result in a new volume, namely Volume III, of Annex 16.[377]

In its thirty-eighth session held in 2013, the ICAO Assembly adopted Resolution A38-18 dealing with climate change, which replaced Resolution A37-19.[378] While most features of Resolution A37-19 were retained, Resolution A38-18 is different from Resolution A37-19 in some important respects. Most importantly, whereas States agreed to *develop a framework* for market-based measures under Resolution A37-19,[379] States decided to *develop* a global market-based measure for international civil aviation under Resolution A38-18.[380] With respect to CO_2 aircraft standard, the Assembly requested the ICAO Council to "develop a global CO_2 Standard for aircraft aiming to finalize analyses by late 2015 and adoption by the Council in 2016."[381]

10.4.10 Basket of measures to reduce emissions

At its thirty-seventh session, the ICAO Assembly defined a basket of measures to achieve ICAO's environmental goals.[382] These measures include technology improvements, operational improvements, sustainable alternative fuels, and market-based measures.[383] The basket of measures is also recognized under Resolution A38-18.[384] According to Resolutions A37-19 and

---

371 ICAO, "Technology," *supra* note 360.
372 See ICAO, "WG3: Emissions," online: www.icao.int/environmental-protection/Documents/CAEP/Images/WG3-Large.png (ICAO, "WG3: Emissions").
373 ICAO, "Technology," *supra* note 360.
374 See ICAO, Press Release, COM 15/12, "New Progress on Aircraft CO_2 Standard" (11 July 2012), online: www.icao.int/Newsroom/Pages/new-progress-on-aircraft-CO2-standard.aspx.
375 See Jane Hupe, "Aviation and Environment: Developments since the Last Assembly" (Presentation delivered at the ICAO Symposium on Aviation and Climate Change, "Destination Green," Montreal, 14–16 May 2013) (unpublished) (Hupe, "Aviation").
376 See ICAO, Press Release, COM 4/13, "ICAO Environmental Protection Committee Delivers Progress on New Aircraft CO_2 and Noise Standards" (14 February 2013), online: www.icao.int/Newsroom/Pages/ICAO-environmental-protection-committee-delivers-progress-on-new-aircraft-CO2-and-noise-standards.aspx.
377 See Hupe, "Aviation," *supra* note 375.
378 See ICAO Res. A38-18, *supra* note 21 at I-70.
379 See ICAO Res. A37-19, *supra* note 21 at I-71.
380 See ICAO Res. A38-18, *supra* note 21 at I-72.
381 Ibid. at I-75.
382 See Jane Hupe, "Towards Environmental Sustainability" in ICAO, *ICAO Environmental Report 2013: Aviation and Climate Change* (Montreal: ICAO, 2013) 11 at 11 (ICAO, *ICAO Environmental Report 2013*).
383 See ibid.
384 See ICAO Res. A38-18, *supra* note 21 at I-72.

A38-18, States are encouraged to submit their action plans "outlining their respective policies and actions, and annual reporting on international aviation CO_2 emissions to ICAO."[385] These action plans "should include information on the basket of measures considered by States."[386]

10.4.10.1 Technology improvements

The principal objective of Working Group 3 of the CAEP is "to keep ICAO engine emissions certification standards [under Annex 16] up to date and effective."[387] Thus, this group has worked on NO_X standards, mentioned above. This working group, in conjunction with other CAEP working groups, is working on ICAO CO_2 aircraft standard and non-volatile PM certification standard,[388] discussed above. Working Group 3 is assigned with the responsibility to assess "advances, within the context of the existing CAEP technology goals, in aircraft and engine design technologies with regard to their impact on fuel burn."[389]

10.4.10.2 Operational improvements

ICAO has been unrelentingly working to facilitate operational improvements in various ways. For example, ICAO, in close conjunction with the International Air Transport Association (IATA) and the Civil Air Navigation Services Organisation, introduced a new aviation system flight plan in November 2012.[390] The new flight plan will enable flight crews and air traffic controllers to optimize routes and diminish flight times as well as reduce noise and emissions.[391] ICAO's CAEP developed and updated the guidance material on operational opportunities to minimize fuel consumption and emissions.[392] The updated guidance material will "provide States and other stakeholders with information on a state-of-the-art variety of measures and best practices to reduce aviation emissions, ranging from weight reduction, to airport operations, as well as other operational improvements."[393] Additional guidance material on conducting communications, navigation, surveillance, and air traffic management (CNS/ATM) environmental

---

385 ICAO Res. A37-19, *supra* note 21 at I-70; ICAO Res. A38-18, *supra* note 21 at I-71.
386 ICAO Res. A37-19, *supra* note 21 at I-70; ICAO Res. A38-18, *supra* note 21 at I-72.
387 ICAO, "WG3: Emissions," *supra* note 372.
388 See ibid.; ICAO, "Technology," *supra* note 360.
389 ICAO, "WG3: Emissions," *supra* note 372.
390 See ICAO, Press Release, COM 19/12, "Aviation Groups Unite to Achieve Instantaneous Global System Upgrade" (15 November 2012) online: www.icao.int/Newsroom/Pages/aviation-groups-unite-to-achieve-instantaneous-global-system-upgrade.aspx.
391 See ibid.
392 See ICAO, "Operational Opportunities to Reduce Fuel Burn and Emissions," Circular 303-AN/176, ICAO Doc. 10013 (2014); ICAO Secretariat, "Overview: Global Emissions" in ICAO, *ICAO Environmental Report 2013*, *supra* note 382 at 96–97 (ICAO Secretariat, "Overview: Global").
393 ICAO Secretariat, "Overview: Global," *supra* note 392 at 96–97. The new manual replaced ICAO Circular 303, and

> contains information on current operational practices being implemented by aircraft operators, airport operators, air navigation service providers (ANSPs), other industry organizations and ICAO Member States. It includes information on airport operations, maintenance, weight reduction, the effect of payload on fuel efficiency, air traffic management, flight and route planning, and other aircraft operations.
>
> ICAO Secretariat, "Operations: Operational Improvements to Reduce Global Emissions" in ICAO, *ICAO Environmental Report 2013*, *supra* note 382 at 112 (ICAO Secretariat, "Operations: Operational Improvements").

assessment, was also developed by the CAEP and endorsed by the ICAO Council.[394] ICAO publishes and updates its Global Air Navigation Plan (GANP) that is "an overarching framework that includes key civil aviation policy principles to assist ICAO Regions, sub-regions and States with the preparation of their Regional and State air navigation plans."[395] The fourth edition of the GANP is "designed to guide complementary and sector-wide air transport progress over 2013–2023 and is approved triennially by ICAO Council."[396] Furthermore, ICAO "continues to develop and make available new tools"[397] to enable States to evaluate the environmental impacts of their aviation operations.[398]

ICAO has developed the Aviation System Block Upgrade (ASBU). The ASBU concept has been developed in collaboration with States, industry, and international organizations to meet the real challenge for the aviation community to achieve "safety and operational improvements on a globally harmonized basis, while also being environmentally responsible and cost-effective."[399] ASBU aims to ensure at reasonable cost that:

- aviation safety is maintained and enhanced;
- ATM improvement programs are effectively harmonized; and
- barriers to future aviation efficiency and environmental gains are removed.[400]

394 See ICAO, "Guidance on Environmental Assessment of Proposed Air Traffic Management Operational Changes," 1st ed., ICAO Doc. 10031 (2014), online: www.icao.int/publications/Documents/10031_en.pdf. The Guidance "focuses on environmental impact assessments (including both engine emissions and noise), related to proposed changes to operational procedures, airspace redesigns, and other related operational aspects." ICAO Secretariat, "Operations: Operational Improvements," *supra* note 393 at 112.

395 ICAO, "Global Air Navigation Plan," 4th ed., ICAO Doc. 9750-AN/963 (2013) at 15, online: www.icao.int/publications/Documents/9750_4ed_en.pdf (ICAO, "Global Air Navigation"). The GANP's objective "is to increase capacity and improve efficiency of the global civil aviation system whilst improving or at least maintain safety. The GANP also includes strategies for addressing the other ICAO Strategic Objectives." Ibid. "The GANP outlines ICAO's ten key civil aviation policy principles" that guide global, regional and State air navigation planning. Ibid. These ten principles are: commitment to the implementation of ICAO's strategic objectives and key performance areas, aviation safety is the highest priority, tiered approach to air navigation planning, global air traffic management operational concept, global air navigation priorities, regional and State air navigation priorities, ASBUs, modules and roadmaps, use of ASBU blocks and modules, cost benefit and financial issues, and review and evaluation of air navigation planning. Ibid. at 17–19.

396 Ibid. at 4. The Plan (ibid.):

> represents a rolling, 15-year strategic methodology which leverages existing technologies and anticipates future developments based on State/industry agreed operational objectives. The Block Upgrades are organized in five-year time increments starting in 2013 and continuing through 2028 and beyond. This structured approach provides a basis for sound investment strategies and will generate commitment from States, equipment manufacturers, operators and service providers.

397 ICAO Secretariat, "Overview: Global," supra note 392 at 97 ("[f]or instance, ICAO recently launched the ICAO Fuel Savings Estimation Tool (IFSET), which was developed to assist States to estimate the fuel savings and corresponding environmental benefits from the implementation of operational improvements").

398 Ibid.

399 ICAO Secretariat, "Operations: ICAO Block Upgrades Minimizing Adverse Environmental Effects of Civil Aviation Activities" in ICAO, *ICAO Environmental Report 2013*, *supra* note 382 at 114 (ICAO Secretariat, "Operations: ICAO Block Upgrades").

400 Ibid. ASBU "forms a critical element of the implementation planning mechanism of" ICAO's GANP. ICAO Secretariat, "Operations: Operational Improvements," *supra* note 393 at 113.

ICAO GANP includes ASBU "framework, its modules and its associated technology roadmaps covering *inter alia* communications, surveillance, navigation, information management and avionics."[401] In order to measure the environmental benefits of the ASBU, the CAEP, in cooperation with the aviation operational community, "is in the process of assessing the first modules of" the ASBU.[402]

At the core of the ASBU concept is a "pragmatic" system of modules.[403] Each module is "comprised of technologies and procedures that are organized towards achieving a specific performance capability. Each of these modules is then linked to one of four specific and interrelated performance improvement areas."[404] These four areas are airport operations, globally interoperable systems and data, optimum capacity and flexible flights, and efficient flight paths.[405] These modules apply several other concepts that include continuous descent operations (CDOs), continuous climb operations (CCOs), collaborative decision making to improve airport operations (A-CDM), and performance-based navigation (PBN).[406]

CDOs feature optimized profiles that permit "aircraft to descend from high altitudes to the airport at minimum thrust settings, thus decreasing noise in local communities and using up to 30% less fuel than standard 'stepped' approaches."[407] CCOs, which do not require a particular air or ground technology and are derived from existing aircraft operating techniques assisted by "the appropriate airspace and procedure design," enable "an aircraft to reach and maintain its optimum flight level without interruption" thus optimizing fuel efficiency and diminishing emissions.[408] The implementation of CDOs and CCOs will largely save fuel since a large amount of fuel burn occurs during the LTO cycle.[409] A-CDM aims to improve surface traffic management, "leading to reduced delays on movement and maneuvering areas."[410] Modules regarding A-CDM provide for "the implementation of a collaborative set of applications and permit the sharing of surface operations data among the different operators at the airport."[411] PBN permits "aircraft to fly even closer to their preferred 4D trajectory. Developed after the improvement of the air navigation system in the vertical plane, PBN improves the efficiency in the horizontal plane."[412] ICAO defines PBN as "[a]rea navigation based on performance requirements for aircraft operating along an [air traffic service] route, on an instrument approach procedure or in a designated airspace" where "[p]erformance requirements are expressed in navigation specifications in terms of accuracy, integrity, continuity, availability and functionality needed for the proposed operation in the context of a particular airspace concept."[413] Among these concepts

---

401 ICAO, "Global Air Navigation," *supra* note 395 at 15 (emphasis added).
402 ICAO Secretariat, "Overview: Global," *supra* note 392 at 97.
403 ICAO Secretariat, "Operations: ICAO Block Upgrades," *supra* note 399 at 114.
404 Ibid.
405 See ibid.
406 See ibid.
407 Ibid. at 115.
408 Ibid.
409 See ibid. at 114.
410 Ibid. at 115.
411 Ibid.
412 ICAO Secretariat, "ICAO's Global Air Traffic Management (ATM): Operational Concept and Global Air Navigation Plan" in ICAO, *ICAO Environmental Report 2010: Aviation and Climate Change* (Montreal: ICAO, 2010) 98 at 100.
413 ICAO, "Performance-based Navigation (PBN) Manual," 3rd ed., ICAO Doc. 9613/AN/937 (2008) at I-(xx); ICAO (2001) 13 International Standards and Recommended Practices: Annex 11 to the Convention on International Civil Aviation: Air Traffic Services: Air Traffic Control Service: Flight Information Service: Alerting Service, at 1–10 (Annex 11).

applied by the modules, PBN is crucial since it is vital to the implementation of ASBU and is an enabler for CDOs and CCOs.[414]

10.4.10.3 Sustainable alternative fuels

With respect to sustainable alternative fuels,

> ICAO is actively engaged in activities to promote and facilitate the emergence of [such] fuels in aviation by exchanging and disseminating of information, fostering dialogue among States and stakeholders, and carrying out dedicated work as requested by ICAO [contracting] States to inform decision making.[415]

In November 2009, the Conference on Aviation and Alternative Fuels endorsed the use of such fuels for aviation.[416] The Conference also established an ICAO Global Framework for Aviation Alternative Fuels.[417] The thirty-eighth session of the ICAO Assembly requested the ICAO Council to, *inter alia*, encourage ICAO contracting States and "invite industry, financial institutions and other international organizations to actively participate in exchange of information and best practices and in further work under ICAO on sustainable alternative fuels for aviation,"[418] and

> collect information on progress of alternative fuels in aviation ... to give a global view of the future use of alternative jet fuels and to account for changes in life cycle [greenhouse gas] emissions in order to assess progress toward achieving global aspirational goals.[419]

In response, ICAO created the Alternative Fuels Task Force in November 2013 within the CAEP, with the mandate "to assess the range of potential emissions reductions from the use of alternative fuels to 2050."[420]

10.4.10.4 Market-based measures

Market-based measures are one of the most important mitigation measures under the basket of measures to address emissions from international civil aviation.[421] Unfortunately, at present, no global market-based measure is in place for international civil aviation, though ICAO has been

414 See P. Paul Fitzgerald and Md Tanveer Ahmad, "Efficient Air Traffic Management: A Precondition for Reducing Hazardous Emissions from Aviation: Is Sovereignty Getting in the Way of Progress?" (2014) 63:3 *ZLW* 386 at 392.
415 ICAO, "Alternative Fuels: Questions and Answers: 7. What is ICAO Doing in the Field of Alternative Fuels?" online: www.icao.int/environmental-protection/Pages/AltFuel-IcaoAction.aspx.
416 See ICAO Res. A38-18, *supra* note 21 at I-69.
417 See ibid.
418 Ibid. at I-75.
419 Ibid. at I-76.
420 See ICAO, "Alternative Fuels: Question 7: What are the Past and Current Achievements of ICAO in the Field of Alternative Fuels?" online: www.icao.int/environmental-protection/Pages/AltFuels-Q7-3.aspx.
421 See generally ICAO Secretariat, "Overview – Market-based Measures: Market-based Measures" in ICAO, *ICAO Environmental Report 2013*, *supra* note 382 at 138 (ICAO Secretariat, "Overview – Market-based").

relentlessly working on such measures for the last decade. A number of studies have been undertaken by ICAO since 2001 that resulted in the preparation of guidance material on these measures.[422] Due to Assembly Resolution A37-19,[423] market-based measures "became a part of a basket of measures that States can use to address CO_2 emissions from international [civil] aviation."[424] However, as mentioned above, the same Resolution requested further work in this area by that same Resolution.[425]

In early 2012, six potential options for a global market-based measure were identified and, in June 2012, the ICAO Council narrowed these options to three, namely, global mandatory offsetting,[426] global mandatory offsetting with revenue,[427] and global emissions trading.[428] Further quantitative and qualitative assessment of these options was requested and performed according-ly.[429] Apart from the market-based measure assessment report, studies on geographic scope of such measures,[430] offsetting mechanism for international civil aviation,[431] and the eligibility of civil aviation projects under the Kyoto clean development mechanism,[432] among others, were conducted. At the thirty-eighth session of ICAO Assembly, an agreement to develop a global

422 ICAO, "Report of the Assessment of Market-based Measures," 1st ed., ICAO Doc. 10018 (2013) at (vii), online: www.icao.int/Meetings/a38/Documents/10018_en.pdf ("Report on Market-based Measures").

423 See ICAO Res. A37-19, *supra* note 21.

424 "Report on Market-based Measures," *supra* note 422 at (vii).

425 See ICAO Res. A37-19, *supra* note 21 at I-69, I-71.

426 Under this measure, "participants acquire emissions units to offset emissions from international avi-ation above an agreed baseline." ICAO Council, "Market-Based Measures (MBMs)," ICAO Assem-bly, 38th Sess., Agenda Item 17, Working Paper No. 29, Doc. A38-WP/29/Ex/24 (4 September 2013) at 2, online: www.icao.int/Meetings/a38/Documents/WP/wp029_en.pdf.

427 This measure

would generally function the same way as the mandatory offsetting scheme. A key difference would be that in addition to offsetting, revenue would be generated by applying a fee to each tonne of carbon, for instance, through a transaction fee. The revenue would be used for agreed purposes, such as climate change mitigation or providing support to developing States to reduce GHG emissions.

Ibid.

428 Under this measure,

total international aviation emissions are capped at an agreed level for a specified compliance period. Aviation allowances (one allowance is equivalent to one tonne of CO_2) would be created for all the emissions under the cap. These allowances would then be distributed among, or auc-tioned to, participants, using an agreed method. At the end of each compliance period, partici-pants would need to surrender sufficient aviation allowances, or other emissions units, such as offsets from other sectors, to cover all the emissions generated during that period. Revenues can be generated by auctioning aviation allowances.

Ibid. See "Report on Market-based Measures," *supra* note 422 at (vii); ICAO Secretariat, "Overview – Market-based," *supra* note 421 at 139.

429 See "Report on Market-based Measures," *supra* note 422 at (vii); ICAO Secretariat, "Overview – Market-based," *supra* note 421 at 139.

430 See ICAO, "Report on Geographic Scope of Market-based Measures (MBMS): Analysis of Proposed Approaches for the Coverage of International Aviation Emissions under a Market-based Measure" (July 2013), online: www.icao.int/Meetings/a38/Documents/REPORT%20ON%20GEOGRAPHIC%20SCOPE%20OF%20MBMs.pdf.

431 See ICAO, "Offsets for International Aviation Emissions" (August 2012), online: www.icao.int/Meetings/a38/Documents/Offsets%20for%20International%20Aviation%20Emissions.v10.14%20August.pdf.

432 See ICAO, "Eligibility of Civil Aviation Projects under the Clean Development Mechanism (CDM)" (June 2012), online: www.icao.int/Meetings/a38/Documents/CDM_Report.pdf.

market-based measure was reached.[433] According to paragraph 19 of Assembly Resolution A38-18,[434] the Assembly requested the ICAO Council, with the support of contracting States, to "finalize the work on the technical aspects, environmental and economic impacts and modalities of the *possible options* for a global"[435] market-based measure, "organize seminars, workshops on a global scheme"[436] for international civil aviation,

> identify the major issues and problems … and make a recommendation on a global [market-based measure] scheme that appropriately addresses them and key design elements, … and the mechanisms for the implementation of the scheme from 2020 as part of a basket of measures … to achieve ICAO's global aspirational goals,[437]

and report the results of all these works for decision by the next session, i.e., thirty-ninth, of the Assembly.[438] Therefore, it is likely that no global market-based measure for international civil aviation will come into effect before 2020.[439]

Since market-based measures can only restrict or reduce emissions to a certain level, no market-based measure can provide any long-term, permanent solution to the issues of climate change and global warming.[440] Only proven technology and policy implementation, which guarantee zero emissions or, at least, zero growth in emissions, can provide a permanent solution to these problems.[441] However, technological improvement, which is a very expensive and time-consuming process, has yet to attain that objective.[442] The other two mitigation measures, namely operational improvements and sustainable alternative fuels, cannot provide a near-term solution in their current state: operational improvements cannot reduce aviation emissions to the extent necessary to lessen significantly aviation's contribution to climate change and global warming; and the use of alternative fuels has not yet become commercially viable.[443] Therefore, market-based measures are considered "to be an important gap filler"[444]

433 See ICAO Res. A38-18, *supra* note 21 at I-72; ICAO, Press Release, "Dramatic MBM Agreement and Solid Global Plan Endorsements Help Deliver Landmark ICAO 38th Assembly" (4 October 2013), online: www.icao.int/Newsroom/Pages/mbm-agreement-solid-global-plan-endoresements.aspx.

434 ICAO Res. A38-18, *supra* note 21 at I-72–I-73. The Resolution has already received a significant number of reservations. See ICAO, "Reservations to Resolution A38-18 (17/2)," online: ICAO www.icao.int/Meetings/a38/Pages/resolutions.aspx.

435 ICAO Res. A38-18, *supra* note 21 at I-72 (emphasis added). It is worth noting that the Resolution does not say three options but possible options. The Russian Federation proposed replacing the word "three" with "possible" and it was replaced accordingly. See Russian Federation, "Proposed Improvements for the Draft Consolidated Statement of Continuing ICAO Policies and Practices related to Environmental Protection: Climate Change," ICAO Assembly, 38th Sess., Agenda Item 17, Working Paper No. 275, Doc. A38-WP/275/Ex/94 (10 September 2013) at 3, online: www.icao.int/Meetings/a38/Documents/WP/wp275_en.pdf.

436 ICAO Res. A38-18, *supra* note 21 at I-72.

437 Ibid.

438 Ibid. at I-73.

439 See Ahmad, "Environmental," *supra* note 12 at 94.

440 See ibid. at 95.

441 See ibid.

442 See generally ibid. at 84–86.

443 See generally ibid. at 86–92; IPCC, "Summary for Policymakers" in Metz, *Climate, supra* note 45 at 13.

444 ICAO Secretariat, "Overview – Market-based," *supra* note 421 at 138. See also ICSA, "Effective," *supra* note 43; Airports Council International (ACI), the Civil Air Navigation Services Organisation (CANSO), the International Air Transport Association (IATA), the International Business Aviation Council (IBAC), and the International Coordinating Council of Aerospace Industries Associations (ICCAIA), "Addressing CO_2 Emissions from Aviation," ICAO Assembly, 38th Sess., Agenda Item 17, Working Paper No. 68, Doc. A38-WP/68/Revision no 3/Ex/33 (17 September 2013), online: www.icao.int/Meetings/a38/Documents/WP/wp068_rev3_en.pdf.

to complement technology, operational, and infrastructure measures.[445] It is now well understood that, without effective global market-based measures, ICAO's goal of achieving carbon neutral growth from 2020 will remain a dream.[446] The forecasts by ICAO CAEP demonstrate that, even after the implementation of technology and operational improvements and assuming 3 percent use of alternative fuels, "the emissions gap from carbon neutral growth in 2020 would be on the order of 500 Mt by 2040"[447] (see Figure 10.1). Hence, ICAO argues that market-based measures are essential "to fill this emissions gap, together with sustainable alternative fuels."[448]

Market-based measures offer the most cost-effective and near-term mechanism for addressing climate change and global warming from the aviation sector.[449] ICAO's study on the market-based measures supports this argument.[450] According to the two quantitative assessments of the three options for a global market-based measure for international civil aviation undertaken in 2012 and 2013, the cost of introducing a market-based measure is relatively small; a market-based measure "could achieve the environmental target of stabilizing CO_2 emissions at a relatively low economic cost."[451] Moreover, the 2012 quantitative assessment demonstrated that the differences between impacts of market-based measure by regions or groups of States were marginal.[452] The qualitative assessment "focused on the design features of the three options ... by identifying and elaborating on the implications of different design choices,"[453] and concluded that:

---

445 IATA, Press Release, 34, "Historic Agreement on Carbon-Neutral Growth" (3 June 2013), online: www.iata.org/pressroom/pr/Pages/2013-06-03-05.aspx; ICSA, "Effective," *supra* note 43; Paul Steele, "Aviation – Benefits Beyond Borders – ICAO Destination Green" (Presentation delivered at the ICAO Symposium on Aviation and Climate Change, "Destination Green," Montreal, 14–16 May 2013) (unpublished) (Steele, "Aviation"); Annie Petsonk, "A Global MBM for Aviation and Climate Change: The Time is Now!" (Presentation delivered at the ICAO Symposium on Aviation and Climate Change, "Destination Green," Montreal, 14–16 May 2013) (unpublished) ("[s]trong economic rationale for MBMs given practical limits to technology improvements or accelerated fleet replacement (high abatement costs relative to other sectors)") (Petsonk, "A Global MBM").

446 See Ahmad, "Environmental," *supra* note 12 at 96; ICAO Secretariat, "Overview – Market-based," *supra* note 421 at 138; Sam Brand, "An Introduction to Market-based Measures" (Presentation delivered at the ICAO Symposium on Aviation and Climate Change, "Destination Green," Montreal, 14–16 May 2013) (unpublished) (Brand, "An Introduction"); Andreas Hardeman, "Reframing Aviation Climate Politics and Policies" (2011) 36 *Ann. Air & Sp. L.* 1 at 16; Petsonk, "A Global MBM," *supra* note 445; Steele, "Aviation," *supra* note 445; ICAO, "Environment: Market-based Measures and Climate Change" (August 2013), online: cfapp.icao.int/tools/38thAssyikit/story_content/external_files/Flyer_US-Letter_ENV_MBMs_2013-08-30.pdf (ICAO, "Environment: Market-based"); Lee, "Mitigating," *supra* note 19. However, Russia does not believe the same as apparent from the working paper submitted during the 38th session of the ICAO Assembly and from the reservation to Assembly Resolution A38-18 submitted by the Russian Federation. See Russian Federation, "Market-based Measures as the Factor of an Increase of Greenhouse Gas Emissions in the Sector of International Civil Aviation," ICAO Assembly, 38th Sess., Agenda Item 17, Working Paper No. 250, Doc. A38-WP/250/Ex/83 (20 August 2013), online: www.icao.int/Meetings/a38/Documents/WP/wp250_en.pdf; Russian Federation, "Statement from the Delegation of the Russian Federation: Re: Report on Agenda Item 17 for the 38th ICAO Assembly (Climate Change Section)," online: www.icao.int/Meetings/a38/Documents/Resolutions/Russia_en.pdf.

447 ICAO, "Environment: Market-based," *supra* note 446.

448 Ibid.

449 See Ahmad, "Environmental," *supra* note 12 at 97; Brand, "An Introduction," *supra* note 446.

450 See "Report on Market-based Measures," *supra* note 422.

451 See ibid. at (vii)–(viii).

452 Ibid. at (viii).

453 Ibid.

- a global mandatory offsetting could be less complex than other two measures due to the existence of emissions units that can be used and tracked through a simple registry;[454]
- a global mandatory offsetting with revenue "could be more complex due to the need to determine how revenue will be collected and used";[455] and
- a global emissions trading scheme "could increase complexity and have higher upfront costs due to the need to administer specific aviation allowances. However, it should offer more flexibility for participants due to the creation of emissions units, which can be traded in the marketplace."[456]

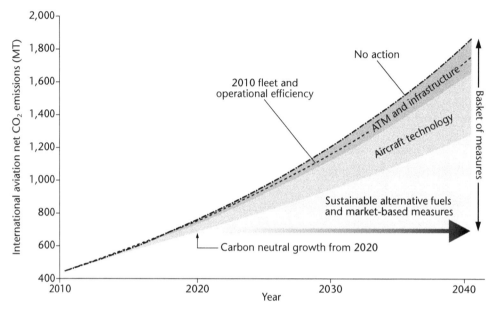

Figure 10.1 Contribution of measures for reducing international civil aviation net CO_2 emissions

Source: ICAO, "Environment: Market-based Measures and Climate Change" (August 2013), online: cfapp.icao.int/tools/38thAssyikit/story_content/external_files/Flyer_US-Letter_ENV_MBMs_2013-08-30.pdf).

454 Ibid. at (ix).
455 Ibid. The "Report on Market-based Measures," ibid. at 7-1, further states:

> Global mandatory offsetting complemented by a revenue generation mechanism could be more complex than global mandatory offsetting, due to the need to establish revenue generation and disbursement mechanisms. It would also be necessary to decide on how revenue will be used. The economic impact on participants is more significant than global mandatory offsetting. However, raising revenue creates a revenue stream that could be used to mitigate the environmental impacts of aircraft engine emissions, including mitigation and adaptation, as well as assistance to and support for developing States.

456 Ibid. at (ix). The "Report on Market-based Measures," ibid. at 7-1, further states:

> Global emissions trading (cap-and-trade system) could be more complex and have higher upfront costs than the offsetting options, due to the need to administer aviation allowances. However, it should offer more flexibility for participants through the creation of additional emissions units, for example, an allowance, which can be traded in the marketplace. Auctioning allowances would create a revenue stream that could be used to mitigate the environmental impacts of aircraft engine emissions, including mitigation and adaptation, as well as assistance to and support for developing States.

The overall results of the quantitative and qualitative assessment of the three options for a global market-based measure showed that these options were "technically feasible and have the capacity to contribute to achieving ICAO's environmental goals."[457] Nevertheless, even after these positive assessment reports, which were made available during the thirty-eighth session of the ICAO Assembly,[458] only an agreement to develop a global market-based measure for international civil aviation was reached at that session.[459]

10.5 National and regional efforts to reduce emissions from international civil aviation

10.5.1 EU emissions trading system

Pursuant to the Treaty on European Union (TEU),[460] the European Union (EU) is obligated "to work for the sustainable development of Europe based on," *inter alia*, "a high level of protection and improvement of the quality of the environment."[461] With respect to the world, the EU acts on behalf of its Member States in the pursuit of, among others, common foreign policies and actions that "ensure sustainable development" and aimed at helping to "develop international measures to preserve and improve the quality of the environment."[462] According to the Treaty on the Functioning of the EU (TFEU), which details the policies of the EU, the EU must share competence with its Member States in the areas of, *inter alia*, environment and transport,[463] i.e., the EU and its Member States "may legislate and adopt legally binding acts" in those areas.[464] The TFEU stipulates that environmental protection measures must be an integral part of the "definition and implementation of the [EU's] policies and activities,"[465] while the EU committed itself to preserve, protect, and improve the quality of the environment, and to promote measures at international level to deal with global environmental problems, in particular, climate change.[466]

The EU approved the UNFCCC in December 1993,[467] which, as noted above, requires stabilization of greenhouse gas concentrations in the atmosphere at a level that would prevent

---

457 Ibid. at (ix). Petsonk, "A Global MBM," supra note 445, states that "[t]he analysis of the policy options for a global MBM indicates that that a global MBM is cost-effective and technically feasible, while having only marginal impacts on future growth (even when revenues are generated)."

458 See ICAO, "Reference Documents," online: www.icao.int/Meetings/a38/Pages/documentation-reference-documents.aspx.

459 See Ahmad, "Environmental," *supra* note 12 at 99–100.

460 Consolidated version of the Treaty on European Union, 7 February 1992 [2012] OJ C326/13, arts. 1, 47 (TEU).

461 Ibid. art. 3(3). "Sustainable development is set out in the Treaty as the overarching long-term goal of the EU." EC, Commission, "Communication from the Commission to the European Parliament, the Council, the European Economic and Social Committee and the Committee of the Regions: Mainstreaming Sustainable Development into EU Policies: 2009 Review of the European Union Strategy for Sustainable Development," COM(2009) 400 final (Brussels: EC, 2009) at 2, online: eur-lex.europa.eu/legal-content/EN/TXT/PDF/?uri=CELEX:52009DC0400&from=EN.

462 TEU, *supra* note 460, art. 21(2)(f).

463 Consolidated version of the Treaty on the Functioning of the European Union, 25 March 1957 [2012] OJ C326/47, art. 4(2) (TFEU).

464 Ibid. art. 2(2).

465 Ibid. art. 11. See also EC, Charter of Fundamental Rights of the European Union, 7 December 2000 [2012] OJ C326/391, art. 37.

466 TFEU, *supra* note 463, art. 191(1).

467 EC, Council Decision 94/69/EC of 15 December 1993 concerning the conclusion of the United Nations Framework Convention on Climate Change, [1994] OJ L33/11 at 11.

dangerous anthropogenic interference with the climate system.[468] This requirement is often referred to in EU legislation dealing with its emissions trading system (ETS).[469] The EU also emphasizes that the Parties to the UNFCCC are required "to formulate and implement national and, where appropriate, regional programs containing measures to mitigate climate change."[470] The EU and its Member States agreed to fulfill their commitments under the Kyoto Protocol jointly.[471] Under the Kyoto Protocol, the EU and its Member States committed to reduce their aggregate anthropogenic greenhouse gas emissions by 8 percent compared to 1990 levels in the 2008–2012 period.[472] To discharge all those responsibilities related to climate change arising under the EU Treaties and international agreements, the EU launched the ETS. Most importantly, the EU ETS was an effort to contribute to meeting the commitments of the EU and its Member States under the Kyoto Protocol more effectively.[473]

The EU has been a pioneer with respect to the adoption of legal and policy measures for the protection of the environment.[474] With the first European Community strategy to limit emissions of CO_2 and improve energy efficiency, the measures dealing with the reduction of greenhouse gas emissions that accelerate climate change and global warming were commenced in 1991.[475] In 2003, the EU adopted Directive 2003/87 that established the ETS of the EU.[476] According to the EU, the ETS is the "cornerstone"[477] of the EU's policy to reduce the anthropogenic emissions of greenhouse gases that accelerate climate change and global warming;[478] it is the EU's "key tool"[479] for reducing such emissions from industrial sources in a cost-effective and economically efficient manner.[480] Launched on 1 January 2005, the EU ETS is the first and largest international market-based measure; it covers more than 11,000 power stations and industrial plants in 31 Member States of the European Economic Area

468 UNFCCC, *supra* note 101, art. 2.
469 See e.g. EC, Directive 2003/87/EC of the European Parliament and of the Council of 13 October 2003 establishing a scheme for greenhouse gas emission allowance trading within the Community and amending Council Directive 96/61/EC, [2003] OJ L275/32 at 32 (Directive 2003/87); EC, Directive 2008/101/EC of the European Parliament and of the Council of 19 November 2008 amending Directive 2003/87/EC so as to include aviation activities in the scheme for greenhouse gas emission allowance trading within the Community, [2009] OJ L8/3 at 3 (Directive 2008/101).
470 Directive 2008/101, *supra* note 469 at 4.
471 See EC, Council Decision 2002/358/CE of 25 April 2002 concerning the approval, on behalf of the European Community, of the Kyoto Protocol to the United Nations Framework Convention on Climate Change and the joint fulfilment of commitments thereunder, [2002] OJ L130/1.
472 Directive 2003/87, *supra* note 469 at 32.
473 Ibid.
474 See also Louise Van Schaik and Simon Schunz, "Explaining EU Activism and Impact in Global Climate Politics: Is the Union a Norm- or Interest-driven Actor?" (2012) 50:1 *J. Common Market Studies* 169 at 169 (Wiley).
475 Giovanni Bo, "The US Challenge to the Inclusion of Aviation Activities within the EU Emissions Trading Scheme: A US–EU Dispute with Global Repercussions," *Law, Justice and Development E-Newsletter* (September 2011), online: go.worldbank.org/TOM5W3VSK0.
476 Directive 2003/87, *supra* note 469.
477 European Commission, "The EU Emissions Trading System (EU ETS)" (October 2013), online: ec.europa.eu/clima/publications/docs/factsheet_ets_en.pdf.
478 Ibid.
479 European Commission, Policy, "The EU Emissions Trading System (EU ETS) Policy," online: ec.europa.eu/clima/policies/ets/index_en.htm (European Commission, "EU ETS Policy").
480 Ibid. See Directive 2003/87, *supra* note 469 at 34.

(EEA),[481] as well as airlines.[482] International civil aviation has been included within the scheme since 1 January 2012 in accordance with Directive 2008/101.[483] A binding obligation was imposed on the EU Member States to bring into force national laws, regulations, and administrative provisions required to comply with Directive 2008/101 before 2 February 2010.[484] Directive 2003/87 was incorporated into the EEA Agreement in October 2007 through EEA Joint Committee Decision 146/2007.[485] The EEA Agreement established the EEA that brings together the EU Member States and three States of the European Free Trade Association (EFTA), namely Iceland, Liechtenstein, and Norway.[486] The agreement further enables these three EFTA States to participate fully in the European Single Market, and provides for the inclusion of EU legislation in all policy areas of the Single Market, including environment.[487] EEA Joint Committee Decision 6/2011[488] incorporated the aviation segment of the EU ETS, i.e., Directive 2008/101, into the EEA Agreement.

Including aviation in the EU ETS was not a sudden and unexpected event.[489] Since the EU ETS was a massive "undertaking for the continent,"[490] and originally included major emitters except the aviation and maritime industries, "a sense of unease"[491] started to develop within the EU, questioning the fairness of such exclusion.[492] According to the European Commission, "[e]missions from aviation are higher than from certain entire sectors covered by the EU ETS, for example refineries and steel production."[493] Hence, in the Sixth Environment Action

481 The Member States of the EEA are all 28 EU Member States and Iceland, Norway, and Liechtenstein. See European Free Trade Association (EFTA), "European Economic Area," online: www.efta.int/eea. According to the EEA Agreement, when a State becomes a member of the EU, it must also apply to become a party to the EEA Agreement. EC, "Agreement on the European Economic Area" [1994] OJ L1/3, art. 128 (EEA Agreement). To learn more about the EEA, particularly on how it works, see EFTA, "The Basic Features of the EEA Agreement," online: www.efta.int/eea/eea-agreement/eea-basic-features (EFTA, "The Basic").
482 European Commission, "EU ETS Policy," supra note 479.
483 Directive 2008/101, supra note 469 at 6, 8–9. See also Md Tanveer Ahmad, "EU Emissions Trading Scheme: Problems Presented to Canada" (Winter 2012) 7:1 European Union Centres of Excellence Newsletter 1 at 1, online: www2.carleton.ca/euce-network-canada/ccms/wp-content/ccms-files/V7-1-EUCE-Newsletter-Winter2012.pdf (Ahmad, "EU Emissions").
484 Directive 2008/101, supra note 469 at 16.
485 EC, Decision of the EEA Joint Committee No 146/2007 of 26 October 2007 amending Annex XX (Environment) to the EEA Agreement, [2008] OJ L100/92 (Decision 146/2007).
486 EEA Agreement, supra note 481; EFTA, "The Basic," supra note 481.
487 Ibid.
488 EC, Decision of the EEA Joint Committee No 6/2011 of 1 April 2011 amending Annex XX (Environment) to the EEA Agreement, [2011] OJ L93/35 (Decision 6/2011).
489 See Jos Delbeke, "A New Flightplan: Getting Global Aviation Climate Measures Off the Ground" (Key Note Speech delivered at the Getting Global Aviation Climate Measures Off the Ground Conference, Norway House, Brussels, 7 February 2012) (unpublished), online: ec.europa.eu/clima/news/docs/speech_en.pdf; M. Vittoria Giugi Carminati, "Clean Air & Stormy Skies: The EU-ETS Imposing Carbon Credit Purchases on United States Airlines" (2010) 37:2 Syracuse J. Intl. L. & Com. 127 at 127 (HeinOnline); Lorand Bartels, "The WTO Legality of the Application of the EU's Emission Trading System to Aviation" (2012) 23:2 Eur. J. Intl. L. 429 at 433. See also Steven Truxal, "The ICAO Assembly Resolutions on International Aviation and Climate Change: An Historic Agreement, a Breakthrough Deal and the Cancun Effect" (2011) 36:3 Air & Space L. 217 (Kluwer Law Online).
490 Doaa Abdel Motaal, "Curbing CO$_2$ Emissions from Aviation: Is the Airline Industry Headed for Defeat?" (2012) 3:1 Climate L. 1 at 8 (IOS Press).
491 Ibid.
492 Ibid. See also Benoît Mayer, "Case C-366/10, Air Transport Association of America and Others v. Secretary of State for Energy and Climate Change," Case Comment (2012) 49:3 C.M.L. Rev. 1113 at 1115–1117.
493 European Commission, Press Release, Memo/11/139, "Questions & Answers on Historic Aviation Emissions and the Inclusion of Aviation in the EU's Emission Trading System (EU ETS)" (7 March 2011) at 4, online: europa.eu/rapid/press-release_MEMO-11-139_en.htm.

Programme 2002–2012,[494] the EU made it clear that it would undertake "to reduce greenhouse gas emissions from aviation if no such action is agreed within the [ICAO] by 2002."[495] Following a review of the policy options, the European Commission adopted a Communication in September 2005 that concluded that a comprehensive approach was necessary.[496] The main conclusion was that the EU ETS should be extended to include aviation.[497]

It is true that ICAO has yet adopted effective measures to reduce emissions from international civil aviation.[498] Most importantly, no global market-based measure is presently in effect for international civil aviation. In 2004, ICAO's CAEP agreed at its sixth meeting that "an aviation-specific emissions trading system based on a new legal instrument under ICAO auspices '…*seemed sufficiently unattractive that it should not be pursued further*'."[499] This outcome of the CAEP meeting has been referred to in the European Commission's proposal to adopt a Directive to include aviation in the EU ETS,[500] which led to the adoption of Directive 2008/101,[501] as well as in the recital to that Directive.[502] As discussed above, although a decision to develop a global market-based measure for aviation was reached at the last ICAO Assembly meeting, such a measure, if agreed to by ICAO contracting States at the next Assembly meeting in 2016, will only become effective in 2020.[503] Such delay at ICAO had always been criticized by the EU and, hence, it included aviation in the EU ETS without waiting for a global solution.[504]

494 EC, Decision 1600/2002/EC of the European Parliament and of the Council of 22 July 2002 laying down the Sixth Community Environment Action Programme, [2002] OJ L242/1 at 1 (Decision No. 1600/2002). See also Dempsey, *Public International Air Law*, supra note 90 at 471.

495 Decision No. 1600/2002, *supra* note 494 at 7.

496 EC, Commission, "Communication from the Commission to the Council, the European Parliament, the European Economic and Social Committee and the Committee of the Regions: Reducing the Climate Change Impact of Aviation," COM(2005) 459 final (Brussels: EC, 2005), online: eur-lex. europa.eu/LexUriServ/LexUriServ.do?uri=COM:2005:0459:FIN:EN:PDF (EC, "Communication," COM(2005) 459 final); European Commission Mobility and Transport, "Air: Climate Change," online: ec.europa.eu/transport/modes/air/environment/climate_change_en.htm.

497 See EC, "Communication," COM(2005) 459 final, *supra* note 496 at 4.

498 See Petersen, "Legality," *supra* note 230 ("[a]lthough the ICAO has not been completely inactive in addressing the climate impact of aviation, it should be noted that these efforts have not led to any effective system to tackle the climate impact of aviation" at 203). See also Barton, "Including Aviation," *supra* note 262 at 184.

499 EC, Commission, "Proposal for a Directive of the European Parliament and of the Council amending Directive 2003/87/EC so as to include aviation activities in the scheme for greenhouse gas emission allowance trading within the Community," COM(2006) 818 final – 2006/0304 (COD) (Brussels: EC, 2006) at 3, online: eur-lex.europa.eu/legal-content/EN/TXT/?uri=CELEX:52006PC0818 (emphasis in original).

500 Ibid.

501 Directive 2008/101, *supra* note 469.

502 Ibid. at 4.

503 See ICAO Res. A38-18, *supra* note 21 at I-72.

504 See Claybourne Fox Clarke and Thiago Chagas, "Aviation and Climate Change Regulation" in David Freestone and Charlotte Steck, eds., *Legal Aspects of Carbon Trading: Kyoto, Copenhagen, and Beyond* (Oxford: Oxford University Press, 2009) 606 at 610; Martin Staniland, "Air Transports and the EU's Emissions Trading Scheme: Issues and Arguments" (2008–2009) 8:2 *Issues in Aviation L. & Policy* 153 at 155 (HeinOnline); Matt Grote, Ian Williams, and John Preston, "Direct Carbon Emissions from Civil Aircraft" (2014) 95:9 *Atmospheric Environment* 214 at 217 (Elsevier). In *ATA v Secretary of State*, the Court of Justice of the European Union and Advocate General Kokott "explicitly explain that the EU ETS regime arose because of the failure of the International Civil Aviation Organisation (ICAO) to evolve a global regulatory scheme." Elain Fahey, "The EU Trading Scheme and the Court of Justice: The 'High Politics' of Indirectly Promoting Global Standards" (2012) 13:1 *German L.J.* 1247 at 1247 (footnote omitted) (HeinOnline). See *Air Transport Association of America and others v Secretary of State for Energy and Climate Change*, C-366/10, [2011] ECR I-13833 at I-13854–I-13856 (*ATA v Secretary of State*); *Opinion*, *supra* note 269 at I-13821.

The EU's continued skepticism about ICAO's ability to address effectively environmental issues involving aviation is evident from the reservations filed by its Member States against ICAO Assembly Resolutions concerning environmental protection. The EU Member States filed reservations against Resolution A36-22,[505] which urged ICAO contracting States "not to implement emissions trading schemes unless it is on the basis of mutual agreement between the States,"[506] and against paragraph 14 of Resolution A37-19, which urged States, *inter alia*, to engage in constructive bilateral and/or multilateral consultations and negotiations with other States to reach an agreement.[507] Most recently, a reservation has been filed against paragraph 16(a) of latest Resolution A38-18,[508] which, like Resolution A37-19, requires States to "engage in constructive bilateral and/or multilateral consultations and negotiations with other States to reach an agreement"[509] when designing new and implementing existing market-based measures.[510] This skepticism is revealed in the latest legislation that amended the EU ETS, namely Regulation 421/2014.[511] This Regulation provides:

> The Commission shall regularly, and at least once a year, inform the European Parliament and the Council of the progress of the [ICAO] negotiations as well as of its efforts to promote the international acceptance of market-based mechanisms among third countries. Following the 2016 ICAO Assembly, the Commission shall report to the European Parliament and to the Council on actions to implement an international agreement on a global market-based measure from 2020, that will reduce greenhouse gas emissions from aviation in a non-discriminatory manner, including on information, with regard to the use of revenues, submitted by Member States in accordance with Article 17 of Regulation (EU) No 525/2013.
>
> In its report, the Commission shall consider, and, if appropriate, include proposals in reaction to, those developments on the appropriate scope for coverage of emissions from activity to and from aerodromes located in countries outside the EEA from 1 January 2017

---

505 "Consolidated Statement of Continuing ICAO Policies and Practices related to Environmental Protection," ICAO Assembly Res. A36-22, 36th Sess., ICAO Doc. 9902, I-54, online: www.icao.int/publications/Documents/9902_en.pdf.

506 Dempsey, *Public International Air Law*, *supra* note 90 at 478. To view the reservation, see EC, Press Release, Memo/07/39, "Written statement of reservation on behalf of the member states of the European Community (EC) and the other states members of the European Civil Aviation (ECAC) [made at the 36th Assembly of the International Civil Aviation Organization in Montreal, 18–28 September 2007]" (2 October 2007), online: europa.eu/rapid/press-release_MEMO-07-391_en.htm?locale=en.

507 See ICAO Res. A37-19, *supra* note 21 at I-71. To view the entire reservation, see Belgium, "Written Statement of Reservation by Belgium on behalf of the European Union (EU), its 27 Member States, and the 17 Other States Members of the European Civil Aviation Conference (ECAC) on Resolution A37-17/2: Consolidated Statement of Continuing ICAO Policies and Practices related to Environmental Protection – Climate Change," online: ec.europa.eu/clima/policies/transport/aviation/docs/reservations_201010_en.pdf.

508 Lithuania, "Written Statement of Reservation by Lithuania on behalf of the Member States of the European Union and 14 other Member States of the European Civil Aviation Conference (ECAC) with regard to ICAO Assembly Resolution A38-18" at 2, online: www.icao.int/Meetings/a38/Documents/Resolutions/Lithuania_en.pdf ("Reservation by Lithuania").

509 See ICAO Res. A38-18, *supra* note 21 at I-72.

510 Ibid. See also Barton, "Including Aviation," *supra* note 262 at 185.

511 EC, Commission Regulation (EU) 421/2014 of the European Parliament and of the Council of 16 April 2014 amending Directive 2003/87/EC establishing a scheme for greenhouse gas emission allowance trading within the Community, in view of the implementation by 2020 of an international agreement applying a single global market-based measure to international aviation emissions, [2014] OJ L129/1 (Regulation 421/2014).

onwards. In its report, the Commission shall also consider solutions to other issues that may arise in the application of paragraphs 1 to 4 of this Article, while preserving the equal treatment of all aircraft operators on the same route.[512]

The EU ETS resembles one of the three market-based measures introduced in the Kyoto Protocol, namely emissions trading. The EU ETS works on the cap and trade principle under which "there is a 'cap', or limit, on the total amount of certain greenhouse gases that can be emitted"[513] by different types of companies, including airline companies.[514] Within this cap, "companies receive emission allowances which they can sell to or buy from one another"[515] as required.[516] Limited amounts of international credits can be purchased as well.[517] Each company is required to surrender enough allowances to cover all of its emissions at the end of each year.[518] If a company reduces its emissions, it can either keep the spare allowances to cover its future needs or sell them to another company that is in need of allowances.[519] Failure to surrender sufficient allowances will lead to a fine of €100 per ton of carbon emitted over the limit set by Directive 2003/87.[520] Failure to comply with these guidelines may lead to an operating ban on the respective company.[521]

Under the EU ETS, each airline company is administered by a single Member State for all of its aviation operations.[522] Originally under Directive 2008/101, 85 percent of emissions allowances were issued free to participating airlines in 2012, which would reduce to 82 percent for the 2013–2020 period.[523] Fifteen percent of allowances have been auctioned off each year since 2012.[524] Although Directive 2008/101 provides guidelines regarding the use of auction proceeds, EU Member States are accorded discretion regarding the use of such revenues.[525]

Originally under Directive 2008/101, all flights by aircraft with a certified maximum takeoff mass of more than 5,700 kg arriving into, or departing from, an aerodrome in the territory of an EU Member State are included unless they satisfy the exemption criteria.[526] In response to intense political pressure – mainly from the non-EU economically strong countries[527] – the European

512 Ibid. at 4.
513 European Commission, "EU ETS Policy," *supra* note 479.
514 Ahmad, "EU Emissions," *supra* note 483 at 1.
515 European Commission, "EU ETS Policy," *supra* note 479.
516 Ahmad, "EU Emissions," *supra* note 483 at 1.
517 European Commission, "EU ETS Policy," *supra* note 479.
518 Directive 2008/101, *supra* note 469 at 11–12.
519 Ahmad, "EU Emissions," *supra* note 483 at 1.
520 See Directive 2003/87, *supra* note 469 at 37; Directive 2008/101, *supra* note 469 at 13.
521 Directive 2008/101, *supra* note 469 at 13.
522 Ibid. at 6.
523 Ibid. at 8; European Commission, Press Release, Memo/11/631, "Questions & Answers on the benchmark for free allocation to airlines and on the inclusion of aviation in the EU's Emission Trading System (EU ETS)" (26 September 2011), online: europa.eu/rapid/press-release_MEMO-11-631_en.htm.
524 Directive 2008/101, *supra* note 469 at 8.
525 Ibid. at 6, 9.
526 Ibid. at 5, 17.
527 See de Mestral, "A Pre-Analysis," *supra* note 314 at 2; Md Tanveer Ahmad, "The CJEU's Radical ETS Judgment: Destabilizing the Chicago Convention System" (2013) 13:1 *Issues in Aviation L. & Policy* 139 at 139–40. See generally EC, Commission, Commission Staff Working Document: Impact Assessment Accompanying the Document Proposal for a Directive of the European Parliament and of the Council amending Directive 2003/87/EC establishing a scheme for greenhouse gas emission allowances trading within the Community, in view of the implementation by 2020 of an international agreement applying a single global market-based measure to international aviation emissions, SWD(2013) 430 final (Brussels: EC, 2013), online: ec.europa.eu/clima/policies/transport/aviation/docs/swd_2013_430_en.pdf (Impact Assessment 2013).

Commission, on 12 November 2012, proposed to defer the requirement for airlines to surrender emission allowances for flights into and out of Europe under the EU ETS until after the thirty-eighth ICAO Assembly meeting held in the autumn of 2013.[528] Consequently, this proposal to suspend was formally approved by the European Parliament and the Council of the EU.[529] Since the thirty-eighth Assembly meeting, where an agreement to develop a global market-based measure for international civil aviation was reached,[530] the EU ETS with respect to aviation has been further amended.[531] According to these new amendments,[532] from 2013 to 2016, "only emissions from flights within the EEA fall under the EU ETS."[533] Due to the latest amendments, the number of free allowances to be issued to airlines for the 2013–2016 period will be reduced in proportion to the decreased scope of the scheme, and the number of allowances to be auctioned for the same period reduced "in proportion to the reduction in the total number of aviation allowances to be issued."[534] Furthermore, "[e]xemptions for operators with low emissions have also been introduced."[535]

In international law, each State possesses the necessary authority to adopt unilateral measures to the extent that these apply to its sovereign territory.[536] This is primarily due to the doctrine of State sovereignty, according to which every State possesses the right to exercise its functions to the exclusion of other States within its territory.[537] Under customary

---

528 European Commission Climate Action, News Release, "Auctions for 2012 Aviation Allowances put on Hold" (16 November 2012), online: ec.europa.eu/clima/news/articles/news_2012111601_en. htm; European Commission Climate Action, News Release, "Commission Proposes to 'Stop the Clock' on International Aviation in the EU ETS pending 2013 ICAO General Assembly" (12 November 2012), online: ec.europa.eu/clima/news/articles/news_2012111202_en.htm.

529 See EC, Decision 377/2013/EU of the European Parliament and of the Council of 24 April 2013 derogating temporarily from Directive 2003/87/EC establishing a scheme for greenhouse gas emission allowance trading within the Community, [2013] OJ L113/1. See also European Commission Climate Action, "Reducing Emissions from Aviation," online: ec.europa.eu/clima/policies/ transport/aviation/index_en.htm (European Commission, "Reducing Emissions from Aviation").

530 See ICAO Res. A38-18, *supra* note 21 at I-72.

531 See Regulation 421/2014, *supra* note 511.

532 See ibid. To learn more about the specific changes, see European Commission, "Frequently Asked Questions: 2013–2016 Regulation amending the EU Emissions Trading System for Aviation" (Brussels, 30 April 2014), online: ec.europa.eu/clima/policies/transport/aviation/docs/faq_aviation_2013-2016_ en.pdf (EC, "FAQ: Amending EU ETS").

533 See also European Commission, "Reducing Emissions from Aviation," *supra* note 529.

534 See EC, "FAQ: Amending EU ETS," *supra* note 532 at 6, 7.

535 European Commission, "Reducing Emissions from Aviation," supra note 529.

536 See Joshua Meltzer, "Climate Change and Trade: The EU Aviation Directive and the WTO" (2012) 15:1 *J. Intl. Econ. L.* 111 at 151–152 (Oxford Journals); Milde, "The EU Emissions," *supra* note 262 at 178; Kati Kulovesi, " 'Make Your Own Special Song, Even if Nobody Else Sings Along': International Aviation Emissions and the EU Emissions Trading Scheme" (2011) 2:4 *Climate L.* 535 at 537. In international law, the "governing principle" is that States cannot adopt measures that have extraterritorial application without the consent of other States or except under the terms of a treaty. See Brownlie, *Principles, supra* note 210 at 309. See also *The Case of the SS "Lotus" (France v Turkey)* (1927), PCIJ (Ser. A) No. 10 at 18.

537 See generally Jean Bodin, *Les Six Livres de la République*, 4th ed. (Paris: Chez Iacques du Puys, 1576) at 125; J.G. Starke, *Introduction to International Law*, 10th ed. (London: Butterworths, 1989) at 157; Sharon Anne Williams and Armand L.C. de Mestral, *An Introduction to International Law: Chiefly as Interpreted and Applied in Canada*, 2nd ed. (Toronto: Butterworths, 1987) at 108; Ruwantissa Abeyratne, *Convention on International Civil Aviation: A Commentary* (London: Springer International, 2014) at 17. However, some authors do not consider that the concept of sovereignty is a useful one to settle disagreements. See James Crawford, "Sovereignty as a Legal Value" in James Crawford and Martti Koskenniemi, eds., *The Cambridge Companion to International Law* (New York: Cambridge University Press, 2012) 117; Jacques Hartmann, "A Battle for the Skies: Applying the European Emissions Trading System to International Aviation" (2013) 82:2 *Nordic J. Intl. L.* 187 at 216.

international law, every State has complete and exclusive sovereignty over the airspace above its territory.[538] The Chicago Convention has codified this principle of airspace sovereignty,[539] and has defined "territory" as "the land areas and territorial waters adjacent thereto under the sovereignty, suzerainty, protection or mandate of such State."[540] Article 2 of the United Nations Convention on the Law of the Sea (UNCLOS) also confirms sovereignty of coastal States over the airspace above their territorial waters or sea.[541] According to Article 3 of UNCLOS, the breadth of territorial sea cannot exceed 12 nautical miles, measured from baselines.[542] In recognition of the principle of airspace sovereignty, Article 6 of the Chicago Convention authorizes every State to regulate the entry of foreign aircraft engaged in scheduled international services into its airspace; special permission or authorization is required for aircraft of one contracting State to operate scheduled international air services over or into the territory of another contracting State and such operation must be performed pursuant to the terms of such permission or authorization.[543]

Therefore, the Member States of the EU possess the necessary authority to adopt unilateral environmental measures applicable within their sovereign airspace. However, the EU ETS was not launched by the Member States but by the EU which is neither a State nor a party to the Chicago Convention. The EU is a union of 28 Member States, all of which are ICAO contracting States. It is a regional organization that is partly intergovernmental and partly supranational, since the Member States have surrendered power in certain areas to the EU.[544] As mentioned above, the EU has been conferred legal personality by the Member States.[545] It acts on behalf of its Member States in the pursuit of, *inter alia*, common foreign policies and actions that "ensure sustainable development" and are aimed at helping to "develop international measures to preserve and improve the quality of the environment,"[546] and has been granted competence to "legislate and adopt legally binding acts" in the areas of environment and transport.[547] Hence, the EU possesses the necessary authority to adopt

538 See *Case concerning Military and Paramilitary activities in and against Nicaragua (Nicaragua v United States of America)*, [1986] ICJ Rep 14 at 111; *ATA v Secretary of State*, *supra* note 504 at I-13885–I-13886; Brownlie, *Principles*, *supra* note 210 at 105.
539 Chicago Convention, *supra* note 303, art. 1. Prior to the Chicago Convention, the principle was codified in art. 1 of the Paris Convention. See Convention Relating to the Regulation of Aerial Navigation, 13 October, 1919, 11 LNTS No. 297 at 173, art. 1 (not in force) (Paris Convention).
540 Chicago Convention, *supra* note 303, art. 2.
541 United Nations Convention on the Law of the Sea, 10 December 1982, 1833 UNTS 3, UKTS 1999 No. 81, 21 ILM 1261, art. 2 (entered into force 16 November 1994) (UNCLOS). Although the term "territorial sea" is now generally accepted, "[o]ther terms employed to denote the same concept include 'the maritime belt', 'marginal sea', and 'territorial waters'." Brownlie, *Principles*, *supra* note 210 at 173 (footnote omitted).
542 UNCLOS, *supra* note 541, art. 3. Art. 5 of UNCLOS provides that "the normal baseline for measuring the breadth of the territorial sea is the low-water line along the coast as marked on large-scale charts officially recognized by the coastal State." Ibid., art. 5.
543 Chicago Convention, *supra* note 303, art. 6.
544 See e.g. Carleton University Centre for European Studies, "Extension: What Are International Organizations?" *EU Learning*, online: carleton.ca/ces/eulearning/introduction/what-is-the-eu/extension-what-are-international-organizations/.
545 See TEU, *supra* note 460, arts. 1, 47.
546 Ibid. art. 21(2)(f).
547 See TFEU, *supra* note 463, arts. 2(2), 4(2).

unilateral environmental measures in the area of transport to the extent that these apply within the sovereign territory of the Member States.[548]

It has to be noted that the EU's authority to adopt unilateral environmental measures is not unlimited. The EU needs to take into consideration, among others, established aviation law principles, several provisions of the Chicago Convention, established international law principles, bilateral and multilateral air transport agreements with non-EEA States, and the World Trade Organization (WTO) rules.

According to Article 11 of the Chicago Convention, laws and regulations of a contracting State concerning admission to or departure from its territory or concerning operation and navigation *"while within its territory"*[549] of aircraft engaged in international air navigation "shall be applied to the *aircraft of all contracting States without distinction as to nationality*, and shall be complied with by such aircraft upon entering or departing from or while within the territory of that State."[550] The EU ETS is administered by the Member States, and not by the EU itself.[551] In this regard, the Member States are required to bring into force national laws, regulations and administrative provision necessary for implementation.[552] Hence, under Article 11 of the Chicago Convention, the EU ETS must apply to all aircraft engaged in international air navigation while within the territory of the EEA Member States.

Under the EU ETS, exemption from the application of the EU ETS is granted to commercial airlines either with fewer than 243 flights per period for three consecutive four-month periods or with flights with total annual emissions lower than 10,000 tonnes CO_2 per year.[553] However, this exemption clause does not violate Article 11 of the Chicago Convention, since the exemption refers to airlines of all nationalities and not to any particular nationality. In fact, Directive 2008/101 applies to airlines, not to States. However, Scott and Rajamani disagree, arguing that the Directive applies to States as well.[554] Acceptance of this claim implies that this exemption is contrary to the equality of opportunity and non-discrimination principles of international aviation law.[555] Several provisions and the preamble of the Chicago Convention provide

---

548 However, the EU does not possess the same authority with respect to the three EEA Member States that are not EU Member States. To be applicable in the EEA, EU legislation must be incorporated into the EEA Agreement through EEA Joint Committee Decisions. Moreover, those EFTA States do not have "formal access to the decision-making process within the EU institutions." However, at the initial stages of preparing a legislative proposal, those States are permitted to participate in shaping a decision. This authority to participate in decision shaping suggests that prior consent, albeit informal, is received from those three EEA Member States before passing any EU legislation that will affect those States. In this way, the EU obtains "informal" approval of those EEA States to adopt unilateral environmental measures applicable within the sovereign area of those States, which will be "formally" approved through incorporation into the EEA Agreement after enactment of such measures. As noted before, Directive 2003/87, which established the EU ETS, and Directive 2008/101, which added aviation to the EU ETS, were incorporated into the EEA Agreement through Decision 146/2007, *supra* note 485, and Decision 6/2011, *supra* note 488, respectively. EFTA, "The Basic," *supra* note 481.
549 Chicago Convention, *supra* note 303, art. 11 (emphasis added).
550 Ibid. (emphasis added).
551 See Directive 2003/87, *supra* note 469; Directive 2008/101, *supra* note 469.
552 Directive 2003/87, *supra* note 469 at 41; Directive 2008/101, *supra* note 469 at 16.
553 See Directive 2008/101, *supra* note 469 at 17.
554 See Joanne Scott and Lavanya Rajamani, "EU Climate Change Unilateralism" (2012) 23:2 *Eur. J. Int. L.* 469 at 480.
555 See Armand de Mestral and Md Tanveer Ahmad, "Time to Support the EU ETS? Some Issues still need to be Resolved," Policy Brief, Carleton University Canada-Europe Transatlantic Dialogue (March 2014), online: labs.carleton.ca/canadaeurope/wp-content/uploads/sites/9/Policy-brief1.pdf (de Mestral, "Time to Support") ("[e]nsuring equality of opportunity and non-discrimination is a general principle of international aviation law").

for these principles.[556] States also recognize such principles, as reflected in several working papers submitted by States at the thirty-eighth session of the ICAO Assembly,[557] ICAO Assembly Resolutions,[558] and reservations to Resolutions.[559] Therefore, it can be argued that the EU ETS violates this general principle of international aviation law.[560]

However, States must appreciate the following facts. The Chicago Convention was signed at a time when environmental costs and benefits were considered incidental to broadly economic concerns, e.g., the exploitation of living natural resources.[561] Emissions from aviation "emerged as a problem in the 1970s,"[562] and, hence, the need to protect the environment was not envisaged at the time of negotiation and drafting of the Convention in 1944. As a consequence, no explicit provisions on environmental protection were incorporated therein.[563] In contrast, international environmental law on the protection of the atmosphere is a relatively new area of international law and is still evolving. The principles of equality of opportunity and non-discrimination are archaic, though established, principles and are enshrined in a treaty, namely the Chicago Convention, which does not address relatively recent global problems – climate change and global warming. Therefore, principles enshrined in this Convention should not appear as barriers to achieving environmental goals – in this case, reducing emissions from aviation that contribute to climate change and global warming.

Article 12 of the Chicago Convention can be put forward to question the validity of the EU ETS. Article 12 provides, *inter alia*, that contracting States have an obligation to adopt measures to ensure that all aircraft (whether national or foreign) flying over or maneuvering within its territory must comply with the rules and regulations concerning the flight and maneuver of aircraft there in force.[564] In these respects, contracting States undertake to keep their own regulations "uniform, to the greatest possible extent, with those established from time to time under this Convention."[565] Since no market-based measure has yet to be established under the Chicago Convention, "the obligation to keep regulations uniform with those established under the Convention cannot be discharged."[566]

556 See e.g. Chicago Convention, *supra* note 303, arts. 7, 9, 11, 15, 35, 44, Preamble.
557 See e.g. United Arab Emirates, "*UAE's Views on Aviation and Climate Change*," ICAO Assembly, 38th Sess., Agenda Item 17, Working Paper No. 258, Doc. A38-WP/258/Ex/85 (9 September 2013), online: www.icao.int/Meetings/a38/Documents/WP/wp258_en.pdf; Lithuania, "A Comprehensive Approach to Reducing the Climate Impacts of International Aviation," ICAO Assembly, 38th Sess., Agenda Item 17, Working Paper No. 83, Doc. A38-WP/83/Ex/38 (31 July 2013), online: www.icao.int/Meetings/a38/Documents/WP/wp083_en.pdf.
558 See e.g. ICAO Res. A38-18, *supra* note 21; "Consolidated Statement of Continuing ICAO Policies in the Air Transport Field," ICAO Assembly Res. A38-14, 38th Sess., ICAO Doc. 10022, III-1, online: www.icao.int/publications/Documents/10022_en.pdf.
559 See e.g. Republic of Korea, "Statement of Reservation of the Republic of Korea Regarding Resolution A38-17/2: Consolidated Statement of Continuing ICAO Policies and Practices related to Environmental Protection – Climate Change" (22 October 2013), online: www.icao.int/Meetings/a38/Documents/Resolutions/Korea_en.pdf; Australia, "Reservation by Australia to Resolution A38/17/2 on International Aviation and Climate Change" (5 November 2013), online: www.icao.int/Meetings/a38/Documents/Resolutions/Australia_en.pdf; United Arab Emirates, "UAE Reservation: Resolution 17/2 Environmental Protection – Climate Change" (4 October 2013), online: www.icao.int/Meetings/a38/Documents/Resolutions/UAE_en.pdf.
560 de Mestral, "Time to Support," *supra* note 555.
561 Redgwell, "International Environmental Law," *supra* note 91 at 687.
562 Dempsey, *Public International Air Law*, *supra* note 90 at 444.
563 See also ICAO, "Annexes 1 to 18," *supra* note 310.
564 Chicago Convention, *supra* note 303, art. 12.
565 Ibid.
566 See Md Tanveer Ahmad, "Evaluating the Effectiveness of the European Union Emissions Trading System to Reduce Emissions from International Civil Aviation" (2015) 11:1 *JSDLP* 115 at 137–138 (Ahmad, "Evaluating").

Several principles of international environmental law, which have attained the status of customary and/or general international law principles, require States to initiate action to reduce emissions from aviation. One of those principles is the established customary international legal principle that States have a sovereign right to exploit their own resources, and simultaneous responsibility to ensure that activities within their jurisdiction or control do not cause damage to the environment of other States or of areas beyond the limits of national jurisdiction.[567] Since emissions from aviation within the territory of States do not respect the national border, and contribute to climate change and global warming wherever they occur, States need to adopt measures to curb such emissions. The international environmental law principle of preventive action, which is a principle of general international law,[568] requires States to adopt measures to prevent "damage to the environment, and otherwise to reduce, limit or control activities that might cause or risk such damage."[569] Therefore, this principle requires States to adopt preventive measures to reduce emissions from aviation. All of these international law principles should be honored by the EU given its responsibilities, as well as power conferred by its Member States, to deal with the issue of environmental protection.

At the thirty-eighth ICAO Assembly meeting, it was resolved in Resolution A38-18 that States need to engage in consultations and negotiations with other States to reach an agreement when designing new – and implementing existing – market-based measures for international civil aviation.[570] Nevertheless, it should be borne in mind that resolutions are not binding per se,[571] and, as mentioned above, EU Member States filed reservations against this provision of the resolution.[572] Nonetheless, the bilateral and multilateral air transport agreements that the EU and the EEA Member States have with other non-EEA States must facilitate the EU's unilateral action in this respect.[573] Therefore, this reservation would not lend any assistance to the EEA States. These States must conclude new bilateral and/or multilateral agreements with non-EEA States, or amend the existing ones, to give way to the application of the EU ETS to non-EEA aircraft, thereby avoiding friction.[574]

---

567 See *Trail Smelter, supra* note 115; *Nuclear Weapons* case, *supra* note 115 at 241–242; *Corfu Channel Case* [1949] ICJ Rep 4; *Iron Rhine Arbitration, supra* note 115; Stockholm Declaration, *supra* note 108, Principle 21; Rio Declaration, *supra* note 99, Principle 2; *Island of Palmas* case, *supra* note 115; *ILC Report of 53rd Session, supra* note 115. See also Michel Adam, "ICAO Assembly's Resolution on Climate Change: A 'Historic' Agreement?" (2011) 36:1 *Air & Space L.* 23 at 28 (Kluwer Law Online).

568 See *Iron Rhine Arbitration, supra* note 115 at para. 59. In the *Pulp Mills* case, the ICJ pointed out "the principle of prevention, as a customary rule." *Case concerning Pulp Mills on the River Uruguay (Argentina v Uruguay)* [2010] ICJ Rep 14 at 55, para. 101. See also Sands, *Principles, supra* note 115 at 200–203.

569 Sands, *Principles, supra* note 115 at 200 (footnotes omitted).

570 See ICAO Res. A38-18, *supra* note 21 at I-72.

571 See e.g. Dinah Shelton, "Soft Law" in David Armstrong, ed., *Routledge Handbook of International Law* (Oxford: Routledge, 2009) 68 at 69–71; Alan Boyle, "Soft Law in International Law Making" in Malcolm D. Evans, ed., *International Law*, 2nd ed. (New York: Oxford University Press, 2006) 141 at 141–143; Milde, "International," *supra* note 306 at 169; Mark Weston Janis, *International Law*, 6th ed. (New York: Wolters Kluwer Law & Business, 2012) at 55.

572 See "Reservation by Lithuania," *supra* note 508.

573 See also Gilbert Schwarze, "Including Aviation into the European Union's Emissions Trading Scheme" (2007) 16:1 *Eur. Envtl. L. Rev.* 10 at 13 (Kluwer Law Online); Pietro Manzini and Anne Masutti, "The Application of the EU ETS System to the Aviation Sector: From Legal Disputes to International Retaliations?" (2012) 37:4–5 *Air & Space L.* 307 at 316 (Kluwer Law Online); Barton, "Tackling Aviation," *supra* note 262 at 319; de Leon, "Enforcement of the EU ETS," *supra* note 307 at 291.

574 See also de Leon, "Enforcement of the EU ETS," *supra* note 307 at 292.

The EU must also ensure the compatibility of the EU ETS with its obligations under the WTO rules.[575] It should be noted that one of the retaliatory actions that the non-EEA States have threatened to adopt against the EU ETS is "[d]etermining the consistency of the EU ETS with the WTO Agreements and taking appropriate action."[576] Hence, ensuring consistency of the EU ETS with the WTO rules is crucial.

Thus, it can be concluded from the above discussion that the existing law does not prohibit the implementation of the EU ETS at its amended form, i.e., applying only within the EEA airspace over which the EEA Member States retain sovereignty, provided that:

1   it does not contravene any provisions of the existing bilateral and multilateral air transport agreements the EU and/or its Member States have with non-EEA States; and
2   it is consistent with WTO rules.[577]

Undoubtedly, the decision to include aviation in the EU ETS is a notable step taken by the EU for a noble cause, namely to reduce emissions from aviation that significantly contribute to climate change and global warming.[578] However, the EU ETS will only be able partially to meet this objective of limiting emissions from aviation.[579] Most importantly, the extraterritorial reach of the decision (as it required carbon credits for the entire flight which landed or took off to or from an EU airport, irrespective of whether the airspace was over an EU member State) was met with opposition and protest from a significant number of governments, airlines, and trade associations which caused the EU significantly to circumscribe its original regulations until at least 2016.[580] Such resistance will hinder the effectiveness of the EU ETS with respect to foreign airlines, the existing friendly relationships among States, and the EU's prospective role as a norm entrepreneur and its ability to influence negotiations.[581] Together, these will result in the limited effectiveness of the EU ETS in reducing emissions from aviation, thereby undermining its environmental value.[582]

---

575 Meltzer, *supra* note 536, and Bartels, *supra* note 489, have comprehensively analyzed the compatibility of the EU ETS with the WTO rules. While Meltzer, *supra* note 536 at 154, "has demonstrated that the application of the [EU ETS] to non-EU airlines raises some important questions about its WTO consistency," Bartels, *supra* note 489 at 437, argues that, although the EU ETS will violate those trade rules, such violations "can be justified on environmental grounds under the general exceptions in these agreements." See also Katelyn E. Ciolino, "Up in the Air: The Conflict Surrounding the European Union's Aviation Directive and the Implications of a Judicial Resolution" (2012–2013) 38:3 *Brook J. Intl. L.* 1151 at 1166 (HeinOnline) ("even if the Directive is justified under GATT Article XX, the EU should refrain from imposing its program on non-EU airlines in the absence of a multilateral agreement on the regulation of aviation emissions" at 1181).
576 Joint Declaration of the Moscow Meeting on Inclusion of International Civil Aviation in the EU-ETS, 22 February 2012, online: www.greenaironline.com/photos/Moscow_Declaration.pdf.
577 See Ahmad, "Evaluating," *supra* note 566 at 140.
578 See Reagan, "Putting," *supra* note 262 (the decision "embodies a progressive and timely regulatory intent to apply a novel regulatory mechanism to a specific manifestation of the climate change effects of a commercial activity, a problem that increasingly attracts global attention" at 380 (footnote omitted)).
579 See Ahmad, "Evaluating," *supra* note 566.
580 See e.g. ibid.
581 See ibid.
582 Environmental effectiveness can be explained as "the extent to which a policy meets its intended environmental objective or realizes positive environmental outcomes." Sujata Gupta, D. A. Tirpak, N. Burger, J. Gupta, N. Höhne, A. I. Boncheva, G. M. Kanoan, C. Kolstad, J. A. Kruger, A. Michaelowa, S. Murase, J. Pershing, T. Saijo, and A. Sari, "Policies, Instruments and Co-operative Arrangements" in Metz, *Climate, supra* note 45 at 751.

The EU ETS is fully successful in one respect. This initiative brought the international actors to the negotiating table and intensified the continuing international efforts to reduce emissions from international civil aviation.[583] This led to an agreement to develop a global market-based measure for international civil aviation, reached at the thirty-eighth session of the Assembly of the ICAO in October 2013. Such enhancement, however, has yet to culminate in a multilateral market-based measure. Moreover, the EU has failed to convince non-EU States to agree to unilateral market-based measures.[584]

10.5.2 Local taxes on emissions

To reduce emissions from aviation, some European States implemented taxes on air passengers. In 1994, the United Kingdom (UK) introduced an "Air Passenger Duty" that is charged "on the carriage on a chargeable aircraft of any chargeable passenger" departing from a UK airport.[585] An aircraft is chargeable if it has an authorized takeoff mass of more than ten tons or more than 20 seats for passengers.[586] The tax was not introduced "as an environmental tax,"[587] and the UK government admitted that the tax does not have any environmental credentials and "none of the approximate £3 [billion] of annual revenues is linked to aviation investment or technological research."[588] Other European States, which charge a similar departure tax on air passengers, include Germany, Austria,[589] France, Bosnia, Serbia, Italy, and Croatia.[590] Among these States, Germany labels the tax an "ecological air travel levy."[591] The rates of charges are:

- €7.50 per passenger for short-haul departure;
- €23.43 for medium-haul services; and
- €42.18 on long-haul flights.[592]

However, the airline industry severely criticized this move from the German government.[593] Giovanni Bisignani, the then director general of IATA, denounced the tax as "the worst kind

---

583 See Ahmad, "Evaluating," *supra* note 566 at 121.

584 See ibid.

585 Finance Act 1994 (UK), c. 9, s. 28(1). For detailed information, see ibid. ss. 28–44.

586 See ibid. s. 29(1).

587 Airport Watch, "Air Passenger Duty," online: www.airportwatch.org.uk/air-passenger-duty/.

588 BAR UK, "Air Passenger Duty (APD)," online: www.bar-uk.org/campaigns/apd/. See also A Fair Tax on Flying, "Get the Facts," online: www.afairtaxonflying.org/facts/.

589 Austria, BMF: Federal Ministry of Finance, "Federal Act Introducing an Air Transport Levy (Air Transport Levy Act – FlugAbgG) Federal as amended by Tax Code Amendment Act 2012," Law Gazette BGBl I No. 112/2012, online: www.bmf.gv.at/steuern/a-z/flugabgabegesetz/Air_Transport_Levy.pdf?3vgwui.

590 See European Business Aviation Association (EBAA), "Aviation Taxes in Europe: A Snapshot" (15 January 2013), online: www.ebaa.org/documents/document/20140116101401-aviation_taxes_in_europe_-_a_snapshot_jan_2014.pdf (EBAA, "Aviation Taxes").

591 See "German Air Passenger Departure Tax linked to Environmental Performance draws Airline Protests," *GREENAIRonline.com* (9 June 2010), online: www.greenaironline.com/news.php?viewStory=1128.

592 See EBAA, "Aviation Taxes," *supra* note 590.

593 See e.g. Kurt Hofmann, "Germany Implements 'Ecological' Tax on Air Travelers," Canadian Union of Public Employees (CUPE), online: accompent.ca/en/news/germany-implements-ecological-tax-air-travelers; Geoffrey Thomas, "Airline Industry blasts Germany's 'Ecological Air Travel Levy'," *ATW Plus* (8 June 2010), online: atwonline.com/operations/airline-industry-blasts-germanys-ecological-air-travel-levy.

of short-sighted policy irresponsibility."[594] According to Bisignani, the tax was "a cash-grab by a cash-strapped government."[595]

10.5.3 Airport emissions charges

Apart from governments, airport authorities also charge airlines for emissions. However, those charges are mainly levied to reduce local air quality pollution from aviation activities. Furthermore, most of these charges are related to emissions of NO_X and/or HC which are already regulated by Annex 16 to the Chicago Convention.

In Germany, the following three airports impose emissions charges: Düsseldorf Airport, Hamburg Airport, and Munich Airport. The Düsseldorf Airport authority levies an NO_X-charge for LTO operation.[596] However, in addition to NO_X emissions, emissions of HC are also considered in the formula for calculating the charge.[597] Similarly, an emission-based charge, where emissions of both NO_X and HC are addressed, is levied per LTO in both the Hamburg Airport and Munich Airport.[598] Three airports in the UK charge airlines for NO_X emissions. The operator of Heathrow Airport levies an NO_X emission charge "on each landing by a fixed wing aircraft over 8,618kg."[599] A similar emissions charge is imposed by the Gatwick Airport authority.[600] In the case of London Luton Airport, an NO_X Levy "applies to all departing aircraft where the Engine NO_X Emission exceeds 400 [grams] per passenger or per 100 [kilograms] cargo."[601] In Sweden, all ten airports operated by the Swedavia AB charge airlines for NO_X emissions.[602] The emission charge applies to aircraft with a maximum takeoff weight exceeding 5,700kg.[603] The charge follows the standard LTO cycle and is based on certified emission values of NO_X in the LTO cycle pursuant to Annex 16 to the Chicago Convention.[604] In Denmark, the Copenhagen Airport authority imposes an emission charge which is payable per takeoff and is calculated on the basis of NO_X generated from the aircraft's idealized LTO cycle.[605]

594 AFP, "Global Airlines slam new German Departure Tax," *Independent* (UK) (9 June 2010), online: www.independent.co.uk/travel/news-and-advice/global-airlines-slam-new-german-departure-tax-1995251.html.
595 Ibid.
596 See Düsseldorf Airport, "Tariff Regulations for Düsseldorf Airport" (valid from 1 January 2015) at 4–5, online: www.dus.com/~/media/fdg/dus_com/businesspartner/aviation/entgelte/tariff_regulations_2015_02-02-2015.pdf.
597 See ibid.
598 See Hamburg Airport, "Airport Charges: Part I" (effective 15 January 2015) at 7–8, online: www.hamburg-airport.de/media/Airport_Charges_Part_I_15-01-2015.pdf; Munich Airport, "Tariff Regulations, Part 1" (effective from 1 January 2015) at 31–32, online: www.munich-airport.de/media/download/bereiche/aviation/charges2015.pdf.
599 Heathrow Airport, "Schedule 5: Charges effective from 1 July 2014," at para. 1.2, online: www.heathrowairport.com/static/HeathrowAboutUs/Downloads/PDF/HAL-Conditions-of-Use-Amendment-SCHEDULE5-Up%20date-25April2014.pdf.
600 See Gatwick Airport, "Gatwick Airport: Conditions of Use 2015/16" (effective from 1 April 2015) at 15, online: www.gatwickairport.com/globalassets/publicationfiles/business_and_community/all_public_publications/2015/2015-16-conditions-of-use---clean-30jan15.pdf.
601 London Luton Airport, "Charges & Conditions of Use 2015/16" (effective from 1 April 2015) at 7.
602 These airports are: Bromma Stockholm Airport, Kiruna Airport, Göteborg Landvetter Airport, Luleå Airport, Umeå Airport, Visby Airport, Stockholm-Arlanda Airport, Malmö Airport, Åre Östersund Airport, and Ronneby Airport.
603 See Swedavia, "Airport Charges: Appendix 1 to Conditions of Services" (valid from 1 April 2015), online: www.swedavia.com/Global/Swedavia/Flygmarknad/Prislista_exceeding5700kg_150401.pdf.
604 See ibid. at 7.
605 See Copenhagen Airports, "Charges Regulations Applying to Copenhagen Airport: In Force during the Period 1 April 2015 to 31 March 2019" (1 April 2015), online: www.cph.dk/en/about-cph/b2b/airline-sales/charges--slot/Copenhagen/.

In Switzerland, emission charges are levied at the following five airports: Basel-Mulhouse Airport, Bern Airport, Geneva International Airport, Lugano Airport, and Zurich Airport. In the case of Basel-Mulhouse Airport, the compulsory landing charge on airlines is adjusted by applying defined factors in accordance with aircraft's engine gas emission classification.[606] Likewise, the Bern Airport authority charges emissions surcharges on landing charges "for every approach with subsequent landing, dependent on the emissions factor of the individual aircraft engines,"[607] the Geneva International Airport authority imposes an emission-related landing charge,[608] the authority of Lugano Airport applies an emission-related landing surcharge,[609] and the Zurich Airport authority levies an emission charge that is charged per landing in accordance with the amount of NO_X emissions.[610] It can be observed that, among these five Swiss airport authorities, only the Zurich Airport authority targets NO_X emissions.

10.6 Summary and conclusions

The current global legal framework to reduce emissions from aviation is insufficient to lessen this sector's environmental impacts. The multilateral environmental agreements do not sufficiently address emissions from aviation. Most importantly, the Kyoto Protocol obliges the Annex I developed State Parties to the Protocol to pursue limitation or reduction of such emissions working through ICAO. The primary source of public international air law, the Chicago Convention, tacitly imposes an obligation on ICAO to reduce such emissions. While ICAO SARPs provide for the reduction of emissions to improve local air quality, they do not provide for the reduction of emissions that contribute to global environmental problems. To reduce effectively aviation's environmental impact, States must agree to global market-based measures for international civil aviation at the thirty-ninth session of the ICAO Assembly, which would become effective from 2020.

At the national and regional level, the EU, a few European States, and operators of a few European airports have attempted to regulate aircraft engine emissions through market-based measures. From an environmental perspective, these efforts deserve admiration. However, these unilateral attempts have come under attack from non-European States and the airline industry, thus affecting their effectiveness.[611] Most airport regulations, with the exception of Swiss airports, only address NO_X and HC emissions. A clean environment is beneficial to the entire globe. Since environmental problems are global problems, and emissions occurring anywhere can intensify these problems, we need a global solution. Furthermore, participation from all sectors is necessitated so that emissions reductions achieved in one sector are not frustrated by inaction from another sector. ICAO contracting States must come forward to adopt effective global measures to reduce aviation's environmental impacts.

---

606 See EuroAirport: Basel-Mulhouse-Freiburg, "Tariff Regulations 2015," ER-TRA-001 V14 (valid from 1 April 2015) at 6–7, online: euroairport.com/en/professionals/tariff-regulations.html. "Engines are classified in five different classes for gas emissions (I to V)." Ibid. at 6.

607 Bern Airport, "Schedule of Fees & Charges" (valid as of 1 July 2014) at 5, online: www.flughafen-bern.ch/images/content/pdf/JUL14Tarifordnung_en_GB.pdf ("[t]he same charge applies for every 'touch and go' and for every 'go around'"). Like the Basel-Mulhouse airport, "[a]ircraft engines are assigned to five emission classes according to their emissions factor." Ibid.

608 See Aéroport International de Genève, "Airport Charges and Services" (last updated 24 March 2015) at 10, online: www.gva.ch/en/Portaldata/1/Resources/fichiers/institutionnels/tarifs/tarifs_GVA_en.pdf.

609 See Lugano Airport, "LSZA – Lugano Airport – Aerodrome Charges: Tariff Regulations at Lugano Airport," arts. 26–29 (19 September 2013), online: www.lugano-airport.ch/files/documents/LS_GEN_4_1_EN_29_05_14.pdf.

610 See Zurich Airport, "Charges," online: www.zurich-airport.com/business-and-partners/flight-operations/charges.

611 For an extensive discussion on the effectiveness of the EU ETS to reduce emissions from aviation, see Ahmad, "Evaluating," *supra* note 566.

11

International air transport agreements

Juan Carlos Salazar and Peter van Fenema

Introduction

This chapter will be devoted mainly to intergovernmental bilateral air transport agreements (often simply referred to as 'bilaterals').

Traditionally, airlines performing international services rely on these agreements as the formal basis for virtually all aspects of their commercial operations. Reciprocal market access is agreed upon bilaterally by aviation authorities for the benefit of their respective national airlines.[1] Market access involving multiple countries requires multiple bilateral agreements. Today, some 4,000 such bilaterals still form the basis for global international air transport and, as a result, approximately 190 individual governmental aeronautical authorities collectively control global commercial activity of the international airline industry.

In the following paragraphs the background and rationale for this bilateral system will be explained, the main provisions of the traditional agreements will be analysed and the effects of this regulatory regime on the industry will be reviewed. Initiatives on the part of primarily the United States (US) and Europe to reduce these governmental controls, resulting *inter alia* in 'open skies' agreements and regional liberalization, will be analysed, and other regional and multilateral approaches to modernization of the 'system' will be discussed. Finally, attention will be paid to the role/initiatives of the International Civil Aviation Organization (ICAO) in this regard.

11.1 The Chicago Convention regime

At the Chicago Conference of 1944 all aspects of post-war international civil aviation were discussed, including the economic-commercial side of operating airlines. But fundamental disagreement on how free airlines should be to 'do business' worldwide resulted in a Convention that regulated in detail the operational and technical aspects of flying aircraft worldwide, but paid precious little attention to international market access and other doing business issues of the (national) airlines.

---

1 An airline or 'carrier' could, alternatively, simply ask for – and receive – permission from foreign authorities to start services to and from the country concerned. However, permission as a unilateral go-ahead may be granted, but also be limited in time or through conditions or may be withdrawn. Airlines that want to exploit (new) markets invest in personnel, offices and technical and operational facilities and do not appreciate the uncertainties connected with unilateral permits. Hence their understandable preference for more official arrangements detailing their long-term rights and obligations as a commercial entity providing international air transport services.

Sure, the lofty principles formulated in the preamble include as a purpose of the Convention 'that international air transport services may be established on the basis of equality of opportunity and operated soundly and economically'. And the aims and objectives of ICAO listed in article 44 of the Convention include the following:

[...]

d   Meet the needs of the peoples of the world for safe, regular, efficient and economical air transport;
e   Prevent economic waste caused by unreasonable competition;
f   Insure ... that every contracting State has a fair opportunity to operate international airlines.

However, when it comes to specific rules that guide the parties when dealing with, let alone fostering, the economics of the airline industry, the Convention remains largely silent. Some provisions that do have a bearing on this aspect will briefly be dealt with in sections 11.1.1–11.1.4 hereafter, followed by two relevant multilateral instruments also developed at Chicago (in 11.1.5 and 11.1.6). In section 11.9, ICAO's efforts through the years to address these economic issues will be reviewed.

11.1.1 Sovereignty over national airspace

The leading principle governing international civil aviation is that of national sovereignty, an already existing principle of international law, reconfirmed in article 1 of the Convention: 'The contracting States recognize that every State has complete and exclusive sovereignty over the airspace above its territory.' Territory extends horizontally to include the territorial waters and thus the airspace above those waters.[2]

The national sovereignty principle is clear and simple: it means there may be no unauthorized access for foreign aircraft to national airspace.

11.1.2 Scheduled air services

The national sovereignty principle is translated into a provision on scheduled air services: 'No scheduled international air service may be operated over or into the territory of a contracting State, except with the special permission or other authorization of that State' (article 6).[3] In other words, without the consent of the national authorities of a country a foreign airline cannot start scheduled operations to/from any destination in its territory; the rule is that all cross-border markets are closed unless an exception has been made. An airline cannot start doing international business without permission given by all relevant foreign authorities.

---

2   Vertically, no specific limitation was considered necessary in 1944: though the appearance of German V-2 rockets had shocked the allied powers, space flight and (spy) satellites would not come into the picture until the late 1950s and early 1960s and therefore did not play a role at Chicago. And even today, the height of the border between air space and outer space, with the concomitant question 'where does sovereign air space end and free outer space begin', is more a space lawyers' concern than one that keeps the air law community awake.
3   For a definition and analysis of 'scheduled international air service' see ICAO Doc. 9587 'Policy and Guidance Material on the Economic Regulation of International Air Transport', 3rd ed. (2008) at I-11; the most important elements are: a series of flights open to the general public and operated according to a timetable; this definition is also relevant for the application of art. 5 on non-scheduled flights.

11.1.3 Cabotage

The national sovereignty principle of article 1 finds another application with economic consequences in the provision of article 7 on *cabotage*. That article allows a state to reserve air transport between points within its territory for its own carriers and to forbid foreign airlines to engage in that type of domestic commercial activity. One could argue that such a right of refusal is inherent in the very concept of sovereignty, but the draftsmen of the Convention in war-year 1944 considered it useful to emphasize this military-relevant right.[4]

11.1.4 Non-scheduled flights

Flights that, at the time of operation, do not fall under article 6 get a somewhat more 'liberal' treatment:

- the right to overfly foreign territory and make a technical – final or intermediate – landing ('technical' meaning a landing *not* for (dis-)embarking paying passengers or (off-)loading cargo) without needing prior permission from the authorities concerned (the Convention does not provide these so-called first and second freedoms (see section 11.1.5) for *scheduled* services);
- the right to transport *paying* passengers and cargo on these flights is however subject to separate conditions of the state of embarkation and/or disembarkation.[5]

11.1.5 Transit Agreement

Subject to the exception in section 11.1.4, national air space worldwide is thus closed, unless opened by the government concerned, for entry by a specific foreign airline. This latter aspect was seen by many delegates at Chicago as an unfortunate regulatory impediment to scheduled international operations. Flying between for instance Europe and Asian destinations at the time involved not only passing through multiple airspaces but also a number of landings for technical purposes, such as refuelling, engine checks and crew changes.

Instead of leaving this non-commercial aspect of aircraft operations to airlines and governments to address in the same way as commercial issues, i.e. through permits or agreements, a number of delegations concluded that this problem should be solved through a multilateral arrangement. The resulting treaty concluded at Chicago on the same day as the Chicago Convention, 7 December 1944, became the International Air Services Transit Agreement, also known as the Transit Agreement.

---

4 The second part of art. 7 provides that

> [e]ach contracting State undertakes not to enter into any arrangements which specifically grant any such privilege on an exclusive basis to any other State or an airline of any other State, and not to obtain any such exclusive privilege from any other State.

This is where sovereignty and the Convention's (underlying) principle of non-discrimination/equal opportunity collide. Through the years states have tended to use their sovereign right to discriminate and grant, though often on an ad hoc basis and without officially excluding others, cabotage to a specific foreign carrier.

5 For an analysis of art. 5, see ICAO Doc. 9587, *supra* note 3, at I-13. Instead of 'non-scheduled flight' the expression 'charter' flight, though denoting a contract between an airline and a tour operator to make an aircraft available for the clients of the latter, is often used. But also private flights would come under art. 5.

The Transit Agreement was – and continues to be – a success: today, 130 states accept its rights and obligations.

The agreement allows each of the parties for the purpose of operating scheduled air services two privileges or 'freedoms' vis-à-vis any other party:

1   to fly across its territory without landing;
2   to land for non-traffic purposes.

These so-called first and second freedoms, or two *technical* freedoms, permit airlines to use the airspace and airports of the states concerned for technical and operational purposes only. The second freedom actually forbids an airline to use the landing for commercial purposes, so neither paying passengers may embark or disembark nor cargo may be (off-)loaded.[6] Overflying and technical landings are not completely free: the state concerned has the right to prescribe routes and determine which airports may be used; and charges may be levied for the airport services and other facilities, e.g. air traffic management, made available.

A substantial number of states are not parties to this agreement, including states with large territories like Canada, Russian Federation, China, Indonesia, Brazil and Saudi Arabia. As a consequence, foreign airlines need to obtain the two freedoms through negotiations with the non-party state concerned through unilateral permits or bilateral agreements.

11.1.6 International air transport agreement

The US and a relatively small number of other participants at the Chicago Conference had aimed for a multilateral regime creating operational and commercial freedom for their respective airlines: the right to fly to any destination and transport passengers and cargo/mail without government-imposed controls on capacity, i.e. number of services, routes and prices. However, fundamental disagreement with countries that demanded a strong government role in protecting the national airlines against – potentially aggressive – foreign competitors resulted in a Chicago Convention that focused primarily on operational and technical aspects of aircraft movements and left the commercial issues and the 'unfreedom' of article 6 untouched.

Unhappy with this clear deviation from its business-oriented philosophy, the US found a number of like-minded states at Chicago prepared to give the airlines more freedom to compete as they deemed fit, at least with respect to both the capacity and the right to transport passengers and cargo on their scheduled services.

The resulting agreement, concluded on the same day as the Convention, repeated the two technical freedoms already laid down in the Transit Agreement and added three *commercial* freedoms in respect of scheduled international air services, the third, fourth and fifth freedoms (hence its nickname the 'Five Freedoms Agreement').

The following examples may explain these freedoms:

1   the third freedom gives a US airline the right to carry traffic (= passengers, freight and/or mail) from the US to the Netherlands;

---

6 Interestingly, a country whose airports are used for this latter purpose may require the airlines concerned 'to offer reasonable commercial service' at these points. One might consider this provision a very early expression of the philosophy that international air transport may serve the economic interests of a country, irrespective of the identity of the airline. It is unknown whether this clause has ever been invoked by any of the states concerned.

2   the fourth freedom gives a US airline the right to carry traffic from the Netherlands to the US;

3   the fifth freedom gives a US airline the right, on a service originating in and returning to the US, to carry traffic between the Netherlands and the next foreign destination of that service beyond the Netherlands, e.g. Ethiopia or Turkey, and vice versa.

Upon acceptance by the first two of the signatory states, the Netherlands and the US respectively, the agreement entered into force on 8 February 1945 between these two countries. The end of that year saw a total score of 11 parties, but, though in the following years some more countries joined, disappointment as to the number and importance of the parties led the US to withdraw from the agreement in 1947, and others followed. The US ideal, a multilateral reciprocal granting of access to important markets, enabling the establishment of a network of profitable routes, had simply not materialized. Put differently, enabling airlines from small parties to benefit from fifth freedom rights between the US and third countries, without – the prospect of – obtaining benefits of comparable value for its own carriers in return was not in the US's national interest.

Of the 11 parties, Greece and Turkey made a reservation with respect to the exchange of fifth freedom rights, further undermining the already limited importance of this agreement for the 'liberalization' of international air transport.

It has to be concluded that the agreement, while promising at the time as to its liberal and pro-competitive aims and contents, failed to obtain critical mass and, though still in force, has become virtually irrelevant.[7] Hence, the regulation of the economic-commercial aspects of international air transport was left to the individual states on behalf and for the benefit of their airlines. The conclusion of bilateral intergovernmental air transport agreements thus became the preferred modus operandi.

11.2 The bilateral system

Two important participants at Chicago, the US and the United Kingdom (UK), represented widely divergent views on how much freedom should be granted to the airlines in post-war international civil aviation to spread their wings. These differences were partly philosophical and partly pragmatic. The US combined its economic philosophy of free competition with the availability of a large number of aircraft (used during the war to transport troops) and airlines eager to use those machines to conquer the world market, whereas the UK saw its own aspirations in this regard hampered by a lack of suitable aircraft (they had specialized in building fighter aircraft during the war), a fear of US dominance and a need for orderly, i.e. government controlled, development of world aviation. Anyhow, the pre-war arrangements of 1935 between the US and the UK had to be thoroughly reviewed and adapted to post-war challenges and opportunities.

11.2.1 The Bermuda agreement

When the two parties met in Bermuda in 1946 to develop rules governing their rights and obligations and those of their respective airlines, the two above approaches kept them fundamentally

---

7 The number (11) and identity of the parties have remained the same for the last three decades:

Bolivia, Burundi, Costa Rica, El Salvador, Ethiopia, Greece, Honduras, Liberia, Netherlands, Paraguay and Turkey. In the mid-1990s the Dutch government invoked the agreement vis-à-vis Ethiopia, but the latter's negative reaction ('it is an old agreement; times have changed'), though incorrect from a legal point of view, prevented KLM from actually starting its planned operations to Addis Ababa on that basis at the time.

apart until compromises could finally be reached. The most important topics to be addressed were *capacity* and *pricing*:

- will the airlines of both parties be free to determine the capacity, expressed in number of services operated and size of the aircraft used, on the routes between the US and the UK or should the governments have a – decisive – say in this matter;
- will those same airlines be allowed to set prices for their products as they deem fit or should the governments have a – decisive – say in this matter?

11.2.1.1 Capacity

The compromise between, roughly, capacity freedom and regulated capacity as laid down in the Bermuda agreement could be seen as a victory for the US's philosophy. Briefly, the agreement does not contain any 'pre-determination' of capacity clause or other requirement for government approval of the number of services prior to them being operated by the airlines concerned.

But the Final Act of the Bermuda Conference attached a number of conditions to the use of the agreement's capacity freedom, allowing the government of an 'affected' airline to demand a reduction of the capacity mounted by its counterparts/competitors:

- the principal rule on capacity is: there shall be 'fair and equal opportunity' for the airlines of both parties to operate on any of the agreed routes any – number of – services they deem justified, *but*:
- there should be a close relationship between the capacity offered and the actual demand for transport, in other words, *no capacity-dumping; and*
- the interest of the carriers of the other party should be taken into account 'so as not to affect unduly the services which the latter provides', in other words, *no cut-throat competition; and*
- a condition included specifically for multi-stop operations: the capacity should have as its *primary objective* the carriage of third and fourth freedom traffic, in other words, adding capacity just or primarily to cater for fifth freedom traffic is frowned upon. To give an example: a US carrier operating a service under the Bermuda agreement from New York to London and onward to Frankfurt may exercise fifth freedom rights between London and Frankfurt, but the capacity, i.e. the number of frequencies and size of aircraft, used for these services should be based primarily on the (expected) traffic carried between New York and London and between New York and Frankfurt. A 'booming' fifth freedom market London–Frankfurt and vice versa cannot in itself justify an increase of capacity of the services operated on the whole route (or on the sector London–Frankfurt and vice versa).[8]

One may safely assume that the regular consultations between the parties on the application of the agreement as foreseen in Bermuda were meant to discourage any of the airlines concerned (but, given the circumstances, primarily the US airlines), to abuse the capacity freedom provided by the 'fair and equal opportunity' clause: in these so-called *ex post-facto* reviews any of the three above conditions could of course be used to underpin a demand for reduced capacity or at least less competitive use thereof by the misbehaving airlines of the other side.

---

8 Agreement between the US and the UK relating to air services. Signed at Bermuda 11 February 1946; entered into force 11 February 1946. 60 Stat. 1499; TIAS 1507; 12 Bevans 726; 3 UNTS 253.

This combination of conditions attached to an, as such liberal-sounding, equal opportunity clause can still be found in today's traditional Bermuda standard bilateral agreements. The de facto interpretation and application of this type of capacity regime depend almost entirely on the competitive positions, needs and concerns of the airlines and their governments. In fact, restrictive interpretations have been the norm rather than the exception (see section 11.2.2).

11.2.1.2 Pricing

A lengthy and detailed provision on 'rates' in the Annex to the agreement made one thing abundantly clear: competition on the prices of the products would be completely in the hands of the aeronautical authorities of the two governments. This so-called *double approval* regime made sure that a passenger or cargo tariff (or 'rate') proposed by one carrier and approved by its government, if considered unfair or uneconomic by its foreign competitor, could be rejected by the latter's government and would then, as a consequence, not be available to the public.

This was a vital concession to allay UK concerns about tariff wars between powerful and well-equipped US carriers and its own fledgling airline. And, like the above capacity regime, it became a standard provision in the agreements signed by other aviation nations around the globe.

The pricing clause included a reference to the 'rate conference machinery' of the International Air Transport Association (IATA) as a multilateral inter-company means to establish fares and rates on all the relevant routes, but neither this method nor bilateral intercompany agreements could lead to definitive tariffs without the approval of the two aeronautical authorities concerned.

11.2.1.3 Other clauses

Apart from the most contentious topics, capacity and pricing, other matters were addressed in the agreement, such as

* the exchange of first and second freedom, plus third and fourth freedom, and special provisions on the exercise of fifth freedom rights (see section 11.2.1.1);
* the conditions which the 'designated airlines' of both parties have to adhere to, including on nationality, through substantial national ownership and effective control, of the airlines concerned;
* the applicability of national laws and regulations to entry by their respective aircraft;
* a 'route annex', detailing the exact routes and route-points made available to the airlines of both parties;
* a provision on 'regular and frequent consultation' to make sure that both parties behave according to the principles of the agreement;
* an article on consultations in case one of the parties seeks modification of the Annex, primarily of the routes prescribed therein.

Most of these and other Bermuda provisions have become part of the standard Bermuda-type agreement that has survived until today; they will be discussed in the following section.

11.2.2 Today's 'traditional' Bermuda-type agreement

11.2.2.1 Grant of rights

A traditional bilateral agreement includes an article that specifies the 'freedoms of the air' made available to the designated airlines of both parties, including the two 'technical' freedoms (also between States that are already parties to the Transit Agreement!) and third and fourth freedoms.

However, the above exchange of traffic rights does not imply any authorization to the airlines of one country to engage in air transport between points in the territory of the other country (cabotage, also called eighth or ninth freedom).[9] In fact, today very few states exchange cabotage rights in their bilateral agreements (an exception is Chile).[10] Ad hoc, temporary permission in emergency situations is a more common approach.

As far as fifth, sixth and seventh freedom rights are concerned, often Civil Aviation Authorities, pressed by their respective national airlines, exclude or restrict the exercise of these freedoms. We referred above to the Bermuda treatment of fifth freedom rights.[11]

The *sixth* freedom is commonly practised today by large and small airlines alike: they carry passengers from their different origins to a 'hub' airport in the home state of the carrier, from where they are then transported by the same airline to their final destination. The airlines concerned see this connecting traffic as simply a combination of third and fourth freedom rights: passengers choose to travel this way because of the geographic location of the hub combined with the fact that this way of channelling traffic flows through a 'hub' sometimes creates additional international services and connections that are not available/viable otherwise (i.e. via direct flights). However others perceive this practice as a thinly 'veiled' fifth freedom traffic right, to which the Bermuda 'primary objective' principles apply, and will, for competitive reasons, (try to) impose restrictions on sixth freedom airlines by limiting the number of their frequencies and the advertising of tariffs for travel between the foreign states involved.[12]

The *seventh* freedom is the right or privilege granted by a state to a foreign airline to transport traffic between the granting state and a third state on a 'stand-alone' basis: the latter means that the airline is not required to connect this service between two foreign countries to its home state in either direction. This right to operate in the 'backyard' of the granting state is rarely granted, as, like the fifth freedom, it competes directly with the third and fourth freedom operations of the carriers of the two foreign countries involved.

11.2.2.2 Designation and revocation

Governments decide how many airlines will be allowed to operate the agreed services. Some countries only have one national carrier and may insist on a 'single designation' clause. However,

---

9 See (text to) note 4. Eighth freedom or consecutive cabotage: a carrier operates an international service to points in a foreign territory and has the right to carry passengers and/or cargo between those points; ninth freedom or stand-alone cabotage: a carrier operates a service and transports traffic wholly within a foreign territory. We may recall that cabotage is not ruled out by the Chicago Convention; however art. 7 of the Convention stipulates that states should not grant cabotage rights on an exclusive basis.

10 By Decree-Law No. 2.564 of 1979 Chile eliminated cabotage restrictions for foreign airlines; more recently, on 29 December 2011 the Civil Aeronautics Board of Chile decided that Chile would not demand reciprocal authorizations in order to authorize cabotage operations to foreign carriers. See www.jac-chile.cl/politica-aerocomercial/transporte-domestico-o-cabotaje.

11 For descriptions and discussion of the nine freedoms of the air, see ICAO, "Manual on the Regulation of International Air Transport', Doc. 9626, 2nd ed. (2004) Chapter 4.1, at 4.1.8–4.1-16 (Traffic rights).

12 In fact it is not very common to find bilateral language explicitly referring to sixth freedom traffic; restrictions are rather imposed implicitly, as for example, when during bilateral consultations one party argues that the amount of third and fourth freedom traffic, sometimes referred to as 'true origin and destination' (TOD) traffic, carried by the airline of the other party does not justify an increase of the number of flights or the number of points (destinations) allowed to the latter. In Netherlands–Israel bilateral relations in the past, two sixth freedom limiting measures alternated: a numerical limit, i.e. a maximum of such passengers to be carried by KLM per summer or winter season, plus a payment per passenger exceeding that maximum, or a limitation of the number of frequencies operated between the two countries. In the relations between the Gulf States/carriers and countries like Canada, Germany and France the latter approach was generally chosen. Japan, traditionally, used the same method. See also section 11.4.2, note 27, on the US–Netherlands sixth freedom conflict.

with the privatization of state owned carriers and increasing liberalization of market access, more and more countries have more than one airline operating international services and therefore ask for 'dual' or 'multiple' designation clauses in their agreements.[13]

11.2.2.3 Nationality (ownership and control)

Historically, for military and political reasons, the question of which state – or its nationals – owned or controlled a foreign airline was an important element for deciding if that airline would be allowed to operate air services into the territory of the receiving state.

Governments are also concerned about the use of 'flags of convenience', a maritime transportation concept that refers to registration of a ship in a country either to circumvent the safety, environmental, taxation, labour and security requirements that may be imposed by its own state, or to gain access to certain markets that otherwise would not be available. Transposed to international air transport, the concept requires ascertaining the nationality of a designated airline, to ensure that its operations are conducted according to international standards and to ensure that market access opportunities go to the airlines of the state with which they were negotiated.

The standard article requires that the designated airline is *substantially* owned and effectively controlled by the designating state and/or its nationals. To avoid problems in practice, the term 'substantial' is usually interpreted as *majority* ownership, i.e. more than 50 per cent equity in the airline. However, 'effective control' is a much vaguer criterion, and may give rise to differing interpretations and application.[14]

It should be noted that (a) the traditional clause requires *both* ownership *and* control to be in national hands, and that (b) the receiving State *may* set conditions or impose sanctions on the foreign airline if it is not *convinced* that that airline meets the nationality requirements; the state's reaction is thus not an automatic response but a matter of *choice*.[15]

---

13 This article in the bilateral agreements normally specifies the formalities applicable to the designation of airlines (e.g. letter from the aeronautical authorities or diplomatic notes), and includes the basic technical and legal requirements to be met for the operation of international services, including compliance with safety and security standards.

14 See e.g. for definition used for licensing purposes in EU Regulation (EC) No. 1008/2008 of 24 September 2008, OJ L293, at 3, on common rules for the operation of air services in the Community (Recast), art. 2.9:

> 'effective control' means a relationship constituted by rights, contracts or any other means which, either separately or jointly and having regard to the considerations of fact or law involved, confer the possibility of directly or indirectly exercising a decisive influence on an undertaking, in particular by: (a) the right to use all or part of the assets of an undertaking; (b) rights or contracts which confer a decisive influence on the composition, voting or decisions of the bodies of an undertaking or otherwise confer a decicive influence on the running of the business of the undertaking.

On ownership and control, see e.g. Isabelle Lelieur, *Law and policy of substantial ownership and effective control of airlines: Prospects for change*, Ashgate (2003).

15 Surprisingly, the national ownership and control clause of 1946 is still present in a vast majority of bilateral agreements. This is more and more a problem for an industry that each day is more dependent on international investors and is increasingly eager to consolidate through international mergers and acquisitions. For those purposes, it has been necessary either to waive the requirement for specific carriers, or to replace the traditional criteria by concepts such as 'principal place of business' (see section 11.4.7 MALIAT), 'effective regulatory control' or 'community carrier' (see section 11.5 on this EU concept). Liberalization of air carrier ownership and control to enable (more) foreign investment in national airlines was a topic discussed at the sixth ICAO Air Transport Conference in 2013. ICAO was mandated to develop an international agreement for state use to liberalize air carrier ownership and control (see section 11.8) and is currently working on a draft multilateral convention to liberalize investment in airlines.

11.2.2.4 Routes

Traditionally, the routes required for the operations of the designated airlines are negotiated individually and, as a result, the Annex (see below) will specify the points to be served, including the points in the territory of the states concerned, and also behind, intermediate and beyond points in other countries. Limiting the number of intermediate etc. points will of course affect the operational and commercial flexibility of the airlines.[16]

11.2.2.5 Tariffs

Nowadays, tariff coordination amongst airlines or through IATA creates competition law concerns, and direct tariff coordination amongst airlines is being avoided as it may constitute a violation of competition law (and in some jurisdictions, a criminal offence). In some cases, IATA tariff coordination continues being used, provided it has been granted immunity or the mechanism has been approved by the relevant competition authorities.

Furthermore, the original double approval pricing formula of Bermuda is rarely used anymore, being replaced by more liberal variations, such as the 'country of origin' regime, which requires only the approval of the State where the transport originates, or 'double disapproval', whereby the rate would go into effect unless the regulatory authorities of both states rejected it. With government control declining, a competition clause may take its place as a safeguard against anti-competitive ('unfair') pricing.

11.2.2.6 'Equal opportunities'

As observed in the previous sub-section, governments, in order to protect their national airlines, have applied restrictive interpretations to the 'fair and equal opportunity' clause.

A common approach has been to read the term as 'equal capacity shares', as a justification for limiting the capacity of the competing foreign airline to exactly the level of the national carrier, expressed in number of frequencies per week operated between the two countries, or in total number of seats offered to the public during a 'traffic season'; the concept is thus reduced to a simple 50/50 capacity sharing regime, a frequent practice in Europe in the decades before 'liberalization' (see section 11.3 hereafter).

Others go a step further and insist on the competing airlines obtaining 'equal benefits'; this may even lead the underperforming airline to request 'compensation' from his more successful competitor, e.g. in the form of a 'pool agreement' (see section 11.3 hereafter).

A more common approach is to maintain the above traditional clauses but, in deviation from the Bermuda principle they contain, simply have the governments pre-determine the capacity permitted to the airlines of both sides, usually in number of frequencies per week, in total or per city-pair.

Obviously, where routes, rights, tariffs and/or capacity are strictly regulated, this clause has little meaning or effect. As a means to guide the behaviour of the competitors it becomes relevant when such specific restrictions are absent. A competition article makes sense when competition is possible. In a more liberal context (see later) this principle has evolved to ensure that parties, when competing in the market, will avoid any form of discrimination or unfair competitive practices.

---

16 Some states will limit the number and 'quality' of intermediate and beyond points for fear that the foreign airline concerned will be tempted to ask for fifth freedom rights in order to use those points commercially.

11.2.2.7 Safety

ICAO has successfully developed technical standards and recommended practices required for the safe operation of air services: air transport agreements provide for the mutual recognition of certificates and licences that are issued according to these international standards.

Bilateral safety provisions describe the rights and obligations of the parties to maintain safe operations, and include recourse to safety consultations in case of concerns. The safety provision is based on the assumption that the States and airlines maintain the minimum safety standards of ICAO. Where ICAO standards are not met, other states are not obliged to accept the certificates of airworthiness issued by the delinquent state, and may therefore ban its airlines from their skies.

11.2.2.8 Security

A security provision was not envisaged in the original Bermuda agreement, but in recent years the concern of states with illegal interference acts against international civil aviation resulted in bilateral security clauses becoming standard.

Such a clause normally refers to the international aviation security conventions applicable to the concerned states, as well as the commitment to comply with international (ICAO) standards. They also require cooperation to prevent or respond to acts of illegal interference with international civil aviation.

11.2.2.9 Codesharing

This is a form of commercial cooperation between one airline, the 'operating partner', flying under its own flight code, and another airline, the 'marketing partner', adding its code to that same flight, and selling it as if it were its own operation. This benefits both airlines: they will no longer compete on the respective route, but will jointly commercialize services that otherwise may not be viable, thus allowing for a more rapid expansion of the airlines' networks.

This practice gives rise to some regulatory concerns, such as the protection of the rights of the consumer and the availability of 'underlying' traffic rights. For this reason it is sometimes required that the participating airlines submit the respective agreement for approval or at least for information purposes to the aeronautical authorities.

11.2.2.10 Leasing

For financial and commercial reasons airlines often prefer to rent, rather than purchase aircraft, without crew (dry lease) or with crew (wet lease). In order to address safety concerns, governments sometimes introduce bilateral or regulatory provisions applicable to aircraft leasing, requiring the compliance with certain safety standards for all parties involved before such operations are allowed. Some countries will, in case of wet lease, require that the foreign lessee and his lessor both possess the traffic rights necessary for the operation of the planned services.

In this connection it should be noted that, in principle, the Chicago Convention assigns the state of registry of an aircraft the responsibility for the compliance with safety standards. Article 83*bis* creates the legal framework to transfer responsibilities pertaining to articles 12, 30, 31 and 32(a) of the Convention from the state of the registry (the lessor air carrier) to the state of the operator (the lessee air carrier); such agreements should be registered with ICAO.

11.2.2.11 Cargo and intermodal transportation

International air transport mobilizes a substantial portion of international trade by value. Cargo flights are often seasonal and cargo movements are uni-directional (whereas passenger movements are usually round-trip), which results in the need for much more operational and commercial flexibility. As a result many bilateral agreements, although restrictive for passenger services, have liberal cargo provisions permitting unlimited services with owned or leased aircraft and unrestricted third, fourth and fifth and sometimes seventh freedom rights. Some countries have gone beyond that to fully liberalize *unilaterally* (e.g. India and Pakistan in their national laws and regulations) the provision of all cargo services.

Another provision normally included in connection with cargo transportation (sometimes also applied to passenger transportation) is one on intermodal transport services allowing the sale of transport by air in combination with one or more modes of surface transportation.

11.2.2.12 Other provisions (change of gauge, taxation, remittance etc.)

Change of gauge is a change of aircraft – usually from large to small – at an intermediate stop while retaining the same flight number. An example would be a US carrier operating a service New York–London–Dusseldorf using a B747 on the first sector and switching to a smaller aircraft in London for the last part of the journey to Dusseldorf and vice versa

Apart from leasing and codesharing, bilateral agreements contain other 'doing business' provisions such as on currency conversion and remittance of earnings, employment of non-national personnel, facilities for sale and marketing activities, airline product distribution, all of which are of tremendous relevance to facilitate the commercial activity of the airlines.

Airlines may face challenges when trying to transfer funds that result from the sale of air transport services abroad. ICAO provides a model bilateral clause on currency conversion and remittance, a matter that is particularly important in cases of countries that have implemented an exchange control regime.[17] Similarly, in some states foreign airlines may have problems employing non-national personnel, thus requiring special authorization from the receiving State to do so; ICAO has developed a model bilateral clause to facilitate the process of employing non-national employees.

Many states require the appointment of a national representative or agent for foreign airlines and the agreements often include provisions enabling foreign airlines to maintain sales offices and to conduct sale and marketing activities directly or through agents. Another aspect that affects the commercial activity of airlines is the use of product distribution systems, such as computer reservation systems (CRS) and the Internet. While some states implemented detailed regulations applicable to CRS, ICAO has developed a set of principles for the provision of CRS services.

11.2.2.13 Annexes and appendices

Most air transport agreements include a 'route annex' with a route schedule for operations by the airlines of each party, and conditions or restrictions to such operations, including traffic rights, routing rights and other operational rights, such as the right to serve two points in one

---

17 For example, the tight exchange controls and restrictions recently imposed by the Venezuelan government on the repatriation of funds by foreign companies. According to IATA, this resulted in the freezing of over $4.1 billion of foreign airlines in Venezuela, with consequential financial losses and resulting in various airlines halting their operations or reducing their capacity to/from that country; see www.iata.org/pressroom/pr/Pages/2014-07-28-01.aspx.

foreign country (co-terminalization) and intermodal transport (e.g. combine air and surface transport like high-speed train).

The rationale for having these in an Annex rather than in the body of the agreement is that the issues included in the Annex are typically discussed in consultations by the aeronautical authorities, and there is more flexibility to amend the Annex to the agreement which generally does not require all the formalities of amendments to the main articles of an international agreement. This makes particular sense where the rights granted have been limited *ab initio*, making it unavoidable for the airline so restricted to negotiate frequently for expanded opportunities.

11.2.2.14 Amendments (including the practice of MoUs)

The bilateral system is maintained alive and relevant by frequent consultations between the aeronautical authorities on such 'bread and butter' matters as the designation of airlines, (waiver of) the application of certain provisions (e.g. of ownership and control), capacity, frequencies and routes for the operation of passenger and (separately) cargo services and sometimes non-scheduled operations. Memoranda of Understanding (MoUs) or Records of Discussions resulting from these meetings will contain any amendment of the agreement or the Annex, or follow-up action, agreed upon.

These documents, though indispensable to understand the contents of a bilateral air transport agreement are, for broader negotiating reasons, frequently kept confidential, making it difficult for governments, airlines and academics confidently to assess aeropolitical developments.

11.2.2.15 Dispute resolution and termination

When a dispute over the interpretation or application of bilateral agreements arises, the parties to the agreement normally meet for discussions. For the case that the parties are not able to resolve their dispute this way, bilaterals provide for third party resolution of disputes, either (in earlier bilaterals) by direct adjudication by ICAO, or (in modern bilaterals) by an ad hoc tribunal of arbiters nominated by the parties. While it is common for parties to an air transport agreement to have different interpretations, third party resolution is not common in such bilateral disputes, and only six cases are known to have been resolved in this way.[18]

As a result, the ultimate remedy available for the concerned party is to take unilateral action or to notify the other party of its intention to terminate the agreement, which normally takes effect 12 months later. Usually, negotiation of differences takes place during the 12-month period, leading ordinarily to a new or amended bilateral air transport agreement. This is clearly a shortcoming of the existing bilateral system, which could benefit from more effective and speedy dispute resolution.

11.3 Liberalization of the bilateral system in Europe

Like elsewhere in the world, aviation relations among the nine members of the European Economic Community[19] in the 1960s and 1970s, were regulated by traditional Bermuda-type

---

18 For an analysis of these cases see Paul Stephen Dempsey, 'Flights of Fancy and Fights of Fury: Arbitration and Adjudication of Commercial and Political Disputes in International Aviation' (2004) 32 *Georgia Journal of International and Comparative Law* 231.

19 The Treaty of Rome of 1957 created the European Economic Community (EEC); reflecting its expanded scope since the Treaty of Mastricht of 1992 it became the European Community (EC); the Lisbon Treaty of 2009 created the present structure and name: European Union (EU). The acronyms will alternate in the text.

bilateral agreements. The control that the governments thus exercised over the development of air transport services between their respective territories was made even more effective through the imposition of *pool*-agreements on the airlines concerned.

The purpose of pool-agreements was primarily to have the airlines of the – usually – two countries concerned review and agree on their respective schedules of operations planned for the coming summer or winter season ('IATA period'). This review would involve both the planned capacity of the aircraft and the total capacity per carrier per period and the scheduled time of operation of the services concerned.

The legal rationale of this check *by proxy* on the competitor's planned capacity was the Bermuda clause on equal opportunity, often interpreted as 'equal capacity shares' and the right of the authorities to disapprove schedules of foreign carriers that would violate either this clause or any of the other capacity-related Bermuda conditions.

A simple 'we do not agree with your planned expansion next summer' expressed during the pool-talks would normally result in the vetoing airline's authorities disapproving the schedule filed by the foreign airline concerned. Though, in fact, this would amount to one airline blocking the expansion of its competitor on the route(s) between their respective home territories, the pool-agreement referred to 'partners' who simply coordinated their schedules to avoid overlap or under-coverage of the market. The partnership suggestion was reinforced by a second standard provision in the agreement, i.e. the pooling of the passenger and freight revenues earned on the routes operated by the carriers between the two countries.[20]

The above combination of – restrictively interpreted – Bermuda bilaterals and compulsory pool-agreements involving state owned and state subsidized airlines was maintained with the firm support of, in particular, France, Italy, Spain and Germany, as the normal post-Chicago order of things, notwithstanding the fact that the Treaty of Rome of 1957 establishing the six-member EEC contained rather clear free competition and free and fair trade principles. However, until the late 1970s these principles were, for political, trade-protectionist and legal reasons, ignored by the member states, when it came to their application to air transport.

Increasing industry and consumer unhappiness with this state of affairs on the one hand and European Commission political and legislative initiatives on the other hand resulted in more and more pressure on the member states to change a system that had brought the air transport user low quality, lack of choice, high prices and stagnation.[21]

But it was the European Court of Justice (ECJ) that forced a dramatic change in the intra-European bilateral system. In its *Nouvelles Frontières* judgment of 1987 it ruled that the competition provisions of the Treaty of Rome did apply to air transport. The bilateral agreements

---

20 The basis for the sharing of the total combined net revenue in an IATA period would be the efforts, expressed in capacity offered, of the two partners. As 50:50 was the usually accepted capacity allocation, a simple example of the effect would be: partner A, who carried 60,000 passengers, put $600,000 into the 'pool' account; its competitor partner B, who carried 40,000 passengers, put $400,000 into the same account. With a 50:50 sharing formula applied, partner A would have to transfer $100,000 as 'pool-payment' to its less successful partner B. Though it was not uncommon to limit these transfers to a percentage of the revenue of the transferring partner, say 5 per cent, in this case resulting in a pool-payment of $30,000, in final analysis the system could be seen as a compulsory royalty payment to be effected by the more successful partner/competitor.

21 Probably the only exception was the relatively liberal capacity regime and multiple designation existing between the UK and the Netherlands since 1974/1978; in 1984 freedom of capacity and of tariff-setting between the two countries was confirmed in an 'Understanding' between the aeronautical authorities. KLM's operations to Hong Kong however, not falling under EEC principles, remained severely restricted.

containing double approval pricing and capacity regimes preventing the airlines from competing on price and capacity, and the compulsory inter-airline pool-agreements with their capacity regimes and sharing of revenue amongst 'partners' thus came under the scrutiny of the European competition authorities.

Between the Commission seeking the immediate and full application of the rules, including those on state aid, and the main member states desperately trying to retain the status quo, a compromise was reached: in order to give the latter and their airlines time to adjust to free and fair competition, that goal would be reached in three steps over a five-year period: the so-called first, second and third liberalization packages of 1987, 1990 and 1992 respectively. These packages successively and increasingly reduced the powers of the member states to restrict or control capacity, pricing, designation, routes and rights. The 'third package' consisting of three Regulations, on licensing, pricing and market access, came into effect on 1 January 1993: it created an internal 'open skies' for all duly licensed Community air carriers.[22] Only domestic cabotage, that is the right of, say, Lufthansa to transport passengers and/or cargo between Paris and Lyon, remained subject to limitations until 1997.

Thus, for all aspects of intra-European air transport the bilaterals between the member states ceased to be relevant. And with the adoption of Regulation 3975/87,[23] dealing with the application of the competition rules to international air transport between Community airports, all commercially relevant cooperative arrangements between the airlines became a matter of Commission concern and scrutiny, with the underlying message: cooperation between competitors, other than of a purely technical nature, will probably be deemed contrary to the public interest.

The advent of free intra-European competition also brought a gradual tightening of the rules on state aid that had been virtually dormant under the bilateral system. The Commission accepted that some airlines had to get used to the concept of competition and needed governmental support to 'get their act together', but saw this as a transitional arrangement only; the message was clear: state subsidization of national airlines distorts competition and has no place in the post-1993 liberal environment. And non-subsidized airlines of Europe made every effort to help the Commission act accordingly.

It should be noted that state *ownership* of airlines as such remained legally acceptable.

And it should be recalled that the above intra-European liberalization did not affect the bilateral agreements and relations of the member states with their non-European counterparts. It would take the 2002 judgment of the ECJ in the so-called 'Open Skies cases' to force the member states to accept Brussels' increasing role in – and influence on – their bilateral aviation relations with the rest of the world. This crucial game change will be further discussed in section 11.6 below.

22 Council Regulation 2407/92 of 23 July 1992 on licensing of air carriers, 1992 OJ L240 at 1, Regulation 2408/92 of 23 July 1992 on access for Community carriers to intra-Community air routes, 1992 OJ L240 at 8 and Regulation 2409/92 of 23 July 1992 on fares and rates for air services, 1992 OJ L240 at 15; in 2008 these three Regulations were repealed and replaced by one updated and expanded Regulation 1008/2008 of 24 September 2008 on common rules for the operation of air services in the Community (recast), 2008 OJ L293 at 3.
23 Regulation (EEC) 3975/87 of 14 December 1987 laying down the procedure for the application of the rules on competition to undertakings in the air transport sector, (1987) OJ L374 at 1; 'sister' Regulation (EEC) 3976/87 of 14 December 1987 on the application of art. 85 (3) of the Treaty to certain categories of agreements and concerted practices in the air transport sector, provided a list of agreements that would, for the time being, be exempted from application of the competition rules ('block exemptions').

11.4 US international deregulation and the 'open skies' model

11.4.1 Domestic deregulation

The US Airline Deregulation Act of 1978, followed by the Civil Aeronautics Board (CAB) Sunset Act of 1984[24] discontinued or 'sunsetted' the CAB effective 1 January 1985, and terminated domestic route and price controls, leaving technical, operational and licensing matters to the Department of Transportation (DOT) and its Federal Aviation Administration (FAA). The result, predicted by such US economists as Alfred Kahn, last chairman of the CAB, was the entry of low(er) cost US carriers into a large number of domestic markets, the opening of new routes and lower prices for the consumer.

11.4.2 Internationalization of deregulation

The UK terminated Bermuda I in 1976 because of what they perceived as excess transatlantic capacity offered by the US carriers. The 'Bermuda II' agreement that resulted from the ensuing negotiations introduced much tighter controls on routes, route entry, capacity and fifth freedom and limited the number of airlines operating to/from London Heathrow to two per party. This bilateral[25] would, unlike its predecessor, not become an international standard. And within the US it triggered a reaction in the opposite direction: in 1978, during the Carter administration, a new US policy *for the conduct of international air transportation negotiations* sought to 'export' the principles and benefits of domestic deregulation: it proposed an end to bilateral capacity and frequency controls, introduced pricing freedom and offered more generous access to points in the US.[26] Of course, it takes two to tango in international aviation, and it is not surprising that two small countries with ambitious airlines, Belgium and the Netherlands were the first to negotiate a new agreement with the US along the above liberal lines.[27] The resulting low fares and unlimited capacity offered by these airlines had the predicted competitive impact on other European airlines and eventually induced a number of the governments concerned, e.g. Germany and France, to follow suit with comparable liberalized agreements.

---

24 Airline Deregulation Act, Pub. L. 95-504, 49 U.S.C. § 1371 *et seq.* Approved October 24, 1978; 98 Stat. 1703 – Civil Aeronautics Board Sunset Act of 1984.
25 Bermuda II of July 23, 1977, 28 U.S.T. 5367 (1976–1977).
26 See www.presidency.ucsb.edu/ws/?pid=31218; this policy received Congressional follow-up with the 1979 International Air Transportation Competition Act, 49 U.S.C. para. 1502 (b), e.i.f. February 15, 1980.
27 In the years before, i.e. between 1974 and 1976, the Dutch government and the US had been in a bitter and prolongued diplomatic fight resulting from PanAm complaints about KLM's sixth freedom traffic and the CAB subsequently ordering KLM to reduce its New York frequencies with more than 50 per cent; the Dutch government instructed KLM to refuse and threatened to cancel its billion dollar order for MDD F-16 fighter jets. This is where Secretary of State Henry Kissinger took over: in a deal with his Dutch counterpart a compromise in the form of a temporary limited reduction of KLM services was reached. See Andreas F. Lowenfeld, 'CAB v. KLM; Bermuda at Bay' (1975) 1:1 *Air Law*, reprinted (2005) 30:1 *Air and Space Law*. This Bermuda-based disagreement on the sixth freedom was not over in 1976/1977 when the imminent termination of Bermuda I (one year after notice of termination) threatened to result in a suspension of services of the US and UK airlines concerned. In that conflict KLM's negotiators Wassenbergh and Mifsud had discrete talks with PanAm on the use of Amsterdam and KLM as a way to accommodate PanAm's US–London traffic. This may have played a role in preparing NL–US relations for the bilateral talks that led to the liberal NL–US agreement of 1978, with free capacity, country of origin pricing and two additional US gateways for KLM; and including an end to the sixth freedom fight; see Protocol relating to U.S.–Netherlands Air Transport Agreement of 1957, March, 31 1978, 29 U.S.T. 3088.

The International Air Transportation Competition Act (IATCA) of 1979[28] codified this essentially liberal US approach towards international aviation relations, based on (more) competition and maximum access to international markets. But many of its larger aviation partners resisted the siren song of free competition because of the risks this entailed for their national airlines.

In the decade that followed there was much less focus on innovative liberal approaches and neither US carriers nor their major foreign competitors seemed inclined to go beyond rather traditional quid pro quo exchanges of traffic rights.[29] And their governments followed suit, with the logical result that only in markets where US carriers looked for increased access, and their counterparts had some unfulfilled wishes as well, were bilateral opportunities expanded for the airlines concerned, with a strong focus on direct services between major gateways.

11.4.3 Underserved cities programme

The introduction in 1990 of an innovative DOT policy on 'underserved airports/cities' ('expanding international air service opportunities to more U.S. cities') heralded a true paradigm shift in US international aviation philosophy. For the first time DOT policy put substantially more emphasis on the economic benefits (to be) brought by international air services to US cities than on the interests of its airlines, at least in the latter's perception. Put differently, the underserved airports policy bluntly told the US carriers: you have to contribute, with air services, to the local, regional and/or national economy, and if you choose not to do so we will invite foreign carriers to assume that vital task.[30] This '(Open) Cities Program' of 30 January 1990[31] created a 'framework for granting eligible foreign air carriers extra-bilateral authority to operate between additional communities in the United States and their homelands'. A number of conditions were attached to meet some of the concerns of the US carriers:

- It is not a permanent 'right' but a – renewable – one-year exemption.
- A US or foreign carrier does not provide nonstop or one-stop single-plane international air service to that US community from the same country.
- There is a pro-competitive bilateral agreement in place with the applicant's homeland country.

---

28 See note 26 *supra*.
29 The IATCA 1980 actually demanded that the US government exchange rights/opportunities of comparable value.
30 In this connection, an important role had been played by reports, commissioned by a number of these airports cooperating in the so-called US-BIAS (US Airports for Better International Air Service) lobby group, which had calculated the economic benefits to be gained by regional US communities once they would be connected with foreign countries through direct international air services irrespective of the identity or nationality of the operating carriers. Understandably US carriers strongly objected to this new approach: offering market access to foreign carriers without asking anything of equal value in return ('equal benefits') went against the carrier-friendly essence of US international aviation policy as adhered to so far. But that policy, said US-BIAS, had resulted in the exchange of 'fat routes' only and had left secondary US cities such as Denver, Charlotte, Las Vegas, New Orleans, Minneapolis and Philadelphia without international services and had thus deprived their local economies of income that expanded tourism, trade, conventions and the accompanying hotel, restaurant, museum and taxi revenues would have brought.
31 DOT Order 90-1-62 of January 30, 1990 in the matter of expanding international air service opportunities to more U.S. cities, 55 FR 4039, February 6, 1990. The programme was made more applicant-friendly with DOT order 91-11-26 of November 20, 1991 (Docket 46534).

- The applicant's proposal 'does not place undue reliance on service to and from third countries': the foreign carrier should not 'operate or hold out single-plane services or any service with single-flight numbers beyond their homelands' and should 'not advertise any third country services in the public media'.

The latter condition was meant to prevent a sixth freedom carrier like KLM Royal Dutch Airlines to promote actively, in third countries, its new services granted under the Program (from the Netherlands) to a new US destination.

In fact, KLM, which had actively participated in the discussions prior to the adoption of the Program, was the first airline to take advantage of these new opportunities. One month after the adoption of the Program, it requested and shortly thereafter obtained an exemption allowing it to start services to Baltimore, Maryland (close to Washington). And soon thereafter it would add Minneapolis and Detroit, allowing the airline to connect Amsterdam to the two main hubs of Northwest Airlines, its new US ally.

The success of the Cities Program should not be determined on the basis of the number of foreign airlines that actually used it to expand services to underserved US cities (apart from KLM, also Swissair, German LTU and Lufthansa and Chilean Ladeco were beneficiaries).

Much more important was the effect it had on the perception of the roles and functions of the two primary stakeholders, the government and the airlines. The authorities have to factor in the national economic interests served by air transport (instead of just taking care of the continued profitability or survivability of 'their' airlines); and the airlines have to realize that their role is largely a *serving* one, and that as a consequence thereof their interests or priorities cannot always come first.

In that sense the Cities Program philosophically paved the way for the market-oriented, non-government interference, survival-of-the-fittest approach that would underpin the US *open skies policy* adopted two-and-a-half years later.

11.4.4 Open skies policy

In March 1992 the US Secretary of Transportation announced that 'we will now offer to negotiate open skies agreements with all European countries willing to permit U.S. carriers essentially free access to their markets'. The Secretary referred to steps already taken by the Bush administration to advance the cause of more open international aviation markets and described his initiative as designed to stimulate interest in creating an even more market-oriented international aviation environment

With an Order Requesting Comments of 29 April 1992 in the matter of defining 'Open Skies' DOT's Assistant Secretary for Policy and International Affairs Jeffrey Shane asked for reactions from US and foreign stakeholders on his definition of 'open skies', designed to establish a framework which would allow both US and foreign carriers 'the greatest flexibility to conduct their business without undue government intervention, benefitting the travelling and shipping public to an extent not possible under traditional bilateral arrangements'. The following basic elements were to be encompassed in the proposed open skies regime:

- open entry on all routes;
- unrestricted capacity and frequency on all routes;
- unrestricted route and traffic rights, that is the right to operate service between any point in the US and any point in the European country, including no restrictions as to intermediate and beyond points, change of gauge (i.e. *change of aircraft – from large to small and/or vice versa – at an intermediate stop while retaining the same flight number*), routing flexibility,

co-terminalization (i.e. *the right when serving a route to combine two points in one foreign territory*) or the right to carry fifth freedom traffic;
- double-disapproval pricing in third and fourth freedom markets, and price leadership in third country markets to the extent that the third and fourth freedom carriers in those markets have it;
- liberal charter arrangement (the least restrictive charter regulations of the two governments would apply, regardless of the origin of the flight);
- liberal cargo regime;
- conversion and remittance arrangement (carriers would be able to convert earnings and remit in hard currency promptly and without restriction;
- open code-sharing opportunities;
- self-handling provisions (right of a carrier to perform/control its airport functions that support its operations);
- procompetitive provisions on commercial opportunities, user charges, fair competition and intermodal rights; and
- explicit commitment to non-discriminatory operation of, and access for, CRS.

Comments from 45 US and foreign stakeholders led to amendment of only one element of this list, i.e. on price leadership in third country markets. For, in the meantime, the EC member states had adopted the third liberalization package, including a Regulation on the establishment of fares and rates for services within the Community. Article 1 paragraph 3 of that Regulation reserved price leadership to Community carriers. The respective element in the Final Order of 5 August 1992[32] thus made a distinction between intra-EC markets – where price *matching* rights would be sought – and non intra-EC markets, where the above original price leadership provision would be requested.

11.4.5 1992 NL–US open skies agreement

From 1–4 September 1992, US and Dutch delegations met to conclude an open skies agreement along the lines of the above elements. Although it was the first of its kind, the parties agreed in a record time on the clauses necessary to turn the existing bilateral of 1957 as amended in 1978 into an open skies model agreement.

Both parties knew what they were doing and were in a hurry: the US wanted to set an example that would convince countries with more attractive markets (for US carriers) to follow suit. The Netherlands needed two things: first, unlimited market access into the US to enable KLM Royal Dutch Airlines to sell, together with its US partner Northwest, transport to all cities in the US served to/from the latter's hubs in Minneapolis and Detroit; and, second, such language in the agreement as would make intensified and far-reaching cooperation between the two airlines (legally) possible.

The latter took the form of the following text in the Memorandum of Consultations (MoC) signed at the close of the negotiations:

In keeping with the spirit of the Netherlands – United States Open Skies negotiations designed to liberalize to the maximum extent, the aviation market between the two countries, the delegations agreed: (a) to give sympathetic consideration, in the context of the Open Skies agreement, to the concept of commercial cooperation and integration of commercial operations between airlines of the Netherlands and United States through

32 Order 92-8-13 of August 5, 1992 (Docket 48130), in the matter of defining 'open skies', Final Order.

commercial agreements or arrangements, provided that such agreements or arrangements are in conformity with the applicable antitrust and competition laws; and (b) to provide fair and expeditious consideration to any such agreements or arrangements filed for approval and antitrust immunity.

With this supportive language the two airlines felt sufficiently confident almost immediately after the completion of the consultations to file their draft cooperation agreement with the DOT;[33] and the latter indeed expeditiously applied the rules on approval and antitrust immunity as laid down in (then) Sections 212 and 214 of the Federal Aviation Act of 1958 to the inter-carrier agreement on the basis of which the airlines would integrate their services and operate as if they were a single carrier.[34] On 11 January 1993 the DOT granted final approval and antitrust immunity for the KL/NW agreement subject to a number of relatively 'light' conditions.[35] The US therewith set the standard for all future intergovernmental and inter-carrier agreements with European partners: no approval and immunity for alliances involving a US carrier would be granted unless accompanied by an open skies agreement between the countries concerned.

That 'deal', i.e. the alliance removes competition between the partners, so, to compensate for that, an open skies bilateral is necessary to open up the relevant markets to more competitors, has stood the test of time. After initial hesitation of EC member states to follow suit, they virtually all did accept the deal for the benefit of their own carriers. The UK however never took the bait as the benefits of an immunized alliance British Airways–American Airlines would, in their view, be offset by the competitive disadvantages of opening up the UK–US market to aggressive US new-comers: the Bermuda II agreement had reserved the US–London market to a relative oligopoly of two US and two UK carriers, with the concomitant benefits derived therefrom.

11.4.6 Standard open skies agreement: main provisions

The main provisions of a standard open skies agreement,[36] in so far as they form a departure from the Bermuda model, are the following:

1   *Designation*: Bermuda-based negotiations would usually produce a lowest common denom-inator outcome (with an 'equal opportunities/benefits' flavour), meaning that the country

33 Joint application of Northwest Airlines, Inc., and KLM Royal Dutch Airlines for approval and antitrust immunity of a Commercial Cooperation and Integration Agreement, DOT Docket 48342 of September 9, 1992. For text of the NL–US agreement of October 14, 1992 see T.I.A.S. No. 11976.
34 The agreement passed both tests:
    • Approval: the agreement was not contrary to public interest, did not violate the Act and did not reduce competition in the markets US–Europe, US–Netherlands; it could reduce competition in the Amsterdam–Detroit and Amsterdam–Minneapolis markets, but that would be outweighed by the agreement's public benefits (which included increased overall competition on the North-Atlantic).
    • Antitrust immunity: the DOT concluded that the public interest, including foreign policy considerations, required the granting of immunity, both because of the spirit of the open skies agreement and the positive language in the MoC and the effect this would have on other EC member countries: they would be encouraged also to conclude open skies agreements with the US. On top of that, the parties had made it clear that they would not proceed with the transaction absent antitrust immunity, because of the risks connected with expensive and lengthy antitrust lawsuits against them.
35 Joint application of Northwest Airlines, Inc., and KLM Royal Dutch Airlines for approval and antitrust immunity of an Agreement pursuant to Sections 412 and 414 of the Federal Aviation Act, as amended, DOT Docket 48342, Final Order, US DOT of January 11, 1993; sections 412 and 414 have since been codified at 49 U.S.C. Sec. 41308 and 41309.
36 For a current model open skies agreement text and a list of US open skies partners, see www.state. gov/e/eb/tra/ata/.

with only one national airline would insist on a 'single designation' clause whether or not its counterpart had two or more airlines interested in operating services. This approach has been replaced by the concept of freedom to designate as many airlines as the country concerned finds appropriate, also referred to as 'multiple designation'.

2   *Routes*: traditional annexes to the bilateral contain routes granted to the designated airlines of the two countries that show carefully negotiated 'mirror' opportunities along the lines of: from all points in the home country of the designated airline via some (specific or unnamed) intermediate points in third countries to one or more specific points in the territory of the other contracting party and – possibly – to one or more points beyond in third countries: also the routes should – operationally and commercially – be of equal value. The open skies model gives the airlines a free choice of routes and route points for their operations between the two countries: from any country/point *behind* the home country via any intermediate point or points to all points in the territory of the other contracting party and to all third countries/points beyond. That allows for unlimited operational flexibility.

3   *Rights*: Bermuda-era bilaterals allowed no fifth freedom rights at all or a carefully negotiated exchange of limited fifth freedom rights to/from intermediate points and/or to/from beyond points, of more or less equal value. In stark contrast, the open skies model allows all designated airlines to use all route points for commercial purposes; in other words, unrestricted *fifth freedom* traffic rights. The new route provision (point 2, above) refers to 'performing scheduled international air transportation between points on the following routes' and thus conveys the message 'we don't care where your traffic comes from or goes to', in other words it legalizes *sixth freedom* traffic. In the first series of open skies agreements concluded by the US since 1992 no mention was made of *seventh freedom* rights, but as from 1996 it became more or less routine to include this right in the agreement, albeit only for all-cargo services. As for *cabotage*, the standard open skies agreement concluded by the US does not provide for this right as the US laws simply forbid granting this right to foreign airlines.

4   *Tariffs*: the Bermuda 'double approval' regime requiring both civil aviation authorities to approve the ticket prices of the designated airlines of both parties before these may be applied has been substituted for a market-oriented system where the airlines autonomously and without government interference whatsoever set prices. Unilateral government action against such airline pricing decisions are not allowed: only in a number of very specific situations may a governmental authority complain about pricing practices in the market but that could only prevent the introduction or continuation of a specific tariff or (cargo) rate if, after intergovernmental consultations, both governments concerned would agree on such a measure 'double disapproval'). Although more than 100 open skies agreements have been concluded since 1992, such a situation has never occurred.

5   *Capacity*: Bermuda's practice of predetermination, in the form of fixed capacity or 'equal opportunities' interpreted as equal capacity shares, has been replaced by a 'fair competition' clause that allows each designated airline 'to determine the frequency and capacity of the international air transportation it offers based upon commercial considerations in the market place'. Restrictions, limitations, financial compensation or filing-for-approval requirements have been outlawed, except, on a non-discriminatory basis, for operational, technical, environmental and other non-commercial reasons.

For those supporting the concept of minimal government intervention in the commercial aspects of international air transport, the open skies model has been a success. The US concluded more than 110 such agreements. Other countries embraced the underlying message that international air transport serves and benefits the national economy and should therefore not be artificially restricted, and concluded their own open skies agreements with likeminded countries.

Nevertheless, fear that the national airline might not survive in a 'free competition' environment has led a number of countries to maintain Bermuda style bilateral controls and restrictions in a number of important aviation relations. It would be too simple to state that they thus choose for the national airline to the detriment of the national economy, or for the producer instead of for the consumer. But, in practice, it is not easy to reconcile these two interests within one model.

11.4.7 MALIAT multilateral open skies agreement

Towards the end of 2000, the US had concluded some 50 open skies agreements, not a bad result as such, but, in the absence of important countries/markets like, in Europe, the UK and France, and outside Europe, Japan, Russia, China, Saudi Arabia, Nigeria and Brazil, not a resounding success either.

A different, multilateral, approach involving Asian-Pacific countries proved a welcome departure from this relative stagnation in the open skies drive. Also here, though, the partners concerned were not of prime air transport market importance: apart from the US, Brunei Darussalam, Chile, New Zealand and Singapore, met in Hawaii from 31 October to 2 November 2000 and concluded the Multilateral Agreement on Liberalization of International Air Transport (MALIAT),[37] which was subsequently signed in Washington DC on 1 May 2001 and entered into force on 21 December 2001.[38] Subsequently, the Cook Islands, Samoa and Tonga acceded. Peru also joined but withdrew early 2005. An amendment in the same year made it possible for Mongolia to accede on a cargo-only basis.

37 The key features of MALIAT copy the traditional bilateral open skies clauses: multiple designation, free routes, all traffic rights including seventh freedom for cargo, unlimited capacity, free tariffs and third-country code-sharing. A novelty is the provision on ownership and control: the traditional substantial ownership and effective control clause, also used in bilateral open skies agreements, was replaced by one that omitted the 'ownership' requirement. The designation clause reads: 'provided that (a) effective control of that airline is vested in the designating Party, its nationals, or both; (b) the airline is incorporated in and has its principal place of business in the territory of the Party designating the airline'. The draftsmen thus created in principle access for the participating airlines to global capital markets: foreign investors are welcome to own more than 50 per cent of the airline as long as control and (economic/safety) oversight remain firmly in national hands. That the airline remains subject to national laws also serves to protect against 'flag of convenience' airlines. It should be realized that this regional arrangement does not bind third countries. In other words, if Chile would buy 80 per cent of the Singapore Airlines shares, this may be agreeable to the other MALIAT parties, but in Singapore's bilateral relations with third countries it may still be seen as a violation of the traditional ownership and control clause in the respective bilateral, requiring consultations. A comparison with the EU community carrier comes to mind.

A Protocol to the agreement of May 2001 added two more novelties: seventh freedom for passenger services and cabotage. Brunei, Chile, Cook Islands, New Zealand and Singapore are parties to that Protocol.

Obviously where a party's domestic law (still) forbids foreign ownership and/or cabotage, i.e. the US situation, that country or the respective airlines will not be able to use these additional opportunities provided by the MALIAT system.

The Agreement is open to accession by any state that is party to the international (ICAO) security conventions. However, after Mongolia's accession in 2008 no other countries joined. Apparently, the generous exchange of *inter alia* fifth freedom rights makes this multilateral less attractive to other Australasian states that continue to believe in bilateral controls.

38 See for text, ratifications etc., www.maliat.govt.nz/.

11.5 EU aviation relations and 'bilaterals' with third countries

11.5.1 EU Commission early initiatives/proposals (1992–2002)

In 1990, the Commission submitted a proposal to the Council of Transport Ministers on the subject of aviation relations between member states and third countries. It received little attention because both the members and the Council were fully occupied by the work on the *internal* liberalization. The adoption of the third package of liberalization measures in July 1992 gave the Commission legal and political arguments to pursue its ultimate goal, i.e. to be the EU member states' sole spokesman and negotiator in the field of aviation relations with third countries. The ECJ, in its Opinion in the so-called 'WTO case' of 1994,[39] held that (air) transport services fell outside the scope of the common commercial policy and were a matter of *shared* competence between the Community and its members. The ECJ Opinion did however confirm the so-called AETR principle dating back to a case of that name judged in 1971, which opened the door to exclusive Community competence in a specific situation, namely, 'insofar as common rules, which have been adopted for the internal market, could be affected by obligations entered into by member states towards third countries'.[40]

With air transport negotiations in particular with the US high on its agenda, the Commission had been unpleasantly surprised by the news of the Netherlands–US open skies agreement of 1992: that agreement 'affected' the third package and undermined the Commission's efforts to obtain a negotiating mandate from the member states. But no action against the Netherlands was taken. The US DOT initiative of 1994 to invite nine other small European countries to conclude similar agreements – which would all come into force at the same time – led to an angry 'don't you dare' letter from the Commission to the respective ministers of transport.[41]

However, national interests prevailed and the member states continued with their open skies negotiations. Faced with the member states' continued hesitation at Council meetings in March and June 1995 to authorize the Commission to start negotiations with the US, the Commission

---

39 ECJ Opinion 1/94 of 15 November 1994; this case revolved around the question of the Community's competence to conclude agreements – in the framework of the GATS Uruguay round – on trade in services.

40 AETR case: *Commission* v. *Council* case 22/70 1971 ECR 263.

41 "The text of the [proposed agreement] is of such a nature and content as to affect internal Community legislation, in particular [the third package]. In addition, the cumulative result of the conclusion of these agreements would be the creation of a network of traffic rights to the benefit of US air carriers within a substantial part of the internal market of the Community."

[...]

"The Commission is extremely concerned that the cumulative effect of a number of new free market aviation agreements will very seriously prejudice any future possibilities to arrive at a more balanced situation in relation to the United States and will de facto create a US/Europe aviation regime. It also considers it unacceptable for the United States to succeed in their objective to increase the pressure on those member States that are at this stage unwilling, or unable, to enter into similar agreement with that country."

"I would like to receive your assurance that you will not negotiate, initial or sign any arrangement of this type with the United States. I should like to receive your answer before 10 March 1995. In the absence of a positive response to this request, the Commission reserves the right to initiate such procedures as are foreseen by the Treaty."

Letter of 28 February 1995 from Neil Kinnock, member of the European Commission to Mr Johann Norrback, Minister for Transport and Communications of Finland (on file with the author); similar letters were sent to Austria, Belgium, Denmark, Luxembourg and Sweden. The other European countries were non-members Norway, Iceland and Switzerland.

in the same and the following year sent out *letters of formal notice* to the 'open skies' countries concerned. With this official start of the Community infringement procedure[42] – leading eventually to action against the offenders of European law before the European Court – it had opted for the legal road to getting a negotiating mandate where political pressure obviously had not worked.

Trying to avoid a legal and political showdown, the member states moved relatively swiftly and approved in June 1996 a mandate for negotiations with the US. But, ill at ease with any role of substance for the Commission, they introduced caveats of such magnitude that the Commission proved seriously handicapped during the two rounds of negotiations that followed in October 1996 (Washington) and April 1997 (Brussels): only *soft rights* could be discussed; *marketing* issues such as CRS, code-sharing and leasing, *access* issues i.e. ownership and control and slot allocation, *competition* issues i.e. antitrust and competition rules, state aid and 'Chapter 11' (US bankruptcy protection), *legal* issue settlement of disputes and, finally, environmental issues and transitional measures. With the US basically only interested in increased market access (to London Heathrow) and other 'hard rights', the talks could not but fail.

A frustrated Commission reopened its infringement procedures, which it had suspended, and on 11 March 1998 sent *reasoned opinions* to seven member states that had concluded open skies agreements since 1995, and to the UK that had concluded a new agreement with the US in 1995 which the Commission also considered in breach of the Rome Treaty and of EU aviation rules.

The response of the countries concerned being unsatisfactory, the Commission on 18 December 1998 took the case to the European Court. The Court's judgment came on 5 November 2002; it gave the Commission substantial powers to – increasingly – involve itself in the member states' bilateral aviation relations.

11.5.2 ECJ 'open skies' decision of 5 November 2002[43]

The Court had to judge two main contentions submitted by the Commission:

1 The Community is exclusively competent to deal with all external aviation relations; and by concluding an open skies agreement with the US the member states concerned violated that Community competence.
2 The national ownership and control provision in the agreements concluded with the US violate the right of establishment and national treatment, in other words the ban on discrimination of, in this case, airlines on the basis of nationality.[44]

---

42 The infringement procedure of then art. 169, renumbered 226, and now 258 of the Treaty on the Functioning of the European Union (TFEU) gives the Commission the power to take legal action against a member state that is not respecting its obligations under EU law. The procedure knows three steps: it begins with a *letter of formal notice*, which is a request for information; if the information received confirms to the Commission that the member state is not complying with its obligations, the Commission may send a *reasoned opinion*, a formal request to the member state to comply with its obligations and inform the Commission about measures taken to that end. If the member state fails to do so, the Commission may refer the member state to the ECJ; see Commission MEMO/12/12 of 17 January 2012.

43 ECJ ruling of 5 November 2002 in cases C-466/98, C-467/98, C-468/98, C-469/98, C-471/98, C-472/98, C-475/98 and C-476/98 against the UK, Denmark, Sweden, Finland, Belgium, Luxembourg, Austria and Germany.

44 Art. 52, later renumbered 43, and now art. 49 TFEU.

The resulting judgment was clear:

Ad (1): the Community is only competent with respect to those aspects/provisions of member states' bilateral agreements with third countries that (may) affect Community legislation in so far as that legislation deals with rights and/or obligations of non-member countries and airlines in those same areas. Put differently, member states are not allowed to enter into international commitments containing rules capable of affecting rules adopted by the Community or of altering their scope. Concrete examples found were the tariff rules of the third package's Regulation 2409/92 (which forbids third country airlines to undercut Community carriers' prices on intra-Community fifth freedom routes) and the CRS Regulation 2299/89 (which applies also to CRS services offered in Community territory by nationals of non-member countries). A member state cannot 'touch' those issues in its bilateral agreements, as they belong to the exclusive competence of the Community.

The importance of this part of the judgment lies in its principle and its increasing scope of application: whenever the member states adopt new European legislation that (also) deals with the rights and/or obligations of third countries and their airlines, the respective topics are effectively *removed* from the bilaterals and only the Commission, or the member state with the explicit approval, and subject to the conditions, of the Commission, may discuss these matters with any third country.

Ad (2): the traditional ownership and control clause does indeed violate European law: it allows the US to reject the designation of, e.g. Lufthansa, by the UK on the grounds that it is a German and not a UK carrier; that is discrimination on the basis of nationality, making it impossible for the German carrier to exercise the same rights vis-à-vis the US as a UK carrier has.

The consequences of this part of the judgment were immediate and far-reaching: all bilaterals of all member states concluded with all third countries contained the same illegal clause, *and thus had to be amended or terminated*, as the Commission was quick to point out.

The Commission also announced that it understood the predicament of the member states where they had to convince the US and other foreign counterparts to replace the national ownership and control clause by a provision that would give carriers of all Community nationalities the same rights under the respective bilateral as the national carrier(s) concerned. And the Commission subtly observed that Community level negotiations could now possibly provide 'added value'.

Early 2003 the Commission proposed three measures to the member States:

- a mandate to negotiate on behalf of the member States a complete bilateral air transport agreement with the US;
- a mandate to engage on behalf of the member states in negotiations with any/all third countries to replace the outlawed national ownership and control clause by a non-discriminatory 'community clause';
- a Regulation that reflected the division – and management – of responsibilities on the basis of the respective areas of competence between the Community and the member states.

On 5 June the Council of Transport ministers approved these measures. And the Commission went to work.

11.5.3 EU–US air transport agreement 2007/2010

The Commission made it clear from the outset that it aimed at accomplishing more than a traditional US-style 'Open Skies' agreement. Additional elements that needed to be included in the agreement in order to create the desired 'Open Aviation Area' were *inter alia*:

- a Community designation clause that would permit all qualified EU carriers to operate from any country in the EU to the US;
- rules on – fair and effective – competition;
- reciprocal open foreign investment, i.e. the possibility for EU airlines to control/take over US carriers;
- cabotage rights;
- high standards of safety, security, environmental and passenger protection.

Between June 2003 and November 2005 eight rounds of negotiations took place, as a result of which a draft agreement was presented which included neither cabotage rights for EU carriers nor the possibility to own and control US carriers.

This was not surprising for at least three reasons: (a) the US carriers on their part were not interested in obtaining these rights vis-à-vis the EU and its airlines, (b) US labour unions feared the effects of EU carriers' intra-US operations on their jobs and (c) both cabotage and foreign ownership and control are effectively forbidden by US law.[45]

The latter, formal, reason proved an insurmountable barrier also for the US delegation as air transport agreements, as 'executive agreements' cannot set aside or overrule an Act of Congress.

The result was the reason for the EU Council of Ministers, after informal consultations and efforts on the US DOT side, to find an acceptable compromise, to send its delegation back to the negotiating table.[46] Three further rounds finally led to the March 2007 signing of an MoU, the signature of the Agreement in April 2007 and consensus on the provisional application of the Agreement as from 30 March 2008.

What did this 'first-stage'[47] EU–US agreement accomplish over and above a traditional open skies agreement?

45 See for cabotage: 49 U.S.C. sec. 41703(c), which permits domestic 'interstate' transportation by foreign carriers in exceptional circumstances and for limited periods only and in the case of US carriers dry-leasing foreign aircraft. Re foreign investment: a US air carrier is defined as 'a citizen of the [US] undertaking ... to provide air transportation'. A citizen of the US means

> an individual who is a citizen of the [US]; ... a [US] corporation of which the president and at least two thirds of the board of directors and other managing officers are citizens of the [US], which is under the actual control of citizens of the [US] and in which at least 75 percent of the voting interest is owned or controlled by persons that are citizens of the [US].

See 49 U.S.C. sec. 40102(a)(2) and (a)(15).
46 On ownership and control, the EU demanded a 'clear, meaningful and robust rule' on actual control of US carriers by foreign carriers. The DOT on 7 November 2005 responded with a Notice of Proposed Rulemaking (NPRM) on 'actual control of US carriers' which redefined control by creating a 'Chinese wall' between control over safety and security matters (to remain in US citizens' hands) and control over all other matters (commercial, day-to-day operations etc.) which could be in foreign hands. This approach pleased neither Congress and labour ('threat to security and to national jobs') nor the Europeans, and a supplemental NPRM (SNPRM) of May 2006 aimed at allaying the fears on the US side only made it worse for the EU and resulted in an impasse, whereupon the Council, accepting defeat on these two issues, instructed its negotiating team in December 2006 to try to otherwise 'restore the balance' in the agreement.
47 With agreement on cabotage and foreign investment not being feasible at this stage, the European side opted for further negotiations at a later stage. The UK in particular was adamant in demanding something of real value in return for the opening up of London Heathrow to additional US competitors.

- An expanded Community designation clause: 'expanded', because the US will not only accept Community airlines that are owned and controlled by member states and/or their nationals, but also if these airlines are owned and/or controlled by any member of the European Common Aviation Area (ECAA) and/or its nationals. ECAA members at the time of signing were, apart from the EU members, Albania, Bosnia and Herzegovina, Croatia, Iceland, the Former Yugoslav Republic of Macedonia, Montenegro, Norway, Serbia and UN Interim Administrative Mission in Kosovo.[48]

- Seventh freedom for all cargo services operated by Community carriers between the US and any other point, and seventh freedom for 'combination services' (passengers + cargo) operated by Community carriers between the US and ECAA countries. US carriers on the other hand did not obtain seventh freedom for combination services and simply kept the seventh freedom cargo rights already available to them under the bilateral open skies agreements previously concluded with the individual member States.[49]

- Ownership and control of third-country airlines:

  a Community *ownership* of a foreign airline does not affect the latter's rights vis-à-vis the US, and US ownership of a foreign airline does not affect the latter's rights vis-à-vis the Community.[50]

  b Community *ownership and control* of an ECAA, Swiss or Liechtenstein airline and of a carrier of any African country that is implementing an open skies agreement with the US on the date of signature of the EU–US Agreement, in other words the acquisition of such an airline, will not affect the latter's rights vis-à-vis the US.[51]

  c If an ECAA state and/or airline acquires a Community/EU carrier, the latter's rights vis-à-vis the US will not be at risk either.[52]

- Under the so-called 'Fly America' programme US federal government financed international passenger and cargo air transport is reserved to US airlines.[53] This prevents EU airlines' access to a large market in the US. As neither the EU nor its member States impose comparable restrictions, the parties agreed, as a first step, on a (very) modest easing of this competition-distorting practice.[54]

---

48 EU–US Air Transport Agreement (hereafter 'EU–US'), arts 4(b) and 5.1(b) and Annex 4, art. 1(3).
49 EU–US, art. 3.1(c)(i) and (ii). Annex 1, Section 3 lists the following seventh freedom cargo rights/ countries for US carriers: Czech Republic, France, Germany, Luxembourg, Malta, Poland, Portugal and Slovak Republic.
50 The MALIAT agreement was an earlier example of this foreign investment-facilitating 'liberalization' of the traditional nationality clause, see section 11.4.7.
51 EU–US, Annex 4, art. 2, para.2; MoC, para. 9 lists the following African countries: Burkina Faso, Cabo Verde, Cameroon, Chad, Gabon, The Gambia, Ghana, Ethiopia, Liberia, Madagascar, Mali, Morocco, Namibia, Nigeria, Senegal, Tanzania and Uganda, plus non-open skies country Kenya.
52 EU–US, art. 4(b), art. 5(1)(b) and Annex 4, art. 1(3).
53 Fly America Act, see 49 U.S.C. 40118; 41 CFR parts 301-10.131 through 301-10.143 (Fed. Travel regulations promulgated by the General Services Administration (GSA)). The programme is seen as a reward for US carriers, which, under the Civil Reserve Air Fleet (CRAF) programme make their fleet available to the government in case of military/emergency needs, e.g. the Gulf War. The GSA annually awards contracts to US carriers to provide discount air fares to government employees on official travel in thousands of domestic and international city-pair markets; these markets are off-limits for EU carriers. Code-shared flights, i.e. flights with a US code operated by a foreign/EU carrier are accepted as US flights. In a number of bilaterals the US has agreed to some other exceptions to the rule.
54 EU–US, Annex 3 and MoC, paras 20–23.

- Wetleasing: the airlines of both parties may, subject to conditions, use aircraft and crew leased from other airlines, for their international operations; important novelty is the absence of the requirement of underlying traffic rights.[55]
- With the EU and the US having different competition laws, policies and practices with respect to (international) aviation issues, it made sense to agree on cooperation to minimize the effects thereof on e.g. transatlantic airline alliances. The parties confirmed that they apply their respective competition regimes to protect and enhance overall competition 'and not individual competitors' and agreed in some detail on the practical aspects of that cooperation between the US DOT and the Commission, in practice its Directorate-General for Competition.[56]
- Other regulatory cooperation, in the areas of safety, security, government subsidies and the environment.[57]
- A Joint Committee reviews the implementation of the agreement, deals with matters of interpretation and application and hears disputes between the parties.[58]
- Commitment to second-stage negotiations: in particular the UK was eager to see something more in return for the opening up of London Heathrow to more US competitors, hence they and the EU saw this first-stage result as one necessitating further negotiations, particularly on cabotage and foreign investment. A threat of sanctions was included in case these matters were not satisfactorily solved before the end of 2010.[59]

11.5.3.1 The second-stage agreement of 2010

After eight rounds of negotiations starting in May 2008, the 'Protocol' to amend the 2007 Agreement was signed on 25 March 2010 in Brussels. As to its contents a US State Department media note issued on that day sums it up succinctly:

> The new agreement affirms that the terms of the 2007 agreement will remain in place indefinitely. It also deepens U.S. – EU cooperation in aviation security, safety, competition, and ease of travel. In addition it provides greater protections for U.S. carriers from arbitrary restrictions on night flights at European airports. It also includes a ground-breaking article on the importance of high labor standards in the airline industry. The new agreement underscores the importance of close transatlantic cooperation on aviation environmental matters in order to advance a global approach to global challenges.[60]

---

55 EU–US, art. 10, para. 9, art. 21 para. 2 (e); MoC, paras 26–33.
56 EU–US, art. 20 and Annex 2, MoC, paras 40–48. One result of this cooperation was the publication of a joint report on the two competition law systems and their application to airline alliances: 'Transatlantic airline alliances: Competitive issues and regulatory appproaches – A report by the [EC] and the [US DOT]', 16 November 2010, see EC press release IP/10/1511 (2010).
57 EU–US, art. 8, MoC, para. 11 (safety); art. 9 and MoC, paras 12–14 (security); art. 14 (subsidies); art. 15 and MoC, paras 35–36, 54 (environment, particularly aircraft noise restrictions at airports and emissions trading).
58 EU–US, art. 18, MoC, paras 37–38.
59 EU–US, art. 21; para. 2 listed the following items of priority interest: (a) further liberalisation of traffic rights; (b) additional foreign investment opportunities; (c) effect of environmental measures and infrastructure constraints on the exercise of traffic rights; (d) further access to government-financed air transportation; and (e) provision of aircraft with crew. Para. 3 provided in part: 'If no second-stage agreement has been reached by the Parties within . . ., each Party reserves the right thereafter to suspend rights specified in this Agreement.'
60 'Statement on U.S.–EU Civil Aviation Agreement', Media Note, U.S. Department of State, Office of the Spokesman, March 25, 2010 (USPOLICY, Embassy of the U.S. Belgium).

The longstanding EU wishes in the field of market access, i.e. cabotage, and foreign investment, i.e. abolishment or relaxation of the ownership and control rules, had not been fulfilled.

A number of new provisions addressed other existing and new concerns of the parties, and provided for – increased – cooperation, such as on:

- Environmental matters: the US continued to disagree with the EU on the latter's 'extra-territorial' application of the emission trading system to international air transport and, under the same heading,
- EU member states' airport night bans: the US had asked for greater transparency on and Commission review of noise-based operating restrictions at national airports, for the benefit of, in particular, its express operators.[61]
- US government procured transportation or 'fly America': EU airlines obtained full access to sell tickets to contractors of the US Government, but other restrictions remain in place.[62]
- *Incentives for regulatory reform*: some seventh freedom passenger rights become available for US carriers after the US laws have been amended to allow for majority EU ownership of US carriers; and some additional seventh freedom passenger rights become available for EU carriers after satisfactory noise restriction rules have been adopted by the European side.
- *Social dimension:* a new provision refers to the importance of high labour standards and states: '[t]he opportunities created by the Agreement are not intended to undermine labour standards or the labour-related rights and principles contained in the Parties' respective laws'.

These principles 'shall guide the Parties as they implement the Agreement'.[63]

11.5.3.2 Some results/effects of the EU–US agreement

The EU–US landmark agreement of 2007 contained in fact only a single prize for US carriers: unlimited entry into London Heathrow. Carriers like Delta, Continental and Northwest however realized, to their dismay, that their ambitions were severely hampered in practice by

61 EU–US, art. 15 ('Environment') has been replaced by a new art. 15, ex Protocol 2010, art. 3 and by (new) MoC, paras 10–17, 21 and Attachment C ('Joint Statement on environmental cooperation'). The provisions related to noise restrictions at EU airports in new art. 15, para. 5, require the EU side to see to it that, when new restrictions are being considered, (a) the authorities enable interested parties to give their views, (b) advance notice and, on request, a report on the reasons, the objectives, the alternatives considered and a cost/benefit analysis are provided, and (c) operating restrictions shall be '(i) non-discriminatory; (ii) not more restrictive than necessary in order to achieve the environmental objective established for a specific airport; and (iii) non-arbitrary.' This has resulted in the adoption of Regulation (EU) No. 598/2014 of 16 April 2014 on the establishment of rules and procedures with regard to the introduction of noise-related operating restrictions at Union airports within a Balanced Approach and repealing Directive 2002/30/EC, OJ L173, 12 June 2014, pp. 65–78; e.i.f. 13 June 2016.
62 New Annex 3 ex Protocol 2010, art. 7 ('US government procured transportation').
63 This provision was introduced because of concerns for 'cheap flag' labour conditions undermining the position of the US workers in the airline industry. It got unexpected relevance in the 2015 'Norwegian' case, involving the Irish subsidiary of a Norwegian low cost airline, which subsidiary was allowed under Irish law to employ cheap Asian personnel for its planned operations to and from *inter alia* the US. US labour and US airlines protested strongly and the DOT delayed granting an authorization pending a full inquiry into this possible violation of the social dimension provision. See DOT Docket No. OST-2014-0063 of May 9, 2014.

the absence of slots at this severely congested airport. So they engaged in a frantic buying, swapping and borrowing of slots from their European alliance partners and from other airlines willing to sell their slots to the highest bidder.[64]

A second interesting effect of the agreement was the entry of European carriers into what formerly would have been called seventh freedom markets: in 2008 Air France started, together – in codeshare – with Delta, operations London–Los Angeles, and British Airways created a subsidiary appropriately named 'OpenSkies', to serve routes between France and the US. These largely symbolic operations underlined one important benefit of the agreement, i.e. that any EU carrier may operate from any point in the EU to any point in the US. In the years thereafter the use of this right by the legacy/network carriers has been rather limited and probably awaits new entrants' innovative transatlantic operating concepts.

The third noteworthy aspect of the EU–US Agreement is its trendsetting character. The EU concluded a comparable agreement with Canada in 2009 and is firmly committed to spread further the 'Open Aviation Area' gospel among its main aviation partners. And third countries have noted the competitive effects of sharply increased transatlantic competition and the ensuing benefits to the economies of the two 'blocks'.

But it cannot be denied that the 2010 Protocol did not add much to the equation and that further progress in the solution of the outstanding issues will be a slow process at best.

11.5.4 EU 'horizontal agreements' with third countries

It should be emphasized that the Commission's mandate to introduce a Community clause in existing bilaterals of member states did not replace the responsibility of the members themselves to renegotiate their bilaterals with the same purpose: it came on top of that. The Commission realized that member states would have a hard time convincing all their bilateral partners to accept a new clause that would enable any 'non-national' European carrier to make use of the rights, so far only reserved for national carriers, contained in the bilateral agreements concerned. And indeed, reactions of surprised third country counterparts faced with this extra point on the negotiating agenda, ranged from 'why should I solve your internal legal problem?' via 'the bilateral is meant to only give benefits to national airlines not to others', to 'what's in it for me?'. The latter question sometimes resulted in requests for additional hard rights or other forms of compensation in return for this concession.

The Commission has two advantages: it has, at least in principle, substantial negotiating clout as it represents all member states and their bilaterals vis-à-vis the selected third country. And it has one 'big stick', i.e. the power to force the member states to terminate their illegal agreements and thus deprive also the third country and its airlines of the legal certainty that a bilateral treaty provides. The preamble delicately refers to this *ultimum remedium* (see below).

The Commission cannot be asked to give anything in return because the mandate does not provide for that: hard rights are not within its remit. The latter absence of bargaining chips may be seen as a disadvantage, which can only be overcome through a different mandate, i.e. to conclude a 'comprehensive', that is all-inclusive, bilateral agreement with the country concerned.

---

64 For example, to provide its partner Northwest with suitable slots, KLM in 2008 terminated services from regional airports (Rotterdam and Eindhoven) to LHR. Alitalia sold slots to Continental, US Airways and British Airways, and Air France reduced its Paris–London flights to enable Delta and Continental to start operations to LHR. Prices quoted ranged from $20–35 million per pair of slots. When Lufthansa took over British Midland, that 2008 deal included 12 per cent of LHR slots making Lufthansa the second largest owner of slots after BA; whether any of these were made available to partner United Airlines or sold to other US carriers is unknown.

The Commission's first 'catch' in 2004 was Chile. The agreement's preamble provided *inter alia* that the provisions in the existing bilaterals which are contrary to EU law must be brought into conformity with that law, 'in order to establish a sound legal basis for air services between the Community and Chile and to preserve the continuity of such air services', i.e. the 'big stick' referred to above.[65]

The Commission's and member states' experience with negotiations in the first years has produced a standard horizontal agreement (HA) that contains provisions on:

- designation (which introduces the crucial concept of *EU carrier*);
- safety oversight;
- intra-EU taxation of aviation fuel;
- tariffs for carriage within the EU;
- compatibility with EU competition rules.[66]

Two important provisions should be highlighted, one of which is the 'Free rider' clause. This clause was inserted at the request of Chile and can be found in many HAs concluded since. The rule established by the Agreement is: Chile cannot reject the designation by a member state of an EU carrier only because the latter has the nationality of another member state. But, in practice, Chile may have serious problems with the operations of that carrier in two situations:

1   The designated carrier uses its new rights to *circumvent* restrictions under its 'own' bilateral with Chile. To give an example: the UK designates LOT Polish Airlines under the UK–Chile bilateral, thus allowing LOT to operate seven services per week between London and Santiago de Chile. The bilateral agreement between Chile and Poland gave LOT only two services per week between Warsaw and Santiago de Chile. By flying Warsaw–London seven times per week and linking these with the seven flights London–Santiago, LOT would in fact offer seven more services between Warsaw and Santiago (with an intermediate stop or stop-over in London) than the two that were bilaterally allowed.[67] The free rider clause gives Chile the right to put a stop to that 'circumvention' by refusing, revoking, suspending or limiting LOT's exercise of its 'UK rights' to/from Chile.

2   In case there is no bilateral agreement in force between, in our example, Poland and Chile, and Poland has refused to grant traffic rights to Chilean carriers; in that case Chile may view

---

65 Other recitals stated:

- The bilaterals concluded with individual member states contain provisions contrary to Community law.
- The EC has exclusive competence with respect to several aspects of those bilaterals.
- Community air carriers established in a member state have the right to non-discriminatory access to air routes between member states and third countries.
- The agreement does not aim at increasing the total volume of air traffic between Europe and Chile, nor does it attempt to affect the balance between Community carriers and the carriers of Chile or to affect the traffic rights exchanged in those bilaterals, see also model agreement, *infra* note 74.

66 See, for latest (2013) model, http://ec.europa.eu/transport/modes/air/international_aviation/doc/draft_horizontal_agreement_en.pdf.

67 An even more flagrant 'circumvention' of the existing restriction would be possible for LOT if the bilateral UK–Chile allowed designated carriers to make an intermediate stop in another European country. This would allow LOT, as airline designated by the UK, to operate seven services per week London–Warsaw–Santiago next to the two existing Warsaw–Santiago services operated under its own (Polish) bilateral with Chile!

LOT's rights to operate out of London as an unjustified reward for Poland's protectionist behaviour. Chile therefore obtained the right to restrict or say 'no' to LOT's use of UK carrier rights.[68]

The standard HA the Commission will submit to its counterpart does not contain a 'free rider' clause. As the clause enables a third country to – one way or the other – distinguish between member states and their airlines, it goes against the principle of non-discrimination and should therefore not be promoted.

Establishment. It is important to note that the non-national carrier wishing to be designated has to be *established* in the designating member state. There is no European rule specifying the national requirements that have to be met to qualify as such. Consequently, establishment criteria and the strictness of the enforcement thereof vary from country to country. Regulation 847/2004 (see 11.5.5, below) gives some guidance[69] on how the authorities should deal with this concept. Though the terms thereof are not very precise they reflect one underlying message: the airline seeking establishment should not be subjected to substantially more complicated or elaborate criteria and formalities than the national carrier had to face: that would amount to illegal discrimination.

The Commission's HA negotiations through the years proved successful: in mid-2014, 46 HAs resulted in 744 amended bilateral agreements with EU member states.[70]

Individual member states were also able to bring their bilaterals with 88 third countries into conformity with EU law, resulting in a total of 298 such amended agreements.

These activities combined resulted, according to the Commission, in a grand total of 1,042 agreements providing for Community/EU designation. All third countries concerned have thus, vis-à-vis the EU, bid farewell to the traditional nationality test and accept merged entities like Air France–KLM, Lufthansa–Austrian and British Airways–Iberia as EU airlines: that creates increased aeropolitical certainty for the smaller partners in those ventures that still rely on their 'own' bilateral agreements.[71] Even more important, the Community designation efforts reinforced globally the trend of reducing the importance of the nationality of designated airlines and of focusing instead on the country of regulatory, i.e. primarily safety, oversight. That has created increased financial, commercial and operational flexibility for the airlines without calling into question the safety of their operations.

---

68 For further HA analysis/examples, see Peter van Fenema, 'EU horizontal agreements: Community designation and the 'free rider' clause' (June 2006) XXXI:3 *Air and Space Law* 172–195.

69 Establishment on the territory of a Member State implies the effective and real exercise of air transport activitiy through stable arrangements; the legal form of such an establishment, whether a branch or a subsidiary with a legal personality, should not be the determining factor in this respect.

Regulation (EC) No. 847/2004 of 29 April 2004 on the negotiation and implementation of air service agreements between Member States and third countries, OJ L157, 30 April 2004, pp. 7–17; e.i.f. 30 May 2004.

70 'Bilateral Air Services Agreements brought into legal conformity since the Court of Justice of the EU judgments of 5 November 2002', updated 24 June 2014 (author's copy); see for earlier info and additional details: http://ec.europa.eu/transport/modes/air/international_aviation/external_aviation_policy/doc/table_-_asa_brought_into_legal_conformity_since_ecj_judgments-_january_2013.pdf. A March 2015 update shows 36 signed HAs of which 23 have entered into force (author's copy).

71 A number of countries, *not* parties to an HA, and possibly encouraged by their own airlines, did not immediately accept KLM's new ownership and control structure and invoked the respective bilateral provision. In the end, most of these 'interpretation' problems could be resolved through clarification and negotiation (KLM info provided to the author).

11.5.5 Regulation 847/2004 on the negotiation and implementation of air service agreements between member states and third countries[72]

To understand the rationale for this Regulation it suffices to quote 'whereas clause' (4) thereof:

> where it is apparent that the subject-matter of an agreement falls partly within the competence of the Community and partly within that of its Member States, it is essential to ensure close cooperation between the Member States and the Community institutions, both in the process of negotiation and conclusion and in the fulfilment of the commitments entered into.

The individual member States have retained the right to (re-)negotiate bilateral agreements in order to obtain new routes/destinations, additional traffic rights, frequencies etc., but

1   They have to notify the Commission and inform the other member states about the issues on the agenda, to allow these 'stakeholders' to make comments and suggestions.
2   In case the agenda lists matters that actually fall under Commission competence, existing standard clauses have to be submitted in the negotiations when these matters are addressed.

A resulting agreement will in principle only be approved by the Commission if it contains all the right clauses and also in other respects conforms fully with EU law. If that is not the case, it will depend on the seriousness of the omissions whether the Commission will ask the national authorities to return to the negotiating table or, alternatively, authorizes the state to sign and provisionally apply the agreement.

The above word 'stakeholders' is used here intentionally: all airlines with an establishment in the member state concerned may ask to be designated and thus benefit from the results of the negotiation. In fact, if the national negotiating team includes a representative of a national airline, all above interested airlines may also ask for a place at the table. In that sense, formally speaking, the days of the EU state negotiating for only its own national airlines are over.

This has interesting and challenging consequences: the outcome of the negotiations may include additional frequencies or new routes which may then be claimed by both the national airlines and the eligible Community airlines; which is a problem if there is not enough to satisfy all interested airlines. As discrimination on the basis of nationality is forbidden, a system to distribute fairly what is available is required. This has been accomplished by the compulsory introduction in national aviation regulations of so-called *procedures for the allocation of limited traffic rights*.[73]

All 28 member states in the meantime have had their national procedures published in the Official Journal of the EU and have thus, with varying success, clarified the conditions to be met by interested airlines in order to qualify for being a beneficiary of the distribution of national traffic rights. It is noteworthy that all procedures have one thing in common: they use the

---

72 Regulation (EC) No. 847/2004, see *supra* note 69.
73 Art. 5 of the Regulation, entitled 'Distribution of traffic rights', reads:

> Where a Member State concludes an agreement, or amendments to an agreement or its Annexes, that provide for limitations on the use of traffic rights or the number of Community air carriers eligible to be designated to take advantage of traffic rights, that Member State shall ensure a distribution of traffic rights among eligible Community air carriers on the basis of a non-discriminatory and transparent procedure.

> By virtue of art. 6, 'Member States shall inform the Commission without delay of the procedures that they shall apply for the purposes of art. 5.'

method of the 'beauty contest'. In other words, the airlines that try to obtain any of the available scarce traffic rights have to meet both quantitative and qualitative criteria, and the national authorities will judge the submissions and select the winner(s).[74]

The alternative to the beauty contest is the *auction*: it is in principle truly objective because the highest bidder gets the traffic rights (which does not mean that the losing airline will be happier!). Qualitative criteria hardly play a role here: the aeronautical authorities have no influence on aspects other than – probably – those related to the type and safety of the aircraft. This lack of control is of course the main reason why none of the member states chose this allocation system. And world-wide only Chile appears to have been using the auction method for that purpose.[75]

11.5.6 EU relations/agreements with other third countries

Approving a Commission Communication on that topic,[76] in 2012, the EU Council agreed on the 'three pillars' of the EU's external aviation policy. The first one, the horizontal mandate, i.e. bringing existing bilateral agreements into line with EU law, has been discussed above.

'Pillar 2' is the creation of a wider 'Common Aviation Area' with neighbouring countries through the conclusion of bilateral agreements which not only provide for market access and other liberal arrangements but also aim at the gradual but complete adoption of all EU aviation legislation, the so-called *acquis communautaire*, by those neighbouring countries. The aim is to have the same aviation rules, whether on safety, passenger rights, licensing, competition, slots or ground handling (etc.) being applied in an area covering the more than 50 States concerned (including the EU and European Free Trade Association (EFTA) member States).

So far, agreements in this category have been concluded with Morocco, the Western Balkans, Jordan, Georgia, Moldova and Israel.[77]

---

74 The UK was one of the very few EU members with experience with that type of allocation system as, for many years, two to three national airlines were fighting for their share of the traffic rights that the UK obtained through bilateral negotiations. In the perception of the UK authorities, the airlines were almost never happy with the results of the allocation, but the system as such worked. Unhappiness on the part of the airlines stems understandably from the fact that weighing and judging the competing offers of the candidates on their (better) contribution to 'consumer interest and the benefit of the public' or 'development of tourism and trade' or 'increased competition in the relevant markets' is never a 'scientific' or completely objective exercise; the losing airline may thus very well conclude that the judgment, given the underlying assessment and arguments, justifies an appeal.

75 See Ley 2564 of 1979 and Decreto Supremo No. 102 (*Reglamenta licitacion publica para asignar frecuencias internacionales a empresas aeras nacionales*) of 17 June 1981. The combination of the HA and this Regulation has produced a regulatory environment in which airlines licensed in one member state may mount operations from the territories of other member states to third countries provided they comply with the 'establishment' criteria in those other member states and traffic rights are – or have been made – available for that purpose. In practice, primarily such low cost carriers as Hungarian Wizzair, Irish Ryanair, British EasyJet and Spanish Vueling have made use of these opportunities; for airlines with hub-and-spokes networks, the move to another member state for the purpose of setting up operations to third countries, appeared less attractive.

76 See http://ec.europa.eu/transport/modes/air/international_aviation/external_aviation_policy/doc/comm(2012)556_en.pdf.

77 At this writing, an agreement with Ukraine awaits signature, whereas negotiations with Lebanon, Azerbaijan, Tunisia and Algeria are ongoing. As further candidates for this type of Agreement the Commission mentions 'neighbours' Armenia, Turkey, Egypt, Libya and Syria. It should be realized that in these negotiations there is always one big – legal and political – hurdle: the partner concerned has to accept the principle of the adoption and application of European aviation legislation. And the real work, actually integrating EU law into national aviation legislation, takes years to accomplish.

'Pillar 3' covers 'comprehensive' bilateral agreements with key aviation partners. The word *comprehensive* denotes a type of agreement that goes one or more steps further than traditional open skies agreements: not only reciprocal free market access, and all other necessary freedoms, but also the removal of investment barriers (ownership and control) and 'regulatory convergence', e.g. with respect to rules on fair competition, environmental issues, licensing.[78]

Two examples of yet different complications concern the relations/negotiations with, first, Russia and, second, the Gulf States (UAE and Qatar).

1   The main bone of contention in the relations with *Russia* is the obligation imposed on EU carriers since Soviet times to pay royalties to, primarily, Aeroflot for each flight operated through Siberian airspace. Negotiations initiated by the EU in 2006 and 2011 to stop this practice never produced an effective result and EU carriers continue collectively to pay more than €300 million per year, a practice which the Commission labels 'anti-competitive' and air lawyers tend to consider in violation of article 15 of the Chicago Convention. The combination of this distortion of competition with the fact that Russia did not sign a horizontal agreement with the EU and thus fails to recognize the concept of Community carrier brought the Commission to launch infringement procedures against the member states concerned.[79] Though this first step in the form of a 'letter of formal notice' might be seen as directed at the wrong entities, it is a logical one in a procedure that, after the next step, a 'reasoned opinion' requesting the member states to amend their bilateral agreements with Russia, could result in action before the European Court requiring the member states to terminate their bilaterals. The infringement procedures provided extra legal and political pressure on all concerned on top of the main negotiating 'big stick': the treat of an EU veto against Russia's accession to the World Trade Organization (WTO). This resulted in an agreement of December 2011 to start the modernization of the royalty system immediately after the acceptance of Russia as WTO member at the end of the year.[80] After the latter had materialized the EU bitterly concluded that the other side had found a new argument to stall the implementation of the agreement, i.e. the imminent application of the EU Emission Trading System (ETS) to air transport to/from and within the EU/European Economic Area (EEA). Although the EU, faced with considerable and vocal opposition from major aviation countries, in the meantime postponed the introduction of the non-EU/EEA air space component of that system,[81] until today progress in this thorny Siberian royalties file remains out of sight.

---

78 See Commission Press release IP/09/1963 of 17 December 2009. The EU–US Agreement was the first in this category, followed by an even more ambitious agreement with Canada signed in 2009. A 'comprehensive agreement' with Brazil was initialled in 2011 but needed further (re)negotiations in 2015. Talks with Australia and New Zealand started in 2008 but have stalled ever since. Other interesting candidates are Russia, UAE, Egypt, China, India, Japan and the ASEAN countries. Some of these are 'hard nuts' to crack, for a variety of reasons, such as the fear for loss of control over the commercial well-being of the national airlines and the prospect of unrestricted competition with the airlines of 28 EU member states, and/or political considerations.
79 See Commission Press releases IP/10/1425 of 28 October 2010 (Austria, Finland, France and Germany), IP/11/74 of 27 January 2011 (Belgium, Denmark, Italy, Luxembourg, Netherlands, Sweden and UK), MEMO 11/46 of 27 January 2011; and Press release IP/11/186 of 16 February 2011 (Cyprus, Ireland, Poland, Portugal, Slovakia and Spain); as only about eight of these member states pay royalties, the average payment per carrier per year is about €40 million.
80 See Commission Press release IP/11/1490 of 1 December 2011.
81 See http://ec.europa.eu/clima/policies/transport/aviation/docs/faq_aviation_2013-2016_en.pdf.

2   Some *Gulf States*, like the UAE, have expressed interest in the negotiation of a 'comprehensive' open aviation agreement with the EU. However, the European Commission
found fierce opposition from some of the main European airline groups: they contended
that the Gulf carriers, Emirates, Etihad and Qatar Airways, while aggressively and successfully offering sixth freedom services in the international market, at the same time benefit
from a multitude of taxation and other state aid advantages and thus engage in unfair competition with their European counterparts. The Gulf carriers postulate that investment by
their state owners as such should not be banned as illegal 'state aid', that they simply benefit
from their superior geographical position and infrastructure and that the EU carriers rather
suffer from the fierce competition of low cost carriers, infrastructure constraints, excessive
tax burdens and regulatory constraints, which is something for which the Gulf carriers
cannot be blamed.

So far the Commission neither started any official investigation[82] nor obtained a mandate
for formal negotiations; however, the 2012 'external aviation policy' communication gave
the Commission a mandate to review or replace EC Regulation 868/2004, to develop a
template for a 'fair competition clause' to be proposed on a bilateral and multilateral basis
and to engage in a dialogue with Gulf States, with a view to enhancing transparency and
safeguarding fair competition.[83]

As a result, the Commission initiated the 'EU–Gulf Cooperation Council (GCC) Aviation Dialogue', the first meeting taking place in 2013. In these meetings the Gulf States
agreed to an agenda proposed by the EC that included matters related to transparency, the
safeguarding of fair competition and cooperation in areas such as aviation safety, security
and air navigation services; in their turn the Gulf States requested some form of commitment to negotiate a comprehensive 'open skies' aviation agreement between the two
regions. The Commission mainly pursued a discussion around a model 'fair competition
clause' to be included in all bilateral agreements, and initially objected to any commitment
with regard to formal aviation negotiations.

An important development took place during the third 'Aviation Dialogue' meeting
held in May 2015,[84] where a draft roadmap included language referring to the possible
negotiation of a comprehensive aviation agreement (major EU concession), which may
include a mutually acceptable fair competition clause and some degree of regulatory convergence (major Gulf States concessions); the parties agreed that 'open, free and fair competition is an important factor in the provision of international air transport'.

82 That action would be based on Regulation (EC) No. 868/2004 of 21 April 2004 concerning protection
against subsidisation and unfair pricing practices causing injury to Community air carriers in the supply
of air services from countries not members of the European Community, OJ L162/1 of 30 April 2004.
It was adopted in reaction to post-9/11 subsidization of US carriers. In the absence of complaints it has
never been used. The Commission is in the course of reviewing this instrument to enhance its
effectiveness in safeguarding fair competiton.
83 See 'EU Council Conclusions on the EU's External Aviation Policy: Addressing the Future Challenges' 3213th Transport, Telecommunications and Energy Council Meeting held in Brussels on 20
December 2012 – paras 22, 23, 24 and 28; see http://ec.europa.eu/transport/modes/air/international_
aviation/external_aviation_policy/doc/comm(2012)556_en.pdf.
84 Joint Statement issued on the occasion of the third EU–GCC Aviation Dialogue, Doha, Qatar, 19 May
2015 (copy of the joint statement with the authors) and Draft EU–GCC Stated Aviation Dialogue
Roadmap attached to the Joint Statement issued at the third Aviation Dialogue Meeting, Doha, Qatar,
19 May 2015 (copy of the draft Roadmap with the authors).

A fourth 'Aviation Dialogue' meeting took place in Europe in late 2015. At the time of writing, the outcome of this 'fair competition/level playing field battle' on two fronts, the US[85] and Europe, was still unclear.

11.6 Other regional approaches to liberalization

In other parts of the world initiatives have been taken aimed at regional liberalization of international air transport.

11.6.1 Latin America: Andean Pact, Fortaleza Agreement, LACAC

Latin America has a longstanding tradition of air transport liberalization at the sub-regional level, although the process has been rather unsuccessful due to improvisation, regional political instability and excessive intervention by governments.

1   *Andean Pact.* One of the first initiatives for air transport liberalization in the region was Decision 297 of 1991 for the 'Integration of Air Transport in the Andean Sub region' that liberalized the exercise of third, fourth and fifth freedom rights for scheduled services among member states of the Andean Pact (Bolivia, Colombia, Ecuador, Peru and Venezuela), and also liberalized tariffs by adopting a country of origin tariff rule. For non-scheduled services, full liberalization was applicable for all-cargo flights, but in passenger services liberalization of non-scheduled flights applied only on routes not connected by scheduled services.[86]

    The present regime[87] dates back to 2004. While the 'open skies' regime in the Andean pact remains in force, after the withdrawal of Venezuela and Bolivia, it is now limited to Colombia, Ecuador and Peru, which *effectively allow the exercise of unrestricted third/fourth and fifth freedom, capacity, country of origin pricing and multiple designation of airlines.*

2   *Fortaleza Agreement.* This agreement of 1996 seeks to liberalize regional air services amongst 'Mercosur' member states (a customs and trade union now grouping Argentina, Brazil, Venezuela, Paraguay and Uruguay). The Agreement aims at promoting new scheduled services on routes not served under traditional bilateral agreements, but also refer to the

---

85 In the meantime also US carriers started to attack the, in their eyes, unfairly privileged position of the Gulf carriers and question the application of open skies agreements signed with certain GCC states, giving additional support to the EU airlines' position. Gulf carriers contended that subsidies allegations are unfounded, quoted industry observers who see a protectionist agenda behind these attacks on their successful model, and referred to the long history of state subsidization and support to the airline industries of both the US and Europe. The US government opened an Information Docket in 2015 to review different arguments concerning these allegations.

86 This Decision was the result of a political mandate adopted by the Presidents in 1990, and, in the view of some critics, reflected an element of improvisation as it was implemented in a very short time, different from the gradual implementation of the three packages of air transport liberalization in Europe. See Sarmiento Garcia, Manuel Guillermo, 'La Politica de Transporte Aereo en la Comunidad Andina de Naciones'. This resulted in delays in its implementation because of differences (financial health/stage of privatization) between the airlines concerned. See ICAO case study of February 2003 on 'Andean open skies pact', referring to Colombia and Venezuela having privately owned airlines and favouring immediate implementation, while Peru, Ecuador and Bolivia deferred the implementation to protect their national state owned airlines.

87 Decision 582; previous versions 320 of 1992 and 360 and 361 of 1994 allowed for multiple designation but left the question of national ownership and control to the domestic laws of the parties.

exercise of fifth and sixth freedom rights *with the consent of involved states*. With regard to tariffs, the agreement introduced a 'country of origin' tariff regime; however, it provides for the revision of tariffs by the Council of Aeronautical Authorities in case any member requests such a review. The Agreement permits multiple designation of airlines; but the airline has to fulfil the legal requirements of the *receiving* party. With regard to capacity, Annex 1 to the Agreement allows the airlines to propose frequencies and type of aircraft, but leaves the decision to the concerned aeronautical authorities to avoid excess capacity; in case of any dispute, the Council of Aeronautical Authorities will analyse the controversy. However, it is important to mention that the Council can only provide recommendations to the member states in regard to controversies arising from the application of the Agreement or anti-competitive practices (Annex 2). As a regional liberalization instrument, this agreement is of very limited importance.

3 *LACAC 'Open Skies' Agreement*. The above limited scope and effect of the existing subregional agreements provided the thrust for the adoption of the more recent Multilateral Agreement for Open Skies amongst Member States of the Latin American Civil Aviation Commission (LACAC Agreement) concluded on 5 November 2010; this multilateral agreement has been signed by Brazil, Chile, Colombia, Dominican Republic, Guatemala, Honduras, Panama, Paraguay and Uruguay.[88] At the time of this writing, the agreement has not yet entered into force.

11.6.2 Africa: the Yamoussoukro Decision

In Africa, the Yamoussoukro Decision adopted by African Ministers of Transport on 14 November 1999 was an ambitious attempt progressively to liberalize air services amongst African states.[89] It provides for the free exercise of the first five freedoms of the air (with a two year transitional period for fifth freedom rights), liberalized tariffs and free capacity (subject to certain fair competition safeguards).

The regime seems to embrace the single designation principle, but allows for the designation of an airline of another African state to operate services on its behalf. The Decision departs from the traditional 'ownership and control' criteria, but lists a number of requisites of eligibility, including to be legally established according to the laws of one state party, to have headquarters, central administration and principal place of business in a state party and to be effectively controlled by a state party.

The legal status and enforceability of the Yamoussoukro Decision is a complex issue, because it was adopted under the Treaty that established the African Economic Community (the Abuja Treaty of 1991), an organization that was replaced by the African Union in the year 2000. The succession of legal regimes and institutions created some legal debate with regard to the parties and enforceability of the provisions of the Yamoussoukro Decision.[90]

The implementation of the Yamoussoukro Decision has been less than satisfactory, as bilateral agreements continue to apply amongst African nations. Furthermore, there has been delay

---

88 Copy of the Agreement and a list of states parties can be found at http://clacsec.lima.icao.int/2013-publicaciones/Acuerdos/Acuerdo-CielosAbiertos/AcuMulCieAbi.pdf.

89 Copy of the Agreement and a list of states parties can be found at www.afcac.org/en/documents/conferences/July2012/yde.pdf.

90 For a complete analysis of the differences between the Abuja Treaty and the African Union Treaty and the impact on the enforceability of the Yamoussoukro Decision, see Charles E. Schlumberger, 'Open skies for Africa: Implementing of the Yamoussoukro Decision', World Bank, Washington, 2010 at ch. 2.

in developing the institutional and legal frameworks required for its implementation, including an executing agency, competition regulations and dispute settlement mechanisms. By virtue of article 12 of the Decision, efforts to liberalize air transport have now shifted to the different sub-regional groups in Africa, of which there are many.[91]

11.6.3 Arab air transport liberalization

In the Arab League member states, the Convention for the Liberalization of Air Transport between Arab states was adopted in 2004 by the Arab Civil Aviation Commission and entered into force in December 2007. Although 16 states signed the Agreement (Algeria, Bahrain, Egypt, Iraq, Jordan, Lebanon, Mauritania, Morocco, Oman, Palestine, Somalia, Sudan, Syria, Tunisia, UAE, and Yemen) only *seven* Arab states are currently party to it (i.e. Jordan, Lebanon, Morocco, Oman, Palestine, Syria, UAE and Yemen).

The Agreement provides for the exchange of the first five freedoms but does not provide for the exchange of cabotage rights. The Agreement allows for free capacity and multiple designation of airlines, but preserves the traditional ownership and control criteria combined with the principal place of business. Interestingly, it opens up the possibility of establishing a 'multinational' air carrier, where 'substantial ownership and effective control are vested in several states parties or their nationals', a practical arrangement since Gulf Air at the time was an airline whose ownership and control was in the hands of four Arab states.

Tariffs can be freely established by the airlines and do not require approval by the aeronautical authorities; but tariffs have to be filed and there is a mechanism to resolve disputes in case of tariff differences.

While the agreement provides a comprehensive framework for the liberalization of air transport amongst Arab states, its low level of ratification, together with political instability in the region and the rapid growth of the Gulf 'Big Three' airlines (Emirates Airline, Qatar Airways and Etihad Airways) have plotted against the full implementation of this instrument. An ongoing debate amongst the parties to the agreement is the need for implementing regulation, which has not yet been adopted. As a result the region, including the seven parties among themselves, still relies on bilateral agreements to govern the provision of intra-regional air services, rendering the convention de facto inapplicable.

11.6.4 ASEAN

The Association of South East Asian States (ASEAN) that currently groups Brunei Darussalam, Cambodia, Indonesia, Lao PDR, Malaysia, Myanmar, Philippines, Singapore, Thailand and Vietnam is also progressing towards the integration of international air transport amongst its member states. In November 2004, the ASEAN Transport Ministers Meeting adopted an 'Action Plan' for air transport liberalization and a 'Roadmap' for the Integration of Air Travel Sector targeting an 'open skies' regime amongst its member states by 2015.

As a result of this process, the following three instruments dealing with the liberalization of air services have been adopted:

1   The 'Multilateral Agreement on Air Services' (MAAS) signed on 20 May 2009; the agreement is accompanied by six protocols staging the incremental liberalization of passenger

91 For a description of the various groups and their membership, and their accomplishments so far, see Schlumberger, ibid.

services, first liberalizing regional services at boundary regions at designated cities and lately pursuing liberalization of air services amongst ASEAN capital cities.

2 The 'Multilateral Agreement on the Full Liberalization of Passenger Air Services' (MAFLPAS) signed on 12 November 2010, includes two protocols (one on the exchange of third and fourth freedom and the other on fifth freedom traffic rights) and complements the MAAS as it pursues liberalization of air services amongst ASEAN cities not covered by MAAS.

3 The 'Multilateral Agreement on the Full Liberalization of Air Freight Services' (MAFLAFS) signed on 20 May 2009 includes two protocols and two implementing MoUs and pursues the progressive liberalization of air *cargo* services including fifth freedom rights among all ASEAN cities.

These agreements pursue relaxation on market access, on airline ownership and control (including the 'principal place of business criterion') and a common policy for user charges, tariffs, capacity, competitive behaviour and other forms of regulation. While the above multilateral agreements have entered into force, ratification by some member states is still pending.[92]

While some steps remain to be taken, in particular re 'seventh' freedom and cabotage rights, in order to finalize the creation of an ASEAN Common Aviation Market similar to the European experience, there is no doubt that it is the most promising regional liberalization project so far.[93]

11.7 GATS and its annex on air transport

The WTO resulted from the Uruguay Round of Multilateral Trade Negotiations concluded on 15 December 1993. The Final Act of the Uruguay Round also encompasses the General Agreement for Trade in Services (GATS) that includes an Annex on Air Transport.

While the focus of GATS is on the liberalization of trade in services, the fact that a sector has been included in the Agreement does not necessarily imply immediate liberalization. A case in point is the Annex on Air Transport, which covers in principle both scheduled and non-scheduled commercial air traffic, as well as any related ancillary services; however, the Annex also specifies that traffic rights (the so-called 'hard rights') and services directly related to them are excluded from the application of GATS disciplines, with the exception of aircraft repair and maintenance, marketing and sales of air transport services and CRS, which are 'included' in GATS.

But even with respect to such services, countries could make exemptions to the application of GATS principles, creating what one author described as 'exemptions from the inclusion provided by the exception to the exclusion to the inclusion'.[94] This broad exemption however, is subject to review by the Council for Trade in Services, to consider the possible expansion of the application of GATS in this sector; however until today, neither of the two reviews conducted have resulted in any concrete proposal for expanding the Annex.

---

92 The Philippines has not ratified MAAS Protocols 5 and 6, whereas Indonesia and Laos so far did not ratify MAFLPAS and its Protocols. Additionally, Indonesia was the only party that did not ratify the (cargo) MAFLAFS and its protocols, see http://agreement.asean.org/search/by_pillar/2.html.

93 See also Alan Tan, 'Air transport integration in the ASEAN region', Report for the World Bank, Washington, DC, October 2013 (copy provided by the author).

94 This paradox was taken from the notes of John R. Byerly, 'Trade law and international aviation' Lecture at the International Aviation Law Institute, De Paul University College of Law, 3 April 2012 (copy provided by the author).

Two of the principles that are the cornerstone of GATS system, namely Most Favoured Nation (MFN) and National Treatment (NT), have created controversy around GATS compatibility with the international aviation system. With respect to MFN, article II (1) of the GATS requires that member states agree on a 'treatment no less favorable than it accords to like services and service suppliers of any other country'; in respect to NT, article XVII (1) of GATS provides that member states agree 'in respect of all measures affecting the supply of services, treatment no less favorable than it accords to its own like services and service providers'. Only MFN provisions apply uniformly to all signatories, while NT is subject to conditions and qualifications of the specific commitments made by a member state.[95]

The view of the majority of the aviation community is that both principles are incompatible with air transport rights or at least impracticable at this time.[96] For some, the application of the MFN principle to hard rights would imply the extension of the most liberal terms to all member states, contrary to the bilateral system, which requires a case-by-case exchange of 'comparable' benefits. However, some authors have noted that article II (2) of GATS allows member states to apply exemptions and others have gone further to provide alternatives for the extension of the MFN principle to hard rights.[97]

11.8 ICAO's role in the liberalization of international air transport

At the centre of the debate on ICAO's role is the limited reference in the Chicago Convention itself to ICAO's responsibilities with respect to the economic regulation of international air transport and the exchange of traffic rights.[98] A majority of the aviation community considers that the sovereignty principle in the Convention and the lack of a specific mandate on economic regulation clearly indicate that this topic was meant to be the exclusive resort of the member states individually. Nonetheless, the Organization has taken various initiatives through the years and has developed policies and guidance material in this area. It is appropriate in this connection to distinguish between ICAO as law-maker/regulator and ICAO as facilitator.

In its first role, ICAO, at least partly in reaction to the WTO/GATS initiatives, embraced the objective of the multilateral liberalization of international air transport at the fourth Air Transport Conference (ATC) in 1994. The member states, though in principle supporting the idea as such, in overwhelming majority insisted on a step-by-step and bilateral-by-bilateral approach, and the ICAO Conferences and symposia that followed, *inter alia* in 2003 (fifth ATC), showed the same behavioural pattern.

---

95 In this regard, see Brian Hindley, *Trade liberalization in aviation services: Can the Doha Round free flight?* AEI Press (2004) at p. 31; also Jason R. Bonin, 'Regionalism in international civil aviation: A reevaluation of the economic regulation of international air transport in the context of economic integration' (2008) *Singapore Yearbook of International Law* 113–131 at p. 119.

96 ICAO concluded as follows:

> Applying the basic GATS principle of MFN to traffic rights remains a complex and difficult issue. While there is some support to extend the GATS Annex on Air Transport Services to include some soft rights as well as some aspects of hard rights, there is no global consensus on whether or how this would be pursued. Whether the GATS is an effective option for air transport liberalization remains in question.

> See ICAO, 'Manual on the Regulation of International Air Transport', *supra* note 11.

97 In general, see Janda papers, and Wolfgang Hubner and Pierre Sauve 'Liberalization Scenarios for International Air Transport'.

98 But model bilateral clauses were agreed at the Chicago Conference, and the Provisional International Civil Aviation Organization in the years thereafter continued its efforts to create a liberal multilateral agreement.

At the sixth ATC held in 2013 it was proposed to expand ICAO's role in this area by way of a new Annex 20 to the Chicago Convention on 'economic development of air transport'. This initiative was ultimately dismissed with the argument that further consideration was required with due regard to the sovereignty of states in this area.[99]

The main vehicle to advise the Council on the development and updating of policies following the sixth ATC is the Air Transport Regulation Panel (ATRP) of governmental experts. As a follow-up to this ATC, the Panel is presently tasked with, *inter alia*, the development of a number of international agreements, i.e. on the further liberalization of cargo-only services, on the liberalization of market access and on the liberalization of air carrier ownership and control (to facilitate foreign investment).[100]

As these latter two agreements, at least in the terms of reference, are qualified as 'for State use', they (also) appear to touch upon ICAO's other, and more successful role, i.e. that of enabler or *facilitator*. In this role, ICAO continues to provide abundant information and documentation on all aspects of – bilateral and multilateral – air transport regulation, both in the context of its Conferences and Colloquia and in the form of guidance material, including on best practices, e.g. Template Air Services Agreements, etc.[101]

An increasingly important issue, arising from the regional and global spreading of the liberalization gospel and practice, is (un-)fair *competition*. This is reflected in European Commission proposals for comprehensive competition provisions in member states and EU agreements. But also ICAO has commissioned further study to collect data and develop policies and guidelines on this issue for its 191 member states.[102]

---

99 Annexes to the Chicago Convention contain standards and recommended practices (SARPs); though they do not have the same legal force as the Convention itself, in particular *standards* are clearly more 'imperative' than templates or guidance material. It is therefore not surprising that member states considered this 'a bridge too far'.

100 See www.icao.int/sustainability/Documents/Panel-StudyGroup-ToRs.pdf. The ATRP/12 Working Group on international agreements (WG1) that met in Dubai on 8–9 June 2015 speaks of 'a multilateral air services agreement and three related protocols (i.e. on commercial rights covering passenger and combination services, on all cargo services, and on waiver of nationality requirements in airline designation'. The meeting recognized that the drafting thereof was a very challenging, complex and delicate exercise, requiring considerable efforts. For that reason, the various drafts including alternative texts may, in the end, become useful 'guidance material' only. The results of WG1 will be discussed at the thirteenth meeting of ATRP in Montreal from 1–4 September 2015 (Doc. ATRP/13-WP/2 of 26 June 2015).

101 ICAO Doc. 9587, see *supra* note 3, deals with the economic aspects of international air transport regulation and includes the ICAO Template Air Services Agreements (TASA) that contain model clauses for both bilateral and multilateral agreements.
     The 'Manual on the Regulation of International Air Transport', see *supra* note 11, which complements and supplements Doc. 9587, describes the existing regulatory processes and structure at the national, bilateral and multilateral levels, as well as regulatory content and key issues. Describing itself as a dictionary, encyclopedia and textbook, it provides very useful reference material for regulatory practitioners, and for training purposes.

102 The ATRP terms of reference include the item 'develop a compendium of current, national and/or regional competition policies and practices'. See also www.icao.int/sustainability/Documents/Compendium_FairCompetition/Compendium.pdf). The ATRP/12 Working Group on competition matters that met in Dubai from 10–12 June 2015 also discussed mechanisms to (i) encourage states to explore the adoption of fair competition policies and practices; and (ii) facilitate exchange of information about such policies and practices. It was noted that fair competition provisions already exist in bilateral agreements and that the ICAO TASA contains relevant model clauses. The planned ICAO Air Transport Symposium on competition of 8–9 December 2015 at Montreal is an example of information sharing in this field. Updating of the above two ICAO Docs, *supra* note 101, is also foreseen, see Doc. ATRP/13-WP/3 of 26 June 2015.

Separately, ICAO facilitates bilateral negotiations through the so-called ICAO Air Services Negotiating Conferences (ICAN): since 2008 ICAO organizes these ICAN events to allow its member states to have multiple bilateral or multilateral negotiations at one venue. This is obviously more efficient and cost-effective for national negotiators than travelling to each of the partner nations separately. Through formal and informal contacts in a neutral, result-oriented setting, agreements may be concluded or amended, and practice shows that the ICAN approach does work.[103]

At a 2014 regional ICAO conference 'economic development of air transport' was mentioned as one of the five strategic objectives of ICAO, making it clear that ICAO is firmly committed to play its role and has no intention of leaving economic issues to other organizations or institutions.[104]

11.9 Conclusions

- The open skies philosophy, with the underlying message that governments should primarily limit themselves to regulating safety and security matters, has become a new standard.
- Still, a substantial number of countries see airlines as more than instruments serving the economy and feel the need to protect these 'national assets' through more traditional bilateral agreements.
- The EU is the only example of successful regional liberalization so far: 28 sovereign states gave up the use of bilateral agreements to regulate international air transport among themselves, and convinced associated countries to do likewise; and slowly but increasingly they negotiate as one bloc.
- EU states were *forced* to liberalize, politically by the *users*, but legally by the European Court's interpretation and application of Rome Treaty-based free trade and non-discrimination principles agreed upon already in 1957 by the six founding member states.
- Without such a legal basis, change comes slowly because national (government and airline) interests will continue to stand in the way: ASEAN may be the only positive exception in the short-to-medium term.
- ICAO's role in this process is understandably severely limited because of the many differences amongst its 191 member states;[105] but it stimulates the development of innovative approaches also by presenting and explaining 'best practices' in this area.
- With governments withdrawing from bilaterally regulating market access, capacity and pricing, such concepts as (un-)fair competition and a (non-)level playing field become increasingly important; in fact, unavoidably, competition laws, policies and practices will be the dominant topic in bilateral and multilateral air transport *fora* in the years to come.

---

103 The first ICAN held in Dubai in 2008 produced 100 bilateral meetings resulting in 20 signed agreements and arrangements; at ICAN no. 6 in Durban (2013) 485 bilateral meetings produced 450 such agreements, see address Benjamin, SG ICAO at ICAN Bali, Indonesia (2014), http://www.icao.int/Meetings/ICAN2014/Documents/SG_Opening-remarks.pdf. Turkey and a Latin-American country will host the 2015 and 2016 events respectively.

104 'Setting the scene', Presentation of Narjess Abdennebi, Chief economic policy and analsysis section, ICAO, at ICAO Regional Air Transport Conference, Montego Bay, Jamaica, 7–9 October 2014; included observations on issues like market access, liberalization and fair competition. See also ICAO strategic objectives 2014–2016 which includes 'the development of a sound and economically-viable civil aviation system … [and] the need for ICAO's leadership in harmonizing the air transport framework focused on economic policies and supporting activities', see www.icao.int/about-icao/Pages/Strategic-Objectives.aspx.

105 According to Hans de Jong, long-time Dutch government ATRP member, the following reasons for resisting change and protecting the flag carrier, as documented by ICAO, are: the desire to have a national carrier, to secure services to/from its territory, concerns about employment, (un-)fair competition, national security/defence needs and (non-)level playing field (information provided to the author).

12

Economic regulation of air transport

P.P.C. Haanappel

12.1 Introduction

Governments have always shown a great interest in aviation, whether *military* or *civil*. The preceding chapters of this book have revealed such interest. Within the domain of civil aviation, as defined by Article 3 of the Chicago Convention on International Civil Aviation,[1] governments have also shown a significant interest in air *transport*, which can perhaps be best described as the *commercial* side of civil aviation: as transport, as carriage 'for hire and reward', as a common lawyer would say; or as carriage 'by onerous title', as a civilian would say.

This interest in *air commerce*, as one could also call air transport,[2] has often translated itself into governmental *economic regulation*. Most industries, in most countries, are to varying degrees subjected to governmental economic controls. What this chapter attempts to do, is to examine such controls, to the extent that they are special to air transport, as compared with industry at large.

First, air transport will have to be more precisely defined, as will the various forms of economic controls.

Air transport is essentially a value chain, consisting of the following links, more or less in chronological order: aircraft manufacturing, maintenance and repair; airlines; airports; ground handling services; and air navigation and air traffic services. This chapter deals essentially with governmental *economic* regulation of *airlines*. *Safety* and *security* regulation of airlines has already been covered in Chapters 3, 4, 7 and 8. This also applies to aircraft manufacturing, maintenance and repair. The same is applicable to airports, which were the subject of Chapter 6; ground handling services, a subject in Chapter 11; and air navigation and air traffic services, the subject of Chapter 5.

Economic regulation of air transport essentially takes two forms: a priori, *ex ante* control, where air transport enterprises need approval from governmental (air) transport authorities before they can implement an economic, a commercial, decision or where such decision is imposed by governmental authorities; and *ex post facto* control, where air transport enterprises take their own commercial decisions, but where such decisions may subsequently be annulled or varied by governmental authorities, whether (air) transport authorities, or antitrust,

---

1 See Chapter 2 of this book.
2 See Chapter 6, 'The Law and Policy of Air Commerce', in: P.P.C. Haanappel, *The Law and Policy of Air Space and Outer Space, A Comparative Approach*, Kluwer Law International, The Hague/London/New York, 2003.

competition law authorities, or increasingly also by consumer law authorities. For antitrust and competition law, reference is made to Chapter 13 of this book; and for consumer law, to Chapter 14. Antitrust and competition laws often protect the air travellers at large; consumer law tends more specifically to protect individual air travellers. *Ex ante* control is most prevalent in the pre-deregulation, pre-liberalization environment of air transport, whereas antitrust, competition and consumer law control is more important in a deregulated, liberalized environment. Deregulation and liberalization are essentially the same, although the former term is more prevalent in the United States and the latter in Europe.

A distinction should also be made between State, publicly owned air transport enterprises and privately owned or privatized air transport enterprises. State or other *public* ownership, whether full or partial, gives governmental or other public authorities the opportunity to control economically air transport enterprises 'from within'; in a pre-deregulated, pre-liberalized air transport environment with *private* or predominantly private ownership of enterprises, *ex ante* or *ex post facto* control by (air) transport authorities is prevalent; in a deregulated or liberalized environment, antitrust, competition and consumer law take on a more important role. Where in the change from a regulated to a deregulated or liberalized environment remnants of old transport law regulation co-exist with forms of new competition and/or consumer law regulation, complaints of overregulation of the industry may be justified.

As previously mentioned, airlines will be principally discussed in detail in this chapter. A few preliminary words need to be said here about the other participants in the value chain, namely the aircraft manufacturers, maintenance and repair enterprises, airports, ground handlers and air navigation service providers.

Aircraft manufacturers may be publicly or privately owned. Increasingly, the aircraft manufacturing industry is becoming concentrated. Where the production of large aircraft is concerned,[3] there is even a question of a duopoly.[4] In such a situation it is not surprising that international trade law plays a role, of the type designed by the World Trade Organization (WTO), especially in situations where claims of unfair direct or indirect State subsidization are made by one competitor against the other.

For aircraft maintenance and repair, it should be noted that in addition to ICAO[5] rules, increasingly EASA[6] rules begin to play a role, also in countries which are not European or not formally associated with EASA.

Airports and air navigation/service providers may hold monopolistic or quasi-monopolistic positions: airports in their natural traffic catchment areas; air navigation or service providers, because, in a given block of air space, there can be only one such provider. Although blocks of air space may be vertically stacked, there can only be one air navigation service provider in each of the following three areas: from bottom up, approach/departure control area; lower air space control area; and upper air space control area. Where airports or air navigation/service providers are commercialized, corporatized or privatized, as is increasingly the case, there may be need for governmental pricing control on various charges, in order to avoid potential abuse of market power. Article 15 of the Chicago Convention prohibiting discrimination against foreign aircraft also plays a role in this context.[7]

---

3 Presently from the Boeing 737 to the Boeing 787, and from the Airbus 318 to the Airbus 380.
4 The Boeing Company from the US and the European Airbus SAS.
5 International Civil Aviation Organization.
6 European Aviation Safety Agency.
7 See reference *supra* footnote 2, and *supra* Chapters 5 and 6.

12.2 Governments and airlines

The first sentence in the Introduction to this chapter reads: 'Governments have always shown a *great*[8] interest in aviation'. Some would use the adjective and noun: *extraordinary* interest. Compared with other modes of transportation – with perhaps, in some countries, the exception of railway transportation – air transport does indeed have the keenest interest of governments and their citizens alike. The public has always been fascinated with aircraft, airlines and airports, and what the public is fascinated with, governments must follow. But there is more: of all now existing modes of transportation, with the exception of the fledgling outer space transportation industry, air transport is the only three dimensional one. This is important to governments and the sovereignty that they exercise over their territories: aircraft, including helicopters, can penetrate national territory, national airspace, more deeply than any other transportation vehicles. This raises issues of sovereignty, national security and national military interests. It also inspires the governmental tendency to get involved with the economic aspects of this form of transportation. It is not only that, transportation, but also an adjunct to military power.[9]

As far as the public is concerned, one should add that air transport has something 'glamorous', although in these populist days in which we now live, with low cost airlines and low promotional air fares, the glamour is waning. The fact remains that, for the public at large, inexpensive air transport has made the world a global village, accessible to all. Where air transport is no longer inexpensive and threatens the accessibility of the global village, the public will call out loud for some kind of governmental economic intervention, be it by consumer law, competition law or other authorities.

Governments have associated themselves very firmly with airlines by creating the 'flag carrier' concept. The concept is not a legal one, but it denotes the situation, as the following will show, that States, through regulatory economic devices, create a situation where only one airline in a particular country is given the right to perform scheduled (international) air services. They thereby create a domestic monopoly, functioning within an international regulatory oligopoly of flag carriers from different countries. National and especially governmental involvement in the flag carrier is reinforced by the so-called substantial ownership and effective control rule to the effect that such airline must be majority owned and effectively controlled by the State and/or its citizens.[10]

The 'extraordinary' interest that governments and the public have shown for airlines is inversely proportional to the profitability of the airline industry. Depending on the economic reports that one consults, since the Second World War, the average rate of return on investment in the airline industry has been only around 3 per cent, whereas airports and especially aircraft manufacturers have been much more profitable.

The interest of governments and citizens in air transport, in airlines, has been a constant factor in the post Second World War period, but the modalities have changed. The decrease in

---

8 Italics supplied.

9 One application thereof is the carriage, by civilian aircraft, by airlines, of military personnel and equipment. See, for instance, in the US, the Civil Reserve Air Fleet (CRAF).

10 On substantial ownership and effective control of airlines, see Chapter 11 of this book; and Haanappel, op. cit. footnote 2, at pp. 145–151. A survey by this author in the mid 1970s, when governmental economic control of airlines was probably at its strongest, showed that, at that time, some 55 per cent of international airlines were fully or more than 50 per cent State owned. See P.P.C. Haanappel, *Ratemaking in International Air Transport*, Kluwer, Deventer, the Netherlands, 1978, at pp. 153–155. In 1983, just before the large scale privatization of airlines began (see below), that percentage stood at about 80: see P.P.C. Haanappel, *Pricing and Capacity Determination in International Air Transport: A Legal Analysis*, Kluwer, Deventer, the Netherlands, 1978, 1984, at pp. 183–186.

'glamour' and the 'global village' have already been mentioned. The watershed in the economic regulation of air transport, and especially of airlines, has not been mentioned yet and that is the move towards deregulation of the airline industry, its liberalization and its large scale privatization, *casu quo* corporatization in many countries having 'flag carriers'. This began in the late 1970s in the US, spread to Europe and other parts in the 1980s and continues to spread today to States in Africa, Asia and Latin America that have not yet been liberalized.

It cannot be stressed enough that the economic regulation of airlines in the pre-deregulation, pre-liberalization period, thus until about 1975–1985, created a world airline industry that does not exist anymore today. It was a world of flag carriers with relatively little competition between them, rather with the opposite, a system of tight regulation by governments and by the International Air Transport Association (IATA), the worldwide association of scheduled international airlines, set up in 1945 and to whom governments, in their bilateral air transport/services agreements, had delegated the function to set air fares and rates on international air routes.[11] Any effective competition in international air transport, especially pricing competition, came from a relatively small group of carriers outside IATA, the non-scheduled, the charter airlines, also called supplemental airlines in the US. By the mid 1970s, this competition had become considerable in size, began to undermine the pricing function of IATA and became one of the impetuses towards deregulation and liberalization of the airline industry. These days, charter airlines have virtually vanished, at least in passenger air transport, in favour of today's so-called low cost, low fare airlines. They operate in the scheduled mode. Charter services still fulfil a function today as a regulatory device in non-liberalized bilateral air transport markets.[12]

However, it has not always been as in the period 1945–1975/1985, as described above. Scheduled (international) air transport began, shortly after the First World War, in 1918/1919, as an initiative of private enterprise, both in the Americas and in Europe. In America, governments soon got involved in the (US) domestic air transport market, by the award of air mail contracts, a form of subsidization to help the fledgling air transport industry develop. In Europe, governments of countries having extensive colonies overseas soon got financially involved in the development of airlines capable of maintaining long lines to and from the colonies. During and following the great depression of the 1930s, State owned airlines, flag carriers, became the model in Europe and the colonies, and would remain so until liberalization of the industry. Notwithstanding liberalization and privatization of airlines as of the 1980s, some of these flag carriers still exist today. In North America, government regulation of airlines, as the following will show, followed a public utility model, initiated in the 1930s and lasting until deregulation of the airline industry in the late 1970s.

Besides the foregoing, there are other considerations which have led governments to get involved with the economics of airlines. First, there is the general difference between free market economies on the one hand and socialist or centrally managed economies on the other. In the former, industry specific government regulation is rather the exception to the rule, whereas in the latter it is the rule. Remnants of that latter approach can still be found today in the Russian Federation and China, for instance, notwithstanding a degree of liberalization of the industry also there.

National prestige also plays a role in the degree to which governments get involved with the economics, with the management of their airlines. When one looks of the lists of airlines in the literature references, mentioned in footnote 10 above, one becomes aware of the fact how many

11 See Chapter 11 of this book.
12 Ibid.

airlines carry the name of their countries, either as a noun or as an adjective, in their corporate names, not to speak of the appearance of the national flag on the tails of the airlines of these countries. National prestige plays a lesser role today than in the past, and this seems to have everything to do with the fact that more and more people view air transport as a 'normal' means of public mass transportation. This is not yet fully applicable to the developing world and its airlines, although there are now a number of developing nations which have shed their loss making flag carriers and largely rely on foreign airlines to serve their territories. Finally, two other considerations for developing nations and their airlines: developing nations' airlines may be an important source of foreign currency earning for their governments. Also, developing nations' governments, whose economies depend significantly on income from foreign tourists may, on the one hand, financially bolster their airlines to carry these tourists, and, on the other, have a liberal policy with respect to the commercial admittance of foreign carriers, whether in the scheduled, non-scheduled or low cost mode.

Finally, a distinction should be made between countries with only an international air transport market, and countries with both a domestic and international market. The latter may either have one system of economic regulation of national airlines, or two, one for the international market, the other for the domestic. Countries with large domestic markets may also segregate their airlines: some for the domestic, some for the international market. The US, in the past, used to be the best example of such airline specialization.[13]

Finally, in this section of this chapter, the question: has the airline industry become a mature, a normal industry, no longer calling for a special system of economic control? The answer is probably: 'mature' yes, 'normal' no. Not 'normal', largely because of the aforementioned national security, adjunct to military power reasons.

12.3 A short history of economic regulation of airlines

Economic regulation of airlines began, indirectly, with the subsidization of the industry: in the US with the subsidization of the aforementioned air mail contracts, for which a solid legal basis was given in the so-called *Kelly Act*.[14] This is because subsidization by governments ordinarily comes with conditions imposed by governments. It was not different in Europe when, during the great economic depression of the 1930s, governments had to subsidize, directly or indirectly, airlines, or had to bail them out in order to ensure their economic survival. This, in Europe, heralded the beginning of the large scale nationalization of airlines. The creation of Air France in 1933 is probably the best example.

The State owned 'flag carrier' soon became the preferred airline model in Europe. The largest European countries, France and the United Kingdom, had more than one major airline.[15] Legal organization of flag carriers varied from country to country, depending on the commercial

---

13 Until deregulation of the airline industry, Pan American World Airways (Pan Am) and Trans World Airlines (TWA) served only international markets, whereas all other US carriers served domestic markets (plus sometimes Canada, the Caribbean and Mexico).

14 Air Mail Act of 1925, 45 Stat. 594.

15 In France, there was State owned Compagnie Nationale Air France and, since the 1960s, also privately owned Union des Transports Aériens (UTA). In addition, for domestic air services (cf. *supra* text to footnote 13), there was Air Inter. In the 1990s, the three national airlines merged into Groupe Air France. In the UK, there were, for many years, State owned British Airways Corporation (BOAC) and British European Airways (BEA). Both merged, under airline privatization in the 1980s, into British Airways.

laws of each country. Some countries, like France and the UK, created airlines as public corporations by special statute. Other countries, like Germany with Lufthansa AG, used the model of a private company, fully owned by the State.

By contrast, the US never created a State owned flag carrier. In the US, there were two privately owned carriers for international air services (i.e. Pan Am and TWA) and a relatively large number of domestic airlines.[16] They both came under a system of 'regulated competition', upon a public utility model, pursuant to the Civil Aeronautics Act of 1938,[17] later reenacted in the Federal Aviation Act of 1958.[18] This situation would continue until the deregulation of the industry in the late 1970s.[19]

International economic regulation of airlines in Europe began piecemeal with the Timetable and Accountancy Conferences, coordinating international air fares and rates, organized by the International Air *Traffic* Association, 1919–1945, not to be confused with the aforementioned International Air *Transport* Association, created in the year 1945.[20]

Following the Second World War, most European States adopted or revised Civil Aviation Laws or Acts, with accompanying secondary legislation, most often in the form of Aviation Regulations. These legal instruments gave broad, most often discretionary powers to national aeronautical authorities to regulate airlines in the fields of air carrier entry, route entry and exit, airline pricing and flight frequencies. The regulation of frequencies, coupled with the existence of commercial pooling agreements between airlines, made the governmental regulation of airlines in Europe, at least on paper, more stringent than the aforementioned public utility regulation in the US, which left the determination of flight frequencies to airlines and forbade commercial pooling of air services. Pricing control in the US, however, was probably more thorough than in Europe, if not on paper, then in practice.

As far as Europe is concerned, this situation would continue until the 1980s, when the European Community began to get involved in air transport matters, including airline matters, culminating in the third EC air transport liberalization package in the 1990s.[21]

12.4 Instrumentalities used by governments for economic regulation

The question here is the organizational form that governments have chosen to regulate civil aviation in general, and air transport in particular, whether that be from the point of view of safety, security, economic regulation or consumer protection. The most common form is a Ministry or a Department of Transport or of Transportation. Sometimes the focus is narrower in the form of a Ministry or Department of Aviation. At other times, and especially in smaller and developing nations, the focus is broader in the form of a Ministry or a Department of Transport(ation) and Communications.

Within large transport ministries, the aviation function is more often than not performed by a Directorate General of Civil Aviation (DGCA) or a Department of the same or similar name. It may be that some functions related to civil aviation lie in other ministries or departments, such as foreign affairs or economic affairs.

---

16 See *supra* footnote 13.
17 52 Stat. 973.
18 72 Stat. 731.
19 See Airline Deregulation Act of 1978, 92 Stat. 1705, and International Air Transportation Act of 1979, 94 Stat. 35.
20 Italics added. Both Associations were and are known by their acronyms IATA.
21 See consolidated EC Regulation 1008/2008.

Increasingly, governments have delegated the regulation of air transport to independent or quasi-independent regulatory bodies, usually under the name of a Civil Aviation Authority (CAA), or Public Authority for Civil Aviation (PACA). Usually these CAAs or PACAs take the legislative form of a statutory, State owned body. Ideally they should be self-financing through fees for services rendered. (Quasi) independence would enhance the competency, efficiency and hiring of staff, and this outside the constraints of the ordinary civil service, including salary constraints.

Next to Authorities, there are also Boards, especially where these bodies perform quasi-judicial functions. The best known example from the past is the Civil Aeronautics Board (CAB) in the US. It functioned under the system of 'regulated competition', as mentioned above, and was active from 1938 to 1985, first under the name Civil Aviation Authority and later as the CAB. It was abolished ('sunsetted') as a result of airline deregulation and its remaining functions were transferred to the US Department of Transportation. The Board model is also often used for aircraft accident investigation, such as currently in the US with the National Transportation Safety Board (NTSB), multimodal, or in Canada with the Transportation Safety Board of Canada.

CAAs or PACAs may have more or less broad regulatory functions, depending on how many and which functions have remained in a ministerial or departmental organization. It is not uncommon to find safety and security in a ministerial or departmental setting, and economic matters in a CAA or PACA. These bodies also frequently carry out consumer protection functions. Some CAAs have broad powers, even beyond the regulatory and into the service provision field. A good example is the Civil Aviation Authority of Singapore (CAAS), which, next to many other things, looks after the provision of air traffic control services.

As efficient as CAAs and PACAs may be, a difficult political and legal point is often their relationship with the Minister responsible for civil aviation, and in particular the question to what extent the quasi-independent CAA or PACA should follow the instructions of the Minister.

Whereas CAAs and PACAs are generally praised for their efficiency, they do not always fit into the general, governmental structures of countries. France and Germany, to mention but two important examples, have kept the regulation of civil aviation, including that of air transport, within traditional ministerial structures.

It is a disputed point whether CAAs or PACAs could ever truly be privatized, beyond their current commercialization and corporatization, or in other words come into the hands of investors, such as airlines, airports, air traffic control authorities, even aircraft manufacturers, somewhat along the lines of the ownership structure of the current National Air Traffic Services (NATS), the air traffic management authority in the UK. Opponents fear conflict of interest situations.

Finally, there is the delegation model of governmental regulation. In the safety field, the private *Bureau Veritas*, operating in 140 countries, for instance, has existed and offered its services since 1928. More importantly for economic regulation of air transport, is the delegation by States, in their bilateral agreements and otherwise,[22] to the aforementioned IATA of ratemaking, that is pricing functions for airlines, engaged in international air services. This will be further discussed below.

12.5 Constraints upon government regulation

Obviously, aeronautical regulators have to abide by the legislative, judicial and executive rules which exist in their respective countries and which may constrain their freedom of action. In air transport, particular attention is to be given to the following:

22 See Chapter 11.

- the federal or unitary organization of a given country;
- the country's system of administrative law and judicial review of administrative action;
- the constraints which may result from bilateral air transport, air services agreements; and
- the constraints which may arise from the nature of the Standards and Recommended Practices (SARPs) in the Annexes to the Chicago Convention.

In federally organized countries, like Australia, Canada, Germany, the US and others, the questions arise whether it is the federal or the 'local' (state, provincial) legislator that is competent to legislate, to regulate civil aviation, air transport; and whether one legislator is thus constrained by another. Different answers apply in different jurisdictions. In unitary countries, like France, the question hardly arises because, as a consequence of the unitary organization, only the central government is competent; but, even then, there may be minor exceptions, such as the partial jurisdiction of communes, states and municipalities in which airports are located. Well known examples of federally organized countries where there is case law in this area, are Canada and the US.

In Canada, one pre-war and one post-war case make it clear that 'aeronautics' is almost entirely a domain of federal jurisdiction: the so-called *Aeronautics reference* from the Canadian Supreme Court to the Privy Council in London,[23] in 1932, and the Canadian Supreme Court decision in *Johannesson* v. *Municipality of West St Paul*, in 1952.[24] Aeronautics would come under the 'peace, order and good government' clause, indicating federal jurisdiction, in the original Canadian constitutional document, the British North America Act, 1867.[25] This has not changed with the so-called 'patriation' of the Canadian Constitution in 1981–1982.[26] There are minor exceptions to the broad federal jurisdiction, such as in the field of private law aeronautical matters, where provinces might be competent to legislate.[27]

In the US, the air space preemption case of *United States* v. *Causby*,[28] congressional debates and the enactment of the Air Commerce Act of 1926[29] make it clear that inter-state aviation, under the US constitutional commerce clause, is of federal jurisdiction. There is room for state jurisdiction in intra-state aviation, but it is narrow. These days it is seldom exercised in the commercial arena, but it was, on occasions, in the pre-deregulation era, when entirely intra-state airlines, like Southwest and Air California, flew important intra-state routes, not controlled by the federal CAB, but by the local Public Utilities Commission.

In the EU, which, for the purposes of this discussion, will be considered as 'quasi-federal', a distinction should be made between intra-European domestic and international air travel on the one hand, and travel to and from the EU, third country traffic, on the other. National aeronautical authorities in the EU, and in associated European Economic Area (EEA) countries, European Common Aviation Area (ECAA) countries, and in Switzerland are 'constrained' by common air transport legislation, coming from the central European legislators.[30] They are basically the local 'executors' of centrally adopted legislation.

---

23 [1932] AC 54.
24 (1952) 1 SCR 292.
25 1867 c. 3 (Regnal. 30 and 31 Vict.).
26 Canada Act, 1982 (UK), Ch. 11.
27 See P.P.C. Haanappel, 'The right to sue in death cases under the Warsaw Convention', VI (1981) *Air Law* 66.
28 326 U.S. 256 (1946).
29 44 Stat. 568 (1926).
30 See the Regulation, referred to *supra* footnote 21.

In third country air transport between points in the EU and countries outside thereof, the legal position is still transitional. Since judgments of the European Court of Justice in the so-called 'open skies cases', on 5 November 2002, external air transport relations between the EU and its member States, on the one hand, and third countries, on the other, is a shared jurisdiction between central EU institutions and individual member States.[31] So long as air transport negotiations with third countries have not been undertaken by the European Commission, individual EU member States may do so themselves, for their own territories, but sometimes 'constrained' by common guidelines from the central EU.

Administrative law and judicial review of administrative action is another matter, and is governed by the constitutional and administrative laws of individual countries. At one extreme, there is the US where a significant number of administrative aeronautical functions take the form of quasi-judicial proceedings, formerly before the CAB, now before the Department of Transportation (DOT). At the other extreme, there are many countries where aeronautical authorities function in a purely civil service context, only constrained by legislation, primary (Laws and Acts) and secondary (Regulations), if existing at all.

Also, to varying degrees, the 'regulated', airlines, airports and others, may be able to appeal from the decisions of aeronautical authorities to the civil or special administrative courts of individual countries: the system of judicial review. In some countries, it does not exist at all and thus does not constrain the regulator.

Another question is the relationship between national aeronautical laws and regulations on the one hand, and bilateral air transport agreements, on the other.[32] Sometimes there are conflicting provisions: a bilateral agreement, for instance, may be more or less stringent than the national laws or regulations. What will prevail? That depends again on the constitutional system of each individual country. What, in a given country, is the status of a treaty? Does it need to be ratified? Does it have to be incorporated into national legislation; does it have to be 'domesticated'? In the UK and most Commonwealth countries, there is a 'dualistic' system: unless bilateral agreements are both ratified and incorporated into national law, which in practice is seldom done, they cannot contravene national laws and regulations.[33] In countries that base their constitutional systems on continental European law, bilateral agreements, if ratified by the Legislators which they most often are, have the status as national laws: the 'monistic' system. In the US, treaties, duly ratified by the US Senate, have the status of 'supreme law of the land'; however, bilateral air transport agreements are in practice not submitted to the Senate for approval, but are dealt with as so-called executive agreements. It is a complex area, the relationship between bilateral agreements and national laws or regulations, but an important one in practice.

Similar constitutional questions arise with respect to the status, in individual countries, of the SARPs contained in the ICAO Annexes.[34] Strictly speaking, only the binding Standards are binding on ICAO member States. SARPs are adopted by a two-thirds majority of the members of the ICAO Council and come into force without ratification by ICAO member States,[35] unless there are very specific exceptions, such as the 'filing of a difference' by a member State.[36] Even though, internationally speaking, SARPs thus come into force without any action on the

31 See also Chapter 11.
32 Ibid.
33 *Pan American World Airways* v. *Department of Trade* [1976] 1 Lloyd's LR 257 (CA) (UK) (Lord Denning, MR).
34 See generally Chapter 2 of this book.
35 Article 90 of the Chicago Convention.
36 Ibid., Article 38.

side of ICAO member States, does this also mean that no national action is required to make them enforceable in member States? This will only be the case in few countries. In most cases, at least the official national publication of the SARPs will be required; sometimes much more, for instance, national ratification, followed by publication. In most Commonwealth countries, the SARPs will have to be 'domesticated', that is re-enacted into national aviation regulations, whereby it must be noted that the authentic text of these regulations prevails over the text of the Annexes.

12.6 Economic regulation and deregulation of airlines

Returning now to the focus of this chapter, the economic regulation of *airlines*: after some preliminary remarks, the following subjects will be addressed: carrier entry; route entry and exit; airline ownership and control; airline pricing; capacity and frequency control of airlines; and some other commercial matters.

Once a potential airline or air carrier[37] has been issued an Air Operator Certificate (AOC),[38] basically a safety certificate, it can apply for an air carrier licence or permit.[39] This is the permission to set up and operate a commercial air transport enterprise, an airline. The two documents should not be confused, and the AOC must always precede the licence. In all countries, national air operators must obtain a national licence; in many countries, foreign carriers need not obtain a permit, if they have already been permitted to fly on the basis of a bilateral air transport/services agreement.[40]

The following discussion will basically examine licensing and other requirements of national authorities for national airlines. To the extent possible, both the pre- and the post-deregulation/situation will be taken into consideration. As already indicated in section 12.2 of this chapter dealing with 'governments and airlines', some countries only have an international air transport market, others both an international and a domestic one. As a consequence some countries may have a single licensing system; others a dual.

Air carrier licensing basically deals with 'carrier entry': how many airlines will be allowed into a domestic and/or international market of a given country? The historical section in this chapter has already outlined how restrictive countries have been in this respect in the past and how some, non-deregulated countries, still are today. Even the US, from the end of the Second World War to deregulation in the mid-1970s, was very conservative in licensing new airlines.

Deregulation and liberalization have dramatically changed that. In American style deregulation, an air carrier need merely be 'fit, willing and able', that is in short managerially and financially sound, and compliant with the law to fly between any domestic points. In European style liberalization, the situation is not much different. The air carrier's operating licence must also satisfy those criteria, with perhaps a little bit more emphasis on the business plan, especially for brand new airlines. New entry into the American airline industry was dramatically high at the beginning of the deregulation era around 1980. In Europe, the new licensing rules made the

---

37 The two terms will be used interchangeably . 'Airline' appears in the definitional Article of the Chicago Convention: Article 96, to wit in (c). But 'air carrier' is the preferred term in, for instance, EU Regulation 1008/2008, *supra* footnote 21.

38 See Chapter 4.

39 Also these terms will be used interchangeably, although 'licence' is the most common one. In some jurisdictions, a distinction is made between the two, for instance 'licence' for a domestic carrier; 'permit' for a foreign one.

40 See Chapter 11.

emergence of low cost carriers possible, a phenomenon which has profoundly changed the nature of the European air transport market.

After air carrier entry, there is route entry. Many AOCs specify which destinations an air operator may serve. Commercial licences may do the same, and the destinations need not be the same, that is: the commercial licence can be more restrictive than the safety certificate. The fewer carriers there are in a country, or in a market, the more important individual route entry may be. In a deregulated or fully liberalized air transport market, there is no limit on route entry: a licensed carrier can serve all possible domestic routes (subject to technical constraints such as congestion and the environment), and all international routes, provided that this is in conformity with bilateral, multilateral or supranational (Europe) air transport agreements or other arrangements.

Next to route entry control, there may also be route exit control. Not all countries have or exercise exit control but, where exerted, it is the regulatory procedure whereby an airline, serving a route and wishing to abandon it, usually for commercial reasons, needs permission to do so. The purpose of the exercise is to protect the public service nature of certain air routes.

Airline ownership and control forms part of both national licensing and international air traffic agreement requirements. The latter have already been discussed.[41] Many countries do not have specific airline ownership and control legislation, especially where they have no significant domestic air transport markets. They then have ownership and control governed by the relevant clauses in the relevant bilateral air transport agreements. The purpose of national ownership and control in bilateral agreements and in national legislation is not quite the same though: in national legislation, it is to promote the national economy and national security. In bilateral agreements, it is to ensure that the airline(s) of the bilateral country partner is/are indeed part of the economy of that country and not of a third one.

Large air transport markets generally have specific airline ownership and control legislation. Well known are the examples of the US and the EU. In the US, foreign ownership of US airlines may not exceed 25 per cent of voting stock, and, in some cases, may go up to 49 per cent of non-voting stock, provided always that control is American. In the EU, the control requirement is less stringent. Foreign ownership of Community (EU) air carriers may go up to 49 per cent. It may exceed that percentage by agreement between the EU as a whole and a third country, but this has not yet occurred.

Foreign ownership and control restrictions hinder the emergence of truly, worldwide multinational airlines. Reform of the requirement has been discussed for many years, but has not yet occurred on any large scale. What has happened though, is that there are a number of countries with domestic air transport markets that allow up to 100 per cent of foreign ownership of strictly domestically operating air carriers, provided also that these are corporate citizens of the country in question. The first example was Australia.

Airline pricing – tariffs, subdivided into passenger fares and cargo rates – is the next subject in regulation and deregulation of airlines. The importance of IATA in this field, in the pre-deregulation, pre-liberalization period, was already mentioned several times in this chapter.[42] Together, liberal airline entry and pricing are the two kingpins of airline deregulation and liberalization. Both in the US and in Europe, prior to about 1975–1985, restrictive airline entry and strict governmental tariff control were the two most important factors, calling for change towards deregulation and liberalization.

41 Ibid.
42 See texts to footnotes 11, 12 and 22.

In a regulated environment, aeronautical authorities usually have the power to approve, disapprove or vary air tariffs. Again, in a regulated environment, international tariffs are proposed to national aeronautical authorities for approval, disapproval or variance by the IATA Tariff Coordinating Conferences.

What happened in the US and in Europe, and later in many other liberalizing jurisdictions, is that governmental tariff control was replaced by airline pricing freedom, subject to only minor *ex post facto* safeguards where sometimes aeronautical authorities may intervene in cases of excessively high prices to consumers, or excessively low prices threatening the financial wellbeing of the airline industry. These safeguards, by the way, have only very seldom been invoked under deregulation and liberalization.

Does this mean that IATA no longer plays a role in international airline pricing? The answer is no, but IATA's role has been greatly reduced. First, in the year 1978, IATA significantly reformed its tariff coordination system so as to make airline participation in it voluntary rather than compulsory, as it had been theretofore, and so as to make it more flexible and competitive.[43] Second, provided that bilateral agreements so permit[44] and antitrust or competition law does not intervene,[45] the use by airlines of the IATA ratemaking machinery is still allowed. However, these days, alliance carriers[46] more often than not do their tariff coordination through their alliances rather than through IATA. Also, through regulatory action on the part of the European Commission, there is no longer IATA tariff coordination on intra-European international air routes.

Next to last, there is capacity and frequency control of airlines.[47] This is the total number and volume of passengers and cargo that an airline may carry, expressed in ton kilometres, but more often as flight frequencies – per day or per week – sometimes even further specified by the type of aircraft to be used. The treatment of this subject in bilateral agreements was already covered in the previous chapter of this book. In a regulated environment, most governmental aeronautical authorities possess(ed) and exercise(d) control in this area. It was basically only the US that has always been opposed to governmental capacity control, both on domestic and international air services, probably to strike a balance between regulation (entry and pricing) and competition (flight frequency and capacity).[48]

Under deregulation and liberalization, both in bilateral agreements and in national law or policy, capacity and frequency control has been eliminated. Airlines may then provide as many flight frequencies as they wish, subject to technical constraints such as congestion and environmental protection, as restricted by airport landing slots and/or flight curfews.

Finally, the governmental regulation of some other commercial airline matters, just some amongst many: first, the airline distribution system, including airline agents. In this area, for which IATA is or was largely responsible, many liberalizing measures have been taken worldwide, amongst others to abolish standard agency commission rates and a system of entry control into the agency market. This has certainly increased competition in airline distribution, but it must be mentioned that distribution through agencies has become far less important

---

43 See, in detail, Haanappel, *Pricing and Capacity Determination in International Air Transport*, op. cit. footnote 10, *passim*.

44 See Chapter 11.

45 See Chapter 13.

46 That is airlines, members of commercial airline alliances and participating in their joint venture agreements.

47 In general, see Haanappel, op. cit. footnote 10, *passim*.

48 See main text, following footnote 20.

in practice now than in the past, as a result of increased use of online airline reservations, directly by travellers.

In Europe especially, through the efforts of EC institutions, there has been a great deal of increase in competition between ground handlers at airports. Except at the smallest airports, ground handling monopolies (flag carriers and airports), have been dismantled in favour of at least two handlers per airport, one of which is a newcomer. Self-handling by airlines has also been promoted.

Much effort has gone, again principally in Europe, through the European Commission, in providing a fair airport slot allocation system, including provisions favouring new entrant airlines. This system can be compared with the somewhat different slot allocation rules that exist in the US at the relatively few High Density Airports.

As a closing remark: in deregulated or liberalized air transport markets, there is the realization that nevertheless some communities can only be adequately served by subsidized programmes: hence some states have adopted public service obligations and subsidized essential air service programmes.

12.7 Conclusion

Government regulation of air transport in general, and of airlines in particular, has not disappeared with airline deregulation and liberalization. Rather, its nature has changed: from largely *ex ante* (air) transportation law control, the move has been towards *ex post facto* (air) transportation law control, and towards enhanced application of antitrust, competition and consumer protection laws.

13

Antitrust and competition law

Kate Markhvida

13.1 Introduction

Since the late 1970s, the airline industry has undergone a major transformation in different parts of the world. The driving forces behind this transformation have been economic deregulation of domestic air transport markets, increased liberalisation of international air transport markets, and emergence and penetration of new airline business models. These changes introduced potent competitive forces in the airline industry, which in turn carried important implications for consumers and airlines. On the one hand, consumers benefited from an increased array of flight choices and reduced fares. On the other hand, fierce competition was a contributing factor to the financial distress suffered by many carriers and the endemic bankruptcies that plagued the industry as a result. The airline industry's response to the financial woes in the past decades has been increased consolidation through mergers and acquisitions or alliances.

In a new free market environment, where carriers have acquired the freedom to set pricing, capacity, schedules and make other commercial decisions, effective competition laws and enforcement play a central role in protecting market competition and consumers from abusive business behaviour. Competition authorities around the world have been preoccupied with cases in the aviation sector, ranging from price conspiracies to mergers and alliances to abusive monopolistic practices by dominant airlines. Integration and increased horizontal cooperation between airlines through cross-border alliances has been the defining dynamic in the industry in the past two decades, presenting serious challenges for competition authorities around the world. The need for the harmonisation and convergence of competition regimes and enforcement policies and practices, especially in reviews of airline alliances, is sharply apparent.

This chapter provides an overview of competition laws that apply to the airline sector and summarises key developments and challenges in airline competition law and enforcement. Case studies are used to illustrate how competition rules are applied in airline cases.

13.2 Economic rationale for the advancement of competition

Market competition is defined as a process of business rivalry between two or more firms where each firm aspires to expand its market share, grow revenues and earn profits. The idea of competitive rivalry relies on the assumption that market agents have the freedom to compete with each other, which in practical terms means that economic agents operate in a free market economy.

Adam Smith, the father of free market economics, put forward strong arguments in favour of free markets and free trade. Smith postulated that in a free market economy with a large number of firms, the "invisible hand" of the competitive marketplace would drive down the price of goods and services to their lowest level, maximising consumer welfare and increasing overall economic prosperity.[1] Competition in a free market economy can bring important benefits to consumers in the form of lower prices, better quality and a greater variety of choices.

One of Smith's many important contributions to our understanding of competitive forces in the marketplace was an identification of the theory of contestable markets. The theory of contestable markets has received much attention in recent years. A contestable market has low barriers to entry (or exit), which means that firms can enter (or exit) the market relatively freely if they observe an opportunity to earn a profit. The very threat of competitive entry in a contestable market acts as a constraint on the ability of incumbent firms to raise prices, ensuring that prices remain at the level that would prevail in a perfectly competitive market.

For many years airline markets had high regulatory and economic entry barriers, where the freedom to compete was hindered by the existence of a vast array of regulatory impediments in domestic and international skies. In the last four decades, airline markets in different parts of the world have undergone a significant transformation with many countries adopting policies to deregulate domestic airline markets. In international markets, governments have increasingly embraced open skies agreements that reduce or eliminate restrictions on competition on international routes. Liberalisation of international air transport markets reflects a general consensus and acceptance of the principle that free trade and commerce is beneficial for countries that engage in it.

Numerous studies and analyses have documented a positive impact of liberalisation in domestic and international air transport on air travellers, airlines, tourists, businesses and the economy more broadly. Government policies aimed at removing restrictions on domestic or international air carriage have the following positive effects:[2]

- growth in international and domestic air passenger and cargo traffic;
- reduced passenger airfares and shipper rates on international and domestic routes;
- increased number of routes and city pairs;
- increased seat capacity and flight frequency; and
- increased competition as a result of a larger number of carriers entering liberalised routes and/or increased penetration by low cost carriers in new markets.

Liberalisation introduced free market forces and injected competition in airline markets. For many carriers, however, intense competition translated into endemic bankruptcies and financial distress in the four decades following deregulation of the airline industry. Competition on price also resulted in a deterioration of service in some markets as carriers attempted to cut costs in order to stay competitive, earn profits or minimise losses.

13.3 Neo-classical economics

Unlike their classical predecessors, neo-classical schools of economic thought believed that due to market imperfections and asymmetries, the perfectly competitive outcome is not feasible without government intervention. The government has an important role to intervene and correct market imperfections where they exist through a wide range of policies including antitrust policy.

---

1 See generally, Adam Smith, *An Inquiry into the Nature and Causes of the Wealth of Nations* (W. Strahan and T. Cadell 1776); Maher R. Dabbah, *International and Comparative Competition Law* (Cambridge University Press 2010) 23–25.
2 See generally, InterVISTAS, *The Economic Impact of Air Service Liberalization* (InterVISTAS 2006).

In the 1930s, Edward Chamberlin and other economists advanced the theory of imperfect markets and markets with product differentiation. Under perfect competition, prices are driven to marginal costs in equilibrium and the economy achieves a socially optimal level of output. In an economy with differentiated products, perfect competition is no longer a miraculous panacea as firms can use branding and marketing to set prices above marginal costs, essentially exploiting consumers' aspiration for a variety of goods and services. The ideal perfectly competitive market outcome is therefore not feasible.[3]

In the 1960s, the structuralist school of economic thought pioneered by Harvard economists received wide acclaim. Structuralist economists treated with suspicion high market concentration and argued that it was likely to lead to increased efficiencies only in a small number of industries. In many industries, market consolidation was deemed anti-competitive and undesirable, particularly in light of the high barriers to entry in many markets and evidence of monopoly pricing in oligopolistic markets even with relatively low concentration levels. The principle of structure-conduct-performance (S-C-P) underpinned the structuralist model of competition, implying that a certain market structure entails a certain type of conduct by market participants that, in turn, reflects on market performance. The key goal of antitrust policy, according to the structuralist school, is to protect market competition by ensuring that many firms with small market shares compete to drive prices down to their optimal levels.[4]

In the late 1970s and 1980s, the Chicago school of economics exerted substantial influence on antitrust policy in the United States. Chicago economists challenged many of the fundamental beliefs held by the proponents of the Harvard school. In particular, increased market consolidation and concentration levels that were perceived anti-competitive by the structuralists were deemed to reflect superior performance in markets. Antitrust policies aimed at breaking mergers and preventing market consolidation were perceived by the adherers of the Chicago school as harmful because they would undermine the ability of firms to attain important economic efficiencies through consolidation of activities.[5]

In the present day, there is a broad consensus that the main goal of antitrust policy is to encourage market efficiency and protect competition in the market rather than protecting individual competitors. Economists agree that promoting market efficiencies is the fundamental goal of antitrust policy and law.[6] A competition authority's principal task is thus to promote competitive markets in order to achieve an efficient market outcome where consumers benefit from competitive prices and a greater variety of product choices.

Other goals of antitrust policy may include promotion of trade, balancing the interests of small and large businesses, improving export competitiveness and consumer protection, among others.

---

3 See generally, Don Bellante, 'Edward Chamberlin: Monopolistic Competition and Pareto Optimality' (April 2004) 2 *Journal of Business and Economics Research*.

4 Herbert Hovenkamp, 'Antitrust and the Close Look: Transaction Cost Economics in Competition Policy' in Ioannis Lianos and D. Daniel Sokol (eds), *The Global Limits of Competition Law* (Stanford University Press 2012) 66.

5 Dabbah 61–62.

6 Economists generally view market efficiency as the main goal of competition policy. The notion of market efficiency encompasses three dimensions: productive, allocative and dynamic efficiency. Productive efficiency means goods and services are produced at the lowest cost, allocative efficiency means goods and services are allocated to the right economic agents who value them most and dynamic efficiency means resources are devoted to research and development to stimulate long-term economic growth. In practice, competition laws and policy have other goals that may include expansion of exports, expansion of world markets, protection of small businesses, protection of competitive prices and product choices. Michael Trebilcock, Ralph A. Winder, Paul Collins and Edward M. Iacobucci, *The Law and Economics of Canadian Competition Policy* (University of Toronto Press 2003) 39.

While it is generally believed that efficient markets will ultimately benefit consumers, the approaches towards protecting consumer welfare differ across jurisdictions. Laws of some countries explicitly require that consumer welfare implications be taken into account in antitrust reviews of market transactions. In other countries, laws are designed to encourage overall market efficiencies that maximise consumer and producer surplus, with no explicit requirement to show an increase in consumer welfare. The latter approach is based on the economic principle that a dollar in the hands of a producer is the same as a dollar in the hands of a consumer. The issue of whether antitrust policy should aim at protecting consumer welfare or maximising overall market efficiencies is a contentious one and is a subject of much debate in global antitrust circles.

13.4 Contemporary antitrust issues in airline markets

The competitive landscape of the airline industry has changed dramatically in the past four decades. Economic deregulation of the industry, which began in the United States with the passage of the 1978 Airline Deregulation Act and spread across other markets around the world, removed controls on carriers' ability to set fares, determine seat capacity and enter or exit routes in domestic markets. Increased liberalisation of air service in international markets created increased opportunities for carriers and stimulated passenger and cargo growth on international routes.

Increased liberalisation of domestic and international markets introduced potent competitive forces in global airline markets. At the same time, these forces opened doors to illegal anti-competitive practices which antitrust laws are designed to curtail. Several important trends in global airline competition are having a profound impact on the marketplace:

- In domestic markets, the rise and rapid penetration of low cost carriers (LCCs) and ultra low cost carriers has led to an increased variety of travel options for passengers at lower prices and undermined the competitive position of full-service network carriers. Currently, approximately 30 per cent of seat capacity on Europe's domestic routes is served by LCCs.[7] In the United States, this figure is similar.[8]
- In international markets, Middle Eastern and Asia-Pacific carriers experience rapid growth, posing a serious competitive challenge for full-service network carriers in international markets. The rise of Middle Eastern carriers is fuelled in part by favourable government policies as governments assign high priority to the development of aviation infrastructure. There is a clear shift of growth in air transport markets to Asia and the Middle East, the fastest growing markets.
- Airlines consolidate domestically and globally by merging or entering into alliances. Larger networks created as a result of consolidation enable important synergies as aligned carriers can optimise networks, exercise capacity discipline by eliminating redundant service, leverage greater bargaining power with suppliers and attract more passengers as a result of added service at existing and new hubs. The impact of increased consolidation on passengers or shippers is not unambiguous. Research has shown that airline alliances and mergers may have both pro- and anti-competitive effects and balancing those impacts on the market and consumers is a key objective of antitrust policy and enforcement.

---

7 Absolute Aviation Advantage, 'LCCs: On the Verge of making it Big in Japan?' (2014) 4.
8 Absolute Aviation Advantage, 'OAG FACTS August 2014' (2014) 3–4.

- A distinct feature of consolidation in international markets is the penetration of new business models and forms of integrated cooperation between carriers, such as metal-neutral joint ventures. Structurally, metal-neutral joint ventures closely resemble mergers, but carriers retain their distinct legal identities. As with mergers, antitrust policy plays a critical role in promoting efficiencies enabled by joint ventures while protecting competition and consumers from potential deleterious effects of increased coordination between joint venture partners.

The following section summarises current and emerging antitrust issues in airline markets, approaches to reviewing competition practices embraced by different jurisdictions and remedies that can be used to address anti-competitive practices and promote market efficiencies.

13.5 Unlawful conduct in the airline industry

In deregulated airline markets, competition law plays an important role in ensuring that competition and consumers are protected from airlines that conspire or abuse their dominant position in the market in order to exclude competition. Jurisdictions around the world apply national competition laws to prevent anti-competitive practices in the airline industry and in the aviation sector more generally.

Business practices in the airline industry that may have a detrimental effect on competition range from various forms of cooperative arrangements between airlines to unilateral actions by a dominant airline. Potentially harmful anti-competitive practices can be broadly grouped into three categories: the first two categories represent cooperative conduct between two or more airlines and the remaining category represents unilateral actions by a dominant airline:

- airline mergers, acquisitions and cross-border alliances;
- collusion between competing airlines (e.g. airline cartels, conspiracies and restrictive agreements); and
- exclusionary conduct by a dominant airline (e.g. predatory pricing, refusal to grant access to essential facilities, use of customer loyalty programmes and use of commission paid to travel agents).

A key question in legal antitrust analysis of airline mergers, acquisitions, conspiracies and various forms of abusive conduct by a dominant airline is to determine the relevant market.[9] Market definition is of paramount importance because different market definitions may lead to different outcomes in the overall competition assessment.

The delineation of a relevant market has two dimensions: geographic and product. In transportation markets, the two dimensions of market definition are interlinked as the provision of product (or service, to be more precise) involves the transportation of passengers or cargo from one geographic location to another.

The geographic dimension of a relevant airline market is typically represented by a city pair, which includes the origin and the destination of a passenger's itinerary or a shipping route for cargo. Airport pairs may also constitute a separate relevant market in antitrust cases where the endpoints of a given route have multiple airports. Where the provision of air transportation at a given airport is unconstrained by the provision of service at another airport, the two airports will be deemed to be in separate geographic markets. The geographic delineation relies on

9 See generally, Dabbah 70–74.

demand-side substitutability; a relevant market will comprise all possible alternatives of getting from the origin to the destination that consumers view as close substitutes. Simply put, if a passenger needs to fly from point A to point B, then the A–B city pair constitutes the relevant market because an alternative route connecting point C to point D is not a viable substitute.

Some jurisdictions use a broader geographic market definition that accounts for competitive effects across an entire network. The US Department of Transport (DOT) has assessed the impact of airline alliances at three levels: network, country pairs and city pairs. In addition to route specific effects, alliances may have broader network implications as alliance carriers re-optimise their networks and adjust pricing and schedules on other routes in the network. A competition assessment focused too narrowly on routes that constitute relevant markets may overlook the detrimental effects of alliances across the entire network of routes.[10]

Case study: the Continental/United/Lufthansa/Air Canada transatlantic alliance

In 2009, the US DOT granted immunity to ten Star Alliance carriers to operate an alliance and, within that broader alliance, it approved an integrated transatlantic joint venture between Air Canada, Lufthansa, United and Continental (Atlantic Plus-Plus or A++).[11] The US DOT generally assesses competitive effects of alliances at three different levels: network, country pairs and city pairs. Network level assessment recognises that when making route specific decisions, the airline will consider the impact on the entire network. In line with this approach, the US DOT determined that the alliance among ten Star members would not reduce competition in any relevant market, and in some cases would improve the competitive position of Star Alliance carriers vis-à-vis other alliances and airlines. The relevant geographic market seems to have been defined as networks operated by three global alliances, as the regulating authority underscored improved competitive position of the Star Alliance compared to other alliances in granting its approval.

The product dimension in airline markets relates to passenger segmentation and depends on passenger characteristics such as time and price sensitivity. Generally, time-sensitive business passengers have distinct demand characteristics compared to time-insensitive leisure passengers; the two classes of passengers may be treated as separate product markets in antitrust analysis. However, increased product differentiation in the airline industry reveals the limitations of this approach, as it does not capture the full spectrum of passenger segmentation. Business travellers can further be segmented according to their price sensitivity, which in turn depends on their company's size and financial performance. Small- and medium-size companies have a higher price elasticity compared to large corporations and are more likely to encourage their employees to use price-competitive air travel options (e.g. economy instead of business class seats or LCCs instead of FSNCs (full service network carriers)).

Given the inherent complexities of market definition in the airline industry, competition authorities examine and evaluate the product and geographic dimensions of the relevant market on a case-by-case basis.

Frequent flyer programmes (FFPs) have attracted antitrust scrutiny due to their potential to distort competition. FFPs are a form of indirect discount for passengers aimed at building brand loyalty, which in turn raises costs for rival airlines to penetrate markets. Passengers especially benefit from participating in FFPs of airlines with extensive route networks, such as networks created by alliances whose members integrate their FFPs, because passengers get access to greater

10 OECD, 'Airline Competition' (2014) 26.
11 US Department of Transportation, Order 2009-7-10 (2009).

opportunities to earn and redeem points. FFPs are an effective tool in building brand loyalty among passengers with higher spending (i.e. business travellers). FFPs act as an indirect rebate from employers to employees: while business travel is paid for by the employer, points are earned and redeemed by the employee. Loyalty programmes of incumbent carriers may effectively act as a constraint, preventing smaller carriers that do not have an FFP with comparable benefits from competing viably in the business segment.

13.6 Mergers and acquisitions

Deregulation of domestic airline markets and liberalisation of international air service agreements injected increased competition on domestic and international routes. Seeking to gain competitive advantage and to capitalise on growth opportunities enabled by liberalisation, airlines have consolidated via mergers in domestic markets and pursued greater cooperation via alliances in international markets. Increased number, variety and complexity of alliances and competition issues that arise from alliance integration render them a topic that deserves closer scrutiny. Alliances are reviewed in detail below.

In antitrust policy and enforcement, merger control is a powerful *ex ante* enforcement tool that enables competition authorities and courts to prevent harmful consolidation before it occurs. Mergers can be vertical or horizontal and involve a partial or complete transfer of ownership. Of particular interest from an antitrust perspective are horizontal mergers involving acquisitions of majority or complete control. The merger review process applicable to mergers between airlines, aircraft manufacturers, computer reservation systems (CRSs) and other entities in the aviation supply chain is reviewed in this section.

A wave of mergers swept the airline industry in the past decade. Major domestic mergers took place following deregulation of domestic markets in the United States, the European Union and other countries around the globe.

- In the United States, the mergers between Delta/Northwest (2008), United/Continental (2010), Southwest/AirTran (2011) and US Airways/American (2013) led to 85 per cent of the US domestic market under control of four carriers.
- In Europe, cross-border mergers were facilitated by the liberalisation of the intra-EU air transport market and led to mega mergers including Air France/KLM (2004), British Airways/Iberia (2011) and Lufthansa's acquisition of Swiss (2005), Austrian Airlines (2009) and Brussels Airlines (2009).
- In Canada, the acquisition of Canadian Airlines by Air Canada (2000) resulted in a near monopoly by the combined carrier on domestic routes.
- In Latin America, the LAN/TAM merger (2011) led to the creation of the largest Latin American airline.
- Middle Eastern carriers have acquired significant minority interests in a number of foreign carriers, most notable are Etihad's acquisitions of a 49 per cent share in Alitalia (2014), 49 per cent share in Air Serbia (2013), 40 per cent share in Air Seychelles (2012), 34 per cent share in Darwin Airline (2014) and 29 per cent share in Air Berlin (2011), among others.

Antitrust analysis of international mergers would typically involve several key stages where competition authorities seek to:

- establish a relevant market and determine markets in which merging airlines have competitive overlap;

- assess whether the merged airline would obtain increased market power in the overlapping markets; and
- assess whether the airline merger would lead to anti-competitive effects and whether competition would be suppressed substantially as a result.

Airline mergers that are likely to have anti-competitive effects may still be allowed to proceed if they result in efficiency gains that outweigh anti-competitive effects (the efficiency defence)[12] or if one of the merging airlines would fail in the absence of the merger (the failing firm defence).[13] While some jurisdictions require merging airlines to show that gains in efficiency would be passed on to consumers in the form of lower prices or better service, other jurisdictions do not require the explicit showing of redistribution of efficiency gains, so long as cost synergies outweigh anti-competitive effects. In airline markets merger efficiencies are frequently observed where the merging carriers' networks are complementary, whereas competition concerns typically arise with respect to overlapping networks.

Case study: the LAN/TAM merger

In 2011, Chile's LAN Airlines and Brazil's TAM SA merged to become the largest airline in South America, LATAM Airlines Group, transporting approximately 42 per cent of passengers and over 30 per cent of cargo in Latin America. The merger raised competition concerns in a number of South American markets, in particular with regards to potential fare increases and service deterioration on the Santiago–Sao Paulo and Santiago–Lima hub-to-hub routes. Chile's Competition Tribunal weighed the anti-competitive effects against potential gains in efficiency, finding that remedies were necessary to address residual competition concerns.

With regards to efficiencies, the Tribunal considered cost synergies that would stem from offering service jointly and from joint procurement activities. In addition, the merged carrier would benefit from revenue synergies as a result of a stronger combined loyalty programme and better scheduling and connectivity offerings for passengers. LATAM is reported to have realised an estimated $200 million in cost savings after the merger. Nevertheless, in its 2013 annual report, LATAM acknowledged that there was a risk that the merged airline would be unable to realise all expected synergies as the airline continued to incur costs related to the integration of commercial operations, such as the merging of FFPs, and that there are uncertainties regarding the ability of LATAM to manage its expanded operations post-merger efficiently.

Increased consolidation through mergers and acquisitions has also been observed in aircraft manufacturing, airline distribution and other segments of the aviation supply chain. There has been a general trend towards greater consolidation in airline distribution in the past two decades. In 1984, there were six CRSs (predecessors of Global Distribution Systems (GDS)) in the United States.[14] By 2012, the GDS industry in the United States came to be dominated primarily by two players (Sabre and Travelport), which together account for roughly 90 per cent of

---

12 International Competition Network, 'ICN Merger Guidelines Workbook' (2006) 63–64.
13 Ibid. 66–69.
14 Sabre, Apollo, PARS, System One, DATAS II and MARS PLUS. These CRSs were developed by US airlines, often in partnership with technology companies. For example, Sabre was developed as a computerised ticket reservation tool by American Airlines and IBM. Airlines later divested CRSs due to financial distress and antitrust concerns regarding flight display bias.

tickets sold through the GDS channels in the United States. Globally, three major providers control the lion's share of all tickets sold through the GDS channels (Amadeus, Sabre and Travelport). The manufacturing of large commercial aircraft is a highly consolidated industry dominated by two global players (Boeing and Airbus).

Case study: the Boeing/McDonnell Douglas merger
The 1997 merger between Boeing and McDonnell Douglas, the first and the third largest aircraft manufacturers at the time, reduced the global manufacturing market of large commercial aircraft to a duopoly and increased Boeing's market share to 70 per cent. In their analysis of the merger the competition authorities on both sides of the Atlantic reached opposite conclusions, illustrating a stark divergence in policy approaches in the United States and the European Union. While the US Federal Trade Commission found that the merger would not result in a lessening of competition and approved the merger, the European Commission opposed it on the grounds that it would create a dominant manufacturer in the global market for large civilian aircraft.[15]

Following an extensive three-month investigation, the European Commission concluded that post-merger Boeing would hold a dominant position in the production of large civilian jet aircraft and a monopoly in aircraft with more than 400 seats. Boeing was compelled to agree to substantial concessions in order to obtain approval from the European Commission. Those included abandoning exclusive supply arrangements, ring-fencing[16] McDonnell Douglas's commercial division and committing not to abuse its relationship with customers. Boeing also agreed to license its non-exclusive patents to competing manufacturers to alleviate the spillover effect of public research funding from McDonnell Douglas's defence to commercial division.[17]

The conflicting assessments exposed the problem of divergent antitrust laws and the inadequacy of the agreement that existed between the United States and the European Union to harmonise competition reviews and avoid conflicting conclusions. This case underscored the need for closer cooperation in antitrust investigations and enforcement.

13.7 Alliances

Airline alliances are cooperative arrangements between airlines that differ widely in depth, breadth and scope. Airlines enter into cooperation agreements ranging from those with limited cooperation such as interline agreements or marketing arrangements which provide reciprocal access to FFPs and lounges to highly integrated forms of cooperation such as metal-neutral joint ventures.[18]

---

15 See generally, Boeing Company and McDonnell Douglas Corporation, Joint Statement closing investigation of the proposed merger and separate statement, of Commissioner Mary L. Azcuenaga, FTC File No. 971-0051, announced 1 July 1997; Boeing/McDonnell Douglas, Case No. IV/M.877, European Commission Decision of 30 July 1997, OJ L336/16 (8 December 1997).

16 Ring-fencing is the separation of a portion of company assets into a separate entity for regulatory, taxation or financing purposes. The entity is not necessarily operated separately. Ring-fencing in the case of McDonnell Douglas would prevent the sharing of information between its commercial and other divisions.

17 See generally, Amy Ann Karpel, 'The European Commission's Decision on the Boeing-McDonnell Douglas Merger and the Need for Greater U.S.–EU Cooperation in the Merger Field' (April 1998) 47 *American University Law Review.*

18 See generally, US Department of Transportation and the European Commission, 'Transatlantic Airline Alliances: Competitive Issues and Regulatory Approaches' (2010).

International alliances are a form of consolidation used by airlines where mergers and acquisitions are not feasible due to legal, regulatory or other restrictions. Limitations on foreign ownership of domestic airlines that exist in the majority of countries and nationality clauses in bilateral Air Service Agreements (ASAs) are the key barrier to transnational mergers in the airline industry. An important benefit of an alliance is access to traffic that, in the absence of the alliance, would not be possible due to limitations established by bilateral ASAs or national laws.

Alliances between air carriers can be broadly divided into two main categories: tactical and strategic alliances. Tactical alliances are designed to address specific gaps in individual carrier networks by enabling better connectivity between the carriers' networks. In contrast, strategic alliances are broader and more comprehensive forms of cooperation between multiple carriers aimed at establishing large worldwide joint networks. Rather than merely close gaps in a network, strategic alliances seek to optimise networks, often changing which carriers operate which routes and with what capacity.[19]

As airline alliances vary broadly in the extent and nature of cooperation, competition authorities review alliances on a case-by-case basis to determine what impacts they have on competition in the marketplace. If net impacts are positive, alliances are approved and granted clearance by the reviewing authority.

From an antitrust perspective, arrangements with limited cooperation such as interline agreements generally pose no concern. The highest degree of cooperation can be observed in metal-neutral joint ventures where carriers engage in revenue, cost and profit sharing; jointly determine prices, capacity and frequency of flights; and cooperate in marketing and sales. These activities have attracted close scrutiny of antitrust agencies around the world. Metal-neutral joint ventures may be reviewed under the merger control or cartel provisions of general competition laws or a separate regulatory regime for antitrust immunity, as they contain elements of integration and coordination that bear a high risk of violating antitrust laws. Carriers are unlikely to pursue merger-like activities through an alliance without antitrust approval because of the high risk that the alliance may be challenged on antitrust grounds.

Institutional frameworks that govern reviews and approvals of airline alliance differ from one jurisdiction to another. In many countries, alliances are reviewed by a designated competition authority. The competition authority will make a decision whether to block or challenge in court an airline alliance based on the law, jurisprudence and its enforcement policy. Canada, Australia and the European Union are examples of jurisdictions where general competition laws are applied by the respective antitrust authorities to review airline alliances. In the United States, a separate regulatory regime exists for reviewing international alliances; the US DOT has the statutory authority to review, approve and immunise international airline alliances from US antitrust laws. In some countries, the responsibility to enforce antitrust laws and implement antitrust policy applicable to alliances is shared by a number of government agencies.

Depending on the degree of integration and the extent of cooperation, alliances may include the following elements:[20]

- coordination of route networks and schedules;
- coordination of prices, inventory and yield management;
- revenue, cost and profit sharing;
- code sharing;

19 Ibid. 4–8.
20 OECD, 'Air Service Agreement Liberalisation and Airline Alliances' (Country-Specific Policy Analysis, 2014) 32.

- joint marketing, advertising and distribution;
- joint procurement (purchase of aircraft, fuel, catering, etc.);
- reciprocal access to FFPs;
- sharing of airport facilities and services (check-in counters, gates, ground handling, etc.);
- coordination of IT platforms;
- coordination of cargo operations.

Regulatory agencies, antitrust authorities, lawyers, consumer groups and industry representatives tend to have mixed views with respect to the effects of joint ventures and highly integrated forms of alliances on competition and consumers. While some underscore pro-consumer and pro-competitive benefits of highly integrated airline alliances, others express concerns about the anti-competitive effects of alliances and potential negative impacts on consumers.

The key antitrust concerns regarding the horizontal foreclosure effects of international alliances are similar to those of mergers and acquisitions and can be grouped into two categories. The first group includes unilateral effects that may arise as a result of reduced or eliminated competition between members of the alliance. The second group includes coordinated effects (or increased potential for collusive behaviour) as a result of reduced competition between alliance members and non-member airlines or reduced competition between alliance members outside the scope of their alliance. In practice, unilateral effects are assigned a much greater emphasis in competition assessments compared to coordinated effects.[21]

Alliances may be particularly problematic on non-stop routes, especially hub-to-hub routes, where carriers have direct competitive overlap. On the one hand, alliances increase barriers to entry, which hinders the ability of competitors to initiate or expand operations in a relevant market, as a result of reduced access to essential infrastructure (airport slots and gates, access to feeder traffic, etc.). On the other hand, competition may be reduced as a consequence of the alliance's enhanced market power and the resulting behaviour (FFP, increased frequency of service, combination of hubs, reputational effects, etc.).[22]

The ultimate goal of competition analysis is to evaluate the impact of an alliance on price and service quality. Airlines have sought antitrust immunity from respective competition authorities to operate alliances on the grounds that alliance networks bring about efficiencies, result in lower fares for consumers, increase the range of routing options and induce traffic growth. These claims, however, have been challenged by independent research and studies conducted by antitrust watchdogs, which found evidence that alliances may be detrimental to consumer welfare in certain circumstances.

Due to the relevant novelty of alliances and the varying extent of cooperation within alliances, there is no single standardised competition enforcement mechanism to address alliances. Alliances can be evaluated under a separate immunity regime or under the merger or cartel provisions of general competition laws. Legal and regulatory mechanisms for assessing alliances in select jurisdictions are briefly reviewed below.

In the United States, airlines can seek immunity from the US antitrust laws by submitting requests for antitrust immunity to the US DOT. The US DOT uses a broad public interest test to review alliances. Essentially, the US DOT undertakes a two-stage analysis when reviewing requests for antitrust immunity. In the first stage, the regulatory agency will determine whether a proposed alliance violates antitrust laws, in other words whether it can negatively affect competition in the air transport market. If the agreement has been found to violate antitrust laws, the regulator will

---

21 OECD, 'Airline Competition' 26.
22 US Department of Transportation and the European Commission 19–20.

undertake further analysis to determine if it is desirable from a public interest perspective. In the second stage, the regulator will consider whether the agreement is in the public interest taking into account such factors as the production of transportation benefits that cannot be achieved without the agreement, and the objectives of foreign policy or obligations under international comity. The US DOT will approve international alliances that substantially reduce or eliminate competition if such alliances are consistent with the broader public interest.[23]

With antitrust immunity, airlines can act as a single carrier, jointly setting prices and schedules, coordinating capacity and jointly marketing and distributing their services. Carriers that have antitrust immunity can effectively eliminate all competition between them without running the risk of antitrust prosecution. Barring the immunity, practices such as joint price, capacity and schedule setting – an inherent feature of metal-neutral joint ventures – would violate US antitrust laws. The US DOT has granted immunity to groups of carriers in all three major international alliances; selected carriers from the immunised groupings have formed metal-neutral joint ventures in regional markets, such as the transatlantic market. As a result, the predominant share of transatlantic passenger traffic between the United States and the European Union is carried by immunised alliances.[24]

Although the US Department of Justice (DOJ) has broad jurisdiction to enforce US antitrust laws, it does not cover international airline alliances. In 1988, the US Congress transferred jurisdiction over airline mergers from the US DOT to the US DOJ. However, the US DOT retained the legal authority to review, approve and immunise agreements relating to international air transportation, and the US DOJ plays a consultative role in such reviews.[25] There is no corresponding authority for the US DOT with regards to domestic alliances or mergers between US carriers, which are ineligible for antitrust immunity.[26] The antitrust division of the US DOJ has commented adversely on alliances that involve a high degree of integration and coordination activities, such as revenue, cost and profit sharing under metal-neutral joint ventures, and cautioned against granting broad antitrust immunity. However, due to the lack of jurisdictional authority over international alliances, the US DOJ is limited in its ability to seek remedies to "mitigate" the impact of anti-competitive international airline alliances.[27] The US DOJ may recommend remedies to alleviate competition concerns, but the ultimate decision whether to apply recommended remedies rests with the US DOT.

The US DOT takes into account several important factors when authorising an alliance as a matter of policy. The regulator would be more likely to grant antitrust immunity if the home States of the alliance partners has concluded an open skies agreement with the United States. In addition, the US DOT has a tendency to grant antitrust immunity to airline alliances that involve at least one or more US carriers.[28]

The United States has a unique legal framework for reviewing international airline alliances that differs from approaches used in other jurisdictions. Many other jurisdictions apply a pure competition test to determine whether an alliance should be authorised.

23 OECD, 'Air Service Agreement Liberalisation and Airline Alliances' 58–59.
24 Ibid.
25 OECD, Latin American Competition Forum, 'Session IV, Competition Issues in the Air Transport Sector; Contribution from the US Federal Trade Commission and the US Department of Justice' (2011) paras 1 and 2.
26 William Gillespie and Richard M. Oliver, 'Antitrust Immunity and International Airline Alliances' (2011).
27 OECD, 'Air Service Agreement Liberalisation and Airline Alliances' 58–59.
28 ICAO, 'Antitrust Immunity for Airline Alliances' (2013) 2.

In the European Union, the European Commission has jurisdiction to review and approve international airline alliances under EU competition laws, laid out in Articles 101 and 102 of the Treaty on the Functioning of the European Union (TFEU). EU competition laws are aimed at promoting a common European market, protecting competition and consumer welfare. Articles 101 and 102 of the TFEU establish competition rules that apply to all industries including air transport markets. Specifically, Article 101 prohibits agreements or concerted practices that distort competition or restrain trade between the EU member States. Article 102 prohibits dominant firms from engaging in abusive practices that restrain trade or distort competition in the EU market. Airline alliance agreements may be reviewed and assessed under either Article 101 or Article 102 of the TFEU. An anti-competitive agreement or concerted practice, such as an airline alliance, may be allowed if parties to the agreement share the benefit they derive from the agreement with consumers, so that consumer welfare is increased as a result.[29]

In Canada, the Competition Bureau has the mandate to review international airline alliances pursuant to the provisions of the Competition Act. The Competition Act is a statute of general application that applies to all industries, including passenger and cargo air transportation. Unlike in the United States, the Competition Bureau has jurisdiction over domestic airline mergers and international airline alliances. The Competition Act has a number of provisions applicable to international airline alliances, which include merger control provision, cartel provisions and provisions that govern collaborative agreements between competitors. Canada does not have a separate immunity regime for airline alliances.[30]

In Australia, the Australian Consumer and Competition Commission (ACCC) is in charge of reviewing and approving international airline alliances. The relevant law applicable to airline alliances and mergers is set out in the Trade Practices Act. The Trade Practices Act is a law of general application that covers a broad range of conduct and applies to all industries, including the airline industry. The ACCC may grant alliance partners a form of immunity called "authorisation", even though the alliance may violate Australian competition laws. Similar to the public interest test used in the United States, carriers must show that the alliance in question is in the public interest in order to obtain authorisation from the ACCC, but authorisations are not limited to specific industries in Australia.[31]

To sum up, alliances can be addressed under a separate immunity regime as well as under merger control or cartel enforcement regimes under general competition laws. The desirability of immunity regimes from an antitrust perspective has been debated, as it effectively shelters airlines from antitrust enforcement.[32] Limitations on antitrust immunity may be applied to leave scope for antitrust enforcement.

13.8 Cartels and conspiracies

Competition laws establish a regime to address collusive or cartel-like behaviour in the airline industry,[33] which may include unlawful coordination of prices, schedules, capacity and other

29 US Department of Transportation and the European Commission 14–15.
30 OECD, 'Air Service Agreement Liberalisation and Airline Alliances' 61.
31 Ibid.
32 OECD, 'Airline Competition' 29.
33 Antitrust law distinguishes between explicit collusion and tacit (implicit) collusion. Tacit collusion occurs when firms adhere to a cooperative pricing strategy without explicitly agreeing to do so. While explicit collusion is prohibited by antitrust law, tacit collusion generally falls outside its scope. Trebilcock et al. 89.

forms of market restriction or customer allocation. Antitrust immunity, if granted, shields air-lines from cartel prosecution and is often sought by carriers on a voluntary basis to enable agreements that include elements of collusive cooperation (e.g. metal-neutral joint ventures).

As the international airline fuel surcharge case reveals, collusive arrangements are difficult to detect and may go on for years before they are exposed. Competition agencies have developed enforcement tools to increase the effectiveness of cartel law enforcement. One such tool that facilitates exposure of conspiracies is an immunity or leniency programme that grants protection from antitrust prosecution to whistle-blowers.

Case study: the airline fuel surcharge cartel

In recent years several jurisdictions around the world launched investigations, brought charges and secured convictions in relation to a fuel surcharge price-fixing scheme that involved over 20 airlines. The airlines conspired to fix the surcharge on fuel, which in turn inflated the final price for air cargo transportation charged to shippers. The conspiracy also involved fixing the surcharge for security and war risk, following the 9/11 attacks in 2001 and the US invasion of Iraq in 2003. Several airlines were also found guilty of fixing the surcharge on fuel for passengers.

Several airlines that brought forward evidence to assist prosecutors in securing convictions received immunity or a reduction in penalties under leniency programmes. Notably, Lufthansa Airlines, which exposed the cartel and sought immunity from antitrust prosecution under the amnesty programme in the United States, received immunity and paid no fines. Other airlines that had been found guilty or had been sued for damages by private plaintiffs in civil courts, faced substantial fines. Sanctions in the United States and the European Union alone totalled respectively $1.6 billion and $1.1 billion (€799 million).[34] In the United States, over a dozen airlines settled private class action lawsuits totalling $485 million. Additional fines and penalties were also imposed in other jurisdictions around the world. Several airline executives were sentenced to prison terms. The success of antitrust prosecutions in the air cargo fuel surcharge price-fixing case was largely due to the effectiveness of immunity and leniency programmes used by competition authorities to expose cartels.

Certain activities of the International Air Transport Association (IATA), an industry association that represents airlines globally, pose a major issue from a cartel law perspective.[35] IATA serves as a natural conduit for discussions between airlines aimed at standardising technological platforms for distribution, marketing and pricing of airline tickets. Coordination of pricing, schedules and IT distribution platforms is problematic from an antitrust perspective, which has forced IATA to adopt a number of changes:

- IATA's Tariff and Schedule Conferences. The Conferences supported the establishment of a multilateral regime for interlining and establishing fares for interlined tickets, essentially enabling a global price coordination regime. At the early stages, the regime was guaranteed by antitrust immunity granted to IATA's Conferences by a number of major jurisdictions. Later, the immunity was lifted and, in response to growing antitrust concerns, IATA modified the process for establishing interlined tariffs and schedules to address those concerns.

34 OECD, 'Airline Competition' 37.
35 Ibid. 39–40.

- IATA's New Distribution Capability (NDC). As part of its mandate, IATA proposed to standardise the distribution of airline tickets via the implementation of the NDC, which would enable airlines to make customised offers to air travellers. The introduction of NDC raised some concerns regarding the accessibility of this platform to airline users. Several regulatory and competition agencies have put in place measures to monitor and control this new standard to ensure that it is used in the interest of consumers and does not restrict competition.

Cartelisation activities and conspiracies reviewed in this section have a global dimension. There exists no single international legal or enforcement regime to address collusive conduct, which presents a challenge as national cartel regimes differ widely in the scope of penalties and remedies.

13.9 Exclusionary and predatory unilateral practices

In addition to various forms of horizontal cooperation (mergers, alliances and cartels), competition laws prohibit business practices exercised by a dominant airline on a unilateral basis that lead to unlawful market monopolisation. A dominant airline may engage in a number of unlawful business practices in order to exclude or significantly diminish the presence of competing airlines in the market including:

- engaging in predatory pricing or other non-price predatory activities (capacity dumping, fighting brands, sham litigation, abuse of government or regulatory processes, etc.);
- precluding or restricting access to essential facilities or infrastructure (airport slots, gates or check-in counters, CRSs, etc.);
- using loyalty programmes and other loyalty inducing marketing and sales strategies to lock in customers.

The types of conduct enumerated above may be problematic from an antitrust point of view only if they are exercised by an airline with market power.[36] An essential element of antitrust assessment is to determine whether the carrier exercises market power in a relevant market. In airline markets, the relevant market is defined on the basis of origin–destination city pairs and, consequently, market power is assessed in relation to the relevant city pair. In determining the extent of market power, competition authorities consider whether the lack of competition is due to the airline's exclusionary conduct or due to the specifics of market or demand structure (e.g. routes may have low traffic density sufficient to sustain no more than one carrier).

Allegations of predatory pricing are frequent in the airline industry; in several jurisdictions, competition authorities brought cases against their major carriers alleging predation. Predation is a response to competitive threat whereby an airline sacrifices profit in the short term in order to induce exit or prevent expansion by its rivals and, consequently, earn monopoly profits in the long term.[37]

The principal challenge in assessing alleged predatory behaviour is to distinguish between illegal conduct and healthy competition. After airline markets were deregulated, airlines began

---

36 Market power refers to the ability of an airline to affect market conditions or, more precisely, to maintain prices above competitive levels for a prolonged period of time.
37 David Greig, 'When does Airline Competition become Predation?' in Peter Forsyth, David W. Gillen, Otto G. Mayer and Hans-Martin Niemeier (eds), *Competition versus Predation in Aviation Markets: A Survey of Experience in North America, Europe and Australia* (Ashgate 2005) 96.

to compete vigorously on price, frequency and capacity. Using price as a tool to stimulate traffic and increase market share at the expense of competitors is an inherent feature of competition. The difficulty in drawing the line between legitimate and illegitimate pricing behaviour is exacerbated by the fact that aggressive competitive behaviour beneficial to consumers often resembles exclusionary conduct detrimental to competition. The legal test used to establish predation varies from jurisdiction to jurisdiction.

As a general rule, allegations of predatory pricing in the airline industry are reviewed under a broader legal prohibition against monopolisation or abuse of dominance. There are five main questions that the competition authority will typically seek to answer to establish whether predation has occurred:[38]

- Does the airline sell at a price below a relevant measure of cost? While there is a general consensus among jurisdictions that an airline should price below an appropriate measure of cost in a predation case, there is considerable debate as to what constitutes the "appropriate" measure. The airline industry is characterised by an extremely complex cost structure, which makes practical application of any price-cost test difficult. Cost measurement has been a central issue in many airline predation cases. One the one hand, a large proportion of airline costs is fixed or joint costs; such costs may be allocated across the entire network of routes. This makes attributing costs to a particular route, flight, freight or passenger inherently difficult, if not impossible. On the other hand, there is much debate about which specific measure of costs should be used; in practice, various jurisdictions have applied different price-cost tests (average avoidable costs, average variable costs, average total costs, opportunity costs etc.).
- Is there evidence that the alleged conduct has an exclusionary effect on competition? Most jurisdictions required the showing of competitive or consumer harm for predation to be illegal.
- Is there a reasonable prospect of recoupment? Recoupment refers to the ability of a carrier to recover the losses sustained during the period of predation through profits earned after the rivals have been disciplined or eliminated. While most jurisdictions require the showing of recoupment to establish liability in predation cases, some jurisdictions consider it irrelevant (e.g. the European Union).
- Does the airline have the intent to exclude or lessen competition substantially? Several jurisdictions require the plaintiff to demonstrate that the predating airline has the intent to harm competition (e.g. Canada, Australia and Taiwan), although in many other jurisdictions proof of subjective intent is considered irrelevant.
- Does the airline have a valid business justification to engage in below cost pricing? Airlines may engage in deep fare discounts for valid business reasons: promotional pricing, inventory and yield management, demand variation, business cycle variation and network optimisation, among others.

Case study: Spirit Airlines *v.* Northwest Airlines[39]
In 2000, Spirit Airlines brought a legal action against Northwest Airlines, alleging predatory pricing on the Detroit–Boston and Detroit–Philadelphia routes during 1995–1996. At the time, Spirit initiated service on those two routes and attempted to expand using low fares aimed at attracting leisure passengers. Spirit, a low cost carrier offering cheap non-refundable

---

38 See generally, Kate Markhvida, 'Enforcement of Anti-Predation Laws in the Airline Industry' (2012) XXXVII *Annals of Air and Space Law.*
39 *Spirit Airlines, Inc.* v. *Northwest Airlines, Inc.* (United States Court of Appeals, Sixth Circuit).

fares, enjoyed high load factors typically exceeding 80 per cent. Northwest responded to Spirit's entry and expansion on its routes with an aggressive pricing reduction and capacity expansion strategy, which caused Spirit's load factors to drop to a low of 31 per cent on Detroit–Philadelphia and to 17–31 per cent on Detroit–Boston. Unable to compete profitably, Spirit exited both routes in 1996. Following Spirit's exit, Northwest raised fares and reduced capacity. Spirit testified that the predatory strategy likely cost Northwest in excess of $10 million in the third quarter of 1996 alone.

The trial court ruled in favour of Northwest on a summary judgment in 2003, essentially signalling that a case of predation could not be established. The decision reflected the general scepticism persisting among US courts that predation could be a rational strategy in the airline industry. While Spirit later won the appeal in 2005 and the case was remanded back to the trial court for a full trial, it later abandoned the legal action after Northwest filed for bankruptcy.

Antitrust laws prohibit exclusionary behaviour whereby the dominant airline precludes or restricts access to essential facilities or infrastructure for competitors. The key issue for competition authorities is to determine whether (1) the essential facility or infrastructure is controlled by a dominant airline and (2) access to the facility or infrastructure is essential for the ability of other airlines to compete viably.

Take off and landing slots at congested or slot-restricted airports are a valuable and essential infrastructural element. Antitrust concerns arise where dominant carriers use "hoarding" strategies to preclude competitors from getting access to airport slots or refuse to sell or lease their slots to competing airlines in secondary slot trading markets. Airport gates are another example of essential facilities; concerns may arise where a dominant airline precludes access to gates for competitors, particularly at hub airports where the dominant airline controls a large share of gates through an exclusive use agreement.

Case study: the US Airways/American Airlines merger[40]

In 2013, US Airways merged with American Airlines creating the largest airline in the world. The US DOJ filed an antitrust lawsuit to block the $11 billion merger on the grounds that it would result in a substantial lessening of competition in many local markets across the United States.

Consistent with the general practice in competition assessments, the relevant geographic market in the merger review was defined as a city pair, and the relevant product market as scheduled air passenger service. An interesting aspect of market delineation is whether connecting service is a viable competitive alternative to non-stop service for a given city pair. At issue in the merger was US Airways' Advantage Fares programme, an aggressive discounting tool that the carrier used to compete effectively against other legacy carriers. US Airways charged substantially lower prices for connecting service to undercut competitors on non-stop routes. In turn, American, Delta and United were observed to charge lower price for their connecting service on routes where US Airways flew non-stop. The US DOJ expressed concern that post-merger US Airways would abandon Advantage Fares, which would eliminate an important source of competition that offered a discount of up to 40 per cent to passengers.[41] The observed pricing dynamics suggest that sometimes

40 *United States of America et al.* v. *US Airways Group, Inc. and AMR Corporation* (United States District Court for the District of Columbia).
41 Ibid. para. 49.

connecting service may be a competitive alternative to non-stop routes, at least for some groups of price conscious passengers.

Another major concern related to flights out of Washington DC's Ronald Reagan National Airport, where US Airways held 55 per cent of the slots prior to the merger and 69 per cent of the slots when combined with American Airlines. The lawsuit alleged that following the merger the combined airline would hold a monopoly on 63 per cent of non-stop routes out of that airport.[42] Ronald Reagan National Airport is one of the four airports in the United States designated as slot constrained. It is difficult to obtain landing and take off rights at the airport; slots are expensive and exchanges of slots between airlines are very rare (i.e. the barriers to entry are substantial).

The concerns were so significant that the US DOJ required unprecedented divestitures as part of a settlement that allowed the merger to proceed. The carriers were required to divest slots at Ronald Reagan Washington Airport and New York LaGuardia Airport as well as gates and other ground facilities at five other major US airports. Slots at the two aforementioned airports were divested to low cost carriers (Southwest Airlines, JetBlue and Virgin America). Market analysis shows that low cost carriers exert greater competitive pressure on price charged by mainline carriers.

Certain marketing and selling strategies, such as the use of loyalty-enhancing programmes, may create exclusionary effects on competitors that do not offer similar benefits to passengers and therefore may trigger scrutiny under the antitrust laws. Loyalty programmes and frequent flyer rewards may result in market foreclosure for competing carriers as passengers are effectively tied to their preferred airline through discounts and additional service enhancements (e.g. airport lounges, priority boarding, complimentary flight changes). Antitrust enforcement against loyalty programmes per se is rare; however, the exclusionary effect of loyalty programmes is often considered in other airline antitrust cases to the effect that it may raise barriers to entry or prevent expansion by competing airlines.

Other exclusionary strategies used by airlines in the past to restrict access to distribution channels included CRS display bias, whereby the flights of the CRS host airlines were given preference over competitors' flights on CRS display, and the use of commissions for travel agents, which served as a disincentive for travel agents to sell flights on competing airlines. If such practices are shown to exclude competitors from accessing a sufficient share of travellers to offer viable service, such strategies may violate antitrust law.

13.10 Antitrust immunity

Antitrust immunity absolves carriers from liability for violating antitrust laws. Some alliances, such as metal-neutral joint ventures, require joint pricing and capacity decisions between competitors – business practices that would be prohibited under antitrust laws in the absence of immunity. In order to enable such alliances, countries may grant authorisation to operate an alliance with inherent anti-competitive features in accordance with their respective antitrust laws or immunity regimes.

No international regime or uniform standard has been put in place to evaluate carriers' requests for authorisation to operate an alliance; each alliance has to obtain immunity from different countries to eliminate the risk of antitrust prosecution. Alliances must comply with different standards to receive immunity, depending on the antitrust laws of the countries where

---

42 Ibid. para. 10.

authorisation is sought. The absence of a unified international antitrust immunity regime is further complicated by the fact that not all countries have laws or regimes in place to grant antitrust immunity to alliances. Some countries do not have a separate regime for granting anti-trust immunity to airline alliances (e.g. Canada, the European Union,[43] Chile and Mexico) and apply general merger control, cartel or civil provisions under their respective antitrust laws to assess the impact of alliances. Other countries (e.g. Australia, Israel, Japan, New Zealand, South Korea and the United States) have laws that vest the regulating agency, the transport or com-petition authority with the statutory power to grant immunity from antitrust laws to alliances, although the regimes differ in review standards, procedural matters, timelines and remedies.[44]

The main rationale for granting immunity to alliances is to encourage efficiency gains and maximise cost synergies that may result from combined operations and joint commercial deci-sion-making. Airlines seeking antitrust immunity often claim that immunised alliances result in lower fares for connecting passengers relative to non-immunised alliances and interline agree-ments, where such lower fares are enabled by cost savings.

The US DOT has leveraged immunisation of airline alliances to promote the overarching objective of the country's foreign aviation policy: liberalisation of international air transport markets and proliferation of open skies agreements. The recent trend in US DOT's policy has been to grant antitrust immunity on the condition that airlines commit to forming and operating a metal-neutral joint venture, the most integrated form of alliance. This policy approach is based on market research and analyses showing that efficiencies are maximised when airlines are indifferent as to which airline operates the aircraft under a joint venture (a form of business organisation referred to as 'metal neutrality'). A metal-neutral joint venture eliminates the incentive to grow individual airline revenue and market share in favour of network optimisation initiatives that allow participating airlines to grow joint or pooled revenue and profit. The US DOT uniquely considers potential efficiencies from an alliance at a broader network level beyond the relevant market (i.e. route), recognising that these benefits may spill over other markets if airlines cooperate across the entire network. However, given the absence of price and service competition, other sources have ques-tioned whether immunised joint ventures enhance consumer welfare.

13.11 Remedies

A variety of remedies have been applied in airline antitrust cases. The choice of remedy depends on the nature of violation and the impact such violation has or is likely to have on the market-place. Remedies may range from an order to cease and desist, to penalties and, sometimes, even prison terms.

Generally, remedies can be classified into two broad categories: structural and behavioural. Structural remedies involve a change in the organisational structure of firms or markets, such as a divestiture, sale or transfer of assets. Behavioural remedies are aimed at regulating conduct of firms, which typically requires monitoring and oversight after the behavioural remedy is put in place.[45]

---

43 In the past, the European Union applied block exemptions from competition law to air transport serv-ices. More recently, the trend has been to align substantive and procedural rules for transport services with those that apply to other sectors and sector-specific competition rules have been removed (only one block exemption regulation applies in maritime shipping). The Directorate General for Competi-tion at the European Commission is charged with the application of EU antitrust and merger rules in aviation.
44 OECD, 'Airline Competition' 32.
45 OECD, 'Remedies in Cross-Border Merger Cases' (Policy Roundtables, 2013) 11.

In airline merger control, competition authorities typically seek a combination of structural and behavioural remedies – where anti-competitive effects are likely to result in the aftermath of the merger – in recognition of the fact that mergers are a permanent and long-lasting form of integration. Structural remedies may include divestiture of airport slots and gates, particularly at congested and slot-constrained airports, or divestiture of routes. Behavioural remedies may include a requirement to interline with competing airlines, provide access to FFPs and distribution channels, restraints on capacity or pricing of merging airlines and other remedies. These remedies are aimed at reducing entry barriers and facilitating entry into affected markets by new airlines or expansion by existing competitors.

Remedies applicable to airline alliances are similar to merger control remedies, where focus is often placed on facilitating greater competition and market entry by way of transferring airport slots or other important assets to existing competitors or new entrants. Behavioural remedies facilitating access of existing or future competitors to feeder traffic, loyalty programmes of alliance carriers, interlining agreements, fare combinability agreements, may be applied in conjunction with structural remedies.

In addition to merger-like remedies, some jurisdictions (e.g. the United States and Canada) have applied carve outs to resolve competition concerns that arise from integrated alliances. This form of restriction prevents alliance partners from coordinating business decisions or integrating operations on routes designated as carve outs. Typically routes where airlines are likely to exercise market power (hub-to-hub or non-stop routes) post-alliance are carved out from antitrust immunity or other forms of alliance authorisation. Alliance members continue operating as competitors on routes carved out from the alliance, at least nominally. Carve outs have attracted criticism due to problematic enforcement and lack of effectiveness, as the existence of an alliance arguably diminishes the incentive for participating airlines to compete on carved out routes. Carve outs may also deplete efficiencies and prevent cost synergies as airlines cannot realise maximum benefits from integrating across their entire networks. The US DOT no longer imposes carve out requirements when conferring antitrust immunity.

The transfer of airport slots to facilitate competitive entry is a remedy that has been widely applied in merger and alliance cases. The mechanism for allocating divested airport slots among competitors differs and may include:

- Market-based slot allocation. Under this scheme competitors are offered to purchase or lease divested slots at a price determined by the current market conditions (e.g. through an auction). This approach has significant drawbacks, however, as there is no guarantee that the acquired slots will be used to initiate service on problematic routes.
- Assigned slot allocation. Under this approach designated competitors are offered released slots on the condition that they will use the slots to offer service on designated routes. In the case of domestic mergers, low cost airlines are likely to be designated users as they are likely to exert significant competitive pressure post-merger. In the case of international alliances, slot allocation may be complicated by restrictions in bilateral air service agreements.

Unlawful airline cartels or collusion arrangements may entail sanctions that range from monetary fines to prison sentences. As discussed above, the fuel price-fixing arrangement between world airlines led to substantive fines in multiple jurisdictions, totalling several billions of dollars. In some jurisdictions, public enforcement of anti-cartel laws may be complemented by private legal action and damage claims. In the United States, injured parties may bring a civil action and, if the action succeeds, receive compensation from the culprit airline(s) in an amount equal to treble damages.

13.12 International coordination of antitrust reviews

Competition law is the fastest growing branch of law; it has experienced geographical expansion at a pace not observable in any other branch of law. Today more than 120 jurisdictions have adopted some form of competition law, although substantive differences in how competition law is viewed and enforcement is administered persist.[46] The continuing trends of market liberalisation and globalisation of the world economy underscore the need for uniformity in applying competition laws and policies.

Cross-jurisdictional uniformity of competition laws and consistent enforcement of competition rules is particularly important for an industry with a global reach such as the airline industry. The standardisation of competition policy and enforcement in the airline industry has been to some extent facilitated by a number of bilateral initiatives and the work of important international organisations.

The fast penetration of international airline alliances has been a defining trend in the airline industry that changed its competitive fabric. Alliances present challenges for reviews undertaken by competition authorities, revealing an urgent need for harmonisation of competition reviews to minimise the risk of conflicting decisions.

- Bilateral initiatives, such as a recent joint study of transatlantic air transportation markets by the US DOT and the European Commission,[47] play an important role in advancing bilateral cooperation aimed at building a compatible regulatory approach to the assessment of competition issues in the airline industry.
- Multilateral cross-jurisdictional studies undertaken by such organisations as the Organisation of Economic Cooperation and Development (OECD), the International Competition Network (ICN) and the International Civil Aviation Organization (ICAO) provide an important comparative perspective of regulatory approaches and contribute to harmonisation by promoting the adoption of best practices in competition law enforcement in the airline sector.

13.13 Conclusion

Effective competition law and enforcement plays a central role in promoting efficiency and innovation in the airline sector and placing safeguards necessary to protect consumers. While many regulatory and economic barriers were removed after the airline industry was deregulated, some formidable barriers still remain in the form of airport infrastructure constraints, and new barriers have evolved in the form of airline strategic behaviour, such as the use of aggressive predatory pricing strategies or FFPs aimed at protecting market share.

The key challenge for competition authorities in the dynamic environment that prevails in the airline sector today is the promotion of benevolent free market competition and timely prevention of airline business behaviour that has detrimental effect on the competitive process and consumers. Antitrust enforcement aimed at addressing inherently harmful forms of airline cooperation, such as price fixing or market restricting cartels, clearly serves this objective. Antitrust reviews of other forms of airline cooperation, such as horizontal airline alliances, present significant challenges as alliance may have pro- and anti-competitive effects. The assessment of alliances is a demanding exercise of weighing their potential efficiencies and cost synergies against the risk of reduced competition.

46 Dabbah 1–3.
47 US Department of Transportation and the European Commission.

The global nature of the airline industry and increased cross-border cooperation between airlines underscores the need for cooperation and harmonisation of approaches between competition authorities. The absence of a global harmonised competition law and enforcement framework creates potential for diverging assessments. Some jurisdictions have undertaken bilateral coordination efforts to promote a more transparent and effective competition regime. While bilateral cooperation is an important step in synchronising competition policy and enforcement approaches, multilateral cooperation under the umbrella of an international organisation holds much promise in advancing global uniformity and harmonisation of competition law in the airline sector.

14

Consumer protection

Martine De Serres

14.1 Introduction

Consumer protection laws in the airline industry have grown exponentially over the past few decades, both in number and in scope. From the traditional body of regulations of safety, security, licensing, navigation, facilitation, noise, etc., governments have begun regulating a wide range of aviation practices, both through targeted industry-specific regulations or case law, as well as through general regulations addressing non–industry-specific issues such as advertising and privacy.

These regulations aim at protecting the consumer at various stages of his or her interaction with the airline, from the time of purchase (e.g. advertising and code share disclosure requirements), to the onset of the itinerary (e.g. baggage allowance determination and disclosure, protection of passengers with a disability, privacy standards in the transmission of a passenger's personal information), and throughout the journey (e.g. flight disruptions regulations addressing delays, cancellations, denied boarding, downgauges, and tarmac delays), and even post-flight (e.g. compensation obligations, obligation to provide a dispositive response to complaints, reporting obligations).

This chapter summarizes these key legislative requirements. The main characteristics of international regimes for the protection of passenger rights during flight disruptions are addressed, as are the principal characteristics of advertising requirements in the airlines industry, including all-inclusive pricing and ancillary fee disclosure, specific distribution and code share disclosure requirements, general principles of privacy in the technological era we live in and advance passenger information regimes, and, finally, rules relating to the determination of baggage allowance.

This chapter is by no means an exhaustive review of consumer protection regimes worldwide. Given its breadth, the growing body of regulations addressing the protection of passengers with a disability is specifically beyond the scope of this chapter.

14.2 Flight delays and cancellations, oversales, and denied boarding

Legislative regimes on this subject began in the United States (US), where consumer rights in the event of irregular flight operations through regulations pertaining to oversales and the resulting denied boarding situations.[1] These regimes are now widespread throughout the globe and have grown to encompass all forms of flight delays and cancellations. Carriers are now faced with a broad spectrum of varying obligations.

---

1 See Paul Stephen Dempsey and William Thorns, *Law and Economic Regulation in Transportation* (Quorum 1986) at pp. 268–273.

The US continues to have a set of regulations specifically targeting oversales,[2] and a separate, more recent regulation addresses long tarmac delays.[3] In the European Union (EU), regulation on denied boarding, delays, and cancellation have been in place since in 2004[4] and have since given rise to a regulatory trend worldwide to regulate irregular operations more generally, thus including delays, cancellations, and downgauges. The fact that this regulation addresses delays, a matter normally considered to be exclusively covered by the Montreal Convention,[5] has been unsuccessfully challenged before the European Court of Justice.[6]

More and more countries are using EC Regulation 261/2004 (the details of which are explained later in this chapter) as a basis for their own national regulation. For example, Switzerland adopted integrally EC Regulation 261/2004 into its national law, per the EU/Swiss Agreement on Air Transport. Some countries, such as Israel,[7] Venezuela,[8] and Turkey[9] also had been inspired by the EU regulatory framework, adopting similar legislation. However, Israel's version has a particular twist – its scope includes departures of flights from other countries, destined to Israel. It has been argued that this is an extraterritorial application of Israeli law.

Other countries, such as Brazil,[10] Mexico,[11] and more recently Chile,[12] also have specific provisions or regulations on the issue, and the Andean Community of Nations passed Decision 619 on 25 July 2005, which contains requirements applicable in its Member States.[13] A number of other countries have been addressing the issue through case law, such as Canada and India.

The resulting body of regulation is fairly harmonized in terms of fundamental principles (e.g. provision of information regarding passenger rights or nature of the irregular operation, requirements to call for volunteers in denied boarding situations, reprotection requirements on other flights

---

2 'Oversales', 14 CFR Part 250.
3 'Enhanced Protection for Airline Passengers', 14 CFR Part. 259 (in particular 'Tarmac Delay Contingency Plans', 14 CFR Part 259.4) and 'Reporting Tarmac Delay Data', 14 CFR Part 244.
4 Regulation 261/2004 of the European Parliament and of the Council of 11 February 2004 Establishing Common Rules on Compensation and Assistance to Passengers in the Event of Denied Boarding and of Cancellation or Long Delay of Flights (EC Regulation No. 261/2004).
5 The Convention for the Unification of Certain Rules for International Carriage by Air (1999), which sets out a specific regime to address damages caused by, *inter alia*, delays, has often been recognized by courts as being applicable to the exclusion of any other (national) law or regime.
6 *IATA* v. *Department for Transport (UK)*, 2006 ECJ CELEX NEXIS 10. See in particular, the reasoning set out at paras 44–48, where it is ruled that the matters covered by EC Regulation 261/2004 are different from those covered by the Montreal Convention, and that the protection afforded by the regulation go above and beyond those of the Convention.
7 Israel's Aviation Services Law (Compensation and Assistance for Flight Cancellation or Change of Conditions), 5772-2012 (ASL).
8 Administrative Order PRE-CJU-002-05 (18 November 2004).
9 Turkey's Regulations on Air Passenger Rights (Shy-Passenger).
10 ANAC Resolution No. 141. Assistance to be provided by carriers in case of flight cancellation, delays, and boarding denials are set out in ANAC's Directive 141/2010. In addition to this directive, proposed changes to the General Air Transportation Conditions (Directive 676/GC-5 of 2000), currently effective, will review and consolidate all rules about passengers' rights and general conditions of carriage into one new directive to be issued, and will also require that carriers provide passengers who have already boarded the aircraft, with the following assistance: (i) information, in intervals of 30 minutes on the reason for the flight delay, as well as the estimated departure time; (ii) food supplies if delays exceeds one hour, unless the departure is imminent; (iii) keep the bathrooms clean and usable; (iv) maintain the climate control, so as to allow thermal comfort; and (v) if the delay exceeds two hours, carrier must disembark the passengers, unless the departure is imminent.
11 Integrated into Mexico's Civil Aviation Law.
12 Integrated into Chile's Aeronautics Code, Article 133.
13 Columbia, Peru, Bolivia, Ecuador.

for irregular operations resulting in long delays, possibility for passengers to obtain a full or partial refund for unused or partially used tickets). However, there remains a substantial lack of harmony in the details and scope of application of these regulations, and in passenger recourses, which causes significant operational challenges for airlines in applying these various requirements.

For example, European regulation applies both to flights departing the EU and to EU carriers, irrespective of where they are operating. US legislation applies to flights departing the US (even to EU carriers operating flights departing from the US), and Israeli law applies to all flights to and from Israel. Important aspects of these regulatory regimes vary widely (levels of compensation, specific information to be provided to passengers, forum for action, etc.), creating confusion for passengers and significant operational challenges for airlines, as well as, in some cases, an unlevel playing field. To ensure compliance, the golden rule for airlines, when faced with a situation where two sets of regulations apply, is to comply with the highest standard.

The International Air Transport Association (IATA), the main industry body in aviation, has adopted a recommended practice regarding denied boarding.[14] As is the case with many of IATA's initiatives, the inherent value lies in its standard-setting effect. When adopted as a voluntary policy, it can provide a reasonable standard by courts in jurisdictions where flight disruptions affecting consumer rights are not directly addressed through local law. As such, the policy may be deemed as providing sufficient protection to consumers, a valuable factor in a regulator's evaluation of the need for additional regulation.

The next section reviews the key components of the most prominent regimes, that is, the European and American regimes, as well as the Canadian regime, where standards exist outside a specific piece of regulation on the issue.

14.2.1 Key denied boarding provisions

Denied boarding occurs when a flight is oversold, that is, when there are more confirmed, checked-in passengers than there are seats available on the aircraft. Airlines tend to overbook flights to account for the no-show factor. Because many airlines offer flexible fares that allow voluntary flight changes and cancellations at little or no charge (a product catered to business or otherwise time sensitive passengers who benefit from the flexibility of being able to modify their travel plans), last-minute changes and passengers who do not show up mean that flights depart significantly emptier than the number of tickets originally sold for that flight would have accounted for. At times, as much as 20 per cent of passengers do not show up for a flight.[15] As such, airlines will oversell flights by a certain factor, to account for the usual no-show factor on a specific route and avoid leaving with empty seats.

Note that the term 'denied boarding', as defined in this section, is not the same as a 'refusal to carry', which is a term more commonly used to describe a situation where a carrier refuses a passenger who, for example, has an unruly behaviour or is improperly documented for travel to the country of destination.

When faced with a denied boarding situation, a carrier is generally required, pursuant to applicable law, to call for volunteers to surrender their reservation.[16] Carriers will often offer cash or travel vouchers as an incentive for volunteers to relinquish their seat rather than having to deny boarding to anyone.

---

14 Recommended Practice 1799.
15 D.G. Wensveen, *Air Transportation: A Management Perspective*, 7th ed. (Ashgate Publishing Ltd 2012) at p. 211.
16 See for example 14 CFR §250.2b; EC Regulation No. 261/2004, Article 4.

Where there are insufficient volunteers, passengers will be denied boarding, in a specific order determined by a carrier's boarding priorities. For example, denial will be based on the order of check-in, whether or not a passenger has an assigned seat, frequent-flyer status.[17] Passengers for which a denied boarding would cause undue hardship, such as passengers with a disability, unaccompanied minors or passengers travelling in groups, are typically never denied boarding.

In addition to calling for volunteers, a carrier's obligations in denied boarding situations is to:

- provide information to passengers regarding their rights;[18]
- compensate them for the inconvenience of being denied boarding (depending on the length of the delay caused by the denied boarding situation, and, in the US and the Andean Community, depending on the value of their ticket);[19]
- re-route them so that they arrive at destination or reimburse them should they choose no longer to travel;[20] and

---

17 Chile's Aeronautic Code, Article 133 and US DOT 14 CFR §2 50.3 both have specific provisions on boarding priorities. US DOT 14 CFR §2 50.3 reads:

  a Every carrier shall establish priority rules and criteria for determining which passengers holding confirmed reserved space shall be denied boarding on an oversold flight in the event that an insufficient number of volunteers come forward. Such rules and criteria shall reflect the obligations of the carrier set forth in §§250.2a and 250.2b to minimize involuntary denied boarding and to request volunteers, and shall be written in such manner as to be understandable and meaningful to the average passenger. Such rules and criteria shall not make, give, or cause any undue or unreasonable preference or advantage to any particular person or subject any particular person to any unjust or unreasonable prejudice or disadvantage in any respect whatsoever.
  b Boarding priority factors may include, but are not limited to, the following:

    1 A passenger's time of check-in;
    2 Whether a passenger has a seat assignment before reaching the departure gate for carriers that assign seats;
    3 The fare paid by a passenger;
    4 A passenger's frequent-flyer status; and
    5 A passenger's disability or status as an unaccompanied minor.

18 In the EU, Switzerland, Turkey, and Israel, there are general information obligations at check-in, and separate obligations for passengers specifically affected by the irregular operation. For example, Article 14 of EC Regulation No. 261/2004 states:

    1 The operating air carrier shall ensure that at check-in a clearly legible notice containing the following text is displayed in a manner clearly visible to passengers: 'If you are denied boarding or if your flight is cancelled or delayed for at least two hours, ask at the check-in counter or boarding gate for the text stating your rights, particularly with regard to compensation and assistance'.
    2 An operating air carrier denying boarding or cancelling a flight shall provide each passenger affected with a written notice setting out the rules for compensation and assistance in line with this Regulation. It shall also provide each passenger affected by a delay of at least two hours with an equivalent notice. The contact details of the national designated body referred to in Article 16 shall also be given to the passenger in written form.
    3 In respect of blind and visually impaired persons, the provisions of this Article shall be applied using appropriate alternative means.

19 EC Regulation No. 261/2004, Article 7; US DOT 14 CFR 250.8, Andean Community Decision 619, Article 8; Israel's ASL First Schedule; Turkey's 'Regulations On Air Passenger Rights (Shy-Passenger)', Article 10; Chile's 'Aeronautical Code', Article 133(2).
20 EC Regulation No. 261/2004, Article 8; Turkey Article 9; Israel's ASL s. 5. In the US, re-routing is not an obligation, but an exception to payment of compensation (14 CFR 250.6(d)):

    The carrier arranges comparable air transportation, or other transportation used by the passenger at no extra cost to the passenger, that at the time such arrangements are made is planned to arrive at the airport of the passenger's next stopover or, if none, at the airport of the final destination not later than 1 hour after the planned arrival time of the passenger's original flight or flights.

- except in the US, provide assistance (Duty of Care)[21] in the form of meals, refreshments, hotel accommodation, ground transportation to hotel, and communication assistance (phone calls, etc.).

14.2.2 EC Regulation 261/2004 and similar legislation

14.2.2.1 Scope

Non-EU carriers are subject to this regulation where the cancellation, delay, or denied boarding occurs from an airport located in a Member State.

EU carriers are subject to this regulation where the cancellation, delay, or denied boarding occurs from an airport located in a Member State or from an airport located in a third country for a flight to an airport in a Member State.

14.2.2.2 Monetary compensation, delays, and extraordinary circumstances

Where reference is made, in the regulation, to compensation per Article 7, compensation is payable as shown in Table 14.1.

Compensation is applicable to cases of denied boarding and cancellations. Per applicable case law, delays above three hours are treated as cancellations,[22] despite no express provision in the regulation to compensate passengers for delay. Passengers are now entitled to the compensation as set out in Article 7 for any delay in excess of *three hours* providing the air carrier cannot raise a defence of 'extraordinary circumstances':

> in view of the fact that the aim pursued by Regulation No 261/2004 is to *increase protection for all air passengers*, passengers whose flights are delayed by three hours or more *cannot be treated differently* from those receiving compensation under Article 5(1)(c)(iii) of that regulation, *since such unequal treatment as between those two groups is not duly justified in the light of the aims pursued by the regulation.*
> [...]
> In the light of the foregoing the answer to question 1 in Case C-629/10 is that Articles 5 to 7 of Regulation No 261/2004 *must be interpreted as meaning that passengers whose flights are delayed are entitled to compensation under that regulation where they suffer, on account of such flights, a loss of time equal to or in excess of three hours*, that is, where they reach their *final destination* three hours or more after the arrival time originally scheduled by the air carrier. Such a delay does not, however, entitle passengers to compensation if the air carrier can prove that the long delay is caused by extraordinary circumstances which could not have been avoided even if all reasonable measures had been taken, namely circumstances beyond the actual control of the air carrier.[23]

---

21 EC Regulation No. 261/2004, Article 9; Israel's ASL s. 3(a)(1).
22 *Nelson* v. *Lufthansa* (C581/10) and *TUI, British Airways, Easyjet and IATA* v. *U.K. Civil Aviation Authority* (C629/10), ECJ, 23 October 2012 (*Nelson and TUI*); *Sturgeon* v. *Condor* (C-402/07) and *Bock* v. *Air France* (C432/07), Fourth Chamber Court, 19 November 2009.
23 *Nelson* and *TUI.*

Table 14.1 Summary of monetary compensation owed pursuant to EC Regulation No. 261/2004

Condition	Flight ≤ 1500 km	1500 km < Flight ≤ 3500 km	Flight > 3500 km
Passenger arrives at final destination on ticket within…	2 hrs of original schedule: €125	3 hrs of original schedule: €200	4 hrs of original schedule: €300
All other instances	€250	€400	€600

There are two exceptions to compensation owed pursuant to Article 7. The first is when a passenger is informed of a cancellation:

- at least two weeks in advance; or
- between two weeks and seven days in advance where they are offered re-routing that allows departure within two hours of originally scheduled time and arrival within four hours of originally scheduled time; or
- less than seven days in advance where they are offered re-routing that allows departure within one hour of originally scheduled time and arrival within two hours of originally scheduled time.

The second exception to compensation is when a cancellation is caused by *extraordinary circumstances* beyond the control of the carrier. Extraordinary circumstances are narrowly interpreted by Courts, and do not include ordinary mechanical issues. Airlines are no longer able to claim that flight disruptions caused by ordinary technical problems (such as wear and tear) are part of the extraordinary circumstances outlined in EU Regulation 261/2004.[24]

The monetary compensation set out in this regulation is viewed as a reasonable amount granted to address the immediate needs of the passengers without them having to suffer the burden of instituting legal proceedings against airlines. However, the regulation clarifies that by accepting this amount, a passenger does not forfeit its rights to full and adequate compensation, based on the particulars of their case.[25]

---

24 *Jet2.com* v. *Huzar* [2014] EWCA Civ 791 (11 June 2014) (Leave to appeal refused); and more recently *Van der Lans* v. *KLM* (C-257-14), 17 September 2015, where the Court left the door open for the extraordinary circumstance defence to apply, (1) where manufacturing defects which would have an impact on multiple aircrafts affected in a fleet, or (2) where the problem could not be detected under ordinary maintenance, which would be considered as normal operations.

25 Article 12: Further compensation

    1 This Regulation shall apply without prejudice to a passenger's rights to further compensation. The compensation granted under this Regulation may be deducted from such compensation.

    2 Without prejudice to relevant principles and rules of national law, including case-law, paragraph 1 shall not apply to passengers who have voluntarily surrendered a reservation under Article 4(1).

Article 13: Right of redress

In cases where an operating air carrier pays compensation or meets the other obligations incumbent on it under this Regulation, no provision of this Regulation may be interpreted as restricting its right to seek compensation from any person, including third parties, in accordance with the law applicable. In particular, this Regulation shall in no way restrict the operating air carrier's right to seek reimbursement from a tour operator or another person with whom the operating air carrier has a contract. Similarly, no provision of this Regulation may be interpreted as restricting the right of a tour operator or a third party, other than a passenger, with whom an operating air carrier has a contract, to seek reimbursement or compensation from the operating air carrier in accordance with applicable relevant laws.

14.2.2.3 Downgrading (Article 10)

Placing the passenger in a lower class than that for which the ticket was purchased would also generate a right to reimbursement, within seven days of:

a   30% of the price of the ticket for all flights of 1500 kilometres or less, or

b   50% of the price of the ticket for all intra-Community flights of more than 1500 kilometres, except flights between the European territory of the Member States and the French overseas departments, and for all other flights between 1500 and 3500 kilometres, or

c   75% of the price of the ticket for all flights not falling under (a) or (b), including flights between the European territory of the Member States and the French overseas departments.[26]

14.2.2.4 Review

EC Regulation No. 261/2004 is currently undergoing a legislative review. Among the changes being addressed are those generated through case law, including: the extraordinary circumstance defence and the length of time of delay that renders the delay akin to a cancellation, thereby triggering compensation; delays causing a missed connection; the duty of care owed where a flight is delayed beyond four hours; and situations under which a reimbursement is payable.

14.2.2.5 Enforcement

EC Regulation No. 261/2004 is interpreted and applied by local courts as well as by consumer protection bodies or aeronautical authorities in EU Member States.

National bodies can a multi-faceted role. They typically perform random inspections or auditing of carriers, advise consumers of their rights, and can assist them in carrying out legal action against carriers. More sophisticated jurisdictions, like the United Kingdom, have audited carriers through questionnaires and published their findings on compliance performance in a report.[27] A public approach of this nature inevitable affects a carrier's reputation and may therefore encourage voluntary compliance or process improvements from carriers.

14.2.3 United States

The US requirements follow the standard key requirements described previously. In terms of monetary compensation, the Table 14.2 provides a comparison of compensation levels between the EU and US requirements for denied boarding (note that no requirements exist in the US for long delays and cancellations, as they do in the EU and other jurisdictions).

Payment of denied boarding compensation must be made by cash or cheque within 24 hours of the denied boarding situation.[28]

---

26 EC Regulation No. 261/2004, Article 10(2).

27 See https://urldefense.proofpoint.com/v2/url?u=http-3A__www.caa.co.uk_docs_33_CAP-25201227-2520Cancellations-2520and-2520Delays.pdf&d=AwIGaQ&c=mOZmNI1OXBXF4QxpF27OnA&r=TpRYtYzp_fTkMOvlJmMnmkyguPqH3lz3j_oY08owFUE&m=h3wsvVBGzP4et7SCZELoeLZq7OsFWss4nRhSc5hApiY&s=tP0SxNzbUqqk2jLaUezcrkKSqY_jT6gF3W8jRTwN1mM&e.

28 14 CFR §250.8.

Table 14.2 Comparison of monetary compensation payable under European and American regulations

EU: EC 261/2004	US: 14 CFR Part 250.5[1]
Flight ≤ 1500 km	Domestic:
0–2 hr delay at arrival: €125.	0–1 hr delay at arrival: $0
>2 hr delay at arrival: €250.	1–2 hr delay at arrival: 200% of one-way fare but no more than US$675.
1500 km < Flight ≤ 3500 km	>2 hr delay at arrival: 400% of one-way fare but no more than US$1350.
0–3 hr delay at arrival: €200	
>3 hr delay at arrival: €400	International:
Flight > 3500 km	0–1 hr delay at arrival: $0
0–4 hr delay at arrival: €300	1–4 hr delay at arrival: 200% of one-way fare but no more than US$675.
>4 hr delay at arrival: €600	>4 hr delay at arrival: 400% of one-way fare but no more than US$1350.

Exceptions to the payment of denied boarding compensation are as follows:[29]

1   compliance with conditions of carriage (e.g. passenger check-in on time);
2   substitution of equipment (for safety or operational reasons);
3   downgrade, but the fare difference must be refunded;
4   provision of comparable transportation arriving within one hour of original planned arrival.

The US Department of Transport (DOT) also has a public approach to compliance. First, it publishes regular reports on carriers' performance levels regarding compliance. Second, its compliance orders against targeted airlines are not only publicly available, but the importance of the monetary penalties imposed tends actually to draw public attention.

14.2.4 Canada

There have been attempts to set-up a regulatory framework for protecting consumer rights the event of denied boarding situations or during delays and cancellations in Canada, but no bill has made it through the House of Commons to date and no legislation to this effect exists in Canada. The last attempt, made in 2009, was a private members' bill[30] heavily inspired from EC Regulation 261/2004. As such, its drafting would not have adequately fit into the existing legislative framework for airline consumer rights in Canada. The absence of formal regulation notwithstanding, a framework has been developed, at least with respect to airlines operating out of Canada, and consumers are not left without rights or a de facto compensatory regime.

14.2.4.1 Transport Canada's guidelines

In 2008, the Government of Canada published guidelines for airlines, Flight Rights Canada,[31] a voluntary code of conduct for airlines operating out of Canada. It outlines rights that air passengers have with respect to air travel, but does not provide or suggest monetary compensation to passengers for denied boarding or delayed or cancelled flights.

---

29 14 CFR §250.6.
30 Bill C-310, An Act to Provide Certain Rights to Air Passengers.
31 See http://travel.gc.ca/air/air-passenger-rights.

Flight Rights Canada resulted in common tariff[32] provisions for Canadian carriers, that set out the usual requirements for flight disruptions. Specifically, they provide for information to be provided to passengers on a regular basis, the reprotection on the carrier's next available flight or on a carrier with which a reprotection agreement exists, the refund of the unused portion of the ticket if the passenger chooses no longer to travel, and assistance in the form of meal vouchers, hotel accommodation, and ground transportation between the airport and hotel.

Even though no compensation obligations are set out, the principles of the Montreal or Warsaw Conventions (as amended) still apply in regards to damages resulting from delay.

14.2.4.2 Canadian Transportation Agency case law

Separately, case law from the Canadian Transportation Agency (CTA) forces specific carriers involved in the relevant cases to apply certain terms and conditions of carriage. Although this body of case law sets the expectation of the CTA in terms of what is deemed reasonable terms and conditions for the compensation of passengers in situations of denied boarding, delays, or cancellations, each case applies to specific carriers, and there is no set legislated standard for all carriers. Arguably, this creates an unlevel playing field for carriers departing Canada, although some carriers, such as European carriers, remain subject to their home legislation wherever they operate.

Through recent case law,[33] the CTA has set a monetary standard by ordering that the following monetary compensation be paid, with increasing amounts depending on the length of the delay, the highest amount being $800 for delays of six hours or more

Previous case law had extended the obligation of carriers to provide accommodation for re-routing on the *next* available flight under certain circumstances, which is a higher standard for airlines to meet than similar requirements in other jurisdictions, where the evaluation of re-routing options is not specifically regulated.[34] These cases also ordered the full refund of entirely unused tickets upon passengers' request if the purpose of travel no longer exists.[35]

14.3 Tarmac delays

The US is the only jurisdiction to have specific tarmac delay regulations.[36] Some regulators, such as China and the EU, are currently looking at implementing rules addressing such situations. Canada has a soft-law through the voluntary tariff provisions implemented by Canadian carriers to reflect Transport Canada's guidelines,[37] to ensure the provision of drinks, snacks, and, for delays exceeding 90 minutes, under certain circumstance, the possibility to disembark.

---

32 An airline's tariff is the document through which regulators allow or disallow an airline's fares, and terms and conditions of carriage, pursuant to the provisions of the applicable bilateral agreement. Most carriers no longer update their tariffs with their applicable terms and conditions of carriage, but, in Canada, there is a legislated requirement for an airline's tariff to contain its terms and conditions of carriage. The CTA's jurisdiction over consumer rights is intimately linked to and often restricted to tariffs.

33 See CTA decision No. 342-C-A-2013 (*Lukacs* v. *Air Canada*) applicable to Air Canada's domestic flights.

34 CTA Decisions No. 248-C-A-2012 (*Lukacs* v. *Transat*), 249-C-A-2012 (*Lukacs* v. *Westjet*), and 250-C-A-2012 (*Lukacs* v. *Air Canada*).

35 Ibid.

36 US DOT 14 CFR Part 244.1, 244.2, 244.3, 259.4.

37 Flight Rights Canada, *supra* note 31.

Tarmac delays occur where there is a lengthy delay while passengers are onboard the aircraft, and can occur at airport of departure, arrival, and during a diversion. A tarmac delay is defined as: 'The holding of an aircraft on the ground either before taking off or after landing with no opportunity for its passengers to deplane.'[38]

For domestic US flights, delays of three hours or more are considered lengthy, the delay being four hours for international flights. The regulation applies both to domestic US and to foreign carriers operating at least one passenger aircraft with capacity of 30 or more seats, for all flights to or from the US and at all airports in the US.

Specific carrier obligations are set out through the main requirement that carriers implement a Contingency Plan for Lengthy Tarmac Delays, and include the provision of:

- adequate food and water must be provided no later than two hours after the delay;
- operable lavatories;
- medical assistance, if needed;
- flight status notifications every 30 minutes, including the reason for the delay;
- notification every 30 minutes of the existence of a deplaning opportunity, should it exist.

Exemptions to the above obligations can arise for safety-related reasons, as determined by the pilot-in-command. This exception is particularly relevant to the opportunity to deplane.

Carriers are required to ensure that their Contingency Plan is coordinated with airport authorities, airport security, and customs. Without this coordination, a carrier may be unable to fulfil its obligation to provide an opportunity to deplane. Such plans must be communicated and made available to customers for consultation and review.

Carriers also have tarmac delay reporting obligations to the US DOT for all delays over three hours, which allow the DOT to investigate reported occurrences.[39] Carriers must retain records for two years following the delay.[40]

In code share situations, the plan of the marketing carrier applies, unless the marketing carrier specifies in its contract of carriage that the operating carrier's plan applies.[41]

Violations to the tarmac delay provisions are considered an 'unfair and deceptive practice' under 49 USC 41712 and are subject to penalties associated thereto, although violations are generally dealt with through a negotiation process with the DOT, resulting in a publicly available consent order published on the DOT's website.

For example, a consent order was issued against Southwest Airlines[42] for failure to offer an opportunity to deplane within three hours of landing at Chicago Midway International Airport on 16 different flights on 2 and 3 January 2014. According to Southwest, this was due to extreme winter weather as well as a malfunctioning of its crew scheduling system. The fine was of $1,600,000 ($600,000 payable immediately, $700,000 credited for compensation paid to passengers and for acquiring a surface management system, and $300,000 payable if there is another violation within one year of the consent order). It is not uncommon for the DOT to order partial payment of the fine, with the remainder reinvested in improving the carrier's systems or processes.

38 14 CFR Part 259.3.
39 14 CFR Part 244.3.
40 14 CFR Part 259.4(e).
41 14 CFR Part 259.4(c).
42 DOT-OST-2015-0002, Order 2015-1-10.

14.4 False and misleading advertising

Misleading advertising regulation in the airline industry was initially implemented to address carrier display discrimination by computer reservation systems (CRSs). These regulations were meant to protect against competitive abuse by airlines that own or control CRSs and to ensure the unbiased display of airfares and travel options, prohibiting controlling airlines from promoting their own flights to the detriment of others when other airlines offer better or equivalent travel options or prices. Such requirements are still in place today in certain jurisdictions, but expired in the US in 2004.[43]

A large number of other, similar regulations have since sprouted worldwide, and now address all manners in which airlines sell and market their products, from the display and sale of airfares (such as full-fare advertising, displaying the name of the operators, disclosing seat availability, providing accessibility information for passengers with a disability) to the display and sale of ancillary products (such as baggage or seat selection fees) and tour packaging (flights sold in conjunction with other products and services, such as car rental, hotels, cruises, etc.).

14.4.1 All-inclusive pricing

The purpose of pricing regulations is to ensure that customers are protected against false and misleading advertising. They prohibit deceptive practices that would distort the actual economic behaviour of an advert and harm the interest of competitors. Such regulations ensure that consumers are in a position to make a clear and informed decision on what type of product they purchase by imposing consistency in pricing throughout a jurisdiction, and allow customers to 'comparison-shop' better.

Today, carriers are subject to all-inclusive pricing regulations in a large number of countries including the US, the EU, Canada and Australia. In those jurisdictions, the airfare must be advertised inclusive of all taxes, fees, charges, and surcharges. All forms of advertising are usual covered by such requirements, that is, print or web advertising, as are all distribution channels, including airlines' call centres. On the Internet, all-in prices must appear on the first public display of a fare during the booking process.

Taxes and fees are generally dependent on a number of parameters such as specific departure and arrival airport (some cities having more than one airport), direction of travel (outbound or

---

43 See for example EC Regulation No. 80/2009 on a Code of Conduct for CRSs (amending and repealing EEC Regulation No. 2299/89). The language used in the now expired US Regulation (14 CFR §255.4 'Display of information') remains informative as it illustrates the type of CRS discrimination issues that were rampant back then. It stated (emphasis added):

 1 Each system must offer an integrated display that uses the same editing and ranking criteria for both on-line and interline connections *and does not give on-line connections a system-imposed preference over interline connections.*
 [...]

 2 Each integrated display offered by a system must either use elapsed time as a significant factor in selecting service options from the database or give single-plane flights a preference over connecting services in ranking services in displays.

  b In ordering the information contained in an integrated display, *systems shall not use any factors directly or indirectly relating to carrier identity.*

   1 *Systems may order the display of information on the basis of any service criteria that do not reflect carrier identity and that are consistently applied to all carriers and to all markets.*

inbound), number of legs (i.e. whether there is a connection or not will change the calculation). This can create significant challenges for carriers, as full fares are difficult to calculate without knowing the full itinerary. Carriers must sometimes be creative in their advertising if they wish to comply while displaying attractive and simple adverts for their services.

The advent of all-inclusive pricing in the aviation industry was a welcome change for consumers, as the base fare charged by airlines can be much lower than the total, final price inclusive of taxes, fees, charges, and surcharges, and the total price sometimes came (and in many jurisdictions, still comes) as a surprise to consumers. The reason for the large difference between the base fare and total price is largely due to the large and costly variety of third-party imposed taxes, fees, and charges (airport fees, security charges, customs fees, agricultural fees, noise taxes, emissions taxes, etc.) and partly to surcharges charged by airlines. These surcharges are not filed by airlines as part of the base fare due to the manner in which airfares are and have historically been filed in fare filing systems and distributed through Global Distribution Systems (GDS). The separate filing of base fares and surcharges allow airlines to make flexible competitive responses to price changes in the market in real time and respond to volatile costs, such as fuel costs, without having to adjust each fare filed individually. With all-inclusive pricing, this entire process is irrelevant to the consumer, who is exposed only to the final price downline from the fare filing and distribution process, thanks to adjustment to price display mechanisms.

14.4.1.1 EU regulation

Under EU regulation,[44] prices offered, whether in print advertising, over the phone, or on the Internet, must be inclusive of all taxes, airport charges, and any other fee, charge, or surcharge. Prices offered cannot automatically include optional services (such as seat selection fees, lounge access fees, fees for frequent flyer points), that would require the customer to opt-out.[45] Moreover, the regulations include a key principle of non-discrimination in pricing, irrespective of point of sale:

> Without prejudice to Article 16(1), access to air fares and air rates for air services from an airport located in the territory of a Member State to which the Treaty applies, available to the general public shall be granted *without any discrimination based on the nationality or the place*

---

44 EC Regulation No. 1008/2008.
45 Ibid., Article 23:

Information and non-discrimination

1 Air fares and air rates available to the general public shall include the applicable conditions when offered or published in any form, including on the Internet, for air services from an airport located in the territory of a Member State to which the Treaty applies. The final price to be paid shall at all times be indicated and shall include the applicable air fare or air rate as well as all applicable taxes, and charges, surcharges and fees which are unavoidable and foreseeable at the time of publication. In addition to the indication of the final price, at least the following shall be specified:

    a air fare or air rate;
    b taxes;
    c airport charges; and
    d other charges, surcharges or fees, such as those related to security or fuel;

where the items listed under (b), (c) and (d) have been added to the air fare or air rate. Optional price supplements shall be communicated in a clear, transparent and unambiguous way at the start of any booking process and their acceptance by the customer shall be on an 'opt-in' basis.

of residence of the customer or on the place of establishment of the air carrier's agent or other ticket seller within the Community [emphasis added].[46]

The regulation reflects similar principles applicable more generally in the EU and not specifically targeting the aviation industry, adopted earlier and in the form of a directive. This means they must be adopted into the national law of Member States before becoming applicable to advertisers as opposed to the regulation targeting airfare advertising, which is directly applicable. However, because of this directive, the national law of each Member State where a person advertises in the EU must still be examined to see how this directive got translated into national law, and analysed to identify specific national requirements:

> Article 7
> Misleading omissions
> 1   A commercial practice shall be regarded as misleading if, in its factual context, taking account of all its features and circumstances and the limitations of the communication medium, *it omits material information that the average consumer needs*, according to the context, to take an informed transactional decision and thereby causes or is likely to cause the average consumer to take a transactional decision that he would not have taken otherwise.
> [...]
> 4   *In the case of an invitation to purchase, the following information shall be regarded as material,* if not already apparent from the context:
> [...]
> c   *the price inclusive of taxes,* or where the nature of the product means that the price cannot reasonably be calculated in advance, the manner in which the price is calculated, as well as, where appropriate, all additional freight, delivery or postal charges or, where these charges cannot reasonably be calculated in advance, the fact that such additional charges may be payable [emphasis added].[47]

This test of material omission of information needed for an average customer to make an informed decision is the key principle and common denominator in misleading advertising regulations in many jurisdictions.

14.4.1.2 United States

The US has similar all-inclusive pricing regulations,[48] as well as a similar prohibition to offer optional services where consumers are automatically opted-in. In addition, as in Canada,

---

46 Ibid., Article 23(2).
47 Directive 2005/29/EC (11 May 2005) concerning unfair business-to-consumer commercial practices in the internal market ('Unfair Commercial Practices Directive').
48 §399.84 'Price advertising and opt-out provisions' (emphasis added):

> a The Department considers any advertising or solicitation by a direct air carrier, indirect air carrier, an agent of either, or a ticket agent, for passenger air transportation, a tour (i.e., a combination of air transportation and ground or cruise accommodations) or tour component (e.g., a hotel stay) that must be purchased with air transportation that states a price for such air transportation, tour, or tour component to be an unfair and deceptive practice in violation of 49 U.S.C. 41712, unless the *price stated is the entire price to be paid by the customer to the carrier,* or agent, for such air transportation, tour, or tour component. *Although charges included within the single total*

charges may be 'broken out' to inform customers of the source of the total price. They must be on a per passenger basis and must not be prominently displayed, or displayed in a font that is large or larger than the total price. This is one of many examples of the detailed regulatory approach taken by the US DOT when interpreting and applying principles of misleading advertising.

The regulation has an additional prohibition to offer one-way prices when a round-trip fare is required to be purchased. In such cases, the advertiser must clearly disclose the requirement of a round-trip purchase, stating that the fare is 'each-way', as opposed to 'one-way'.

The US DOT also issues notices that impact advertisement practice and that must be referred to for a full understanding of US advertising requirements. For example, surcharges and percentage-based taxes are to be included in the fare. Airlines cannot advertise airfares for 'free' if any taxes, fees, charge, or surcharge is levied. The carrier must ensure that, during the overall period within which the fare is offered, there is reasonable availability and no lengthy period of time when no seats are available at the advertised price.

As with tarmac delays, violations of these US regulations are deemed to be an unfair and deceptive practice, under 49 USC 41712. This is a broad prohibition against unfair and deceptive practices, including violations to the application of advertising standards and regulations.

The US DOT has been very active in enforcing compliance with advertising requirements in recent years.

For example, in consent order DOT-OST-2014-0001, 13 May 2014, Southwest was fined for running a television advertisement advertising $59 fares between Atlanta and New York, Chicago, and Los Angeles. However, no seats were actually available at that price. The fine was $200,000.

In consent order DOT-OST-2014-0001, 7 July 2014, issued against Delta, Delta was fined for having advertised 'each way' pricing on its booking flow where a round trip purchase was required (disclosure was noted by an asterisk to the bottom of the page). The fine was $100,000.

---

price listed (e.g., government taxes) may be stated separately or through links or 'pop ups' on websites that display the total price, such charges may not be false or misleading, may not be displayed prominently, may not be presented in the same or larger size as the total price, and must provide cost information on a per passenger basis that accurately reflects the cost of the item covered by the charge.

b The Department considers any advertising by the entities listed in paragraph (a) of this section of an each-way airfare that is available only when purchased for round-trip travel to be an unfair and deceptive practice in violation of 49 U.S.C. 41712, unless such airfare is advertised as 'each way' and in such a manner so that the disclosure of the round-trip purchase requirement is clearly and conspicuously noted in the advertisement and is stated prominently and proximately to the each-way fare amount. *The Department considers it to be an unfair and deceptive practice to advertise each-way fares contingent on a round-trip purchase requirement as 'one-way' fares, even if accompanied by prominent and proximate disclosure of the round trip purchase requirement.*

c When offering a ticket for purchase by a consumer, for passenger air transportation or for a tour (i.e., a combination of air transportation and ground or cruise accommodations) or tour component (e.g., a hotel stay) that must be purchased with air transportation, a direct air carrier, indirect air carrier, an agent of either, or a ticket agent, may not offer additional optional services in connection with air transportation, a tour, or tour component whereby the optional service is automatically added to the consumer's purchase if the consumer takes no other action, i.e., if the consumer does not opt out. *The consumer must affirmatively 'opt in' (i.e., agree) to such a service and the fee for it before that fee is added to the total price for the air transportation-related purchase. The Department considers the use of 'opt-out' provisions to be an unfair and deceptive practice in violation of 49 U.S.C. 41712.*

14.4.1.3 Canada

The Canadian Competition Bureau has a general jurisdiction over misleading advertising in Canada. Separately, the CTA has a specific jurisdiction over airfare.

Pricing requirements specific to the airline industry are found in section 86.1 of the Canada Transportation Act[49] and sections 135.5–135.92 of the Air Transportation Regulations (ATRs):[50]

> 86.1 (1) The Agency shall make regulations respecting advertising in all media, including on the Internet, of prices for air services within, or originating in, Canada.
>
> (2) Without limiting the generality of subsection (1), regulations shall be made under that subsection *requiring a carrier who advertises a price for an air service to include in the price all costs to the carrier of providing the service and to indicate in the advertisement all fees, charges and taxes collected by the carrier on behalf of another person in respect of the service, so as to enable a purchaser of the service to readily determine the total amount to be paid for the service* [emphasis added].

The ATR requirements apply only if a price is listed. They contain specific requirements on total price advertisements (inclusive of all air transportation and third party charges) and on price breakdown on carrier websites. The key requirements are as follows:

> 135.8 (1) Any person who advertises the price of an air service must include in the advertisement the following information:
>
> a the *total price* that must be paid to the advertiser to obtain the air service, expressed in Canadian dollars and, if it is also expressed in another currency, the name of that currency;
>
> b *the point of origin and point of destination* of the service *and whether the service is one way or round trip;*
>
> c *any limitation on the period during which the advertised price will be offered and any limitation on the period for which the service will be provided at that price;*
>
> d *the name and amount of each tax, fee or charge* relating to the air service that is a third party charge;
>
> e *each optional incidental service offered for which a fee or charge is payable* and its total price or range of total prices; and
>
> f *any published tax, fee or charge that is not collected by the advertiser but must be paid* at the point of origin or departure by the person to whom the service is provided.

The ATRs specifically prescribe how third party charges must be displayed.[51] The total price can be advertised for one-way journeys only, so long as it is clearly indicated that the advertised price relates to only one direction of the service and applies only if both directions are purchased.[52]

---

49 S.C. 1996, c. 10.
50 SOR/88-58.
51 ATR s. 135.8(2) and (3):

   2 A person who advertises the price of an air service must set out all third party charges under the heading 'Taxes, Fees and Charges' unless that information is only provided orally.
   3 A person who mentions an air transportation charge in the advertisement must set it out under the heading 'Air Transportation Charges' unless that information is only provided orally.

52 ATR s. 135.8(4).

The ATRs distinguish between non-interactive and interactive advertisements. Interactive advertising includes online booking systems and booking systems over the phone, where all prescribed information must be available pre-purchase. Non-interactive advertising includes print ads, television, radio, Internet banners, social media announcements, emails, and newsletters. There is no need to provide prescribed information set out in 135.8(d) to (f) for such advertisements. However, advertisements must mention a location where such information is readily accessible.[53]

Apart from the ATRs, which are specifically targeted to aviation, it is important to keep in mind that the Federal Competition Act[54] and provincial consumer protection legislation also contain provisions that would be relevant to advertisers. Indeed, the Competition Bureau has jurisdiction to review misleading and deceptive acts and practices in Canada. Section 52 of the Competition Act contains a criminal provision regarding misleading representations:

> No person shall, for the purpose of promoting, directly or indirectly, the supply or use of a product or for the purpose of promoting, directly or indirectly, any business interest, by any means whatever, knowingly or recklessly make a representation to the public that is false or misleading in a material respect.

The equivalent civil provision, section 74.01(1)(a), states:

> A person engages in reviewable conduct who, for the purpose of promoting, directly or indirectly, the supply or use of a product or for the purpose of promoting, directly or indirectly, any business interest, by any means whatever ... (a) makes a representation to the public that is false or misleading in a material respect

'Material' does not refer to value; it refers to a representation that could be reasonably expected to influence a person to buy the product or service. It is not necessary that a person be misled or deceived; it is sufficient that the representation be capable of misleading. As always in advertising, one must look at the overall impression that the advertisement conveys to the consumer.

Moreover, the Supreme Court of Canada has determined that the applicable standard is that of the 'credulous and inexperienced' and 'ordinary hurried purchasers', as opposed to that of a prudent and diligent consumer.[55]

14.4.2 Ancillary fees

Just as airfare must be advertised inclusive of applicable taxes, fees, and charges, the advertising of ancillary fees must also be all-inclusive, a general requirement in many jurisdictions with all-inclusive pricing regulations. This requirement often covers the first, or initial display of an ancillary fee during the booking process, whether online or over the phone.

---

53 ATR s. 135.8(5):

> A person is exempt from the requirement to provide the information referred to in paragraphs (1)(d) to (f) in their advertisement if the following conditions are met:
>
> a the advertisement is not interactive; and
> b the advertisement mentions a location that is readily accessible where all the information referred to in subsection (1) can be readily obtained.

54 R.S.C., 1985, c. C-34.
55 Supreme Court of Canada's interpretation of the Quebec Consumer Protection Act's provisions on the protection against false and misleading advertisement in *Richard* v. *Time* [2012] 1 SCR 265.

In Europe, for instance, EC Regulation No. 1008/2008 requires that the price of ancillary services be disclosed up front to the customer.

Canadian ATRs require that the total price of ancillary services be disclosed on the carrier's website. Specific baggage fees must also be disclosed on the itinerary/receipt.[56]

In the US, 14 CFR Part 399.85 addresses baggage and ancillary fee disclosure requirements, and is quite detailed. For example, baggage fee increases must be displayed on a carrier's homepage for at least three months. Carriers must disclose (1) that bag fees apply, on the first page on which there is a fare quotation, and (2) the location where customers can see these fees. Carriers must also include on an e-ticket confirmation, the precise bag fees including those of code share carriers, if applicable.

In May 2014, the DOT proposed another rulemaking on enhancing passenger rights, one that would require carriers to make ancillary service fees (carry-on baggage, checked baggage, and seat selection fees) available through all sales channels, including through ticketing agent channels. Although there is no actual requirement for airlines to sell ancillary products through third parties (airlines can choose to restrict the sale of these products through their own sales channels), this consequence is inevitably implied given the manner in which airlines distribute fares. This would therefore force carriers to distribute ancillary fee information to all ticketing agents, including GDS, and allow consumers to compare fares that are inclusive of the options that are tailored to their needs.

The US Notice of Proposed Rulemaking for Enhancing Airline Passenger Protections (EAPP) III received widespread opposition from industry associations representing airlines (IATA and A4A) and from the GDS. The arguments raised against the rule is that it is an unprecedented interference of government into the way airlines distribute fares, in contractual relationships between airlines and GDS, it would be incredibly costly (in fact, the DOT has recognized that the potential IT costs would exceed quantifiable benefits), and complex to implement. The rule would dampen airlines' competitive edge and ability to differentiate their product and stifle innovation.

At the time of writing, the EAPP III rule is still not final.

14.5 Code sharing

Code sharing is a marketing arrangement in which a carrier (the marketing carrier) sells seats using its own airline code on a flight operated by another carrier. For example, Air Canada markets and sells a flight between Toronto and Frankfurt operated by Lufthansa, with flight number AC1234 (code share flight numbers usually have four digits). Lufthansa sells the same flight, which it operates, with flight number LH567.

Regulations worldwide require that the operating carrier be disclosed to consumers who purchase air services. In the US, the requirements are extremely detailed, specifically requiring that both the corporate name and the 'doing business as' name of the operating carrier be disclosed, which can make for a fairly lengthy disclosure. The example provided in the regulation is 'Service between XYZ City and ABC City will be operated by Jane Doe Airlines d/b/a QRS Express'.[57]

US regulations also go as far as specifying the manner in which disclosure must be made, unlike other regulations of this type. In flight schedules, for instance, each flight sold with a

---

56 CTA Decision 144-A-2014.
57 14 CFR Part 257.5.

designator code other than that of the operating carrier must be 'identified by an asterisk or other easily identifiable mark', with the corporate name and 'doing business as name' of the operating carrier. In print advertisement, reasonable font type must be used:

> the advertisement shall prominently disclose that the advertised service may involve travel on another carrier and clearly indicate the nature of the service in reasonably sized type and shall identify all potential transporting carriers involved in the markets being advertised by corporate name and by any other name under which that service is held out to the public.[58]

The US DOT's new proposed rulemaking, EAPP III, furthers the code share disclosure requirements and the level of detail imposed. The DOT is considering setting minimum standards on the text size of the disclosure, and requiring that disclosure be done earlier in the booking process, on the first webpage following an itinerary search, with a code share disclosure either immediately adjacent to the entire itinerary or immediately adjacent to each code share flight.[59] Although many airlines already comply with such requirements, the mere imposition of such levels of detail in code share disclosure supports arguments in favour of alleviating regulatory burden where the burden, complexity, or level of intervention into free market dynamics outweigh the benefits.

The US DOT's jurisdiction is over the sales aspect of the air services, irrespective of the nationality of the air carrier. This type of regulation is commonly referred to as 'point-of-sale regulation'. Until recently, the regulation could also have been deemed to apply to all air services purchased in the US even if the code share flight takes place between points outside the US. However, in the new proposed regulations, EAPP III, the DOT clarifies that the requirements apply to advertisements for services operated within, to, or from the US that are marketed to consumers in the US.

Code share disclosure requirements exist in many other countries and airlines applying for code share approval in other countries will often be approved on the condition that consumers be advised of who the operator of the flight is. Requirements worldwide are usually much simpler and not as detailed and onerous as in the US.

In the EU, for instance, EC Regulation No. 2299/1989 states more generally that notice of the operating carrier must be included on schedules, timetables, electronic displays, or other public advertising. Disclosure must be made to customers before the reservation is made as well as at the time of check-in. Requirements in Canada are similar.[60]

Another key requirement regarding code share operations is that the marketing carrier's contract of carriage applies to the customer. This is in line with general principles of contractual

---

58 14 CFR part 257.5 'Notice requirement'.
59 Notice of Proposed Rulemaking at 29986–29988.
60 Air Transportation Regulations (SOR/88-58), s. 8.5:

> The licensee shall give notification that the air service referred to in subsection (1) is being operated using an aircraft and a flight crew provided by another person, and shall identify that person and specify the aircraft type
>
> a on all service schedules, timetables, electronic displays and any other public advertising of the air service; and
> b to travellers
>
>> i before reservation, or after reservation if the arrangement for the air service has been entered into after a reservation has been made; and
>> ii on check-in.

law; the contract of carriage is made with the marketing carrier, based upon that carrier's terms and conditions of carriage, and those are therefore the conditions of carriage that should apply to the entire travel itinerary.

The principle of 'marketing carrier rules apply' is expressly recognized in many jurisdictions. In Canada, for instance, the CTA will approve code share arrangements on the basis that the airlines 'shall apply their published tariffs, in effect, to the carriage of their traffic', 'their' being a reference to the traffic of the airline selling the traffic. Additionally, CTA conditions state that 'nothing in any commercial agreement between the air carriers relating to limits of liability shall diminish the rights of passengers as stated in such tariffs'.[61]

However, the application of this principle is not always straightforward from an operational perspective. Indeed it is operationally unfeasible for an operating carrier to apply different conditions of carriage to different passengers on its flight, depending on which carrier each passenger purchased their ticket from. Carriers involved in code share agreements prefer having service standards that are of a similar calibre, so the issue does not arise regularly in practice. Additionally, in cases where a passenger is subject to more advantageous terms and conditions when travelling with the operating carrier than those provided for by the marketing carrier's terms and conditions, the passenger will have no complaints.

Unfortunately, the dichotomy cannot be eliminated completely since anti-trust principles prohibit airlines from aligning their products, services, and terms and conditions of carriage. The customer service issues that arose in the context of baggage allowance and fees for complex itineraries eventually prompted the development of an industry-wide solution, which is detailed in the next section.

14.6 Baggage allowance for multi-carrier journeys

IATA Resolution 302 and the associated elaboration of a baggage allowance calculation system serve to ensure that one single baggage allowance applies to an entire itinerary, regardless of the number of carriers involved the itinerary, and of their varying conditions of carriage.

Historically, airlines established baggage rules and other terms and conditions of carriage through IATA's tariff conference mechanism, setting a number of standards, including standards for baggage allowance (weight, dimensions, number) and charges. This allowed for uniformity across the industry, thereby facilitative interline travel for consumers. Customers therefore knew that, for example, two free pieces of checked baggage allowance weighing a maximum of 20 kg each was permitted in economy class on all carriers.

However, this approach was deemed anti-competitive by the US DOT, and airlines began changing their baggage allowance, charging for the first or second checked bag, and consumers travelled on journeys where different baggage rules applied to different parts of the itinerary.

IATA therefore established a process, through Resolution 302, that allows the determination of baggage allowance and charges applicable throughout a 'journey', so that one set of rules apply in any given 'journey'. The process involved significant IT changes and solutions developed through GDS and travel agents.

IATA Resolution 302 uses the concept of Most Significant Carrier (MSC) to determine the baggage allowance applicable to an interline itinerary where many operating carriers are involved, irrespective of whether there is a different marketing carrier on each segment.

---

61 See as an example condition no. 2 of Decision No. 318-a-2015 (Westjet and AeroMexico).

The US DOT and CTA deemed that the approach conflicted with the principle mentioned in the code share section above, whereby the marketing carrier's terms and conditions apply, as the marketing carrier is the carrier with which the customer has a contract, irrespective of who the operating carrier is.

Accordingly, both the US and Canada expressed reservations with IATA Resolution 302. As further explained below, the US has implemented 14 CFR Part 399.87 to address the issue, and Canada issued CTA Decision 144-A-2014.

14.6.1 The IATA Resolution 302 logic

MSC is determined, under IATA Resolution 302, by establishing the carrier that crosses tariff conference areas or sub-areas, divisions of the world's main geographical areas as defined by IATA. It resets at each stopover, a stopover being defined as a stop of 24 hours or more.

The first step in the process of establishing the applicable baggage allowance is to determine if the published baggage provisions among all participating carriers are the same; if so, these provisions will apply. Second, where one or more published baggage provisions differ between participating carriers, one must apply any common provisions and where provisions differ, the published baggage provisions of the MSC apply. As previously stated, in case of code share flights, this will be those of the operating carrier, unless that carrier publishes a rule stipulating that it will be the marketing carrier, or unless the US DOT or CTA reservation applies (in which case the MSC is the marketing carrier).

The third step applies if the MSC does not publish baggage provisions for the journey concerned, in which case the published baggage provisions of the carrier accepting the baggage at check-in apply. If the carrier accepting the baggage at check-in does not publish baggage provisions for the interline journey concerned, the next published baggage provisions apply.

The following is an example using pure IATA methodology:

Outbound:
• AA9876, operated by BA123 between New York and London;
• BA456 between London and Johannesburg.

Inbound:
• BA8765, operated by SN908 between Johannesburg and Brussels;
• BA367 between Brussels and London;
• BA1234, operated by AA956 between London and New York.

IATA uses the 'bound' approach to the journey, meaning, in this example, that there are two separate journeys, the outbound and the inbound segments. A journey, under Resolution 302, is defined as travel from a point of departure to the next stopover (24 hour rule).

A Tariff Conference Area is crossed between North America and Europe, and a sub-area is crossed between Europe and Africa. The MSC on the outbound is therefore BA, as the operating carrier between New York and London. The MSC on the inbound portion is AA, as operating carrier between London and New York. The passengers on this itinerary would therefore be exposed to two different sets of baggage rules: BA's on the entire outbound journey, and AA's on the entire inbound journey.

14.6.2 The US DOT and CTA approach

The US DOT's rules[62] establish the applicable baggage allowance and fees on interline itineraries where the ultimate ticketed origin or destination is the US. Pursuant to industry consultation, the CTA then followed suit, following the US logic, and the result is a coherent approach for all itineraries beginning or ending in Canada or the US.[63]

The US DOT and Canadian approach are similar to IATA's approach, with the following two exceptions:

1   For itineraries where the ultimate origin or destination of a ticket is a US or Canadian point, the baggage rules established at the beginning of an itinerary must apply throughout the journey, irrespective of stopovers. In other words, the baggage rules applicable to the inbound portion of a round-trip itinerary are those that were applicable to the outbound portion.
2   In the case of code share flights, as previously stated, the MSC is not the operating carrier, but the marketing carrier.

Under this revised approach, the baggage logic of the first marketing carrier will apply. The first marketing carrier (this carrier is the 'Selecting Carrier' under the Canadian approach) must choose to apply either their own baggage policy or the baggage policy of the MSC, per IATA Resolution 302 as conditioned by the DOT/CTA. All participating carriers (i.e. downline carriers, including the check-in carrier at each point of stopover) must apply the baggage rules as specified by the Selecting Carrier

In the example given above, therefore, AA's baggage rules would apply to the entire itinerary, both outbound and inbound portions. Indeed, as first marketing carrier, AA would choose to apply its own rules or that of the MSC. The MSC on the outbound is also AA (it would be BA under IATA Resolution 302, but it is AA pursuant the US DOT's reservation).

Disclosure requirements under US DOT Part 399.85 require all carriers operating within, to, and from the US to set out the applicable baggage allowance information as determined by the first marketing carrier, on all e-ticket confirmations, the summary page at the completion of the online purchase, and in any post-purchase email confirmation. These requirements ensure that passengers are made aware of which baggage allowance applies to the itinerary.

Because the journey-based approach does not allow the baggage allowance to reset at points of stopovers or for return flights, the returning check-in carrier must assess the baggage allowance and fees as applied by the first marketing carrier. Airlines are therefore extremely reliant on information systems to retrieve the accurate baggage allowance information, and on information filed by all airlines through the Airline Tariff Publishing Company.

62 14 CFR Part 399.87:

> For passengers whose ultimate ticketed origin or destination is a U.S. point, U.S. and foreign carriers must apply the baggage allowances and fees that apply at the beginning of a passenger's itinerary. In the case of code-share flights that form part of an itinerary whose ultimate ticketed origin or destination is a U.S. point, U.S. and foreign carriers must apply the baggage allowances and fees of the marketing carrier throughout the itinerary to the extent that they differ from those of any operating carrier.

63 Decision 144-A-2014.

14.7 Summary and conclusions

When ICAO was established through the Chicago Convention in 1944, there was an overwhelming international recognition of a need for uniformity and standards in rules and regulations for the aviation industry. This imperative still exists, as it is fundamentally driven by the international nature of the industry, where a single operation commonly crosses many national borders and is consequently subject to various bodies of differing regulations.

The growing body of regulations being developed outside of ICAO's founding jurisdiction are mostly aimed at consumer protection, whether of the type described in this chapter, in other chapters (e.g. competition laws), or yet other regulations affecting the core of air passengers services, such as regulation on the carriage of passengers with a disability, privacy laws affecting advance passengers' information requirements, or privacy, anti-spam, and IT laws affecting the marketing and advertising of airfare.

The result is a gigantic set of rules with a substantial lack of cohesion, that are sometimes inconsistent or even conflictual, and that generate significant operational challenges for airlines and confusion for consumers.

While industry efforts to standardize requirements have often yielded positive results, antitrust prohibitions set a clear limit to what the industry can achieve on its own, particularly in terms of standards pertaining to terms and conditions of carriage. There is an unequivocal need for governments to clear a path towards uniformity and simplification of these rules.

Multilateral international agreements between countries can be difficult to coordinate, negotiate, and altogether achieve. But governments in the airline industry are regularly renegotiating bilateral air services agreements. These provide a perfectly adequate forum to begin developing a framework for the establishment of a common and uniform regulatory approach to consumer protection laws in the aviation industry.

Index

Page numbers in **bold** denote figures, those in *italics* denote tables.

noise certification, of aircraft 187–90; Effective Perceived Noise Decibels (EPNdB) 188; non-noise certificated (NNC) aircraft 188; procedures for 190

noise production in aviation, mechanisms of: aircraft engine noise 182; airframe noise 182–3; airport noise 182–3

non-scheduled flights 12, 254, 288

Open Aviation Area 276, 281

Open skies agreement 15, 269–70, 276; between US and The Netherlands 270–1; main provisions of 271–3; Memorandum of Consultations (MoC) 270; Multilateral Agreement on Liberalization of International Air Transport (MALIAT) 273

operational flight plan 42, 45

overflight, rights of 10, 14–15, 114, 130

ozone 201, 209; ozone-depleting substances 211

Paris Agreement (2015) 222

Paris Convention (1919) 6, 9, 11, 114, 186n35, 195

Paris Peace Conference Agreements 9

persistent organic pollutants (POPs) 208

personnel licensing 34–40; aeronautical station operator licence (ASOL) 40; air traffic controller licence (ATCL) 39; aircraft maintenance licence (AML) 39; airline transport pilot licence (ATPL) 37; commercial pilot licence (CPL) 37; definitions and general rules 34–5; flight dispatcher licence (FDL) 40; flight engineer licence (FEL) 39; flight instructor and 38; flight navigation licence (FNL) 39; glider pilot licence (GPL) 38; instrument flight rating 38; language requirements and specifications 34–5; Licensing Authority 35; medical provisions for 40; multi-crew pilot licence (MPL) 37; for other flight crew members 38–9; for other operational personnel 39–40; private pilot licence (PPL) 36–7; and ratings for pilots 35–8; student pilot 36; training for 34–5; validity of 34–5

pilots, ratings for: airline transport pilot licence (ATPL) 37; commercial pilot licence (CPL) 37; flight instructor and 38; free balloon pilot licence (FBPL) 38; glider pilot licence (GPL) 38; instrument flight rating 38; licences and 35–7; multi-crew pilot licence (MPL) 37; private pilot licence (PPL) 36–7; student pilot 36

Planning and Implementation Regional Groups (PIRGs) 102

powered-lift, flight instructions requirements for 36

predatory pricing 322–5; marketing and selling strategies 325; Spirit Airlines v. Northwest

Airlines 323–4; US Airways/American Airlines merger 324–5

pressurized aeroplanes 44, 46

Private International Air Law 4

private pilot licence (PPL) 35, 36–7

Procedures for Air Navigation Services (PANS) 21, 33, 96, 101, 191

Provisional International Civil Aviation Organization (PICAO) 9–10

Public Authority for Civil Aviation (PACA) 301

public international air law 1, 5, 222, 251

public utility 6, 298, 300

public–private partnership (PPP) 118–20

radio communication equipment 45

Records of Discussions 264

reduced vertical separation minimum (RVSM) operations 45

regional air navigation plans 101, 102

Regional Economic Integration Organizations (REIOs) 30, 216, 222

Regional Safety Oversight Organization (RSOO) 76

Regional Supplementary Procedures (SUPPs) 21, 33, 101

registration of aircraft 2, 5, 139; transfer of 13n23, 52

remedies, in antitrust cases 326–7

remote pilot 62

remote pilot station 62

remote piloted aircraft 113

remote piloted aircraft systems (RPAS) 61–2

Rio Declaration (1992) 204n93, 205, 211–13

Roadmap for Integration of Air Travel Sector (RIATS) 125n54

Rome, Treaty of (1957) 265

safe operation of air services, practices required for 262

Safety Assessment of Foreign Aircraft (SAFA) 83

safety audits: EU safety list (air carriers operating ban) 83–4; FAA International Aviation Safety Assessment (IASA) Program 80–1; Safety Assessment of Foreign Aircraft (SAFA) 83

safety management: acceptable level of safety performance (ALoSP) 58; Effective Implementation (EI) score 60; EU aviation safety list 60–1; International Aviation Safety Assessments (IASA) Program 60; proactive 58; risk-based approach for 60; Safety Management System (SMS) 23, 61; safety oversight 59–61; safety-related requirements 59–60; Significant Safety Concerns (SSC) 60; state responsibilities 58–9; State Safety Programme (SSP) 58–9; States safety risk profiles 60; Universal Safety Oversight Audit Programme (USOAP) 7, 17, 23–4, 32

For Product Safety Concerns and Information please contact our EU
representative GPSR@taylorandfrancis.com
Taylor & Francis Verlag GmbH, Kaufingerstraße 24, 80331 München, Germany